Semantic Web for Business:

Cases and Applications

Roberto García
Universitat de Lleida, Spain

A volume in the Advances in E-Business Research (AEBR) Book Series

Director of Editorial Content:	Kristin Klinger
Director of Production:	Jennifer Neidig
Managing Editor:	Jamie Snavely
Assistant Managing Editor:	Carole Coulson
Typesetter:	Sean Woznicki
Cover Design:	Lisa Tosheff

Published in the United States of America by
Information Science Reference (an imprint of IGI Global)
701 E. Chocolate Avenue
Hershey PA 17033
Tel: 717-533-8845
Fax: 717-533-8661
E-mail: cust@igi-global.com
Web site: http://www.igi-global.com

Library of Congress Cataloging-in-Publication Data

Semantic Web for business : cases and applications / Roberto Garcia, editor.
p. cm.
Includes bibliographical references and index.
Summary: "This book provides simple costs and benefits analysis showing that the Semantic Web is prepared for e-business"--Provided by publisher.
ISBN 978-1-60566-066-0 (hbk.) -- ISBN 978-1-60566-067-7 (ebook) 1. Management information systems. 2. Semantic Web. 3. E-commerce. I.Garcia, Roberto, 1976-
HD30.213.S46 2009
025.04--dc22

2008010306

This book is published in the IGI Global book series Advances in E-Business Research (AEBR) Book Series (ISSN: 1935-2700; eISSN: 1935-2719)

British Cataloguing in Publication Data
A Cataloguing in Publication record for this book is available from the British Library.

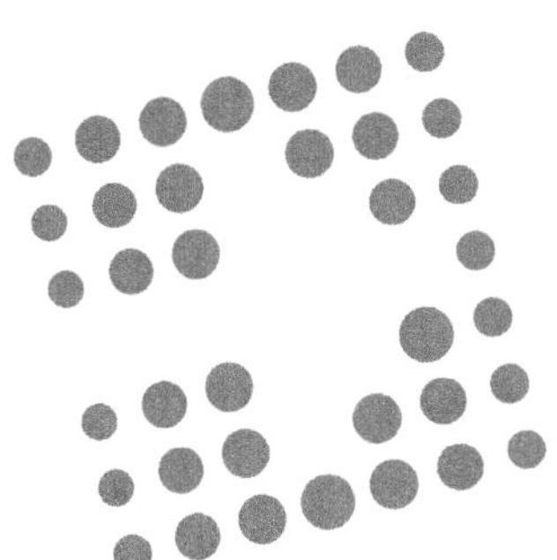

Advances in E-Business Research (AEBR) Book Series

In Lee (Western Illinois University, USA)

ISSN: 1935-2700
EISSN: 1935-2719

Mission

Technology has played a vital role in the emergence of e-business and its applications incorporate strategies. These processes have aided in the use of electronic transactions via telecommunications networks for collaborating with business partners, buying and selling of goods and services, and customer service. Research in this field continues to develop into a wide range of topics, including marketing, psychology, information systems, accounting, economics, and computer science.

The **Advances in E-Business Research (AEBR)** series provides multidisciplinary references for researchers and practitioners in this area. Instructors, researchers, and professionals interested in the most up-to-date research on the concepts, issues, applications, and trends in the e-business field will find this collection, or individual books, extremely useful. This collection contains the highest quality academic books that advance understanding of e-business and addresses the challenges faced by researchers and practitioners.

Coverage

- E-Business Management
- E-Business Models and Architectures
- E-Business Systems Integration
- E-Business Technology Investment Strategies
- E-CRM
- E-Marketing
- Global E-Business
- Outsourcing and E-Business Technologies
- Semantic Web
- Sustainable E-Business
- Virtual Organization

IGI Global is currently accepting manuscripts for publication within this series. To submit a proposal for a volume in this series, please contact our Acquisition Editors at Acquisitions@igi-global.com or visit: http://www.igi-global.com/publish/.

The Advances in E-Business Research (AEBR) Book Series (ISSN 1935-2700) is published by IGI Global, 701 E. Chocolate Avenue, Hershey, PA 17033-1240, USA, www.igi-global.com. This series is composed of titles available for purchase individually; each title is edited to be contextually exclusive from any other title within the series. For pricing and ordering information please visit http://www.igi-global.com/book-series/advances-business-research-aebr-book/37144. Postmaster: Send all address changes to above address.

Titles in this Series

For a list of additional titles in this series, please visit: www.igi-global.com

Interdisciplinary Perspectives on Business Convergence, Computing, and Legality
Himanshu Khurana (NCSA, University of Illinois, USA) and Rashimi Aggarwal (Institute of Management Technology-Ghazibad, India)
Business Science Reference • copyright 2013 • 354pp • H/C (ISBN: 9781466642096) • US $165.00 (our price)

Research and Development in E-Business through Service-Oriented Solutions
Katalin Tarnay (University of Pannonia, Hungary & Budapest University of Technology and Economics, Hungary) Sandor Imre (Budapest University of Technology and Economics, Hungary) and Lai Xu (Bournemouth University, UK)
Business Science Reference • copyright 2013 • 328pp • H/C (ISBN: 9781466641815) • US $185.00 (our price)

Mobile Services Industries, Technologies, and Applications in the Global Economy
In Lee (Western Illinois University, USA)
Information Science Reference • copyright 2013 • 368pp • H/C (ISBN: 9781466619814) • US $190.00 (our price)

Strategic and Pragmatic E-Business Implications for Future Business Practices
Karim Mohammed Rezaul (Glyndwr University, UK)
Business Science Reference • copyright 2012 • 496pp • H/C (ISBN: 9781466616196) • US $185.00 (our price)

Emergent Strategies for E-Business Processes, Services and Implications Advancing Corporate Frameworks
In Lee (Western Illinois University, USA)
Information Science Reference • copyright 2009 • 424pp • H/C (ISBN: 9781605661544) • US $195.00 (our price)

Semantic Web for Business Cases and Applications
Roberto Garcia (University of Lleida, Spain)
Information Science Reference • copyright 2009 • 444pp • H/C (ISBN: 9781605660660) • US $195.00 (our price)

Cyberlaw for Global E-business Finance, Payments and Dispute Resolution
Takashi Kubota (Waseda University, Japan)
Information Science Reference • copyright 2008 • 318pp • H/C (ISBN: 9781599048284) • US $180.00 (our price)

E-Business Models, Services and Communications
In Lee (Western Illinois University, USA)
Information Science Reference • copyright 2008 • 464pp • H/C (ISBN: 9781599048314) • US $180.00 (our price)

www.igi-global.com

701 E. Chocolate Ave., Hershey, PA 17033
Order online at www.igi-global.com or call 717-533-8845 x100
To place a standing order for titles released in this series, contact: cust@igi-global.com
Mon-Fri 8:00 am - 5:00 pm (est) or fax 24 hours a day 717-533-8661

Editorial Advisory Board

Marcos Ruano Mayoral
Universidad Carlos III de Madrid, Spain

Maria João Viamonte
Polytechnic of Porto, Portugal

Marta Oliva
Universitat de Lleida, Spain

Martin Bryan
CSW informatics, UK

Martin Hepp
Digital Enterprise Research Institute, Innsbruck, Austria

Mick Kerrigan
University of Innsbruck, Austria

Mills Davis
Project10X, USA

Mustafa Jarrar
University of Cyprus, Cyprus

Nuno Silva
Polytechnic of Porto, Portugal

Oscar Corcho
Universidad Politécnica de Madrid, Spain

Paavo Kotinurmi
Helsinki University of Technology, Finland

Paola Hobson
Motorola Labs, UK

Ricardo Colomo
Universidad Carlos III de Madrid, Spain

Sergio Bellido
Bankinter, Spain

Sören Auer
University of Leipzig, Germany

Tomás Pariente Lobo
ATOS Origin SAE, Spain

Tommaso Di Noia
Technical University of Bari, Italia

Table of Contents

Foreword xviii

Preface xx

Acknowledgment xxix

Section I
Introduction

Chapter I
Semantic Web Take-Off in a European Industry Perspective 1
Alain Léger, France Telecom R&D, France
Johannes Heinecke, France Telecom R&D, France
Lyndon J.B. Nixon, Freie Universität Berlin, Germany
Pavel Shvaiko, University of Trento, Italy
Jean Charlet, STIM, DPA/AP-Hopitaux Paris & Université Paris 6, France
Paola Hobson, Motorola Labs, UK
François Goasdoué, LRI, CNRS et Université Paris Sud XI, France

Section II
Semantic Web E-Business Cases

Chapter II
Applying Semantic Web Technologies to Car Repairs 31
Martin Bryan, CSW Group Ltd., UK
Jay Cousins, CSW Group Ltd., UK

Chapter III
Semantic Integration for B2B Service Assurance 50
Alistair Duke, BT Group Chief Technology Office, UK
Marc Richardson, BT Group Chief Technology Office, UK

Detailed Table of Contents

Foreword xviii

Preface xx

Acknowledgment xxix

Section I
Introduction

Chapter I
Semantic Web Take-Off in a European Industry Perspective 1
Alain Léger, France Telecom R&D, France
Johannes Heinecke, France Telecom R&D, France
Lyndon J.B. Nixon, Freie Universität Berlin, Germany
Pavel Shvaiko, University of Trento, Italy
Jean Charlet, STIM, DPA/AP-Hopitaux Paris & Université Paris 6, France
Paola Hobson, Motorola Labs, UK
François Goasdoué, LRI, CNRS et Université Paris Sud XI, France

The first chapter presents an overview of the penetration of Semantic Web technology in industry, which is progressing slowly but accelerating as new success stories are reported. The authors report on the ongoing work in the cross-fertilization between industry and academia. In particular, they present a collection of application fields and use cases from European enterprises which are interested in the promises of Semantic Web technology. The spectrum of applications is extremely large, e.g. corporate portals and knowledge management, e-commerce, e-work, e-business, healthcare, e-government, natural language processing, search, data and services integration, social networks, business intelligence, etc. The chapter ends with the presentation of the current state of the technology and future trends as seen by prominent actors in the field.

Chapter II presents the European Commission MYCAREVENT research project, which brought together European vehicle manufacturers, vehicle repair organisations, diagnostic tool manufacturers and IT specialists, including Semantic Web technologists, to study how to link together the wide range of information sets they use to identify faults and repair vehicles. These information are integrated and accessed through a service portal by using a 'shared language' for the project, a reference terminology to which the disparate terminologies of organisations participating in the project can be mapped. This shared vocabulary is materialised as a Semantic Web ontology.

This chapter describes an approach to support operational support system (OSS) integration across organisation boundaries. The requirement for such business-to-business (B2B) interfaces is expected to increase as is the need to carry out integration in much more flexible way. Existing approaches for integration tend to be implementation specific, operate at the syntactic level and are realised by programme code. Consequently they are inflexible due to their highly coupled nature and are costly to setup and maintain. An approach to decouple B2B interfaces is introduced, which allows them to be flexibly coupled as required with the use of scalable, semantic mediation. An initial prototype is described based on an Assurance Integration scenario for BT Wholesale's B2B gateway.

Chapter IV deals with one of the most difficult problems dealing with applications interoperation, protocol mediation. This kind of mediation is concerned with non-matching message interchange patterns in applications interaction. The proposed solution focuses on solving the interoperation issues between two heterogeneous logistic provider systems, which use two different standard protocols: RosettaNet and EDIFACT. It includes an ontology for interaction choreography description and the software that implements the bridging mechanisms between these two protocols based on the knowledge captured by the ontology.

In this chapter, authors report their practical experiences in building an ontology-based eRecruitment system. This case study confirms previous findings in ontology engineering literature. First, to build ontology-based systems is still a tedious process due to the lack of proved and tested methods and tools supporting the entire life cycle of an ontology. And second, to reuse existing ontologies within new application contexts is currently related to efforts potentially comparable to the costs of a new implementation. These findings are used to further elaborate existing best practices towards a list of recommendations for the eRecruitment domain.

Chapter VI also presents a European Research project, SEEMP. This project promotes increased partnership between labour market actors and the development of closer relations between private and public Employment Services. The need for a flexible collaboration gives rise to the issue of interoperability in both data exchange and share of services. SEEMP proposes a solution that relies on semantic services based collaboration among public and private Employment Services. Each actor in the marketplace has to care only about integrating with the marketplace and the Reference Ontology. The marketplace will offer services to support the interaction with other actors.

This chapter presents an ontology for customer complaint management, which has been developed in the EU funded project CCFORM, with the aim of establishing an European customer complaint portal.

The objective is that any consumer can register a complaint against any party about any problem, at this portal. The portal should be multilanguage and sensitive to cross-border business regulations. A customer complaint ontology, which underpins the CC portal, makes all these features possible. The CContology comprises classifications of complaint problems, complaint resolutions, complaining parties, complaint-recipients, ''best-practices", rules of complaint, etc.

Chapter VIII
A Semantic Web-Based Information Integration Approach for an Agent-Based Electronic Market 150
Maria João Viamonte, GECAD – Knowledge Engineering and Decision Support Research Group, Porto Polytechnic Institute, Portugal
Nuno Silva, GECAD – Knowledge Engineering and Decision Support Research Group, Porto Polytechnic Institute, Portugal

In this chapter, authors face the problem of the growth of e-commerce using software agents to support both customers and suppliers in buying and selling goods and services. The diversity of the actors involved leads to different conceptualizations of the needs and capabilities, giving rise to semantic incompatibilities between them. Authors propose an ontology-based information integration approach, exploiting the ontology mapping paradigm, by aligning consumer needs and the market capacities, in a semi-automatic mode and based on Semantic Web technology. The approach is improved by the application and exploitation of the information and trust relationships captured by the social networks.

Chapter IX
Semantic Web for Media Convergence: A Newspaper Case 170
Ferran Perdrix, Universitat de Lleida, Spain & Diari Segre Media Group, Spain
Juan Manuel Gimeno, Universitat de Lleida, Spain
Rosa Gil, Universitat de Lleida, Spain
Marta Oliva, Universitat de Lleida, Spain
Roberto García, Universitat de Lleida, Spain

Chapter IX studies the case of media convergence in newspaper media houses, which are evolving to highly dynamic and multi-channel communication mediums, where the different channels converge into a unified news editorial office. In order to cope with the new requirements arising from this change, machines must be aware of a greater part of the underlying semantics. Ontologies are a clear candidate to put this semantics into play, and Semantic Web technologies a good choice for Web-wide information integration. However, newspapers have made great investments in their current systems so a smooth transition is preferred. The chapter proposal is to build an ontological framework based on existing journalism and multimedia standards and to translate existing metadata to the Semantic Web.

Chapter X
Ontologically Enhanced RosettaNet B2B Integration 194
Paavo Kotinurmi, Helsinki University of Technology, Finland
Armin Haller, National University of Ireland - Galway, Ireland
Eyal Oren, Vrije Universiteit Amsterdam, The Netherlands

This chapter describes the OERN ontological extension to RosettaNet and shows how this extension can be used in business integrations to resolve data heterogeneities. RosettaNet is an industry-driven e-business process standard that defines common inter-company public processes and their associated business documents. The usage of Web ontology languages in RosettaNet collaborations can help accommodate partner heterogeneity in their set-up phase and can ease back-end integrations, enabling for example more competition in the purchasing processes.

Chapter XI
Towards an Operational REA Business Ontology 222
Frederik Gailly, Ghent University, Belgium
Geert Poels, Ghent University, Belgium

The authors of this chapter present the development of a formal representation, based on an OWL Semantic Web ontology for the Resource Event Agent (REA), which is a business ontology for ontology-driven enterprise system development. The objective is to overcome the limitation of the current specification, which is neither sufficiently explicit nor formal, and thus difficult to use in ontology-driven business information systems. The chapter discusses the choices made in redesigning REA and illustrates how this new formal representation can be used to support ontology-driven supply chain collaboration.

Chapter XII
Towards Semantic Business Processes: Concepts, Methodology, and Implementation 244
Muhammad Ahtisham Aslam, University of Leipzig, Germany & COMSATS Institute of Information Technology, Pakistan
Sören Auer, University of Leipzig, Germany & University of Pennsylvania, USA
Klaus-Peter Fähnrich, University of Leipzig, Germany

In this chapter, semantic extensions for Web services are presented as a mean to overcome business processes interoperability limitations due to purely syntactic approaches. Another drawback is that services cannot be discovered and composed dynamically by other semantic enabled systems slowing down the process of interaction between business partners. OWL-S is a suite of OWL ontologies and can be used to describe the compositions of Web services on the basis of matching semantics as well as to expose semantically enriched interfaces. The aim of this chapter is to describe an approach and its implementation that can be used to enable business processes for semantic based dynamic discovery, invocation and composition by translating BPEL process descriptions to the OWL-S suite of ontologies.

Chapter XIII
Experiences in Building Mobile E-Business Services: Service Provisioning and Mobility 275
Ivano De Furio, AtosOrigin Italia S.p.A., Italy
Giovanni Frattini, AtosOrigin Italia S.p.A., Italy
Luigi Romano, AtosOrigin Italia S.p.A., Italy

Chapter XIII analyses how telecommunications operators can improve their partnership networks and provide new services by solving the interoperability limitations of service-oriented architectures (SOA). The idea is to use Web services technology to create service providers federations and ontologies to

support advanced matchmaking mechanisms based on a semantic metadata store. In particular, the proposal includes a Service Registration Authority that controls and enforces annotation policies in order to avoid the lack of uniformity in service descriptions. Furthermore, this solution enables enhanced service/component discovery and validation, helping software engineers to build services by composing building blocks.

Chapter XIV
Towards the Use of Networked Ontologies for Dealing with Knowledge-Intensive Domains:
A Pharmaceutical Case Study 298
Germán Herrero Cárcel, ATOS Origin SAE, Spain
Tomás Pariente Lobo, ATOS Origin SAE, Spain

The case study presented in this chapter is about how networked ontologies satisfy the needs of such a knowledge intensive sector as the pharmaceutical one. The use of semantics helps bridging the gap between the different representations that different stakeholders have. The problem arises when the ontologies used to model the domain become too large and unmanageable. Networked ontologies can solve these problems. The particular case scenario considered by this chapter is the nomenclature of products in the pharmaceutical sector, which is currently under development in the EC funded FP6 project NeOn in order to develop a common Reference Ontology about drugs.

Chapter XV
Semantic Competence Pull: A Semantics-Based Architecture for Filling Competency Gaps
in Organizations 321
Ricardo Colomo-Palacios, Universidad Carlos III de Madrid, Spain
Marcos Ruano-Mayoral, Universidad Carlos III de Madrid, Spain
Juan Miguel Gómez-Berbís, Universidad Carlos III de Madrid, Spain
Ángel García-Crespo, Universidad Carlos III de Madrid, Spain

The authors of this chapter highlight one of the key problems that the software industry has been facing due to the lack of alignment between the curricula offered by Universities and other kinds of education and training centres and the professional profiles demanded by companies and organizations. The chapter proposal is to provide a set of mechanisms and an intermediary system that allows companies to define and express their competency gaps and, at the same time, allow education centres to analyse those gaps and define the training plans to meet those needs.

Chapter XVI
Using Semantic Web Services in E-Banking Solutions 336
Laurent Cicurel, iSOCO, Spain
José Luis Bas Uribe, Bankinter, Spain
Sergio Bellido Gonzalez, Bankinter, Spain
Jesús Contreras, iSOCO, Spain
José-Manuel López-Cobo, iSOCO, Spain
Silvestre Losada, iSOCO, Spain

In this chapter an e-Banking case is presented, concentrating on how to offer a public access to efficient transactional stock market functionalities. Traditional service oriented architectures (SOA) succeed at providing reasonable good Web-based brokerage solutions but may lack on extensibility possibilities. By introducing Semantic Web Services (SWS) as a way to integrate third party services from distributed service providers, authors propose an innovative way that combines ontologies and SWS in order to allow different users to define their own stock change strategies regardless of the provider of information.

Chapter XVII
Formal Ontology for Media Rights Transactions 353
Adam Pease, Articulate Software, USA
Godfrey Rust, Rightscom/Ontologyx, UK

The last chapter presents a large-scale data integration and transaction management system for media rights, called Ontologyx. Previous versions of this system have utilized lightweight schema and conventional Semantic Web technologies such as OWL. The current version employs formal ontology development in the SUO-KIF logical language and involves reuse an extension of a large formal ontology, the suggested upper merged ontology (SUMO). In particular, authors argue that extending from a large ontology will give the model greater coverage of more domains and expand business opportunities to expand into supporting more kinds of transaction management applications.

Compilation of References 374

About the Contributors 400

Index 414

Foreword

This book is about the business value of semantic technologies. Specifically, it reports case studies that have applied Semantic Web standards and methodologies to a range of business applications and infrastructure needs, including many European Union funded research programs. The results are encouraging, and worthy of consideration by both business executives and IT professionals. The future of e-business lies in this direction.

As discussed in this book and as demonstrated by the case studies presented here, the Semantic Web for business is a work in progress. Most work to date has focused on issues of data integration, system interoperability, and process plumbing. There is significant value in this. But, it is only the beginning. Much more business value will be harvested from semantic technologies in the coming decade.

To set the stage, let us talk for a moment about the business value of semantic technologies. We estimate that over the next ten years semantic technologies have the potential to drive 2-3 order of magnitude improvements in capabilities and life cycle economics of business solutions through cost reductions, improved efficiencies, gains in effectiveness, and new functionalities that were not possible or economically feasible before now.

The business value of semantic technologies has three dimensions or axes[1]: capability, performance, and life cycle economics.

1. **New capabilities:** Semantic technologies enable new capabilities that tap new sources of value. Sources of new value include: value from knowledge modeling, value from adding intelligence, value from learning and value from semantic ecosystem.
2. **New performance:** The classic motivations for new investments in technology are: efficiency gain, effectiveness gain, and strategic edge. We call these the 3-Es.
3. **New life cycle economics:** Semantic technologies improve economics and reduce risks across all stages of the solution life cycle: "Research and Development", "Deployment and Operations" and "Maintenance and Evolution".

The value drivers for semantic technologies in business are strong. As you read the research case studies presented in this book, you will find many aspects of business value discussed and demonstrated, although not to the full extent that can be anticipated for full deployment of production solutions exploiting commercialized products and services. Collectively, however, these case studies make a compelling case for the adoption of semantic technologies in business.

ENDNOTE

1 Davis, M. (2008). *Semantic Wave 2008 Report: Industry Roadmap to Web 3.0 and Multibillion Dollar Market Opportunities*. Retrieved from http://www.project10x.com

Mills Davis, Project10X, USA
February 2, 2008

Mills Davis *is founder and managing director of Project10X — a Washington, DC based research consultancy specializing in next wave semantic technologies and solutions. The firm's clients include technology manufacturers, global 2000 corporations, and government agencies. Mills served as principal investigator for the Semantic Wave 2008 research program. A noted consultant and industry analyst, he has authored more than 100 reports, whitepapers, articles, and industry studies. Mills is active in both government and industry-wide technology initiatives that are advancing semantic technologies. He serves as co-chair of the Federal Semantic Interoperability Community of Practice (SICoP). Mills is a founding member of the AIIM interoperable enterprise content management (iECM) working group, and a founding member of the National Center for Ontology Research (NCOR). Also, he serves on the advisory boards of several new ventures in the semantic space.*

Preface

INTRODUCTION

The Semantic Web is what the World Wide Web was initially intended to be by its inventor, Tim Berners-Lee:

The first step is putting data on the Web in a form that machines can naturally understand, or converting it to that form. This creates what I call a Semantic Web, a Web of data that can be processed directly or indirectly by machines. (Berners-Lee, 2000)

However, due to the Web deployment challenges, this very ambitious vision was simplified in order to facilitate its take-off. Then, why this vision is being retaken now? And why is this important for e-business?

The Semantic Web is not just for the World Wide Web. It represents a set of technologies that work equally well on internal corporate intranets because it tries to solve several key problems in current information technology architectures.

In the context of e-business, the key contribution of the Semantic Web is integration. The Internet and the World Wide Web have made it possible to interconnect information systems worldwide. The result is a global market where enterprises have the potential of carrying out business with any partner by electronic means.

However, exploiting this potential is difficult due to the communication barriers among information systems, e.g. different operating systems, legacy systems, proprietary information schemes, etc. The key to break these barriers is integration. A lot of effort has been invested to achieve it and two initiatives can be highlighted due to their tight relation to the Web and their impact in the e-business world: XML and Web Services.

The former provides a common data model and the latter the global channel through which systems can communicate. Both constitute a good foundation for systems integration but something more is needed if we want to scale it to a worldwide framework. Each system has its own history, development team, etc., which make they lay on different conceptual models that impede a meaningful communication among them, though they might all be based on XML and Web Services. In other words, there is a common syntax but disparate semantics, i.e. meanings, and computers do not have the means to manage them.

Manual intervention might lower the semantic barrier. In any case, it is not sustainable if developers are forced to analyse each potential conversation and develop a particular adapter that makes it understandable. There are also standardisation efforts that establish common frameworks that facilitate communication in concrete domains. However, they have proliferated so much and are based on the same syntactic-level interoperability principles that, in most cases, they have just moved the barriers slightly down.

The Semantic Web focuses on interoperability at the conceptual level. It provides the building blocks that facilitate establishing connections among the meanings of the things managed by computers. These connections tell computers simple facts such as that two pieces of data refer to the same thing or, more complex ones like that everything of one kind is accompanied by something of another kind so, when something of the first kind is seen, it can be assumed that the accompanying thing is from the second kind.

Computers are not able to deduce these connections on their own; it is still necessary that we teach them the roots from which they can start integrating data automatically. However, although this implies a great initial effort, it scales to Web wide environments. In fact, as more and more connections among concepts are added, computers have more paths to follow as they try to realise if two pieces of data match or the kind of product an invoice is referring to.

The research community has placed great efforts in the Semantic Web initiative and we are starting now to see its practical benefits in many domains, especially in one with great impact that is e-business. The main opportunities are anticipated in information systems interoperation and range from inter to intra-organizational links. The question is then if the Semantic Web will help the takeoff of a webbed economy where, in spontaneous inter-organizational relations, the involved parties share data and integrate their internal business processes in a transparent and trustful way.

Mill Davis strongly supports this idea in his Semantic Wave report (Davis, 2007). He anticipates that semantic technologies are going to carry multi-billion dollar opportunities in the next decade. For instance, it is foreseen a 50 billion dollars market of information and communication semantic technologies. It also estimates that the R&D investment in semantic technologies will reach more than 2 billion dollars per year by the end of the decade.

The objective of this book is also to provide more evidences about the Semantic Web takeoff in e-business, but from an innovative point of view compared to existing related books. The approach is to present a compendium of business cases that show the application of Semantic Web technologies in e-business problems. Business cases allow considering not only technological issues, as it is common in other Semantic Web and e-business books (Salam, & Stevens, 2007). Other issues that are relevant from the business point of view are also covered, such as strengths, weaknesses, opportunities and threats analysis (SWOT).

The aim of this combination of technological and business perspectives is to make the book also appealing to IT managers and decision makers that. Apart from technological and methodological issues, the book also sketches costs and benefits analysis showing that the Semantic Web is prepared to do business. Consequently, in addition to Semantic Web researchers and developers, the intended audience of the book is also IT professionals, IT researchers, business executives, consultants and students (undergraduate, graduate, PhD and MBA).

Thanks to this cross-discipline approach, the hope is that this book will encourage and facilitate the transfer of technologies and methodologies from the Semantic Web to the e-business world. The next section provides a small introduction to Semantic Web technologies together with some pointers for further reading. Then, Section presents the business case structure followed by each case description chapter and Section details the contents of the book with a small summary for each chapter. Finally, there is a conclusions section that ends this preface.

SEMANTIC WEB TECHNOLOGIES OVERVIEW

The Semantic Web is rooted on a data model, a way to represent data, geared towards interoperability. It is based on a directed graph, i.e. a set of nodes connected by edges with a direction, from node A to node B. This graph model constitutes the first building block for semantic interoperability because a graph can be used to represent many other kinds of data structures.

For instance, it is easy to model a tree using a graph -it is just a graph without cycles- or a table -each row is represented by a node that is connected to the different row values by edges labelled after each column name. This makes it easier to integrate data coming from XML documents or relational databases into the Semantic Web. Moreover, it easier to mash-up data from disparate sources into a graph because the result is always a graph.

The Semantic Web graph model is named RDF, Resource Description Framework (Tauberer, 2008). However, this is not enough. We can put it all into a graph but, how do we tell the computer that one part of the graph can be joined to another part because they refer to the same thing? And, what is even more important, how do we put restrictions on how the graph is built in order to make it model interesting things and avoid that it becomes a messy bunch of nodes?

It is possible to accomplish these features using schemas and ontologies. First of all, they guide graph construction by providing restrictions on how nodes are connected to other nodes using different kinds of edges, called properties. For instance, it is possible to say that a node represents a person and that it is related through properties called "name", "e-mail" or "friend" to nodes providing the corresponding values for them.

RDF Schema is the simplest tool that allows modelling these restrictions (Daconta, Obrst, & Smith, 2003). It provides primitives similar to those from object oriented programming so it is possible to define classes with defined sets of properties and appropriate values. Classes are then used to categorise the things represented by nodes, called the resources, in order to apply the corresponding restrictions to them.

For instance, there is a class "Person", associated to the relevant properties for persons, which is applied to a node representing a given person. From this point, it is possible to guide how that person is described by the graph and, more importantly, the computer can interpret a description for that resource following the guidelines provided by the "Person" class.

Ontologies also provide ways to restrict how the graph is modelled, and how it should be interpreted by the computer (Fensel, 2004). They are a more sophisticated way to do so and are based on logic formalisms. This makes it possible to use logic reasoners in order to deduce new things about the data being managed. These kinds of deductions are a key feature in order to enable scalable data integration by computerised means. Computers use the clues and rules captured by ontologies in order to make sophisticated data integration at the semantic level, such as realising that two pieces of data match together or the kind of product that an invoice is referring to, e.g. from what the ontology says about the invoice, the customer, etc.

The Web Ontology Language (OWL) is used in order to define Semantic Web ontologies (Lacy, 2005). There are three sublanguages with different levels of complexity, which require increasing computation power but provide more expressive ways to pose restrictions. The simpler is OWL Lite and the more complex and expressive OWL Full. In the middle there is OWL DL, which is based on Description Logics (Baader, Calvanese, McGuinness, Nardi, & Patel-Schneider, 2003) and provides a trade-off between complexity and expressiveness.

The technologies previously described provide the means for semantic interoperability at the data level. Additionally, interoperability is also required at the operational level and, nowadays, Web services are the common approach to solve this issue. However, the foreseen Web of services where applications can be built from the combination of services published all over the world in an almost automatic way has not yet come true.

The barrier continues to be the difficulties to integrate the disparate data models that services process and the different ways to describe their functionality. It might be the case that two services that can be used interchangeably, but the different terms used to describe what they do make it impossible for the computer to realise that one can be used in place of the other. The Semantic Web approach for this problem is also to use semantic descriptions of the services, called Semantic Web Services (Cardoso, 2007).

There are some approaches (Yu, 2007) to Web services description that allow to say what they do, how they do it, what kind of data they get as input and what is the output, etc. The simpler way is to put semantic annotations into the Web Service Description Language (WSDL). This proposal is called semantic annotation for WSDL (SAWSDL). There are also two Web Services Ontologies that provide richer ways to describe them, an OWL-based Web Dervice Ontology (OWL-S) and the Web Service Modelling Ontology (WSMO).

All these technologies are put into practice in the different Semantic Web in e-business application scenarios included in this book. The reader can follow the references provided in this section in order to get deeper into Semantic Web technologies. Each chapter also provides relevant references and additional readings that help getting into the details.

THE BUSINESS CASE STRUCTURE

In order to make the book more practical and appealing for IT decision makers, chapters follow a business case structure. The idea is to make it easier to read for the managers that would at last decide to put Semantic Web technologies into practice in enterprises. Many information systems managers are used to business cases and they are a common teaching resource in management masters (e.g. MBA).

The objective is to make more people aware of the benefits that Semantic Web technologies can carry to e-business information systems, focusing on the people that would have the last word in this process. There is still room in the case for the technical details, but it is also important to highlight the opportunity or problem and to make the benefits of the proposed solution clear and justifiable from a costs and benefits point of view.

This approach pretends also to make chapter more practical and less theoretic. Each business case presents a current e-business situation where Semantic Web technologies are being applied producing some benefits and opportunities that justify the cost.

Some question business cases should answer are:

- Why the project is needed? Existing issues and opportunities.
- How will the effort solve the issues or opportunities facing the organisation?
- What is the recommended solution(s)?
- How does the solution address the issues or opportunities (benefits)?
- What are the risks if the issues or opportunities are not faced?
- Qualitatively, how much will all this cost? Is it worth compared to the benefits?

The proposed business case is shown in Table 1. Authors have used it as the starting point for organizing their chapters, though authors have adapted it to their particular needs.

A part from the abstract, chapters begin with a description of the current situation. The scenario is described paying special attention to how the things were before Semantic Web methodologies and technologies are applied. Then, from the previous situation description, the current problem is highlighted. This statement should make it clear that there are issues that are limiting how e-business is conducted and that there is an opportunity for the Semantic Web.

Table 1. Proposed business case structure

Business Case
Abstract
1. Current Situation
1.1. Problem Statement
2. Solution Description
2.1. Objectives
2.2. Overview
3. Solution Details
4. Alternatives
5. Cost and Benefits
6. Risk Assessment
7. Future Trends
8. Conclusions

Once the opportunity has been signaled, there is the description of the proposed solution. First of all, the objectives of the proposed solution are stated and an overview of the solution is given. Then, we get into details and the technicalities of the proposed solution are presented, i.e. approach, architecture, components, implementation, etc.

Then there are the alternatives. This is a related work section that introduces some alternative solutions, either based on the Semantic Web or not. In other words, this section shows the competitors of the proposed solution.

Next, the costs and benefits are analyzed. The idea is to provide an overview of the costs associated to the solution. There is no need to enter into detailed economic costs, just some sketches of the implications associated to development costs, additional infrastructure requirements, etc. compared to the current situation. The objective is to make clear that the proposed solution has benefits that surpass the costs, but from a qualitative perspective, i.e. operational savings, improved customer and employee satisfaction, etc.

Another section also related to business aspect is risk assessment. The aim of this section is to document the critical assumptions that have been made in order to develop the solution, e.g. technical assumptions about scalability or future evolution of Semantic Web technologies. This section also includes a discussion of the proposed solution strengths, weaknesses, opportunities and threats (SWOT). Finally, the risks associated with implementing and not implementing the solution are presented.

The chapter ends with the future trends and the conclusions. Trends provide insight about the future of Semantic Web and e-business from the perspective of the business case topic. The closing conclusions reiterate the key issues that caused the solution to be proposed and restate the solution at a high-level. The overall benefits of the solution are also reminded, together with the main risks of doing nothing and continuing with a Semantic Web agnostic situation. Finally, the authors highlight the conclusions the reader should draw from the business case and the proponents' recommendations for next steps.

SEMANTIC WEB E-BUSINESS CASES

Now, it is time for an overview of the book structure. All chapters but the first one present different Semantic Web and e-business application scenarios. The first chapter presents an overview of the penetration of Semantic Web technology in industry. The authors report on the ongoing work in the cross-fertilization between industry and academia. In particular, they present a collection of application fields and use cases from European enterprises which are interested in the promises of Semantic Web technology. The chapter ends with the presentation of the current state of the technology and future trends as seen by prominent actors in the field.

Chapter II presents the European MYCAREVENT research project, which brought together European vehicle manufacturers, vehicle repair organisations, diagnostic tool manufacturers and IT specialists, including Semantic Web technologists, to study how to link together the wide range of information sets they use to identify faults and repair vehicles. Information is integrated and accessed through a service portal by using a 'shared language' for the project, a reference terminology to which the disparate terminologies of organisations participating in the project can be mapped. This shared vocabulary is materialised as a Semantic Web ontology.

The next chapter describes an approach to support operational support systems (OSS) integration across organisation boundaries. The requirement for such business-to-business (B2B) interfaces is expected to increase as is the need to carry out integration in much more flexible way. Existing approaches for integration tend to be implementation specific, operate at the syntactic level and are realised by programme code. Consequently they are inflexible due to their highly coupled nature and are costly to setup and maintain. An approach to decouple B2B interfaces is introduced, which allows them to be flexibly coupled as required with the use of scalable, semantic mediation.

Chapter IV deals with one of the most difficult problems dealing with applications interoperation, protocol mediation. This kind of mediation is concerned with non-matching message interchange patterns in applications interaction. The proposed solution focuses on solving the interoperation issues between two heterogeneous logistic provider systems, which use two different standard protocols: RosettaNet and EDIFACT. It includes an ontology for interaction choreography description and the software that implements the bridging mechanisms between these two protocols based on the knowledge captured by the ontology.

In the next chapter, authors report their practical experiences in building an ontology-based e-Recruitment system. This case study confirms previous findings in ontology engineering literature. First, to build ontology-based systems is still a tedious process due to the lack of proved and tested methods and tools supporting the entire life cycle of an ontology. And second, to reuse existing ontologies within new application contexts is currently related to efforts potentially comparable to the costs of a new implementation. These findings are used to further elaborate existing best practices towards a list of recommendations for the e-Recruitment domain.

Chapter VI also presents a European Research project, SEEMP. This project promotes increased partnership between labour market actors and the development of closer relations between private and public Employment Services. The need for a flexible collaboration gives rise to the issue of interoperability in both data exchange and share of services. SEEMP proposes a solution that relies on semantic services based collaboration among public and private Employment Services. Each actor in the marketplace has to care only about integrating with the marketplace and the Reference Ontology. The marketplace will offer services to support the interaction with other actors.

Chapter VII presents an ontology for customer complaint management, which has been developed in the EU funded project CCFORM, with the aim of establishing a European customer complaint portal. The objective is that any consumer can register a complaint against any party about any problem, at this portal. The portal should be multilanguage and sensitive to cross-border business regulations. A customer complaint ontology, which underpins the CC portal, makes all these features possible. The CContology comprises classifications of complaint problems, complaint resolutions, complaining parties, complaint-recipients, ''best-practices'', rules of complaint, etc.

In the following chapter, authors face the problem of the growth of e-commerce using software agents to support both customers and suppliers in buying and selling goods and services. The diversity of the actors involved leads to different conceptualizations of the needs and capabilities, giving rise to semantic incompatibilities between them. Authors propose an ontology-based information integration approach, exploiting the ontology mapping paradigm, by aligning consumer needs and the market capacities, in a semi-automatic mode and based on Semantic Web technology. The approach is improved by the application and exploitation of the information and trust relationships captured by the social networks.

Chapter IX studies the case of media convergence in newspaper media houses, which are evolving to highly dynamic and multi-channel communication mediums, where the different channels converge into a unified news editorial office. In order to cope with the new requirements arising from this change, machines must be aware of a greater part of the underlying semantics. Ontologies are a clear candidate to put this semantics into play, and Semantic Web technologies a good choice for Web-wide information integration. However, newspapers have made great investments in their current systems so a smooth transition is preferred. The chapter proposal is to build an ontological framework based on existing journalism and multimedia standards and to translate existing metadata to the Semantic Web.

The next chapter describes the OERN ontological extension to RosettaNet and shows how this extension can be used in business integrations to resolve data heterogeneities. RosettaNet is an industry-driven e-business process standard that defines common inter-company public processes and their associated business documents. The usage of Web ontology languages in RosettaNet collaborations can help accommodate partner heterogeneity in their set-up phase and can ease back-end integrations, enabling for example more competition in the purchasing processes.

The authors of the following chapter present the development of a formal representation, based on an OWL Semantic Web ontology for the Resource Event Agent (REA), which is a business ontology for ontology-driven enterprise system development. The objective is to overcome the limitation of the current specification, which is neither sufficiently explicit nor formal, and thus difficult to use in ontology-driven business information systems. The chapter discusses the choices made in redesigning REA and illustrates how this new formal representation can be used to support ontology-driven supply chain collaboration.

In Chapter XII, semantic extensions for Web services are presented as a mean to overcome business processes interoperability limitations due to purely syntactic approaches. Another drawback is that services cannot be discovered and composed dynamically by other semantic enabled systems slowing down the process of interaction between business partners. OWL-S is a suite of OWL ontologies and can be used to describe the compositions of Web services on the basis of matching semantics as well as to expose semantically enriched interfaces. The aim of this chapter is to describe an approach and its implementation that can be used to enable business processes for semantic based dynamic discovery, invocation and composition by translating BPEL process descriptions to the OWL-S suite of ontologies.

The authors of Chapter XIII analyse how telecommunications operators can improve their partnership networks and provide new services by solving the interoperability limitations of service-oriented architectures (SOA). The idea is to use Web services technology to create service providers federations and ontologies to support advanced matchmaking mechanisms based on a semantic metadata store. In particular, the proposal includes a Service Registration Authority that controls and enforces annotation policies in order to avoid the lack of uniformity in service descriptions. Furthermore, this solution enables enhanced service/component discovery and validation, helping software engineers to build services by composing building blocks.

The case study presented in Chapter XIV is about how networked ontologies satisfy the needs of such a knowledge intensive sector as the pharmaceutical one. The use of semantics helps bridging the gap between the different representations that different stakeholders have. The problem arises when the ontologies used to model the domain become too large and unmanageable. Networked ontologies can solve these problems. The particular case scenario considered by this chapter is the nomenclature of products in the pharmaceutical sector, which is currently under development in the EC funded FP6 project NeOn in order to develop a common Reference Ontology about drugs.

The authors of the next chapter highlight one of the key problems that the software industry has been facing due to the lack of alignment between the curricula offered by Universities and other kinds of education and training centres and the professional profiles demanded by companies and organizations. The chapter proposal is to provide a set of mechanisms and an intermediary system that allows companies to define and express their competency gaps and, at the same time, allow education centres to analyse those gaps and define the training plans to meet those needs.

In Chapter XVI an e-Banking case is presented, concentrating on how to offer a public access to efficient transactional stock market functionalities. Traditional service oriented architectures (SOA) succeed at providing reasonable good Web-based brokerage solutions but may lack on extensibility possibilities. By introducing Semantic Web Services (SWS) as a way to integrate third party services from distributed service providers, authors propose an innovative way that combines ontologies and SWS in order to allow different users to define their own stock change strategies regardless of the provider of information.

The last chapter presents a large-scale data integration and transaction management system for media rights, called OntologyX. Previous versions of this system have utilized lightweight schema and conventional Semantic Web technologies such as OWL. The current version employs formal ontology development in the SUO-KIF logical language and involves reuse an extension of a large formal ontology, the suggested upper merged ontology (SUMO). In particular, authors argue that extending from a large ontology will give the model greater coverage of more domains and expand business opportunities to expand into supporting more kinds of transaction management applications.

CONCLUSION

To sum up, the book includes a nice overview of the Semantic Web in e-business and a compendium of comprehensive business cases that illustrate, from a practical point of view, how Semantic Web is growing inside organizations. The call for contributions had a great success among enterprises that are leading Semantic Web research and development, chapters have been contributed by authors from Articulate Software, ATOS Origin, Bankinter, British Telecom, CSW Informatics, Diari Segre, France Telecom, Intelligent Software Components, Le Forem and Motorola. There has been also a great participation of academic and research institutions, in some cases coauthoring with authors coming from the industry.

On the other hand, an unintended outcome is a clear bias towards the European Semantic Web scenario, thought the call for contributions was distributed worldwide. The reason does not seem to be a more evolved market of Semantic Web solutions in Europe, thought the European Framework Program for research funding is playing an important role in supporting many projects pioneering Semantic Web in e-business scenarios. In fact many of the business cases come from European Framework Program research projects.

On the contrary, the European bias seems to be due to the editor's origin. This fact is also supported by the impressive participation of Spanish authors. At the end, it seems that we have not become as global as the World Wide Web and the Internet might make us think we are ;-)

REFERENCES

Baader, F., Calvanese, D., McGuinness, D., Nardi, D., & Patel-Schneider, P. (2003). *The Description Logic Handbook: Theory, Implementation and Applications*. Cambridge University Press.

Berners-Lee, T. (2000). *Weaving the Web*. New York, NY: HarperBusiness.

Cardoso, J. (2007). *Semantic Web Services: Theory, Tools and Applications*. Hershey, PA: IGI Global.

Daconta, M. C., Obrst, L. J., & Smith, K. T. (2003). *The Semantic Web: A Guide to the Future of XML, Web Services, and Knowledge Management*. Indianapolis, IN: Wiley.

Davis, M. (2008). *Semantic Wave 2008 Report: Industry Roadmap to Web 3.0 and Multibillion Dollar Market Opportunities*. Retrieved from http://www.project10x.com

Fensel, D. (2004). *Ontologies: A Silver Bullet for Knowledge Management and Electronic Commerce*. Heidelberg, DE: Springer.

Lacy, L. W. (2005). *Owl: Representing Information Using the Web Ontology Language*. Trafford Publishing.

Salam, A., & Stevens, R. (2007). *Semantic Web Technologies and e-business: Toward the Integrated Virtual Organization and Business Process Automation*. Hershey, PA: IGI Global.

Tauberer, J. (2008). *What is RDF and what is it good for?* Retrieved from http://www.rdfabout.com/intro

Yu, L. (2007). *Introduction to Semantic Web and Semantic Web services*. Boca Raton, FL: Chapman & Hall/CRC.

Roberto García, Editor

Acknowledgment

First of all, I would like to thank my family, especially Víctor and Rosa, for their comprehension and support during the book edition. Without them, this adventure would have been impossible to pursue.

A special thank goes to all the authors that have contributed their effort to make this book possible, and to all the reviewers that helped improve the quality of the contributions.

Roberto García, Editor

Section I
Introduction

Chapter I
Semantic Web Take-Off in a European Industry Perspective

Alain Léger
France Telecom R&D, France

Johannes Heinecke
France Telecom R&D, France

Lyndon J.B. Nixon
Freie Universität Berlin, Germany

Pavel Shvaiko
University of Trento, Italy

Jean Charlet
STIM, DPA/AP-Hopitaux Paris & Université Paris 6, France

Paola Hobson
Motorola Labs, UK

François Goasdoué
LRI, CNRS et Université Paris Sud XI, France

ABSTRACT

Semantic Web technology is being increasingly applied in a large spectrum of applications in which domain knowledge is conceptualized and formalized (e.g., by means of an ontology) in order to support diversified and automated knowledge processing (e.g., reasoning) performed by a machine. Moreover, through an optimal combination of (cognitive) human reasoning and (automated) machine processing (mimicking reasoning); it becomes possible for humans and machines to share more and more complementary tasks. The spectrum of applications is extremely large and to name a few: corporate portals and knowledge management, e-commerce, e-work, e-business, healthcare, e-government, natural language understanding and automated translation, information search, data and services integration, social networks and collaborative filtering, knowledge mining, business intelligence and so on. From a social and economic perspective, this emerging technology should contribute to growth in economic wealth, but it must also show clear cut value for everyday activities through technological transparency and efficiency. The penetration of Semantic Web technology in industry and in services is progressing slowly but accelerating as new success stories are reported. In this chapter we present ongoing work in the cross-fertilization between industry and academia. In particular, we present a collection of application fields and use cases from enterprises which are interested in the promises of Semantic Web technology.

The use cases are focused on the key knowledge processing components that will unlock the deployment of the technology in industry. The chapter ends with the presentation of the current state of the technology and future trends as seen by prominent actors in the field.

CURRENT SITUATION

As a result of the pervasive and user-friendly digital technologies emerging within our information society, Web content availability is increasing at an incredible rate but at the cost of being extremely multiform, inconsistent and very dynamic. Such content is totally unsuitable for machine processing, and so necessitates too much human interpretation and its respective costs in time and effort for both individuals and companies. To remedy this, approaches aim at abstracting from this complexity (i.e., by using ontologies) and offering new and enriched services able to process those abstractions (i.e., by mechanized reasoning) in a fully – and trusted - automated way. This abstraction layer is the subject of a very dynamic activity in research, industry and standardization which is usually called "Semantic Web" (see for example, DARPA, European IST Research Framework Program, W3C initiative, OASIS). The initial application of Semantic Web technology has focused on Information Retrieval (IR) where access through semantically annotated content, instead of classical (even sophisticated) statistical analysis, aimed to give far better results (in terms of precision and recall indicators). The next natural extension was to apply IR in the integration of enterprise legacy databases in order to leverage existing company information in new ways. Present research has turned to focusing on the seamless integration of heterogeneous and distributed applications and services (both intra- and inter-enterprise) through Semantic Web Services, and respectful of the legacy systems already in place, with the expectation of a fast return on investment (ROI) and improved efficiency in e-work and e-business.

This new technology takes its roots in the cognitive sciences, machine learning, natural language processing, multi-agents systems, knowledge acquisition, automated reasoning, logics and decision theory. It can be separated into two distinct – but cooperating fields - one adopting a formal and algorithmic approach for common sense automated reasoning (automated Web), and the other one "keeping the human being in the loop" for a socio-cognitive Semantic Web (automated social Web) which is gaining momentum today with the Web 2.0 paradigm[1].

On a large scale, industry awareness of Semantic Web technology has started at the EC level with the IST-FP5 thematic network Ontoweb[2] [2001-2004] which brought together around 50 motivated companies worldwide. Based on this experience, within IST-FP6, the Network of Excellence Knowledge Web[3] [2004-2008] made an in-depth analysis of the concrete industry needs in key economic sectors, and in a complementary way the IST-FP6 Network of Excellence REWERSE[4] was tasked with providing Europe with leadership in reasoning languages, also in view of a successful technology transfer and awareness activities targeted at the European industry for advanced Web systems and applications. This impetus will continue and grow up in the EU IST-FP7 [2007-2013][5].

The rest of the chapter is organized as follows. Four prototypical application fields are presented in Section 2, namely (1) healthcare and biotechnologies, (2) knowledge management (KM), (3) e-commerce and e-business, and finally, (4) multimedia and audiovisual services. Finally, Section 3 reports on a current vision of the achievements and some perspectives are given.

Overall Business Needs and Key Knowledge Processing Requirements

Use Case Collection

In order to support a large spectrum of application fields, two EU FP6 Networks of Excellence NoE-Knowledge Web and NoE-REWERSE are tasked with promoting transfer of best-of-the-art knowledge-based technology from academia to industry. The networks are made up of leading European Semantic Web research institutions that co-ordinate their research efforts while parallel efforts are made in Semantic Web education to increase the availability of skilled young researchers and practitioners and last but not the least, in pushing the take-up in Business and Industry.

In order to accelerate the transfer from research to industry, the objective of an Industry-Research co-operation is to establish a working relationship between Semantic Web researchers and an industry partner, in which research results being produced in an area of Semantic Web research will be prototypically applied to the industry partner's selected business case. The co-operation not only seeks to achieve an individual success story in terms of some specific research and a given business case, but also to establish the value of Semantic Web technologies to industrial application in a more general sense. It achieves this by demonstrating the use of Semantic Web technology in a business setting, exploring their usefulness in solving business problems and ensuring future applicability by directing researchers towards meeting industrial requirements in their work.

In NoE-Knowledge Web, an Industry Board was formed at the beginning of the network to bring together potential early adopters of Semantic Web technologies from across a wide spread of industry sectors. Industry Board members have been involved in many initiatives of the Knowledge Web Industry Area, including the collection of business use cases and their evaluation. In order to more directly achieve close co-operation between researchers and industry, each research activity in the network was invited to select a use case whose requirements closely correlated to what would be achieved in their research work. Results have been collected and reported in July 2007[6].

Currently in 2007, this Industry Board consisted of about 50 members (e.g., France Telecom, British Telecom, Institut Français du Pétrole, Illy Caffè, Trenitalia, Daimler AG, Thalès, EADS, ...) from across 14 nations and 13 economic sectors (e.g., telecoms, energy, food, logistics, automotive,...).

The companies were requested to provide illustrative examples of actual or hypothetical deployment of Semantic Web technology in their business settings. This was followed up with face-to-face meetings between researchers and industry experts from the companies to gain additional information about the provided use cases. Thus, in 2004, a total of 16 use cases were collected from 12 companies. In 2007, through many workshops and Industry forum sessions at major Semantic Web conferences, more than a hundred use cases were available or illustrative of the current trend to introduce Semantic Web technology in the main stream.

As shown in Figure 1, where the use cases are broken down according to the industry sector, collected cases are from 9 industry sectors, with the highest number of the use cases coming from the service industry (19%) and media & communications (18%) respectively. This initial collection of use cases can be found in (Nixon L. et al., 2004), and an updated selection is available on the Knowledge Web Industry portal[7].

The co-operations have been a very challenging activity, given the early state of much cutting edge Semantic Web research and the differences in perspective between academia and business.

Figure 1. Breakdown of use cases by industry sector

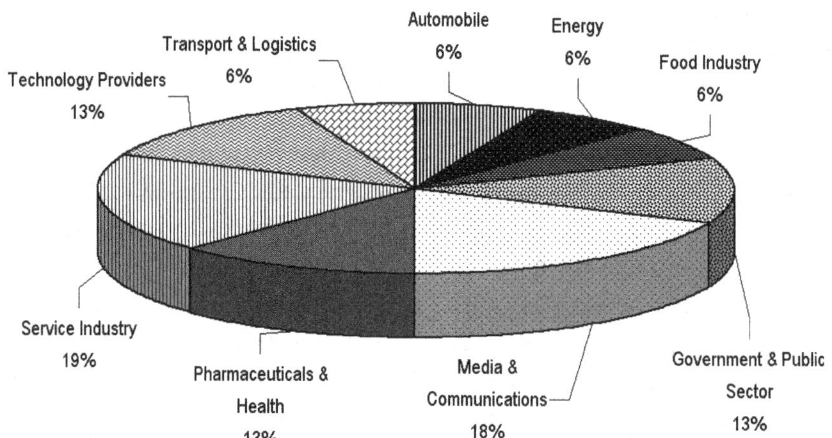

However, successes have been reported, not only in the production of some prototypical solutions and demos which can be shown to industry and business top managers, but also in making researchers more aware of the importance of their work to solving business problems and the earlier recognition by academics of industry needs and expectations and so integrating them to their research agenda.

Hence, the Industry-Research co-operations in NoE-Knowledge Web and NoE-REWERSE must be seen as a significant first attempt to align the ambitious cutting edge work on Semantic Web technologies done by leading researchers in Europe and the real world business problems encountered by the European industry which may find a potential solution in those same Semantic Web technologies. Given a continued rise in awareness among Semantic Web researchers of the applicability of their work to industry and the continued rise in awareness among industry of the potential of the work of Semantic Web researchers, which has been begun in IST-NoEs, in IST-R&D projects, but also clearly in industry (SMEs and large companies), the technology transfer is gradually evolving.

Use Case Analysis

A preliminary analysis of the use cases has been carried out in order to obtain a first vision (end of 2004) of the current industrial needs and to estimate the expectations from knowledge-based technology with respect to those needs. The industry experts were asked to indicate the existing legacy solutions in their use cases, the service functionalities they would be offered and the technological locks they encountered, and eventually how they expected that Semantic Web technology could resolve those locks. As a result, this analysis has provided an overview of:

- Types of business or service problems where the knowledge-based technology is considered to bring a plausible solution.
- Types of technological issues (and the corresponding research challenges) which knowledge based technology is expected to overcome.

Figure 2 shows a breakdown of the areas in which the industry experts thought Semantic Web technology could provide a solution. For example, for nearly half of the collected use cases, data integration and semantic search were areas

Figure 2. Breakdown of use cases by industry sector

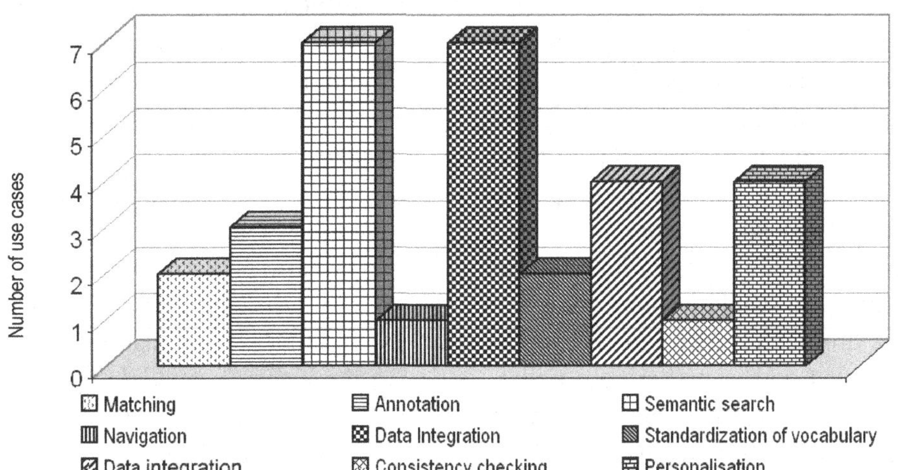

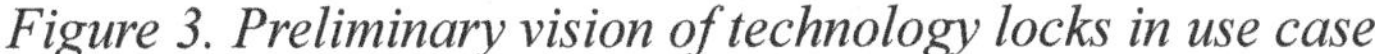

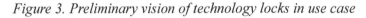

Figure 3. Preliminary vision of technology locks in use case

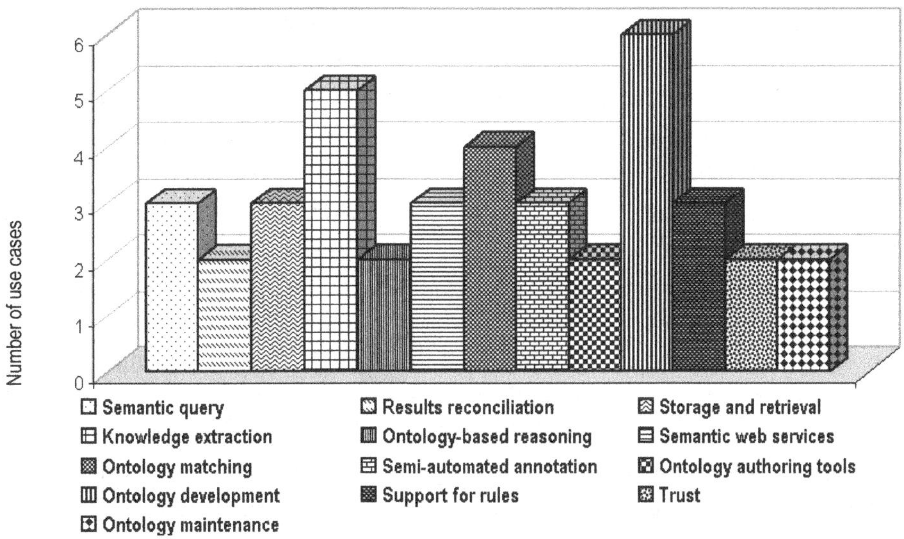

where industry was looking for knowledge-based solutions. Other areas mentioned, in a quarter of use cases, were solutions to data management and personalization.

Figure 3 shows a breakdown of the technology locks identified in the use cases. There are three technology locks which occur the most often in the collected use cases. These are: (1) ontology development, i.e., modeling of a business domain, authoring, reusing existing ontologies; (2) knowledge extraction, i.e., populating ontologies by extracting data from legacy systems; and (3) ontology mapping, i.e., resolving semantic heterogeneity among multiple ontologies.

Below, an illustration is given, with the help of a use case from the collection, how a concrete business problem can be used to indicate the technology locks for which knowledge-based solutions potentially might be useful. This use case addresses the problem of intelligent search of documents in the corporate data of an international coffee company.

The company generates a large amount of internal data and its employees encounter difficulties in finding the data they need for the research and development of new solutions. The aim is to improve the quality of the document retrieval and to enable personalization services for individual users when searching or viewing the corporate data. As technology locks, the expert mentioned here the corporate domain ontology development and maintenance, and semantic querying.

Eventually, this analysis (by experts estimations) has provided with a preliminary understanding of scope of the current industrial needs and the current concrete technology locks where knowledge-based technology is expected to provide a plausible solution. However, to be able to answer specific industrial requirements, there is the need to conduct further a detailed technical analysis of the use cases, thereby associating to each technology lock a concrete knowledge processing task and a component realizing its functionalities.

Knowledge Processing Tasks and Components

Based on the information processing needs identified during the technical use cases analysis (Shvaiko P. et al., 2004), a typology of common knowledge processing tasks and a library of high level components for realizing those tasks, was built, see Table 1. The first tentative typology includes twelve processing tasks. Let us discuss knowledge processing tasks and components of Table 1 in more detail:

- *Ontology management, ontology merging and ontology manager.* These tasks and component are in charge of ontology maintenance (e.g., reorganizing taxonomies, resolving name conflicts, browsing ontologies, editing concepts) and merging multiple ontologies (e.g., by taking the union of the axioms) with respect to evolving business case requirements, see (Dou D. et al., 2005) (McGuiness D. et al., 2000) (Protégé[8]), OAEI-2007 Ontology Alignment Evaluation Initiative[9], NeOn[10] (Networked Evolving Ontologies) and Ontology Matching survey site[11].
- *Ontology matching, matching results analysis, producing explanations and match manager.* These tasks and component are in charge of (on-the-fly and semi-automatic) determination of semantic mappings between the entities of multiple schemas and ontologies, see (Rahm E. et al., 2001) (Shvaiko P. and Euzenat, 2005), (Euzenat J. and Shvaiko P., 2007). Mappings are typically specified with the help of a similarity relation which can be either in the form of a coefficient rating match quality in the (0,1] range (i.e., the higher the coefficient, the higher the similarity between the entities, see (Billig A. et al., 2002) (Ehrig M. et al., 2004) (Euzenat J. et al., 2004) (Do H. H. et al., 2002) (Zhong J. et al., 2002) or in the form of a logical relation (e.g., equivalence, subsumption), see (Giunchiglia F. et al., 2003) (Giunchiglia F. et al., 2004). The mappings might need to be ordered according to some criteria, see (Di Noia T. et al., 2003) (Do H. H. et al., 2002).

  Finally, explanations of the mappings might be also required, see (Dhamankar R. et al., 2004) (Shvaiko P. et al., 2005). Matching systems may produce mappings that may not be intuitively obvious to human users. In order for users to trust the mappings (and thus use them), they need information about them. They need access to the sources that were used to determine semantic correspondences between terms and potentially they need to understand how deductions and manipulations are performed. The issue here is to present explanations in a simple and clear way to the user.

Table 1. Typology of knowledge processing tasks & components

N°	Knowledge processing tasks	Components
1	Ontology Management	Ontology Manager
2	Ontology Matching	Match Manager
3	Ontology Matching results Analysis	Match Manager
4	Data Translation	Wrapper
5	Results Reconciliation	Results Reconciler
6	Composition of Web Services	Planner
7	Content Annotation	Annotation manager
8	Reasoning	Reasoner
9	Semantic Query Processing	Query Processor
10	Ontology Merging	Ontology Manager
11	Producing explanations	Match Manager
12	Personalization	Profiler

- *Data translation and wrapper.* This task and component is in charge of automatic manipulation (e.g., translation, exchange) of instances between heterogeneous information sources storing their data in different formats (e.g., RDF, SQL DDL, XML …), see (Hull R. 1997) (Petrini J. et al., 2004) (Velegrakis Y. et al., 2005) (Halevy A. et al., 2006). Here, mappings are taken as input (for example, from the match manager component) and are the support for generating query expressions that perform the required semantic and syntactical manipulations with data instances coming from heterogeneous environment.
- *Results reconciliation and results reconciler.* This task and component is in charge of determining an optimal solution, in terms of contents (no information duplication, etc.) and routing performance, for returning results from the queried information sources, see (Preguica N. et al., 2003).
- *Composition of Web services and planner.* This task and component is in charge of automated composition of Web services into executable processes (Orchestration). Composed Web services perform new functionalities by specific on demand interaction with pre-existing services that are published on the Web, see surveys from (Chan et al., 2007) (Berardi et al., 2005) (Hull et al., 2005) (Pistore et al., 2005) (Roman et al., 2005) (Traverso P. et al., 2004) (Cardoso et al., 2003) (McIlraith et al., 2001). From a business viewpoint, it remains a key challenge to be overcome, as the businesses react very positively to the need for a very effective integration technology and for more agility in a very competitive worldwide economy. In the meantime, reducing interoperability problems will open opportunities for easier innovative solutions and for the increase in cooperation between enterprises. This should result in re-combinations of businesses the technology provides and so will have a profound impact on business and economic workflows.
- *Content annotation and annotation manager.* This task and component is in charge of automatic production of metadata for the contents, see aceMedia[12] for multimedia annotation. Annotation manager takes

as input the (pre-processed) contents and domain knowledge and produces as output a database of content annotations. In addition to the automatic production of content metadata, prompt mechanisms offer the user the possibility to enrich the content annotation by adding extra information (e.g., title, name of a location, title of an event, names of people) that could not be automatically detected.

- *Automated reasoning.* This task and component is in charge of providing logical reasoning services (e.g., subsumption, concept satisfiability, instance checking tests), see (Haarslev V. et al., 1999-2007). For example, when dealing with multimedia annotations, logical reasoning can be exploited in order to check consistency of the annotations against the set of spatial (e.g., left, right, above, adjacent, overlaps) and temporal (e.g., before, after, during, co-start, co-end) constraints. This can certify that the objects detected in the multimedia content correspond semantically to the concepts defined in the domain ontology. For example, in the racing domain, the automated reasoner should check whether a car is located on a road or whether the grass and sand are adjacent to the road.
- *Semantic query processing and query processor.* This task and component is in charge of rewriting a query posed by a human being or a machine, by using terms which are explicitly specified in the model of domain knowledge in order to provide semantics preserving query answering, see (Mena E. et al., 1996) (Halevy et al., 2001) (Calvanese et al., 2002) (IST-IP aceMedia 2004). Examples of queries are "Give me all the games played on grass" or "Give me all the games of double players", in the tennis domain. Finally, users should be able to query by sample content e.g. an image. In this case, the system should perform an intelligent search of images and videos (e.g., by using semantic annotations) where, for example, the same event or type of activity takes place.
- *Personalization and profiler.* This task and component is in charge of tailoring services available from the system to the specificity of each user, see (Antoniou G. et al., 2004). For example, generation and updating of user profiles, recommendation generation, inferring user preferences, and so on. For example users might want to share annotations within trusted user networks, thus having services of personal metadata management and contacts recommendation. Also, a particular form of personalization, which is media adaptation, may require knowledge-based technology and consistent delivery of the contents to a broad range user terminals (e.g., PDA, mobile phone, portable PC).

KEY APPLICATION SECTORS AND TYPICAL TECHNOLOGY PROBLEMS

Healthcare and Biotechnologies

The medical domain is a favourite target for Semantic Web applications just as the expert system was for artificial intelligence applications 20 years ago. The medical domain is very complex: medical knowledge is difficult to represent in a computer format, making the sharing of information even more difficult. Semantic Web solutions become very promising in this context.

One of the main mechanisms of the Semantic Web - resource description using annotation principles - is of major importance in the medical informatics (or sometimes called bioinformatics) domain, especially as regards the sharing of these resources (e.g. medical knowledge on the Web or genomic database). Through the years, the IR area has been developed by medicine: medical thesauri are enormous (e.g., more than 1,600,000 terms in Unified Medical Language System, UMLS[13]) and are principally used for bibliographic indexation. Nevertheless, the MeSh thesaurus (Medical Subject Heading) or UMLS have been used to provide data semantics with varying degrees of difficulty. Finally, the Web services technology allows us to imagine some solutions to the interoperability problem, which is substantial in medical informatics. Below, we will describe current research, results and expected perspectives in these biomedical informatics topics in the context of Semantic Web.

Biosciences Resources Sharing

In the functional genomics domain, it is necessary to have access to several databases and knowledge bases which are accessible separately on the Web but are heterogeneous in their structure as well as in their terminology. Among such resources, we can mention SWISSPROT[14] where the gene products are annotated by the Gene Ontology[15], Gen-Bank[16], etc. When comparing these resources it is easy to see that they propose the same information in different formats. The XML language, which acts as a common data structure for the different knowledge bases, provides at most a syntactic Document Type Definition (DTD) which does not resolve the semantic interoperability problem.

One of the solutions comes from the Semantic Web with a mediator approach (Wiederhold G., 1992) which allows for the accessing of different resources with an ontology used as the Interlingua pivot. For example and in another domain than that of genomics, the NEUROBASE project (Barillot C. et al., 2003) attempts to federate different neuro-imagery information bases situated in different clinical or research areas. The proposal consists of defining an architecture that allows the access to and the sharing of experimental results or data treatment methodologies. It would be possible to search in the various data bases for similar results or for images with peculiarities or to perform data mining analysis between several databases. The mediator of NEUROBASE has been tested on decision support systems in epilepsy surgery.

Ontologies for Coding Systems

The main usage of ontologies in medical domain is as index of coding system: after using thesauri for indexing medical bibliography (PubMed with the Mesh[17]), the goal is to index Electronic Health records with medical concept in order to enhance information retrieval or to allow epidemiological studies. For that purpose, several countries intend to use the SNOMED, an international classification of concepts organized in eight axes (Spackman et al., 2002). Except the problem of languages, this classification exists in two versions: a classification of 160,000 concepts (SNOMED-I V3.5) and an ontology, which is the evolution of the preceding one, of 330,000 concepts, SNOMED CT. The use of ontologies of such a size is difficult. Some authors describe them as *Reference Ontology* which cannot be accessed without an *interface ontology* (Rosenbloom et al., 2006). Notwithstanding, UK national health system (NHS) is integrating SNOMED CT and it will be interesting to examine the results of this industrial deployment[18].

Web Services for Interoperability

The Web services technology can propose some solutions to the interoperability problematic. We describe now a new approach based on a "patient envelope" and we conclude with the implementation of this envelope based on the Web services technology.

The patient envelope is a proposition of the Electronic Data Interchange for Healthcare group (EDI-Santé[19]) with an active contribution from the ETIAM[20] society. The objective of the work is on filling the gap between "free" communication, using standard and generic Internet tools, and "totally structured" communication as promoted by CEN (in the Working Group IV "Technology for Interoperability"[21]) or HL7[22]. After the worldwide analysis of existing standards, the proposal consists of an "intermediate" structure of information, related to one patient, and storing the minimum amount of data (i.e. exclusively useful data) to facilitate the interoperability between communicating peers. The "free" or the "structured" information is grouped into a folder and transmitted in a secure way over the existing communication networks (Cordonnier E. et al., 2003). This proposal has reached widespread adoption with the distribution by Cegetel. rss of a new medical messaging service, called "Sentinelle", fully supporting the patient envelope protocol and adapted tools.

After this milestone, EDI-Santé is promoting further developments based on ebXML and SOAP (Simple Object Access Protocol) in specifying exchange (see items 1 and 2 below) and medical (see items 3 and 4 below) properties:

1. *Separate what is mandatory* to the transport and management of the message (e.g., patient identification from what constitutes the "job" part of the message.
2. *Provide a "container" for the message*, collecting the different elements, texts, pictures, videos, etc.
3. *Consider the patient as the unique object of the transaction.* Such an exchange cannot be anonymous. It concerns a sender and an addressee who are involved in the exchange and who are responsible. A patient can demand to know the content of the exchange in which (s)he is the object, which implies a data structure which is unique in the form of a triple {sender, addressee, patient}.
4. *The conservation of the exchange semantics.* The information about a patient is multiple in the sense that it comes from multiple sources and has multiple forms and supporting data (e.g., database, free textual document, semi-structured textual document, pictures). It can be fundamental to maintain the existing links between elements, to transmit them together, e.g., a scanner and the associated report, and to be able to prove it.

The interest of such an approach is that it prepares the evolution of the transmitted document from a free form document (from proprietary ones to normalized ones as XML) to elements respecting HL7v3 or EHRCOM data types. In France, the GIP-DMP[23] retains such an approach (in conjunction with the Clinical Document Architecture of HL7[24]) for the implementation of the exchanges of the *Dossier Médical Personnel* (a future national electronic health record).

What is Next in the Healthcare Domain?

These different projects and applications highlight the main consequence of the Semantic Web being expected by the medical communities: the sharing and integration of heterogeneous information or knowledge. The answers to the different issues are the use of mediators, a knowledge-based system, and ontologies, which should be based in the mid term on normalized languages such as RDF, OWL but also in addition to come OWL-S, SAWSDL, WSML, SWRL, or RuleML. The work of the Semantic Web community must take into account these expectations, see for example the FP6 projects[25,26,27]. Finally, it is interesting to note that the Semantic Web is an integrated vision of the medical community's problems (thesauri, ontologies, indexation, and inference) and provides a real opportunity to synthesize and reactivate some research directions (Charlet J. et al., 2002).

Knowledge Management

Leveraging Knowledge Assets in Companies

Knowledge is one of the key success factors for enterprises, both today and in the future. Therefore, company knowledge management (KM) has been identified as a strategic tool. However, if for KM, information technology is one of the foundational elements, KM in turn, is also interdisciplinary by its nature. In particular, it includes human resource management as well as enterprise organization and culture[28]. KM is viewed as the management of the knowledge arising from business activities, aiming at leveraging both the use and the creation of that knowledge for two main objectives: capitalization of corporate knowledge and durable innovation fully aligned with the strategic objectives of the organization.

Conscious of this key factor of productivity in an ever faster changing ecosystem, the European KM Framework (CEN/ISSS[29], KnowledgeBoard[30]) has been designed to support a common European understanding of KM, to show the value of this emerging approach and to help organizations towards its successful implementation. The Framework is based on empirical research and practical experiences in this field from all over Europe and the rest of the world. The European KM Framework addresses all of the relevant elements of a KM solution and serves as a reference basis for all types of organizations, which aim to improve their performance by handling knowledge in a better way.

Benefits of Knowledge-Based KM

The knowledge backbone is made up of ontologies that define a shared conceptualization of an application domain and provide the basis for defining metadata that have precisely defined semantics, and are therefore machine-interpretable. Although the first KM approaches and solutions have shown the benefits of ontologies and related methods, a large number of open research issues still exist that have to be addressed in order to make Semantic Web technology a complete success for KM solutions:

- Industrial KM applications *have to avoid any kind of overhead as far as possible. A seamless integration of knowledge creation* (i.e., content and metadata specification) and knowledge access (i.e., querying or browsing) into the working environment is required. Strategies and methods are needed to support the creation of knowledge, as side effects of activities that are carried out anyway. These requirements mean emergent semantics that can be supported through ontology learning, which should reduce the current time consuming task of building-up and maintaining ontologies.
- *Access to as well as presentation of knowledge has to be context-dependent.* Since the context is setup by the current business task, and thus by the business process being handled, a tight integration of business process management and knowledge management is required. KM approaches can provide a promising starting point for smart push services that will proactively deliver relevant knowledge for carrying out the task at hand more effectively.
- *Conceptualization has to be supplemented by personalization.* On the one hand, taking into account the experience of the user and his/her personal needs is a prerequisite in order to avoid information overload, and on the other hand, to deliver knowledge at the right level of granularity and from the right perspective at the right time.

The development of knowledge portals serving the needs of companies or communities is still a manual process. Ontologies and related metadata provide a promising conceptual basis for generating parts of such knowledge portals. Obviously, among others, conceptual models of the domain, of the users and of the tasks are needed. The *generation of knowledge portals* has to be supplemented with the (semi-) automated evolution of portals. As business environments and strategies change rather rapidly, *KM portals have to be kept up-to-date in this fast changing environment.* Evolution of portals should also include some mechanisms *to 'forget' outdated knowledge.*

KM solutions will be based on a combination of intranet-based functionalities and mobile functionalities in the very near future. Semantic technologies are a promising approach to meet the needs of mobile environments, like location-aware personalization and adaptation of the presentation to the specific needs of mobile devices, i.e., the presentation of the required information at an appropriate level of granularity. In essence, employees should have access to the KM application *anywhere* and *anytime.*

Peer-to-peer computing (P2P), social networking (W2.0), combined with Semantic Web technology, will be a strong move towards getting rid of the more centralized KM approaches that are currently used in ontology-based solutions. W2.0 scenarios open up the way to derive consensual conceptualizations among employees within an enterprise in a bottom-up manner.

Virtual organizations are becoming more and more important in business scenarios, mainly due to decentralization and globalization. Obviously, semantic interoperability between different knowledge sources, as well as trust, is necessary in inter-organizational KM applications.

The integration of KM applications with *e-learning* (e.g., skill management in companies) is an important field that enables a lot of synergy between these two areas. KM solutions and e-learning must be integrated from both an organizational and an IT point of view. Clearly, interoperability and integration of (metadata) standards are needed to realize such integration.

Knowledge management is obviously a very promising area for exploiting Semantic Web technology. Document-based portals KM solutions have already reached their limits, whereas semantic technology opens the way to meet KM requirements in the future.

Knowledge-Based KM Applications

In the context of geographical team dispersion, multilingualism and business unit autonomy, usually a company wants a solution allowing for the identification of strategic information, the secured distribution of this information and the creation of transverse working groups. Some applicative solutions allowed for the deployment of an Intranet intended for all the marketing departments of the company worldwide, allowing for a better division of and a greater accessibility to information, but also capitalisation on the total knowledge. There are four crucial points that aim at easing the work of the various marketing teams in a company: (1) Business intelligence, (2) Skill and team management[31], (3) Process management[32] and (4) Rich document access and management[33].

Thus, a system connects the "strategic ontologies" of the company group (brands, competitors, geographical areas, etc.) with the users, via the automation of related processes (research, classification, distribution, knowledge representation). The result is a dynamic semantic system of navigation (research, classification) and collaborative features.

At the end from a functional point of view, a KM system organises skill and knowledge management within a company in order to improve interactivity, collaboration and information sharing. This constitutes a virtual workspace which facilitates work between employees that speak different languages, automates the creation of work groups, organises and capitalises structured and unstructured, explicit or tacit data of the company, and offers advanced features of capitalisation (Bonifacio M. et al., 2005) (Brunschweig B. et al., 2005) (Nordheim D. et al., 2005).

Eventually, the semantic backbone makes possible to cross a qualitative gap by providing cross-lingual data.

E-Commerce and E-Business

Electronic commerce is mainly based on the exchange of information between involved stakeholders using a telecommunication infrastructure. There are two main scenarios: business-to-customer (B2C) and business-to-business (B2B).

B2C applications enable service providers to promote their offers, and for customers to find offers which match their demands. By providing unified access to a large collection of frequently updated offers and customers, an electronic marketplace can match the demand and supply processes within a commercial mediation environment.

B2B applications have a long history of using electronic messaging to exchange information related to services previously agreed among two or more businesses. Early plain-text telex communication systems were followed by electronic data interchange (EDI) systems based on terse, highly codified, well structured, messages. A new generation of B2B systems is being developed under the ebXML (electronic business in XML) heading. These will use classification schemes to identify the context in which messages have been, or should be, exchanged. They will also introduce new techniques for the formal recording of business processes, and for the linking of business processes through the exchange of well-structured business messages. ebXML will also develop techniques that will allow businesses to identify new suppliers through the use of registries that allow users to identify which services a supplier can offer. ebXML needs to include well managed multilingual ontologies that can be used to help users to match needs expressed in their own language with those expressed in the service providers language(s) see (Guarino N. 1999) (Zyl J. et al., 200) (Lehtola A. et al., 2003) (Heinecke J. et al., 2003) (Benatallah B et al., 2005).

Knowledge-Based E-Commerce and E-Business Value

At present, ontology and more generally knowledge-based systems appear as a central issue for the development of efficient and profitable e-commerce and e-business solutions. However, because of the actual situation i.e. the partial standardization of business models, processes, and knowledge architectures, it is currently difficult for companies to achieve the promised ROI from knowledge-based e-commerce and e-business.

Moreover, a technical barrier exists that is delaying the emergence of e-commerce, lying in the need for applications to *meaningfully share information*, taking into account the lack of reliability, security and eventually trust in the Internet. This fact may be explained by the variety of e-commerce and e-business systems employed by businesses and the various ways these systems are configured and used. As an important remark, such *interoperability problems* become particularly severe when a large number of trading partners attempt to agree and define the standards for interoperation, which is precisely a main condition for maximizing the ROI indicator.

Although it is useful to strive for the adoption of a single common domain-specific standard for content and transactions, such a task is often difficult to achieve, particularly in cross-industry initiatives, where companies co-operate and compete with one another. Some examples of the difficulties are:

- *Commercial practices* may vary widely, and consequently, cannot always be aligned for a variety of technical, practical, organizational and political reasons.
- *The complexity of a global description* of the organizations themselves: their products and

services (independently or in combination), and the interactions between them remain a formidable task.
- It is not always possible to establish *a priori rules* (technical or procedural) governing participation in an electronic marketplace.

Adoption of a single common standard may limit business models which could be adopted by trading partners, and therefore, potentially reduce their ability to fully participate in e-commerce.

A knowledge-based approach has the potential to significantly accelerate the penetration of electronic commerce within vertical industry sectors, by *enabling interoperability at the business level*. This will enable services to adapt to the rapidly changing business ecosystem.

Knowledge-Based E-Commerce and E-Business Applications

The Semantic Web brings opportunities to industry to create new services[34], extend markets, and even develop new businesses since it enables the inherent meaning of the data available in the Internet to be accessible to systems and devices able to interpret and reason at the knowledge level. This in turn leads to new revenue opportunities, since information becomes more readily accessible and usable. For example, a catering company whose Web site simply lists the menus available is less likely to achieve orders compared to one whose menus are associated with related metadata about the contents of the dishes, their origin (e.g., organic, non-genetically modified, made with local produce), links to alternative dishes for special diets, personalised ordering where a user profile can be established which automatically proposes certain menu combinations depending on the occasion (e.g., wedding banquet, business lunch). The latter case assumes that both provider-side knowledge generation and knowledge management tools are available, such that the asset owner can readily enhance their data with semantic meaning, and client-side tools are available to enable machine interpretation of the semantic descriptions related to the products being offered, such that the end user can benefit from the available and mined knowledge. Examples of some possible application areas were studied by the Agent Cities project[35].

In the e-business area Semantic Web technology can improve standard business process management tools. One prototypical case is in the area of logistics. The application of knowledge technology on top of today's business management tools enables the automation of major tasks of business process management[36] see (Semantic Web Case Studies for eBusiness 2005).

In one of the Knowledge Web Industry-Research co-operations, a number of scenarios within the **B2B integration scenario** were identified, involving data mediation, discovery, and composition of services. All of these use cases have been evaluated according to a community-agreed methodology defined by the SWS challenge methodology with satisfying success levels defined by the methodology. This is an important step when proving the added value of the Semantic Web service technology applied to B2B integration domain. In addition, the standardization process has been partially finalized within the OASIS Semantic Execution Environment Technical Committee (OASIS SEE TC) and W3C Semantic Annotations for WSDL and XML Schema (W3C SAWSDL WG). However, the standardization process in both groups is still ongoing, but under business pressure has concluded respectively on SAWSDL in 2007 and SESA framework early 2008.

The Industry-Research co-operation has *demonstrably solved a business case from the B2B domain*. We have shown how the technology deals with requirements from B2B domain and how this technology reacts to changes in back-end systems which might occur over the system's lifetime.

The research is not yet ready for industry. It must be shown how the technology is layered on the existing infrastructure and how it interacts with existing systems. For this purpose some parts of the technology need to be standardized (such as grounding mechanisms built on SAWSDL or the architecture). In particular, the grounding mechanism built on SAWSDL provides a "common interface" between semantic descriptions and non-semantic descriptions (in our case WSDL). The standardization is still ongoing while at the same time, the alignment of service semantics with this grounding mechanism must be further finalised. While it has been demonstrated how this is possible to be done and what the added value of this approach is, *the complexity of business standards still needs to be addressed.*

In addition, a prototype is available[37] and has been provided to NoE-Knowledge Web industry partners see Figure 4.

The following scenarios have been realised as part of the Semantic Web Services Challenge:

- **Mediation Scenario** (http://sws-challenge.org/wiki/index.php/Workshop_Budva). Addressing the mediation scenario for B2B integration when proprietary back-end systems of one company needed to be integrated with a partner using RosettaNet standard. Whole scenario has been successfully addressed.
- **Discovery Scenario** (http://sws-challenge.org/wiki/index.php/Workshop_Athens). Addressing discovery scenario when a supplier needed to be discovered and selected from suitable ones. Whole scenario has been successfully addressed.
- **Composition Scenario** (http://sws-challenge.org/wiki/index.php/Workshop_Innsbruck). Addressing composition scenario when more services can satisfy the user need. Whole scenario has been successfully addressed.

Work will continue and the co-operation plans to address additional scenarios of the SWS challenge, namely scenarios when services can be filtered based on non-functional properties (QoS, financial, etc.). In addition, a tutorial was given on SWS in the context of business process management at ICWS'07 conference, and the authors co-organize the workshop on service composition and SWS challenge held at the Web Intelligence

Figure 4. Semantic Web services integration in B2B

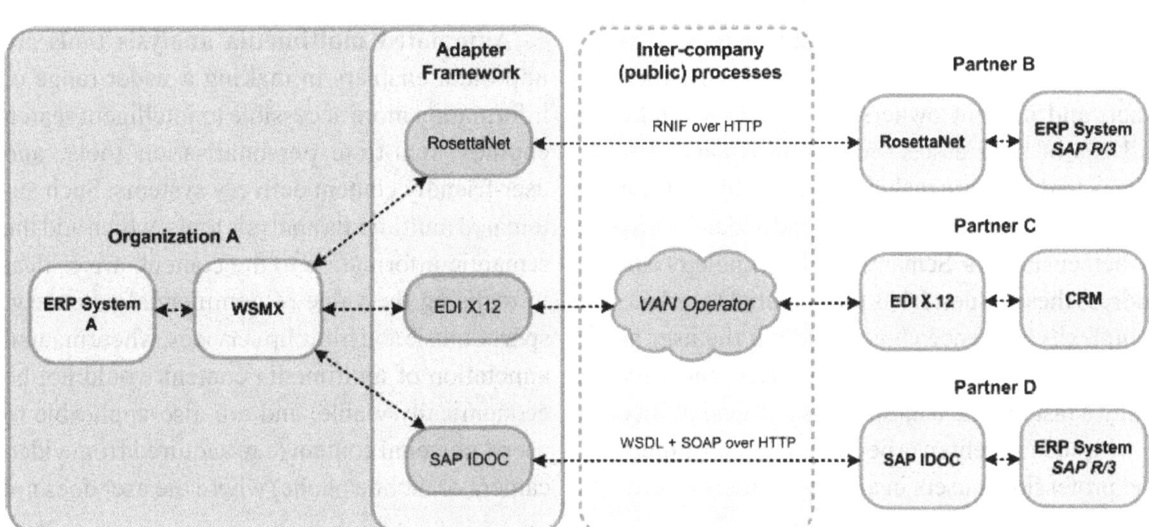

conference[38] (Vitvar T. et al., 2007a) (Vitvar T. et al., 2007b) (Hasselwanter T. et al., 2007).

Multimedia and Audiovisual Services

Practical realisation of the Semantic Web vision is actively being researched by a number of experts, some of them within European collaborative projects, and others within company specific initiatives. Earlier projects such as SEKT[39] and DIP, mainly focused on enhancing text based applications from a knowledge engineering perspective. Although significant benefits in unlocking access to valuable knowledge assets are realised via these projects, in various domains such as digital libraries, enterprise applications, and financial services, it was soon recognised that there was a challenging and potentially highly profitable area of research into the integration of multimedia and Semantic Web technologies for multimedia content based applications. Projects such as aceMedia, BOEMIE, and MESH are examples of initiatives aiming to advance the use of semantics and reasoning for improved multimedia applications such as automated annotation, content summarisation, and personalised content syndication.

The drive for application of semantic technologies in the multimedia and content domains comes from a proliferation of audiovisual devices and services which have led to an exponential growth in available content. Users express dissatisfaction at not being able to find what they want, and content owners are unable to make full use of their assets. Service providers seek means to differentiate their offerings by making them more targeted toward the individual needs of their customers. Semantic Web technology can address these issues. It has the potential to reduce complexity, enhance choice, and put the user at the center of the application or service, and with today's fast mobile data services and availability of wifi, such benefits can be enjoyed by consumers and professional users in all environments using all their personal devices, in the home, at work, in the car and on the go.

Semantic Web technologies can enhance multimedia based products to increase the value of multimedia assets such as content items which are themselves the articles for sale (songs, music videos, sports clips, news summaries, etc) or where they are used as supporting sales of other goods (e.g. promotional images, movie trailers etc). Value is added in search applications, such that returned items more closely match the user's context, interests, tasks, preference history etc, as well as in proactive push applications such as personalised content delivery and recommendation systems, and even personalised advertising. However, applications such as content personalisation, where a system matches available content to the user's stated and learned preferences, thereby enabling content offerings to be closely targeted to the user's wishes, rely on the availability of semantic metadata describing the content in order to make the match. Currently, metadata generation is mostly manual, which is costly and time consuming. Multimedia analysis techniques which go beyond the signal level approach to a semantic analysis have the potential to create automatic annotation of content, thereby opening up new applications which can unlock the commercial value of content archives (Stamou et al., 2006) (Stamou et al., 2005).

Automated multimedia analysis tools are important enablers in making a wider range of information more accessible to intelligent search engines, real-time personalisation tools, and user-friendly content delivery systems. Such automated multimedia analysis tools, which add the semantic information to the content, are critical in realising the value of commercial assets e.g. sports, music and film clip services, where manual annotation of multimedia content would not be economically viable, and are also applicable to users' personal content (e.g. acquired from video camera or mobile phone) where the user does not have time, or a suitable user interface, to annotate all their content.

Multimedia ontologies are needed to structure and make accessible the knowledge inherent in the multimedia content, and reasoning tools are needed to assist with identification of relevant content in an automated fashion. Although textual analysis and reasoning tools have been well researched, and despite the projects funded by the European Commission in the 6th framework, fewer tools are available for semantic multimedia analysis, since the problem domain is very challenging. However, automated multimedia content analysis tools such as those being studied within aceMedia[40] are a first step in making a wider range of information more accessible to intelligent search engines, real-time personalisation tools, and user-friendly content delivery systems.

Furthermore, interoperability of multimedia tools is important in enabling a wide variety of applications and services on multiple platforms for diverse domains. The W3C Multimedia Semantics Incubator Group reported on interoperability issues[41] and it is clear that a common framework using Semantic Web languages tools is essential for full exploitation of the potential of multimedia assets. Interoperability is essential in achieving commercial success with semantic multimedia applications, since it enables multiple manufacturers, content providers and service providers to participate in the market. This in turn enables consumer confidence to be achieved, and a viable ecosystem to be developed.

Knowledge Enhanced Multimedia Services

In aceMedia the main technological objectives are to discover and exploit knowledge inherent in multimedia content in order to make content more relevant to the user; to automate annotation at all levels (see Figure 5) ; and to add functionality to ease content creation, transmission, search, access, consumption and re-use.

Users access multimedia content using a variety of devices, such as mobile phones and

Figure 5. Automated semantic annotation in aceMedia

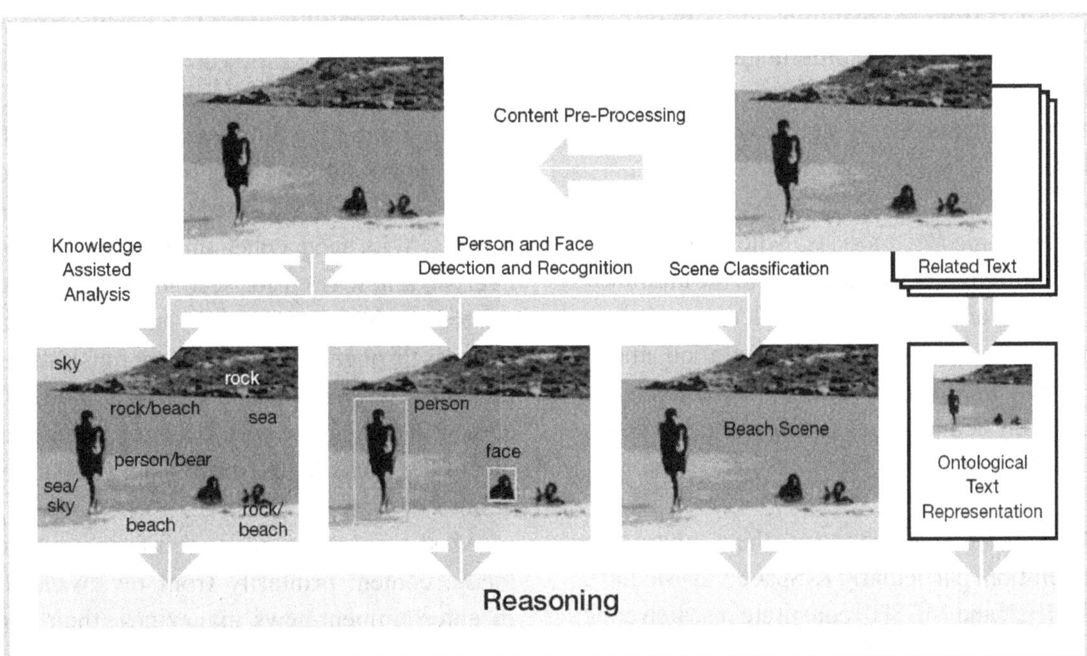

set-top-boxes, as well as via broadband cable or wireless to their PC. Through exploitation of Semantic Web tools, aceMedia has created a system which provides new and intuitive ways for users to enjoy multimedia content, such as intelligent search and retrieval, self-organising content, and self-adapting content. For example, using aceMedia's automatic metadata generation, a user can annotate content taken with her mobile phone, then seamlessly upload it to her PC where further automatic metadata generation takes place. aceMedia tools enables the content to be automatically organised into thematic categories, according to the user's preferences, and using extensions to DLNA/UPnP (networked digital home) standards, the content can be automatically pushed to other users (as specified by the content owner) according to chosen rules. For example, our user might automatically receive new pictures of herself on her mobile phone or PC which were acquired and annotated on the device of one of her friends or family.

The aceMedia use case highlighted a number of future direction, issues and new challenges with respect to semantic multimedia content analysis and manipulation within a Semantic Web framework. Apart from the requirements with respect to formal uncertainty representations and more effective reasoning and management tools support, two dimensions of significant importance include:

- *Cross-media analysis*, where additional requirements are posed due to the multimodality of knowledge considered, and their semantic modelling and integration, and
- *Non-standard approaches to reasoning*, as purely deductive reasoning alone proves not sufficient

Other projects which can use the results of this co-operation: particularly K-Space[42], X-Media[43], BOEMIE[44] and MESH[45] constitute research consortiums working on the same topic. As, in the case of aceMedia, the main research directions focus on the exploitation of formal explicit knowledge and (possibly extended) inference services for the extraction of semantic descriptions from multimedia content. Additional aspects include among other scalability, logic programming and DL-based reasoning integration for non-standard inference support, and ontology evolution (Stoilos G. et al, 2005) (Petridis K. et al., 2006) (Dasiopoulou S. et al., 2007).

Leveraging Social Network Knowledge for Movie Recommendations

Another interesting reported multimedia experiment is MediaCaddy (Garg S. et al., 2005) aiming at providing *movie or music recommendations* based on published online *critics, user experience and social networks*. Indeed, for the entertainment industry, traditional approaches to delivering meta-content about movies, music, TV shows, etc. were through reviews and articles that were done and published in traditional media such as newspapers, magazines and TV shows. With the introduction of the Internet, non-traditional forms of delivering entertainment started surfacing. The third quarter of 2003 in the U.S was the best ever for broadband penetration bringing such services as content on-demand and mobile multimedia. As of today more than 5000 movies and 2,500,000 songs are available on line. In the next couple of years this figure is expected to grow in leaps and bounds. With such a phenomenal rise in content over IP, a new need for secondary metacontent related to the movies/music emerged. Initially this was through movie reviews or music reviews published on Web portals such as Yahoo, MSN and online magazine portals as well as entertainment sales sites such as Netflix.com and Amazon.com.

Most consumers today get information about media content primarily from reviews/articles in entertainment/news magazines, their social network of friends (one user recommends a song or movie to a friend), acquaintances and advertisements. In most of the cases, one or all of the above influence user's opinion about any content (s)he chooses to consume. In addition, a new breed of customizable meta-content portal has emerged, which specifically targets the entertainment industry. Examples of such portals include Rotten Tomatoes[46] and IMDB[47]. However, these services today are typically accessed via Web portals thereby limiting the interactions and access to the information for a user in a non-PC environment.

MediaCaddy is a recommendation and aggregation service built around a self-learning engine, which analyzes a click stream generated by user's interaction and actions with meta-content displayed through a UI. This meta-content (Music /Movies/ TV reviews/ article/ synopsis/ production notes) is accessed from multiple Internet sources and structured as an ontology using a semantic inferencing platform. Figure 6 illustrates the conceptual model of MediaCaddy

This provides multiple benefits, both allowing for a uniform mechanism for aggregating disparate sources of content, and on the other hand, also allowing for complex queries to be executed in a timely and accurate manner. The platform allows this information to be accessed via Web Services APIs, making integration simpler with multiple devices and UI formats. Another feature that sets MediaCaddy apart is its ability to achieve a high level of personalization by analyzing content consumption behaviour in the user's personal Movie/Music Domain and his or her social net-

Figure 6. Conceptual model of content navigation system from the MediaCaddy project

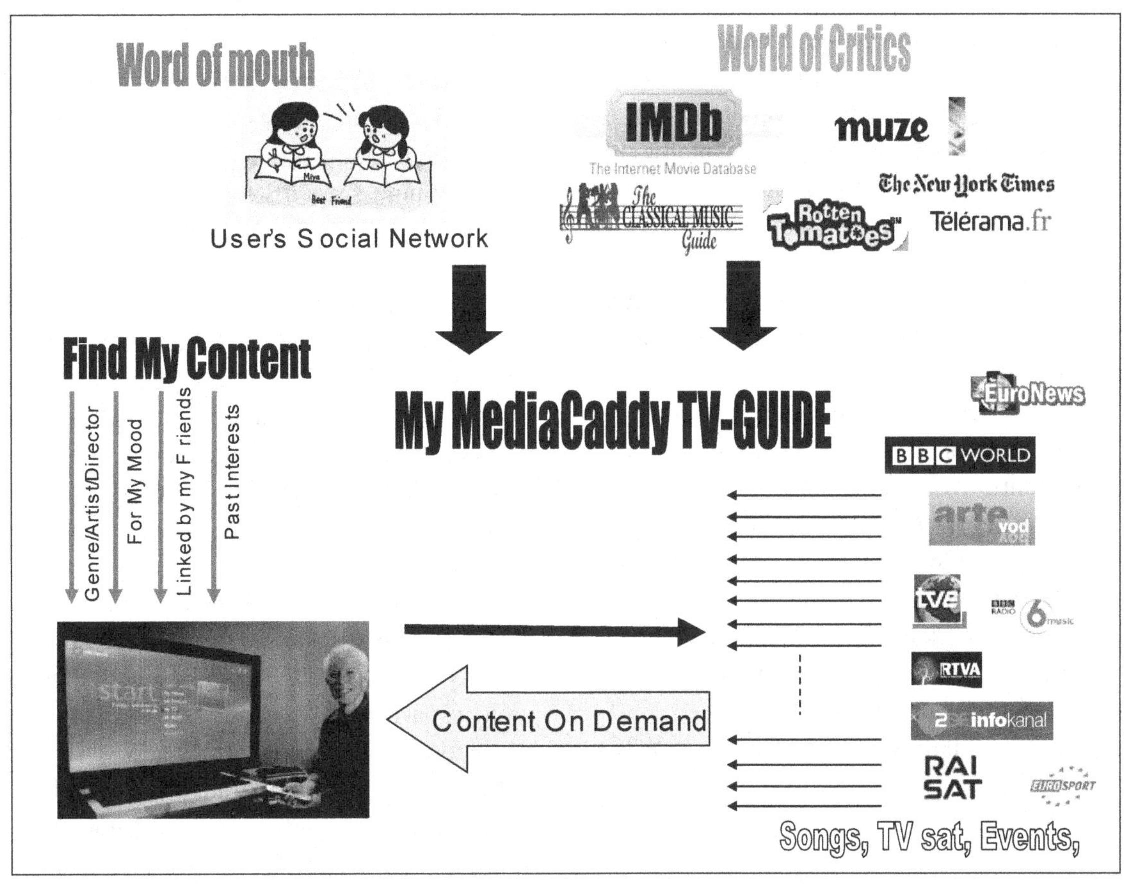

work and using this information to generate music and movie recommendations.

Prominent Applications

Finally we list some excellent illustrations of the applications of Semantic Web technology, as selected from a worldwide competition[48] which offers participants the opportunity to show the best of the art.

- Multimedia e-culture demonstrator, is to demonstrate how novel semantic-Web and presentation technologies can be deployed to provide better indexing and search support within large virtual collections of cultural heritage resources, 1st Prize 2006, http://e-culture.multimedian.nl/demo/search
- CONFOTO, Essen, Germany. CONFOTO is an online service which facilitates browsing, annotating and re-purposing of photo, conference, and people descriptions. 1st Prize 2005: http://www.confoto.org/
- FungalWeb, Concordia University, Canada. "Ontology, the Semantic Web, Intelligent Systems for Fungal Genomics".2nd Prize 2005: http://www.cs.concordia.ca/FungalWeb/
- Bibster – A semantics-based Bibliographic P2P system. http://bibster.semanticweb.org
- CS AKTive space – Semantic data integration. http://cs.aktivespace.org (Winner 2003 Semantic Web challenge)
- Flink: SemWeb for analysis of Social Networks. http://www.cs.vu.nl/~pmika (Winner 2004 Semantic Web challenge)
- Museum Finland: Sem. Web for cultural portal. http://museosuomi.cs.helsinki.fi (2nd prize 2004 Semantic Web challenge)
- Also see Applications and Demos at W3C SWG BPD. http://esw.w3.org/mt/esw/archives/cat_applications_and_demos.html

CONCLUSION AND FUTURE TRENDS

In 2000, three prominent authors in the Semantic Web activity expounded in a seminal Scientific American paper (Berners-Lee T. et al., 2001) the Semantic Web vision. In the time since then, the Semantic Web has become real. Currently, there are hundreds of millions of RDF triples, on tens of thousands of Web pages, and thousands of ontology pages have been published using RDF schema and OWL, with a growing level of industrial support. This very active support from industry is witnessed at worldwide key conference[49] very focused on the applications of the Semantic Web Technology. Indeed, about 100 talks on industry experience in testing and deploying the technology and about 30 technology showcases and 10 workshops or tutorials were actively followed by hundreds of attendees (300 at STC 05, 700 at STC 06, 730 at STC 07 and 210 at the 1st ESTC 2007) mostly from the industry.

However, the Semantic Web is still in its early days and there are many exciting innovations on the horizon.

A keynote speech[50] foresaw (Hendler J. & Lassila O., 2006) a "re-birth of AI" (or the end of the AI-winter) thanks to big-AI applications (Deep Blue, Mars Rover, Deep Space 1, Sachem-Usinor) and Web AI (IR, NLP, Machine Learning, Services, Grid, Agents, social nets) needed due to the tremendous amount of data continuously available on the Web and the emergence of new ways of doing things (loose coupling of distributed applications or services, new business models, etc.).

From 2000 to 2007, three major endeavours have paved the way for the future: DARPA, W3C and EU IST where DARPA and EU IST funded projects particularly were clearly forces towards production of recommendations to W3C (RDF-S, OWL, Rules, …), for fast adoption in industry. In the meantime, 2003 saw early government adoption and emerging corporate interest, in

2005 the emergence of commercial tools, lots of open source software and even good progress in the problem of scalability (tractable reasoning over 10 million triples has already been claimed by Oracle[51]).

So, *significant corporate activity is clearly noticeable today compared to 7 years ago*:

- Semantic (Web) technology companies are starting and growing: Cerebra, Siderean, SandPiper, SiberLogic, Ontology Works, Intellidimension, Intellisophic, TopQuadrant, Data Grid, Software AG, OntoText, Autonomy, FAST, Exalead, iSoco, Jouve, Mondeca, Sirma, Pertim, Biovista, etc.
- Semantic Web technology appears in the strategic plans of large corporations: Nokia, SAP AG, IBM, HP, Adobe, Cisco, Oracle, Sun, Vodaphone, Renault, AGFA, Cable and Wireless, Novartis, JP Morgan Chase Bank, Wells Fargo, Swiss Life, Boeing, Audi, Elsevier etc.
- Outreach to industry is also demonstrated through a newly launched W3C initiative (2007): "Semantic Web Education and Outreach Interest Group - Case Studies and Use Cases". Case studies include descriptions of systems that have been deployed within an organization, and are now being used within a production environment[52].
- Government projects in and across agencies: US, EU, Japan, Korea, China, FAO, etc.
- Life sciences/pharma is an increasingly important market, e.g. the Health Care and Life Sciences Interest Group at W3C[53]
- Many open source tools are available: Kowari, RDFLib, Jena, Sesame, Protégé, SWOOP, Wilbur etc. see the W3C SWAD initiative[54]
- Related technologies are taking off: Google Base (taxonomies for resource descriptions), Web 2.0 initiatives for mash-up applications, etc.
- Enterprise Web 2.0 can be the catalyst for a more collaborative business environment[55]. The BBC World Service had done a lot of work to try to create a more collaborative work environment. As it turned out, the BBC's internal forums, which only cost the company about 200 pounds, got the company to be more collaborative than the more formal initiatives did.

Then, it is also witnessed that adding a few semantics to current Web applications - meaning "not harnessing the full picture at once but step by step" – gives a significant push in applications: richer metadata, data harvesting and visualization, Web-based social network, digital asset management, scientific portals, tools for developers, and so gradually closing the semantic gap.

What has been Learned from AI?

- Cross-breeding with AI succeeded, standalone AI did not!
- Tools are hard to sell (needed too much skill and education)
- Reasoners are a means, not an end (a key component but not the end)
- Knowledge engineering bottleneck (Ontology development and management)

What has been Learned from the Web?

- The magic word: Distribute, interconnect and Share Roadmap!
- PC era [1980-1990] – autonomous computing and Ethernet
- Internet 1st generation [1990-2000] - Web 1.0), "read-only Web", Web sites and Companies' portals
- Social Networks [2000-2010] - Web 2.0, corporate Knowledge Management and social nets

- Semantic Web [2007 – 2020] - Web 3.0 – merging social net with automated Semantic Web
- Web OS [2020-2030] - Web 4.0

However, it must be clear that there are still **key technology locks** identified today that needs academic research and R&D investments for a full uptake of the technology (Cuel et al., 2007):

- **Ontology and reasoning:**
  - **The development of medium size to large ontologies is a challenging task:** e.g. modelling of business domains, unified and industry-grade methodology, best practices and guidelines, re-use of existing ontologies and simple tools to use.
  - **Automated update of ontologies and knowledge bases:** e.g. ontology maintenance by extraction of new knowledge facts and concept reasoning (abduction, learning), knowledge base population from legacy databases, data warehouse and data on the Web, consistency checking.
  - **Ontologies interoperability:** Overcome inevitable heterogeneity in spite of KR standards via e.g. automated mapping (concepts, properties, rules, graphs, …) in particular in the open context of the Web and the social Web (Web 2.0).
  - **Scalability:** Be capable to process business and real applications needs e.g. approximate reasoning, reasoning on inconsistent ontologies, ontology and reasoning modularization, distribution and cooperation.
  - **KR expressivity and tractability trade-off:** Maintaining the just needed KR expressivity to avoid tractability and decidability issues, there are many open problems in this area. Look for reasoning algorithm optimizations (!), measure experimental complexity and lastly may be relax the completeness property.
  - **Rules - Logic Programming and KR:** Moving towards a deeper and broader automation of business process intra- and inter-enterprise require the addition of semantic rules technology. e.g. Rules in communicating applications, Rules to describe / represent service process models, Rules for policies and contracting, etc. (see e.g. RuleML W3C[56])
- **Semantic Web Services and sevices oriented computing** (Papazoglou et al., 2006):
  - **Discovery:** Automated service discovery, reasoning on non functional parameters like QoS and cost.
  - **Composition:** Business and industrial processes automated. I/O signature and behavioural composition (Inputs, Outputs, pre-conditions, effects and message protocols). Robustness in a versatile and inconsistent context. Composition driven by high level business needs (Business Rules).
  - **Management:** Web services supervision, self-healing service, self-optimizing service, self-configuring service, self-protecting service.
  - **Design tools:** Unified design principles for engineering service applications, associating a service design methodology with standard software development and business process modelling techniques, service governance, test and proof checks.
  - **Pilots and standard platforms**. The most prominent (2007):
    - *WSMX*[57] (Fensel et al., 2005) probably the most complete architecture to date, experimented on business cases and in transfer to OASIS

- *SAWSDL*[58]: some running prototypes, industrial pilots and transfer to W3C (Sivashanmugam, 2003) (METEOR-S[59])
- *OWL-S*[60] (Ankolenkar, 2004) (OWL-S MX[61])
- *SWSF*[62]

In summary, the Semantic Web is "an interoperability technology", "a architecture for interconnected communities and vocabularies" and "a set of interoperable standards for knowledge exchange"[63]. Firstly, layman users facing the unmanageable growth of data and information, and secondly companies facing the huge amounts and volatility of data, applications and services, all require urgently automated means that master this growing complexity. In such de-facto context, no individual is able to identify knowledge patterns in their heads, no company (and employees!) is able to always shorter its products and service lifecycle and self adapt rapidly enough to survive.

The performance of semantic technologies clearly shows efficiency gain, effectiveness gain and strategic edge. Those facts are based on a survey[64] of about 200 business entities engaged in semantic technology R&D for development of products and services to deliver solutions and also recently witnesses at the ESTC 2007 industry oriented major event. From an academic and technological viewpoint, most things that have been predicted have happened - the semantic chasm is closing. Some things happened faster than anticipated like – triple store scaling, cooperation tools, enhanced SOA middleware, meta-data tagging tools, semantically-aware development environments and last but not the least, the unpredicted huge rise of Web 2.0 user-oriented technology[65] – and others still need to be realized: ontologies are there (but very little interlinking and the need is huge especially in the healthcare domain), public information sources and public re-usable ontologies (as RDF, OWL, etc.), standard Rules (SWRL, WSML, etc.) and Logic Programming integration to Ontology languages, scalable and robust reasoners, technology transparency for the final user and the practitioners, and these technologies must mature into enterprise-class products, etc.

Pervasive computing is just emerging.

ACKNOWLEDGMENT

This work has been possible thanks to the three large European consortia REWERSE, Knowledge Web and aceMedia. Acknowledgements are also for the large gathering of international conferences mixing research results and prospects from academia and industry: ESWC, ISWC, ASWC, ICWS, WWW, STC etc. Lastly, credits go also directly to the numerous people, in research labs in academia and in industry who are contributing so strongly to make semantic technology a real momentum in industry.

IST-REWERSE is a NoE supported by the European Commission under contract FP6-506779 http://rewerse.net

IST-Knowledge Web is a NoE supported by the European Commission under contract FP6-507482 http://knowledgeweb.semanticweb.org

IST-aceMedia is an Integrated Project supported by the European Commission under contract FP6-001765. http://www.acemedia.org

REFERENCES

Ankolenkar A., Paolucci M., Srinivasan N., and Sycara K., (2004). *The owl services coalition, owl-s 1.1 beta release*. Technical report, July 2004.

Antoniou G., Baldoni M., Baroglio C., Baumgartner R., Bry F., Eiter T., Henze N., Herzog M., May W., Patti V., Schindlauer R., Tompits H., Schaffert S. (2004). Reasoning Methods for Personalization on the Semantic Web. *Annals of Mathematics, Computing & Telefinformatics*, 2(1), 1-24.

Benatallah B., Hacid M. S., Léger A., Rey C., Toumani F. (2005). On automating Web services discovery. *VLDB Journal* 14(1): 84-96.

Berners-Lee, T., Hendler, J., Lassila, O. (2001). The Semantic Web. *Scientific American Journal* (May 2001).

Barillot C., Amsaleg L., Aubry F., Bazin J-P., Benali H., Cointepas Y., Corouge I., Dameron O., Dojat M., Garbay C., Gibaud B., Gros P., Inkingnehun S., Malandain G., Matsumoto J., Papadopoulos D., Pélégrini M., Richard N., Simon E. (2003). Neurobase: Management of distributed knowledge and data bases in neuroimaging. *Human Brain Mapping*, 19, 726-726, New-York, NY.

Berardi D., Calvanese D., De Giacomo G., Lenzerini M., and Mecella M. (2005). Automatic Service Composition based on Behavioral Descriptions. *International Journal of Cooperative Information Systems*, 14(4): 333-376.

Billig A. and Sandkuhl K. (2002). Match-making based on semantic nets: The xml-based approach of baseweb. *1st workshop on XML-Technologien fur das Semantic Web*, 39–51.

Bonifacio M. and Molani A. (2005). Managing Knowledge needs at Trenitalia. *Proceedings of the Second European Semantic Web Conference* ESWC 2005, Industry Forum proceedings. http://www.eswc2005.org/industryforum.html

Brunschweig B. and Rainaud J.F. (2005). Semantic Web applications for the Petroleum industry. *Proceedings of the 2nd European Semantic Web Conference,* ESWC 2005 Industry Forum http://www.eswc2005.org/industryforum.html

Cardoso J. and Sheth A. (2003). Semantic e-workflow composition. *Journal of Intelligent Information Systems*, 21(3): 191–225. Technical description of the composition of a workflow.

Chan May K.S., Bishop Judith and Baresi Luciano (2006). *Survey and Comparison of Planning Techniques for Web Services Composition.* Technical Report.

Charlet J., Cordonnier E., Gibaud B. (2002). Interopérabilité en médecine: quand le contenu interroge le contenant et l'organisation. *Revue Information, interaction, intelligence*, 2(2), 37-62.

Cordonnier E., Croci S., Laurent J.-F., Gibaud B. (2003). Interoperability and Medical Communication Using "Patient Envelope"-Based Secure Messaging. *Medical Informatics Europe Congress*, 95, 230-235.

Cuel R., Deleteil A., Louis V., Rizzi C. (2008). *Knowledge Web Technology Roadmap: The Technology Roadmap of the Semantic Web.* To appear early 2008.

Dasiopoulou S., Saathoof C., Mylonas Ph., Avrithis Y., Kompatsiaris Y., Staab S. (2007). Introducing Context and Reasoning in Visual Content Analysis: An Ontology-based Framework. In Paola Hobson, Ioannis Kompatsiaris (Editors), *Semantic Multimedia and Ontologies: Theories and Applications.* Springer-Verlag.

Description Logics for Information Integration, (2002). *Computational Logic: Logic Programming and Beyond.* LNCS; Vol. 2408, pp 41 – 60. London, UK: Springer-Verlag.

Dhamankar R., Lee Y., Doan A., Halevy A., Domingos P. (2004). iMAP: Discovering complex semantic matches between database schemas. *Proceedings of the 2004 ACM SIGMOD international conference on Management of data*, pages 383 – 394.

Di Noia T., Di Sciascio E., Donini F. M., Mongiello M. (2003). A system for principled matchmaking in an electronic marketplace. *Proceedings of the 12th international conference on World Wide Web*, WWW 2003, 321–330.

Do H.H. and Rahm E. (2002). COMA - a system for flexible combination of schema matching approaches. In *Proceedings of Very Large Databases* VLDB 2002, 610–621.

Dou D., McDermott D., Qi P. (2005). Ontology translation on the Semantic Web. *Journal on Data Semantics*, 3360, 35–57.

Ehrig M. and Staab S. (2004). QOM: Quick ontology mapping. *Third International Semantic Web Conference,* ISWC 2004, LNCS 3298, 683–697.

Euzenat J. and Valtchev P. (2004). Similarity-based ontology alignment in OWL-lite. *Proceedings of European Conference on Artificial Intelligence* ECAI 2004, 333–337.

Euzenat J. and Shvaiko P. (2007). *Ontology Matching.* Springer-Verlag.

Fensel, D., Kifer, M., de Bruijn, J., Domingue, J. (2005). *Web service modeling ontology (wsmo) submission.* w3c member submission.

Garg S., Goswami A., Huylebroeck J., Jaganathan S., Mullan P. (2005). MediaCaddy - Semantic Web Based On-Demand Content Navigation System for Entertainment. *Proceedings of the 4th International Semantic Web Conference*, ISWC 2005. LNCS 3729, 858 – 871.

Giunchiglia F. and Shvaiko P. (2003). Semantic matching. *Knowledge Engineering Review Journal*, 18(3), 265–280.

Giunchiglia F., Shvaiko P., Yatskevich M. (2004). S-Match: an algorithm and an implementation of semantic matching. In *Proceedings of the First European Semantic Web Symposium*, ESWS2004, LNCS 3053, 61–75.

Guarino N., Masolo C., Vetere G. (1999). OntoSeek: Content-Based Access to the Web. *IEEE Intelligent System*, 14(3), 70-80, (May 1999).

Haarslev V., Moller R., Wessel M. (1999-2007). *RACER: Semantic middleware for industrial projects based on RDF/OWL, a W3C Standard.* http://www.sts.tu-harburg.de/~r.f.moeller/racer/

Halevy A. (2001). Answering Queries Using Views: A Survey. *VLDB Journal*, Vol. 10, Issue 4.

Halevy A., Rajaraman A., Ordille J. (2006). Data Integration: The Teenage Years. 10-year best paper award. *VLDB.*

Hasselwanter T., Kotinurmi, P., Moran M., Vitvar T., Zaremba M. (2006). WSMX: a Semantic Service Oriented Middleware for B2B Integration. In *Proceedings of the 4th International Conference on Service Oriented Computing*, Springer-Verlag LNCS series, Chicago, USA.

Heinecke, J. and Cozannet, A. (2003). Ontology-Driven Information Retrieval. a proposal for multilingual user requests. *Workshop on Ontological Knowledge and Linguistic Coding at the 25th annual meeting of the German Linguistics*, Feb. 26-28, 2003.

Hibbard, J. (1997). Knowledge management-knowing what we know. *Information Week* (October 20).

Hull R., (1997), Managing Semantic Heterogeneity in Databases: A Theoretical Perspective, Tutorial at *PODS 1997.*

Hull R. and Su J. (2005). Tools for composite Web services: A short Overview. *ACM SIGMOD Record*, Vol. 34, 2.

Lehtola, A., Heinecke, J., Bounsaythip, C. (2003). Intelligent Human Language Query Processing in mkbeem. Workshop on Ontologies and Multilinguality in User Interface, in the *Proceedings of Human Computer Interface International*, HCII 2003, 4, 750-754.

McGuinness D. L., Fikes R., Rice J., Wilder S. (2000). An environment for merging and testing large ontologies. Proceedings of the *Seventh International Conference on Principles of Knowledge Representation and Reasoning* (KR2000), Breckenridge, Colorado, 483–493.

Mcllraith S.A., Son T.C., and Zeng H. (2001). Semantic Web services. *IEEE Intelligent Systems, Special Issue on the Semantic Web*, Volume 16, pages 46–53.

Mena E., Kashyap V., Sheth A., Illarramendi A. (1996). Observer: An approach for query processing in global information systems based on interoperability between pre-existing ontologies. *Proceedings of the First International Conference on Cooperative Information Systems* CoopIS'96, 14–25.

Nixon L., Mochol M., Léger A., Paulus F., Rocuet L., Bonifacio M., Cuel R., Jarrar M., Verheyden P., Kompatsiaris Y., Papastathis V., Dasiopoulou S. & Gomez Pérez A. (2004). *Prototypical Business Use Cases.* (Technical report Deliverable 1.1.2), Knowledge Web IST-NoE.

Norheim D. and Fjellheim R. (2006). Knowledge management in the petroleum industry. *Proceedings of the 3rd European Semantic Web Conference*, ESWC 2006 Industry Forum. http://www.eswc2006.org/industry.html

Papazoglou M., Traverso P., Dustdar S. and Leymann F. (2006). *Service-oriented computing research roadmap.* Technical report.

Petridis K., Bloehdorn S., Saathoff C., Simou N., Dasiopoulou S., Tzouvaras V., Handschuh S., Avrithis Y., Kompatsiaris I., Staab S. (2006). Knowledge Representation and Semantic Annotation of Multimedia Content. *IEEE Proceedings on Vision Image and Signal Processing, Special issue on Knowledge-Based Digital Media Processing*, Vol. 153, No. 3, pp. 255-262, June 2006.

Pistore M., Roberti P., and Traverso P. (2005). Process-Level Composition of Executable Web Services: "On-thefly" Versus "Once-for-all" Composition. The Semantic Web: Research and Applications. *Proceedings of ESWC 2005*, Heraklion, Crete, Greece. LNCS 3532, Springer Verlag.

Preguica N., Shapiro M., Matheson C. 2003). Semantics-based reconciliation for collaborative and mobile environments. In *Proccedings of the Eleventh International Conference on Cooperative Information Systems,* CoopIS 2003, LNCS 2888, 38-55.

Petrash G. (1996). Managing knowledge assets for value. *Proceedings of the Knowledge-Based Leadership Conference*, Linkage Inc., Boston, MA, October 1996.

Petrini J. and Risch T. (2004). Processing queries over RDF views of wrapped relational databases. In *Proceedings of the 1st International workshop on Wrapper Techniques for Legacy Systems*, WRAP 2004, Delft, Holland, 2004.

Rahm E. and Bernstein P. (2001). A survey of approaches to automatic schema matching. *Very Large Databases Journal*, 10(4), 334–350, (Dec. 2001).

Dumitru Roman, Uwe Keller, Holger Lausen, Jos de Bruijn, Ruben Lara, Michael Stollberg, Axel Polleres, Cristina Feier, Christoph Bussler, Dieter Fensel (2005). *Web Service Modeling Ontology, Applied Ontology Journal*, Volume 1, Number 1, Pages 77-106

Rosenbloom ST, Miller RA, Johnson KB. (2006). Interface terminologies: facilitating direct entry of clinical data into electronic health record systems. *Journal of the American Medical Informatics Association.*

Semantic Web Case Studies and Best Practices for eBusiness (SWCASE). At *ISWC 2005*, online version http://sunsite.informatik.rwth-aachen.de/Publications/CEUR-WS/Vol-155/

Shvaiko P., Giunchiglia F., Pinheiro da Silva P., McGuinness D. L. (2005). Web explanations for semantic heterogeneity discovery. In *Proceedings of the Second European Semantic Web Conference*, ESWC 2005, 303-317.

Shvaiko P., Léger A., Paulus F., Rocuet L., Nixon L., Mochol M., Kompatsiaris Y., Papastathis V., & Dasiopoulou S. (2004). *Knowledge Processing Requirements Analysis.* Technical report Deliverable D 1.1.3, Knowledge Web IST-NoE.

Shvaiko P. and Euzenat J. (2005). A survey of schema-based matching approaches. *Journal on Data Semantics* (JoDS) 4, 146–171.

Spackman K. A., Dionne R., Mays E., Weis J. Role grouping as an Extension to the Description Logic of Ontylog Motivated by Concept Modeling in SNOMED. *Proceedings of the AMIA Annual Symposium 2002*, San Antonio, Texas, p. 712-6, November, 9-13, 2002.

Stamou G. and Kollias S. (2005), *Multimedia Content and the Semantic Web: Standards, Methods and Tools.* Wiley.

Stamou, Giorgos, Jacco van Ossenbruggen, Jeff Pan and Guss Schreiber. (2006). Multimedia annotations on the Semantic Web. *IEEE Multimedia*, 13(1):86-90.

Stoilos G., Stamou G., Tzouvaras V., Pan J.Z., Horrocks I. (2005). A Fuzzy Description Logic for Multimedia Knowledge Representation. In *Proc. of the International Workshop on Multimedia and the Semantic Web*, pp 12-19, ESWC 2005, Heraklion, Grece, June 2005 .

Traverso P. and Pistore M. (2004). Automated composition of Semantic Web services into executable processes. In *Proceedings of the Third International Semantic Web Conference,* ISWC 2004, 380–394, 2004.

Velegrakis Y., Miller R. J., Mylopoulos J. (2005). Representing and querying data transformations. *Proceedings of the 21st International Conference on Data Engineering* ICDE 2005, 81-92.

Vitvar T., Zaremba M., Moran M. (2007a). Dynamic Service Discovery through Meta-Interactions with Service Providers. In *Proceedings of the 4th European Semantic Web Conference* (ESWC2007), Springer-Verlag LNCS series, Innsbruck, Austria.

Vitvar, T. Zaremba M., Moran M., Haller A., Kotinurmi P. (2007b). Semantic SOA to Promote Integration of Heterogeneous B2B Services. *The 4th IEEE Conference on Enterprise Computing, E-Commerce and E-Services* (EEE07), IEEE Computer Society, July, 2007, Tokyo, Japan.

Zhong J., Zhu H., Li J., Yu Y. (2002). Conceptual graph matching for semantic search. In *Proceedings of the 10th International Conference on Computational Science*, 2393 (2002), 92-106

Zyl J., and Corbett D. (2000). A framework for Comparing the use of a Linguistic Ontology in an Application. *Workshop Applications of Ontologies and Problem-solving Methods*, ECAI'2000, Berlin Germany, August, 2000.

Wiederhold G. (1992). Mediators in the architecture of future information systems. *IEEE Computer*, 25(3), 38-49.

Wiig K. (1997). Knowledge management: where did it come from and where will it go? *Journal of Expert Systems with Applications*, 13(1), 1–14.

ADDITIONAL READINGS

The Semantic Web: research and Applications LNCS series: LNCS 2342 (ISWC 2002), LNCS 2870 (ISWC 2003), LNCS 3053 (ESWS 2004), LNCS 3298 (ISWC 2004), LNCS 3532 (ESWS 2005), LNCS 4011 (ESWC 2006), LNCS4273 (ISWC 2006), LNCS 4519 (ESWC 2007), LNCS 4825 (ISWC 2007).

Journal of Web semantics (Elsevier)

Annual Semantic Web applications challenge: http://challenge.semanticweb.org

W3C http://www.w3.org/2001/sw/

ENDNOTES

1. http://www.web2con.com
2. http://www.ontoweb.org
3. http://Knowledge Web.semanticweb.org
4. http://rewerse.net
5. http://cordis.europa.eu/fp7/home_en.html
6. Knowledge Web Deliverable D 1.1.4v3 http://knowledgeweb.semanticweb.org/semanticportal/deliverables/D1.1.4v3.pdf
7. http://knowledgeweb.semanticweb.org/o2i/
8. http://protege.stanford.edu/index.html
9. http://oaei.ontologymatching.org/2007/
10. http://www.neon-project.org
11. http://www.ontologymatching.org/
12. http://www.acemedia.org
13. http://www.nlm.nih.gov/research/umls/umlsmain.html
14. http://us.expasy.org/sprot/
15. http://obo.sourceforge.net/main.html
16. http://www.ncbi.nlm.nih.gov/Genbank/index.html
17. http://www.ncbi.nlm.nih.gov/sites/entrez
18. http://www.connectingforhealth.nhs.uk/
19. http://www.edisante.org/
20. http://www.etiam.com/
21. http://cen.iso.org/ and http://www.tc251wgiv.nhs.uk/
22. http://www.hl7.org/
23. http://www.d-m-p.org/docs/EnglishVersionDMP.pdf
24. http://www.hl7.org/Special/Committees/structure/index.cfm#Mission
25. http://www.cocoon-health.com
26. http://www.srdc.metu.edu.tr/webpage/projects/artemis/index.html
27. http://www.simdat.org
28. Some of the well-known definitions of KM include: (Wiig 1997) " Knowledge management is the systematic, explicit, and deliberate building, renewal and application of knowledge to maximize an enterprise's knowledge related effectiveness and returns from its knowledge assets"; (Hibbard 1997) "Knowledge management is the process of capturing a company's collective expertise wherever it resides in databases, on paper, or in people's heads and distributing it to wherever it can help produce the biggest payoff"; (Pettrash 1996) "KM is getting the right knowledge to the right people at the right time so they can make the best decision".
29. http://www.cenorm.be/cenorm/indcx.htm
30. http://www.knowledgeboard.com
31. Semantic Web, Use Cases and Challenges at EADS, http://www.eswc2006.org Industry Forum.
32. See for example in the Petroleum industry (Nordheim D. et al., 2005)
33. See for example Use of Ontology for production of access systems on Legislation, Jurisprudence and Comments (Delahousse J. et al., 2006) http://www.eswc2006.org/industry.html
34. E.g. see the EU Integrated project "DIP Data, Information, and Process Integration with Semantic Web Services", http://dip.semanticweb.org/
35. agentcities RTD project http://www.agentcities.org/EURTD/
36. Semantic Business Automation, SAP, Germany http://www.eswc2006.org Industry Forum
37. http://sws-challenge.org/2006/submission/deri-submission-discovery-phase3/ http://sws-challenge.org/2006/submission/deri-submisson-mediation v.1/ http://sws-challenge.org/2006/submission/deri-submisson-mediation v.2/
38. http://events.deri.at/sercomp2007/
39. Semantically Enabled Knowledge Technologies http://www.sekt-project.com/
40. http://www.acemedia.org
41. http://www.w3.org/2005/Incubator/mmsem/
42. http://www.kpace-noe.net

[43] http://www.x-media-project.org

[44] http://www.boemie.org

[45] http://www.mesh-ip.eu

[46] http://www.rottentomatoes.com

[47] http://www.imdb.com/

[48] Annual Semantic Web applications challenge: http://challenge.semanticweb.org

[49] Semantic Technology Conference http://www.semantic-conference.com/; European Semantic Technology Conference http://www.estc2007.com/

[50] SemWeb@5: Current status and Future Promise of the Semantic Web, James Hendler, Ora Lassila, STC 2006, 7 March 2006, San José, USA

[51] Oracle Database 10g using RDF natively supported by the 10g Enterprise Edition

[52] http://www.w3.org/2001/sw/sweo/public/UseCases/

[53] http://www.w3.org/2001/sw/hcls/

[54] Semantic Web Advanced Development for Europe http://www.w3.org/2001/sw/Europe/

[55] Forester, Erica Driver, October 2007

[56] http://www.w3.org/2005/rules/wg/wiki/RuleML

[57] http://www.oasis-open.org/committees/semantic-ex/faq.php, http://www.wsmx.org http://sourceforge.net/projects/wsmx

[58] http://www.w3.org/TR/sawsdl/

[59] http://lsdis.cs.uga.edu/projects/meteor-s/

[60] http://www.w3.org/Submission/OWL-S/

[61] http://www-ags.dfki.uni-sb.de/~klusch/owls-mx/index.html

[62] http://www.w3.org/Submission/SWSF/

[63] ESTC 2007 Keynote speech from Susie Stephens (Oracle)

[64] Semantic Wave 2006, Part-1 Mills Davis

[65] Web 2.0 and its related phenomena becomes increasingly interesting for businesses. In January 2007 a research programme conducted by the Economist Intelligence Unit and sponsored by FAST gauged the relevance of Web 2.0 to large corporations throughout the world and across a wide range of industries. The research, which consisted of an online survey plus follow-up interviews with senior executives at large public corporations, found that Web 2.0 now has significant implications for big business across a wide range industry sectors. By 2006, and even earlier at some companies, the world's multinationals began to see many Web 2.0 technologies as corporate tools. In fact, according to the survey, 31% of companies think that use of the Web as a platform for sharing and collaboration will affect all parts of their business (Economist Intelligence Unit (2007): Serious business. Web 2.0. goes corporate. A report from the EIU sponsored by FAST. Also to mention two majors initiatives: MySpace with 300 million users (Dec 2007) http://www.myspace.com and Facebook with 60 millions users (Nov 2007) http://www.facebook.com

Section II
Semantic Web E-Business Cases

Chapter II
Applying Semantic Web Technologies to Car Repairs

Martin Bryan
CSW Group Ltd., UK

Jay Cousins
CSW Group Ltd., UK

ABSTRACT

Vehicle repair organizations, especially those involved in providing roadside assistance, have to be able to handle a wide range of vehicles produced by different manufacturers. Each manufacturer has its own vocabulary for describing components, faults, symptoms, etc, which is maintained in multiple languages. To search online resources to find repair information on vehicles anywhere within the European Single Market, the vocabularies used to describe different makes and models of vehicles need to be integrated. The European Commission MYCAREVENT research project brought together European vehicle manufacturers, vehicle repair organisations, diagnostic tool manufacturers and IT specialists, including Semantic Web technologists, to study how to link together the wide range of information sets they use to identify faults and repair vehicles. MYCAREVENT has shown that information sets can be integrated and accessed through a service portal by using an integrated vocabulary. The integrated vocabulary provides a 'shared language' for the project, a reference terminology to which the disparate terminologies of organisations participating in the project can be mapped. This lingua franca facilitates a single point of access to disparate sets of information.

CURRENT SITUATION

Repair scenarios for resolving a vehicle breakdown are varied, and can take place in a garage (repair by a qualified mechanic in a franchised or independent workshop) or by the roadside (repair by a qualified mechanic working for a Road Side Assistance (RSA) organisation, or a repair by a vehicle driver). For legal liability reasons, 'driver-assisted' repair scenarios only cover minor or temporary repairs of the type covered in owner's manuals, such as changing a vehicle wheel or a fuse.

In workshop scenarios, access to repair information may be provided through online access to repair information systems. Information may be provided publicly by a manufacturer for all users, or specifically to franchised dealers who are provided with access to information systems that are specific to the makes and models they retail.

Access to repair information in roadside scenarios is more complicated. A vehicle driver may not have access to the vehicle's owner's manual. In the context of a roadside repair by a mechanic working for an RSA, the mechanic might have access to repair information through a computer located in their van. RSA organisations, however, rely heavily on the detailed knowledge of their highly trained staff to diagnose faults without the aid of documentation. RSA mechanics aim to repair as many vehicles as possible at the roadside, but need to identify as early as possible if a car will need to be taken to a garage for repair. If the repair requires specialist equipment the RSA must be able to identify the nearest garage with suitable equipment that the car may be taken to for repair.

Fault diagnosis precedes vehicle repair in both repair scenarios. Details of the type of fault are ascertained at the point of contact with the customer, be this through direct conversation with the vehicle owner at a service centre, or by conversation through a call centre operator when a motorist initially reports a problem. When contact is made through a phone call it is important that call centre operators analyze the customer's situation in as much detail as possible. They have to be able to identify whether the problem is one that might be repairable at the roadside or whether a recovery vehicle is likely to be needed from the responses received to an ordered set of questions.

Customer contacts rarely lead to a detailed fault diagnosis because vehicle owners typically have insufficient knowledge of their vehicles to identify the cause of a problem. At best they can describe the symptoms produced by the fault and the conditions in which the symptoms manifest themselves (e.g. won't start when it is too cold). In many cases these descriptions can be used to identify the type of diagnostic tests that may have to be carried out before the cause of the problem can be identified.

PROBLEM STATEMENT

With the ever increasing use of electronics in vehicle components, identifying and correcting faults at the roadside or in an independent workshop is becoming a challenge. While the use of on-board diagnostic tools to report faults electronically via dashboard messages can assist mechanics, identifying the cause of a fault from such messages is not always a simple process. When faults are reported over the phone from remote locations sufficient diagnostic information may only be obtainable if the vehicle can be connected directly to the call centre information centre using tools such as personal digital assistants (PDAs) or mobile phones that can be connected to the vehicle's diagnostic ports.

A roadside assistance vehicle cannot contain the wiring schematics for all models of vehicles. Although, under European Union Block Exemption Regulation (European Commission, 2002), manufacturers provide access to all their repair information, repairers at the roadside are not always easily able to find the repair information that they need, particularly if this is related to a previously unreported fault, while physical and business constraints impose restrictions on the set of spare parts, tools, etc, that can be available in the workshop or repair van at any one time.

Consequently, the following problem areas can be identified:

- Practical limitations exist on the level of information that can be provided in any repair context. There is variability in the amount and quality of information that is available to describe a fault and its associated symptoms and conditions in order to support fault diagnosis.
- Environmental variables such as geographical location, repair equipment, and spare part availability may combine to constrain the speed with which a repair can be affected, and determine the location at which the repair takes place.
- Logistics and supply chain management and facilitation can provide advance warning of required spare parts or repair equipment at the point of initial fault diagnosis, supporting decision processes such as the direction of a vehicle to an appropriate repair location or the triggering of inventory supply processes to pre-order required parts and arrange their delivery to the repair location.
- Maintenance of acceptable response times that meet customer expectations.

The MYCAREVENT project addresses these issues by facilitating the diagnosis of faults and the provision of repair information at the location where the fault is first described, be this in a workshop or at the roadside.

The MYCAREVENT project provides a single point of entry – a portal – through which a user can access services to support the description and diagnosis of a fault, and to search for and retrieve repair information from a variety of content providers. For this to be achievable, however, it must be possible to associate the terms used by the vehicle owner to describe the problem that has occurred with the terms used by the content provider to describe content or how to detect and solve the fault causing the problem. It should be noted that content can be of variable quality and scope – for example, repair information from a vehicle's manufacturer will typically apply to specific makes of vehicle, whereas information from third parties like technical specialists working for RSAs, or technical data for an automotive part or content from a third party information provider, may be more generic in application.

SOLUTION DESCRIPTION

The Mobility and Collaborative Work in European Vehicle Emergency Networks (MYCAREVENT) research project was sponsored by the IST (Information Society Technology) program of the European Commission. The 3-year project brought together leading manufacturers from the automotive sector, academic researchers and commercial IT suppliers to develop facilities for the provision of repair information to remote users in the automotive aftermarket. Remote access, for example a roadside repair, is enabled by the use of mobile services. Research focused on service development, process and organization management, e-business, communication networks and human-computer interaction.

Work in MYCAREVENT has been organized in nine work packages:

WP 1: Project Management
WP 2: Use Case and Business Model
WP 3: Ontologies
WP 4: Mobile Communication
WP 5: Remote Services
WP 6: Service Portal
WP 7: Mobile Applications
WP 8: Training
WP 9: Demonstration and Dissemination

The relationships between these packages are illustrated in Figure 1.

WP1 supported project management, establishing and monitoring the administration and leadership of the MYCAREVENT project. It needs no further discussion here.

Figure 1. MYCAREVENT work package relationships

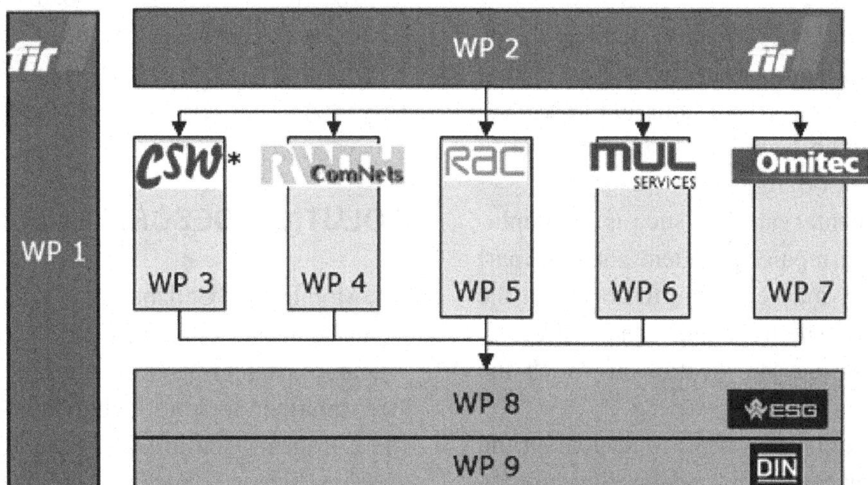

WP2 developed the fundamental business model and use cases that scope the project requirements and identify the customers, actors, processes, and the constraints on the legal and organisational environment within which the project solution operates.

The project scope can best be understood by looking at the project's three pilot scenarios, which demonstrate the functionality provided by the solutions and identify their targets:

- **Pilot I** was designed to demonstrate possible solutions for original equipment manufacturer (OEM) workshops and OEM roadside technicians who require remote access to the MYCAREVENT service portal to obtain instructions for specific repairs.
- **Pilot II** was designed to demonstrate how the concept of access to car repair information via the MYCAREVENT service portal could be extended to help mechanics working in independent workshops and roadside assistance services to identify faults.
- **Pilot III** was designed to demonstrate the concept of "Driver Self Help" in those scenarios where the driver can carry out simple repairs using advice provided by the MYCAREVENT service portal.

The ontology work package (WP3) defines the information structures that enable cross-system interoperability and the integration of content from disparate sources and heterogeneous databases.

The mobile communications and devices work package (WP4) provides a secure and reliable communication service between users (roadside assistants, drivers, and mechanics) and the service portal. These services are intended to enable the exchange of fault codes and repair information from remote locations, such as those required to carry out roadside repairs.

The remote services work package (WP5) allows a driver to search for self- help information, such as that provided in the owner's handbook, using standard Web browser software that resides on their smart-phone or PDA.

The service portal work package (WP6) defines the core project portal, the gateway for accessing repair information.

The mobile applications work package (WP7) allows the MYCAREVENT Service Portal to be used to deliver automated diagnostic tests to trained mechanics. This requires the application of additional access security and other middleware services within the portal interface.

The role of WP3 Ontology and WP6 Service Portal work packages is explained further in the following sub-sections.

OBJECTIVES

The MYCAREVENT Service Portal acts as a *gateway* to technical information on automotive diagnosis, repair and maintenance that is available from automotive manufacturers and independent organisations supporting the aftermarket.

To ensure high user acceptance, the MYCAREVENT work packages use innovative *state-of-the-art technologies* to find the 'right' information for user needs. To make this possible the service portal includes the following subsystems:

- *Core e-business infrastructure* for the flexible implementation of workflow and business processes.
- *Service data backbone* providing secure links to services as well as manufacturer and third party information repositories.
- An ontology-based *advanced query service (AQS)* for guided navigation through different data resources and terminologies.
- *Expert system hub* combining the capabilities of distributed (specialised) expert system nodes.
- *Authoring tools* for specific types of technical information, such as the interactive circuit diagrams (IACD) used to identify faults in electronic systems.

The remainder of this section explains how the ontology-based advance query service applies Semantic Web technologies to identify solutions to repair problems.

OVERVIEW

The MYCAREVENT Ontology work package was responsible for the development of the models, data structures and terminology sets used to support the work carried out by the service portal. The work package drew on the expertise of data modelling specialists, implementers and content providers (including OEM and RSA organisations) to build an agreed set of 'information artefacts' to be used across all MYCAREVENT services.

The Ontology work package developed:

- A *Generic and integrated information reference model (GIIRM)* (MYCAREVENT, 2005), providing a high-level conceptual model of the MYCAREVENT mobile service world.
- A set of W3C XML Schemas derived from the GIIRM, which are used for the representation of data in messages, metadata and interfaces.
- Terminology for populating the GIIRM, enabling repair information, symptoms and faults to be described in a generalized way.
- A W3C Web ontology language (OWL) (McGuinness, 2004) ontology, derived from the GIIRM and the terminology, in which data sources can be registered for access by MYCAREVENT applications.

DETAILS

Since the publication of Tim Berners-Lee's futuristic paper on The Semantic Web in *Scientific American* in May 2001 (Berners-Lee, 2001) the concepts that form the backbone of a system that can add semantics to Web resources has begun to form. As was pointed out in that paper:

For the Semantic Web to function, computers must have access to structured collections of informa-

tion and sets of inference rules that they can use to conduct automated reasoning.

The goal of the MYCAREVENT ontology work was to link together collections of information created by different vehicle manufacturers, component suppliers and repair organizations in such a way that we can use the collected information to conduct automated reasoning wherever possible.

The start point for the work package was the development of a formal model that could record the relationships between the information components used to identify and repair faults. This top-level model was designed to be generalized enough to apply to any type of repairable product.

Figure 2 shows a diagrammatic representation of the *MYCAREVENT Generic and Integrated Information Reference Model (GIIRM)* which was developed to manage the inter-relationship between information message components exchanged between information suppliers and the service portal. The diagram is expressed in the Object Management Group's Unified Modeling Language (UML) (Object Management Group, 2007).

The information required to populate the classes defined in this model are supplied by information providers in the form of Information Bundles that conform to the ISO/IEC 14662 Open-EDI Reference Model (ISO/IEC 14662, 2004). In this standard Information Bundles are defined as:

The formal description of the semantics of the recorded information to be exchanged by parties in the scenario of a business transaction. The Information Bundle models the semantic aspects of the business information. Information bundles are constructed using Semantic Components.

A Semantic Component is defined as:

A unit of information unambiguously defined in the context of the business goal of the business transaction. A Semantic Component may be atomic or composed of other Semantic Components.

The model allows, therefore, for simple (i.e. 'atomic') and composite (i.e. 'non-atomic') attribute values, represented in the model using the concept of the 'representation class' which can be either an atomic datatype or a non-atomic composite data type as defined by the 'Naming and design principles' established in Part 5 of the ISO Metadata Registries (MDR) standard (ISO/IEC 11179-5, 2005). The GIIRM has foundations in abstract concepts and existing standardisation work. This design philosophy and layer of abstraction provides a generic model independent of any detail specific to implementation. It is, therefore, a platform-independent model.

To simplify the process of identifying relevant information sources, the model includes the concept of a Term. Terms can be used to describe a vehicle instance, its build specification, a system or subsystem used in the build specification, a condition under which a problem was detected, a symptom of the problem or a detected fault. Terms can be grouped into Terminologies that can be applied by different manufacturers within their documentation and information delivery systems.

Users of the MYCAREVENT Service Portal may or may not be aware of the terms used by manufacturers within their documentation. Users need to be able to enter terms that they are familiar with for describing problems, etc. The MYCAREVENT Advanced Query Service (AQS) needs to be aware of the relationships between the terms applied by a particular user community and the terms applied by a particular manufacturer. Terminology, and the mapping of terms in one terminology to terms in another terminology, is central to the AQS as it enables the querying of disparate information sources. The parameters of a search query can be established by a user

Figure 2. MYCAREVENT generic and integrated information reference model

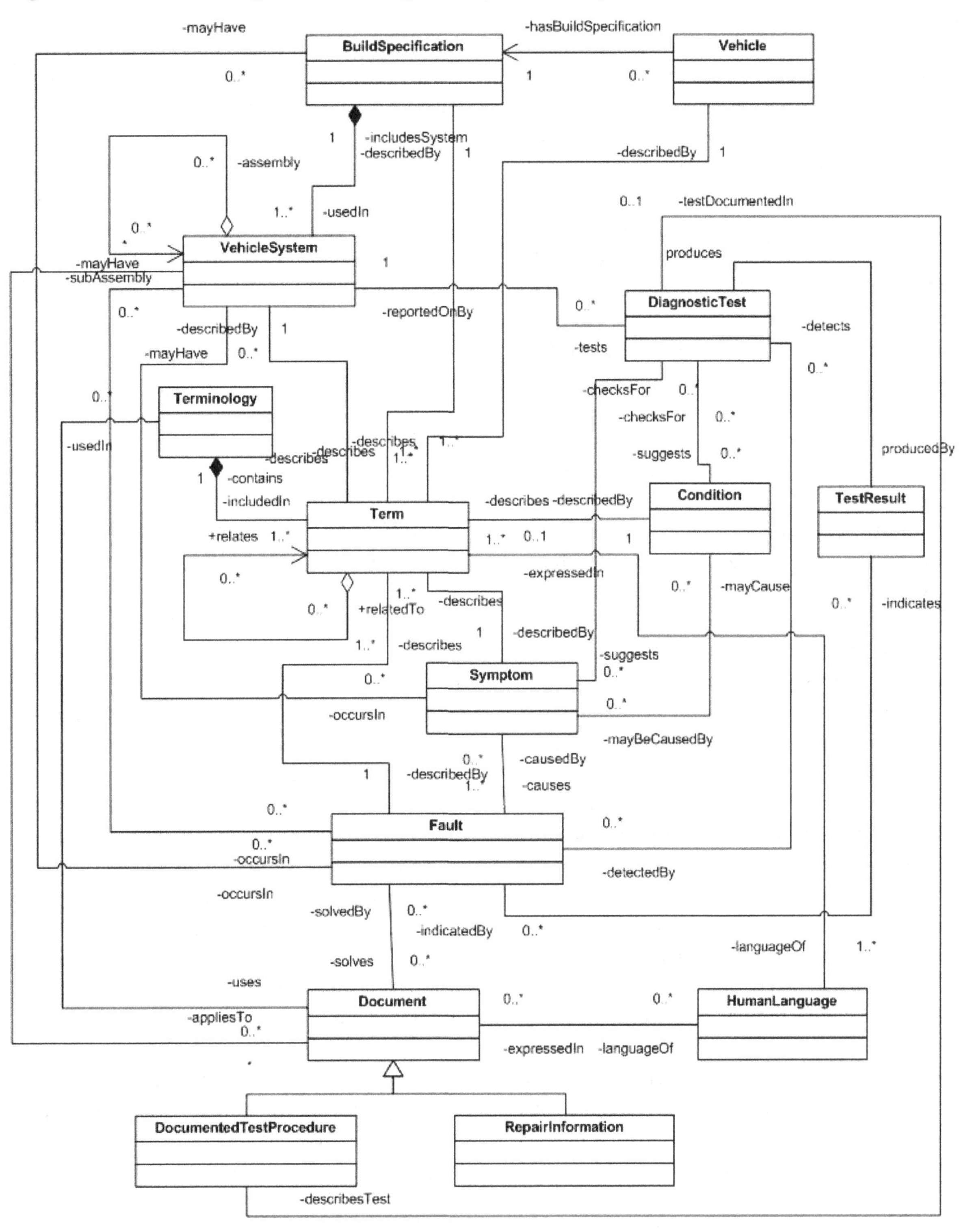

using their preferred terminology, which may be manufacturer-specific or generalized using a MYCAREVENT specific term set. This search context is then passed to the AQS, which translates the MYCAREVENT terminology into the terminology used to describe the content that will be searched to retrieve information. This level of indirection allows disparate corpora of information to be searched using their own terminology. From an integration perspective, the AQS enables content integration using metadata describing repair information content created by OEMs or third parties, or through direct interface to a vehicle information source system.

The AQS has been developed using open-source technology to enable the latest developments in Semantic Web technology to be adopted. It uses the Jena RDF triple store ("Jena", n.d.) to record OWL classes and individual occurrences of these classes. The Jena 2 Database Interface allows W3C Resource Description Framework (RDF) (Klyne, 2004) triples to be stored in MySQL, Oracle, PostgreSQL or Microsoft SQL databases, on both Linux and WindowsXP platforms.

An important feature of Jena 2 is support for different kinds of inference over RDF-based models (for RDFS, OWL, etc). Inference models are constructed by applying *reasoners* to models (Dickinson I, 2005). The statements deduced by the reasoner from the model can appear in the inferred model alongside the statements from the model itself. RDF Schema (RDFS) (Brickley, 2004) reasoning is directly available within Jena: for OWL an external reasoner needs to be linked to the Jena engine through a Reasoner Registry. The Pellet reasoner (Clark & Parsia, 2007) is used within MYCAREVENT to ensure that all inferred relationships are identified prior to searching. Jena includes an OWL Syntax Checker that can be used to check that OWL files are correctly formed.

Jena includes an implementation of the SPARQL query language (Prud'hommeaux, 2007) called ARQ. SPARQL has been developed as part of the World Wide Web Consortium (W3C) Semantic Web activity to provide a transportable technique for RDF data access that serves a similar purpose to the structured query language (SQL) used to access information held in a range of relational databases. The MYCAREVENT AQS generates SPARQL queries, based on the objects in the GIIRM, which are used to identify the concepts being referred to by terms entered by users. Because the query service is based on RDF it can query the contents of any OWL data property used to record information about an individual class member within the MYCAREVENT ontology, or any language-specific RDF label associated with a class or individual, irrespective of whether or not it is a term that has been specifically declared within a terminology.

SEARCHING AND RETRIEVING REPAIR INFORMATION

The key to the success of the MYCAREVENT portal is to allow users to ask questions using terms that they are familiar with and to use these questions to generate alternative versions of the question that OEM and other information provision systems associated with the portal can answer. The workflow steps used to establish a search query are described in the following sections.

MYCAREVENT queries are implemented in a controlled, context sensitive, manner to provide guidance to users as they enter information into the service portal. Figure 3 shows the information components used to identify the type of vehicle to be repaired within the portal.

Users complete each field in turn. As they do so the options available to them in the next field are restricted using the ontology. So, for example, as soon as the user identifies the make of vehicle to be repaired, the set of options that can be used to complete the model field is reduced to the set of models appropriate for the entered make. Completing the model field restricts the range of years that can be entered in the Year field, select-

Figure 3. MYCAREVENT Repair Information Form

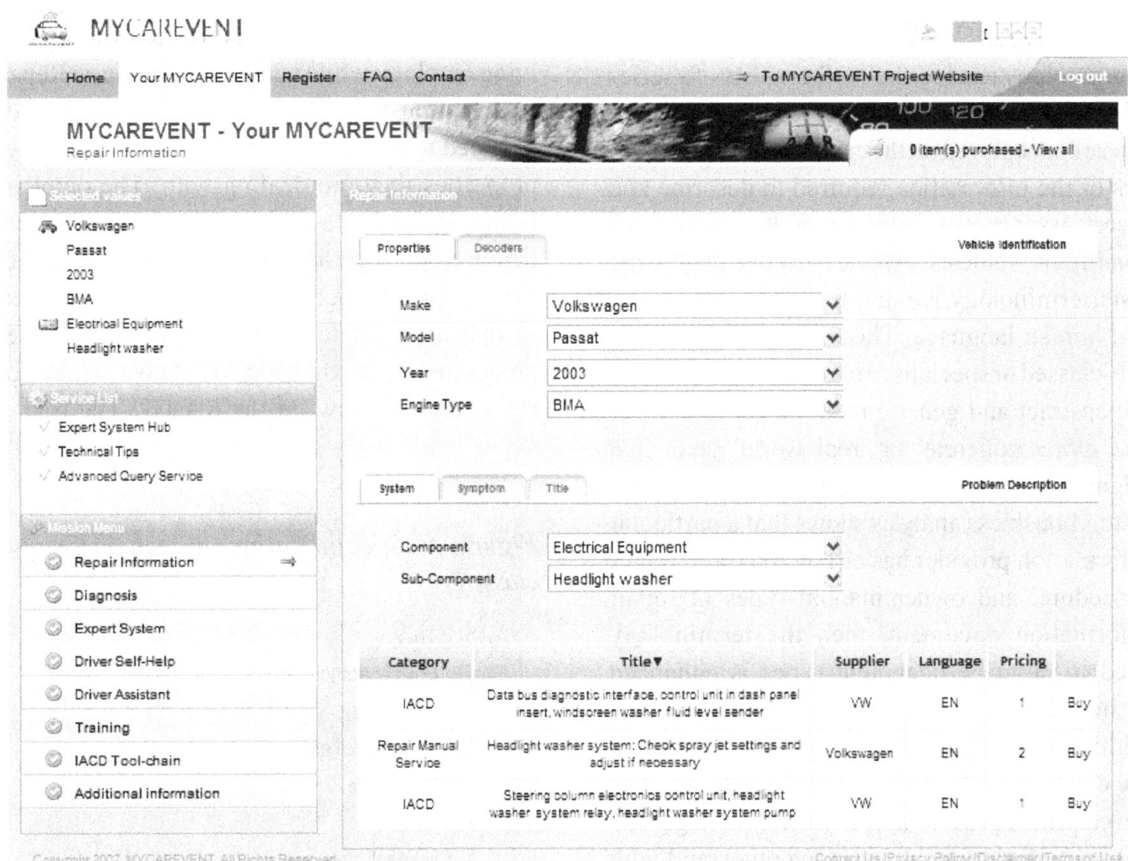

ing a year restricts the set of Series that can be selected, and so on.

For countries such as the UK where a vehicle registration number decoder is accessible it is possible to enter the vehicle registration number (VRN) into a field displayed under the Decoder tab and have the entered number return information that has been recorded about the year of manufacture, engine type, fuel type, etc, by the vehicle registration authority. Alternatively the manufacturer's vehicle identification number (VIN) can be used to automatically identify system components. Where a decoding service is not available each field in the vehicle description has to be completed in turn.

When as much information on the vehicle as is available has been recorded the user can be shown a list of available services, which can range in complexity from a set of online technical tips through the use of the advanced querying system to identify relevant information resources to the use of an expert system to diagnose problems.

By reducing the set of selectable options at each stage to that recorded in the ontology we not only refine the search criteria but also reduce the likelihood that subsequent queries will be rejected. Only those services that are relevant to the type of vehicle to be repaired and the service that is being employed to repair it are offered to users so that, for example, users are not prompted to carry out tests using diagnostic equipment that is not fitted to the vehicle or accessible to the repairer, and are prompted to carry out all tests that must be performed to identify a specific fault.

THE ROLE OF THE MYCAREVENT ONTOLOGY

The ontology used by the AQS consists of a series of specializations of the concepts in the GIIRM. These concepts reflect the core classes and properties of the information required to describe and assert associations between faults, symptoms, conditions, vehicles, vehicle systems, diagnostic tests, terminology, repair information documents and human language. These classes are further sub-classed or specialised to refine concepts from the abstract and generic model level to a lower and more 'concrete' or 'real world' level that aligns with the business requirements. To illustrate, if business analysis shows that a particular information provider has circuit diagram, repair procedure, and owner manual types of repair information document, then the terminology used to describe document types is enhanced to include these new kinds of document, and within the ontology new document sub-classes are created to reflect these document types. The development process keeps the terminology and ontology in alignment with each other, and with the GIIRM which defines the base model and so ensures interoperability across the portal and database(s) accessed by it.

Figure 4 shows how the Vehicle System class is specialized into two levels of sub-class. Each class has associated with it multilingual labels, and a set of properties. Figure 5 shows the properties associated with the Vehicle class as they are displayed using the Protégé ontology editor used to maintain the MYCAREVENT ontology.

As a value is assigned to each of these properties within the MYCAREVENT System Identification form, the set of related properties that can be found by querying the triple store is reduced. Only those entries that are used in matched terms need to be displayed to users when they are required to select options for a currently empty field. The order in which responses are requested can be optimized to ensure that the minimum set of options is provided at each response point.

In MYCAREVENT users never see the underlying ontology while completing the basic Repair Information form shown in Figure 3. They do not need to browse the class tree, or know which properties they are dealing with. The ontology is simply used as a Web service by applications that need to request data from users, so that they can restrict the set of choices offered to users to that appropriate for the currently identified processing context, which is shown in the top right-hand window on the display. The role of

Figure 4. Specialization of generic model classes

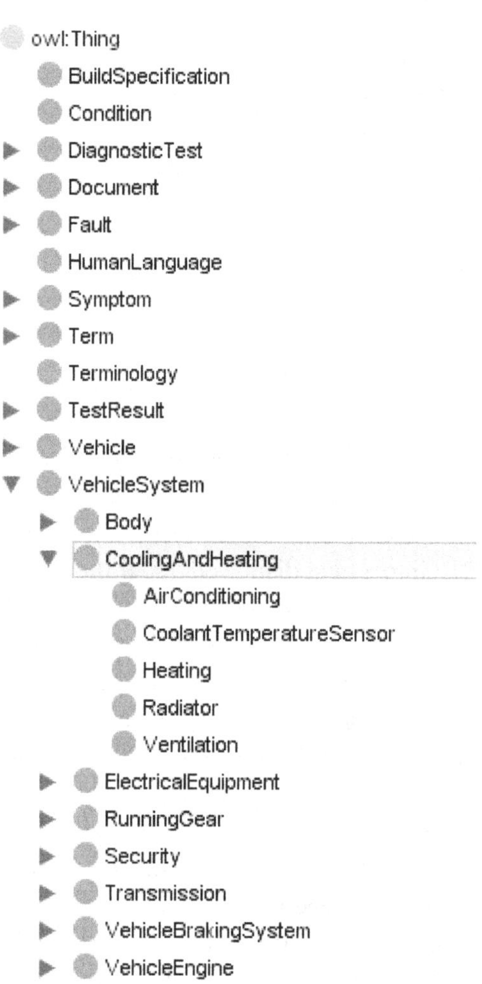

Figure 5. Properties of a vehicle

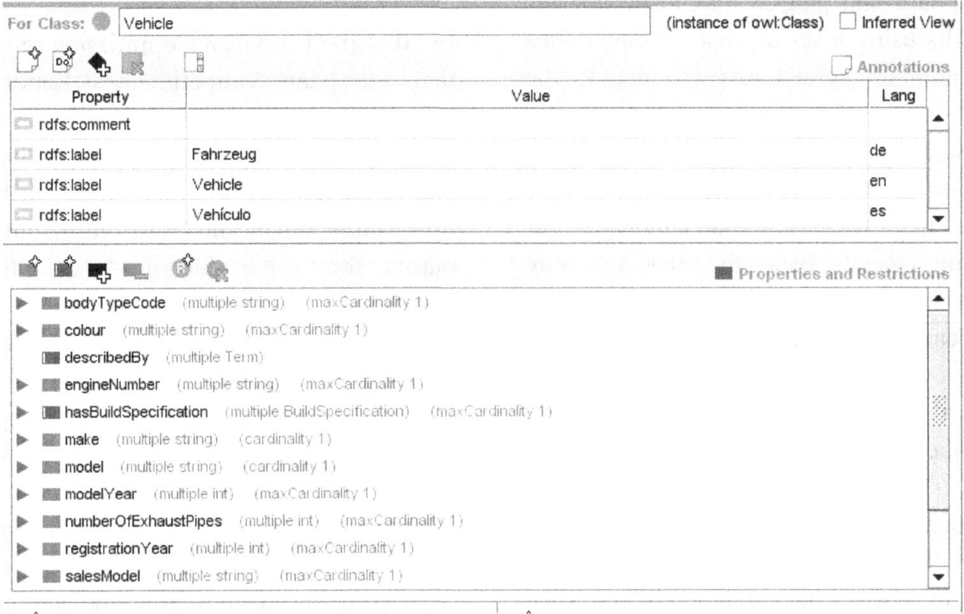

the ontology is, therefore, to reduce information overload for users.

In later stages of the process, when accessing data using the Symptoms and Title tabs, users are prompted to enter keywords that are searched against lists of symptoms or the titles of documents. In these scenarios matches can only be made in those situations where the title contains relevant wording, or where the symptoms entered match symptoms recorded in one of the terminologies.

ALTERNATIVES

On-line access to information for vehicles is available from a variety of sources, including individual OEMs and third party automotive data suppliers. Subscription models vary, but typically documents are only available to paying subscribers and may require the installation of specialist software or training in the use of a specialized information retrieval system. For an individual user requiring access to information for a variety of vehicles, the availability of a single portal through which multiple sources of information can be accessed and queried is an attractive option. Rather than paying multiple subscriptions and having the burden of maintaining integration with multiple information access points, the portal provides a central point of access from which a user can search for and retrieve information.

Each manufacturer and third party information provider maintains their own vocabulary of terms for describing components, faults, symptoms, etc, in multiple human languages. If a trained mechanic knows which terms a manufacturer has applied to the fault they have identified then it is possible to search the manufacturer's database using a free text search. But if a mechanic is not familiar with the terms used by a specific manufacturer, there are unlikely to be any synonyms for them provided by information suppliers.

The issue of understanding the meaning of a particular terminology is not confined to metadata describing different types of vehicle systems, but applies to data recorded as codified values as well. On-board and plug-in diagnostic devices report faults using a set of codes. Some codes are internationally agreed, and will identify the same fault in a number of vehicles. Other codes are manufacturer specific. As with terminology, descriptions and names for fault codes may be maintained in a variety of human languages. For manufacturer specific codes the same code may be used to identify different problems in different makes of cars. Without access to a decoder that turns the codes into meaningful descriptions of faults for a specific vehicle build specification, knowing the code does not necessarily help the repairer.

Manufacturers of diagnostic tools need to ensure that their decoders are always up-to-date, providing the correct interpretation of codes for the latest models. Users of such tools need to be able to update their tools regularly to ensure the correct analysis of faults. While many OEMs already provide an up-to-date tool set for their vehicles through their BER portals, the extent of this is not consistent across manufacturers, and so a central point for updating information online provides one approach to addressing any gap which may arise between the release of new vehicle types and the availability of tools to diagnose their problems, other than those provided by the vehicle manufacturer.

By providing a central point for searching for repair information, issues such as the need to ensure this content is up-to-date, and legal liability for any claim arising from errors, need to be taken into account. For access across the single European market, irrespective of language and affiliation, however, centralized diagnostic services of the type that can be supplied using the MYCAREVENT service portal provide a viable alternative once agreement can be obtained from OEM and other content providers for making the information available online through the service portal.

COST AND BENEFITS

In 2004 the European Commission reported, in their European Competitiveness Report (European Commission, 2004a) that the automotive industry, as one of Europe's major industries, contributes about 6% to total European manufacturing employment and 7% to total manufacturing output. Total value added produced in the motor vehicles industry in the EU-15 in 2002 was roughly the same as in the US, some €114 billion.

With 209 million passenger cars in use in 2002 the European Union (EU-25) is by far the largest single market for cars in the world. It accounts for roughly 38% of all cars on major international markets. On average, four out of ten EU inhabitants own a car. According to the ACEA, the European Automobile Manufacturers Association, 15 million new passenger cars were registered in the EU and EFTA in 2006.

According to the EU report, it is expected that 90% of all future innovation in vehicle manufacturing will be driven by IT. This affects both the electronics dominated spheres of multimedia entertainment and navigation systems and the traditional mechanical components such as the chassis, body, engine or brakes. For instance, the percentage of electronics in the chassis is expected to increase from 12% to 40% in the next decade. Similar developments are expected for safety features, e.g. pedestrian protection, traction control, backward driving cameras, night-view display on the windscreen, sensor controlled brakes or fuel economy regulation. Product differentiation will be increasingly driven by electronics: for example, performance tuned variants of the same engine will differentiate suppliers. The value of electronic components in vehicles could rise from its current 20% today to 40% by 2015.

Since October 2002 motor vehicle distribution and servicing agreements within the EU have come under the new Block Exemption Regulation (BER). Under the new regulations repairers cannot be required to use original spare parts.

Only if repair costs arise which are covered by the vehicle manufacturer, for example warranty work, free servicing and vehicle recall work, can the vehicle manufacturer insist on the use of original spare parts. Other than that, matching quality spare parts of other manufacturers or of independent suppliers can be used.

The automotive aftercare market had a turnover of around €84 billion per annum at the end of the 20th century; automotive replacement parts account for around half of this figure, some 45% of which is supplied by independent aftermarket (IAM) suppliers (European Commission, 2004b). The 210 million motorists in the EU spend on average €400 each per year and approximately €5,000 during the average vehicle lifetime on repair and maintenance.

Major service providers in the automotive industry are franchised dealers (120,000 dealers employing 1.5 million people in 1999) and independent repair shops (160,000 garages employing about 600,000 people). In addition, 18,000 roadside service vehicles fulfil 14 million missions a year.

By providing a single access point through which details of electronically available information can be searched, using generic Semantic Web technologies rather than manufacturer-specific solutions, the MYCAREVENT Service Portal simplifies and speeds up the task of finding information on how to repair vehicles with specific problems. With over a million potential customers it provides a cost-effective solution to information distribution.

By using ontologies to establish relationships between the terms used by vehicle owners and repairers to describe faults and the terms used by manufacturers to classify and describe faults, the MYCAREVENT Advanced Query Service can provide a more flexible solution to finding information, resulting in a higher likelihood of mechanics being able to find the information they need in a timely manner.

RISK ASSESSMENT

Each manufacturer produces thousands of models, each of which can have many build specifications. Model details and build specifications have to be defined prior to manufacture, but cannot be used within the service portal until the product is released. Unless the release date is known in advance, data relating to vehicle models, build specifications, system components, etc, cannot be added to the ontology at the time they are captured by the manufacturer, but need to be made available at the point when relevant documentation is released.

Manufacturers are naturally reluctant to maintain two sets of information, which could get out of step with one another. It must be possible to automatically convert information in local systems into the form that can be used by the AQS. As an alternative it should be possible to turn a query to the AQS into a query to the manufacturer's product database.

Another area of risk is in the level at which data is described, and the equivalence of terminology at different levels. A constraint on the MYCAREVENT ontology is that it currently only recognizes two levels in the system component hierarchy, system and sub-system. If a manufacturer uses a multi-level system hierarchy this needs to be flattened into a two level hierarchy for reference within the service portal. This means that entries at lower levels in the hierarchy have to become members of the appropriate higher level sub-system, thus restricting the level of refinement that can be applied to queries. This restriction is necessary because otherwise it would not be easy to convert AQS queries to queries that could be applied to manufacturer-developed services that can only handle two levels of querying.

Where diagnostic information is a requirement for identifying build specifications and associated repair information, obtaining the necessary information without access to OEM-provided diagnostic equipment can be a problem, especially in roadside breakdown scenarios. Unless the repairer can send appropriate information to the portal it will not be possible to retrieve relevant repair instructions. For this reason, other MYCAREVENT work packages have concentrated on how to get information from on-board diagnostic devices to a portal, diagnostic tool or expert system capable of identifying the cause of the problem.

Not all concepts are applicable to all makes, or to all models made by a specific manufacturer. Where a feature is specific to a particular manufacturer it is not to be expected that other content providers to the portal (be they manufacturers or third party information providers) will have equivalent terms in their terminology. If a user requests information on this subject for another make of vehicle the system will not be able to match the term. In such cases a number of strategies can be adopted to find appropriate terms, including:

- Identifying the term in the terminology of another manufacturer and informing the user that this term is manufacturer-specific
- Identifying the sub-system with which the term is associated by the originating manufacturer and offering a set of terms associated with the same sub-system that are used by the manufacturer of the vehicle being repaired
- Identifying other terms that include one or more of the words in the entered term, which may or may not identify higher-level concepts
- Identify other terms that include the largest identifiable substring of the entered term in compound nouns such as those used in German.

Expanding terminologies to cover all European languages, particularly agglutinative languages such as Finnish and Hungarian, where there are many compound words that could be derived from a term, will make identifying potential matches much harder. For such languages it will be vital to be able to define relationships between alternative references to a term within terminologies.

Identifying which terms have significance in which documents is another problem area. Unless the sub-systems that documents refer to are unambiguously recorded in either the data or metadata associated with a document, and the faults that can be solved using a document are recorded in the ontology or manufacturer's information base, refining queries down to the level of identifying documents that are specific to a particular problem with a given sub-system will not be possible. The best that can be achieved is to identify the set of documents that refer to a particular sub-system and allow users to determine from metadata describing the type of document, etc, whether it may be suitable for solving the problem.

Relying on user selection of suitable documents introduces another risk. Manufacturers want to be paid for preparing and supplying data. Users only want to pay for information that they know will solve their problem more efficiently than alternative solutions. If the cost of information is too high users will not risk purchasing something that may not solve the problem. If the cost of information is too low manufacturers, or third party documenters, supplying the information will not be able to recover the cost of preparing the information for distribution. Because of legal liability concerns, and the requirements by the BER, manufacturers are reluctant to supply information units which do not contain all the legally required warnings, safety notices, etc, that can apply to the repair scenario. OEMs want to supply units of information that are known to contain all relevant details for the sub-system(s) that are connected with the fault.

The rate at which documents change is also a concern to information suppliers. It is not possible to maintain an up-to-date repository that includes all repair information generated by all vehicle manufacturers, even if an efficient enough content management system was available to store and access them. The best a service portal can expect is to receive metadata about which documents are available for which sub-systems, and the roles those documents serve. If the metadata supplied with each document fails to identify the type of faults that the document can help to correct, it will not be possible to associate faults with the documents that can be used to repair them. These risks were identified and confirmed by the OEMs involved in the project, and in some cases would prevent them from being able to integrate their content with MYCAREVENT.

The key strength of using an ontology-based approach to service portal management is that it reduces information overload on users, who otherwise would find it difficult to find their way through the maze of specifications and information types supplied by different manufacturers. By minimizing the set of options provided at each stage in the process, the MYCAREVENT advanced query service makes it possible to identify information resources provided by a range of manufacturers through a single reference point.

Until manufacturers are able to provide information as to which faults can be solved using which documents a weakness of the service portal is that it will necessarily rely on users making the final choice between a range of information resources that cover a particular component. Where diagnostic tests are available their results can be used to narrow down the range of possibilities. When diagnostics are implemented an associated problem is that of identifying the relationships between symptoms, the conditions they can occur under and the diagnostic test results that can be used to identify specific faults. At present this information is generally not available from manufacturers. Until it is systematically recorded the efficient identification of faults within the portal will be difficult.

The recording of the symptoms reported when a particular fault has occurred is, however, also an opportunity for the service portal. By recording the symptoms reported by users, the conditions under which they occur and the fault that was eventually identified as the cause of the problem within the service portal it should become possible, over time, to generate statistics that can be used to predict the likelihood of a particular fault being the cause of an exhibited symptom.

The size of the European automotive industry is another major risk. If all vehicle suppliers adopted the system, and it covered all cars in current production, the potential user community could be as many as 2,000,000 people. Several portals would be required to cope with such a load. To keep the systems synchronised it would be necessary to adopt a time-controlled update system, with updates being scheduled for early in the morning when system use is low. A separate system would have to be assigned the task of receiving information from manufacturers and accumulating them ready to carry out a single daily update of online portals. The downside of these process integration issues would be that any changes made to documentation, build specifications, etc, would not be available on the day they were recorded by the manufacturer. This risk can be managed using Trading Partner Agreements and Service Level Agreements between the portal and the information providers, following standard practices for managing business relationships.

Expanding the proposed system to cover all vehicles would also require significant expansion of system functionality, because commercial vehicles have a much wider range of build specifications. One vehicle manufacturer reported to have 93,000 build specifications for trucks. Part of the reason for this is that there are more distinguishing features, such as type of steering, number of axles, body type, couplings, etc, used to define the build of a commercial vehicle. For such vehicles it becomes important to use the unique vehicle identification number (VIN) rather than its vehicle registration number (VRN) to obtain accurate details of the build specification.

FUTURE RESEARCH DIRECTIONS

As Tim Berners-Lee pointed out in his seminal paper on the Semantic Web (Berners-Lee, 2001):

Traditional knowledge-representation systems typically have been centralized, requiring everyone to share exactly the same definition of common concepts such as "parent" or "vehicle". But central control is stifling, and increasing the size and scope of such a system rapidly becomes unmanageable.

Two important technologies for developing the Semantic Web are already in place: eXtensible Markup Language (XML) and the Resource Description Framework (RDF). XML lets everyone create their own tags—hidden labels such as <author> or <title> that annotate Web pages or sections of text on a page. ... Meaning is expressed by RDF, which encodes it in sets of triples, each triple being rather like the subject, verb and object of an elementary sentence. These triples can be written using XML tags.

An ontology is a document or file that formally defines the relations among terms. ... We can express a large number of relations among entities by assigning properties to classes and allowing sub-classes to inherit such properties. ... Ontologies can enhance the functioning of the Web in many ways. They can be used in a simple fashion to improve the accuracy of Web searches—the search program can look for only those pages that refer to a precise concept instead of all the ones using ambiguous keywords. More advanced applications will use ontologies to relate the information on a page to the associated knowledge structures and inference rules.

The real power of the Semantic Web will be realized when people create many programs that collect Web content from diverse sources, process the information and exchange the results with other programs. ... The Semantic Web, in naming every concept simply by a URI, lets anyone express new concepts that they invent with minimal effort. Its unifying logical language will enable these concepts to be progressively linked into a universal Web.

In a follow-up paper entitled *The Semantic Web Revisited* (Shadbold, 2006) it was noted that:

The need has increased for shared semantics and a Web of data and information derived from it. One major driver has been e-science. For example, life sciences research demands the integration of diverse and heterogeneous data sets that originate from distinct communities of scientists in separate subfields. ... The need to understand systems across ranges of scale and distribution is evident everywhere in science and presents a pressing requirement for data and information integration.

The need to integrate data across a range of distributed systems is by no means restricted to the scientific community. It is a fundamental characteristic of any e-business scenario that needs to be linked to back-office systems or to systems, such as those used for payment management, run by other companies. OWL allows the UML-based modelling techniques that are fundamental to the design and maintenance of back-office systems to be swiftly integrated with the XML-based messaging approach that has been widely adopted for inter-system communication.

The trend towards globalisation that characterises today's business environment is established and set to continue. Increasingly, demands are placed upon organisations to integrate information from diverse sources and to deliver new products and value propositions in narrower timescales. To meet these demands IT organisations need to evolve towards loosely coupled systems where services can be assembled to support the execution of business processes in a flexible way. A service oriented architecture (SOA) is not the only answer, though – for an SOA to be effective, a common view on to the data of the organisation needs to be available, so that data can be provided when and where needed to the processes consuming that data.

RDF-based data integration has a lot to offer because it provides a way to access information held in disparate systems without imposing a new structure on source data. If metadata is available, or can be generated, a metadata-based approach provides a framework structuring, processing and querying information sources.

The use of OWL and Semantic Web technologies moves us beyond simple metadata to structures where additional rules that determine the logical meaning of the data can be layered on top of existing data by the application of an ontology. Ontologies allows rules to be specified which can be reasoned over using methodologies such as description logics, allowing inferred models of data to be constructed. Not only is the explicit meaning of the data recorded, but the implicit meaning of the data can also be inferred and exposed by applying such rules to data.

The use of ontology-based approaches is another step along the path from the computer to the conceptual world used by humans. Now programming has progressed from binary assembler languages to 4th generation object-oriented paradigms, ontologies allow knowledge to be encoded as data structures in a way that reflects the understanding and semantics of the domain and of human users. Data can be modelled in a manner that is more intuitive and conceptually closer to the way humans think. Ontologies allow humans to use their own terminology to model the domain in a way that reflects how they understand it and speak about it. Furthermore, they can now encode knowledge and logic about the data structure, moving it out of application logic.

In this chapter we have said nothing about how OWL's limited set of description logic (DL) rules can be used to constrain the values assigned to ontology properties or to infer membership of a class from the presence or absence of property values. MYCAREVENT has not identified any points at which rules more complex than those needed to constrain cardinality or to ensure that all object properties are members of a given class or set of classes need to be applied to repair scenarios. But in many business scenarios more complex rules, including access control rules and permissions management, will be needed to ensure that business constraints can be met. The presence of an alternative, expert-system based approach to rule definition and application within MYCAREVENT has meant that the service portal team has not fully investigated the role that inferencing rules might play in the development of e-business applications, though a number of possibilities have been identified, including ones related to digital rights management and skill-based access control to information resources.

Work began in 2006 on a W3C Rule Interchange Format (RIF), an attempt to support and interoperate across a variety of rule-based formats. RIF (see www.w3.org/2005/rules for details) will eventually address the plethora of rule-based formalisms: Horn-clause logics, higher-order logics, production systems, and so on. Initially, however, the Phase 1 rule semantics will be essentially Horn Logic, a well-studied sublanguage of first-order logic which is the basis of logic programming. Among the deliverables scheduled from the RIF Working Group for the end of 2007 is:

A W3C Recommendation on using this rule interchange format in combination with OWL. This document is needed to help show implementers and advanced users how these technologies overlap and the advantages and limitations around using them together. This document must clearly state which features of OWL can be mapped to (or otherwise interoperate with) Phase 1 rules and which cannot, and software using this mapping must be demonstrated during interoperability testing. The document may also discuss rule language extensions to cover the excluded OWL features.

A second phase, scheduled to be completed in 2009, will extend rule processing to provide full first-order logic, negation, scoped negation-as-failure and locally closed worlds.

Until RIF tools are readily available, OWL users will have to make use of proposals such as that for a Semantic Web Rule Language (SWRL) (Horrocks, 2004) that extends OWL's built-in set of simple rule axioms to include Horn-like rules. While MYCAREVENT has not currently identified any rules it needs to deploy within the AQS which cannot be implemented using predefined SPARQL queries, it is anticipated that there will be other applications based on the GIIRM for which more complex queries of the type provided by SWRL may be needed. It will be interesting to see, as RIF develops, whether the additional functionality offered by adopting Horn-clause or higher-order logics provides a simpler solution to the type of reasoning currently being performed by the expert system currently used to identify the causes of problems within MYCAREVENT.

CONCLUSION

The automotive market has become one of the most important and complex industries in the EU, due to the rapid development and change in electronics, electrics, software and hardware. Economically, it is a major contributor to the EC economy, accounting for circa 6% of total European manufacturing employment and 7% of total manufacturing output.

Due to the EU Block Exemption Regulation, service providers have the right to access different kinds of repair information, training material and tools.

The MYCAREVENT project gathered partners from across Europe to establish a model of excellence leveraging innovative applications and state-of-the-art technologies, to offer a way for making the market more transparent, competitive and lucrative. It developed and implemented new applications and services which could be seamlessly and securely accessed by mobile devices deploying Semantic Web technologies. These tools allow us to provide manufacturer-specific car repair information that matches problems identified by Off/On-Board-Diagnostic systems.

Breakdown information is presented in different languages. Mobile workers in different countries can interact with service portals of independent service suppliers as well as those of car manufacturers. Using the MYCAREVENT Service Portal it becomes possible to provide a single point of access to information for any make of car, so ensuring that any car manufactured in Europe can be repaired in any European workshop or by any European roadside assistance organisation, irrespective of the preferred language of the owner or the mechanic.

REFERENCES

Berners-Lee, T (2001). The Semantic Web. *Scientific American*, May 2001. http://www.sciam.com/article.cfm?articleID=00048144-10D2-1C70-84A9809EC588EF21

Brickley, D and Guha, R (2004). *RDF Vocabulary Description Language 1.0: RDF Schema*, W3C. http://www.w3.org/TR/rdf-schema/

Clark & Parsia LLC (2007). *Pellet: The Open Source OWL DL Reasoner.* http://pellet.owldl.com/

Dickinson, I (2005). *HOWTO use Jena with an external DIG reasoner.* http://jena.sourceforge.net/how-to/dig-reasoner.html

European Commission (2002). *EC Regulation 1400/2002; Application of Article 81(3) of the Treaty to categories of vertical agreements and concerted practices in the motor vehicle sector.*

http://ec.europa.eu/comm/competition/car_sector/distribution/

European Commission (2004). The European Automotive Industry: Competitiveness, Challenges, and Future Strategies, *European Competitiveness Report 2004*, http://ec.europa.eu/enterprise/library/lib-competitiveness/doc/ european_competitiveness_report%202004_en.pdf

European Commission (2004). *Proposal for a Directive of the European Parliament and of the Council amending Directive 98/71/EC on the Legal Protection of Designs.* Extended Impact Assessment. http://register.consilium.eu.int/pdf/en/04/st12/st12555-ad01.en04.pdf

Horrocks, I. et al. (2004). *SWRL: A Semantic Web Rule Language Combining OWL and RuleML.* http://www.w3.org/Submission/2004/SUBM-SWRL-20040521/

ISO/IEC 11179-5:2005. *Information technology -- Metadata registries (MDR) -- Part 5: Naming and identification principles.* http://www.iso.org/iso/iso_catalogue/catalogue_tc/catalogue_detail.htm?csnumber=35347

ISO/IEC 14662:2004. *Information technology -- Open-edi reference model.* http://www.iso.org/iso/iso_catalogue/catalogue_tc/catalogue_detail.htm?csnumber=37354

Jena – A Semantic Web Framework for Java. http://jena.sourceforge.net/

Klyne, G and Carroll, J (2004). *Resource Description Framework (RDF): Concepts and Abstract Syntax*, W3C. http://www.w3.org/TR/rdf-concepts/

McGuinness, D & van Harmelen, F (2004). *OWL Web Ontology Language Overview*, W3C. http://www.w3.org/TR/owl-features/

MYCAREVENT Deliverable D3.2 (2005) *Generic and Integrated Information Reference Model.* http://www.mycarevent.com/Deliverables/ DL.3.2_Generic_and_Integrated_Information_Reference_Model_DT_v01.00.pdf

Object Management Group (2007) *Unified Modeling Language (UML).* http://www.omg.org/technology/documents/formal/uml.htm

Prud'hommeaux, E & Seaborne, A (2007) *SPARQL Query Language for RDF*, W3C. http://www.w3.org/TR/rdf-sparql-query/

Shadbolt, N, Berners-Lee T and Hall, W (2006) The Semantic Web Revisited. *IEEE Intelligent Systems, 21,* pp. 96-101. http://eprints.ecs.soton.ac.uk/12614/01/Semantic_Web_Revisted.pdf

Chapter III
Semantic Integration for B2B Service Assurance

Alistair Duke
BT Group Chief Technology Office, UK

Marc Richardson
BT Group Chief Technology Office, UK

ABSTRACT

This chapter describes an approach to support operational support system (OSS) integration across organisation boundaries. The requirement for such business-to-business (B2B) interfaces is expected to increase as is the need to carry out integration in much more flexible way. Existing approaches for integration tend to be implementation specific, operate at the syntactic level and are realised by programme code. Consequently they are inflexible due to their highly coupled nature and are costly to setup and maintain. An approach to decouple B2B interfaces is introduced, which allows them to be flexibly coupled as required with the use of scalable, semantic mediation. An initial prototype is described based on an Assurance Integration scenario for BT Wholesale's B2B gateway.

CURRENT SITUATION

The number of companies in the telecommunications industry has increased rapidly in recent years. The industry has been transformed by changes in regulation and the emergence of the Internet and mobile technologies. The days of one organisation providing end-to-end services to customers are gone. Supply chains now involve many players of differing size and function. Companies now need to efficiently provide service fulfillment, assurance and billing across organisational boundaries (Evans et al., 2002). The problem is exacerbated by today's fast moving market and dynamic business-to-business (B2B) relationships. Getting a new service to market quickly involves close integration of data with existing and new partners. The integration of heterogeneous operational support systems (OSS) of all parties is crucial. However, this can be a costly process. A Forrester survey (Koetzle et al., 2001) found that average annual spending on integration by the top 3500 global companies was $6.3 million and 31% was spent on integrating with external trading partners. In the telecommunications sector, costs of OSS integration can rise to 70% of the total OSS budget (McKenna, 2002).

Like many companies, BT is transforming its systems with the adoption of a service orientated architecture (SOA) (Strang, 2005) which can be defined as a system in which resources are made available to other participants in the network as independent services that are accessed in a standardized way – allowing more flexible, loose coupling of resources than in traditional systems architectures. The business goals are to increase speed to market (organisational agility), to reduce overall IT costs (through greater reuse and reduced integration costs), to improve the alignment of IT with the business, but also to differentiate themselves in their customer service (e.g. through improved responsiveness, leaner/faster support processes, quicker delivery, etc.). SOA components can be exposed to business partners allowing service-chains to be developed across organisational boundaries.

BT Wholesale's B2B Gateway is provided to Internet Service Providers (ISPs) to allow them to integrate their own operational support systems with those of BT. Without such a system the ISP would either need to manually coordinate with BT via a BT contact centre or operate a system separate to its own OSS that communicated with BT's – thus requiring information to be entered twice.

The B2B Gateway exposes an interface whose behaviour is a combination of transport technologies such as SOAP, security protocols such as SSL, messaging middleware such as ebXML and the process behaviour of back end systems. Messages formats are expressed using XML Schema[1] (XSD) which has the advantage of availability of tools and the increased possibility of integrating with newer transport standards such as Web Services.

The Gateway currently exposes a number of interfaces concerned with service fulfilment and assurance. These are generally concerned with regulated services. The interfaces allow Service Providers to manage faults (i.e. raise and manage faults, request, confirm and cancel repair appointments and receive status fault status notifications) and carry out diagnostics (i.e. request tests and handle the response to these).

Currently the process involved in granting access to the Gateway for a new service provider is lengthy and complex. It commences with a communication phase where partners assess their technical suitability, receive documentation and consider the level of fit with their existing OSS. A development phase follows this during which support is provided by BT. During the testing phase, the partner is given access to a test environment provided by BT where they can test the validity of their messages and their transport and security mechanisms. Firewalls, proxies, etc. must be configured by both parties to ensure that communication can occur. Once the testing phase is complete and documented the partner can move to a pilot phase where terms must first be agreed regarding volumes, frequency and support arrangements before access is given to the live system. Transactions are monitored during the pilot phase to ensure validity.

Problem Statement

The process described in the previous section can take several months from start to finish. One of the major issues is the level of manual effort required firstly to interpret the documentation and secondly to generate adaptation software that allows the systems of the parties involved to interoperate. Related to this are the inherent disconnect between the documentation and the XML descriptions of the interfaces. An approach that can reduce development time, improve the quality of development through enhanced understanding and as a result avoid significant problems during the testing and pilot phases will naturally save BT and its partners significant time and money.

PROPOSED SOLUTION

The proposed solution is to enable the Broadband Diagnostics interfaces, for both BT and one of its partners, to be represented semantically allowing them to exist as decoupled entities that can then be coupled as appropriate in a flexible, ad hoc manner via mediation.

Objectives

The key objective is to support OSS integration by using semantic descriptions of the system interfaces and messages which allows semi-automatic mediation to be carried out between the data and process requirements of the interacting parties. This permits greater automation in the integration process and will allow Service Providers to better meet the needs of the end customer. This is of great importance since without such automation, we argue that the benefits of the SOA approach will not be fully realised since the need for manual intervention will remain high. The aim of the semantic approach is to not only reduce the time and cost involved in establishing and maintaining integration but to allow a more flexible approach to integration to prevail where partners and services can be dynamically discovered and integrated at (or at least very close to) run-time.

Semantic Mediation

This section introduces the concept of mediators which, although in existence for a number of years, has recently been adopted by the Semantic Web community in efforts to apply semantics to a Service Orientated Architecture.

Mediators are components which enable heterogeneous systems to interact. In a practical sense, mediators have generally been realised as pieces of program code that perform point-to-point, low-level translations. Although such mediators satisfy the short-term goal in that they allow two systems to talk to each other, they suffer from maintainability and scalability problems and prospects for automating their application in a dynamic environment are low due to their close coupling with the implementation. An alternative view of mediation which attempts to address these issues was proposed by Wiederhold (1992) who saw mediators as modules occupying an explicit, active layer between the users' applications and the data resources with the goal: a sharable architecture containing inspectable, declarative elements. The key role of the mediator is to "...exploit encoded knowledge about some sets of subsets of data to create information for a high level of applications" (Wiederhold, 1992). Knowledge represented in an implementation neutral manner can more readily be used and re-used in different applications. Such a representation can be achieved using techniques adopted by the Semantic Web (Berners-Lee et al., 2001) effort which is aiming to make the Web more machine processable. Central to the vision of the Semantic Web are ontologies (Fensel, 2001) which provide a consensual and formal conceptualisation of a given domain. Mediators can be used to represent the interface requirements of a source implementation as knowledge that can be transformed as appropriate before being converted to satisfy the requirements of a target interface.

Mediation can be classified as acting on both data and process. The following two sections describe this in more detail.

Data Mediation

Data mediation is required when even though the semantic content of a piece of data or message provided by one system and required by another is the same, the syntactic representation is different. This may be due to differing naming or formatting conventions employed by the partner systems. In order to overcome these mismatches, a graphical mapping tool can be applied at design time. Such tools can be used to map source elements to target elements on a one-to-one or many-to-one basis using a simple drag and drop approach. Where more complex mappings are required such as those that are dependent upon content, a declarative mapping language may be necessary to describe them. Once a data mediator has been developed it should expressed in a declarative form such that other users (be they humans or computers) can inspect it and determine whether they can make use of it.

Process Mediation

Process mediation is required when the semantic content of a process is shared by both parties but when the messages or message exchange patterns of the parties required to achieve that process differ.

The process mediator must ensure that the message exchange required by each party is adhered to. As a result the mediator may need to, for example, create new messages that appear to come from the source party and send these to the target. The content of such created messages will have been obtained from the source by the mediator either by explicitly asking for it or by retaining it until it was required by the target. An example of process mediation is shown in Figure 1. This simple example is based upon the TestRequest message exchange between an ISP Trading Partner and BT Wholesale. The Trading Partner's message exchange is shown on the left-hand-side. It sends a TestRequest for which it expects an acknowledgement. It then later expects to receive the result of the test including whether it was accepted or rejected. BT's message exchange is shown on the right-hand-side. It expects to receive a TestRequest message but does not send an acknowledgement. It then either rejects or accepts the test and sends an appropriate message for this decision. If the test was accepted the TestResult message is sent following the completion of the test.

The process mediator has two tasks to perform in order to allow the process to be carried out successfully. Firstly, it is aware that an acknowledgement is required by the trading partner but is not sent by BT, so it creates a suitable acknowledgement and sends this to the trading partner. No data is contained in the acknowledgement other that

Figure 1. Process mediation

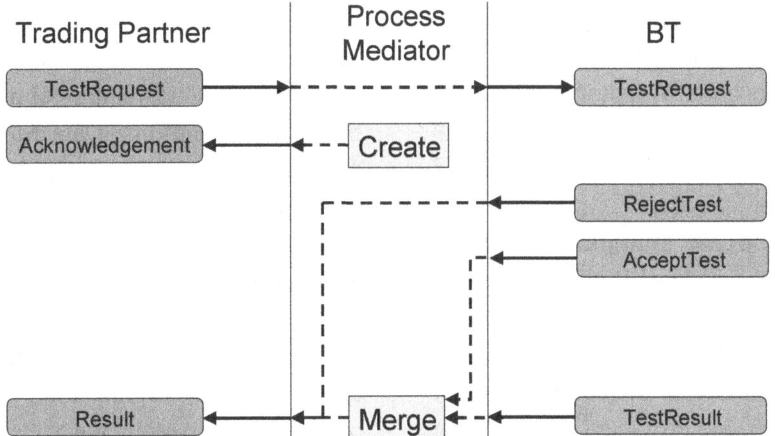

the fact that the TestRequest message has been received by BT. Of course, there is no guarantee that the message has been received but this must be assumed by the process mediator in order to allow the process to complete. The second task is to mediate the response to TestRequest. In the case of a test that is rejected by BT, the message can be immediately forwarded to the trading partner (some data mediation may be required) since no further interaction is required. When a test is accepted the process mediator absorbs the AcceptTest message and awaits the TestResult. Upon receiving the Test Result it merges its content with the content of the AcceptTest message into the Result message required by the Trading Partner.

Prototype Overview

The prototype system – The B2B Integration Platform - has been developed to allow mediation to occur between the ISP systems and the B2B Gateway. The prototype is based upon the Web Services Modeling Ontology[2] which provides the conceptual underpinning and a formal language for semantically describing Web services in order to facilitate the automation of discovering, combining and invoking electronic services over the Web (Roman et al, 2005). WSMX[3], the execution environment of WSMO, is used to build the prototype. The components of this architecture include Process Mediation and Choreography (which is required by process mediation to conform to the message exchange patterns of the partners), Data Mediation and Invocation. Adaptor components have been added to allow low level message to be represented in WSML – WSMO's associated language.

In the specific use case, multiple Service Providers are interfacing with one Wholesale Provider (BT). As such, the diversity is at one end only. However, outside of the use case, the scenario could easily be expanded to include diversity at both ends where Service Providers interact with multiple Wholesale Providers (depending on location, technology, (e.g. ADSL, cable, satellite) etc.). In that scenario, extra benefit is provided to the Service Providers as they are able to more easily reconfigure their systems and processes to interact with alternative Wholesale Providers.

SOLUTION DETAILS

This section provides further detail on the prototype system including a description of the approach, architecture and implementation. The section begins with a description of the steps that must be carried out at design-time prior to usage of the system at runtime.

Design-Time

The prototype relies upon a number of design-time activities that must be carried out in order for mediation to occur at run-time. From BT's point of view, the key design-time task is to represent its interfaces semantically. This includes adapting the messages descriptions to the language of the platform – WSML. It is envisaged that a library of adaptors will exist to convert to and from popular messaging formats such as XML, UBL, etc. No intelligence is required in this adaptation step and the result is an ad-hoc messaging ontology that simply represents the descriptions of the various messages in WSML. Following the adaptation, the elements within these descriptions can then be referenced against a domain ontology, perhaps using an industry standard approach such as the Shared Information / Data Model (SID) of the TeleManagement Forum[4] (TMF). These references provide context to the data and allow their semantic meaning to be inferred. For example the SID defines two concepts `Party` and `PartyRole`. The concept `Party` is used to explicitly define an organisation or individual and `PartyRole` allows an organisation/individual to take on a particular role during a business transaction.

On the B2B Gateway these concepts fit nicely, as there are a number of organisations that use the Gateway (such as BT and other third party providers) and they take on different roles depending on the operation being undertaken and thus the `Party` that represents them can be associated with an appropriate `PartyRole`. If a third party provider wishes to carry out a `testRequest` operation, then the Concept `Party` is used to describe their organisation, and `PartyRole` is used to define their role in this transaction as "Conductor". Similarly BTs `PartyRole` in this operation is "Performer" as they are performing the actual test.

The final design-time task for BT is to semantically describe the message-exchange pattern that it expects – in WSMO this description is known as the choreography. The choreography relates the semantic content of the messages to a semantic description of the process. This can be used by a process mediator to reason about how to mediate to a target choreography. It may be possible to automatically generate the choreography description with a suitable process description approach for the native interface (such as the Business Process Specification Schema[5] of ebXML). The outcome of the design-time tasks for BT is illustrated in Figure 2. This represents the process of applying the WSMX adapter to the ebXML messages in order to create equivalent messages in WSML. The message elements reference the appropriate domain and choreography ontologies.

From the perspective of the Trading Partner, the design-time activities include applying an appropriate adaptor to their messages descriptions, defining its own semantic choreography description and defining a data mediator between its data representation and that of BTs. This final step is perhaps the most important and labour intensive, however the open architecture should allow discovery and reuse of mediators should they already exist. The end result of this mediation step is that the ad hoc messaging ontology of the Trading Partner is mapped to the domain ontology enabling semantic equivalence. A data mediator is produced that is stored and applied at run-time. The mediator acts as a declarative transform that can be dynamically discovered and applied in other (perhaps closely related) scenarios. As such, it should be stored in such a way that other parties can later discover it. These tasks are illustrated in Figure 3.

The semantically described choreography of the Trading Partner can be considered against that

Figure 2. Outcome of BT design-time tasks

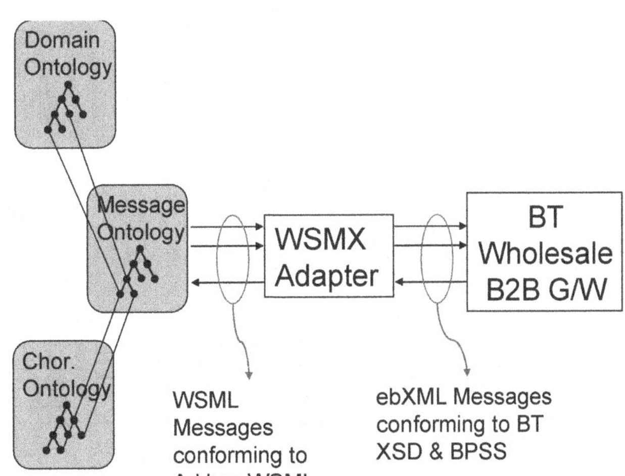

of BT by the Process Mediation system which can reason whether it is possible to mediate (based on the content of the messages in the choreographies and whether that content can be provided at the required time and in the required format of the target choreographies) and if so, automatically generate a process mediator. This reasoning step can be carried out at design-time if the two parties are known at this stage (as is the case here) or at run-time if one of the parties discovers the other in a dynamic run-time scenario. This latter case is only feasible if data mediation has already occurred or a suitable data mediator can be discovered.

Run-Time

The sequence of events at runtime is:

1. The trading partner OSS generates a message in its native format e.g. XML and forwards this to the B2B Integration Platform (i.e. the prototype).
2. The Integration Platform applies the appropriate adaptor to convert the message to WSML.
3. A description of the appropriate target interface is retrieved from the data store of the platform. This can either be predetermined at design-time or discovered at run-time in a more flexible scenario.
4. The choreography engine identifies suitable process and data mediators for the message exchange which has been determined based upon the nature of the first message.
5. If it is appropriate to send an outgoing message to the target system at this stage the choreography engine applies the data mediator to generate a message that the target will understand.
6. The outgoing message is adapted to the native format of the target interface. In the case, that of the B2B Platform which is ebXML.
7. The outgoing message is forwarded to the intended destination.

Of this sequence, steps 2-6 are platform dependent in that they are carried out by the WSMX architecture. However, it is worth pointing out that the key benefit is obtained by the explicit relation

Figure 3. Outcome of trading partner design time tasks

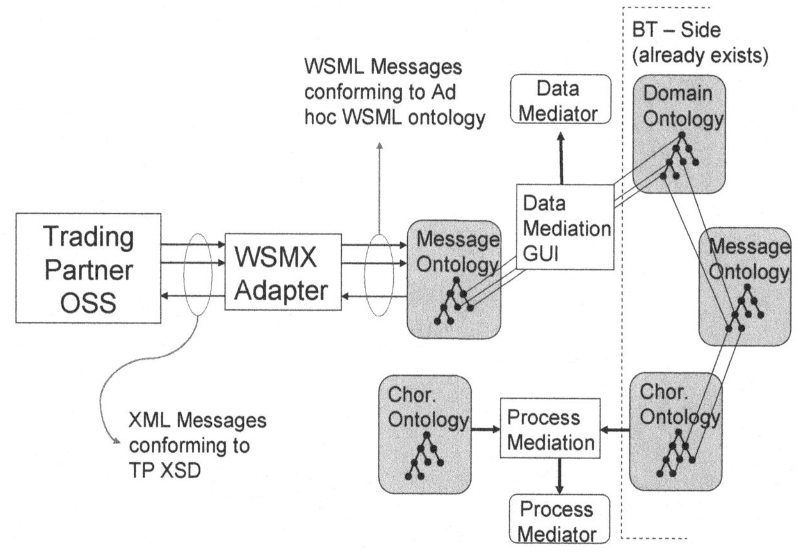

Figure 4. Prototype architecture

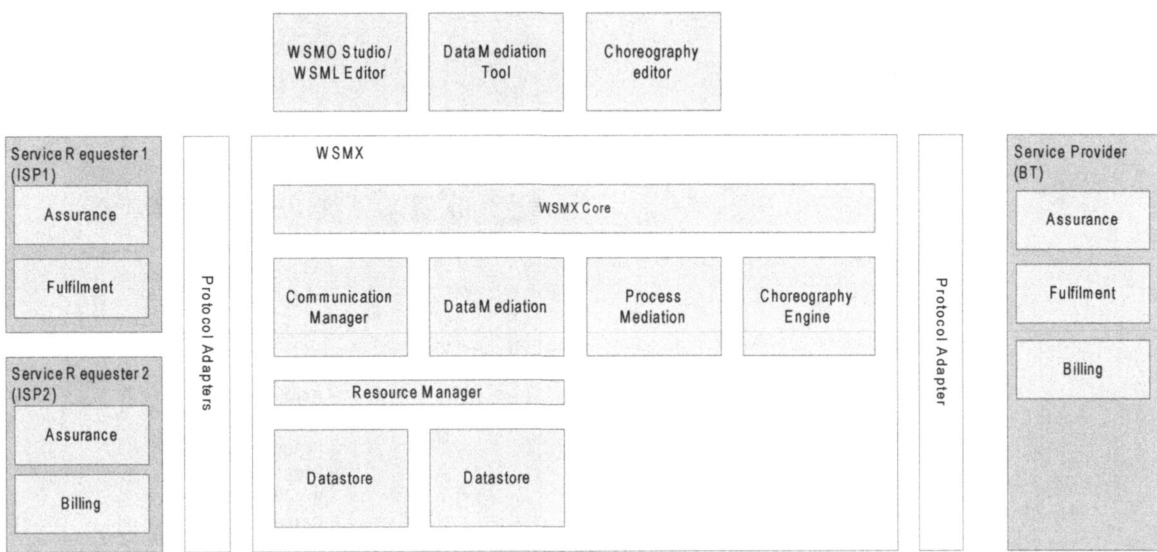

that is made between the low-level messages and the domain ontology. Any platform that was able to interpret this relationship would be able to apply mediation and transform the data and process to that required by the target.

B2B Integration Platform Architecture

Figure 4 shows the high level architecture for the prototype including the necessary components from the WSMX architecture. This includes a set of design-time tools to create the semantic descriptions of the services and mediators, the WSMX core, choreography engine, communication manager and resources manager to manage storage and interaction and the adaptor framework to convert to and from WSML and mediator components to apply the WSMO mediators at run-time.

Prototype Implementation

The prototype has been implemented using WSMX components to form the B2B Integration platform with Web-based GUIs backed by appropriate Web Services to simulate the OSS of the ISP and BT Wholesale. The Web Services mimic the behaviour of the working systems in that actual message formats and exchange patterns have been utilised. The following describes the RequestTest process that has been implemented for the Assurance Integration scenario. A screenshot from a trading partner GUI is shown in Figure 5.

1. A Customer informs his ISP of an error occurring in one of his products through a form on the ISP's Web site. The error is passed to the ISP's trouble ticketing system.
2. The ticketing system raises the problem with an operator who requests that a test should be carried out on the customer's line using the GUI of the ISP's OSS (as shown in Figure 5). The OSS system produces a message in a specific XML format (including the data payload, describing the error and the Customer's product).
3. The message is sent to the B2B Integration Platform which carries out the steps described in Section 4.2 resulting in a test request being forward to BT.

Figure 5. Screenshot from prototype UI

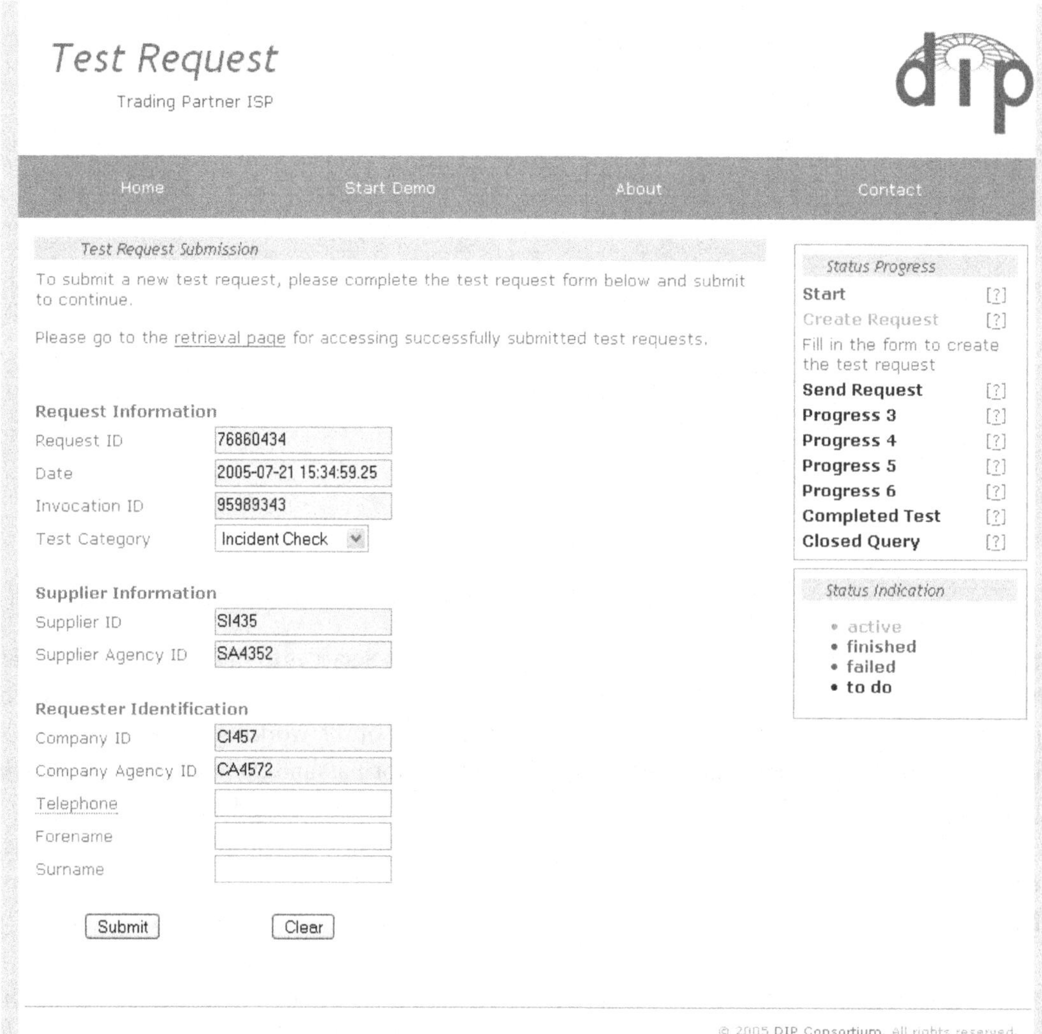

4. BT's OSS receives the message and handles it appropriately, updating its internal records with details and status of the test.
5. Upon completion of the test, the status is updated and an appropriate message is returned to the B2B Integration Platform which again carries out the steps described in Section 4.2 resulting in a test request response being sent to the ISP which then updates its GUI allowing the operator to see the result and act on it.

ALTERNATIVES

This section identifies related alternative approaches to semantic technology for improving B2B integration.

Web Services

The most common method for creating B2B gateways is to expose a set of Web Services which partners invoke to send and receive data. The interfaces and communication of Web Services is done with XML, and they are based on a number of standards:

- **Simple object access protocol (SOAP):** An XML-based, extensible message envelope format, with "bindings" to underlying protocols. The primary protocols are HTTP and HTTPS, though bindings for others, including SMTP and XMPP, exist.
- **Web services description language (WSDL):** An XML format that allows Web Service interfaces to be described, along with the details of their bindings to specific protocols, such as SOAP. Typically used to generate server and client code, and for configuration.
- **Universal description, discovery and integration (UDDI):** UDDI is a protocol for publishing and discovering metadata about Web services, to enable applications to find Web services, either at design time or runtime.

There are various other layers that can be added to Web Service to implement, authorization security, policies and trust and are part of the family of Web Service standards in OASIS.

There are many backend application servers that natively support Web Services, such as BEA WebLogic[6], JBoss[7] and IBM WebSphere[8]. This means that code can be created in a programming language such as Java or C# and the server automatically publishes a Web Service interface for it. The application server is then responsible for managing the data flow between the Web Service and the executable code.

Web Services mean that B2B interfaces can be accessed easily over the Web with standard protocols. What Web Services do not do is give much information on *how* to access a service and what the result will be after invoking it. They give basic information of the correct type of inputs and outputs (such as Integer or String) and they can be linked to XML schema definitions for more complex data types, but usually there is still quite a lot of manual work involved to correctly interact with the Web Service. Typically a set of Web Services in a B2B gateway will come with a substantial amount of documentation to describe what each services does, what the inputs/outputs mean and the correct way to invoke them.

Some effort has been made to define standards for common business interactions, as many B2B gateways perform similar tasks (e.g. product ordering, fault reporting). There has been effort to define generic industry wide standards (such as ebXML and RosettaNet[9]), and some domain specific ones such as the telecommunications eTOM and SID from the TMF. While these standards have helped in gateways where they have been adopted, there is still a lack of richness in the definitions of the data and process described in them. For example the telecommunications SID data model is based on UML and as such is not directly machine interpretable and suffers from brittleness due to the enforced hierarchical structure of the model. Also solutions that have tried to be too generic have suffered from lack of granularity, forcing users to create custom extensions which are not part of the shared standard.

Semantic Web Service approaches such as WSMO can overcome the deficiencies described above by supporting machine interpretable descriptions that enables an agile, flexible architecture for integration.

Open Source Approach

Increasingly, companies that need to interact electronically are working together on common open source systems. The current approach of single organisations having bespoke internal software applications and then defining a B2B gateway onto them means there is a lot of work interpreting and translating from the different organisations' systems into the B2B gateway format. Open source development allows all parties to contribute to the system and make sure their specific requirements are included, and can integrate with their current systems. BT has adopted an open source approach for the BT global services open application server (OAS). This is a platform which sits on top of the telephone network and offers services such as private networks for corporate companies and '0800 freephone' number services. Amongst other benefits, a recent paper (BT, 2006) describes one of the advantages of the open source approach: "Its flexibility also allows the OAS to work with numerous networks from different vendors in a way traditional software doesn't".

COST AND BENEFITS

Costs

'Semantic Tax'

Semantic technology involves the creation of richer descriptions of data and processes that are interpretable by computers to allow increased automation. These rich descriptions, in the form of ontologies are immensely useful once created, but there is an initial cost in the development of ontologies and some ongoing effort to maintain and update them.

Computational Resources

The increase in automation that can be achieved with semantic technologies inevitably leads to an increase in computational resources required compared to classical approaches. This is largely down to the reasoning carried out over ontologies when certain tasks need to be performed. Reasoning is the process of interpreting the semantic descriptions and inferring new knowledge as a result. For example, when mediation is carried out across the prototype, if there are complex data mediation mapping rules between two ontologies, the reasoning engine will have to interpret these and make the transformations dynamically as messages pass through the data mediator. In a classical system these transformations would be carried out with a hard-wired approach, which would require less computation at run time (but is more manually intensive and brittle, as discussed below).

Currently most reasoners use an 'in memory' model to reason over ontologies. This means that all the ontological statements that need to be reasoned about have to be loaded into a computer's RAM. This presents some issues when dealing with very large ontologies. More pragmatic solutions are emerging where data is persisted in a database. Such an approach increases the amount of data that can be reasoned over but is inherently slower.

Benefits

Automation

As discussed in the section above there are some additional computational resources and some initial manual resource required for a semantic technology based approach. However this should be greatly outweighed by the increase in automation achieved, and hence a decrease in overall effort and cost. In the prototype, semantic mediation allows a declarative approach to mapping between data and processes expressed in an ontology. This means that once these high level mapping have been made, all the run time mappings of actual messages are carried out automatically and dynamically at run-time. The current approach is to program manual mappings between each individual message, which is time consuming and results in brittle point to point mappings. If the format of the incoming message changes evenly slightly these mappings will break and will have to be manually re-programmed. In the semantic mediation prototype this problem would only require changes to the declarative mappings between the ontologies and the low-level messages transformation will be dealt with automatically. The key point here is that a non-programmer is able to carry out the change using a graphical mapping tool.

Open Data Models

It has been long recognised that developing open standards for data and process representation in computing is beneficial. The Semantic Web encourages people to work together and develop ontologies, which are by their nature open and accessible over the Web. The prototype described in this chapter is based upon ontologies and declarative mappings which rather than relying upon representing the domain with programme code. Although one could represent a domain in a multitude of ways, the use of open standards such as WSMO and OWL should further promote reuse and increased automation. One of the reasons for the success of the Web was due to the open standard of HTML that allowed people to develop Web technologies around a stable open model and create Web pages that everyone could view and access. If there had been 20 competing formats for creating Web pages, it would have severely limited the growth of the Web. The same can be said about other data and process formats using the Semantic Web. As the use of ontologies grows and people develop applications based on the same open ontologies the process of communicating and sharing data over the internet will be achieved much more effectively.

RISK ASSESSMENT

The development of the Semantic Web and semantic technologies has made great progress since the original article by Tim Berners Lee et al. (2001). It was quickly realised that the goal of encouraging greater automation in the processing and exchange of data over the Web would be highly useful in the area of B2B interactions, where the high degree of manual intervention required currently makes connecting to gateways expensive. Although we have showed in principle that a B2B system based on semantic technology has many advantages over the current methods, there are still a number of risk factors that need to be taken into account when assessing the feasibility for adopting a full scale B2B solution. The prototype was based on a subset of the functionality of the B2B gateway, and its current state has not been tested extensively for performance in a real scenario. There are some assumptions that the benefits we see in the proof of concept can be scaled up to a full B2B system. At the same time we acknowledge that there is still significant ongoing work in the area of reasoner optimisation and addressing scalability issues for large ontologies. The section below gives a full SWOT analysis

Strengths

- **Good tool support.** The current prototype is built on WSMX, which is an open source semantic execution environment initially developed with funding from the EU DIP project[10]. The system has a strong active development community and has continued funding for development under a number of active and forthcoming EU 6th and 7th framework projects. As well a good number of active Open Source SW tools, a number of commercial SW applications have started to emerge recently, such as Progress DataXtend Semantic Integrator.[11]
- **Standards support.** The W3C and OASIS have been strong supporters of the Semantic Web and have pushed through a number of standards around the Semantic Web (including RDF[12] and OWL[13]) that has helped create

stability and encourage companies to begin using the technology

- **Increasing maturity.** Much of the initial work on the Semantic Web was done by the academic community, or by industrial researchers with funding from government agencies such as DARPA and the EU. We are now beginning to see a wave of venture capital funding for new SW startups (Schenker, 2007), and also some buyouts of early adopters e.g. Unicorn was recently acquired by IBM[14]. This is a sign that the technology is maturing and that SW solutions can be delivered to meet the robust requirements of real industrial settings.

Weaknesses

- **Scalability.** The prototype presented in this chapter is a proof-of-concept system, so there was not a rigorous trial to test the system on a larger industrial scale. There are, however, some known issues around scalability when dealing with large ontologies. The reasoner used in the prototype currently has an in-memory model to reasoner over ontologies, so there is an upper limit to the size of the ontology that it can deal with. There is significant research in attempting to address this.
- **Reusability.** One of the cited advantages of semantic mediation is that once a mediator has been created, it can be stored in a mediation library and adapted/reused in other situations when needed (as common mismatches in ontological concepts are likely so occur, such as Zip Code – Post Code). In the course of the prototype development we did not have the variety of ontologies to test this reusability. It may be the case that attempting to adapt a current mediator for a new situation will be at least as time consuming as creating a new one from scratch. More research needs to be carried out to assess the assumptions of reusability.
- **Performance.** The advantages of using semantic mediation are the increase in automation and the ability to dynamically map between messages at run time. The disadvantage to this is that more processing is required at run time to analyse the mapping rules and perform the mediation, thus increasing latency. In some situations this may cause a problem (e.g. in a stock market trading gateway). This problem is likely to diminish over time as reasoning improves and computing power increases
- **Validation.** Since the mediation approach is new, validation is perhaps not as vigorous and well understood as is now the case with traditional software engineering. Further work is required to better understand how to ensure that the output of mapping and mediation tools is indeed as the user intended and workable in practice.

Opportunities

The prototype presents a semantic mediation solution for a B2B gateway dealing with telecommunications assurance related tasks. Generally there is the opportunity to apply this type of solution to any scenario where two parties need some form of automated communication, and there is a difference in data or process representations that need to be resolved. Integration problems are present in many places, whether it is internal OSS system integration, legacy system integration, B2B/B2C integration or SOA service integration.

Threats

- **Resistance to change.** With any new technology the largest barriers to adoption are often non-technical. There is a need to convince people of the benefits and to encourage them to embrace ontologies and meta-data when creating new applications. By design, semantic technologies can cope with heterogeneous data sources, but applications that conform to existing ontologies and data standards are much easier to integrate. It is still common for developers to create applications in isolation, and then worry about integration problems at a later date. There is also an upfront cost to develop ontologies and deploy the new SW infrastructure, and this may also be a barrier to take-up.

FUTURE TRENDS

The prototype described in this chapter is a first step in applying semantic mediation to the B2B integration problem. A number or areas require further attention, principally due to the fact that the prototype currently considers only the technical aspects of the mediation process. Further work is required to address other requirements. For example, in the current prototype, a sample message exchange format for a trading partner has been created. Engaging a trading partner in a trial would allow an evaluation of the mediation process to be carried out using an authentic message exchange and determining the time and costs associated with the appropriated design-time activities. Further evaluation of run-time performance is also required. In tandem, these activities will provide a measure of the overhead that WSMX introduces versus the potential benefits in cost and time savings. From the purely technical point-of-view, further work is required to establish a semantically explicit choreography representation that enables all appropriate message exchange patterns to be described. Reasoning over these potentially complex descriptions with the aim of constructing a process mediator is required.

Looking ahead, many more players within the industry are expected to expose their interfaces for integration. These will include service, wholesale and content provider. When that occurs, semantic technologies have real value since the economies of scale are greater. The initial effort required in creating ontologies, describing interfaces semantically and relating the two together is much less than the total integration effort. It is also likely that certain ontologies will flourish while others will not resulting in de facto standard ways of describing things. Mediation will be important both to map low level messages and data to the ontologies and since new services will emerge requiring integration between the services (and ontologies) of players in previously unimagined fields. In this more fluid environment the customer is given more power since he or she is the one who is able to choose the components in their service bundles and can even start to create integrated bundles that providers had previously been considered unviable or perhaps not considered at all.

CONCLUSION

The requirement for flexible B2B interfaces with Telecommunications has increased due to regulatory impact and the emergence of the converged ICT sector. Existing approaches for integration tend to be implementation specific, operate at the syntactic level and are realised by programme code. Consequently they are inflexible due to their highly coupled nature and are costly to setup and maintain. This chapter describes an approach to decouple B2B interfaces allowing them to be flexibly coupled as required with the use of scalable, semantic mediation. A prototype based on an Assurance Integration scenario for BT Wholesale's B2B gateway is described. The prototype uses the execution environment of the Web Services modeling ontology and demonstrates how the OSS of partner organisation can be integrated.

REFERENCES

Berners-Lee. T., Hendler, J. & Lassila, O. (2001). The Semantic Web. *Scientific American*. May.

BT plc. (2006). *Open Source Discussion*. Retrieved July 30th, 2007, from http://www.btplc.com/Innovation/Strategy/Open/Open.pdf

Evans, D., Milham, D., O'Sullivan, E. & Roberts, M. (2002). Electronic Gateways — Forging the Links in Communications Services Value Chains. *The Journal of The Communications Network*, 1, Part 1.

Fensel, D. (2001). *Ontologies: Silver Bullet for Knowledge Management and Electronic Commerce*. Springer-Verlag.

Koetzle, L., Rutstein, C., Liddell, H. & Buss, C. (2001). *Reducing Integration's Cost*. Forrester Research Inc. December 2001.

McKenna, T. (2002). *Telecommunications One-track minds: providers are integrating software to manage service delivery*. Retrieved July 30th, 2007, from http://www.findarticles.com/p/articles/mi_m0TLC/is_5_36/ai_86708476

Roman, D., Keller, U., Lausen, H., de Bruijn, J. Lara, R., Stollberg, M., Polleres, A., Feier, C., Bussler, C., & Fensel, D. (2005) Web Service Modeling Ontology. *Applied Ontology*, 1(1): 77 - 106, 2005.

Shenker, J.L. (2007). Battle for the Future of the Net. *Business Week*. Retrieved July 30th, 2007, from http://www.businessweek.com/globalbiz/content/jul2007/gb20070725_335895.htm

Strang, C. (2005). Next Generation systems architecture – the Matrix. *BT Technology Journal*. 23(1), 55-68.

Wiederhold, G. (1992). Mediators in the Architecture of Future Information Systems. *IEEE Computer*, March 1992, 38-49.

ENDNOTES

1 http://www.w3.org/XML/schema/

2 http://www.wmo.org/

3 http://www.wsmx.org/

4 http://www.tmforum.org/

5 http://www.ebxml.eu.org/process.htm

6 http://www.bea.com/framework.jsp?CNT=index.htm&FP=/content/products/weblogic/server/

7 http://www.jboss.org/

8 http://www.ibm.com/websphere

9 http://www.rosettanet.org/

10 http://dip.semanticweb.org/

11 http://www.progress.com/dataxtend/dataxtend_si/index.ssp

12 http://www.w3.org/RDF/

13 http://www.w3.org/TR/owl-features/

14 http://www-306.ibm.com/software/swnews/swnews.nsf/n/hhal6pgmpm?OpenDocument&Site=software

Chapter IV
Semantic Web-Enabled Protocol Mediation for the Logistics Domain

Oscar Corcho
Universidad Politécnica de Madrid, Spain

Silvestre Losada
Intelligent Software Components, S.A., Spain

Richard Benjamins
Intelligent Software Components, S.A., Spain

ABSTRACT

Among the problems that arise when trying to make different applications interoperate with each other, protocol mediation is one of the most difficult ones and for which less relevant literature can be found. Protocol mediation is concerned with non-matching message interaction patterns in application interaction. In this chapter we describe the design and implementation of a protocol mediation component that has been applied in the interoperation between two heterogeneous logistic provider systems (using two different standards: RosettaNet and EDIFACT), for a specific freight forwarding task.

CURRENT SITUATION

Logistics is defined as the art and science of managing and controlling the flow of goods, energy, information and other resources like products, services and people from the source of production to the marketplace. As pointed out by Evans-Greenwood and Stason (2006) the current trend in logistics is to divide support between planning applications, which compute production plans overnight, and execution applications, which manage the flow of events in an operational environment. This disconnection forces users to deal with business exceptions (lost shipments, for example), manually resolving the problems by directly updating the execution and planning applications. However, this human-dependency problem can be ameliorated by using Web technology to create a heterogeneous composite application involving all participants in the process, providing a complete Third-Party Logistics solution, and giving users a single unified view into the logistics pipeline. This consolidated logistics solution greatly simplifies the task of identifying and correcting business exceptions (e.g., missing shipments or stock shortages) as they occur. Therefore, logistics management is a typical business problem where the use of a service oriented architecture is clearly suited.

Furthermore, Evans-Greenwood and Stason (2006) also talk about the possibility of combining multiple Third-Party Logistics solutions into a single heterogeneous virtual logistics network. With such a virtual network, each shipment is assigned a route dynamically assembled from one or more individual logistics providers, using dynamically created virtual supply chains. Most of these business functions are still manual and offline, but most of them can be automated with the use of service oriented architectures, as will be presented in this chapter. Obviously, the main advantages of using such solutions are the decreases in cost and speed in transactions, which influence in a better quality of the service provided to customers.

The main barrier to set up a business relationship with a company in the logistics domain is that it usually requires an initial large investment of time and money. This is ameliorated by the emergence of some industry standards like EDIFACT (EDIFACT), AnsiX12 (AnsiX12) or RosettaNet (RosettaNet), which ease the integration tasks between information systems that comply with them. However, given that these standards have some flexibility in what respects the content and sequencing of the messages that can be exchanged, the integration of systems is still time and effort consuming. Besides, there is sometimes a need to integrate systems that use different standards, what makes the integration task even more time and effort consuming.

This is the focus of one of the four case studies developed in the context of the EU project SWWS[1] (Semantic-Web enabled Web Services), a demonstrator of business-to-business integration in the logistics domain using Semantic Web Service technology. All the features of this demonstrator are described in detail by Preist and colleagues (2005), including aspects related to the discovery and selection of relevant services, their execution and the mediation between services following different protocols.

In this chapter we will focus on the last aspect (mediation) and more specifically on protocol mediation, which is concerned with the problem of non-matching message interaction patterns. We will describe the design and implementation of the protocol mediation component applied in this case study to show how to make logistic provider systems using two different standards (RosettaNet and EDIFACT) interoperate for a specific freight forwarding task.

The chapter is structured as follows. The rest of this section introduces a motivating example, focusing on the needs for protocol mediation, and gives some background on how the problem of mediation can be characterised in general and on the approaches for mediation proposed in the context of Semantic Web Service research. Section 2 summarises the protocol mediation approach followed for this case study and the main elements to be considered inside the approach. It also describes the ontology used for the description of the abstract and concrete protocols used by the entities involved in the message exchange. Section 3 provides an overview of the API of the protocol mediation component and gives details about how to configure it for deployment. Finally, section 4 gives some conclusions.

An Example in the Logistics Domain

Let us imagine that we have a manufacturing company in Bristol, UK, which needs to distribute goods internationally. The company outsources transportation into other companies, which offer *Freight Forwarding Services*. These companies may be providing the transportation service by themselves or just act as intermediaries, but this is not important for the manufacturing company. However, the manufacturing company still needs to manage relationships with these service providers, as a *Logistics Coordinator*, being responsible for selecting the service providers, reaching agreements with them with respect to the nature of the service that they will provide, coordinating the activity of different service providers so as to ensure that they link seamlessly to provide an end-to-end service (e.g., if a ship company transports a goods to a port, then the ground transportation company should be waiting for those goods with a truck to transport them to an inland city), etc.

The manufacturing company uses EDIFACT for its exchange of messages with the service providers. However, not all of them use this standard, but in some cases RosettaNet. So the situation can be that two different companies that can offer the same service (e.g., road transportation inside Germany) are using two different standards and the logistics coordinator should be able to use any of them, independently of the protocol that they use in their information systems, taking only into account the business requirements that the parcel delivery may have (quality of service, speed, price, insurance, etc.). In this situation there is a need for a seamless integration of a mediation component that is able to capture the EDIFACT messages sent by the Logistics Coordinator into RosettaNet ones that are sent to the corresponding Freight Forwarding Service, and vice versa, without any change to the information systems of any of the parties involved.

Mediation in Service Oriented Architectures and in Semantic Web Services

In **service oriented architectures**, mediation services are middleware services that are in charge of resolving inconsistencies between the parties involved in a sequence of message exchanges. Mediation can be considered at different levels:

- **Data mediation:** Transformation of the syntactic format of the messages.
- **Ontology mediation:** Transformation of the terminology used inside the messages.
- **Protocol or choreography mediation:** Transformation of sequences of messages, to solve the problem of non-matching message interaction patterns.

All types of mediation are important to achieve a successful communication between the services involved in an application, and each of them poses different challenges. In this chapter we will focus on aspects related to the last type of mediation, which is the one aimed at ensuring that, from a high-level point of view, the services involved in a message exchange achieve their overall goals. In other words, it aims at mapping the patterns of conceptually similar, but mechanically different interaction protocols sharing a similar conceptual model of a given domain.

The atomic types of mismatches that can be found between a set of interaction patterns are (Cimpian and Mocan, 2005):

- **Unexpected messages:** One of the parties does not expect to receive a message issued by another. For instance, in a request for the delivery of a parcel the logistics provider sends the parcel weight and size, the departure place and the arrival place, while the freight forwarding service does not expect the parcel weight and size, since it will not use this information.

- **Messages in Different Order:** The parties involved in a communication send and receive messages in different orders. In the previous case the sender may send the messages in the order specified above while the receiver expects first the arrival place and then the departure place.
- **Messages that Need to be Split:** One of the parties sends a message with multiple informations inside it, which needs to be received separately by the other party. In the previous example, the sender sends the arrival and departure places in one message, while the receiver expects it as two messages.
- **Messages that Need to be Combined:** One of the parties sends a set of messages that the receiver expects as a single message with the multiple information. We can think of the inverse situation to the one aforementioned.
- **Dummy Acknowledgements or Virtual Messages that Have to be Sent:** One of the parties expects an acknowledgement for a certain message, but the receiver does not issue such acknowledgement; or the receiver expects a message that the sender is not prepared to send.

One of the purposes of the work on **Semantic Web Services** is the automation of some of the tasks involved in the development of applications that follow a service oriented architecture. As a result, some work on mediation has been done in the area. If we focus on protocol mediation, we can find the following two approaches:

Priest and colleagues (2005) and Williams and colleagues (2006) describe the approach followed in the context of SWWS, and which will be described in more detail in the next section. This approach is based on the use of a general abstract state machine that represents the overall state of the communication between parties, and a set of abstract machines for each of the parties in the conversation, which specify their state and the sets of actions to be performed when they receive a set of messages or when they have to send a set of messages.

In the context of the WSMO initiative, Cimpian and Mocan (2005) describe the approach taken for the design and implementation of the process mediator for the Semantic Web Service execution engine WSMX. This approach is similar to the previous one, since it is also based on the use of an abstract machine with guarded transitions that are fired by the exchange of messages and the definition of choreographies for each of the parties involved in the communication.

PROPOSED SOLUTION: THE SWWS APPROACH FOR PROTOCOL MEDIATION

This section describes briefly the main components involved in our protocol mediation approach. A more detailed explanation is provided in (Williams et al., 2006), and Figure 2 shows an example of the use of all these components in the logistics domain described in the introduction.

Communicative Acts

Communicative acts are the basic components of the communication. They are modelled as sequences of four events that are exchanged between systems and the underlying communication infrastructure when sending a message (see Figure 1), as follows:

- `.request`. The initiator sends a message to the communication infrastructure.
- `.indication`. The responder receives the message from the communication infrastructure.
- `.response`. The responder acknowledges the receipt of the message.

- `.confirm`. The initiator receives the acknowledge receipt.

Both the `.response` and `.confirm` primitives model an acknowledgement that the communication has reached its intended recipient. Any substantive response motivated by the communicative act itself is modelled as a subsequent communicative act in the opposite direction.

At the initiator, the outcome of a communicative act may be a success (the initiator knows that the communication has reached the intended recipient), an exception or failure (the initiator knows that the communication has failed to reach the intended recipient), or indeterminate (the initiator does not know the outcome of the communication).

Abstract Protocols and Roles

When we described protocol mediation, we commented that systems involved in a message exchange have conceptually similar interaction protocols. This high-level conceptual protocol is described by means of an abstract protocol.

The abstract protocol can be then defined as a multi-party choreography that describes the constraints that govern the sequencing of communicative acts between the systems engaged in an interaction. Each system takes on one or more roles (e.g., buyer, seller, logistics provider, freight forwarder, etc.) with respect to a choreography. The choreography then describes each of these roles in terms of the sequencing constraints on the exchange of primitives between the communication infrastructure and the system adopting the role.

Concrete Protocols

Each of the systems involved in a message exchange may have different mechanics by which communicative acts are managed. For each communicative act event in each system we will have then a concrete protocol that describes this behaviour.

Hence concrete protocols describe what happens at an initiating system in response to an admissible `.request` primitive and prior to (and after) the corresponding `.confirm` primitive. Likewise, at a responding system in response to the stimuli that give rise to an `.indication` primitive, the behaviours that occur between that and the corresponding `.response` and the behaviours that occur after that.

Figure 1. A communicative act and its four events (Williams et al., 2006)

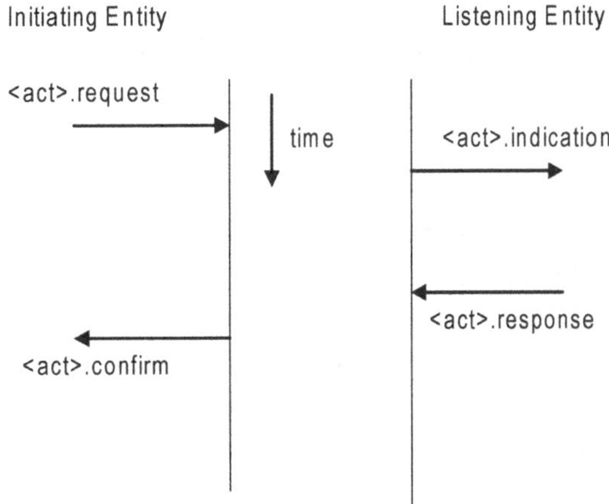

Processes as Abstract State Machines

The abstract and concrete protocols are described by means of processes, which in our approach are implemented by concurrent finite state machines. For abstract protocols a state represents the state of the high-level conversation in the context of the common multi-party choreography (e.g., a request for payment has been issued by the freight forwarding service and received by the logistics coordinator). For concrete protocols a state represents some intermediate state in the behaviours associated with the issuing of `.request` and `.confirm` primitives or issuing `.indication` and `.response` primitives.

Transitions between states may be driven by different internal and external actions, as follows:

1. *PrimitiveDriven transitions*. In abstract protocols they can be any of the primitives of a communicative act. In concrete protocols, they can be only `<act>.request` or `<act>.response` primitives, since these primitives can initiate the state machines associated to a concrete protocol.
2. *EventDriven transitions*. They are used to communicate between concurrent processes (a process may raise an event that is being waited for by another process). They are normally used in communication exchanges between more than 2 parties and in concrete protocols (e.g., two processes are waiting for the same payment under different payment procedures, credit card or cheque, and one of them is satisfied).
3. *TimeDriven transitions*. They occur on the expiry of a time interval following the entry to the state that has the time driven transition associated. They can be used in any type of protocol (e.g., in an abstract protocol, the system will have a timeout feature to send another communicative act if a response has not been received in a given time).
4. *MessageDriven transitions*. They occur only in concrete protocols, when a message is received from the communication infrastructure and filtered according to a template, so that the relevant information is extracted (e.g., for a freight forwarding service, if a request for a shipment service is broadcasted through the communication infrastructure, this could activate it so that it provides its service to the logistics provider).

All the transitions have associated a transition condition guard (a Boolean expression that determines whether the transition can be actually performed given the state where the state machine is and the external and internal conditions) and a transition behaviour. Transition behaviours model the actual transition logic to be done besides moving from one state to another. They include (both for abstract and concrete protocols): raising `.indication` or `.confirm` primitives, raising events to concurrent processes, and instantiate concurrent processes. For concrete protocols they may also include: perform transformations on received message structures, generate message structures for transmission, and extract, maintain and manipulate information taken from message fields.

An Ontology for Describing Abstract and Concrete Protocols

Figure 3 and Figure 4 show different parts of the very simple choreography language (VSCL) ontology, which is available at http://swws.semanticweb.org/. This ontology can be used to describe the abstract and concrete protocols presented in the previous section, together with all their components, and is used to configure the protocol mediation component described in the next section.

Figure 2. Abstract and some concrete protocols in the logistics domain (adapted from Williams et al., 2006)

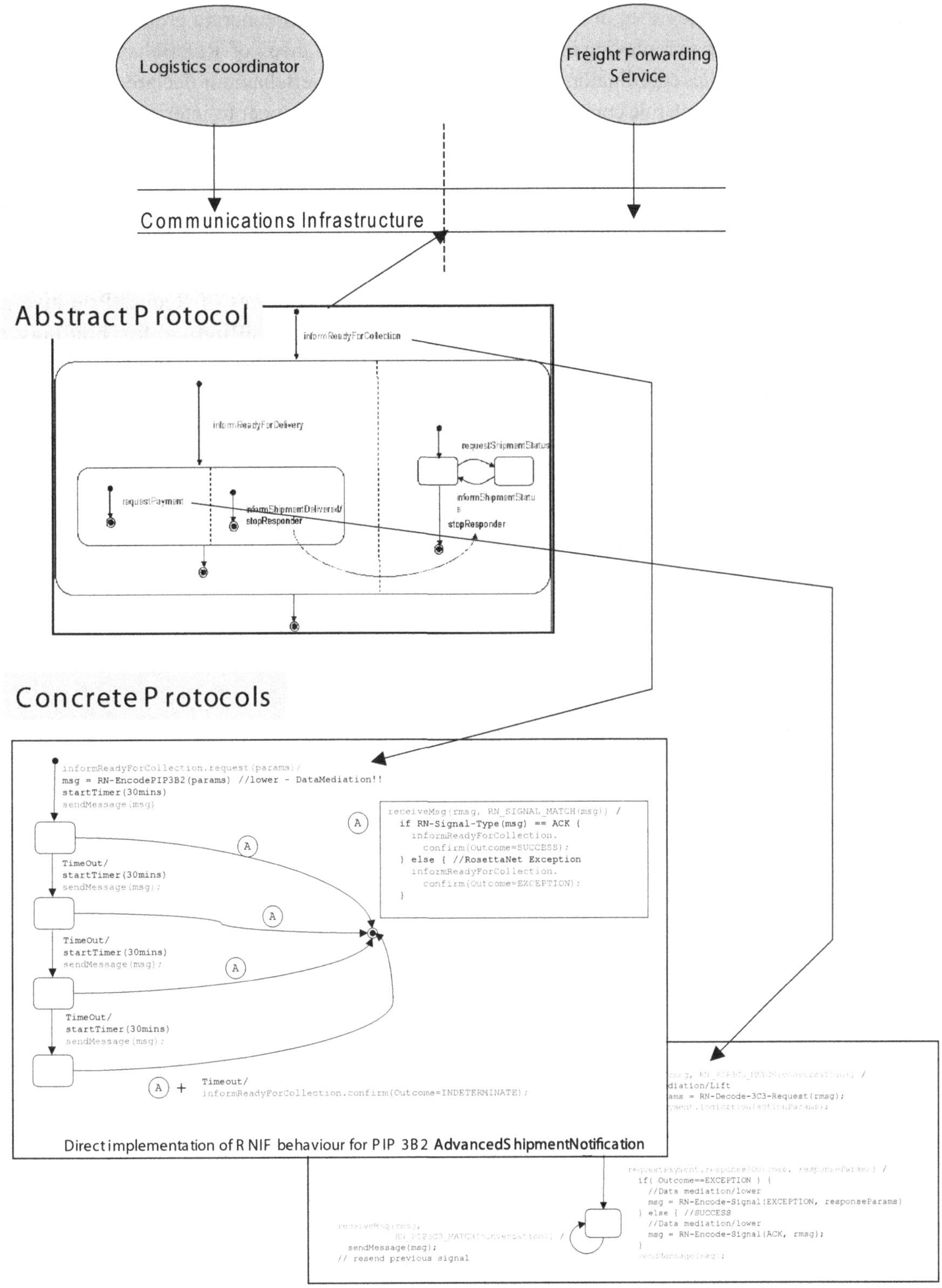

As shown in Figure 3, choreographies are divided into abstract and concrete protocols. An abstract protocol specifies a set of roles that identify the role that a system is playing in an exchange of messages (logistics coordinator, freight forwarding service, etc.). Each role contains a set of communicative acts that are considered in the shared abstract protocol and that allow defining the shared conceptual model of the message exchange patterns to be followed by all the systems participating in a conversation. For each of these roles in each abstract protocol and with each specific implementation of any of the systems involved there is one role behaviour, that implements a set of concrete protocols that correspond to the behaviour that the actual system for the different communicative acts that are defined for it.

The admissible sequences of communicative acts are specified in what we call a process, whose common implementation will be a state machine, as we will see in the next figure. The primitives that are considered are those that were described when we discussed communicative acts: request, indication, confirm and response.

Finally, each concrete protocol contains one or more instances of RoleBehaviour. Each instance of RoleBehaviour declare a role that may be adopted by a peer to interact with the service provider agent via its interface. Each RoleBehaviour and carries a PrimitiveBinding for each RequestPrimitive and IndicationPrimitive associated with the role. This divides PrimitiveBinding into two subclasses, InitiatingPrimitiveBinding for binding instances of RequestPrimitive and ListeningPrimitiveBinding for bindings associated with instances of IndicationPrimitive. Each instance of PrimitiveBinding associates an instance of Process with the corresponding primitive. The Process(es) associated with an InitiatingPrimitiveBinding are instantiated when an admissible invocation of the corresponding RequestPrimitive occurs. The Process(es) associated with a ListeningPrimitiveBinding are instantiated either when the corresponding conversation is

Figure 3. Ontology excerpt related to abstract and concrete protocols and communicative acts

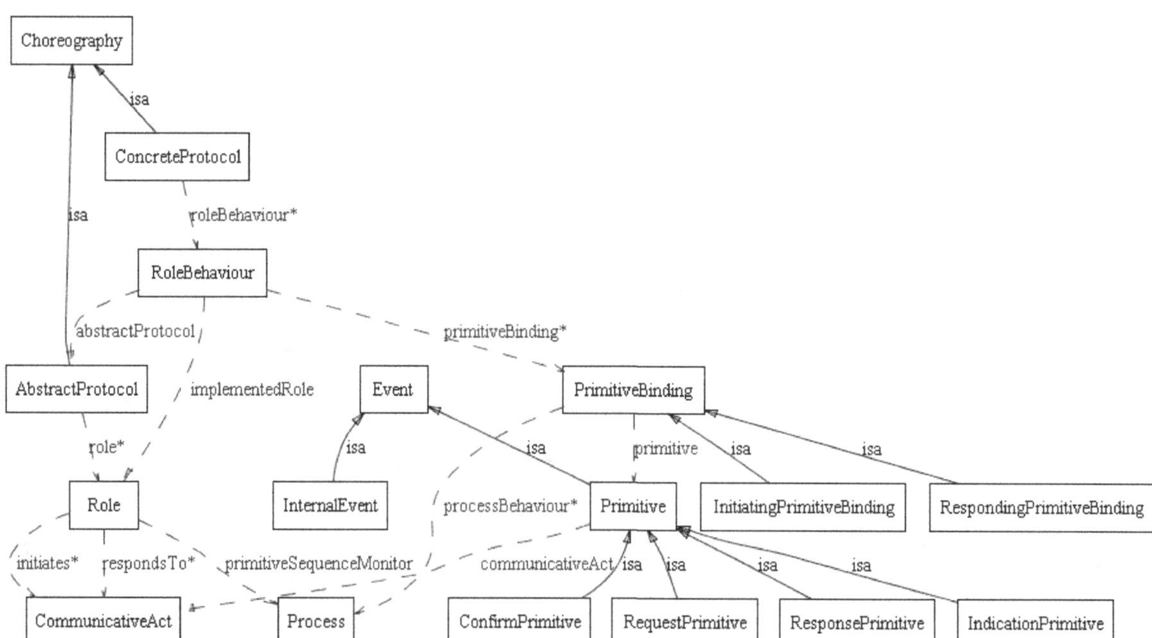

instantiated or as the conversation progresses and the IndicationPrimitive associated with the binding becomes admissible.

Figure 4 illustrates the classes used to represent state machines in VSCL. A state machine is a type of process that is composed of a set of states (some of which can be end states). Each state can have a set of associated transitions, which specify the next state, a set of guards and a set of transition behaviours. Transitions can be of different types, as described in the previous section (event driven, time driven, or message driven). The primitive driven transitions were already specified in Figure 3 as initiating and responding primitive bindings, since they are responsible for starting a state machine.

Transitions behaviours are of different types, as pointed out in the previous section. From them, the most relevant is the script, which can be provided by a reference to a URL (external) or as part of the instance values (internal). We will analyse them in more detail later, when we discuss the component API.

In our logistics application we have a state machine for each of the protocols aforementioned.

Figure 4. Ontology excerpt related to the state machine descriptions

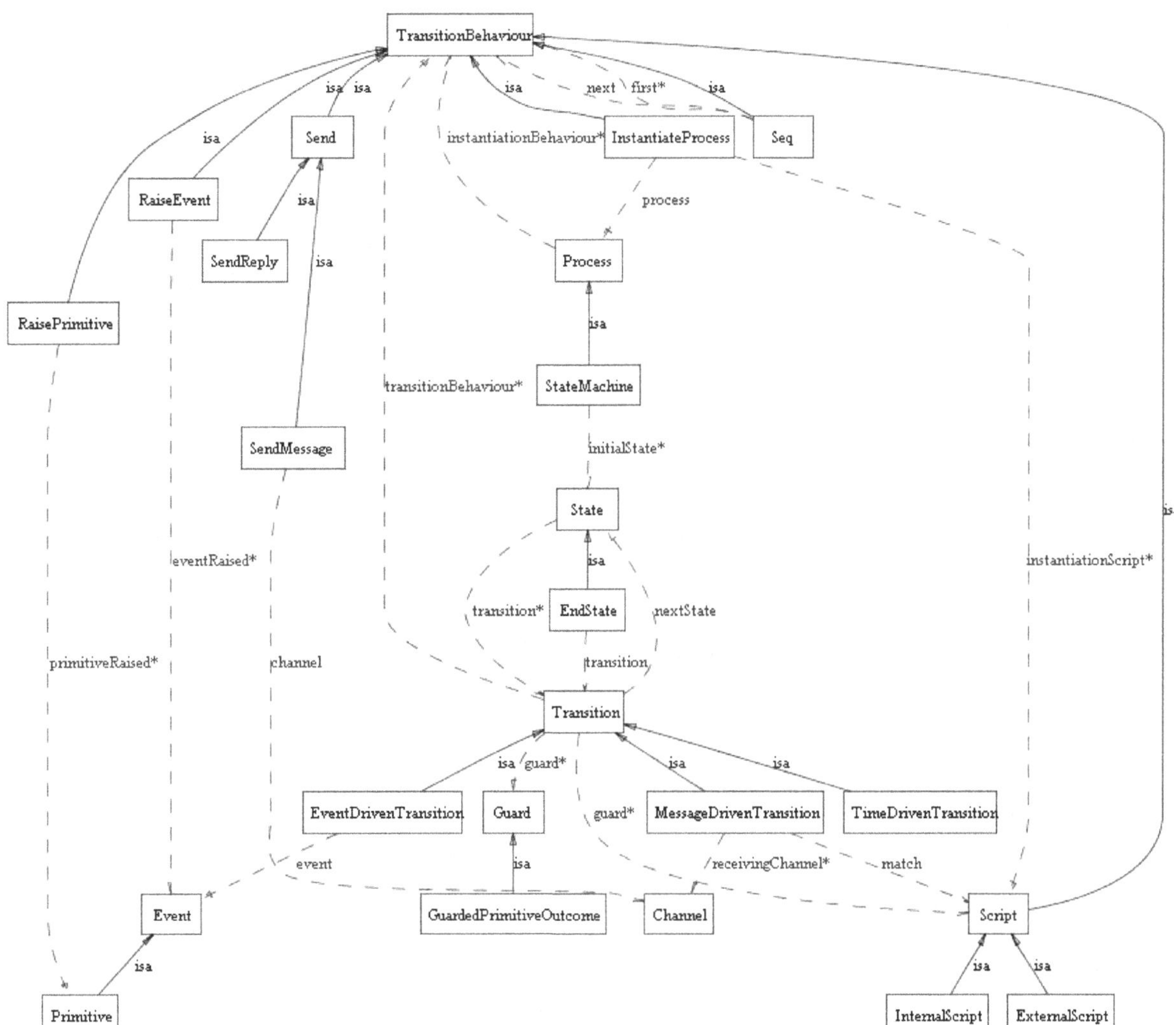

In summary, in our logistics application we have the following instances of this ontology (available at *http://swws.semanticweb.org/*):

- One abstract protocol with two roles defined for it: FreightForwardingServiceConsumer and FreightForwardingServiceProvider.
- 14 processes (state machines) for concrete protocols.
- Six communicative acts: InformReadyForCollection, RequestShipmentStatus, InformShipmentStatus, InformReadyToDeliver, InformShipmentDelivered, and RequestPayment, with their corresponding primitives (four for each of them).
- 10 event driven transitions with 20 scripts for their transition behaviours.

SOLUTION DETAILS: THE SWWS PROTOCOL MEDIATION COMPONENT

Here we provide a general description of the protocol mediation component architecture and of important implementation details, including a broad description of the component API, so that it can be used in other similar applications with protocol mediation needs.

Though the usual deployment of a protocol mediation component would be as part of the communication infrastructure between services in a service-oriented application, in our case this component has been deployed as shown in Figure 5: A consumer application incorporates the protocol mediation component inside its environment in order to control the exchange of messages with the provider application. In our logistics application, the selection of one system or another as consumer or provider is arbitrary. Our decision has been to use the logistics coordinator as a consumer and the freight forwarding service as a provider.

The protocol mediation component has 5 essential subcomponents, which are described in detail in the next sections:

- **Local agent** (package com.isoco.swws.conversation.local_agent). It is the subcomponent directly used by the final user. Basically, the component allows creating conversations, initiating them in an active or a passive mode and later, by means of the ConversationManager, explicitly invoking the different CommunicativeActs and tracing the interactions with the remote conversation partner.
- **Protocol** (package com.isoco.swws.conversation.abstractprotocol). It is the internal representation of the protocols (either abstract or concrete) that rule the conversation. This is based on the ontology described in the previous section.
- **ChoreographyHandler** (package com.isoco.swws.conversation.mediation.vscl). It is the bridge between the application and the external choreography that is included in the VSCL ontology.

Figure 5. Location for the deployment of the protocol mediation component

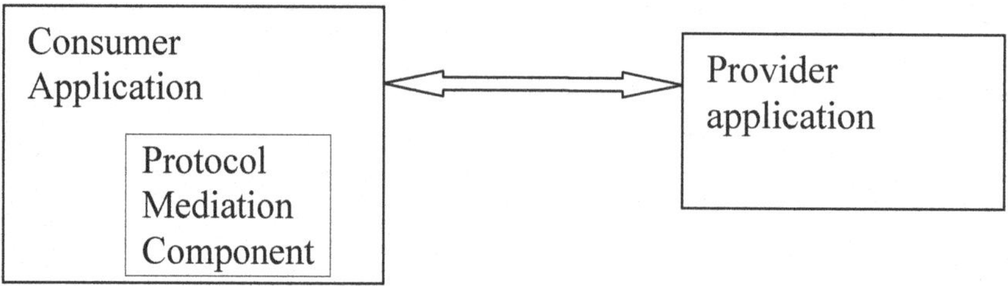

- **Message transfer plugin** (package com.isoco.swws.conversation.plugins). Internally, a specific communication protocol (HTTP, SMTP, etc.) is used for the communication between the consumer and the provider. This plugin serves as an interface for the protocol. This implementation of the component includes an HTTP plugin, but other plugins could be easily created and deployed.
- **Rhino facilites** (package com.isoco.swws.conversation.environment). They are used to execute the Javascript scripts included in the choreography. The mechanism used in the component is Rhino (Mozilla) and there is an abstraction layer to ease its use and to adapt it to the application needs.

Local Agent

The local agent groups the collection of classes that the Consumer needs to create and control a conversation. A conversation is initiated with the creation of a *ConversationManager*, which receives the following parameters in its constructor:

- A set of roles (the systems involved in a conversation). The InterfaceRole contains the *remoteInterface*, the URL that holds the address of the conversation's partner, and the *localRole,* the URL of the role adopted by the local agent with respect to the choreography and this conversation.
- The URL where to find the choreography (that is, the place where the VSCL ontology instances are stored).
- An indication handler, which is used in the case that an external system has to contact this system or send it and event. Normally this handler is used when the system receives a message from the provider that causes a <CommunicativeAct>.indication. This is the way that the protocol mediation component has to inform an application that an indication has arrived. It is also responsibility of the IndicationHandler to respond to the indication of the CommunicativeAct. Responding to the .indication means to model the .response. The user must calculate the outcome and the results of that CommunicativeAct.

The implementation of the IndicationHandler is robust enough to deal with situations where it could be blocked or fail, where the response will be launched again.

A conversation consists in the coordinated exchange of communicativeActs. The local agent can send CommunicativeActs either in a **synchronous** or an **asynchronous** way. In the synchronous exchange the communicative act is sent and the system waits for the confirmation of the remote partner. In the asynchronous exchange the communicative act is launched and the control is returned back to the application. When the confirmation from the user is received, the *confirm* method of the ConfirmHandler interface that has been specified as a parameter is invoked.

The creation of a new ConversationManager implies the following tasks: initializing the abstract and concrete protocols and initializing of the ChoreographyHandler for the successive uses of the choreography. A conversation that has been created can be initiated in two modes: **active** and **passive**:

- In the active mode, the Consumer can invoke the *synchSay* and the *asynchSay* methods (for synchronous and asynchronous exchanges of messages) to start the exchange of CommunicativeAct with the remote partner.
- In a passive mode, the *listen* method must be invoked to initiate a conversation in a passive mode. This action prevents the use of the *synchSay* and the *asynchSay* methods and the conversation waits for an indication

from the remote partner. It should be noted that once the *listen* method is invoked, the conversation will only be activated by a remote message from the partner. There is no explicit method to transfer the conversation to the active mode.

Figure 6 shows how this works in an active mode: the .request primitive is created for a CommunicativeAct. This primitive is sent to the abstract protocol to know if the CommunicativeAct can be initiated in the current context of the conversation.

- If it cannot be initiated, the execution is aborted and Outcome.INVALID is returned to the entity to inform that it is impossible to execute that action in the current situation.
- If it can be initiated, the primitive is sent to the concrete protocol in order to execute the set of scripts and other relevant actions associated to this primitive. It is important to emphasize that the primitive is sent, that is, there is no explicit communication from the abstract protocol to the concrete protocol. The idea is that the abstract protocol allows executing the primitive but it does not consume it. Afterwards, we wait to receive the .confirm primitive and the Outcome associated to the CommunicativeAct of the primitive is returned. The outcome can be: Outcome.SUCCESS, Outcome.EXCEPTION, or Outcome.INDETERMINATE.

When the entity is waiting for an indication, the process is different. When a message arrives, it is evaluated in the MessageDrivenTransitions of the active processes of the concrete protocol.

Figure 6. Usual process followed for a communicative act being sent

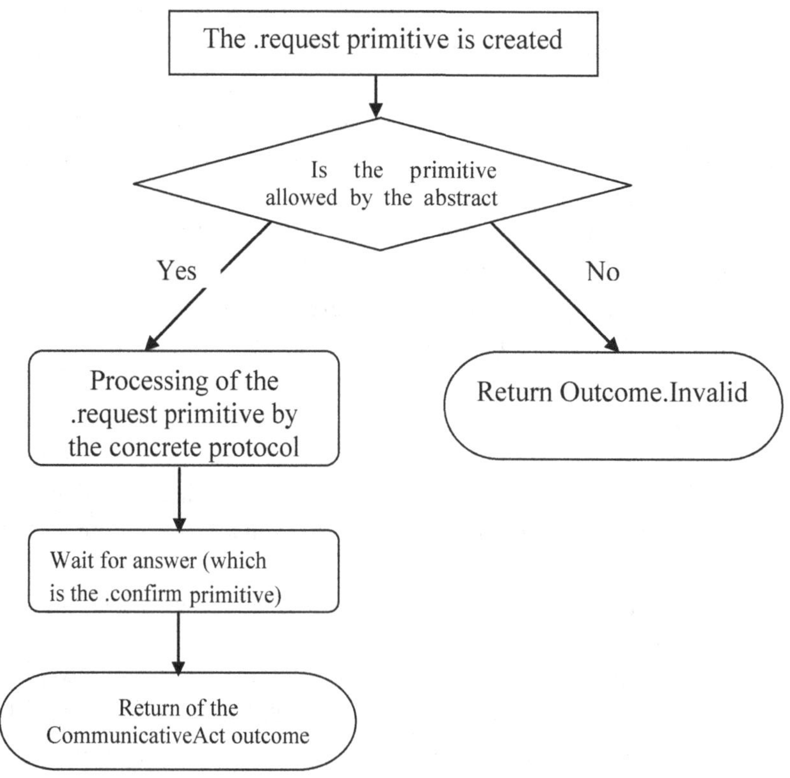

If any of them matches, that transition is executed and it will be its responsibility, among other responsibilities, to launch an .indication primitive to the abstract protocol to check if in the context of this conversation that primitive is allowed. If the primitive is allowed, the entity will be informed about it by the indication method of the IndicationHandler.

Multiple Conversations

The exchange of messages between the consumer and the provider is executed in a multiple simultaneous conversations scenario. To know which conversation should process each message, the protocol mediation component associates a unique conversation id to each ConversationManager.

Whenever a conversation is initiated by a partner, a message is sent with a parameter that informs that it is a new conversation. A new conversation id is created for this conversation and the following messages of this conversation must include this id.

The ConversationDispatcher class is responsible for registering all the existing conversations. Basically there are two lists: a list of active conversations and a list of potential conversations (those that are waiting to receive a message to start, by the invocation of the method *listen*). When a message to start a conversation arrives, all the conversations that are waiting are checked to inquire which one can process it. If a conversation can process it, that conversation is moved to the list of active conversations.

The ConversationDispatcher is also responsible for initializing all the available plugins once a conversation starts.

Protocols

Conversations are ruled by a choreography, which contains two types of protocols (abstract and concrete). Both protocols are specified by means of the ontology described in section 2.5. For each class in the ontology there is a Java class in this package, including the states and transitions.

Each ConversationManager has references to its own abstract and concrete protocols. When a conversation is created, the ConversationManager loads the initial processes with all their associated structure, using those Java classes (as explained in the following section). The list of processes and active states is updated as the transitions are executed.

Transitions are modelled with the `Transition` Java class and its subclasses. The following methods are called for a transition:

- **Evaluate initTransition.** This function must be redefined by all the subclasses of Transition. It has two responsibilities: verify that the object that it receives is the instance that it knows how to process. For example, the EventDrivenTransition must guarantee that the object type is 'Event'. Not only must it guarantee that it has the correct type, but also that it is the instance that sets off the transition (for example, that it is the RequestShipmentStatus.request primitive). Its other responsibility is to initiate whatever is necessary to execute the transition. For example, to set some variable in the RhinoEnvironment or some other task.
- **Evaluate initGuard.** The transitions can have an associated guard that must be satisfied to continue with the transition. In general, it is a method that does not have to be redefined by the subclasses.
- **Execute doBehaviours.** As a consequence to the execution of the transition, a set of TransitionBehaviours must be executed. These behaviours represent what the transition does. This method should not be modified. As we will see, transition behaviours are specified in Javascript and executed by the RhinoEnvironment.
- **Execute advanceToNextState.** A change to the new state is performed in order to end

the execution of a transition. This process entails several tasks such as the loading of all the structure of the new state from the choreography, the initialization of the associated TimeDrivenTransitions, etc.

Choreography Handler

It serves as a bridge between the application and the choreography. It is used to create instances of the classes included in the Protocols package from the choreography information available in a URL. As aforementioned, the whole choreography is not loaded completely from the start but incrementally according to the transitions done through the abstract and concrete protocols. Two significant methods from this class are:

- *createProcessByName*, which creates a state machine from the information available in its location (URL). It returns the state machine and all the structure associated to it (states, transitions, transition behaviours, scripts, etc.).
- *createStateByName*, which creates a state from its name (URI). It returns the state and all the structure associated to it (transitions, transition behaviours, scripts, etc.).

This component uses the KPOntology library[2] to navigate the RDF graph that models the choreography.

Message Transfer Plugin

This component deals with the specific communication protocol (HTTP, SMTP, etc.) used for the communication between consumers and providers. An HTTP plugin is included with the current implementation, and other plugins can be also created.

The HTTP plugin provided is made up of the HttpPlugin class and an auxiliary Web application that manages the queue of received messages, with two services:

- Receive a message. This service is used when a remote partner, e.g. the provider, must send a message to the consumer. The Web application receives the message and puts it in the queue of received messages.
- Recover the message. This service allows the HttpPlugin class to recover the messages received from the Web application.

The HttpPlugin class has two main objectives:

- Send messages to remote partners, using the sendMessage method. This method receives a remote address where to send the message, the conversation id, and the message.
- Transfer messages from the Web application to the component. The HTTP plugin has a thread that is constantly polling the Web application for the arrival of new messages.

The Web application always responds to the petition of messages by means of an XML that contains the following elements:

- **conversationId:** id of the conversation under way.
- **newConversation:** it indicates if it is a new conversation.
- **Message:** Depending on the types of message, it will have different types of structures. For instance, in the case of the RosettaNet messages, it will be divided into: "Preamble", "DeliveryHeader", "ServiceHeader" and "Content".

It is the responsibility of the plugin to find the appropriate Conversation Manager from the conversation id, to build the internal structure of the protocol for the representation of the messages and to send the resulting message to the Conversation Manager for its processing.

Messages and Filters

All messages are vectors of XML structures, so that they can accommodate multi-part messages that are typical in B2B interactions. The underlying messaging system plugins are responsible for encoding/decoding between the internal XML structures (typically XML DOMs or more abstractly XML Infosets) and the packaged and encoded wire format - this includes XML validation of inbound messages against the relevant DTDs and/or XML schema. Directly or indirectly the concrete interface descriptions MUST provide message DTD/Schema and lift/lower transformations.

In addition, received message structures also carry low-level connection and endpoint information. Typically this will not be used directly in processing the message, but is essential for the plugins to correctly formulate a response message - in particular if a response/reply needs to be returned on the same connection as a given received message.

Message are filtered and classified according to the various pieces of typing information that they carry: internet media type, XML DOCTYPE and XML root element type of the primary part of the message; and identification of the endpoint via which they were received. This associates a received message with a collection of processes which serve messages of a given kind. Concrete Role behaviour descriptions contain a static description of the message types they are able to receive.

Messages with the same conversation id are bound to a particular conversation and queued to be processed by the concrete role behaviours associated with that process - in particular messages are consumed by message driven transitions. When a message matches a message filter in the initial transition of a listening role behaviour, a factory behaviour is invoked which instantiates a new instance of a conversation (controller) and passes that new message to that controller - a new conversation id value becomes associated with the new conversation.

So coarse filtering is used to associate messages with a class of conversational role where they may either be queued at an existing conversation or used to instantiate a new conversation. Messages queued at a conversation are then visible to the processes that realise the concrete role behaviours for that conversation. As discussed earlier these may or may not be processed in strict arrival order.

Message Filtering

This component eases the use of Rhino, the Javascript interpreter used by the protocol mediation component to express message filters, transition pre-conditions and some (scripted) transition behaviours. Each process specified in the choreography has a Rhino Environment, and each environment will have a defined scope. This scope has a set of variables and functions defined in the scripts. In this way, the processes do not share the execution environment when they execute the scripts.

The abstraction layer of Rhino is achieved through the RhinoEnvironment class. The most distinguishable of its functions are:

- *execute*, which receives a script as a parameter and executes it.
- *match*, which receives a script that returns a Boolean value, executes it and returns that Boolean value.
- *setMessage*, which receives a variable name and its value, and is in charge of creating in the Javascript environment a variable with that value.
- *getMessage*, which returns the value of a variable name in the Javascript environment.

Deployment and Installation

The protocol mediation is a framework designed to be used by a client application. The typical scheme for its use would be:

- Initialize the ConversationDispatcher.
- Create a ConversationManager, specifying the choreography, the participating agents and the Indicationhandler. The implementation of the IndicationHandler must guarantee that all the possible .indication communicative acts that the remote partner can send are processed and for each one of them, it must compute the Outcome and the adequate results.
- Initiate the exchange of CommunicativeActs with the remote partner.

Next, we show an example on how to use the component in Box 1. The objective of this example is to give a guidance on the use of the component. The typical use must be by means of an application that should keep the evolution of the conversation as well as the CommunicativeActs that have been sent and received by the remote partners.

The first thing to do is the initialization of the ConversationDispatcher. This initialization also includes the initialization of the plugins. In the previous example, the URL is the address of the local Web application that uses the HTTP-Plugin.

The second thing to do is the creation of the ConversationManager. In the previous example we talk to the partner that we can reach at "http://provider:8080/". In the conversation we adopt the role of the FreightForwardingServiceConsumer. The choreography is found in http://swws.semanticweb.org/logistics.owl. We also have the IndicationHandlerImpl which is an implementation of the IndicationHandler.

Afterwards, a CommunicativeAct is created (in this case: InformReadyForCollection) and we send it in a synchronous way.

To keep the example simple we do not send any parameter in the comunicativeAct, but it would be usual practice.

ALTERNATIVES, COST AND BENEFITS

The proposed solution to protocol mediation be-

Box 1.

```
String logisticsNamespace = "http://swws.semanticweb.org/logistics#"
ConversationDispatcher.init("http://consumer:8080/");
interfaceRole = new InterfaceRole( new URI("http://provider:8080/"),
    new URI(logisticsNamespace + "FreightForwardServiceConsumer"));
IndicationHandlerImpl indct = new IndicationHandlerImpl();
ConversationManager conversationManager = new ConversationManager(
    new InterfaceRole[]{interfaceRole},
     new URI("http://swws.semanticweb.org/logistics.owl"), indct);
CommunicativeAct communicativeAct = new CommunicativeAct(
  new URI(logisticsNamespace + "InformReadyForCollection"));
conversationManager.synchSay(communicativeAct);
communicativeAct = new CommunicativeAct(
  new URI(logisticsNamespace + "RequestShipmentStatus"));
conversationManager.synchSay(communicativeAct);
```

tween heterogeneous applications can be applied not only to the logistics domain, which is the one that has been described in this chapter, but also to other similar domains where applications are already deployed and have to interoperate with each other in order to support a specific set of added-value functionalities.

While work on the area of data mediation in service exchanges is quite widespread and there are tools available in the mainstream market for solving these issues, most of the approaches for protocol mediation have been based on ad-hoc solutions that are tightly related to the applications where they are being applied. No easy configurable toolkit exists yet for solving this problem, hence the main alternative for the work proposed here is to create an ad-hoc solution that solves the interaction problem between applications or services for a specific set of functionalities.

Though our approach still requires a lot of effort to be done, and requires more maturity and further evaluations to be applied in production systems, the main advantages with respect to the current state of the art are related to the reusability of the abstract representations of message exchanges for each of the systems involved, as well as the reusability of message filters across different types of applications, what can benefit the agility of developing new added-value applications in the future. Besides, the model is easily extensible and fully declarative, what influences in the lowering of maintenance costs.

CONCLUSION AND FUTURE TRENDS

In this chapter we have motivated the need to use some form of protocol mediation to make it possible to different systems in the logistics domain to communicate successfully with each other, even if they use different protocols (RosettaNet and EDIFACT). Furthermore, we have described the approach for protocol mediation developed in the context of the SWWS project, including the ontology used to describe the choreography (that is, how the systems interact with each other) and the software that implements the component that has been developed.

Though this is a first approach to solve the protocol mediation problem between systems, there is still much work to be done in the future to convert this prototype into a production-quality component. Among them, we have to add new message transfer plugins to allow message transfer using other communication protocols, such as SMTP, FTP, etc., which is what it is used by many of the current systems. Besides, a tighter integration and evaluation with existing systems has to be provided, and a library of common interaction patterns should be also implemented, so that the task of protocol mediation is as simple as possible for those developers that want to develop a mediation solution for their systems.

ACKNOWLEDGMENT

This work was supported by the EU under the SWWS and DIP consortia. In addition we want to thank Stuart Williams, for his ideas that have been the basis for this work and for providing good comments to improve this chapter, to Jorge Pérez Bolaño for making part of the component implementation, to Juan Miguel Gómez for the work on the VSCL ontology, and the other members of the consortium, who contributed to the use case and to the ideas presented here.

REFERENCES

AnsiX12 (n.d.). *National Standards Institute Accredited Standards Committee X12.*

Cimpian E, Mocan A (2005). *Process Mediation in WSMX.* WSMO Working Draft D13.7 v0.1.

http://www.wsmo.org/TR/d13/d13.7/v0.1/

EDIFACT. ISO 9735. (2002). *Electronic data interchange for administration, commerce and transport (EDIFACT) – Application level syntax rules*. International Standards Organisation.

Evans-Greenwood P, Stason M (2006). Moving Beyond Composite Applications to the Next Generation of Application Development: Automating Exception-Rich Business Processes. *Business Integration Journal*, May/June 2006.

Preist C, Esplugas-Cuadrado J, Battle SA, Grimm S, Williams SK (2005). Automated Business-to-Business Integration of a Logistics Supply Chain Using Semantic Web Services Technology. In Gil et al. (eds), *Proceedings of the 4th International Semantic Web Conference (ISWC2005)*. Lecture Notes in Computer Science, Volume 3729, Oct 2005, Pages 987-1001

RosettaNet Implementation Framework: Core Specification Version 2.00.01. March 2002. http://www.rosettanet.org/

Williams SK, Battle SA, Esplugas-Cuadrado J (2006). Protocol Mediation for Adaptation in Semantic Web Services. In Domingue and Sure (eds), *Proceedings of the 3rd European Semantic Web Conference (ESWC2006)*. Lecture Notes in Computer Science, Volume 4011, June 2006, Pages 635-649.

ADDITIONAL READING

We recommend reading WSMO deliverables about mediation, in general, and about process mediation in particular. They can be found at http://www.wsmo.org/. Efforts on process mediation are also being done in the context of the SUPER project (http://www.ip-super.org/).

ENDNOTES

1. http://swws.semanticweb.org/
2. http://kpontology.sourceforge.net

Chapter V
A Case Study in Building Semantic eRecruitment Applications

Elena Simperl
University of Innsbruck, Austria

Malgorzata Mochol
Free University of Berlin, Germany

ABSTRACT

Ontology-based technology has achieved a level of maturity which allows it to become a serious candidate for the resolution of several major IT problems in contemporary businesses, be that enterprise application integration, data modeling or enterprise search. As it implies considerable additional efforts, building and deploying ontologies at industrial level has to be supported by elaborated methodologies, methods and tools, which are available to a large extent and at feasible quality to date. However, sophisticated methods alone are not sufficient for the industrial purposes. They have to be accompanied by extended case studies and comprehensive best practices and guidelines, which are of benefit in particular in real-world situations and in the absence of deep knowledge engineering expertise. In this chapter we report our practical experiences in building an ontology-based eRecruitment system. Our case study confirms previous findings in ontology engineering literature: (1) building ontology-based systems is still a tedious process due to the lack of proved and tested methods and tools supporting the entire life cycle of an ontology; and (2) reusing existing ontologies within new application contexts is currently related to efforts potentially comparable to the costs of a new implementation. We take this study a step further and use the findings to further elaborate existing best practices towards a list of recommendations for the eRecruitment domain, which, far from claiming completeness, might speed-up the development of similar systems.

CURRENT SITUATION

Ontology-based technology has achieved a level of maturity which allows it to become a serious candidate for the resolution of several major IT problems in contemporary businesses, be that enterprise application integration, data modeling or enterprise search. This trend is confirmed by the wide range of international projects with major industry involvement exploiting the business potential of ontologies, by the increasing interest of small and medium size enterprises requesting consultancy in this domain or by recent surveys by established ICT advisory companies such as Gartner.[1]

Enterprise IT systems nowadays need to handle an explosively growing amount of information and the variety of forms in which this information might be available or might be required to be processed. Ontology-driven technology improves traditional IT systems as those used in the areas mentioned above as it extends the functionality of these systems by replicating to a certain extent the human-specific "understanding" of the business domain being dealt with. Besides acting as a means to formally represent knowledge and to model data, ontologies can be viewed as mediators between applications operating within and among enterprises. In this way they enable application interoperability as applications in heterogeneous environments are provided with an instrument to communicate to each other using a commonly agreed vocabulary with a machine-unambiguous meaning.

Despite the acknowledged potential of this novel technology across businesses its feasibility from an implementability perspective needs to receive equal attention both from the research community and from technology vendors and consultants. As ontology engineering activities usually imply considerable additional efforts in extending conventional systems into semantics, building and deploying ontologies at industrial level has to be supported not only by elaborated methodologies, methods and tools but also by extended case studies and comprehensive best practices and guidelines. Such empirical knowledge is of non-negligible benefit in real-world situations, in the absence of deep ontology engineering expertise and under limited resource and time constraints.

In this chapter we report on our practical experiences in building an ontology-based eRecruitment system, which can be seen as a case study on current ontology reuse technology. In the last years, the Web has advanced into being a fundamental technology for many recruitment applications, be that job portals, personal service agencies or official employment initiatives. While the advantages of using the Web as a dissemination medium are widely recognized by job applicants and employing companies, current job search engines are far from offering job seekers high-quality access to job offer resources. Apart from the fact that a significant number of job offers are still published on proprietary, non-publicly accessible company sites, the quality of the results of a job search - performed by using either general-purpose or specialized search heuristics - depends on a great extent on various characteristics of the job descriptions available on the Web, such as form, language and purpose. Furthermore, the free text representation of these descriptions considerably restricts the precision and recall of the underlying retrieval engines, which, in absence of a machine-understandable representation of the semantics of the content, are restricted to flavors of keyword- and statistics-based techniques.

In this case study we analyzed the possibility of extending existing job search engines into business semantics represented through ontologies. In doing so, domain-relevant ontologies termed as *"Human Resources/HR ontologies"* are aimed at being used as semantic indices, by which job descriptions and applications in the selected sector are classified and matched, thus enhancing the search engine with semantics-aware retrieval functionality. In developing the target application ontology we investigated the possibility of reusing the impressive body of domain knowledge available in the form of ontologies and ontology-like structures on the Web. Our experiences confirm previous findings in the ontology engineering literature (e.g. in (Uschold et al, 1998), (Antoniou, 2000), (Lopez, 2002), (Paslaru, 2005), (Fernández et al, 2006), and (Lisi, 2007)): (1) building ontology-based applications is still a tedious process due to the lack of proved and tested tools and methods supporting particular activities within the life cycle of an ontology; and (2) reusing existing ontologies within new application contexts is currently related to efforts, potentially comparable to the costs of a new implementation.

We argue that the business scenario discussed in this chapter can be considered as a typical scenario for the deployment of Semantic Web technologies, with respect to the application type (*semantic search*) and the business sector (*eRecruitment*). Given the complexity of the application domain correlated with the lack of operational experience as regarding ontologies within enterprises, practice-oriented case studies and guidelines for building semantic HR applications are core requirements for a serious impact of ontology-driven technology in this promising field. Therefore, a second goal of this work was to use the experiences gained during the project to further elaborate existing best practices towards a list of recommendations for the eRecruitment domain, which, far from claiming completeness, might speed-up the development of similar systems.

The rest of the chapter is organized as follows: in the remaining of this section and in Section 2 we introduce the application scenario, emphasizing the use cases to be addressed with the help of ontologies and ontology-based services. Then in Section 3 we describe the main steps, activities and results of the ontology development process. The case study is complemented by a comparison of our approach with alternative technologies (Section 4) and an analysis of its costs, benefits and risks (Sections 5 and 6). Based on the results of this analysis we elaborate a series of guidelines for building ontology-based applications in the Human Resources sector in Section 5. We conclude with a summary of future trends and outline further directions of research of development in Sections 7 and 8, respectively.

Problem Statement

It is a well-known fact that people are a key asset of an organization. For businesses to compete effectively it is therefore fundamental to be able to optimally fill vacancies and to develop and leverage the skills and capabilities of the employees. Furthermore, the employer has to maximize the impact of training and educational efforts, to align the activities of the employees with the overall corporate objectives as well as to retain top performers by an effective incentive management (Ferris et al, 1999). The Internet has more and more advanced to a core instrument for personal management purposes, and in particular for job recruitment. According to (wwjGbmH, 2005) 47 % of Internet users in Germany and 28% of European Internet users read online job postings. Furthermore over 50% of the new hires in 2005 were sourced from the Internet.

This trend has nevertheless several limitations. Although a large number of (commercial) online job portals have sprung up, competing to publish job postings for a fee and dividing the online labor market into information islands, employers either publish their job postings on a rather small number of portals in order to keep costs and administrative effort low, or they distribute their openings over the company's own Website (Ferris et al, 1999). The latter, however, makes it difficult for job portals to locate, gather and integrate job postings into their database since job offers lack semantically meaningful descriptions. Furthermore, the offers published only on corporate Websites reach a very limited audience, because the indexing capabilities of current search engines are too imprecise to support searches for open positions. Beside this, meta-search engines are restricted in their ability to identify those offers that match the precise needs of the job seekers since job postings are written in free text form using uncontrolled vocabularies and heterogeneous formats. Several dedicated search engines are entering into the market to cope with this problem. They allow for detailed queries - as opposed to keyword-based ones traditionally used in general-purpose search engines. However, the quality of the search results depends not only on the search and index methods applied. Influential factors include the processability of the Web technologies utilized and the quality of the automated interpretation of company-specific terms occurring in the job descriptions. In other words the problems related to the quality of job search engines can be traced back to the incapacity of current Web technologies to understand the semantics of the business domain associated to the content they process.

To increase transparency of the job market while decreasing the duration of job procurement, national public bodies such as the German Federal Employment Office (BA)[2] and the Swedish National Labor Market Administration[3] have initiated projects to integrate open positions into centralized repositories. To give an example, in December 2003 the German office launched the platform *"virtual employment market"*. Despite of the high investments the project partially failed as all participants in the virtual market were assumed to align to the proprietary data exchange format officially issued, whilst the quality of the query results in terms of precision and recall was suboptimal. An additional, more technical problem with such projects is the fact that the entire virtual market depends on a single point of failure, a centralized repository storing the job-related content (Crosswater, 2003).

Due to the strained labor market situation employers receive a large number of applications for an open position and, since the costs of manually pre-selecting potential candidates are constantly rising, means to automate some parts of the eRecruitment process (cf. Figure 1) such as the publishing of job postings (applicants' profiles) and the pre-selection of candidates (search for suitable opening) are an important cost factor.

To conclude, as this brief analysis clearly shows, the information flow in the (online) labor market is far from being optimal. The publishing behavior of companies not only makes it almost impossible for a job seeker to get an overview of all the appropriate openings, but also complicates or even prevents job offers from reaching a greater range of potential employees. Furthermore, employers experience difficulties in processing the incoming applications in an efficient manner due to the lack of appropriate automated tools providing search and match features on job openings and candidate profiles. We now turn to a description of our approach which utilizes semantic technologies to overcome major technical issues behind these drawbacks.

Figure 1. General eRecruitment Process (HeMoOl, 2007)

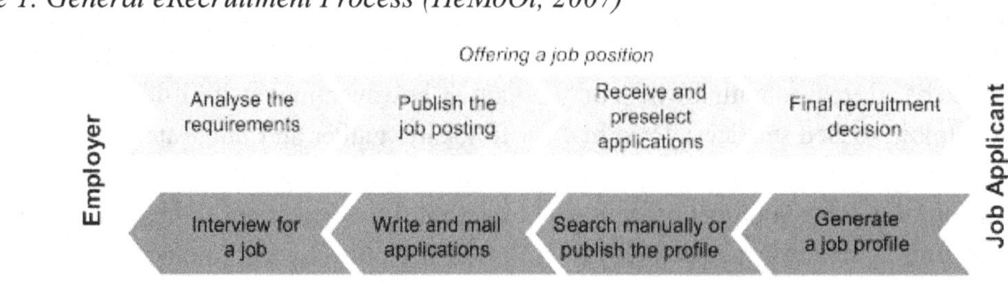

PROPOSED SOLUTION

In the next sections we describe in detail the objectives and the goals of the project and the development process of the semantic job portal including possible extensions.

Objectives

The work described in this chapter was performed within the project *Wissensnetze (Knowledge Nets)*[4] in cooperation with a German job portal. The project explores the potential of Semantic Web from a business and a technical perspective and examines the effects of the deployment of semantic technologies for particular application scenarios and market sectors. Every scenario includes a technological component which makes use of the achievements of the Semantic Web community prospectively available within several years, and a deployment component assuming the availability of the required information in machine-readable form. The combination of these two projections allows us, on the one hand, to build eBusiness scenarios for analysis and experimentations and, on the other hand, to make statements about the implications of the new technology on the participants of the scenario in the current early stage of development.

In this chapter we focus on the eRecruitment scenario studied in this project and analyze the costs and benefits of applying ontology-based technologies to cope with the limitations of the current solutions which have been briefly introduced in the previous section.

Overview

We propose an approach to eRecruitment which takes advantage of the newly emerging Semantic Web to enhance job postings and applications into semantics as a preliminary step towards the realization of business domain-aware search engines in the field. Concretely, our proposal utilizes *ontology-based technology* that supports the main steps of the recruitment process:

- **Publishing** job postings and applicant profiles enriched through domain ontologies/controlled vocabularies.
- **Pre-selection** of the candidates based on semantic matching techniques implemented on top of these ontologies and the associated automated reasoning.
- **Delivering interview recommendations** to employers or **suitable open positions** to job seekers based on the semantic matching of the annotated applicant profiles with the job postings (cf. Figure 2).

Since we take into account both process participants - the employer and the job seeker - the job portal, in turn, must deal with two types of information:

Figure 2. Semantic eRecruitment (Bizer et al, 2005)

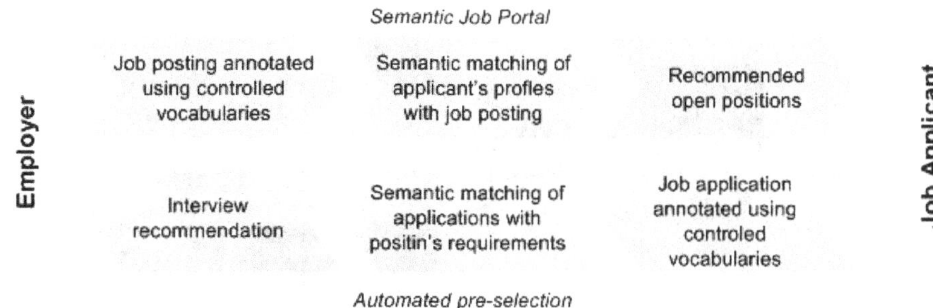

- **Job postings/offers** consisting of typical metadata information and an extended job description.
- **Job applications/profiles** describing the capabilities and level of experience of individual job seekers.

The technical setting of the case study (cf. Figure 3), which shares many commonalities with what is called a "typical'" job search engine, implies three basic roles:

- **Information providers** who publish open positions using controlled vocabularies,
- **Aggregators** who crawl the published information and present it to the information users, and
- **Consumers** who use the information delivered by the aggregators.

From an architectural point of view the portal infrastructure consists of the following components (Bizer et al, 2005):

- A **crawler** component seeking for domain-relevant information across the Web or on pre-defined company sites and collecting data from the different providers.
- A **mapping engine** to integrate data published using different vocabularies.
- A **semantic matching engine** to match applicant's profiles and job postings based on the knowledge included in the ontologies and the available market data.
- A Web **user interface** presenting the information according to the user's preferences.

Job seekers register to the portal and insert their application profile to a repository, thus being automatically taken into consideration in future recruitment tasks. Job descriptions are matched against incoming job candidates on the basis of a pre-defined schema, while the results of this comparison flow into a ranking function used to present the job search results to the users.

Ontologies are used as a means to represent domain knowledge in a machine-processable manner and as a basis for the implementation of semantic search techniques which use them for indexing, query rewriting and query matching. Their usage has several benefits compared to traditional solutions:

- A fine grained, domain narrow classification of the information items increases the precision of user queries and consequently, of the search heuristics. Furthermore, by means of the domain ontology the system is provided with additional, explicitly rep-

Figure 3. Architecture of the Job Portal (Bizer et al, 2005)

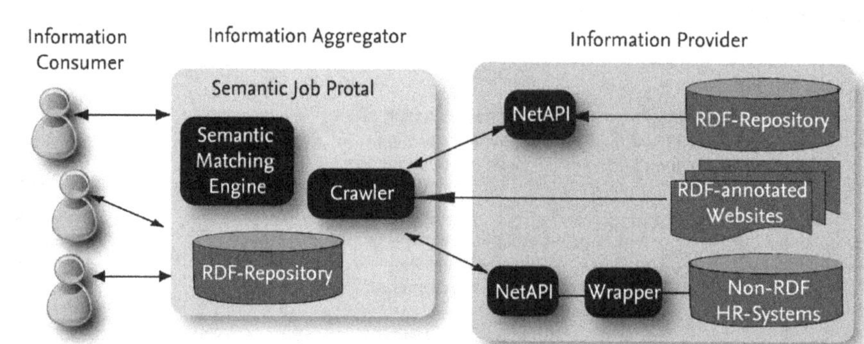

resented domain knowledge, thus being able to semantically rewrite user queries: a search request on, for instance, "programming languages"} could be in this way automatically extended with more specific concepts subsumed by this category, such as *"object-oriented programming"* or *"Java"* in order to improve the recall of the system. The precision value can be improved through the usage of pre-defined search terms, described by the ontology. As an example, consider a job search specified by the name of particular companies: the ontology can be used to extend the user query with standard company identifiers, thus avoiding ambiguities as those emerging through the usage of slightly different spellings.

- Besides its primary role as an index structure for system-relevant information, the ontology could be involved in the methods applied to (semi-)automatically classify this information by (ontologically) pre-defined dimensions. An ontology-driven information extraction procedure has the advantage that the domain specificity of the classification heuristics is stored separately from the system implementation, which can be easily customized to new domains of interest. Given the explicitly represented domain knowledge, the system can automatically decide on new, domain-relevant information types, which are then extracted from the free text job descriptions.
- A third use case for an ontology-driven job portal is the search and ranking functionality. Information items can be compared using ontology-based similarity measures, which take into account domain-specific matching concept labels or taxonomical structures.

In our prototypical implementation (Oldakowski, & Bizer, 2005), the domain-specific knowledge is represented by concept hierarchies covering areas such as skills, occupations, qualifications and industrial sectors. Based on this knowledge the engine is able to compare job descriptions and applicant profiles using semantic similarity measures (Poole, & Campbell, 1995) instead of merely relying on the containment of keywords as most of the contemporary search engines do. The content of job postings and candidate profiles is structured into *"thematic clusters"*, e.g. information about skills, information regarding industry sector and occupation category, and finally job position details like salary information or travel requirements, which form the basis for matching between job descriptions and candidate profiles. The overall similarity is then calculated as the average of the cluster similarities. The cluster similarity itself is computed based on the similarities of semantically corresponding concepts the plain content is annotated with. The latter makes use of the taxonomical hierarchy within an ontology. The taxonomic similarity between two concepts is determined by their distance within the taxonomical hierarchy altered by their exact position within the hierarchy, under the assumption that the granularity of the concept modeling is finer at lower levels within the hierarchy than towards the top. Since we also provide means for specifying competence levels (e.g. expert or beginner) we compare these levels as well in order to find the best match (Bizer et al, 2005). The result is a ranking list of the best fits of openings for the job seeker and likewise a ranking list of job applicants for the employer, including an explanation of the rationales behind the rankings. Explanations of this kind are absent in current job search portals and Websites - For more details on our semantic matching approach, its application to the eRecruitment and matching results the reader is referred to (OlBi, 2005), (HeMoOl, 2007) and the Website of the semantic matching framework (SemMF).[5]

This basic matching algorithm can be further enhanced towards a more sophisticated processing of very specific or inconsistent queries. If the description of the job requirements is too specific, the algorithm presented above might deliver a very restricted number of hits, a situation which might negatively impact the acceptance of the portal. To tackle this problem we extend the initial approach with a set of query rewriting rules capturing domain and user-specific knowledge which are then used for query relaxation purposes. To order the results of each of the resulting queries we can again use the semantic similarity function. The query rewriting approach provides a high-level relaxation including grouping the results according domain knowledge and user preferences, whereat the similarity function is useful to fine-tune the results within one group. The rewriting relaxes the over-constraint query based on rules in the order defined by conditions. It starts with the strongest possible query that is supposed to return the "best" answers satisfying most of the conditions. If the returned result set is either empty or contains unsatisfactory results, the query is modified either by replacing or deleting further parts of the query. For further details on this technique the reader is referred to (Mochol, Wache, & Nixon, 2006), (Mochol, Wache, & Nixon, 2007) and (Mochol, Jentzsch, & Wache, 2007).

The architecture of the portal implementing this functionality is depicted in Figure 4. The requirements defined by the employers are converted into a SeRQL query and forwarded to the *Approx System*[6], which is responsible for the relaxation of the queries and maintains the rewriting rules. The system consists of two core components:

- **Approx controller** that controls the search process, and
- **Approx rewriter** which is responsible for applying the rewriting rules to a query.

The controller asks the rewriter for all possible relaxation of an incoming query. The returned relaxed queries are checked by the controller if they return answers. The controller uses for this purpose its interface to the RDF Repository Sesame[7] where the developed HR ontology together with the instance data regarding candidate profiles is stored. All queries with zero hits are maintained in a list by the controller and are further relaxed with the help of the rewriter until the rewriter can not relax the query any more or the relaxed query returns at least one answer.

The idea of rewriting rules is quite simple and not really new but, as shown in context of the eRecruitment, just in the combination with semantic technologies has evolved into a powerful and helpful technique. The query approximation is useful in areas where restrictive queries needs to be loosened in order to allow users to find best matches rather than simply receive no results at all.

In the following we turn to the description of the ontology engineering process, which was

Figure 4. Extended Semantic Job Portal

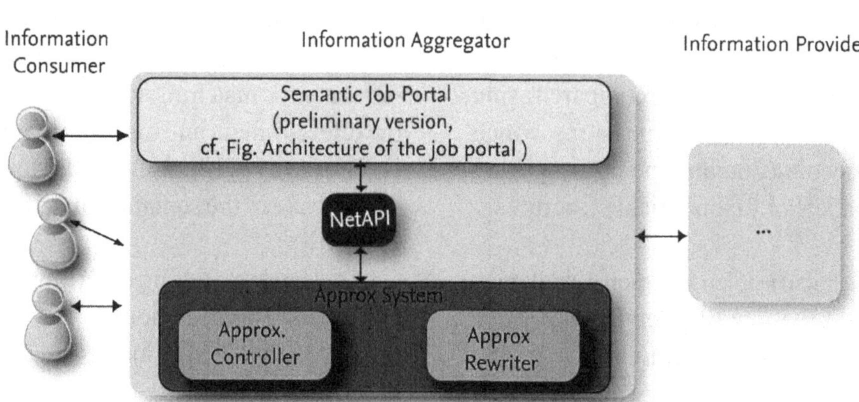

an essential part of our work. We describe the generation of the HR-ontology and introduce a preliminary set of guidelines for building semantic vertical retrieval applications (OntoWeb, 2002) according to the empirical findings of the project.

SOLUTION DETAILS

The need for comprehensive classification systems describing occupational profiles has been recognized at an early stage of the eRecruitment era by many interested parties. In particular major governmental and international organizations strove for the creation of standard classifications comprising unambiguous and well- documented descriptions of occupational titles and associated skills and qualifications. The result is an impressive inventory of classification systems, mostly with national impact, ready to be deployed in job portals to simplify the management of electronically available job postings and job seeker profiles and to encourage application interoperability. Standards such as O*NET (Occupational Net), ISIC (International Standard Industrial Classification of Economic Activities), SOC (Standard Occupational Classification) or NAICS (North American Industry Classification System), to name only a few, are feasible building blocks for the development of eRecruitment information systems. In the same time they are valuable knowledge resources for the development of application-specific ontologies, which can inject domain semantics-awareness into classical solutions in this field, as described below. These were the main rationales for following an ontology reuse approach – as opposed to building from scratch - approach to engineer our HR ontology.

The reuse process was performed in three phases:

1. **Discovery of the reuse candidates:** In this step the ontology engineering team conducted a survey on potentially reusable ontological sources.
2. **Evaluation and selection of the ontological sources:** The result of the previous step was analyzed with respect to its domain and application relevance, as well as its general quality and availability.
3. **Customization of the ontologies to be reused:** The relevant fragments of the (to some extent) very comprehensive sources were extracted and integrated into a single target ontology.

Discovery of the Reuse Candidates

In order to compute a list of existing ontologies or ontology-like structures potentially relevant for the human resources domain we carried out a comprehensive search with the help of ontology location support technologies available at present:

1. **General-purpose search engines:** We used conventional search tools and pre-defined queries combining implementation and content descriptors such as *"filetype:xsd human resources"* or *"occupation classification"*.
2. **Ontology search engines and repositories:** Resorting to existing dedicated search engines and ontology repositories clearly pointed out the immaturity of these technologies for the Semantic Web.
3. **Domain-related sites and organizations:** A third search strategy focused on international and national governmental institutions which might be involved in standardizations efforts in the area of human resources. Discussions with domain experts complemented by Internet research led to the identification of several major players in this field: at national level the Federal Agency of Employment (Bundesagentur für Arbeit), at foreign level the American, Canadian, Australian and Swedish correspondents,

and at international level institutions like the United Nations/UN or the HR-Consortium. These organizations make their work, which is proposed for standardization, publicly available in form of domain-relevant lightweight, HR ontologies. The result of the discovery procedure—which was performed as manual Google-based searches on pre-selected keywords in correlation with the investigation of the Websites of international and national employment organizations—was a list of approximately 24 resources covering both descriptions of the recruitment process and classifications of occupations, skills or industrial sectors in English and German.

Evaluation and Selection of the Reuse Candidates

The engineering team decided to reuse the following resources:

1. **HR-BA-XML**[8]: which is the official German translation of Human Resources XML, the most widely used standard for process documents like job postings and applications. HR-XML is a library of more than 75 interdependent XML schemas defining particular process transactions, as well as options and constraints ruling the correct usage of the XML elements.
2. **BKZ**[9]: Berufskennziffer, which is a German version of SOC System, classifying employees into 5597 occupational categories according to occupational definitions.
3. **SOC**[10]: Standard Occupational Classification, which classifies workers into occupational categories (23 major groups, 96 minor groups, and 449 occupations).
4. **WZ2003**[11]: Wirtschaftszweige 2003, which is a German classification standard for industrial sectors.
5. **NAICS**[12]: North American Industry Classification System, which provides industry sector definitions for Canada, Mexico, and the United States to facilitate uniform economic studies across the boundaries of these countries.
6. **KOWIEN**[13]: Skill Ontology from the University of Essen, which defines concepts representing competencies required to describe job position requirements and job applicant skills.

The selection of the 6 sources was performed manually without the usage of a pre-defined methodology or evaluation framework. The documentation of the 24 potential reuse candidates was consulted in order to assess the relevance of the modeled domain to the application setting. The decision for or against a particular resource was very effective due to the small number of reuse candidates covering the same or similar domains and the simplicity of the evaluation framework, which focused on provenance and natural language aspects. Nevertheless the resulting ontologies required intensive ex post modifications in order to adapt them to the requirements of the tasks they were expected to be involved in at application level. The importance of these application-oriented dependencies has been underestimated by the engineering team at that point. In the absence of an appropriate methodology for this purpose they were not taken into account during the evaluation. For the German version of the ontology the BKZ and the WZ2003 were the natural choice for representing occupational categories and industrial sectors, respectively. The same applies for the English version, which re-used the SOC and NAICS classifications. As for occupational classifications in the English language, the SOC system was preferred to alternative like NOC or O*NET due to the availability of an official German translation[14]. The same applies for the choice between industry sector classifications: by contrast to ISIC[15] the NAICS system is provided with a German version, while being used in various applications and classifications in the human resources area.

Customization and Integration of Relevant Sources

The main challenge of the eRecruitment scenario was the adaptation of the 6 reusable ontologies to the technical requirements of the job portal application. From a content oriented perspective, 5 of the sources were included to 100% to the final setting, due to the generality of the application domain. The focus on a particular industrial sector or occupation category would require a customization of the source ontologies in form of an extraction of the relevant fragments.

To accomplish this task for the KOWIEN ontology we compiled a small conceptual vocabulary (of approx. 15 concepts) from various job portals and job procurement Websites and matched these core concepts manually to the source ontology. The candidate sources varied with respect to the represented domain, the degree of formality and the granularity of the conceptualization. They are labeled using different natural languages and are implemented in various formats: text files (BKZ, WZ2003), XML-schemas (HR-XML, HR-BA-XML), DAML+OIL (KOWIEN). While dealing with different natural languages complicated the process, human readable concept names in German and English were required in order to make the ontology usable in different job portals and to avoid language-specific problems. Another important characteristic of the candidate ontologies was the absence of semantic relationships among concepts. Except for the KOWIEN ontology, which contains relationships between skill concepts, the remaining ones are confined to taxonomical relationships at most. Consequently we had to focus on how vocabularies (concepts and relations) can be extracted and integrated into the target ontology. The usage of the ontology in semantic matching tasks requires that it is represented in a highly formal representation language. For this reason the implementation of the human resources ontology was realized by translating several semi-structured input formalisms and manually coding text-based classification standards to OWL.

The remaining of the chapter focuses on an analysis of this approach as opposed to alternative technologies and ontology engineering strategies.

ALTERNATIVES

Job Search without Domain Semantics

As mentioned before recruitment tasks have been increasingly supported by Web technologies in the last years, however with rising unemployment and strained satiation of the job market the number of applications received by an employer is growing in equal measure. In the following we describe the main phases of the recruitment process and the problems on the nowadays eRecruitment solutions in more detail.

From the point of view of the employer there are presently three main possibilities (which are not mutually exclusive) to find the suitable candidates for an opening on the Web (cf. Figure 5). The recruitment process can be divided into four steps: analysis of the job requirements, publishing of the job posting, receiving and pre-selection of the applications and decision regarding the hiring of the most suitable candidate.

- **Analysis of the job requirements:** Job analysis identifies and determines in detail the particular job duties, skills, abilities, credential and experience and the relative importance of these characteristics for a given job. The requirements for an opening are usually conceived by the operating de-

Figure 5. Recruitment over the Internet (extended, cf. Grund, 2006)

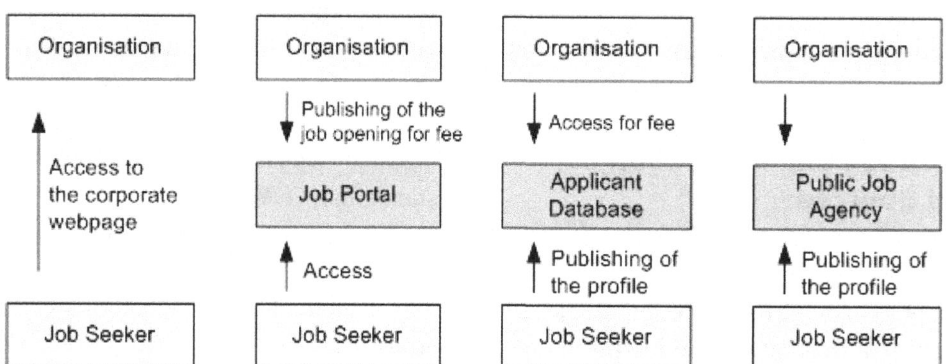

partment together with the human resource department. The resulting job posting description is basically an outline of how the job fits in the company and should point out in broad terms the job's goals, responsibilities and skills. Nowadays the description containing the requirements for an opening is written in free text which limits the machine processability of postings in the later phases of the recruitment process.

- **Publishing of the job posting:** There are as many ways to post a job offer on the Web as there are places where an applicant can look for a job. There is a large number of commercial online portals financed by publishing fees like Monster[16], JobPilot[17] or StepStone[18] and portals set up by state job centers (German Federal Employment Office, Swedish National Labour Market Administration). Job exchange portals differ substantially according to location in terms of geographical areas as well as specific industries or occupation groups. Further differentiation criteria are the range of online functionality and the scale of integration of job exchange portal and employer/employee. As publication fees easily add up, employers publish their postings only on a limited number of portals. Another publication channel for job postings is the employer's own Website. Publishing postings on the corporate Website is cheap but reaches only a very limited audience, because the indexing capabilities of current search engines like Google are too imprecise to support directed searches for open positions (cf. Section 1.1).
- **Receiving and pre-selection of the applications:** In order to reduce processing costs employers have begun to prefer online applications over classic paper applications. Other companies like IBM[19] or Volkswagen[20] have set up Web forms to obtain applications, where applicants have to constantly re-enter the basic facts of their application. This data is used for the semi-automated pre-selection of candidates fulfilling the basic requirements and thus reducing pre-selection costs.
- **Final decision regarding the hiring of the most suitable candidate:** Face-to-face interviews with the candidates are indispensable for the final recruitment decision. This phase of the recruitment process, where candidates are interviewed and in which not only their technical and languages skills but also their soft skills are evaluated in face-to-face meetings or in assessment centers, will continue to be in person in the future.

As stated in (Grund, 2006), in comparison e.g. with a newspaper announcement, the employee search over the Internet has many advantages regarding time savings and abolition of spatial and temporal borders. However, the current solutions do not fully exploit the potential of the information on the Web and can not take into account the semantics of the underlying business domain to improve the quality and the costs of the selection process.

Job Search with Semantic Web Services

The Single European Employment Market Place (SEEMP)[21] project aims to provide an infrastructure for enabling interoperability between public and private actors in the employment market across European borders (EEM). The approach is based on two main concepts, namely services and semantics. Web services are quickly becoming the standard for B2B integration, allowing for the development of loosely coupled architectures. In the EEM developed in this project the services exposed by the marketplace participants are modeled as a unique consistent set of Web services. The semantics of the content managed by the EEM is captured in ontologies, while Web services are annotated with a semantic description of their functionality and of the user goals. Mediation services handle the heterogeneity of the existing applications. Each marketplace participant has its own local dictionary of terms and its own classification, i.e. a Local Ontology. The ontology is used as a base for exchanging data, in other words the structure and content of the exchanged messages are classes or instances in the ontology, and describes at a semantic level the capabilities and the interfaces of the exposed Web services. Compared to our approach SEEMP has a clear focus on the heterogeneity of the eRecruitment landscape, which is handled using Semantic Web Services. The results are complementary to the work presented in this chapter, which emphasizes the usage of ontologies for semantic search purposes.

COST AND BENEFITS

In this section we compare the costs and the benefits of an ontology-based approach to realize a semantic job portal. The analysis is focused on the ontology engineering process, a focus which is justified through the core role played by the HR ontology in the implementation of our solution.

Typically ontology reuse starts with the selection of a set of knowledge sources presumably adequate for the application setting. Once their relevance has been positively evaluated, these ontologies are subject of further customization and integration activities. In an arbitrary setting the reuse candidates differ with respect to content, implementation and provenance. They might model various domains from a multitude of viewpoints or optimize the domain representation to particular scopes and purposes. Furthermore, they might not share a common level of formality or the same implementation language, might be used in accordance to specific license conditions, still be under development or at least subject to frequent updates and changes. An automatic integration of the source ontologies means not only the translation from their initial representation languages to a common format, but also the matching and merging of the resulting schemas and the associated data. Our findings during the presented ontology engineering study showed that the aforementioned activities can not be performed optimally due to the incapacity of current ontology-based technology to deal with this diversity to a satisfactory extent. Selecting appropriate ontologies is a non-trivial task not only because the lack of flexible and fine-grained evaluation frameworks, but because of the difficulties attested by humans when dealing with the extreme heterogeneity of the assessed resources. Furthermore, the tools employed for ontology management are inherently targeted at particular classes of ontologies, while their user-friendliness and real-world feasibility is still improvable.

A wide range of standards for process modeling and classification schemas for occupations, skills and competencies have been developed by major organizations in the human resources field. Using these standards was a central requirement for the simplification of the communication between international organizations accessing the portal and for interoperability purposes. Besides, reusing classification schemas like BKZ, WZ2003 and their English variants, which have been completely integrated into the target ontology, implied significant cost reduction. They guaranteed a comprehensive conceptualization of the corresponding sub-domains and saved the costs incurred by intensively collaborating with domain experts. Furthermore, due to the generality of the application domain—the final application ontology provided a (high-level) conceptualization of the complete human resources domain—and to the manageable number of pre-selected reuse candidates, the ontology evaluation step did not imply major development costs. This is indicated by the distribution of the efforts in each of the enumerated process stages. Solely 15% of the total engineering time was spent on searching and identifying the relevant sources. Approximately 35% of the overall efforts were spent on customizing the selected source ontologies. Due to the heterogeneity of the knowledge sources and their integration into the final ontology up to 40% of the total engineering costs were necessary to translate these sources to the target representation language OWL. Lastly, the refinement and evaluation process required the remaining 10%. The aggregation of knowledge from different domains proved to be a very time consuming and tedious task because of the wide range of classifications available so far. The second cost intensive factor was related to technological issues. Translating various representation formats to OWL was tedious in the current tool landscape. Though non-trivial, the manual selection of relevant parts from the KOWIEN ontology and the HR-BA-XML standard was possible in our case thanks to the high connectivity degree of the pruned fragments and to the relatively simple, tree-like structure of the sources. However, we see a clear need for tools which assist the ontology engineer during this kind of tasks on real world, large scale ontologies with many thousands of concepts and more complicated structure. Despite the mentioned problems, our experiences in the eRecruitment domain make us believe that reusability is both desirable and possible. Even though the ontology is still under development, it already fulfills the most important requirements of the application scenario, which are related to interoperability and knowledge share among job portals. Reusing available ontologies requires, however, a notably high amount of manual work, even when using common representation languages like XML-Schema or OWL. The reuse process would have been significantly optimized in terms of costs and quality of the outcomes with the necessary technical support.

The case study emphasized once more the need for extensive methodological support for domain experts with respect to ontology reuse. In the absence of fine-granular, business-oriented process descriptions the domain experts—possessing little to no knowledge on ontologies and related topics—were not able to perform any of the process steps without continuous guidance from the side of the ontology engineers. The lessons learned in the eRecruitment scenario are summarized in form of a set of guidelines for ontology reuse which might aid ontology developers in similar situations in Table 1. These results are complemented by the SWOT analysis in Section 6.

RISK ASSESSMENT

In order to improve the feasibility of the proposed solution and the associated prototype in real life

Table 1. List of guidelines

Process Step	*Lessons Learned and Guidelines*
Ontology discovery	Finding an appropriate ontology is currently associated to considerable efforts and is dependent on the level of expertise and intuition of the engineering team. In absence of fully-fledged ontology repositories and mature ontology search engines the following strategies could be helpful: • Use conventional search engines with queries containing core concepts of the domain of interest and terms like ontology, classification, taxonomy, controlled vocabulary, and glossary (e.g., "*classification AND skills*"). • Identify institutions which might be interested in developing standards in the domain of interest and visit their Websites in order to check whether they have published relevant resources. • Dedicated libraries, repositories and search engines are still in their infancy. The majority of the ontologies stored in this form are currently not appropriate for the human resources domain. This applies also for other institutional areas such as eGovernment or eHealth. • Large amounts of domain knowledge are available in terms of lightweight models, whose meaning is solely human-understandable and whose representation is in proprietary, sometimes unstructured formats. These conceptual structures can be translated to more formal ontologies if appropriate parsing tools are implemented, and are therefore a useful resource for building a new ontology. The benefits of reusing such resources usually outweigh the costs related to the implementation of the parser, however, the development team needs to the check whether the semantics of the original model and of the target ontology (language) are compatible. • Additional input such as standard lists and codes of countries and administrative regions, lists of currencies, lists and codes of languages are available on the Web and can be easily integrated to the target HR ontology.
Ontology Evaluation	Due to the high number of classifications proposed for standardization in the HR domain the evaluation methodology should take into consideration the high degree of content overlapping between the reuse candidates and the impact of the originating organization in the field. The evaluation methodology should be aware of the following facts: • A complete evaluation of the usability of the reuse candidates is extremely tedious, if not impossible. The same domain is covered to a similar extent by several ontologies, while there are no fundamental differences among them with respect to their suitability in a semantic job portal. Eliminating candidate ontologies which are definitely not relevant is sometimes more feasible than an attempt to a complete evaluation. • An important decision criterion is the provenance of the ontology, since this area is dominated by several emerging standards. Many standards situated at international institutions such as the EU or the UNO are likely to be available in various natural languages. • Many high-quality standards are freely available. • As the majority of HR ontologies are hierarchical classifications, the evaluation process requires tools supporting various views upon the vocabulary of the evaluated sources. • These considerations apply for further application scenarios such as eGovernment and eHealth.
Ontology Merging and Integration	Existing HR ontologies have a considerable size, but a relatively simple structure. Adapt your integration methodology to their particularities: • Matching and merging ontologies with overlapping domains imposes serious scalability and performance problems to the tools available at present. Nevertheless, using simple algorithms (e.g. linguistic and taxonomic matchers) considerably increases the efficiency of this activity. • The merging results are to be evaluated by human experts. Due to the size of the ontologies, the merging methodology should foresee a flexible and transparent involvement of the users during the process in order to avoid the complexity of a monolithic evaluation. • Dedicated tools extracting lightweight ontological structures from textual documents or Websites are required. • The integration step requires means to translate between heterogeneous formats (XML to OWL and RDFS, data base schemas to OWL and RDFS etc.). • The customization of these structures with respect to particular domains of interest (e.g. HR ontology for the chemical domain) causes additional efforts as all HR standards are independent of any industrial sector.

Table 2. SWOT analysis

Strengths	***Opportunities***
• open n:m communication → employers reach more potential applicants • employers save publication fees • the proposed solution can use (be based on) the existing infrastructure • more accurate and precise search results through query relaxation in combination with semantic matching • flexible configuration	• higher market transparency → it raises new strategic questions for the market participants which will ultimately determine their willingness to participate → job seekers use a single portal to access all relevant information → employers reach more potential applicants • inadequate information about job postings and applications can be substantially reduced • search engines can reliably crawl and index job postings • advantages of the semantic matching → search engines can use semantic matching to increase the precision of matching of open positions and applications → employers can use semantic matching to automate the pre-selection of candidates • the three-phase development (cf. Sec. 7) can allow to convince the employers and job seekers to use the controlled vocabularies • more efficient and faster job procurement • the content of job postings and applicant profile of employees can be used for company-internal HR-management
Weaknesses	***Threats***
• small changes in the information flow • changes in business models of job portals are needed • still some performance problems	• unsolved problem with financing of maintaining the controlled vocabularies • controlled vocabularies may not gain acceptance

settings we performed a SWOT analysis which is summarized in Table 2.

The extended prototype shows the use of query relaxation defined by rules in providing further semantic matching functionality which is relevant to industrial application:

- Providing answers even to over-specified queries.
- Supporting relaxation of queries in meaningful ways.
- Scaling query answering by providing less exact answers.

Conceptually, the work demonstrates that the ideas are sound and implementable, however it cannot be said that the work is mature to be adopted in commercial settings, particularly with respect to scalability.

FUTURE RESEARCH DIRECTIONS

As stated in DirectEmployers (2006) the employers must exploit the technical opportunities to increase the corporate Websites' technical capabilities and stronger recruitment marketing to a specific segment. Furthermore, they definitely need a better applicant tracing system. Regarding these needs expressed by the domain experts the development path towards the Semantic Web in the HR domain, in our opinion, will occur in three main phases: simple annotation, richer annotation and replacement of free text with RDF.

1. **Simple annotation:** Using RDF and a shared vocabulary derived for example from HR-XML, employers can mark a webpage as a job posting that allow search engines to identify job postings on the Web (cf. Figure 6). Knowing that a page is a job posting in-

Figure 6. Simple annotation

```
<html>
   <head>
      <rdf:RDF xmlns:rdf="...#" xmlns:jpp="...#">
         <jpp:JobPositionPosting rdf:about="http://www.example.org/jp1.html"/>
      </rdf:RDF>
   </head>
   <body>
      ...Job posting in free text...
   </body>
</html>
```

Figure 7. Richer annotation

```
<html>
   <head>
      <rdf:RDF xmlns:rdf="...#" xmlns:jpp="...#" xmlns:skills="...#">
      <jpp:JobPositionPosting rdf:about="http://www.example.org/jp1.html"/>
         <jpp:requiredCompetence>
            <skills:Java>
               <skills:hasCompetenceLevel rdf:resource="...#expert"/>
            </skills:Java>
         </jpp:requiredCompetence>
      </rdf:RDF>
   </head>
   <body>
      ...Job posting in free text...
   </body>
</html>
```

creases the precision of linguistic methods and leads to better indexing.

2. **Richer annotation:** When employers recognize that simple annotation already leads to a better ranking of their posting, they may be willing to use richer annotation. They can use the existing specifications, classifications and standards (e.g. for job titles - BKZ or SOC System and for industry WZ2003 or NAICS) to annotate their openings (cf. Figure 7).
3. **Replacement of free text with RDF:** The endpoint of this three-phase development will be the complete replacement of job postings using free text with posting using controlled vocabularies (cf. Figure 8).

Our vision regarding the online job market in about 10 years time is based on the three-phases-process, as described above. We assume that (i) employers and job seekers will use common, controlled vocabularies for annotating job posting and applications, (ii) the job postings will be published directly on the employers' Websites, (iii) the semantic search engines will be able to detect the relevant Websites, collect the appropriate information and offer semantic matching services, and (iv) both job seekers and employers will able to get an overview of all relevant information on the market.

CONCLUSION

In this chapter we gave an overview of a Semantic Web-based application scenario in the eRecruitment sector. We described the realization of a prototypical semantic job search engine and

Figure 8. Replacement of free text with RDF

```
<?xml version="1.0" encoding="UTF-8" ?>
<rdf:RDF xmlns:rdf="…#" xmlns:jpp="…#" xmlns:skills="…#">
   <jpp:JobPositionPosting rdf:about="#JobPositionPostingId-inf-44">
      <jpp:hasHiringOrganisation>
         <org:Organisation>
            <org:name>Freie Universität Berlin</org:name>
         </org:Organisation>
      </jpp:hasHiringOrganisation>...
      <jpp:requiredCompetence>
         <skills:Java>
            <skills:hasCompetenceLevel rdf:resource="…#expert"/>
         </skills:Java>
      </jpp:requiredCompetence>...
   </jpp:JobPositionPosting>...
</rdf:RDF>
```

the development of HR ontology at the core of this engine. We analyzed the advantages and disadvantages of our solution and provided a set of preliminary guidelines whose focus is on the reuse of existing knowledge sources to develop Semantic Web ontologies.

Since semantic technologies are moving towards large-scale industrial adoption, practice-oriented case studies and guidelines for building applications based on these new Internet technologies are fundamental requirements for the realization of a fully developed Semantic Web. A significant factor for the success of Semantic Web and ontology technologies in the industrial sectors is cost management. Considering this, we strive to leverage the empirical findings we have gained in this work into a technology roadmap covering reuse-oriented activities within the life cycle of an ontology to be used by the ontology engineering community and technology vendors in shaping their future R&D plans and improving their products. These efforts could be aligned with similar initiatives such as the W3C Semantic Web Best Practices and Deployment Working Group[22] and the KnowledgeWeb Network of Excellence[23].

ACKNOWLEDGMENT

The project Wissensnetze is a part of the InterVal Berlin Research Centre for the Internet Economy funded by the German Ministry of Research (BMBF) and comprises two academic institutions located in the region Berlin-Brandenburg, Germany: the Humboldt Universität zu Berlin represented by the working group "Databases and Information Systems" at the Department of Computer Science (http://dbis.informatik.hu-berlin.de) and the Freie Universität Berlin, represented by the working group "Networked Information Systems" at the Department of Computer Science (http://www.ag-nbi.de) and the working group "Produktion, Wirtschaftsinformatik und OR" at the Department of Economics (http://wiwiss.fu-berlin.de/suhl/index.htm).

REFERENCES

Antoniou, G., Kehagias, A. (2000). *A note on the refinement of ontologies*, International Journal of Intelligent Systems 15(7), pp. 623-632.

Bizer, C., Heese, R., Mochol, M., Oldakowski, R., Tolksdorf, R., Eckstein, R. (2005). *The Impact of Semantic Web Technologies on Job Recruitment Processes.* Proc of the 7. Internationale Tagung Wirtschaftsinformatik 2005, Bamberg, Germany.

CrosswaterSystems. (2003). *Der Virtuelle Arbeitsmarkt der Bundesanstalt für Arbeit. Anspruch und Wirklichkeit - das Millionengrab.*

Direct Employers. (2006). *Recturing Trends Survey.*

Fernández, M., Cantador, I., Castells, P. (2006). *CORE: A Tool for Collaborative Ontology Reuse and Evaluation*, Proc. of the 4th International Evaluation of Ontologies for the Web (EON2006) Workshop located at the 15th International World Wide Web Conference WWW 2006.

Ferris G.R., Hochwarter W.A., Buckley M.R., Harrell-Cook G., Frink D.D. (1999). Human resources management: some new directions. *Journal of Management*, 25(3), pp. 385-415.

Grund, C. (2006). Mitarbeiterrekrutierung über das Internet. *Marktanalyse und empirische Untersuchung von Determinanten und Konsequenzen für die Arbeitnehmer, 76*(5), pp. 451-472.

Heese, R., Mochol, M., Oldakowski, R. (2007). Semantic Web Technologies in the Recruitment Domain, in *Competencies in Organizational E-Learning: Concepts and Tools.*

Lisi, F. A. (2007). *An ILP Approach to Ontology Refinement for the Semantic Web*, Proc. of the 4th European Semantic Web Conference (ESWC2007), Poster Session.

Lopez F. M. (2002). Overview and analysis of methodologies for building ontologies, in *Knowledge Engineering Review*, 17(2).

Mochol, M., Jentzsch, A., Wache, H. (2007). *Suitable employees wanted? Find them with semantic techniques*, Making Semantics Work For Business, European Semantic Technology Conference 2007 (ESTC2007), 2007.

Mochol, M., Wache, H., Nixon, L. (2006). *Improving the recruitment process through ontology-based querying*, Proc. of the 1st International Workshop on Applications and Business Aspects of the Semantic Web (SEBIZ 2006), collocated with the 5th International Semantic Web Conference (ISWC-2006).

Mochol, M., Wache, H., Nixon, L. (2007). *Improving the accuracy of job search with semantic techniques*, Proc. of the 10th International Conference on Business Information Systems (BIS2007).

Oldakowski, R. Bizer, C. (2005). *SemMF: A Framework for Calculating Semantic Similarity of Objects Represented as RDF Graph;* Poster at the 4th International Semantic Web Conference (ISWC 2005), 2005.

OntoWeb European Project. (2002). *Successful scenarios for ontology-based applications.*

Paslaru, E.B. (2005). *Context-enhanced Ontology Reuse.* Doctoral Consortium at the 5th International and Interdisciplinary Conference on Modeling and Using Context CONTEXT05.

Poole, J., Campbell, J. A. (1995). A Novel Algorithm for Matching Conceptual and Related Graphs. *Conceptual Structures: Applications, Implementation and Theory, 954*, pp. 293 – 307.

Uschold, M., Healy, M., Williamson, K., Clark, P. and Woods, S. (1998). *Ontology Reuse and Application.* Proc. of the International Conference on Formal Ontology and Information Systems - FOIS'98, pp. 179–192.

wwjGbmH. (2005). *Online-Rekrutierung I/2005.*

ADDITIONAL READING

Human Resource

Della Valle, E., D., Cerizza, I. Celino, J. Estublier, G. Vega, M. Kerrigan, J. Ramirez, B. Villazon-Terrazas, P. Guarrera, G. & Zhao G. (2007). *Monteleone: SEEMP: a Semantic Interoperability Infrastructure for e-government services in the employment sector*, Proc. of the 4th European Semantic Web Conference (ESWC).

Keim, T. et al. (2004). *Recruiting Trends 2004.* Working Paper No. 2004-5. efinance Institut. Johann-Wolfgang-Goethe-Universität Frankfurt am Main.

Keim, T. et al. (2005). *Recruiting Trends 2005.* Working Paper No. 2005-22. efinance Institut. Johann-Wolfgang-Goethe-Universität Frankfurt am Main.

Nixon, L., & Mochol, M. (2005). Prototypical Business Use Cases. Deliverable 1.1.2 in the *Knowledge Web EU Network of Excellence*, pp. 11-15 & 53-56.

Sure, Y., Maedche, A., & Staab, S. (2000). *Leveraging Corporate Skill Knowledge – From ProPer to OntoProPer.* Proc. of the 3rd International Conference on Practical Aspects of Knowledge Management, 2000.

Wright, P.M., & McMahan, G.C. (1992). Theoretical perspectives for strategic Human resource management. *Journal of Management*, 18, pp. 292-320.

Semantic Web

Davies, J., Studer R., & Warren P. (2006). *Semantic Web Technologies: Trends and Research in Ontology-based Systems.* Wiley.

Fensel, D., Hendler, J.A., & Lieberman, H. (2005). *Spinning the Semantic Web. Bringing the World Wide Web to Its Full Potential.* MIT Press.

Hitzler P., & Sure Y. (2007) *Semantic Web.* Grundlagen, Springer.

T. Berners-Lee, J. Hendler, & O. Lassila. (BeHeLa, 2001) The Semantic Web. *Scientific American*, 284(5), pp. 34–43.

Ontologies & Ontology Engineering

Gomez-Perez, A., Fernandez-Lopez, M., & Corcho, O. (2004). Ontological Engineering – with examples from the areas of Knowledge Management, e-Commerce and the Semantic Web. *Advanced Information and Knowledge Processing.* Springer.

Gruber, R.T. (1995). Toward principles for the design of ontologies used for knowledge sharing. *International Journal Hum.-Comput. Stud.*, 43(5-6), pp. 907–928.

Grüninger M. & Fox M. (1995). *Methodology for the Design and Evaluation of Ontologies.* Proc. of the Workshop on Basic Ontological Issues in Knowledge Sharing, IJCAI95.

Pinto, H.S., & Martins, J.P.. (2001) *A methodology for ontology integration.* K-CAP 2001: Proc. of the International Conference on Knowledge capture, ACM Press.

Russ, T., Valente, A., MacGregor, R., & Swartout, W. (1999). *Practical Experiences in Trading Off Ontology Usability and Reusability.* In Proc. of the KAW99 Workshop.

Staab, S., & Studer R. (2003). *Handbook on Ontologies. (International Handbooks on Information Systems)* Springer.

Uschold, M. & King, M. (1995). *Towards a Methodology for Building Ontologies.* Proceedings Workshop on Basic Ontological Issues in Knowledge Sharing, IJCAI95, 1995.

Uschold M. and Grüninger M. (1996). ONTOLOGIES: Principles, Methods and Applications. *Knowledge Engineering Review*, 11(2).

Uschold M. and Jasper R. (1999). *A Framework for Understanding and Classifying Ontology Applications*. KRR5-99, Stockholm, Sweden.

Ontology Matching, Merging, and Alignment

Euzenat, J. & Shvaiko P. (2007). *Ontology Matching*. Springer.

Giunchiglia, F. & Shvaiko, P. (2004). Semantic Matching. *Knowledge Engineering Review*, 18(3), pp. 265–280.

Mochol M., Jentzsch A., & Euzenat J. (2006). *Applying an Analytic Method for Matching Approach Selection*. Proc. of the International Workshop on Ontology Matching (OM-2006) collocated with the 5th International Semantic Web Conference (ISWC-2006), Athens, Georgia, USA.

Noy, F. & Musen, N. (1999). *An Algorithm for Merging and Aligning Ontologies: Automation and Tool Support*, Proc. of the Workshop on Ontology Management at the Sixteenth National Conference on Artificial Intelligence (AAAI-99). Orlando, FL: AAAI Press.

Rahm, E., & Bernstein, P. A. (2001). A survey of approaches to automatic schema matching. *VLDB Journal: Very Large Data Bases*, Vol. 10, Nr. 4, pp. 334-350.

Shvaiko, P. (2004). *A Classification of Schema-Based Matching Approaches*. Technical Report DIT-04-09, University of Trento. Retrieved, December 2004, from http://eprints.biblio.unitn.it/archive/00000654/01/093.pdf

Query Relaxation and Processing

Dolog P., Stuckenschmidt H., & Wache H.. (2006). *Robust query processing for personalized information access on the Semantic Web*. In 7th International Conference on Flexible Query Answering Systems (FQAS 2006), Nr. 4027 in LNCS/LNAI, Springer, Milan, Italy.

ENDNOTES

1. http://www.gartner.com/
2. http://www.arbeitsagentur.de
3. http://www.ams.se
4. http://wissensnetze.ag-nbi.de
5. http://sites.wiwiss.fu-berlin.de/suhl/radek/semmf/doc/index.html
6. Approx System is based on the SWI-Prolog, available at http://www.swi-prolog.org/
7. http://www.openrdf.org/
8. http://www.hr-xml.org, retrieved on 14.12.2007
9. http://www.arbeitsamt.de/hst/markt/news/BKZ_alpha.txt, retrieved on 05.12.2007
10. http://www.bls.gov/soc/, retrieved on 05.12.2007
11. http://www.destatis.de/allg/d/klassif/wz2003.htm, retrieved on 05.12.2007
12. http://www.census.gov/epcd/www/naics.html, retrieved on 05.12.2007
13. http://www.kowien.uni-essen.de/publikationen/konstruktion.pdf, retrieved on 14.12.2007
14. http://www23.hrdc-drhc.gc.ca/2001/e/generic/matrix.pdf, http://www.onetcenter.org/ , retrieved on 05.12.2007
15. http://unstats.un.org/unsd/cr/registry/regcst.asp?Cl=17&Lg=1, retrieved on 05.12.2007
16. http://www.monster.com, retrieved on 12.12.2007
17. http://www.jobpilot.com, retrieved on 13.12.2007
18. http://www.stepstone.com, retrieved on 13.12.2007
19. https://forms.bpfj.intronet.com/ibm/Forms/emea/expro/GeneralApp.jsp, retrieved on 10.12.2007

[20] https://www.vw-personal.de/content/www/de/bewerbung/onlinebewerbung.html, retrieved on 10.12.2007

[21] http://www.seemp.org/, retrieved on 10.12.2007

[22] http://www.w3.org/2001/sw/BestPractices/, retrieved on 12.12.2007

[23] http://knowledgeweb.semanticweb.org/, retrieved on 13.12.2007

Chapter VI
The SEEMP Approach to Semantic Interoperability for E-Employment

E. Della Valle
CEFRIEL – Politecnico of Milano, Italy

D. Cerizza
CEFRIEL – Politecnico of Milano, Italy

I. Celino
CEFRIEL – Politecnico of Milano, Italy

M.G. Fugini
CEFRIEL – Politecnico of Milano, Italy

J. Estublier
Université Joseph Fourier, France

G. Vega
Université Joseph Fourier, France

M. Kerrigan
University of Innsbruck, Austria

A. Gómez-Pérez
Universidad Politécnica de Madrid, Spain

J. Ramírez
Universidad Politécnica de Madrid, Spain

B. Villazón
Universidad Politécnica de Madrid, Spain

G. Zhao
Le Forem, Belgium

M. Cesarini
Università di Milano-Bicocca, Italy

F. De Paoli
Università di Milano-Bicocca, Italy

ABSTRACT

SEEMP is a European Project that promotes increased partnership between labour market actors and the development of closer relations between private and public Employment Services, making optimal use of the various actors' specific characteristics, thus providing job-seekers and employers with better services. The need for a flexible collaboration gives rise to the issue of interoperability in both data exchange and share of services. SEEMP proposes a solution that relies on the concepts of services and semantics in order to provide a meaningful service-based communication among labour market actors requiring a minimal shared commitment.

CURRENT SITUATION

European Member States have introduced major reforms to make the labour market more flexible, transparent and efficient, in compliance with the European Employment Strategy guidelines. Such major reforms include decentralization, liberalization of the mediation market (competition between public and private actors), and quality monitoring of Employment Service (ES) staff and services. As an effect, ESs understood the need for making available on-line a one-stop shop for employment. This results in an increased used of information communication technology (ICT) and a boost in differentiating and personalizing the services they offer (e.g., Borsa Lavoro Lombardia, Le FOREM, EURES[1], etc.).

The current employment market is characterized by high heterogeneity of models and actors; in particular we can distinguish between Public Employment Services (PES) and Private Employment Services (PRES)[2]. The ICT systems in ESs can serve different purposes: facilitating job-matching and job mobility for job seekers and employers; improving the functioning of labour markets; coordinating the exchange of information; allowing a more efficient management of ES internal services; monitoring of local market trends; personalized services, etc. The need for reconciling local, regional and national policies is increasing and it concerns the combination of services and data provided by different actors.

SEEMP project (IST-4-027347-STP) aims to design and implement a prototype of an Interoperability infrastructure for PESs and PRESs. More specifically, SEEMP is developing an EIF-compliant Architecture (EC, 2004) to allow collaboration between the Employment Services that exist in Europe. The resulting European Employment Marketplace will overcome the national barriers complying, at the same time, with the local policies of each Member State. Job-seekers and employers will have better services that operate at European scale thanks to SEEMP, which promotes increased partnership between labour market actors and the development of closer relations between private and public Employment Services. For instance, the matching of Job Offers and CVs across European borders will become possible, eventually increasing labour hiring and workforce mobility.

PROBLEM STATEMENT

In order to fulfil SEEMP's ambitious goals several problems must be solved at an organizational and technical level.

At an organizational level, the business model of SEEMP has to be catchy for all ESs. The main reason for an ES to buy in is by creating added value for its local users (both job seekers and employers) by offering interconnections with other ESs. Today it is normal for users to insert their CV or Job Offers into many ESs and collect, laboriously, the results by hand. With SEEMP in place, each ES will be able to collaborate with other ESs. From the perspective of the end user, the add-value is the outreach to other niches of the job market without 'being stretched out'. End users will be able insert their CV or Job Offer into one ES and collect pan-European results. From the ESs perspective it will result in an increase in both the number of users and their faithfulness to each ES, thus an increase in transaction volume.

At a technical level, the need for a flexible collaboration between ESs, gives rise to the issue of interoperability in both data exchange and share of services. The technical approach of SEEMP relies on the concepts of Web services and semantics. Web services, exploited in a Software Engineering manner, enable an easier maintenance of the integration. Semantics, encoded in the systems by the means of ontologies and mediators, allow for the reconciliation of hundreds of local professional profiles and taxonomies.

The SEEMP solution will expose, following the well established Software Engineering approach of Mélusine (Estublier, J., Vega, G., 2005),

Figure 1. The running example of distributed matching of CVs and job offers

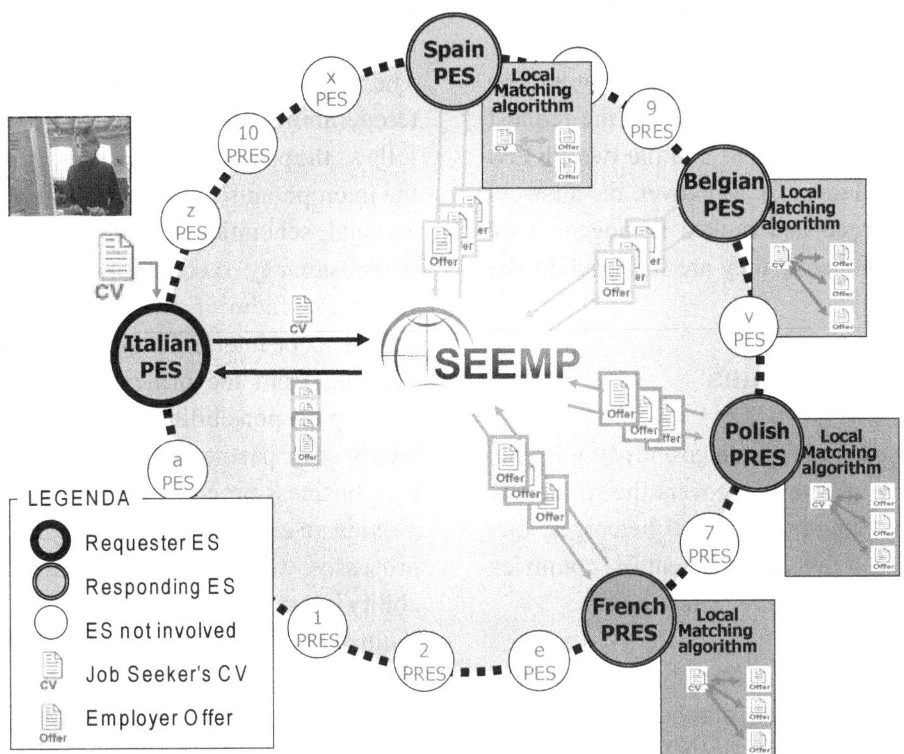

a single consistent set of abstract services each ES can invoke. Such abstract services will provide a multilateral interoperability solution that delegates the execution of the services to the local ESs (in accordance with the subsidiary principle) and aggregates the results before sending the response back to the invoker. Moreover, following the innovative Web Service Modeling Ontology (WSMO) (Fensel et al. , 2006) approach, we will capture the semantics shared among ESs in a single consistent model. Such a model includes a Reference Ontology to which the local semantics is mapped, as well as a semantic description of the local Web services for their automatic use. A set of tools will be provided to each ES for modelling its Local Ontology and for mappings its Local Ontology to the Reference Ontology. As a technical result SEEMP will enable a meaningful service-based collaboration among ESs.

An e-employment running example. For the discussion of this chapter we will consider a running example derived by the user requirements of the SEEMP project:

Job seekers (companies) put their CVs (Job Offers) on a local PES and ask to match them with the Job Offers (CVs) other users put in different PESs and PRESs through SEEMP.

It may look like a fairly simple example, but to reach its potential EU-wide audience, this e-Employment running example (see Figure 1) needs to fulfil a wider set of requirements than the respective local ES service. A local matching service is designed for national/regional requirements only (i.e., central database, single professional taxonomy, single user language, etc.). SEEMP has to be able to send the request, which an end-user submits to the local PES (the Italian ES on the left of Figure 1), to the other PESs and PRESs in the marketplace. In order to avoid asking "all" ESs, it has to select those that are most likely will be able to provide an answer and send the request only to them (the two PESs and the two PRESs on the right of Figure 1). Moreover, the answers should be merged and ranked homogeneously by the SEEMP before they are sent back to the local ES.

Interoperability Issues

The running example presented above highlights the need for a system that covers the whole EU and subsumes hundreds of real heterogeneous systems existing in many different EU countries and regions. It implies the resolution of:

- Language heterogeneity, e.g., an Italian Java Analyst Programmer may be looking for Job Offers written in all the different European languages.
- CVs and Job Offers structural heterogeneity, i.e. the use of standards like HR-XML is not wide spread and a multitude of local formats exists.
- CVs and Job Offers content description heterogeneity, i.e., European level occupation classifications like ISCO-88 exist, but they do not reflect legitimate differences and perspectives of political economic, cultural and legal environments.
- System heterogeneity in terms of service interface and behaviour, i.e., no standard exists for e-Employment services thus each ES implements its own external interfaces and behaviour.

These issues are typical interoperability issues that SEEMP helps to solve. The need for interoperability at European Level among e-Government services has been perceived since 1999 (1720/1999/EC) with the adoption of a series of actions and measures for pan-European electronic interchange of data between administrations, businesses and citizens (IDABC) (2004/387/EC). The main result of IDABC is the European Interoperability Framework (EIF) (EC, 2004). EIF follows the principle of subsidiarity in addressing the interoperability problem at all levels: organizational, semantic and technical. The principle of subsidiarity recommends that the internal workings of administrations and EU Institutions should not be interfered with. One crucial aspect, deriving from the principle of subsidiarity, is to keep responsibility decentralized; in other words each partner should be able to keep its own business process almost unchanged and to provide an external point for interacting with its processes, which EIF terms Business Interoperability Interfaces (BII). Quoting from IDABC: "it is unrealistic to believe that administrations from different Member States will be able to harmonize their business processes because of pan-European requirements". EIF itself does not prescribe any technical solution, but rather it recommends the principles to be considered for any e-Government service to be set up at a pan-European level, namely accessibility, multilingualism, security, privacy, use of open standards and of open source software (where possible) and, last but not least, use of multilateral solutions. SEEMP proposes itself as an implementation of EIF in the domain of e-Employment.

PROPOSED SOLUTION

SEEMP relies on the concept of Service. Web services are quickly becoming the standard for Business to Business integration, allowing for loose, decoupled architectures to be designed and built. Following the EIF, each PES and PRES must expose its Business Interfaces as Web services. SEEMP uses Mélusine (Estublier, J., Vega, G., 2005) as a tool for modelling abstract services and orchestrating the process of delegating the execution to distributed independent service providers. SEEMP, as a marketplace, models a unique consistent set of Web services out of those exposed by the PESs and PRESs. Therefore the services exposed by SEEMP become the actual standard for the distributed independent service providers.

SEEMP relies on the concept of semantics. Data semantics is captured in ontologies and the semantics of heterogeneity is captured in mediators. As for services, each local PES and PRES has its own local dictionary of terms and its own classification, which are regarded in SEEMP as a Local Ontology. Such an ontology provides a means for exchanging data (i.e., structure/content of the exchanged messages are classes/instances of such ontologies). All these ontologies differ but share a common knowledge about employment. SEEMP models a unique consistent ontology, called the Reference Ontology (RO), made up of those exposed by the PESs and PRESs. An extension of the METHONTOLOGY (Gomez-Pérez, 2003) is employed as a methodology for developing and maintaining both the local and Reference Ontologies. This extension includes methods and techniques for reuse and reengineering non ontological resources.

SEEMP combines Services and Semantics. The semantics of a given service is captured in semantic descriptions of Web services and user Goals; SEEMP adopts the Web Service Modeling Ontology (WSMO) (Fensel et al. , 2006) as the conceptual model for described Services and the data they exchange. WSMO is used to semantically describe the data model for data exchanged between SEEMP services, the SEEMP Web services exposed by ESs, the requirements of service requestors as Goals, and Mediators for resolving heterogeneity issues. The Web Service Modeling Language (WSML) (de Bruijn, 2006) provides a concrete syntax for encoding these semantic descriptions using the WSMO model.

Minimal Shared Commitment

In the domain of e-Employment, different Employment Services, both public and private, collect CVs and Job Offers in order to match demand with supply. Each ES covers either a region or an occupational sector. As a result, the employment market is severely fragmented and many ESs perceive the need of sharing information in order to provide a better service to their customers. However, they would never exchange CVs or Job Offers, since they contain sensitive information (like contact details). Instead, the ESs use "anonymized" versions of CVs and Job Offers, which we have named Candidacies and Vacancies, respectively. Therefore, if an ES exchanges a Candidacy/Vacancy with another ES, it potentially enlarges the possibilities of finding a match, without giving the peer the chance to by-pass it by directly contacting the Job Seeker/Employer.

The prerequisite of the employment domain can be generalized to a common industrial need: parties agree on general principles, but then they only commit to a subset of the possible implications of these principles and keep for themselves all their disagreements. Therefore, we draw the conclusion that the common notion of shared agreement is not enough to manage the complexity of the industrial scenarios we face. We believe that two important notions have to be made explicit: commitment and disagreement. It is worth noting that usually when parties provide ontology commitment the intended meaning is that all parties commit to the "entire" ontology. On the contrary, we propose to give a "subjective" meaning to commitment and disagreement, which does not presume a common knowledge (Lewis, 1969 and Aumann, 1976) among all the parties: two parties may commit to (or disagree with) different parts of the agreement.

In order to move from the problem statement to the solution conception, we need to find appropriate methods and technologies. We need conceptual elements to capture the notions of agreement, commitment and disagreement, to make them operational and to express the respective relations among them. Ontologies have been used and are good for formalizing and sharing the agreement. The notion of commitment is usually associated to the notion of ontology, and this is certainly true in the context of agent communication. In agent-based systems, all agents usually share a single ontology. The Semantic Web vision, however, foresees an ecosystem of ontologies, because of the very nature of the Web which is "fractal" (Berners-Lee, 1998). Ontologies can be co-invented, they can partially overlap and, in developing a new ontology, the importing of existing ones is encouraged (Shadbolt et al., 1998). We believe that the "practical" meaning of ontological commitment in the Semantic Web is slightly different from the original one. In formal terms, committing to an ontology that imports several other ones is the same as committing to one big ontology obtained by the union of all of them; however, in practical terms, committing to the ontology that includes the import annotations is partially an "unconscious" commitment, in that it means trusting the knowledge engineer who decided which ontologies to import.

Therefore, our best practice is to distinguish between the RO, which captures the shared agreement, and the Local Ontologies, which captures the commitment and the disagreement of the various parties. We propose to build the RO including all the details that are needed to allow for a meaningful communication between each pair of parties, thus including also details that most of the parties would consider either inessential or not sharable. Then, each party can develop its Local Ontology, partially by importing parts of the Reference Ontology, and partially by developing its own point of view. Every time a Local Ontology imports a part of the RO, the party is considered to commit to the imported parts of the RO. Moreover, every time a part of the Local Ontology is aligned to a part of the RO (e.g., by the means of ontology-to-ontology mediators (de Bruijn et al., 2006b)), the party is also said to commit to that part of the RO. A particular attention should be given in capturing also the source of disagreement within the Local Ontology. Finally, each party should make available to all other actors the part of the Local Ontology that explains its different point of view without causing conflicts.

The SEEMP Solution

The SEEMP solution is composed of a reference part (all the dark components in Figure 2), which reflects the "minimal shared commitment" both

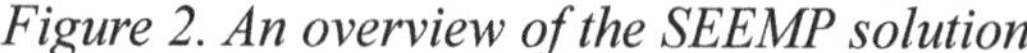
Figure 2. An overview of the SEEMP solution

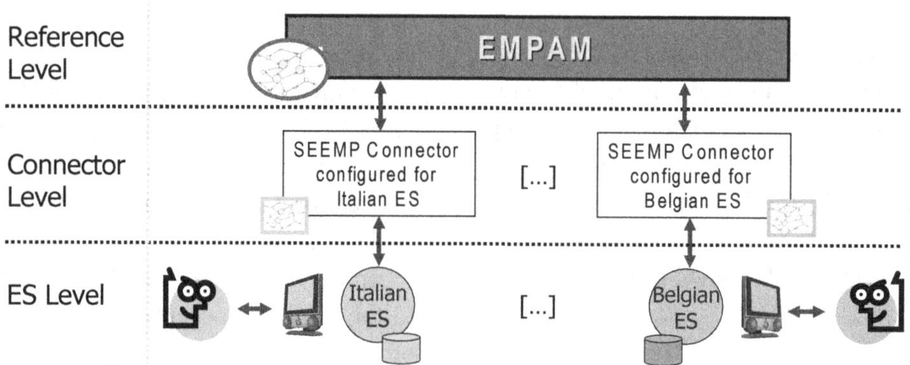

in terms of services and semantics, and by the connectors toward the various local actors (the components in shading colors in Figure 2).

Structural Overview

The reference part of SEEMP solution is made up of the central abstract machine, named EMPAM (Employment Market Place Abstract Machine) and a set of SEEMP services.

The EMPAM is an abstract machine, in that it does not perform directly any operations, but rather offers abstract services that are made concrete by delegation: when the abstract service is invoked, the EMPAM delegates its execution to the appropriate ES by invoking the correspondent concrete services. It acts as a multilateral solution (as request by EIF), in which all the services connected to the EMPAM are made available to all other ESs, i.e. they ensure a pan-European level of services without interfering with the Business processes of each ES.

The SEEMP services are meant to support EMPAM execution. The running example requires two SEEMP services, namely discovery and ranking. The discovery service is offered by Glue (Della Valle et al., 2005). The EMPAM invokes Glue Discovery Engine before delegating the execution to the concrete services exposed by the ESs. Glue analyzes the CV sent by the invoking ES and it selects among all ESs those that are most likely to be able to return relevant Job Offers. The ranking service is invoked by the EMPAM after all the concrete services have answered and it merges the results providing a homogeneous ranking of the returned Job Offers. It also deletes duplicated Job Offers that are returned from different ESs.

The SEEMP connectors enable the collaboration that occurs between the EMPAM and a given ES. A SEEMP connector will exist for each of the ESs that are connected to the EMPAM and has two main responsibilities:

- **Lifting and lowering:** When communicating with the ES any outgoing (or incoming) data which is exchanged by the means of Web services must be lifted from the syntactic XML level to the semantic WSML level in terms of the Local Ontologies of the ES (or lowered back to the syntactic XML level from the semantic WSML level).
- **Resolving heterogeneity:** Each ES has its own Local Ontology that represents its view on the employment domain. The SEEMP connector is responsible for resolving these heterogeneity issues by converting all the ontologized data (the data lifted from the XML received from the ES) into data in terms of the Reference Ontology shared by all partners and vice versa.

Functional Overview

By combining the EMPAM and the connectors, the SEEMP solution enables a meaningful service-based collaboration among ESs. Figure 3 illustrates how such a meaning collaboration occurs when executing the example from section 1.1:

1. The user inserts a CV into the Italian PES and requests relevant Job Offers.
2. The Italian ES invokes the matching service of the marketplace providing the CV in XML.
3. The SEEMP connector lifts the XML CV to the semantic level in terms of the Italian Local Ontology and then translates the CV from the Italian ontology to the Reference Ontology.
4. The discovery service in the EMPAM analyzes the CV and selects among all ESs those that are most likely to be able to return relevant Job Offers.
5. The EMPAM invokes in parallel the local matching service of the selected ESs.
6. The various connectors translate the CV from the Reference Ontology to the Local

Figure 3. How SEEMP solution enables meaningful service-based collaboration

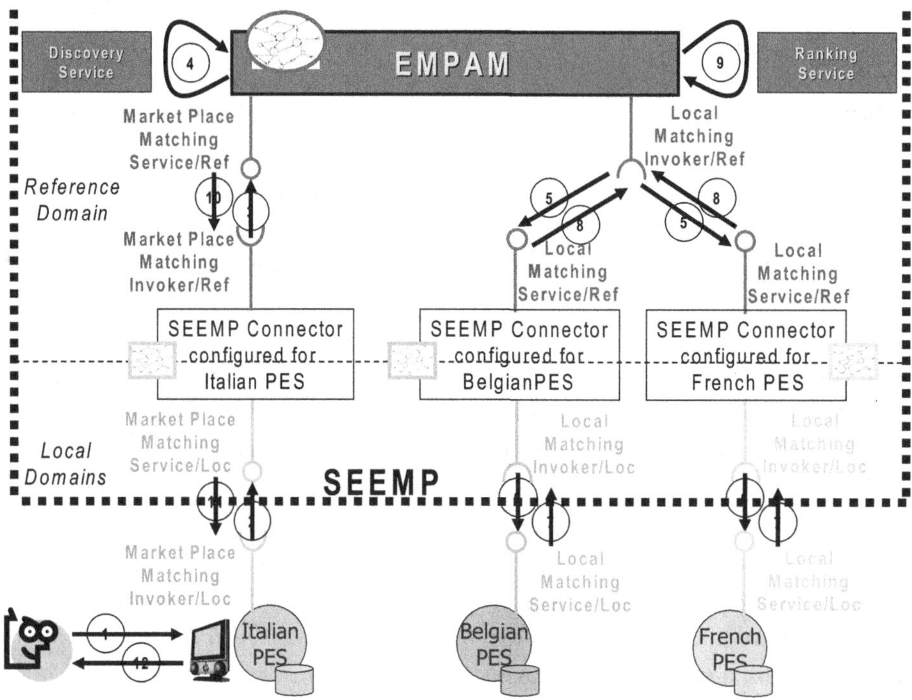

Ontology (i.e., the Belgian and French ESs), lower the Local Ontology instances to the local ES XML format and invoke the local service with the CV.

7. The Belgian and French PESs match the provided CV with their local repository of Job Offers, with all the processing occurring locally, and return those that match to the connector.
8. The respective connector lifts the Job Offers from XML to the Local Ontology and translates the Job Offers from each Local Ontology to the reference one.
9. The ranking service in the EMPAM merges, at a semantic level, the responses and ranks the Job Offers homogeneously.
10. The Job Offers are sent back in terms of the Reference Ontology to the Italian connector that translate them in the Italian ontology and lower them back to XML.
11. The connector responds to the Italian ES.
12. Finally the ES displays the Job Offers to the user.

SOLUTION DETAILS

The SEEMP Reference Ontology for E-Employment

The Reference Ontology (RO) is a core component of the system. It acts as a common "language" in the form of a set of controlled vocabularies that describe the details of the employment sector. The Reference Ontology has to be rich enough to support the semantic needs of all the Employment Services involved currently and in the future, i.e. it must be possible for an Employment Service to map a meaning full amount of its own Local Ontology to the Reference Ontology. The Reference Ontology also has to be a scalable, adaptable and maintainable ontology. For these reasons it was developed following the METHONTOLOGY approach (Gomez-Pérez, 2003) including methods and techniques for reuse and reengineering of non ontological resources.

The specification of the RO is based on international standards (like NACE, ISCO-88 (COM), FOET, etc.) and codes (like ISO 3166, ISO 6392, etc.). The RO is composed of thirteen sub-ontologies: competence, compensation, driving license, economic activity, education, geography, job offer, job seeker, labour regulatory, language, occupation, skill and time. The main sub-ontologies are the Job Offer and Job Seeker ontologies, which are intended to represent the structure of a Job Offer and a CV respectively. While these two sub-ontologies were built starting from the HR-XML recommendations, the other sub-ontologies were derived from the available international standards/codes and ES classifications, chosen according to criteria that will be explained in the following of the chapter.

In order to choose the most suitable human resource management standards for modelling CVs and Job Offers, the degree of coverage needed in the desired domain has been considered, taking into account the scope and size of the standards; However, too broad a coverage may move us further away from the European reality; therefore we have tried to find a trade-off between coverage and the following concerns:

- **The current European need:** It is important that the Reference Ontology focuses on the current European reality, because the Employment Services involved in SEEMP are European, and the Employment Marketplace will be used in a European context.
- **Employment service recommendations:** In order to assess the quality of the Reference Ontology, the opinion of existing Employment Services is crucial as they have a deep knowledge of the employment domain.

When choosing the standards, we selected the ICT domain as a "proof of concept" for prototyping the SEEMP marketplace. Hence, the chosen standards should cover the ICT domain to an acceptable degree. Narrowing the focus for prototype purposes results in a more focused Reference Ontology that can be validated more easily than modelling the entire employment domain, also modelling even a subsection of the employment involves the modelling of all primitives that will be needed across the entire domain. In the case of the Occupation ontology, for example, we have chosen one standard (ISCO-88 (COM)), but have also taken into account concepts coming from other classifications, in order to obtain a richer classification for the ICT domain.

When specifying Job Offers and CVs, it is also necessary to refer to general purpose international codes such as Country codes, currency codes, etc. For this aim, the chosen codes have been the ISO codes, enriched in some cases with classifications provided by individual Employment Services. Finally, the representation of Job Offers and CVs also requires temporal concepts such as Interval and Instant. So, in order to represent these concepts in the final RO, the DAML time ontology was chosen among the most relevant time ontologies found in the literature on ontologies.

Developing Local Ontologies for SEEMP

We propose two possible approaches to building the Local Ontologies for a given Employment Service:

1. **Taking the Reference Ontology as a seed:** In this case, the concepts in the Local Ontologies are an extension in depth of the concepts already present in the RO; the consequence is that the effort required to transform instances between the local and Reference Ontologies is low, while the complexity of translating

between the Local Ontologies and the local schemata is higher.

2. **Reverse engineering from ES schemas:** This is the easiest way for ontologizing the data of an ES, since each concept in a Local Ontology is the semantic expression of a relevant concept in the respective ES's schema; the consequence is that the translation between Local Ontologies and local schemata is not complex, while the creation of mappings between the Reference and Local ontologies can be difficult and costly to maintain.

The suggested best practice is to use the first option when few ESs are present in the marketplace, and, when further ESs join the marketplace, to move progressively towards the second option. The balance between the two options is a trade off between allowing for meaningful communication and requiring minimal shared commitment.

Since each ES talks in its own "language", i.e. the Local Ontology that represents its view on the employment domain, its respective connector is responsible for resolving these heterogeneity issues, by translating the local content into the terms of the Reference Ontology. In this way, all the ESs in the marketplace speak the same language, and heterogeneity issues are resolved. Crucially each of the Employment servcies is responsible for managing its own mappings to the Reference Ontology, rather than managing mappings between every other possible Local Ontology in the SEEMP. Thus the addition of a new Employment Service to SEEMP represents no cost to exist members, reducing the barriers to entry for new ESs.

As a result of the introduction of a RO, a set of Local Ontologies and the various ontology-to-ontology mediators it is possible to support scenarios in which parties agree while disagreeing (see section 5). For instance each European Country has its own regulation in terms of job legislation and skills/certifications required to apply for a job. This is especially relevant for some professions, such as physician, lawyers, teachers, and so on. Those

Figure 4. The levels that make up the EMPAM as a Mélusine application

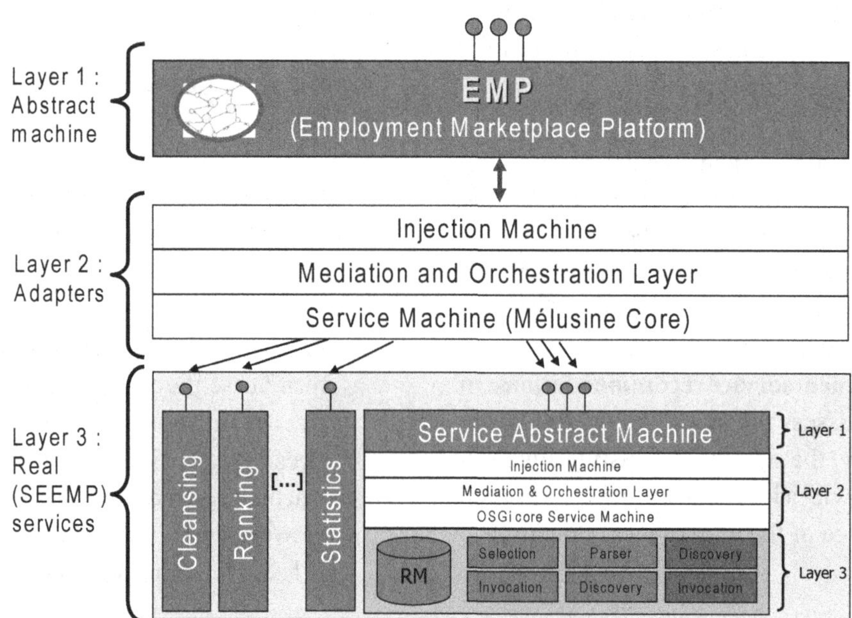

regulations are mandatory for each Country, but, being "local", they cannot fall within the shared agreement (i.e., the RO). As a concrete example, let us consider a Swiss ES and an Italian ES. Both express a positive commitment on the concepts related to jobs related to Academic Positions. However, the legislation about the prerequisites to apply for a University Professor position is different between Switzerland and Italy: the two Countries disagree on the necessity of holding a Ph.D. title. Therefore, the Swiss ES also makes explicit in its Local Ontology that each candidate for a Professor position should hold a Ph.D. title (whereas in Italy this is not mandatory).

The Employment Market Place Abstract Machine (EMPAM)

The EMPAM machine is implemented as a Mélusine application, which means it is structured following the Mélusine three layers approach (cf. Figure 4).

Layer 1—Abstract Machine: The higher EMPAM machine layer is a Java abstract program where abstract classes represent the concepts present in our SEEMP public Employment Service. EMPAM acts as an ES covering the whole of Europe, i.e. it acts as if all the CV and vacancies were present in its repositories. However the EMPAM is abstract since, in fact, it does not have any information locally, but delegates the responsibilities of storing and matching CVs and Job Offers to real ESs. The EMPAM program defines functions like repository access and matching that are not implemented at all or are only sketches of the functions behaviour.

Layer 2—Adapters: The responsibility of the second layer if to link the abstract services in the first layer with the real services provided by the Employment Services. To that end this layer is itself structured in three layers:

- *The Injection Machine*, whose duty is to capture those methods that need to be completed or implemented, and to transfer the call to the mediation and orchestration layer
- *The Mediation and Orchestration Layer,* which is responsible for transforming a single abstract method call into a potentially complex orchestration of real lower level services that together will perform the required function
- *The Service Machine*, whose duty is to transparently find and load the required SEEMP service and to call it. In SEEMP, this service machine is the core Mélusine service machine (an open source implementation of OSGi).

Layer 3—SEEMP Services: SEEMP Services are OSGi services, and are called accordingly by Mélusine. Using OSGi ensures the optimal performance of the EMPAM, while leaving the system open to future extension with new SEEMP Services and even dynamic changes, such as the dynamic loading/unloading of services. Two classes of services have been identified:

- **Services for interacting with ESs:** Most of the issues raised by EMPAM are related to discovering, selecting, parsing, and finally invoking a remote Employment Services connector. This functionality is delegated to a specific service, namely the service abstract machine (SAM), which is itself a Mélusine application and therefore contains an abstract machine that defines the fundamental concepts and functions of a service machine. This layer is captured and delegated to an orchestration layer that calls local services, which in the scope of SEEMP, are WSMX components (Haller et al., 2005) , wrapped as OSGi services.
- **Services of the marketplace:** These services include the cleansing, ranking and

statistic functions, and will include, in the future, the implementation of specific functions and repositories of the EMPAM machine i.e. those functions and information not available in the ESs. Functions and information available in ESs are made available by calling the SAM service.

SEEMP Connectors

All communication between the EMPAM and a given ES occurs through the given ESs' SEEMP Connector and has two main responsibilities:

- **Lifting and lowering:** Current Employment Services only deal in terms of structured XML content and do not deal in terms of ontologies. Within the SEEMP marketplace it is important that all content is ontologized so that it can be reasoned over, thus the SEEMP connector must lift all messages received from a given ES to the semantic level. This is done by converting the XML content received from the ES to WSML in terms of the Local Ontologies of the ES. Likewise when communicating with the ES, any outgoing data must be lowered back to the XML level so that the ES can understand the content. Since WSMO elements can be serialized in an RDF format, this task could be done by converting XML content to RDF first, and then converting RDF to WSML. In SEEMP this task is achieved by the means of X_2O, which is an extension of the R_2O language (Barrasa et al., 2004), it can be used to describe mappings between XML schemas and ontologies, and to its related processor XMapster, based on ODEMapster (Rodriguez et al., 2006).
- **Resolving heterogeneity:** Each Employment Service has its own view of the employment domain. The SEEMP connector is responsible for resolving heterogeneity issues that may exist between a given ESs' view of the employment domain and the EMPAMs' view of the employment domain. This is achieved by transforming the data received from for the terms of the Local Ontology into the terms of the Reference Ontology. Of course when the EMPAM wishes to send data back to a given ES the reverse process must be performed such that data in the terms of the Reference Ontology is transformed into the terms of the ESs Local Ontology.

As described in section 7.1 the Reference Ontology represents the bridge, or common vocabulary, that the ESs communicate through. Rather than managing mappings between every possible ontology pair, which essentially becomes unmanageable as the number of ESs in the marketplace grows, each ES need only maintain mappings to and from the Reference Ontology.

Figure 5. Converting between two Local Ontologies via the Reference Ontology

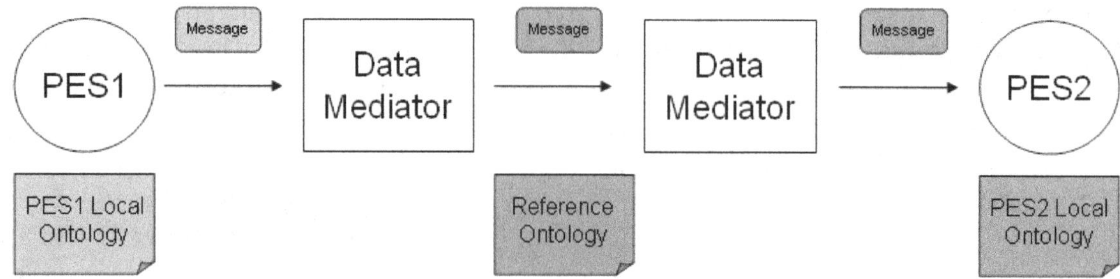

These mappings represent a set of rules describing how to convert an instance from the Local Ontology to an instance of the Reference Ontology and vice versa. This process can be seen in Figure 5, when PES1 wishes to communicate with PES2 it is necessary to convert the message from PES1s' Local Ontology to the Reference Ontology and then to convert the message to PES2s' Local Ontology.

Technologically this is achieved using the WSMX Data Mediation (Mocan et al., 2006). This work is made up of two components, the first being a design time component, within which the ES can describe the mappings between their Local Ontology and the Reference Ontology, and the second being a run time component, which is responsible for executing the mappings at run time to transform the messages between ontologies.

A reusable SEEMP connector is built by bringing together the functionality described above. The architecture of the SEEMP Connector outlined in the Figure 6 shows the ES communicating with the connector using XML via the exposed Web services. This XML is then lifted to the Local Ontology using the X_2O mappings stored in the repository and furthermore converted to the Reference Ontology using the data mediation mappings. Ultimately the EMPAM is invoked using messages in the Reference Ontology via its exposed Web services. Communication also occurs in the opposite direction.

Each of the ESs joining the marketplace will require its own SEEMP connector, however the only difference between any two connectors is the code for executing the ESs exposed Web services as each ES will expose services in a different way. The need for individual SEEMP connectors could be removed through the use of WSMO Choreography (Fensel et al., 2006) to describe the interfaces of the ES services and the integration of the WSMX choreography engine (Cimpian et al., 2005) and invoker into the

Figure 6. The SEEMP Connector internal architecture

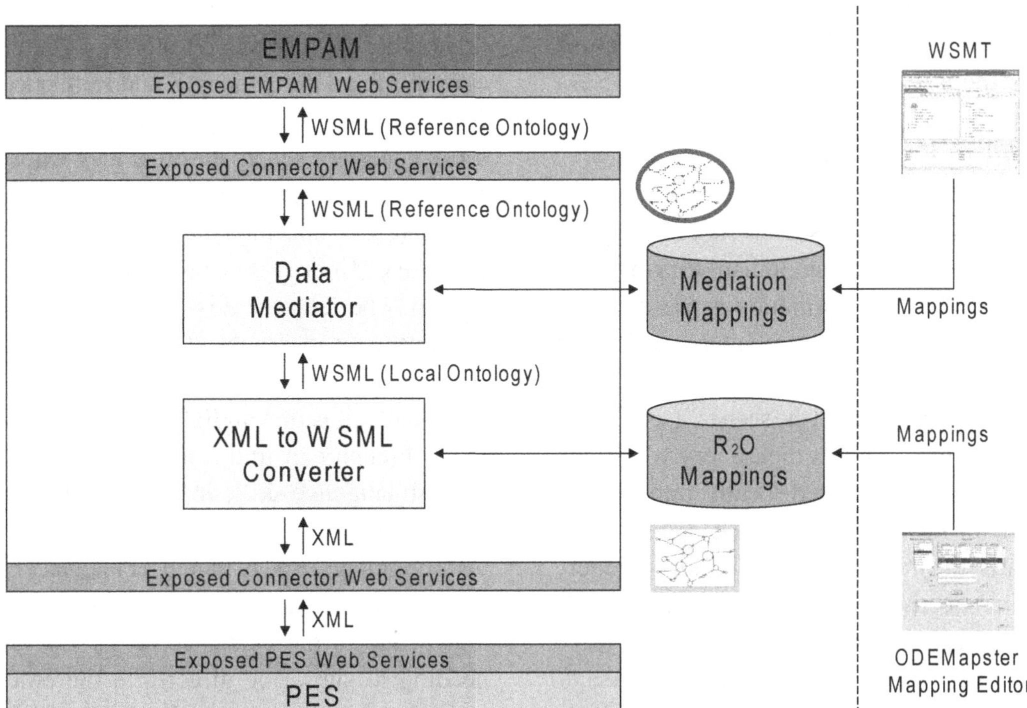

Figure 7. How the Job Offers SEEMP got from all EU are presented to an Italian User

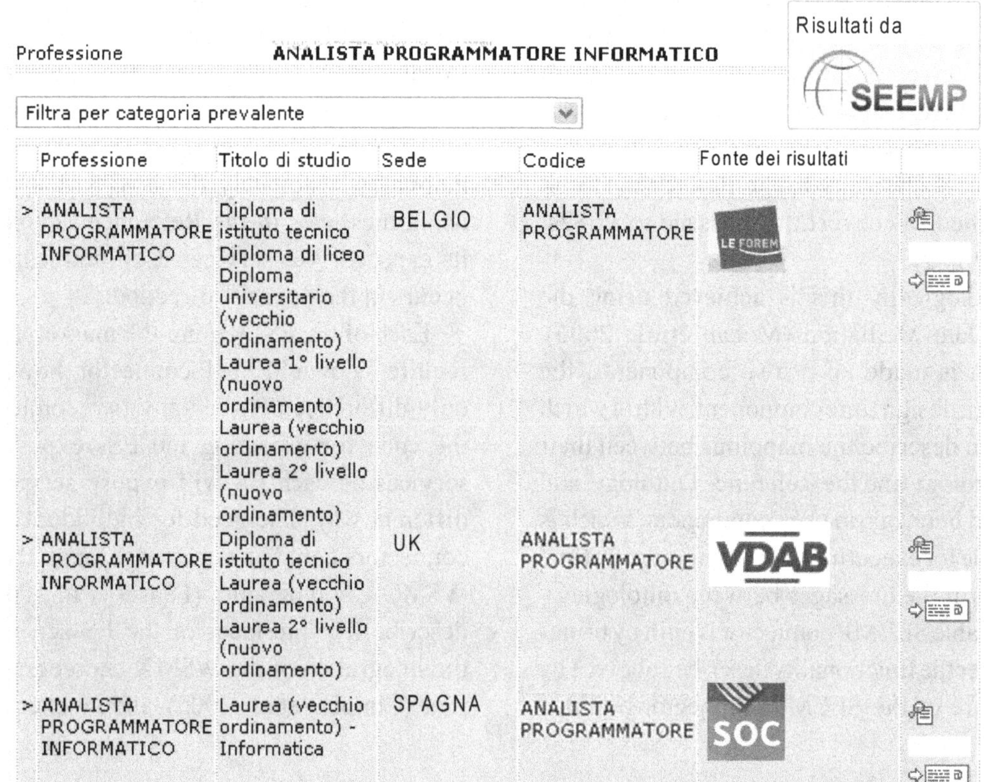

SEEMP Connector. This is considered as future work for the SEEMP Connector.

A Running Example

In Figure 7 we provide a screen-shot of the page receive when users of an Italian PES ask for SEEMP results. All information is presented in Italian even if they were originated by different ESs in different languages.

What happens "behind the scenes" (see Figure 8) is that the user submits their query with their profile, which is translated locally into a message with the local Italian code (e.g., Code_X-it); afterwards, the Italian SEEMP Connector generates the respective ontological message, which refers to the Local Ontological concept (e.g., Concept_X-it) and then translate the message into the reference version, which contains indications about the respective Reference Ontological concepts (e.g., RefConceptY and RefConceptX). Once the message is expressed in the reference format, it can be sent to the other ESs, whose connectors can translate it into the Local Ontological format (e.g., Concept_Y-be) and then in the local codes (e.g., Code_Y-be), processable by the local system. The receiver ESs can finally send back their response messages, if any, by following the same process.

The result is that an Italian user that does not speak French can find a job that requires only English language skills in Belgium, from an ES that was not previously accessible to him because of the language used in their user interface. Moreover, he can access this information without the knowledge of the existence of the ES, without needing to subscribe directly to the other ESs system and without re-posting his profile.

Figure 8. Translated a message from one ES to another using Local and Reference Ontologies

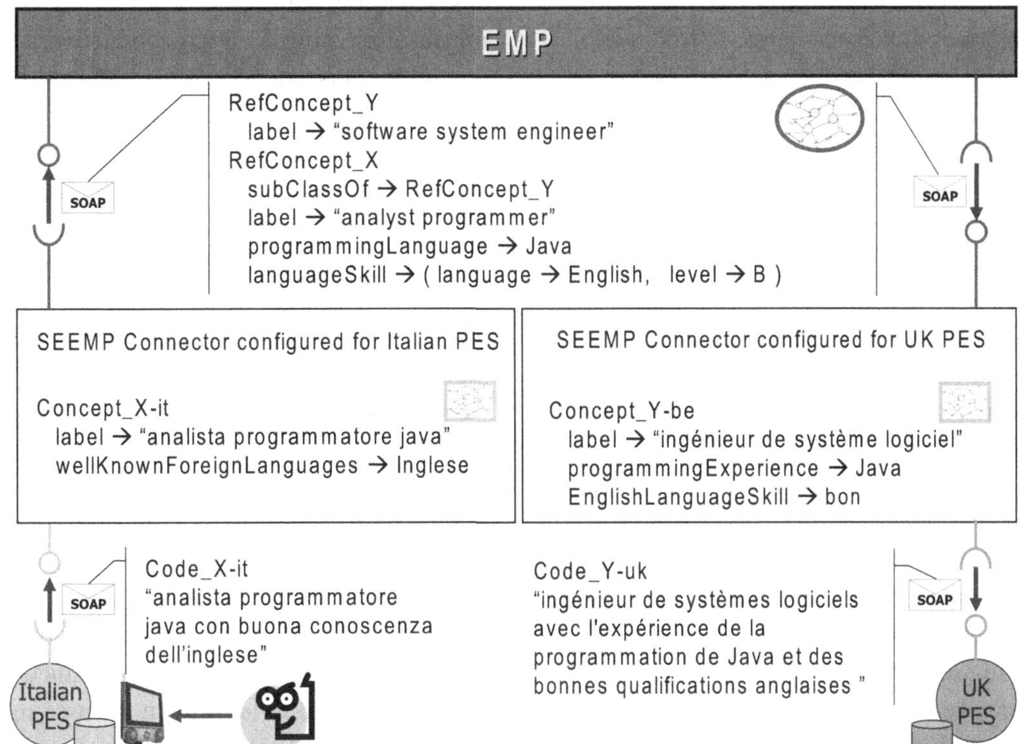

ALTERNATIVES

In order to draw a comparison between SEEMP and other approaches we selected two case studies: private employment networks (e.g. Adecco) and hierarchical networks (e.g. Borsa Lavoro Lombardia, EURES). Moreover we consider the differences from the point of view of both the CEO and the CTO, i.e. the decision makers and the IT experts.

Compared to other approaches the SEEMP solution offers the CEO a way to enforce the subsidiarity principle, therefore valuing the contribution of each ES to the marketplace. In private networks the subsidiarity principle is not applicable, while in hierarchical networks most of the nodes are passive actors. Moreover the marketplace creates added value by increasing the number of interconnections, hence resulting in more faithful users (more JO/CV accessible using the user language) and in more transactions. Many Job Offers that can only be found today by inserting a CV into multiple ESs and gathering the results manually by hand, now become available through the interface of each ES., with no additional effort on behalf of the user.

For the CTO the SEEMP solution enables an easier maintenance of the integration with other ESs and minor integration costs. It has been proven that Web services used in a service oriented architecture eases the effort of integration and maintenance. Moreover semantics makes the process of mapping different terminology easier because tools (such as the WSMT) can analyze local and Reference Ontologies, by comparing sub-structures and by searching for synonyms, and can guide the IT Administrator in creating the mappings. Thank to this support, the mapping definition process requires less time or provides more precise mappings in the same amount of time.

Normally to achieve this benefit the CEO has to develop a "partnership", i.e., the ability to collaborate with other peers, ES or staffing industries. The partnerships are different in the two case studies. In private network everything is agreed in advance. In hierarchical network partnership are necessary, but no peer to peer decision taking is possible. Decisions are institutionally imposed top-down. Moreover SEEMP supports the CTO by providing a comprehensive set of tools and methodologies for service and semantic interoperability.

Concerning services the CTO has to expose his ES APIs as Local Web services and has to provide support for invoking EMPAM services. However, they don't have to understand interfaces and behaviour of other ES (as in hierarchical solutions) because the connector presents the market place as if the ES was invoking its own services. Concerning semantics the CTO has to model his data structures and content and has to defining mappings with the Reference Ontology, but as discussed above, this is made easier through the provision of good tool support.

What has to be built, and which SEEMP alone is unable to achieve, is a comprehensive Reference Ontology and abstract service machine that encompasses the entire employment domain. Developing and maintenance this reference part of SEEMP is not a ICT problem; it is a matter of reaching agreement at organizational level. As already discussed in section 4 the goal of SEEMP is reaching a "minimal shared commitment" in which ESs agree on high-level aspects, allowing for collaboration among them, while disagreeing on minor details that differentiate one ES from the others.

COST AND BENEFITS

As described in section 2.1, there is a minimum level of commitment required from a given ES if they wish to join the SEEMP network of Employment Services. This commitment is design to ensure that the joining of a new ES has no negative impact on existing ESs within the network and the commitment is kept to a minimal level to ensure that barriers to entry for new ES are as low as possible. The SEEMP architecture revolves around two main themes, namely Services and Semantics, and there exists a minimum commitment with respect to both of these themes. As can be seen in section 3, the SEEMP architecture is broken up into three levels and here we are concerned with the interaction between the EMP and a given ES through the Connector. The EMP assumes that each ES exposes a standardized set of services that can be invoked to achieve some specified functionality. The EMP also assumes that all data exchanged by these services are ontological data, formalised in the SEEMP Reference Ontology. Therefore we can define the minimum level of commitment for a given ES as the functionality that it needs to provide so that the assumptions, upon which EMP is based, are true.

At the ES level, each Employment Service will exist in its own non standardised world, with each ES having a different level of technological advancement in terms of how data is stored and exchanged with outside parties (if external sharing of data happens at all). The process of meeting the minimum level of commitment in terms of Service and Semantics should not involve any change to the internal processes of the Employment Service (unless they choose to make such a change). Thus the SEEMP Connector is designed as a mechanism to layer on top of the existing architecture of the ES and provide the services expected by the EMP that exchange data in terms of the SEEMP Reference Ontology. A SEEMP Connector is thus a piece of software that exposes the services expected by the EMP and communicates in terms of instances of the Reference Ontology.

There are two main tasks that must be undertaken by the engineer wishing to build a connector between the Web services exposed by the ES and the Web services expected by the EMP. Firstly, the engineer must identify the mapping between the ESs services and those expected by the EMP and link these together via some code. In other words when the EMP invokes the matchCV interface of the connector, this invocation must result in the invocation of one or more of the interfaces of the ES. Of course the reverse mapping must also be made such that invocations from the ES are translated into invocations to the EMP. Thus the connector must expose services upwards towards the EMP and downwards towards the ES. While the services exposed to the EMP are standardized, the choice of the services to expose to the ES is at the discretion of the connector architecture. However, it is recommended to mirror the services that the ES itself already exposes, such that the ES views the connector as if communicating with itself as is shown in Figure 8-a. Such an approach to exposing services to the ES ensures the minimal change to the functionality of the ES when it wishes to invoke the connector and ensures that ES engineers, who are already familiar with their own interfaces, can successfully work with the connector services with minimum effort. Secondly the XML data exchanged by the ES Web services must be lifted to the instances of the Reference Ontology in order to meet the minimum commitment of semantics. There are a number of approaches to performing this lifting:

Direct Mapping of XML to the Reference Ontology

Performing this step involves the use of technologies like XSLT or X_2O Mappings to define a set of syntactic mappings between the XML received from the ES to the instances of the Reference Ontology expected by the EMP and vice versa. Integrating this approach with Figure 9-a results in an architecture like that depicted in Figure 9-b. This approach is only feasible in cases where the XML data is semantically very close to the Reference Ontology. In cases where a big gap between the two formats exists, the mappings would quickly become too complicated for such a simple approach. If an ES decides to adopt this type of connector, the following figure reports on an estimation of the integration costs to be sustained.

The solution based on the Syntactic Connector is very simple at the beginning since it doesn't require any particular know-how or deep understanding of the interoperability problem. The development may become harder than expected but acceptable in those situations where the XML data is semantically very close to the Reference Ontology. However, with this solution there is a risk of increased cost during the maintenance phase and, in particular, it's infeasible when important changes in the ES are required (see Figure 9).

Two Step Syntactic XML Translation

To break the problem into a more manageable one, an additional XML format can be included in the translation from local XML format to the Reference Ontology. This second XML format would be very similar to the semantics of the Reference Ontology allowing for the complexity of the mappings to be broken into two steps. The translation from the Local XML format to the new XML format would resolve semantic issues between the two XML formats (although it should noted that this would be done syntactically via a technology like XSLT) and the second step of lifting the new XML format to the Reference Ontology would be relatively trivial, achieved using a syntactic transformation. Again with this approach a large difference between the two XML formats in terms of semantics would result in large amounts of mappings being created and resulting in the need to maintain these mappings as the XML formats and Reference Ontologies evolve. Integrating this approach with Figure 9-a results in an architecture like that depicted in Figure 9-c.

Figure 9. Architecture of the possible SEEMP connectors

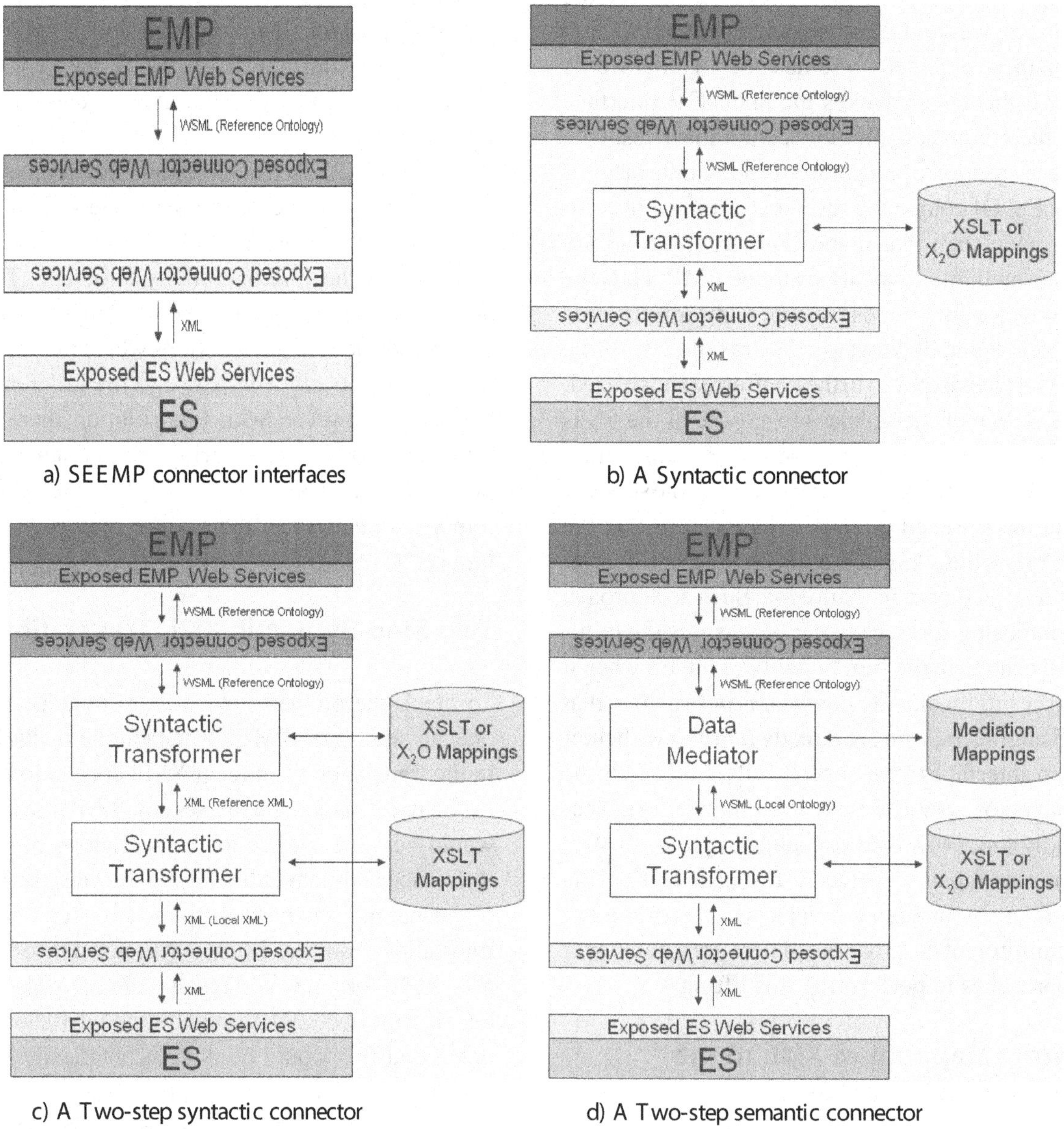

a) SEEMP connector interfaces

b) A Syntactic connector

c) A Two-step syntactic connector

d) A Two-step semantic connector

The initial costs and the development are higher than the previous solution (see Figure 10). This is because this solution requires the engineer to understand the problem related to the heterogeneity gap early in the process (both syntactic and semantics) and to develop a syntactic transformation between the local XML and the reference XML. However, thanks to a clear separation between these gaps, this solution promises to be more flexible in terms of maintenance and changes. Nevertheless, whenever the changes become critical, the integration costs may become more expensive.

Figure 10. Estimating integration costs for the possible SEEMP connectors

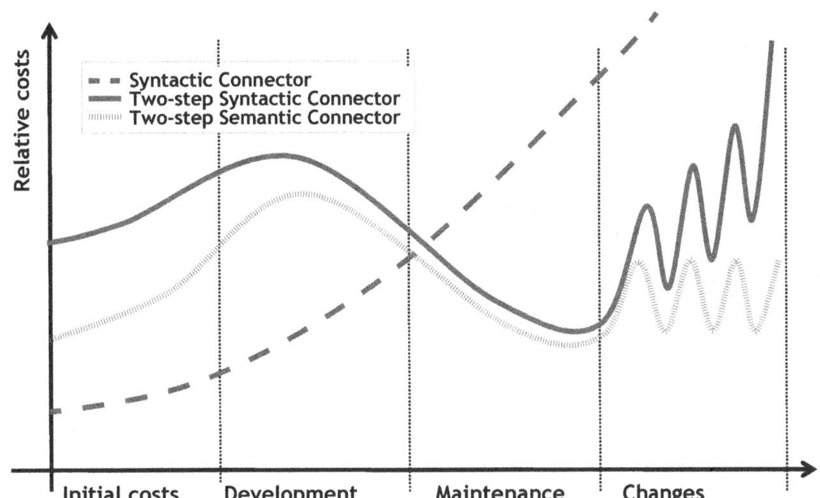

Two-Step Semantic XML Translation

One of the major problems with the previous designs, especially in cases where the Employment Services schemas are semantically very different from the Reference Ontology, is that they try to use syntactic technologies to resolve a problem with semantics and this results in the creation of many complex mappings that are difficult to create and harder to maintain. The inclusion of a semantic transformation step in the process helps alleviate this problem as semantic transformation involves fewer and less complicated mappings. In this method a Local Ontology is built that represents the local ESs view of the employment domain. The Local XML received from the ESs Web services is translated to the Local Ontology using XSLT or X_2O mappings. The remaining problem to be solved is the transformation of the instances of the Local Ontology to instances of the Reference Ontology, which can be solved by technologies such as the WSMX Data Mediation component with the accompanying design time environment in the Web Service Modeling Toolkit (WSMT) (Kerrigan et al. , 2007). This approach provides the cleanest and most maintainable solution for performing the translation of local XML to instances of the Reference Ontology, however it does have the overhead of maintaining the ES Local Ontology. Integrating this approach with Figure 8-a results in an architecture like that depicted in Figure 9-c. In the three above approaches to translation two specific technologies are mentioned, namely R_2O mappings for translating from XML to Ontologies and WSMX Data Mediation for performing the transformation of instances of one ontology into instances of another ontology.

This solution follows a progress similar to the previous architecture and it's slightly cheaper in the initial phases since the SEEMP technology is shipped with a specific tool for designing mappings. Moreover, thanks to the fact that the tool can leverage the semantic expressiveness for creating mappings, this solution promises to be more flexible in the face of changes without increasing the cost when the changes become critical. For example, in the case that the Local Ontology will evolve by detailing some parts and the Reference Ontology remains stable in those parts, the semantic mappings will not be affected thanks to the subsumption features.

RISK ASSESSMENT

A SWOT analysis (see Table 1) for SEEMP was performed in order assess strengths, weaknesses, opportunities and threats of the marketplace. In the rest of the chapter we gave a detailed explanation of the benefits of SEEMP. The most remarkable weaknesses of SEEMP are related to costs.

The initial costs for starting the SEEMP community would be considerable in relation to the actual benefits. However, these benefits are essential to the public sector and EC actors so SEEMP be targeted first to Public Sector stakeholders and to educational providers. We consider that the first experimentations of SEEMP are relevant for a pool of Public actors, with a few selected pool of private actors, e.g., some large companies for example operating in the ICT market.

Once a SEEMP community exists, it would be much easier to attract private services and provide better ROI reports. However, even for the public integration with the private sector is necessary and thus even at the initial stage SEEMP should incorporate in the business plans the private sector.

CONCLUSION

This chapter presented the SEEMP approach in supporting meaningful service based collaboration among public and private Employment Services. The following results have been shown:

- *Services and Semantics* are the key concepts for abstracting from the hundreds of heterogeneous systems already in place that are evolving separately. They provide a straightforward way to implement the subsidiarity principle of EIF.
- *The combination of an abstract service machine with a Reference Ontology* is a technically sound Multi-lateral approach for marketplace implementation. Each actor in the marketplace has to care only about integrating with the marketplace. The marketplace will offer services to support the interaction with other actors.
- *A mix of Software Engineering and a Semantic approach* is required to achieve flexibility. The two approaches nicely complement each other. By means of "conventional" software engineering design SEEMP built an abstract machine that can run on "conventional" technology and at the same time embeds semantics both in the form of ontologies and

Table 1. SEEMP SWOT analysis

Strengths	**Weaknesses**

• No competitors;
• Respond to a need from current market agencies (Public + Private) by increasing:
  ○ Geographical scope in an extending EU;
  ○ The quality through mapping technologies based on ontologies and Web services
	• Entrance costs;
	• Kick-off costs
	• Management of semantic protocols

Opportunities	**Threats**
• Enlargement of the EU; • Increasing of regions prerogatives regarding the employment policy (no more national only anymore); • Obligation for PES to respond to programs like : e-administration; modernisation of PES,… • Mobility framework at EU level • Shortage of skills with highly mobile profiles	• Laws regarding privacy

mediators, and in the form of semantic-aware components (i.e. ODE mapster, WSMX data mediation, Glue).

Currently the SEEMP consortium is running a pilot that shows the integration of EURES and Borsa Lavoro Lombardia. This integration has so far allowed for the testing of the functional aspects of SEEMP approach. The next step is integrating with the Le FOREM ES as a validation case. We expect, the Reference Ontology and the abstract machine to be so well designed that Le FOREM introduction would have no impact on the existing services.

FUTURE TRENDS

Future work includes extending the number of abstract services included in the EMPAM and the respective concepts in the reference and Local Ontologies. For instance, one essential service of SEEMP should be the possibility to have regularly (monthly, weekly, daily, . . .) a set of key indicators regarding labour market in all participant regions (job seekers, Job Offers, training, etc.), in a common and comparable language, both in terms of methods (definitions, calculation of indicators, etc.) and in terms of technical requirements.

ACKNOWLEDGMENT

This research has been partially supported by the SEEMP EU-funded project (IST-4-027347-STREP). We thank all the colleagues that work in SEEMP for the for the fruitful discussions that lead to this work.

REFERENCES

1720/1999/EC. *Decision of the European Parliament and of the Council* of 12 July 1999

2004/387/EC. (2004). *Decision of the European Parliament and of the Council on Interoperable Delivery of pan-European Services to Public Administrations.*

Aumann, R.J. (1976). Agreeing to Disagree. *The Annals of Statistics*, 4(6) 1236–1239.

Barrasa, J., Corcho, O., Gomez-Pérez, A. (2004). *R2O, an extensible and semantically based database-toontology mapping language.* In: Second International Workshop on Semantic Web and Databases.

Berners-Lee, T (1998). *The Fractal Nature of the Web*, working draft.

Cimpian, E., Mocan, A. (2005). *WSMX Process Mediation Based on Choreographies.* In: Business Process Management Workshops. 130–143

de Bruijn, J., Ehrig, M., Feier, C., Martìns-Recuerda, F., Scharffe, F., Weiten, M. (2006b). *Ontology Mediation, Merging, and Aligning* In: Semantic Web Technologies: Trends and Research in Ontology-based Systems. John Wiley & Sons, Ltd. 95–113

de Bruijn, J., Lausen, H., Polleres, A., Fensel, D. (2006). *The Web Service Modeling Language: An overview.* In: Proceedings of the 3rd European Semantic Web Conference (ESWC2006), Budva, Montenegro, Springer-Verlag

Della Valle, E., Cerizza, D. (2005). *The mediators centric approach to automatic Web service discovery of glue.* In: MEDIATE2005. Volume 168 of CEUR Workshop Proceedings., CEUR-WS.org 35–50

EC (2004). European Communities: *European interoperability framework for pan-european e-government services.* Technical report, Office for Official Publications of the European Communities.

Estublier, J., Vega, G. (2005). *Reuse and variability in large software applications.* In: ESEC/SIGSOFT FSE. 316–325

Fensel, D., Lausen, H., Polleres, A., de Bruijn, J., Stollberg, M., Roman, D., Domingue, J. (2006). *Enabling Semantic Web Services – The Web Service Modeling Ontology*. Springer

Gomez-Pérez, A., Fernandez-Lopez, M., Corcho, O. (2003). *Ontological Engineering*. Springer Verlag

Haller, A., Cimpian, E., Mocan, A., Oren, E., Bussler, C. (2005). *A Semantic Service-oriented architecture*. In: ICWS. 321–328

Kerrigan, M., Mocan, A., Tanler, M., and Fensel, D. (2007). *The Web Service Modeling Toolkit - An Integrated Development Environment for Semantic Web Services (System Description)*, Proceedings of the 4th European Semantic Web Conference (ESWC2007), June 2007, Innsbruck, Austria

Lewis, D. (1969). *Convention: A Philosophical Study*. Oxford: Blackburn

Mocan, A., Cimpian, E., Kerrigan, M. (2006). *Formal model for ontology mapping creation. In: International Semantic Web Conference*. 459–472

Rodriguez, J.B., Gomez-Pérez, A. (2006). *Upgrading relational legacy data to the Semantic Web*. In: WWW '06: Proceedings of the 15th international conference on World Wide Web, New York, NY, USA, ACM Press 1069–1070

Shadbolt, N., Berners-Lee, T., Hall, W. (2006). *The Semantic Web Revisited*. IEEE Intelligent Systems 21(3) 96–101

ADDITIONAL READING

E. Della Valle, M.G. Fugini, D. Cerizza, I. Celino, P. Guarrera, G. Zhao, G. Monteleone, A. Papageorgiou, J. Estublier, J. Ramìrez, B. Villazon, M. Kerrigan (2007) *SEEMP: A marketplace for the Labour Market* - In Proceedings of e-challenges 2007, 24 - 26 October 2007, The Hague, The Netherlands

E. Della Valle, D. Cerizza, and I. Celino, J. Estublier, G. Vega, M. Kerrigan, J. Ramirez, B. Villazon, P. Guarrera, G. Zhao and G. Monteleone (2007) *SEEMP: an Semantic Interoperability Infrastructure for e-government services in the employment sector* – In Proceedings of 4th European Semantic Web Conference, ESWC 2007, LNCS 4519, Innsbruck, Austria

E. Della Valle, D. Cerizza, and I. Celino, J. Estublier, G. Vega, M. Kerrigan, J. Ramirez, B. Villazon, P. Guarrera, G. Zhao and G. Monteleone (2007) *SEEMP: Meaningful Service-based Collaboration Among Labour Market Actors* – In Proceedings of 10th International Conference on Business Information Systems, BIS 2007, LNCS 4439, Poznan, Poland

IDABC and Capgemini (2004). *Architecture for delivering pan-European e-Government services*

ENDNOTES

1. See respectively http://www.borsalavorolombardia.net/, http://www.leforem.be/ and http://europa.eu.int/eures/
2. In the rest of the chapter we use ES when we refer both to public and private actors, whereas we us PES and PRES referring respectively to public and private actors.

Chapter VII
Towards Effectiveness and Transparency in E-Business Transactions:
An Ontology for Customer Complaint Management

Mustafa Jarrar
HPCLab, University of Cyprus, Cyprus & Vrije Universiteit Brussel, Belgium

ABSTRACT

This chapter presents an ontology for customer complaint management, which has been developed in the CCFORM project. CCFORM is an EU funded project (IST-2001-38248) with the aim of studying the foundation of a central European customer complaint portal. The idea is that any consumer can register a complaint against any party about any problem, at one portal. This portal should: support 11 languages, be sensitive to cross-border business regulations, dynamic, and can be extended by companies. To manage this dynamicity and to control companies' extensions, a customer complaint ontology (CContology) has to be built to underpin the CC portal. In other words, the complaint forms are generated based on the ontology. The CContology comprises classifications of complaint problems, complaint resolutions, complaining parties, complaint-recipients, ''best-practices'', rules of complaint, etc. The main uses of this ontology are (1) to enable consistent implementation (and interoperation) of all software complaint management mechanisms based on a shared background vocabulary, which can be used by many stakeholders. (2) to play the role of a domain ontology that encompasses the core complaining elements and that can be extended by either individual or groups of firms; and (3) to generate CC-forms based on the ontological commitments and to enforce the validity (and/or integrity) of their population. At the end of this chapter, we outline our experience in applying the methodological principles (Double-Articulation and Modularization) and the tool (DogmaModeler) that we used in developing the CContology.

INTRODUCTION AND MOTIVATION

Current Situation

The use of the Internet for cross-border business is growing rapidly. However, in many cases, the benefits of electronic commerce are not exploited fully by customers because of the frequent lack of trust and confidence in online cross-border purchases. To achieve fair trading and transparency in commercial communications and transactions, effective cross-border complaint platforms need to be established and involved in e-business activities (Claes, 1987) (Cho et al, 2002) (ABA, 2002).

The CCFORM project aims to study and *reach a consensus* about the foundation of online customer complaint mechanisms by developing a general but extensible form (called CC-form[1]) which has widespread industry and customer support. This CC-form must facilitate cross-language communication to support cross-border e-commerce and should be easy to implement in software tools. The CC-form will raise the basic agreement about complaint handling, and should be extended in vertical markets (e.g. hotels, banks, factories, or even governments) to provide sector-wide solutions to allow service providers to gain competitive advantages (see Figure 1).

Problem Statement

There are several challenges involved in establishing and agreeing on such a CC-form: (1) Legal bases: the sensitivity of cross-border business regulations and privacy issues. (2) The diversity of language and culture: controlling and agreeing on the semantics of the complaint terminology so that the intended meaning of the term gets across, even in the different languages. (3) Consumer sensitivity and business perspectives. (4) Extensibility: the flexibility of extending the CC-form (perhaps dynamically) according to market needs and standards. This would mean for example, extending the kinds of problems that a complainant can complain about, extending the kinds of complaint resolutions, managing who may extend what, etc.

Figure 1. Depiction of the CCform design

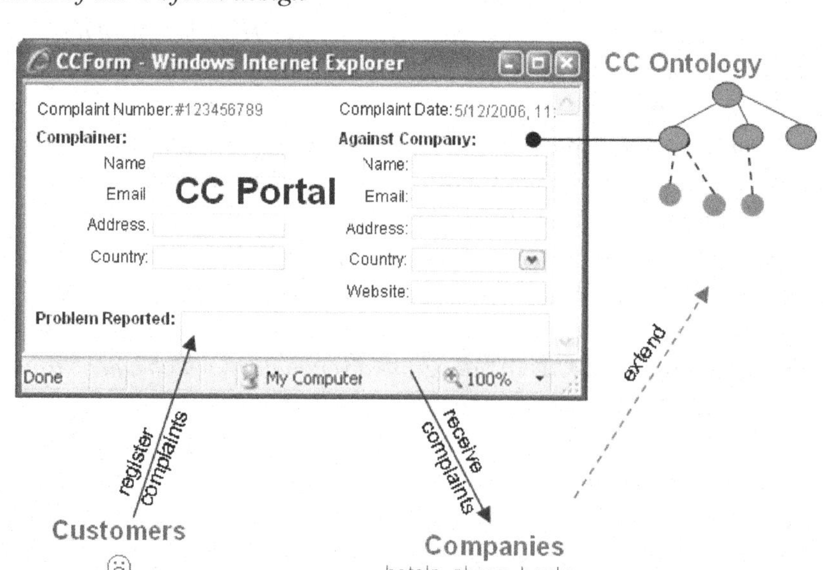

Proposed Solution

In order to tackle such challenges and to perfect the reference model for a CC-form, the research has been divided into six interest groups, each consisting of 10-15 highly specialized members. Each group has been intensively discussing different issues: SIG1- Legal Affairs, SIG2- Consumer Affairs, SIG4 - Standards for SMEs, SIG5 -Alternative Dispute Resolution Systems, SIG6 - Ontology and Extensibility, SIG7 - Vertical markets.

The work presented in this chapter outlines our main achievements in the "Ontology and extensibility" group, including multilingual and cultural issues (Jarrar et al, 2003). The mission of this group, SIG6, is to undertake extensibility and multilingual demands. To approach this, a customer complaint ontology (CContology) has been developed and lexicalized in 11 European languages. *This CContology is developed and reviewed by the six interest groups, and is seen as a conceptual framework that is necessary to develop such a CC-form.*

In the following section, we present the CContology itself and the methodology we applied to engineer it. In section 3, we provide some lessons learnt and a discussion about our applied engineering solutions. Section 4 presents a multilingual lexicalization methodology. To end, section 6 presents our conclusions and directions for future work.

CUSTOMER COMPLAINT ONTOLOGY

In this section we introduce the *customer complaint ontology* (CContology) that is intended to capture the main concepts in the "customer complaint management" domain. Its core covers a semantic description of complaints that could be issued by any legal person against any other legal person (NGO, company, natural person, etc.). The CContology comprises classifications of complaint problems, complaint resolutions, complainant, complaint-recipient, "best-practices", rules of complaint, etc.

The intended impact of this research is the future initiation of a European online complaint platform that will provide a trusted portal between consumers and business entities. In this respect, the ontology is intended to become the basis for a future *core ontology* in the domain of customer complaint management (for both humans and machines). Applying the CContology in such an European online complaint platform will facilitate further refinements of the CContology.

The main uses of such an ontology are (1) to enable consistent implementation (and interoperation) of all software complaint management mechanisms based on a shared background vocabulary, which can be used by many stakeholders. (2) to play the role of a *domain ontology* that encompasses the core complaining elements and that *can be extended by either individuals or groups of firms*; and (3) to generate CC-forms based on the *ontological commitments* and to enforce the validity (and/or integrity) of their population.

Although this CContology has been developed and reviewed by six specialized groups, in its current state, it can only be considered a proposal. The CCFORM community is representative of a sizable cross-section of the domain but is not a standardization body. Nor is it in the position to insist on a *de facto* enforcement of this ontology as a generally agreed semantic specification. However, the approach presented in this chapter is designed to initiate and drive such a process.

The Applied Engineering Methodology

The CContology is developed according to the two methodological principles that we developed in (Jarrar, 2005): (1) ontology double articulation, and (2) ontology modularization. See Figure 2.

Figure 2. Depiction of applied methodology (Jarrar, 2005) (Jarrar et al, 2003c)

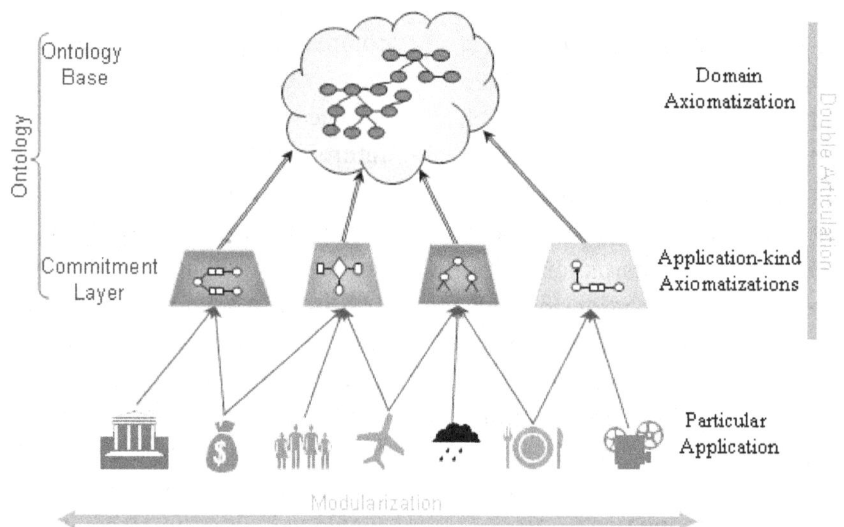

The ontology double articulation principle suggests, in nutshell, that: *an ontology is doubly articulated into: domain axiomatization and application axiomatizations. While a domain axiomatization is mainly concerned with characterizing the "intended models" of a vocabulary at the domain level (typically shared and public), an application axiomatization (typically local) is mainly concerned with the usability of this vocabulary according to certain application/usability perspectives. An application axiomatization is intended to specify the legal models (a subset of the intended models) of the application(s)' interest.*

To simplify the double articulation principle, in other words, one can imagine WordNet as a domain axiomatization, and an application axiomatization built in OWL (or RDF, ORM, UML, etc). The double articulation principle then suggests that all vocabulary in the OWL axiomatization should be linked with word-senses (i.e. concepts) in WordNet. In this way, we gain more consensus about application axiomatizations as it is rooted at the domain level; we improve the usability of application axiomatizations as they are specific, and the reusability of domain axiomatizations as the are generic; application axiomatizations that are built in the same way (i.e. commit to the same domain axiomatization) will be easier to integrate, and so forth. See (Jarrar, 2005), (Jarrar et al, 2008b), and (Jarrar, 2006) for more details.

The modularization principle suggests that application axiomatizations be built in a modular manner. Axiomatizations should be developed as a set of small modules and later composed to form, and be used as, one modular axiomatization. A composition operator is defined for a full automatic composition of modules (see Jarrar, 2005 and Jarrar, 2005b). It combines all axioms introduced in the composed modules. As shall be discussed later, the idea of the modularization principle is that modules are easier build, maintain, use, and reuse.

The CContology is built according to the above methodological principles. It consists of a domain axiomatization (the lexons, context, and the term glossary) and seven application axiomatization modules, (Complaint Problems, Complaint Resolutions, Complaint, Complainant, Complaint-Recipient, Address, and Contract). See Figure 3. Applications (such as the CCform) use the composition of these 7 modules. Notice that

Figure 3. Depiction of CContology components

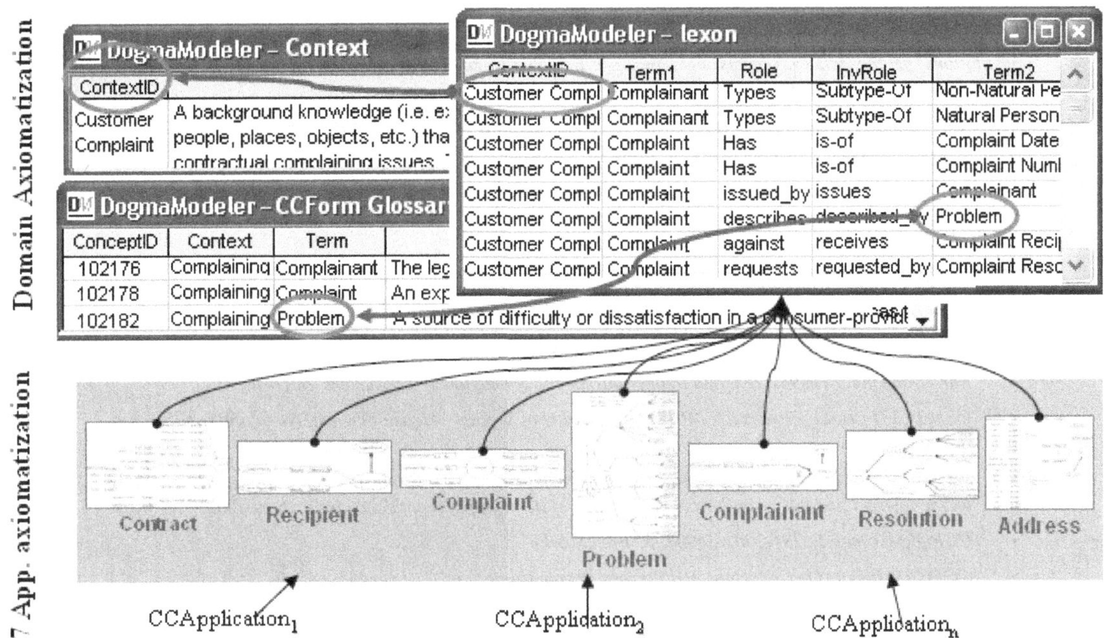

the CCform (as an application) is committing to the domain ontology through this composition (i.e. the 7 application axiomatizations). The advantages of this methodology will be discussed in later sections. In the following we present each component of the CContology. The full content of the CContology can be accessed from the CContology-webpage[2]. In the following we present some samples of this ontology.

The Domain Axiomatization

This part of the CContology consists of three representation units: 1-the "customer complaint" context, 2-domain vocabularies and their glosses, and 3- the set of lexons. A lexon is a binary relationship between context-specific linguistic terms, or in other words, a lexical rendering of a binary conceptual relation.

The "Customer Complaint" Context

The notion of context is the first building block in our methodology for developing a domain axiomatization. It plays a *scoping role*, through which the interpretation of the intended meaning of the ontology terminology is bounded. We say a term *within* a context refers to a concept, or in other words, *that context is an abstract identifier that refers to implicit (or maybe tacit) assumptions, in which the interpretation of a term is bounded to a concept.* In practice, we define context by referring to a source (e.g. a set of documents, laws and regulations, informal description of "best practices", etc.), which, by *human understanding*, is assumed to "contain" those assumptions.

In the CContology, the "Content ID" is called the "*Customer Complaint*" context, or the *CCcontext in short*. The "Context Description" is defined in Table 1.

We have learned during the definition process that it is not an easy task to create such a context, and a context cannot be defined rigidly in the early phases of the development of such an ontology. As none of our team was an ontology expert, we provided a draft definition and investigated by providing many different examples of applica-

Table 1. The definition of the "Customer Complaint" context

Background knowledge (i.e. explicit, implicit, or tacit assumptions) about all (activities, communications, institutions, people, places, objects, etc.) that are involved in consumer-provider relationships, regarding contractual and non-contractual complaining issues.

These assumptions can be understood (i.e. can be found explicitly or intuitively) in the following sources:

- *European Distance Selling Directive (97/7/EC), on the promotion of consumers in respect of distance contracts.*
- *European e-Commerce Directive (2000/31/EC) on certain legal aspects of information society services, in particular, electronic commerce, in the Internal Market.*
- *European Data Protection Directives (95/46/EC and 97/66/EC) on the protection of individuals with regards to the processing of personal data and on the free movement of such data.*
- *European Directive (99/44/EC) on aspects of the sale of consumer goods and associated guarantees.*
- *European Directive (98/27EC) on Injunctions for the Protection of Consumers' Interests.*
- *CEN/TC331 Postal Services EN 14012:2002 Quality of Service – Measurement of complaints and redress procedures.*
- *"Best practice" guidelines, The Nordic Consumer Ombudsmen's position paper on trading and marketing on the Internet and other similar communication systems(http://econfidence.jrc.it, June 2002)*
- *CCFORM Annex 1, (IST-2001-34908, 5th framework).*
- *CCFORM Report On Copyright And Privacy Recommendations (Deliverable D.5.3).*
- *CCFORM user guide and business complaints (Deliverable D.5.1.1).*
- *CCFORM Company user guide (Deliverable D.5.1.2).*
- *CCFORM Web publication of CCform User Guides in 11 languages (Deliverable D6.11).*
- *Code of Conduct (CCFORM deliverable).*

Remark: For the sake of brevity, many resources (regulations at the European and national levels, best practices, existing online complaining (plat)forms, etc.) are not mentioned here. However, references to these resources can be found inside the resources listed above.

tion scenarios that this context should cover. This investigation was done to prevent the CContology from being dependent on the CC-form application scenario which the team had in mind during the early phases. For example, we questioned whether the context should cover applications such as customer-relationship-management, market analyses, sales force automation and so forth; whether it should cover all consumer regulations in any country or only in Europe; whether it should cover all commercial activity, in any place and at any time; which documents, laws and regulations should be our main references, etc. Such questions led not only to the CCcontext definition (which was achieved after several iterations), but also propelled the team to discuss deeply and even redefine the scope of the research goals.

Vocabularies and their Glosses

Within the "Customer Complaint" context, we define 220 terms. A sample of these terms and their glosses (Called the CCglossary) is provided in Table 2. This CCglossary was developed (and reviewed) over several iterations. The first iteration was accomplished by a few (selected) experts before the lexon modeling process was started (lexons are the third component of the CContology). Further iterations have been carried out in parallel with the lexon modeling process. The final draft was reviewed and approved by several groups. It is probably worth noting that intensive discussions were carried out (by legal experts, market experts, application-oriented experts) for almost every gloss. We have found that the

Table 2. A sample of the "Customer Complaint" glossary

The CCglossary (*Sample*)	
Term	Gloss
Address	A construct describing the means by which contact may be taken with, or messages or physical objects may be delivered to; an address may contain indicators for a physical or virtual (i.e. accessed electronically) location or both.
Complainant	The legal person who issues a complaint.
Complaint	An expression of grievance or resentment issued by a complainant against a compliant-recipient, describing a problem(s) that needs to be resolved.
Complaint Recipient	A legal person to whom a complaint is addressed.
Complaint Resolution	A determination for settling or solving a problem in a consumer-provider relationship.
Contract	A binding agreement between two or more legal persons that is enforceable by law; an invoice can be a contract.
Contract Problem	Problem linked to a contract in a customer-provider relationship, it may occur before or after the contract effective date.
Contract Termination Problem	A problem concerned with the proper termination or completion of the contract.
Data Collection Problem	A privacy problem regarding all activities and purposes of private data collection
Delivery and Installation Problem	A purchase phase problem related to dissatisfaction regarding delivery or Installation of goods or services.
Delivery problem	A purchase phase problem related to dissatisfaction regarding the delivery of goods or services.
Evidence	(WordNet) all the means by which any alleged matter of fact whose truth is investigated at judicial trial is established or disproved
Guarantee Problem	An after sales service problem related to a legal or contractual guarantee; particularly a problem related to a responsibility on the recipient consequent to the guarantees directive.
Guarantee refused	Refusal to apply a legal or contractual guarantee.
Legal Person	An entity with legal recognition in accordance with law. It has the legal capacity to represent its own interests in its own name, before a court of law, to obtain rights or obligations for itself, to impose binding obligations, or to grant privileges to others, for example as a plaintiff or as a defendant. A legal person exists wherever the law recognizes (as a matter of policy). This includes the personality of any entity, regardless of whether it is naturally considered to be a person. Recognized associations, relief agencies, committees, and companies are examples of legal persons
Mailing Address	The address where a person or organization can be communicated with for providing physical objects. It is broadly equivalent to a postal address as described in standards CEN 14132 or UPU S42, but has different functional definition
Privacy Problem	A problem related to the collection, storage, handling, use or distribution of private data, violating the data protection directives.
Problem	A source of difficulty or dissatisfaction in a consumer-provider relationship.
Product delivery delayed	A delivery problem related to delay in product delivery.
Registration	A certification, issued by an administrative authority or an accredited registration agency, declaring the official enrolment of an entity. Typically, it includes the official name, mailing address, registration number, VAT number, legal bases, etc.
	....

gloss modeling process is a great mechanism for brainstorming, domain analyses, domain understanding and for reaching (and documenting) consensus. Furthermore, it allowed non-ontology experts to participate actively in the ontology modeling process. Some partners have remarked that the CCglossary is the most useful and reusable component in the CContology.

As shall be discussed later, this CCglossary, which has been developed in English, has played the role of *the key* reference for lexicalizing the CContology into 11 other European languages. The translators have acknowledged that it guided their understanding of the intended meanings of the terms and allowed them to achieve better translation quality. The following are the guidelines (Jarrar, 2006) that we used to deciding what should and should not be provided in a gloss:

1. It should start with the *principal/super type* of the concept being defined. For example, "Search engine: A computer program that ...", "Invoice: A business document that..."University: An institution of ...".
2. It should be written in the form of propositions, offering the reader inferential knowledge that helps him to construct the image of the concept. For example, instead of defining 'Search engine' as *"A computer program for searching the internet"*, or *"One of the most useful aspects of the World Wide Web. Some of the major ones are Google, Galaxy... ."*. One can also say *"A computer program that enables users to search and retrieve documents or data from a database or from a computer network..."*.
3. More importantly, it should focus on distinguishing characteristics and intrinsic properties that differentiate the concept from other concepts. For example, compare the following two glosses of a 'Laptop computer': (1) *"A computer that is designed to do pretty much anything a desktop computer can do. It runs for a short time (usually two to five hours) on batteries"*; and (2) *"A portable computer small enough to use in your lap..."*. Notice that according to the first gloss, a 'server computer' running on batteries can be seen as a laptop computer; also, a 'Portable computer' that is not running on batteries is not a 'Laptop computer'.
4. The use of supportive examples is strongly encouraged: (1) to clarify true cases that are commonly known to be false, or false cases that are known to be true; and (2) to strengthen and illustrate distinguishing characteristics (by using examples and counter-examples). The examples can be types and/or instances of the concept being defined. For example: "Legal Person: *An entity with legal recognition in accordance with law. It has the legal capacity to represent its own interests in its own name, before a court of law, to obtain rights or obligations for itself, to impose binding obligations, or to grant privileges to others, for example as a plaintiff or as a defendant. A legal person exists wherever the law recognizes, as a matter of policy, the personality of any entity, regardless of whether it is naturally considered to be a person. Recognized associations, relief agencies, committees and companies are examples of legal persons*".
5. It should be consistent with the formal axioms in the ontology. As glosses co-exist in parallel to the formal axioms, both should not contradict each other; any change on side should be reflected on the other.
6. It should be sufficient, clear, and easy to understand.

Lexons

Stemming from the 220 terms within the "Customer Complaint" context, we have developed 300 lexons. A sample of these lexons can be found in Table 3. As we mentioned earlier, a lexon is a lexical rendering of a binary conceptual relation.

A lexon (Jarrar, 2005) (Jarrar, 2002) (Meersman, 1999) is described as a tuple of the form: <*ContextID*: $Term_1$, *Role*, *InvRole*, $Term_2$>. Where $Term_1$ and $Term_2$ are linguistic terms from a language *L*; *Role* and *InvRole* are lexicalizations of the pair roles of a binary conceptual relationship R; *InvRole* is the inverse of the *Role*. For example, the pair roles of a *subsumption* relationship could be: "Is a type of" and "Has type"; the pair roles of a *parthood* relationship could be: "is a part of" and "has part", and so forth. See Table 3 for examples.

Table 3 shows a sample of lexons for the CCo-ntology[3]. Notice that "Customer Complaint" is defined in section 2.2.1, and that each term used in these lexons has a gloss as described in section 2.2.2. The first draft of the CC lexons has been developed based on presentations and discussions between the members of SIG 6 (Ontology and Extensibility). Most of these lexons represent taxonomies of complaint problems, complaint resolutions, complainant, complaint recipient, and addresses. One of the most important inputs, for the first draft, was the complaint categorization survey (Vassileva, 2003) that was performed by two of the group members. Further, refinements and investigations were performed during meetings and workshops that we organized in cooperation with other SIGs.

The CC Application Axiomatizations

Given the previously presented "customer complaint" domain axiomatization, seven application axiomatization modules have been developed. *The intended meaning of the terminology used in these modules (i.e. application axiomatizations) is restricted to the terminology defined at the domain axiomatization level.* Figure 4 depicts this relationship between a concept used at the

Table 3. A sample of the "Customer Complaint" lexons

Context	Term1	Role	InvRole	Term2
Customer Complaint	Problem	Types	Subtype-Of	Contract Problem
Customer Complaint	Problem	Types	Subtype-Of	Non-Contract Problem
Customer Complaint	Problem	Types	Subtype-Of	Privacy Problem
Customer Complaint	Complaint	against	receives	Complaint Recipient
Customer Complaint	Complaint	describes	described_by	Problem
Customer Complaint	Complaint	issued_by	issues	Complainant
Customer Complaint	Complaint	requests	requested_by	Complaint Resolution
Customer Complaint	Contact Details	comprised_of	comprises	Address
Customer Complaint	Contact Details	Has	is-of	Name
Customer Complaint	Contract Problem	Types	Subtype-Of	Post-purchase Phase Problem
Customer Complaint	Contract Problem	Types	Subtype-Of	Pre-purchase Phase Problem
Customer Complaint	Contract Problem	Types	Subtype-Of	Purchase Phase Problem
Customer Complaint	Complaint Resolution	Types	Subtype-Of	Economic Resolution
Customer Complaint	Complaint Resolution	Types	Subtype-Of	Information Correction
Customer Complaint	Complaint Resolution	Types	Subtype-Of	Symbolic Resolution
Customer Complaint	Conduct	Types	Subtype-Of	Lewd or Immoral conduct
Customer Complaint	Conduct	Types	Subtype-Of	Untruthlness
	...			

Figure 4. An example of three different applications specializing a domain concept

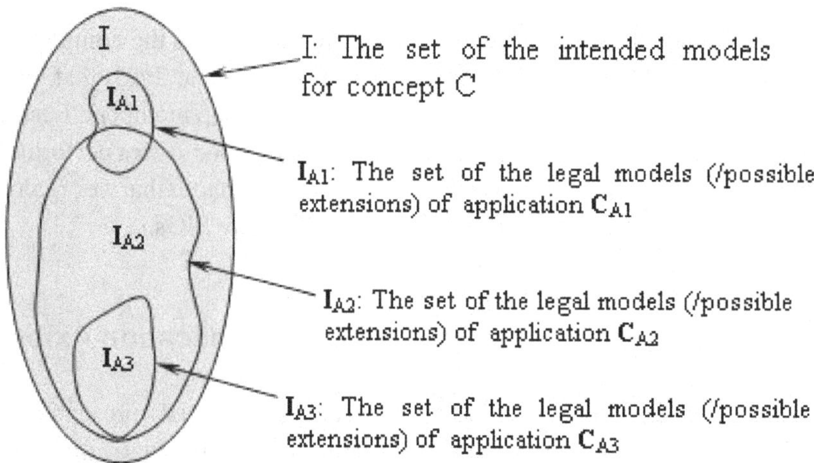

application level and its general meaning at the domain level (this way of expressing knowledge is called *double-articulation*; Jarrar, 2005).

Given a concept **C** as *a set of rules (e.g. described by lexons and glosses) in our mind about a certain thing in reality*, the set **I** of "all possible" instances that comply with these rules are called the *intended models* of the concept **C**. According to the ontology double articulation principle, such concepts are captured at the domain axiomatization level. An application A_i that is interested in a subset $\mathbf{I}_{Ai}$ of the set **I** (according to its usability perspectives), is supposed to provide some rules to specialize **I**. In other words, every instance in $\mathbf{I}_{Ai}$ must also be an instance in **I**. We call the subset $\mathbf{I}_{Ai}$: the *legal models* (or extensions) of the application's concept $\mathbf{C}_{Ai}$. Such application rules are captured at the application axiomatization level[4].

The application axiomatization modules are intended to play the role of conceptual data schema(s) for CC-forms development. Any CC-form, including its population, should be based on (i.e. commit to) the CContology through those modules. A CC-from can be constructed manually or generated automatically; nevertheless, the semantics of all elements in this CC-from (i.e. the data fields) is defined in the CContology. See (section 6.7.1 in Jarrar, 2005) on how to generate a Web form automatically out of a given ORM schema

As stated earlier in this chapter, the seven application axiomatization modules are: Complaint problems, Complaint resolutions, Contract, Complaint, Complainant, Complaint Recipient, and Address. Depending on an application's usability requirements, these modules can be used individually or composed to form a modular axiomatization(s). In the following, we provide a brief description of each module.

These application axiomatization modules below are represented using the ORM (Object Role Modeling) notation. We have found this notation is not only expressive, but also from a methodological viewpoint, ORM can be verbalized into natural language sentences (Jarrar et al, 2006b). This verbalization capabilities was a great help for our community (who are not IT savvy) to still be able to build and review the CContology without needing to know its underpinning logic or reasoning (Jarrar et al, 2006) (Jarrar et al, 2008). ORM has well-defined semantics (Halpin, 1989) (Halpin, 2001) in first order logic, and recently we have mapped ORM into the SHOIN/OWL (Jarrar, 2007b) (Jarrar et al, 2007) and the DLR (Jarrar, 2007) description logics.

Figure 5. The "Complaint Problems" application axiomatization module, in ORM[5]

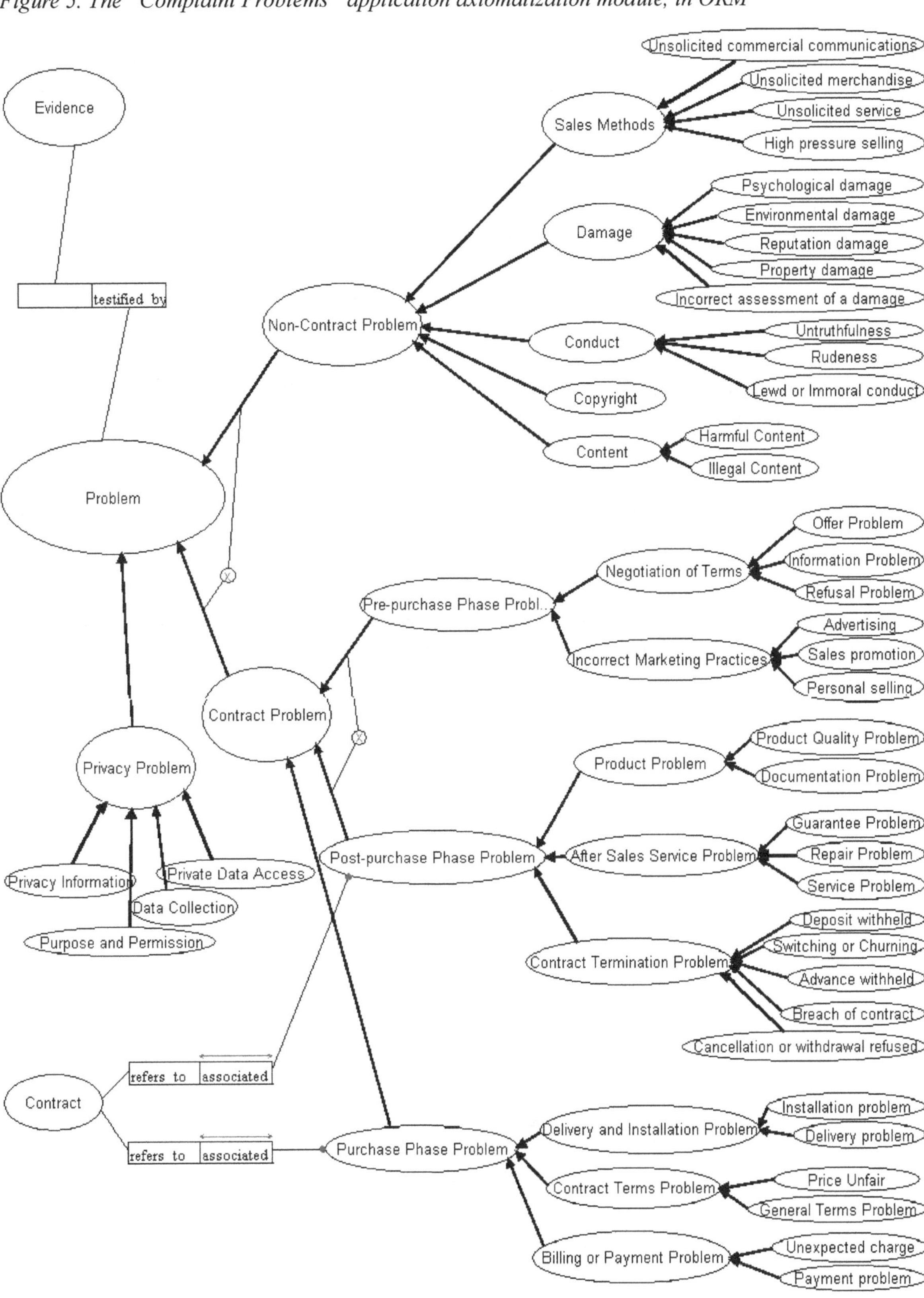

Complaint Problems

Figure 5 shows the "Complaint Problems" axiomatization module. It is a taxonomy of complaint problems.

We distinguish between a 'Complaint' and a 'Problem'. A 'Complaint' *describes* one or more 'Problems'. While the concept 'Problem' is defined as "A source of difficulty or dissatisfaction", the concept 'Complaint' is defined as "An expression of grievance or resentment issued by a complainant against a compliant-recipient, describing a problem(s) that needs to be resolved".

Within the "customer complaint" domain, a 'Problem' can be a 'Privacy Problem', or either a 'Contract Problem' or a 'Non-contract Problem'. A 'Contract Problem' can be a 'Purchase Phase Problem', or either a 'Pre-purchase Phase Problem' or a 'Post-purchase Phase Problem'. It is mandatory for both 'Purchase Phase Problems' and 'Post-purchase Phase Problems' to be associated with a 'Contract'[6]. For any type of problem, 'Evidence' might be provided for investigation purposes.

Remark: In this "Complaint Problems" module, only four classification levels are presented, all of which are the popular categories in most CC-forms. Further classifications of complaint problems can be found at the ontology base level.

Complaint Resolutions

Figure 6 illustrates the "Complaint Resolution" module, which presents a taxonomy of 'Complaint Resolutions'. A 'Complaint Resolution' is defined in the CCglossary as "A determination for settling or solving a complaint problem(s)". It can be requested by a complainant or offered by a complaint-recipient. A 'Complaint Resolution' can be an 'Economic Resolution', a 'Symbolic Resolution', or an 'Information Correction'.

Contract

A 'Contract' is defined in the CCglossary as "a binding agreement, between two or more legal persons, that is enforceable by law". Under this definition, an invoice can also be a contract.

Figure 6. The "Complaint Resolutions" application axiomatization module, in ORM

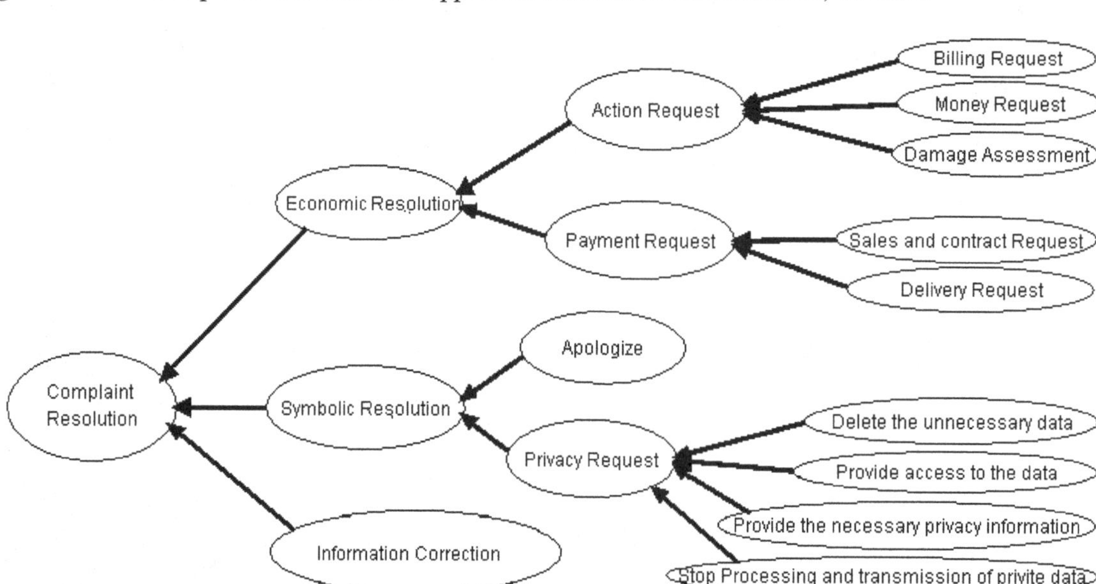

Figure 7 illustrates the "Contract" module, which specifies the information that should be provided for a contract associated with a 'Purchase Phase Problem' or 'Post-purchase Phase Problem'. Notice that, for a CC-form, we speak of a 'Contract' from the moment there is a 'Contract Order Date'.

Complaint

A 'Complaint' is defined in the CCglossary as "An expression of grievance or resentment issued by a complainant against a compliant-recipient, describing a problem(s) that needs to be resolved".

Figure 8 illustrates the "Complaint" axiomatization module, which specifies the main concepts that can be associated with the concept 'Complaint'. A 'Complaint' must be issued by a 'Complainant' against a 'Complaint-Recipient', on a certain 'Date'. It must describe at least one 'Problem', and may request one or more 'Complaint Resolutions'. A 'Complaint' *might*

Figure 7. The "Contract" axiomatization module, in ORM

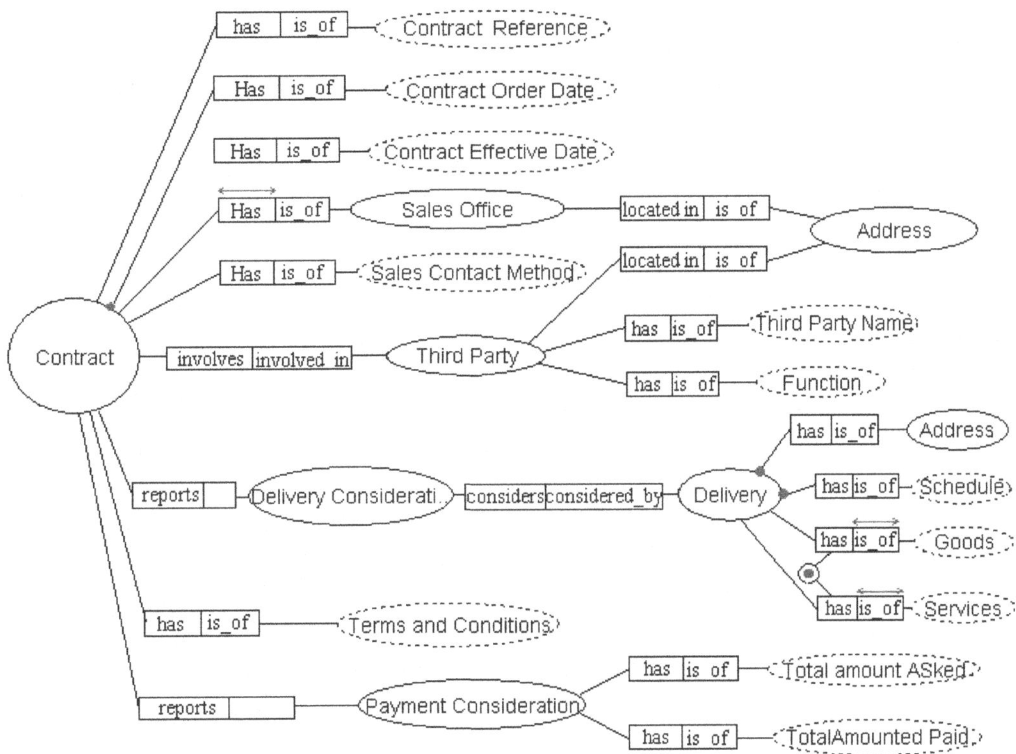

Figure 8. The "Complaint" application axiomatization module, in ORM

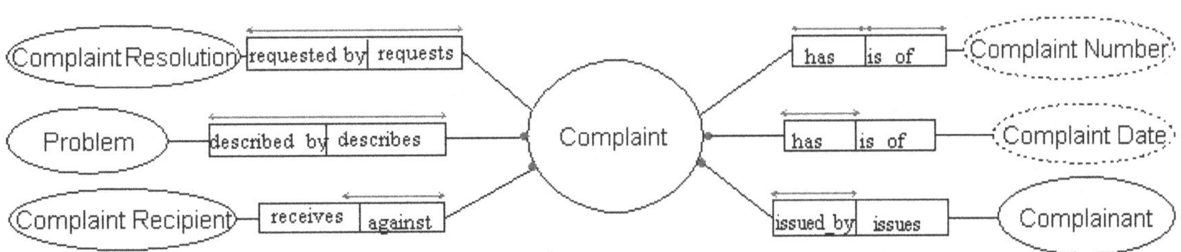

be identified by a 'Complaint Number', which is typically used as a unique reference in a court or a complaint system.

Complainant

Figure 9 illustrates the 'Complainant' axiomatization module. A 'Complainant' is defined in the CCglossary as "A legal person who issues a complaint". In the customer complaint context, and as commonly understood in most consumer regulations, a complainant must either be a 'Natural Person Complainant' or a 'Non-Natural Person Complainant', each implying a different legal basis for the handling of the complaint.

The distinction between natural and non-natural person complainants is not only based on the variation of their complaint handling regulations, but also on the legal preference (in any CC-from) for not obligating the inquiry of private information about the 'Natural Person Complainant', such as his/her 'Name', 'Birth Date', 'Mailing Address', 'Religion' etc. Each 'Natural Person Complainant' must have 'Contact Details'. The mandatory contact details (as agreed with the "customer complaint" community, but which cannot be generalized for all communities) are an 'eMail' and his/here 'Country' of residence. A 'Non-Natural Person Complainant' must be denoted by a certain 'Registration' that identifies him in a CC-form. See the definition of 'Registration' in the CCglossary.

Complaint recipient

Figure 10 illustrates the "Complaint Recipient" axiomatization module. A 'Complaint Recipient' is any legal Person to whom a complaint is addressed. Typically, when a 'Complaint' is issued against a 'Complaint Recipient', the 'Contact

Figure 9. The "Complainant" application axiomatization module, in ORM

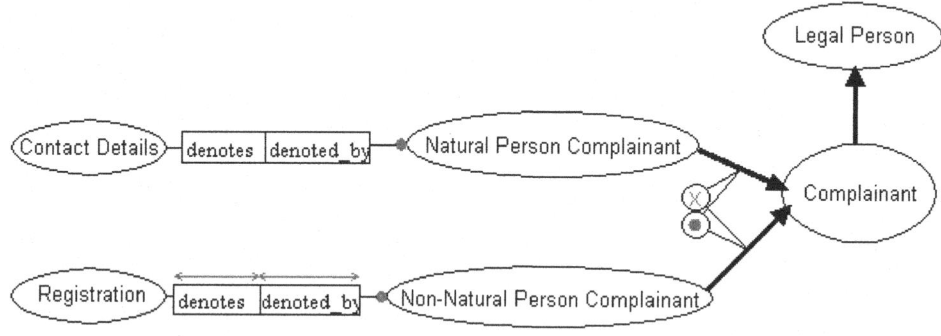

Figure 10. The "Recipient" application axiomatization module, in ORM

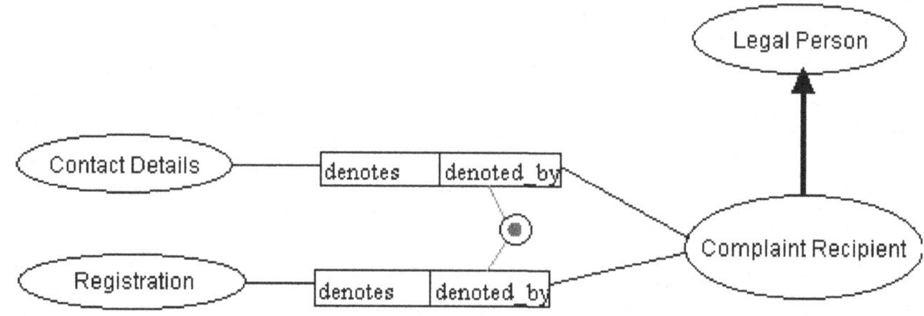

Details' *or* the 'Registration' of this 'Complaint Recipient' should be denoted. Usually, all online customer complaint platforms provide a searchable database of many "Complaint Recipients", which enables complainants to easily find the official names and addresses of 'complaint recipients'.

Address

Figure 11 illustrates the "Address" axiomatization module. The concept 'Contact Details', which is a channel of communication, is attributed by both 'Name' and 'Address'. An 'Address' must be either an 'Electronic Address' or a 'Mailing Address'. An 'electronic Address' can be either a 'Web Site', 'Telephone', 'eMail', or 'Fax'. A 'Mailing Address' can have all the traditional information of postal addresses in the European Union.

Remark: Due to epistemological differences, the notion of 'Address' can be specified in many different ways, especially since each country has its own postal information structure. Hence, this "Address" axiomatization module is considered an "unsteady" module, and should be replaced by a more sophisticated module – one that does, for example, consider the compatibility with online national, European, or international address servers[8].

DISCUSSION AND LESSONS LEARNED

This section provides a further discussion on the application of our methodological principles for the development and engineering of the CContology.

Figure 11. The "Address" application axiomatization module, in ORM

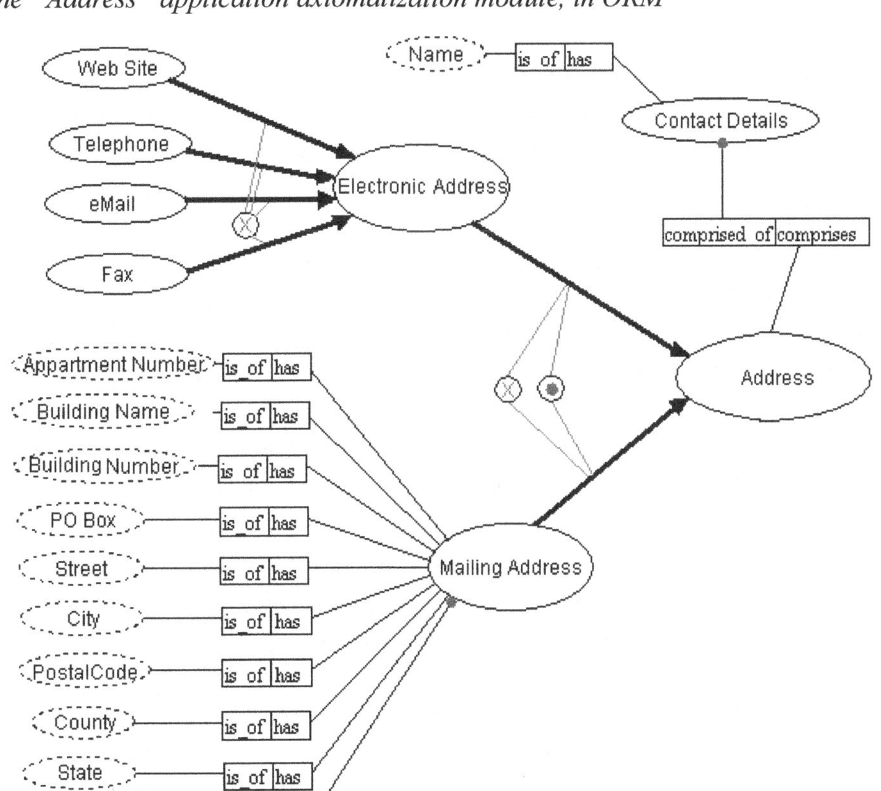

Extensibility is one of the main requirements (and one of the most challenging issues) for the development of any CC-form. As we have mentioned earlier, our main goal is to reach consensus about the foundation of a trusted customer complaint portal. Once such a portal is implemented as a centralized CC-form between customers and companies, companies may wish to extend "their" CC-form to inquire about more specific complaint details, e.g. delivery conditions, certain product attributes, or they might wish to offer the customer a particular resolution, etc[9]. Such extensions may be a necessity not only for individual companies but also in so called vertical markets applications (discussed by the "vertical market" group, SIG7). The idea is to allow companies to extend the CC-form content themselves. On the one hand, this will help to achieve a wider adoption of complaint mechanisms in e-commerce applications. On the other hand, this will create new challenges such as keeping the new extensions consistent with the existing CC-form and preventing the misuse of the CC-form. For example, a company might try to misuse the CC-form by inquiring about private information that violates the privacy regulations, or it may introduce new terminology and rules that are semantically inconsistent with the existing content terminology and rules.

As a solution, we propose that the CC-form not be altered directly. Instead, extensions should be introduced first into the CContology, the base of CC-form (see Figure 1). Moreover, our modularization of the application axiomatization part of the CContology offers simplified methodologies for extending, maintaining, and managing the CC-form:

- *Extensions will not be allowed on all axiomatization modules.* For example, the "Complainant" and "Address" axiomatization modules may be "locked", so companies will be prevented from, for example, asking privacy-rule-violating questions. Or perhaps, we can only allow extensions to be made into the "Complaint Problems" and "Complaint Resolutions" modules. In this way, we can achieve a "relatively" systematic management of the kinds of extensions allowed.
- *Extensions can be made and treated as separate modules.* If a company wishes to extend one of the seven core modules to inquire details about, for example, a certain kind of product, a new module can be constructed to capture these details. Both the core module(s) and the new module can be composed automatically. Notice that the specification of our composition operator (see section 4.4.2 in (Jarrar, 2005)) guarantees that the constraints and the complaining details introduced in a core module will never be dismissed or weakened. In other words, the constraints and complaint details in the resultant composition will always imply the constraints and the complaint details in the core module[10].
- *Efficient maintenance and management.* A CC-form platform may need to manage a large number of extensions that target many different complaining issues. Releasing and treating these extensions as separate modules will make managing, maintaining, and indexing them more scalable.
- *The development of the modules can be distributed among ontology experts, domain experts and application-oriented experts.* In the case of a vertical market application where one wishes to develop a set of extensions (i.e. modules), the development and the review processes can be distributed according to the expertise of the developers and the subject of the modules. In the development of the seven core modules we have distributed the development and review between several specialized groups in accordance with their expertise. Bistra Vassilev acted as domain expert for the development of the complaint problem and

resolutions modules, even though she was based several thousand kilometers away. Members from SIG1 (legal affairs) have contributed to the development and review of the "Complaint", "Complainant", "Complaint Recipient", "Address" and "Contract" modules. Members from SIG2 (consumer affairs) have similarly contributed to the development and review of the "Complaint", "Complainant", "Complaint Problem" and "Complaint Resolution" modules, etc.

- *Reusability of domain axiomatizations.* Notice that our methodology requires domain knowledge (lexons and glosses) to be developed first, then this knowledge can be used at the application level. In this way we improve the reusability of the domain knowledge because application developers will be forced to investigate and use what already exists at the domain level.
- *Reusability of the Module.* Modularizing the application axiomatization of the CContology indeed simplifies the reusability of this axiomatization. One may wish to reuse some of these axiomatization modules in application scenarios other than the CC-form. For example, the 'Address' module can easily be reused for tasks in other domains such as Mailing, Marketing and Sales Force Automation. The 'Complaint Problems' module is in the domains of market analysis, qualitative statistics, etc.

MULTILINGUAL LEXICALIZATION OF THE CCONTOLOGY

As our role SIG-6 was also to undertake the multilingual and cultural demands of customer complaint forms, a methodology for multilingual lexicalization of ontologies had to be developed. This methodology has been applied to lexicalize the CContology into several natural languages in order to support the development of a software platform providing cross-language CC-forms. For complaint platforms, this helps to systematize the translation of all terms in the generated and filled-in CC-forms that do not contain "free" text.

As shall be clear later in this section, we distinguish between a *multilingual ontology* and *multilingual lexicalization of an ontology*. The former refers either: (1) to different monolingual ontologies with an alignment layer to map between them. Such an alignment layer may include different kinds of relationships (e.g. 'equivalence', 'subtype-of', 'part-of', etc.) between concepts across the aligned ontologies. All of these ontologies, in addition to the alignment layer, form a multilingual ontology. A multilingual ontology can also be (2) a one ontology in which the terminology (i.e. concept labels) is a mixture of terms from different languages. For example, some concepts are lexicalized in language L_1, and others are lexicalized in language L_2, or maybe even in both L_1 and L_2. Yet other concepts may not have terms to lexicalize them. See (Kerremans et al, 2003) for a methodology (called "termontography") that supports such a process of multilingual ontology engineering. The processes of modeling, engineering, or using multilingual ontologies are still open (and difficult) research issues. Some related works can be found in (Lauser et al, 2002) (Agnesund, 1997) (Vossen, 1998) and (Bryan, 2001).

Multilingual lexicalization of an ontology is our aim in this section. It is an ontology lexicalized in a certain language (we call this the "native language") and a list of one-to-one translations of the ontology terms into other languages. *This list is not seen as part of the ontology itself*; rather, it belongs at the application level or to a group of users.

Our approach to the multilingual lexicalization of ontologies is motivated by the belief (Guarino, 1998) that *an ontology is language-dependent*, and by Avicenna's argument (980-1037 AC) (Qmair, 1991) that "*There is a strong relationship/dependence between concepts and their linguistic terms, change on linguistic aspects may affect the intended meaning... Therefore logicians should consider linguistic aspects 'as they are'. ...".* Indeed, Conceptual equivalence between terms in different languages is very difficult to find at the domain level. Hence, from an engineering viewpoint, multilingual lexicalization (i.e. one-to-one translation) of ontology terms should not be preserved or generalized at the domain level. Instead, such translations can be fairly established at the application level for a certain application (e.g. CC-form) or group of users.

The main goal of providing the multilingual lexicalization of an ontology is to *maximize the usability of this ontology for several cross-language applications*. We believe that this is of ever increasing importance in today's global, networked economy. In the following paragraphs, we describe our approach to the multilingual lexicalization of ontologies using the CContology as an illustrative example.

Our approach requires *an ontology to be built and lexicalized completely in one language*, namely, the ontology's *native language*. In the case of the CContology, English is chosen as the native language that then acts as *the* reference for translating ontology terms into other languages. Given the CCglossary (all the terms in the CContology and their glosses), and given the CC-form as a certain application scenario, the CContology has been lexicalized into 11 European languages[11]. Notice that changing this application scenario may yield different translations. In Figure 12, we provide a sample of these translations, illustrating one-to-one translation between terms in English, Dutch, and French languages. A CC-form can easily switch between different natural languages by substituting the terms and using the corresponding terms in such a translation list (Jarrar et al, 2003b).

It is important to note that the CCglossary has played a critical role during the translation process of the CContology. The CCglossary has been used as the principal reference, by the translators, for understanding the intended meaning of the terms, and thus achieving better quality translations. It is maybe worth mentioning that the translation process has been subcontracted to a translation company whose personnel have been trained to follow our approach.

While it is a scalable, pragmatic, easy to use, and systemized approach, one-to-one translations are not as simple as they appear – they do sometimes yield imperfect translations. The translator needs to perform further searches in order to acquire more elegant translations. In the following, we present some issues and guidelines for greater convenience and accuracy in the multilingual lexicalization of ontologies:

- *Cultural issues.* There is a great interdependency between the language and culture (social activities, religion, region, weather, interests, etc.) of a people. Thus, within a community of people speaking the same language, we can find different usage of terms, even within the same context and situation. For example, within the "Customer Complaint" and CC-form application

Figure 12. An example of multilingual lexicalization of the CContology

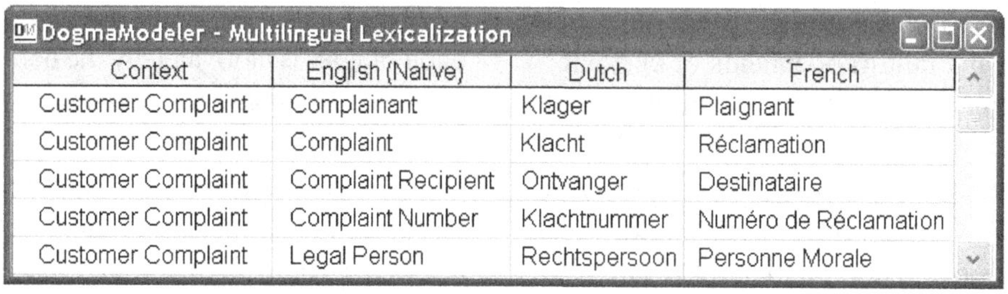

DogmaModeler - Multilingual Lexicalization

Context	English (Native)	Dutch	French
Customer Complaint	Complainant	Klager	Plaignant
Customer Complaint	Complaint	Klacht	Réclamation
Customer Complaint	Complaint Recipient	Ontvanger	Destinataire
Customer Complaint	Complaint Number	Klachtnummer	Numéro de Réclamation
Customer Complaint	Legal Person	Rechtspersoon	Personne Morale

scenario, when translating the term "Complaint" into Arabic, there are two possible terms: "Mathaalem" and "Shakaoa". In Palestine, the most commonly used term is "Shakaoa", while in Saudi Arabia, people prefer the term "Mathaalem". Seemingly, the ideal solution for such a problem is to provide a set of rules for the usage of each term, considering *all* cultural issues (see (Chalabi, 1998)). However, this does not yield a scalable approach for our purposes. Thus, we advise that if such cultural variations are important for a certain application scenario, it is better to treat each variation as a distinct language e.g. English-UK, English-USA, Dutch-Belgium, Dutch-Netherlands, Old-Arabic, Modern-Arabic.

- *Word to word translation is not our goal.* Usually, the purpose of building an ontology is to formally represent an agreed conceptualization of a certain domain, and share it among a community of users. Thus, lexicalizing the concepts in an ontology into multiple languages is a way of maximizing the *usability* of this ontology. It does not result in a multilingual lexicon. In lexicons or dictionaries, the purpose is to list only the common *words* (e.g. based on the corpus of a language) with a description and some lexical information. In ontologies, it is normal to find a concept lexicalized by an expression. For example, "Total Amount Paid", "Trying to obtain data improperly", etc. Such concepts cannot, in general, be lexicalized into one word - at least not in English.

To conclude, with the methodology we have presented in this chapter, we aim to maximize the usability of an ontology over several cross-language applications. We believe this methodology would be useful and easily applicable in information systems that comprise forms, database schemes, XML and RDF tags, etc. However, this methodology might not be suitable for ontology-based information retrieval and natural language processing applications. For such application scenarios, multilingual ontologies might be more suitable. See (Gilarranz et al, 1997) (Bonino et al, 2004).

CONCLUSION AND FUTURE DIRECTIONS

We have presented an ontology for customer complaint management, with the aim of improving the effectiveness and transparency in e-business transactions. Using ontologies as a foundation for cross-border online complaint management platforms can indeed improve the effectiveness, scope and extensibility of such platforms. While offering individual companies, organizations or associations the possibility of advanced customization (by including ontology extension capabilities) semantic consistency is maintained through the complaint management terminology. Furthermore, by restricting extensions to certain parts of the ontology, some legal constraints such as privacy regulations may be enforced systematically.

The proposed methodology for the multilingual lexicalization of ontologies is a pragmatic one. It offers a scalable way of offering multilingual services –a necessity for cross-border complaint management within the EU. An important goal in our future research is to develop a formal approach for developing multilingual ontologies which would for example, allow computers to interpret and disambiguate terms in different languages.

Remark: The ontology presented in this chapter has been implemented and applied in the CC-form demo portal[12]. Furthermore, the results of this research are being disseminated by FEDMA (the Federation of European Direct and Interactive Marketing) into its wide consortium.

However, we are not aware of any realization of this portal *yet*.

ACKNOWLEDGMENT

I dedicate this work to the memory of Peter Scoggins, the CCFORM project coordinator. Peter did not only contribute himself to the development of the ontology, but also he was the person who opened my eyes on the importance of this topic. I am in debt to Robert Meersman, Andriy Lisovoy, and Ruben Verlinden for their comments, discussion, and suggestions on the earlier version of this work. I would like to thank all members of SIG-6 for their cooperation, and particularly Alastair Tempest, Bistra Vassileva, Albert Bokma, Milos Molnar, Céline Damon, Christophe Benavent, Martin Ondrusek and Bernard Istasse, Anne Salaun, Yves Poullet, Sophie Louveaux, Bob Schmitz, Brian Hutchinson and many other partners for their comments on the early draft of the CContology.

REFERENCES

ABA Task Force on Electronic Commerce and Alternative Dispute Resolution. *Final Report.* (2002)

Agnesund, M. (1997). Representing culture-specific knowledge in a multilingual ontology. *Proceedings of the IJCAI-97 Workshop on Ontologies and Multilingual NLP.*

Bonino, D., Corno, F., Farinetti, L., Ferrato, A. (2004). Multilingual Semantic Elaboration in the DOSE platform. *ACM Symposium on Applied Computing, SAC'04.* Nicosia, Cyprus. March.

Bryan, M. (eds.) (2001). MULECO -Multilingual Upper-Level Electronic Commerce Ontology. MULECO draft CWA. *The CEN/ISSS Electronic Commerce Workshop.*

Chalabi, C. (1998). Sakhr Arabic-English Computer-Aided Translation System. *AMTA'98.* pp. 518–52.

Cho, Y., Im, I., Hiltz, S., Fjermestad, J. (2002). An Analysis of Online Customer Complaints: Implications for Web Complaint Management. *Proceedings of the 35th Annual Hawaii Int. Conf. on System Sciences.* Vol. 7.

Claes, F., Wernerfelt, B. (1987). Defensive Marketing Strategy by Customer Complaint Management: A Theoretical Analysis. *Journal of Marketing Research,* No. 24. November pp. 337–346

Gilarranz, J., Gonzalo, J., Verdejo, F. (1997). Language-independent text retrieval with the EuroWordNet multilingual semantic database. *The 2nd WS on Multilinguality in the Software Industry.*

Guarino, N. (1998). Formal Ontology in Information Systems. *Proceedings of FOIS'98,* IOS Press. pp. 3–15

Halpin, T. (1989). *A logical analysis of information systems: static aspects of the data-oriented perspective.* PhD thesis, University of Queensland, Brisbane. Australia.

Halpin, T. (2001). *Information Modeling and Relational Databases.* 3rd edn. Morgan-Kaufmann.

Jarrar, M., & Meersman, R. (2002). Formal Ontology Engineering in the DOGMA Approach. In *proceedings of the International Conference on Ontologies, Databases, and Applications of Semantics (ODBase 2002).* Volume 2519, LNCS, Pages: 1238-1254, Springer. ISBN: 3540001069.

Jarrar, M. (2005). *Towards Methodological Principles for Ontology Engineering.* PhD thesis, Vrije Universiteit Brussel.

Jarrar, M. (2005b). Modularization and Automatic Composition of Object-Role Modeling (ORM) Schemes. In *OTM 2005 Workshops, proceedings of the International Workshop on Object-Role Modeling (ORM'05).* Volume 3762, LNCS, Pages (613-625), Springer. ISBN: 3540297391.

Jarrar, M. (2006). Towards the Notion of Gloss, and the Adoption of Linguistic Resources in Formal Ontology Engineering. *Proceedings of the 15th International World Wide Web Conference (WWW2006).* Edinburgh, Scotland. Pages 497-503. ACM Press. ISBN: 1595933239.

Jarrar, M. (2007). Towards Automated Reasoning on ORM Schemes. -Mapping ORM into the DLR_idf description logic. *Proceedings of the 26th International Conference on Conceptual Modeling (ER 2007).* Volume 4801, LNCS, Pages (181-197), Springer. ISBN:9783540755623. New Zealand.

Jarrar, M. (2007). Mapping ORM into the SHOIN/OWL Description Logic- Towards a Methodological and Expressive Graphical Notation for Ontology Engineering. *OTM workshops (ORM'07).* Portogal. Volume 4805, LNCS, Pages (729-741), Springer. ISBN: 9783540768890.

Jarrar, M., Verlinden, R., & Meersman, R. (2003). Ontology-based Customer Complaint Management. *OTM 2003 Workshops, proceedings of the 1st International Workshop on Regulatory Ontologies and the Modeling of Complaint Regulations.* Italy. Volume 2889, LNCS, pages: 594-606, Springer. ISBN: 3540204946.

Jarrar, M., Lisovoy, A., Verlinden, R., & Meersman, R. (2003b). *OntoForm Ontology based CCForms Demo.* Deliverable D6.8, The CCFORM Thematic Network (IST-2001-34908), Brussels.

Jarrar, M., Demey, J., & Meersman, R. (2003c). On Using Conceptual Data Modeling for Ontology Engineering. *Journal on Data Semantics, Special issue on Best papers from the ER/ODBASE/COOPIS 2002 Conferences,* 2800(1):185-207. Springer, ISBN: 3540204075.

Jarrar, M., & Heymans, S. (2006). Unsatisfiability Reasoning in ORM Conceptual Schemes. *Proceeding of International Conference on Semantics of a Networked World.* Germany. Volume 4254, LNCS, Pages (517-534), Springer. ISBN: 3540467882.

Jarrar, M., Keet, M., & Dongilli, P. (2006b). *Multilingual verbalization of ORM conceptual models and axiomatized ontologies.* Technical report. STARLab, Vrije Universiteit Brussel.

Jarrar, M., & Eldammagh, M. (2007, August). *Reasoning on ORM using Racer.* Technical Report. STAR Lab, Vrije Universiteit Brussel, Belgium.

Jarrar, M., & Heymans, S. (2008). Towards Pattern-based Reasoning for Friendly Ontology Debugging. *Journal of Artificial Tools,* Volume 17, No.4. World Scientific Publishing.

Jarrar, M. & Meersman, R. (2008b, in press). Ontology Engineering -The DOGMA Approach. (Chapter 3). *Advances in Web Semantic.* Volume 1, IFIP2.12. Springer.

Kerremans, K., Temmerman, R. and Tummers, J. (2003). Representing multilingual and culture-specific knowledge in a VAT regulatory ontology: support from the termontography approach. *OTM 2003 Workshops.*

Lauser, B., Wildemann, T., Poulos, A., Fisseha, F., Keizer, J., Katz, S. (2002). A Comprehensive Framework for Building Multilingual Domain Ontologies. *Proceedings of the Dublin Core and Metadata.*

Meersman R. (1999). Semantic Ontology Tools in Information System Design. *Proceedings of the ISMIS 99 Conference,* LNCS 1609, Springer Verlag. pp. 30–45

Qmair, Y. (1991). *Foundations of Arabic Philosophy.* Dar al-Shoroq. Bairut.

Vossen, P. (eds.) (1998). *EuroWordNet: A Multilingual Database with Lexical Semantic Networks*. Kluwer Academic Publishers, Dordrecht.

Vassileva, B., Scoggins, P. (2003). *Consumer Complaint Forms: An Assessment, Evaluation and Recommendations for Complaint Categorization*. Technical report, CCForm Project (IST-2001-34908). Brussels.

ENDNOTES

1 We refer to the project name as "CCFORM" and to a customer complaint portal as "CC-form". One may imagine a CC-form as several pages of Web forms, which can be dynamic and filled in several steps.

2 http://www.starlab.vub.ac.be/staff/mustafa/CContology

3 The full content of the CContology can be downloaded from http://www.jarrar.info/CContology

4 The differences between the legal models of these application-types illustrate their different usability perspectives: (First) the intersection between the legal models of C_{A2} and the legal models C_{A3} shows that I_{A3} is a subset of I_{A2}. An example of this case could be the difference between notions of 'book' in an axiomatization of bookstores and libraries: all legal instances of the bookstores' notion are legal instances for the libraries, but not vice versa. For libraries, the instances of e.g. 'Manual' or 'Master Thesis' can be instances of a 'book'; however, they cannot be instances of 'book' for bookstores, unless they are published with an 'ISBN'. (Second) The difference between I_{A1} and I_{A3} shows an extreme case: two types of applications sharing the same concept C while their legal models are completely disjoint according to their usability perspectives. An example of this case could be the difference between notions of 'book' in an axiomatization of bookstores' and museums': Museums are interested in exhibiting and exchanging instances of old 'books', while bookstores are not interested in such 'books', unless for example, they are re-edited and published in a modern style.

5 In ORM: Concepts are represented as ellipses, and relations as rectangles. Each relation consists of one or more roles, e.g. the relationship between the concepts *Contract* and *Purchase Phase Problem* consists of the two co-roles *Refers* and *AssociatedWith* The thick arrow between *Contract Problem* and *Problem* denotes a subsumption. The ⊗ between subtypes is called exclusive constraint, it means that the intersection of their population is empty. The dot • on the line connecting *Purchase Phase Problem* and *Contract* represents a mandatory constraint. The arrow ←→ on a role represents a uniqueness constrain. Other ORM constraints will be explained later.

6 Notice that the mandatory constraint cannot be generalized at the domain level, because there might be other types of applications where it is not mandatory to be associated with a contract, at least explicitly.

7 The ORM exclusion constraint ⊙ states that each *Delivery* should be at least *Goods* or *Services*, or both.

8 Such address servers are: http://www.afd.co.uk/tryit/ (July 2007), http://www.post-direkt.de (July 2007), http://www.usps.com, (July 2004).

9 One can imagine a company providing a link to the CC-form portal in their own webpage. When the link is clicked, the CC-form appears with the company's information filled and the details of the complaints (that are specific to this company) attached to the basic complaint questions.

10 This is in fact a clear illustrative application of our composition mechanism, especially in

the legal domain. From a "legal" viewpoint, our composition operator means that when including a module into another module (that has a higher authority, or also called *legal weight*), all rules and fact-types in the included module will be inherited by (or applied in) the including module.

11 These translations are not provided in this chapter as the distribution of the knowledge is restricted, and its intellectual property is owned by the CCFORM project.

12 This portal (which was not an official deliverable in the project) is no longer available due to copy-right issues.

Chapter VIII
A Semantic Web-Based Information Integration Approach for an Agent-Based Electronic Market

Maria João Viamonte
GECAD – Knowledge Engineering and Decision Support Research Group, Porto Polytechnic Institute, Portugal

Nuno Silva
GECAD – Knowledge Engineering and Decision Support Research Group, Porto Polytechnic Institute, Portugal

ABSTRACT

With the increasing importance of e-commerce across the Internet, the need for software agents to support both customers and suppliers in buying and selling goods/services is growing rapidly. It is becoming increasingly evident that in a few years the Internet will host a large number of interacting software agents. Most of them will be economically motivated, and will negotiate a variety of goods and services. It is therefore important to consider the economic incentives and behaviours of e-commerce software agents, and to use all available means to anticipate their collective interactions. Even more fundamental than these issues, however, is the very nature of the various actors that are involved in e-commerce transactions. This leads to different conceptualizations of the needs and capabilities, giving rise to semantic incompatibilities between them. Ontologies have an important role in Multi-Agent Systems communication and provide a vocabulary to be used in the communication between agents. It is hard to find two agents using precisely the same vocabulary. They usually have a heterogeneous private vocabulary defined in their own private ontology. In order to provide help in the conversation among different agents, we are proposing what we call ontology-services to facilitate agents' interoperability. More specifically, we propose an ontology-based information integration approach, exploiting the on-

tology mapping paradigm, by aligning consumer needs and the market capacities, in a semi-automatic mode. We propose a new approach for the combination of the use of agent-based electronic markets based on Semantic Web technology, improved by the application and exploitation of the information and trust relationships captured by the social networks.

CURRENT SITUATION

As the result of technological developments, e-commerce, namely business-to-consumer (B2C), is emerging as the new way of doing business.

In most current (first generation) e-ecommerce applications, the buyers are generally humans who typically browse through a catalogue of well-defined commodities (e.g., flights, books, compact discs, computer components) and make (fixed price) purchases (often by means of a credit card transaction). However, this modus operandi is only scratching the surface of what is possible. By increasing the degree and the sophistication of automation, on both the buyer's and the seller's side, e-commerce becomes much more dynamic, personalized, and context sensitive.

We believe that over the course of the next decade, the global economy and the Internet will merge into a global market with a large amount of autonomous software agents that exchange goods and services with humans and other agents. Agents will represent, and be, consumers, producers, and intermediaries.

When interactions among agents become sufficiently rich, a crucial qualitative change will occur. New classes of agents will be designed specially to serve the needs of the other agents. However, in order to harness the full potential of this new mode of e-commerce, a broad range of social, legal, and technical issues need to be addressed. These issues relate to things such as security, trust, payment mechanisms, advertising, logistics, and back office management. Even more fundamental than these issues, however, is the very nature of the various actors that are involved in e-commerce transactions.

In an efficient agent-mediated electronic market, where all the partners, both sending and receiving messages have to lead to acceptable and meaningful agreements, it is necessary to have common standards, like an interaction protocol to achieve deals, a language for describing the messages' content and ontologies for describing the domain's knowledge.

The need for these standards emerges due to the nature of the goods/services traded in business transactions. The goods/services are described through multiple attributes (e.g. price, features and quality), which imply that negotiation processes and final agreements between seller and buyers must be enhanced with the capability to both understand the terms and conditions of the transaction (e.g. vocabulary semantics, currencies to denote different prices, different units to represent measures or mutual dependencies of products). A critical factor for the efficiency of the future negotiation processes and the success of the potential settlements is an agreement among the negotiating parties about how the issues of a negotiation are represented and what this representation means to each of the negotiating parties. This problem is referred to as the ontology problem of electronic negotiations (Ströbel, 2001). Distributors, manufactures, and service providers may have radically different ontologies that differ significantly in format, structure, and meaning. Given the increasingly complex requirements of applications, the need for rich, consistent and reusable semantics, the growth of semantically interoperable enterprises into knowledge-based communities; and the evolution; and adoption of Semantic Web technologies need to be addressed. Ontologies represent the best answer to the demand for intelligent systems that operate closer to the human conceptual level (Obrst, Liu, and Wray, 2003).

To achieve this degree of automation and move to new generation e-commerce applications, we believe that a new model of software is needed.

PROBLEM STATEMENT

In order to make possible the interaction between agents in a Multi-Agent Systems, it is necessary to have a communication platform, a communication language and a common ontology.

With respect to communications, there are some implications:

- There are many different ontology languages.
- Different ontology languages are sometimes based on different underlying paradigms.
- Some ontology languages are very expressive, some are not.
- Some ontology languages have a formally defined semantics, some do not.
- Some ontology languages have inference support, some do not.

However, even if the exact same language is used, the resulting ontologies can be incompatible in various ways:

- People or agents may use different terms for the same thing.
- People or agents may use the same term for the different things.
- A given notion or concept may be modeled using different primitives in the language.
- A given notion or concept may be modeled with very different fundamental underlying primitives.

Once we take this problem as a challenge, representing these differences in a common ontology becomes essential. The ontology includes the entire domain's knowledge, which is made available to all the components active in an information system (Huhns & Singh, 1997). The use of a common ontology guarantees the consistency (an expression has the same meaning for all the agents) and the compatibility (a concept is designed, for the same expression, for any agent) of the information present in the system. However, we cannot assume that all the agents will use a common ontology. In fact, as stated in (Hepp, 2007), the adoption of ontologies in e-commerce has some drawbacks, namely concerning the comprehension and correct use of the adopted ontology which is a difficult and time consuming task, often leading to conflicting interpretations and eventually wrong use of the ontology and data. Usually, each agent has its heterogeneous private ontology and it cannot fully understand another agent's ontology, giving rise to semantic incompatibilities between them. Consequently, different actors involved in the marketplace must be able to independently describe their universe of discourse, while the market is responsible for providing a technological framework that promotes the semantic integration between parties.

However, it is necessary to consider that the solution proposed to overcome theses problems, has to take into consideration the technological support already existent, namely a well-proven e-commerce platform, where agents with strategic behaviour represent consumers and suppliers.

PROPOSED SOLUTION

We propose an agent-based electronic market with an ontology-based information integration approach, exploiting the ontology mapping paradigm, by aligning consumer needs and the market capacities throughout the negotiation conversations in a semi-automatic mode, improved by the application and exploitation of the information and trust relationships captured by the social networks.

To study our proposal we will combine the use of ISEM and MAFRA Toolkit into a novel electronic marketplace approach, together with the exploitation of social semantic network services.

ISEM – Intelligent System for Electronic MarketPlaces (Viamonte, Ramos, Rodrigues & Cardoso, 2006) is a simulation platform developed at our research group. ISEM is a multi-agent market simulator, designed for analysing agent market strategies based on a complete understanding of buyer and seller behaviours, preference models and pricing algorithms, considering user risk preferences and game theory for scenario analysis. Each market participant has its own business objectives and decision model. The results of the negotiations between agents are analyzed by data mining algorithms in order to extract knowledge that gives agents feedback to improve their strategies. The extracted knowledge will be used to set up probable scenarios, analyzed by means of simulation and game theory decision criteria.

The main objectives of ISEM are: first, the ISEM system addresses the complexities of on-line buyers' behaviour by providing a rich set of behaviour parameters; second, the ISEM system provides available market information that allows sellers to make assumptions about buyers' behaviour and preference models; third, the different agents customise their behaviour adaptively, by learning each user's preference models and business strategies. The learning agent capacity is achieved through data mining techniques applied on-line during the market sessions within the ISEM system.

MAFRA Toolkit is the instantiation of the MAFRA-MApping FRAmework (Maedche, Motik, Silva & Volz, 2002), addressing the fundamental phases of the ontology mapping process. In particular, it allows the identification, specification and representation of semantic relations between two different ontologies. These semantic relations are further applied in the execution phase of the interoperation, by transforming the data (messages' content) as understood by one of the actors into the data understood by the other. In this sense, ontology mapping allows actors to keep their knowledge bases unchanged while supporting the semantic alignment between their conceptualizations (ontologies).

On the other hand, social network repositories aim to capture collaboratively created information and trust relationships between individuals according to different subjects (e.g. business, family, music, sport, travel, and hobbies). Social networks together with security oriented technologies form the basic infrastructure to encompass collaboration and trust relationships in many internet based activities, including e-commerce transactions and information integration.

Objectives

The proposed approach introduces a novel agent-based marketplace architecture that will be deployed within the ISEM simulator in order to assure that different agents can establish deals in a more flexible and evolved form. In order to judge the feasibility and relevance of the approach, we will use the Consumer Buying Behaviour model (CBB) as a reference (Runyon & Stewart, 1987).

Another important goal is to support the identification stage of the CBB model using ontologies to construct the most accurate model of the consumer's needs. Moreover, at the product brokering, buyer coalition formation, merchant brokering and negotiation stages, the ontology mapping process will provide the integration of the seller and consumer's models (HarmoNet, 2007).

Complementarily, the repository of relationships provided by emergent social networks will support establishing more accurate trust relationships between businesses and customers, as well as providing a better alignment (mapping) between their models. This new information is very important to feed the agents' knowledge bases to improve their strategic behaviour. Market participant's strategic behaviour is very significant in the context of competition.

Overview

In the following sections, we will describe the electronic market objectives and model, the ontology mapping features and the proposed ontology-based, socially-driven information integration approach.

Our ontology-based services will be provided through an additional Market service provided by a specific agent, the Market Facilitator agent. This agent will be responsible for providing structural and semantic relationships between different vocabularies, which carry appropriate conversations and make agreement possible.

The Marketplace Objectives

Agents can be used in many ways in the electronic commerce applications and for this it will be necessary to create a scenario where they can interact with each other. The Marketplace function is to permit and facilitate the interaction between the agents. We support the idea of a Web site where users go to trade items. All agents are notified by the market about existing buying agents and selling agents and about what they want to sell and what they want to buy. We expect that we have agents interested in buying and selling the same category of commodities. At any time, we can have a variable number of partners in our market and every transaction has specific parameters.

A language support for inter-agent communication has to be defined; we need to ensure that all the agents participating in the market use the same language, or that the languages in use can be translated; and an ontology-based information integration to ensure transparent semantic interoperability.

Another objective is supporting some of the stages of the CBB model:

- *Need Identification*, "the consumer can be stimulated through product information". Although all the buyer agents are notified by the market about existing selling agents and about their products, the marketplace needs some additional expertise to notify the users about products available based on their profiles and last deals.
- *Product Brokering*, "the evaluation of product alternatives based on consumer-provided criteria." The agent system must be able to assist consumers in deciding which products best fit their personal criteria, they must act as recommendation agents, make predictions based on profiles and "business intelligence", possibly derived by data mining techniques and based on social-driven information.
- *Buyer Coalition Formation*, "having determined the product to buy, customers may move directly to the merchant brokering phase (see below) or they may interact with other similar buyers to try and form a coalition before moving to the merchant brokering phase. Here, a coalition is viewed as a group of agents cooperating with each other in order to achieve a common task. In these "buyer coalitions," each buyer is represented by their own agent and together these agents try to form a grouping in order to approach the merchant with a larger order (in order to obtain leverage by buying in bulk). Normally a buyer coalition model is composed of five stages: negotiation, leader election, coalition formation, payment collection, and execution stages. It is essential to have a trustworthy and reliable agent that will collect the buyer's information, divide the agents into coalitions, and negotiate with sellers (refer to Yamamoto & Sycara, 2001 and Tsvetovat & Sycara, 2000 for a full discussion of these issues).

- *Merchant Brokering*, "who to buy from, includes the evaluation of merchant alternatives based on consumer-provided criteria". Having selected the desired product, and perhaps after having formed a buyer coalition, merchant brokering involves the agent finding an appropriate seller to purchase the item from. The customer agent must be able to find several providers for each item, taking into account different user preferences and based on past events and users satisfaction with certain providers.
- *Negotiation*, "this stage is about how to determine the terms of the transaction". Having selected a merchant (or set of merchants), the next step is to negotiate the terms and conditions. We believe that this is one of the major changes that will be brought about by agent-mediated e-commerce. The agents negotiate with each other by using strategies based on rule systems and users' criteria, searching for an agreement on multiple goals and considering tradeoffs between the goals.

The Marketplace Model

Our Marketplace facilitates agent meeting and matching, besides supporting the negotiation model. In order to have results and feedback to improve the negotiation models and consequently the behaviour of user agents, we simulate a series of negotiation periods, D={1,2,…,n}, where each one is composed by a fixed interval of time T={0,1,…,m}. Furthermore, each agent has a deadline $D_{\max}^{Agt} \in D$ to achieve its business objectives. At a particular negotiation period, each agent has an objective that specifies its intention to buy or sell a particular good or service and on what conditions. The available agents can establish their own objectives and decision rules. Moreover, they can adapt their strategies as the simulation progresses on the basis of previous efforts' successes or failures. The simulator probes the conditions and the effects of market rules, by simulating the participant's strategic behaviour.

Our simulator was developed based on "A Model for Developing a MarketPlace with Software Agents (MoDeMA)" (Viamonte, 2004). MoDeMA is composed of the following steps:

- Marketplace model definition, that permits doing transactions according to the CBB model.
- Identification of the different participants, and the possible interactions between them.
- Ontology specification, that identifies and represents items being transacted.
- Agents' architecture specification, and information flows between each agents module.
- Knowledge Acquisition, defining the process that guarantees the agent the knowledge to act in pursuit of its role.
- Negotiation Model, defining the negotiation mechanisms to be used.
- Negotiation Protocol, specification of each of the negotiation mechanism rules.
- Negotiation Strategies, specification and development of several negotiation strategies.
- Knowledge Discovery, identification and gathering of market knowledge to support agents' strategic behaviour.

ISEM is flexible; the user completely defines the model he or she wants to simulate, including the number of agents, each agent's type and strategies.

The Negotiation Model and Protocol

The negotiation model used in ISEM is bilateral contracting where buyer agents are looking for sellers that can provide them with the desired products at the best conditions.

We adopt what is basically an alternating protocol (Fatima, Wooldridge & Jennings, 2004 and Osborne & Rubinstein, 1994).

Negotiation starts when a buyer agent sends a request for proposal (RFP) (Figure 1). In response, a seller agent analyses its own capabilities, current availability, and past experiences and formulates a proposal (PP).

Sellers can formulate two kinds of proposals: a proposal for the product requested or a proposal for a related product, according to the buyer preference model.

On the basis of the bilateral agreements made among market players and lessons learned from previous bid rounds, both agents revise their strategies for the next negotiation round and update their individual knowledge module.

The negotiation protocol of the ISEM simulator (Figure 2) has three main actors:

- *Buyer* (B) is the agent that represents a consumer or a buyer coalition. Multiple Buyers normally exist in the marketplace in an instant.
- *Seller* (S) is the agent that represents a supplier. Multiple Sellers normally exist in the marketplace in an instant.
- *Market Facilitator agent* (MF), usually one per marketplace, coordinates the market and ensures that it works correctly. MF identifies all the agents in the market, regulates negotiation, and assures that the market operates according to established rules. Before entering the market, agents must first register with the MF agent.

The Ontology

Ontologies, as knowledge representation artefacts, allow the "explicit formal specification of

Figure 1. Sequence of bilateral contracts

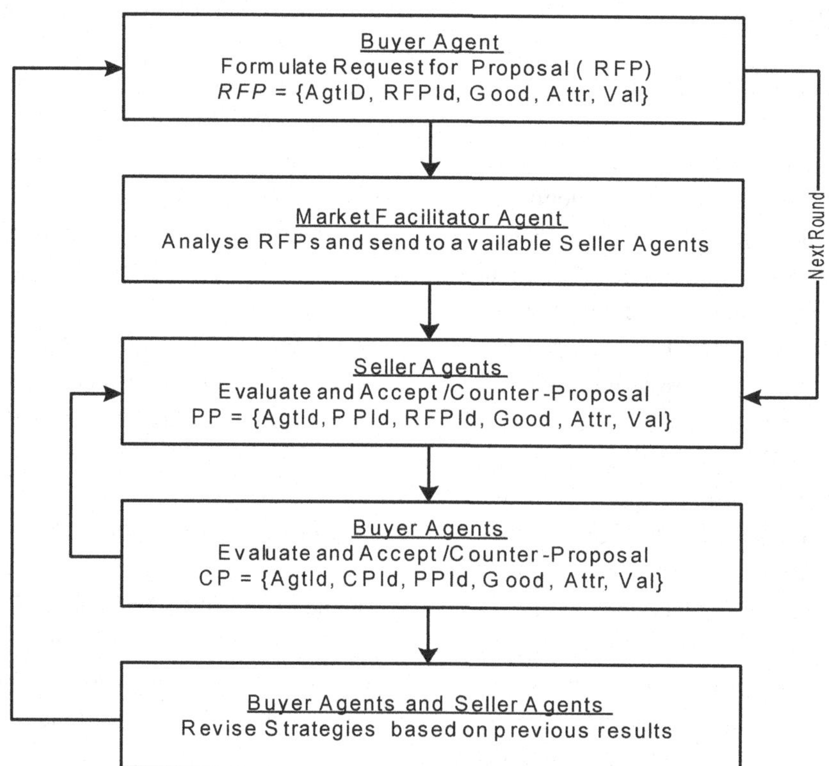

Figure 2. ISEM bilateral contract protocol

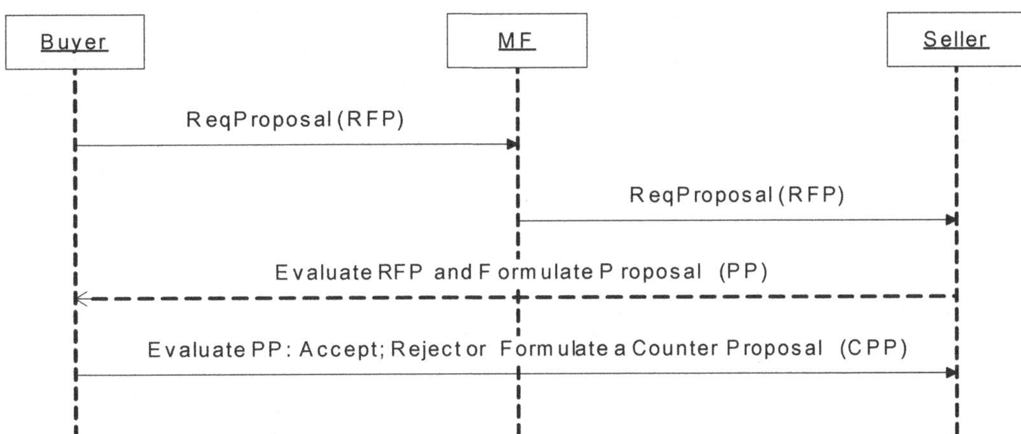

a shared conceptualization" (Studer, Benjamins & Fensel, 1998). Ontologies raise the level of specification, incorporating semantics into the data, and promoting its exchange in an explicit understandable form. The resulting artefact is then shared between interoperating actors and is used for querying and reasoning about each others knowledge base. Ontologies are therefore fully geared as a framework for capturing, specifying, representing and sharing the domain of discourse in the scope of distinct types of e-commerce, namely B2C or business-to-business (B2B).

However, ontologies per se are not able to overcome information interoperability incompatibilities and it is hardly conceivable that a single ontology can be applied to all kinds of domains and applications. Information integration mechanisms are necessary in order to identify, represent and apply the diverse relationships between concepts and relations of two or more ontologies. Ontology Mapping is one of the most successful information integration paradigms used in the Internet and in particular in the Semantic Web. Despite a more holistic description of the Ontology Mapping Process (Maedche et al., 2002), ontology mapping is primarily the process whereby semantic relations are defined at an ontological level between source ontology entities and target ontology entities and then further applied at instance level, transforming source ontology instances into target ontology instances (Figure 3).

Therefore, unlike other information integration paradigms (e.g. Merging and Integration) (Pinto, Gómez-Pérez & Martins, 1999) that lead to definitive semantics and information loss, through ontology mapping, repositories are kept separated, independent and distinct, maintaining their complete semantics and contents.

The approach followed in MAFRA Toolkit adopts a declarative specification of semantic relations through the use of the SBO-Semantic Bridging Ontology, itself an ontology. When instantiated it becomes the description of the syntactic and semantic relations between entities of two ontologies. MAFRA Toolkit's support of the SBO manipulation hides the procedural complexity of specification and execution of relations. Additionally, its open Service-oriented architecture allows the incorporation of new types of mapping relations into the system (Services), improving the expressive power and mapping capabilities of the system. Additionally, Services play the important role of driving the semi-automatic specification of semantic relations, releasing the user from this time consuming and difficult task. Instead, the user is invited to supervise the

Figure 3. Informal representation of ontology mapping

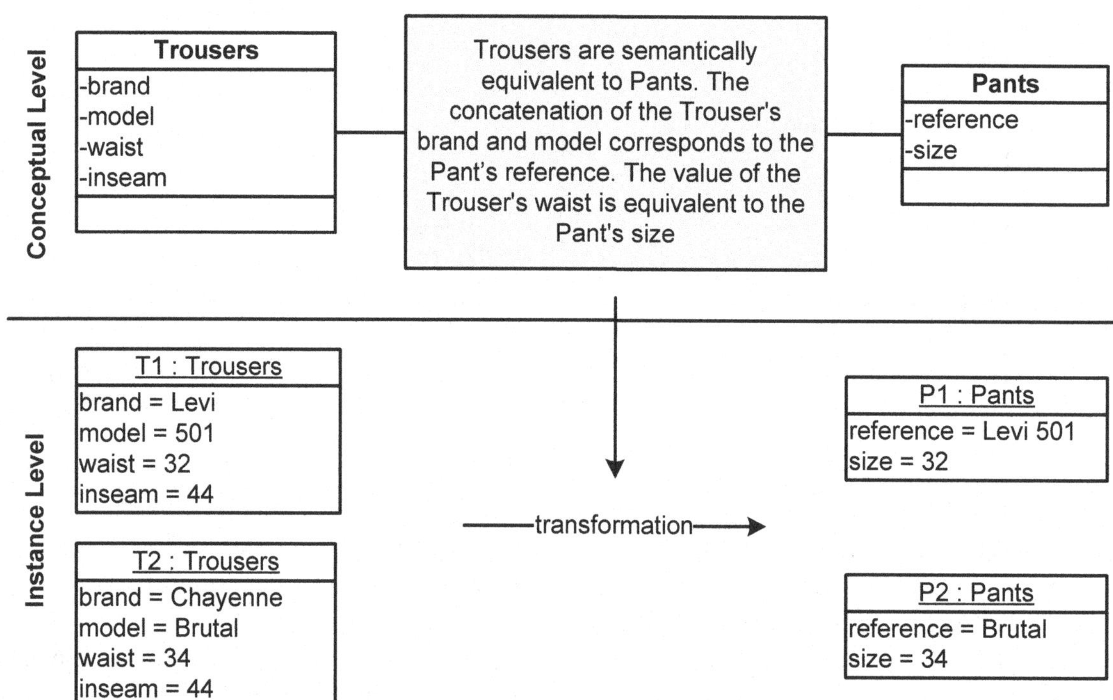

services' process and confirm the automatically generated proposals.

MAFRA Toolkit has been successfully adopted in the EU-funded project Harmo-Ten (www.harmo-ten.org) devoted to the exchange of information in tourism. The outcome of this project is now being applied in the HarmoNet initiative (HarmoNet, 2007).

The Social Networks

Social Networks are one of the grounding theories behind the promotion and success of Web 2.0. Social Networks connect people around issues or causes. Different interests give rise to and promote different communities (e.g. music, sports, technology, religion, fashion), which simplify many customer target initiatives such as pricing, marketing, advertising and selling. Social Network Analysis (SNA) unveils clusters of users with similar interests, even when such relations are vague or implicit. Based on users' manually created relationships, SNA provides important formal metrics such as Activity, Betweenness and Closeness. Yet, either explicit social relationship expressed through social network tools (e.g. LinkedIn, MySpace, Friendster) or through email analysis, the so called social network mapping tools are emerging that are capable of exposing relevant links between users (e.g. InFlow) and generate statistics on almost anything. As often stated in many blogs and editorials, business managers expect that Web 2.0 will bring more information about users, customers and their trends, allowing business efforts to focus on specific target communities.

Through tagging and social bookmarking, folksonomies are emerging as a valuable classification mechanism of documents and goods. Moreover, folksonomies, seen as very simple ontologies (Van Damme, Hepp & Siorpaes, 2007) are perceived as an important social interrelation mechanism allowing systems to track the relationships between individuals and groups across the social networks. This assumption is based on empirical evidence showing that users follow the tendencies originated by specific users (or groups of users). With this approach, i.e. decentralized, cooperative and intuitive development (Siorpaes & Hepp, 2007), folksonomies tend to better represent the conceptualization of a community, while at the same time the community is able to cooperatively participate in other ontology-based processes, such as information integration and evolution. This permeating process promotes discussion about future communities' tendencies, their similar desires, interests and knowledge patterns, supporting the idea of exploiting the intrinsic social knowledge for improving the e-commerce interactions.

It is expected that social network services will soon provide automatic access to SNA metrics, improved content classification and many statistical reports. For that, API, agent-based or Web Services will be used instead of the traditional Web page interaction. The Web-Of-Trust and PKI (Public Key Infrastructure) (Aberer, Datta & Hauswirth, 2005) infrastructures will be combined with such services in order to assure identity, trust and no repudiation between users and systems. Kondifi and FOAFRealm are two examples of such systems. The FOAFRealm aims to integrate several types of social semantic information sources through the same infrastructure, and its access control rules are based in FOAF data (http://www.foaf-project.org/). Kondifi deploys and exploits relations between the formal identification mechanisms available through PKI infrastructure, and RDF-based (Resource Description Framework) information provided by accessed documents.

SOLUTION DETAILS

While the use of ontologies allows e-commerce actors to describe their needs and capabilities into proprietary repositories, the use of the ontology-mapping paradigm allows transparent semantic interoperability between them. This is the technological basis for the alignment between needs and capabilities of consumer and supplier, even when they use different ontologies. Based on this approach we can obtain the minimal requirements to support our proposed solution.

Minimalist Approach

The first proposed version of the protocol (Figure 4) models the simplest interactions between the three types of agents, minimizing the changes in interactions between B (Buyer) and S (Seller) agents with the MF (Market Facilitator) agent, based on the ISEM protocol (Figure 2).

This minimal approach aims to overcome the simplest information integration problems mentioned above.

In this protocol, the MF agent is responsible for the specification of the mapping between the B and S ontologies. When the B requests a proposal (ReqProposal), the MF agent generates (or queries) the ontology mapping repository for a mapping between the two agents' ontologies, and proposes it to the agents. The agents are free to accept or reject the mapping, but in case both accept, the messages' content will be transformed between agents according to that ontology mapping specification.

The changes to the original protocol are minimal. In fact, most of the changes affect the MF agent only, in the sense that the ReqMapping and ReqTransf messages will trigger MF's internal processes.

Extended Approach

However, this system infrastructure is too simple to be effective especially because:

- It neglects the complexity and subjectivity of the ontology mapping process.

Figure 4. The information integration basic protocol

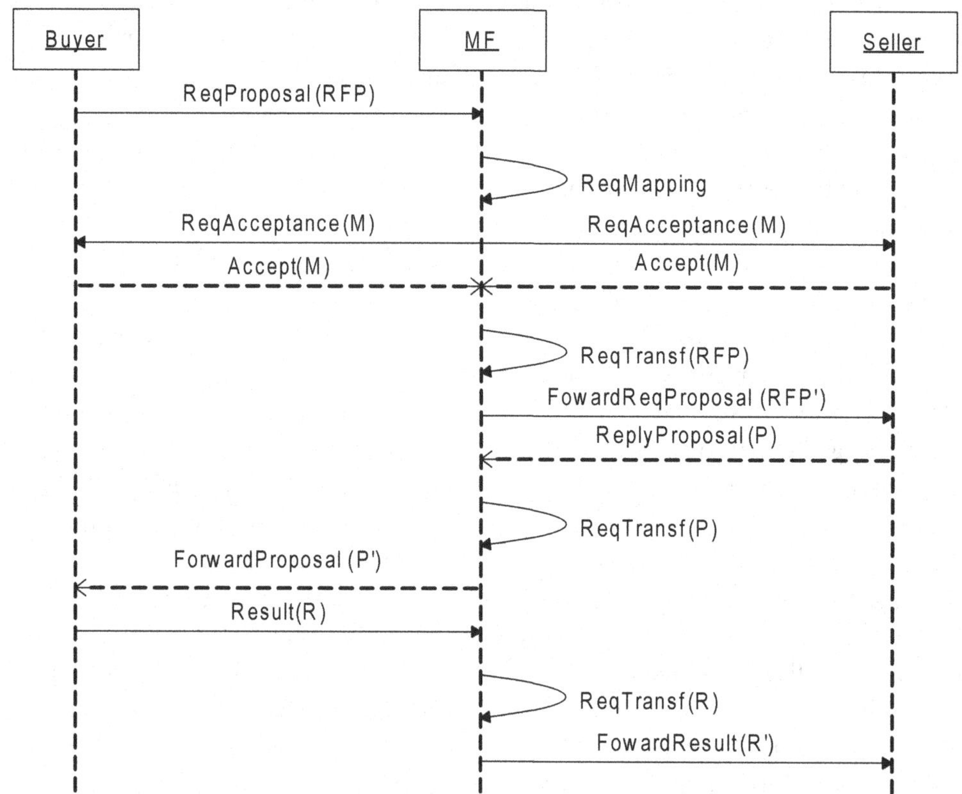

- It does not consider the social relationships emerging in the Web and their potential in disambiguation and decision-making processes.

As a consequence, a new system infrastructure is proposed, recognizing two new types of actors:

- *Ontology Mapping Intermediary* (OM-i), is the agent that supports the information integration process during the market interoperability, typically one per marketplace.
- *Social Networks Intermediary* (SN-i), is the agent that provides trust relationship information holding between B, S and other agents that undertake similar experiences (e.g. a trader agent), typically one per marketplace.

These actors deploy a set of relationship types whose goal is to automate and improve the quality of the results achieved in the e-commerce transactions. Figure 5 depicts the types of interactions between the marketplace supporting agents (i.e. MF, OM-i and SN-i agents) and the operational agents (i.e. B and S).

Considering the previous descriptions, a more complete and complex protocol is now detailed, including the OM-i and SN-i agents in the system (Figure 6).

The integration starts when the B agent sends a request for proposal message (ReqProposal) to the MF agent. In response, the MF sends to the OM-i a request for mapping message (ReqMapping) between B and S's ontologies.

Once OM-i receives the ReqMapping message, it will start the ontology mapping specification process, with the support of other entities, includ-

Figure 5. Marketplace's actors and interactions

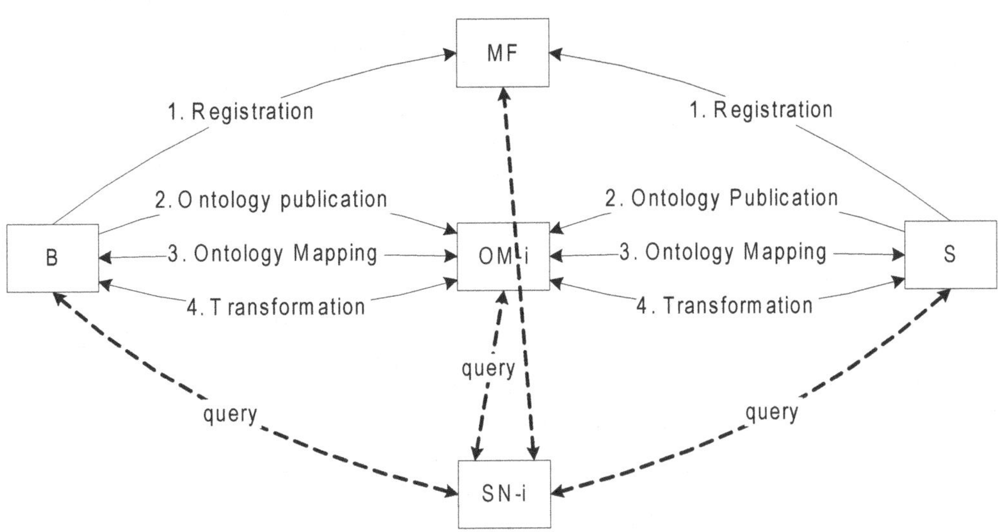

1. *The Registration phase is initiated by the B or S agent, and allows these agents to identify themselves to the marketplace and specify their roles and services.*
2. *The Ontology Publication phase is the set of transactions allowing B and S to specify their ontologies to the marketplace.*
3. *The Mapping phase is the set of transactions driven by OM-i to align the ontologies of B and S.*
4. *The Transformation phase is the set of information transactions through OM-i that transforms (i.e. converts) the interaction data described in two different ontologies.*

ing matching agents, ontology mapping repositories and SN-i. SN-i is responsible for retrieving the relevant information from ontology mapping repositories and social networks. Past similar ontology mapping experiences undertaken by agents with trust relationships with B and S will be used by SN-i to compile the social network repository information (i.e. SNInf(Inf)). Because the ReqSNInf is the sole responsibility of OM-i, both B and S are advised to perform a similar verification (eventually using other SN-i) once the ontology mapping is submitted for acceptance (i.e. ReqAcceptance(M)). Despite the fact that figure 6 represents only the acceptance scenario, a rejection scenario is also possible, in which case no further interaction will occur between B and S. In case the mapping is accepted, MF resumes the protocol by requesting to OM-i the RFP data transformation. Using the ontology mapping document, RFP data represented according to B's ontology is transformed into data represented according to S's ontology. The transformed data (RFP') is forwarded to S, which will process it and will reply to MF. MF will then request the transformation of the proposal data (P) and will forward P' to B. B processes it and will accept or formulate a counter-proposal (CP). As can be seen, once a mutually acceptable ontology mapping is established between B's ontology and S's ontology, all messages exchanged between B and S through MF are forwarded to OM-i for transformation.

Notice that Figure 6 represents one single S in the system, but in fact multiple S's capable of replying to the request may exist in the marketplace. In such case, the protocol would replicate the previous protocol for as many capable S's. In order to decide which S's are capable of answering the request, a simple approach based on a keyword matching algorithm is taken. The B agent speci-

Figure 6. The integration protocol

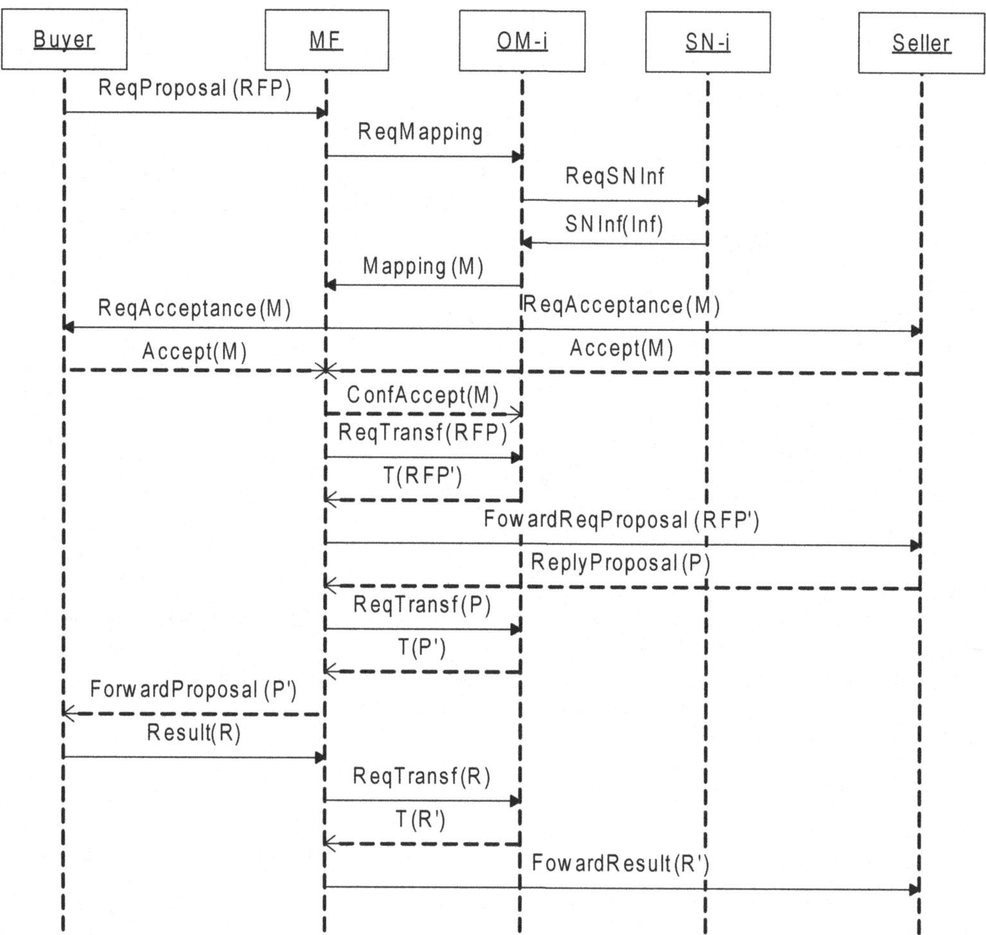

fies a few keywords along with its formal request (RFP). The MF, with the aid of SN-i, matches this list against every S's publicized keyword list. In case the match succeeds to a certain level, the S is classified as capable.

The interaction protocol just described emphasises the information integration problem occurring in the negotiation stage of the CBB model. However, other interaction protocols are needed to improve the marketplace in accordance to the objectives stated in section 2.1. In fact, in every stage of the CBB model, both the SN-i and OM-i are major players in the proposed solution. Notice that the social network information and trust component of the system is orthogonal to previous processes, as depicted in Figure 5. Also notice that the trust component of the system is orthogonal to previous processes, as depicted in Figure 7.

In particular, the Social Network component is envisaged as a source of information for disambiguation and decision-making to the other processes, along with trust relationships between users and groups:

- The Registration process will profit from the Trust component in several ways. For example, the S agents can better decide which Services to provide in a marketplace, depending on the segment of customers

Figure 7. Marketplace's ontology-based services

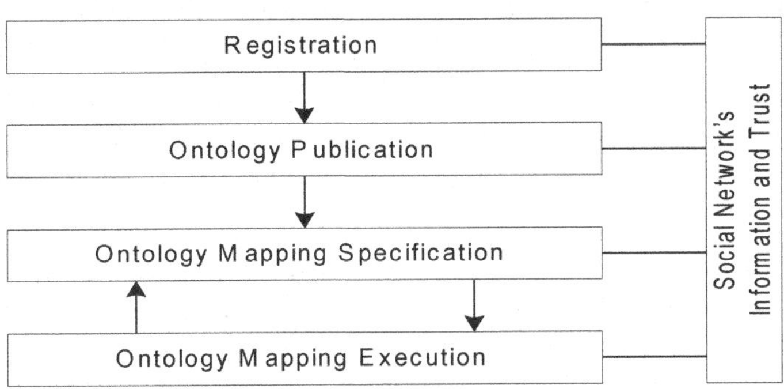

traditionally found in specific marketplace. This is achieved by the social characterization of the B agents according to the social networks they belong to. In the same sense, B agents can more accurately choose the marketplaces to register to, depending on the social network advice, based on a social characterization of the other marketplace participants (i.e. Buyers and Sellers);

- During the Ontology Publication process, agents need to decide which ontologies are advisable in that particular marketplace (e.g. simple or more detailed). The agent is able to choose the ontology that conveniently describes the semantics of its data in a certain context. In order to decide the more convenient ontology, S agents require a social characterization of the marketplace. Similar decisions are taken by B agents. Notice however, that the agent's published ontology should not be understood as the complete representation of its internal data, but the semantics the agent intends to exteriorize through the Ontology Publication process. As a consequence, the agent should encompass the mechanisms allowing the internal transformation between the internal data semantics (e.g. data schema) and the external semantics (ontology), and vice-versa;
- The Ontology Mapping Specification process is typically very ambiguous, thus it can potentially profit from the social characterisation and social trust relationships provided by SN-i. This process is understood as a negotiation process, in which B and S try achieving a consensus about the ontology mapping. The SN-i agent participates in this process as an information provider to the OM-i in order to disambiguate the ontology mapping achieved through automatic mechanisms and protocols. A possible approach for this negotiation can be found in (Silva, Maio & Rocha, 2005);
- The Ontology Mapping Execution process is very systemic (in accordance to the ontology mapping specification document). Yet, the messages' data may be inconsistent in respect to the B's and S's data repository. In such cases, social knowledge is often required in order to decide/correct the consistency of the data. Through the use of social relationships, SN-i is a facilitator of this process.

ALTERNATIVES

Some approaches to agent-based applications for competitive electronic markets are more targeted or limited than our proposal: some of them not address a multi-issue negotiation type; do not consider behaviour dependent dynamic strategies, or expected future reactions. Others, although considering behaviour dependent dynamic strategies, frequently assume that agents have complete information about market, such as the distribution of buyer preferences or its competitor's prices like (Dasgupta & Das, 2000) and (Sim & Choi, 2003), and, in general, all of them assume that actors be aware of understand each other. Nevertheless, we can find approaches where the semantic problems are been considered.

For example, in (Malucelli, Rocha & Oliveira, 2004) ontology-based services are proposed to be integrated in the ForEV architecture in order to help in the Virtual Enterprise formation process (B2B). ForEV is an appropriate computing platform that includes and combines a multi-issue negotiation method in the context of Multi-Agent Systems, which makes the platform more open, enabling the establishment of the negotiation process between agents with different ontologies although representing the same domain of knowledge. They propose an ontology-based services Agent which is responsible for providing the ontology-based services. However we are interested in studying Multi-agent systems for B2C domain where other stages, as advocated by the CBB model, need to be contemplated in order to represent real situations. We are interested in studying how the identification stage of the CBB model can be supported by using ontologies to construct the most accurate model of the consumer's needs. Moreover, at the product brokering, buyer coalition formation, merchant brokering and negotiation stages, the ontology mapping process will provide the integration of the seller and consumer's models and guarantee the agent's heterogeneity. On the other hand, they don't explore the repository of relationships provided by emergent social networks, which can carry out the establishment of more accurate trust relationships between businesses and customers, as well as providing a better alignment (mapping) between their models.

In (Paolucci, Sycara, Nishimura & Srinivasan, 2003) authors present a capabilities matchmaker for applications in the Web, wrapped by Web Services. DAML-S is an ontology of capabilities that is instantiated for describing the capabilities of Web Services, which are then matched against other Web Services' capabilities. Thus a semantic matchmaking approach is adopted, ahead of the syntactic description approach commonly adopted. A very important limitation of the approach is the lack of a decision-making mechanism. In fact, as stated by the authors, "DAML-S requires applications that look more like intelligent software agents than traditional e-commerce applications".

Instead, the approach proposed in this chapter suggests the adoption of an orthogonal information and trust and social relationship service, capable of supporting the overall e-commerce processes, especially the decision-making and disambiguation processes.

A similar concept is adopted by the on-going myOntology project (http://www.myontology.org), in which the ontologies are perceived as socially evolving descriptive artefacts of a domain of discourse, namely that of e-commerce. This project aims to create infrastructures capable of capturing the social interactions in developing/evolving the ontologies, and exploit such information "to improve the expressiveness and disambiguity of informal concept definitions in an ontology".

Therefore, this project is complementary to the approach we propose, in the sense that it is focused on capturing, populating and systematizing the repository with the ontology changes carried by the social groups. The approach suggested in this chapter will profit form this technology as a social information and Web-of-trust source of information. It is up to the SN-i to conveniently exploit such information in e-commerce scenarios.

COST AND BENEFITS

In an efficient agent-mediated electronic market it is necessary to have common standards: an interaction protocol to achieve deals; a language for describing the messages' content; and ontology for describing the domain's knowledge.

The interaction protocol is usually announced at the marketplace and composed of a set of interaction phases. The language for describing the messages' content is usually provided by the communication platform used to develop the e-commerce application. Platforms for distributed agent's communication are also available, however, an ontology for describing the domain's knowledge needs to be incorporated and represent the best answer to the demand for intelligent systems that operate closer to the human conceptual level.

With regard to ontologies, many studies are being done but, currently, there is neither a standard ontology language nor a standard ontology knowledge representation. This lack of standardization, which hampers communication and collaboration between agents, is known as the interoperability problem. However, *ontologies per se* are not able to overcome information interoperability incompatibilities and it is hardly conceivable that a single ontology can be applied to all kinds of domains and applications. Information integration mechanisms are necessary in order to identify, represent and apply the diverse relationships between concepts and relations of two or more ontologies. Ontology Mapping is one of the most successful information integration paradigms used in the Internet and in particular in the Semantic Web. The use of a common ontology guarantees the consistency and the compatibility of the information present in the system.

In this work, the different actors involved in the marketplace are able to independently describe their universe of discourse, while the market is responsible for providing a technological framework that promotes the semantic integration between parties through the use of ontology mapping.

On the other hand, we propose an approach where the agents are free to accept or reject the mapping done by the marketplace. With this approach we can test several scenarios and explore a valid future agent-based platform for B2C. Additionally, through the integration information process carried out in the different stages, the searching space is enlarged, promoting the access to goods/services otherwise inaccessible.

Nevertheless, this solution has some drawbacks related to development and deployment. The development problems are specially related with the heterogeneity of the main technology requirements. The deployment issues are related with the configuration of the agent according to the user's constraints and strategic behaviours.

RISK ASSESSMENT

During this chapter, several assumptions were considered in order to support the proposed system. In particular, it is assumed that the social network paradigm will continue growing and that processing mechanisms will be provided. In particular it has been assumed that:

- The social participation in the Web will continue growing, namely tagging, social bookmarking and collaborative activism;
- The capabilities of the social network infrastructures will increase, providing and promoting services exploiting the information brought online by each individual;
- The relation (dependency) between Web-Of-Trust systems and Social Networks (based on FOAF or other representation mechanism) will tighten. This relation will be of fundamental importance in the effective development of the proposed infrastructure since it will provide the identification and

trust infrastructure between communities and systems.

- The social network concept will evolve in order to encompass some explicit semantics, turning into semantic social networks. More than an enabler, such evolution would facilitate the adoption of the proposed approach.

According to what has been stated, the proposed approach has several internal strengths and weaknesses.

Strengths:

- The CBB reference model is widely recognized as a correct interaction model in B2C.
- The proposed approach adopts concepts and behaviours not supported by traditional agent-based approaches.
- Permeation of ideas, domain modelling and content characterization between individuals and communities leads to socially supported decisions and disambiguation.

Weaknesses:

- Intrinsic semantic ambiguity of the proposed approach, which might lead to users having difficulty in accepting the decisions recommended by the system.
- Novelty of the suggested model, which might lead to poor results which are not fully geared and tweaked.

At the same time, the proposed approach profits and suffers from the technological, social and economic context.

Opportunities:

- Limitations of the user-driven portal-based and of the traditional agent-based B2C.
- Social network relationships, giving rise to communities of interests with some degree of mutual trust.
- SNA metrics and statistics, enabling the characterization of (implicit) communities, and hence promoting business activities according to target community.
- Social network engagement, promoting the cooperation between individuals, thus facilitating technological solutions, such as information integration and decision support.

Threats:

- Maturity of the Social Networks and related technologies.
- Lack of the supposed social network services.
- Lack of social network services accessibilities for software agents (e.g. API, Web Services).

FUTURE TRENDS

One of the largest problems this approach faces is related to the access and processing of social relationships. Despite the fact that the social networks and social network analysis are well established concepts, their implementation in the scope of the Internet started a couple of years only. As a consequence, some of the available services supporting online social communities (e.g. LinkedIn, MySpace, FaceBook) are now facing relevant problems, such as duplication of registers inside and across services, abandoned registers, ghost (virtual) registers. Instead, the evolution seems to follow the specialization trend (e.g. one service is used to create music relationships, another one is used for sports relationships) and respecting the age of user (i.e. one service is mostly used by young people, while another is used by middle age people). Additionally, organizations are now creating their own business-oriented social networks, either for employers or customers. Social networks are spreading on the Web, which will require an immense effort of integration. Our approach would profit from this characterization as it will be possible to better characterize the customer needs in respect to buyers and other customers.

We need to develop our approach and test several scenarios in order to obtain and explore new market information, which will be used to feed agent's knowledge-bases and the social networks repositories.

CONCLUSION

The meaningful interaction between distributed, heterogeneous computing entities (e.g. software agents), in order to be both syntactic and semantically compatible, needs to follow appropriate standards well understood by all participants. Some standards are being developed with regard to ontologies specially the Ontology Web Language (i.e. OWL) in the context of Word Wide Web Consortium.

Several problems involved in the overcoming of syntactic and semantic heterogeneity are difficult to be solved, at least nowadays. However, some efforts have been made in order to find possible ways to resolve parts of this complex problem.

A big challenge for communicating software agents is to resolve the problem of interoperability. Through the use of a common ontology it is possible to have a consistent and compatible communication. However, we maintain that each different actor involved in the marketplace must be able to independently describe their universe of discourse, while the market has the responsibility of providing a technological framework that promotes the semantic integration between parties through the use of ontology mapping. In addition, we think that the solution to overcome theses problems has to take into consideration the technological support already existent, namely a well-proven e-commerce platform, where agents with strategic behaviour represent consumers and suppliers.

This chapter has proposed the use of agents and Multi-Agents Technology as a platform for B2C. We propose an agent-based electronic market with an ontology-based information integration approach, exploiting the ontology mapping paradigm, by aligning consumer needs and the market capacities, in a semi-automatic mode, improved by the application and exploitation of the trust relationships captured by the social networks. Additionally we explore the repository of relationships provided by emergent social networks, which can carry out the establishment of more accurate trust relationships between businesses and customers, as well as providing a better alignment (mapping) between their models. Social networks form the basic infrastructure to encompass trust in many internet based activities, including B2C transactions and information integration.

REFERENCES

Aberer, K., Datta, A., & Hauswirth, M. (2005). A decentralized public key infrastructure for customer-to-customer e-commerce. *International Journal of Business Process Integration and Management*, 1, 26-33.

Dasgupta, P., & Das, R. (2000). Dynamic Service Pricing for Brokers in a Multi-Agent Economy. *Proceedings of the Third International Conference for Multi-Agent Systems* (ICMAS), pp. 375-76.

Fatima, S., Wooldridge, M., & Jennings, N. (2004). An agenda-based framework for multi-issue negotiation. *Artificial Intelligence*, 152(1), 1-45.

HarmoNet (2008). HarmoNET - the Harmonisation Network for the Exchange of Travel and Tourism Information. Retrieved January 11, 2008, from the World Wide Web: http://www.etourism-austria.at/harmonet.

Hepp, M. (2007). Possible Ontologies: How Reality Constrains the Development of Relevant Ontologies. *IEEE Internet Computing*, 11(7), 96-102.

Huhns, M. N., & Singh, M. P. (1997). *Readings in Agents*. San Francisco, CA: Morgan Kaufmann Publishers.

Maedche, A., Motik, B., Silva, N., & Volz, R. (2002). MAFRA-A MApping FRAmework for Distributed Ontologies. *Proceedings of the 13th International Conference on Knowledge Engineering and Knowledge Management,* LNCS, 2473, 235-250.

Malucelli, A., Rocha, A., & Oliveira, E.. (2004). B2B Transactions enhanced with ontology-based services. *Proceeding of the 1st International Conference on E-business and Telecommunication Networks*. Setúbal, Portugal.

Obrst, L., Liu, H. & Wray, R. (2003). Ontologies for Corporate Web Applications. *AI Magazine*, 24(3), 49-62.

Osborne, M. J., & Rubinstein, A. (1994). *A Course in Game Theory*. Cambridge, MA: MIT Press.

Paolucci, M., Sycara, K., Nishimura, T., & Srinivasan, N. (2003). Toward a Semantic Web e-commerce. *Proceedings of the 6th International Conference on Business Information Systems*. Colorado Springs (CO), USA.

Pinto, H., Gómez-Pérez, A., & Martins, J. P. (1999). Some issues on ontology integration. *Proceedings of the Workshop on Ontology and Problem-Solving Methods: Lesson learned and Future Trends at IJCAI'99*, 18, 7.1-7.11.

Runyon, K., & Stewart, D. (1987). *Consumer Behavior* (3rd ed.). Merrill Publishing Company.

Silva, N., Maio, P., & Rocha J. (2005). An approach to ontology mapping negotiation. *Proceedings of the Third International Conference on Knowledge Capture Workshop on Integrating Ontologies*. Banff, Canada.

Sim, K. M., & Choi, C. Y. (2003). Agents that React to Changing Market Situations. *IEEE Transactions on Systems, Man and Cybernetics*, Part B, 33(2), 188-201.

Siorpaes, K., & Hepp, M. (2007). myOntology: The Marriage of Ontology Engineering and Collective Intelligence. *Proceedings of the ESWC 2007 Workshop "Bridging the Gap between Semantic Web and Web 2.0"*. Innsbruck, Austria.

Ströbel, M. (2001). Communication Design for Electronic Negotiations on the Basis of XML Schema. *Proceedings of the Ten'th International Conference on World Wide Web*. Hong-Kong, pp. 9-20.

Studer, R., Benjamins, R., & Fensel, D. (1998). Knowledge Engineering: Principles and Methods. *Data & Knowledge Engineering*, 25(1), 161-197.

Tsvetovat, M., & Sycara, K. (2000). Customer Coalitions in the Electronic Marketplace. *Proceedings of the Fourth International Conference on Autonomous Agents*, pp. 263-264.

Van Damme, C., Hepp, M., & Siorpaes, K. (2007). FolksOntology: An Integrated Approach for Turning Folksonomies into Ontologies. *Proceedings of the ESWC 2007 Workshop "Bridging the Gap between Semantic Web and Web 2.0"*. Innsbruck, Austria.

Viamonte, M.J. (2004). *Mercados Electrónicos Baseados em Agentes – Uma Abordagem com Estratégias Dinâmicas e Orientada ao Conhecimento*. Doctoral dissertation, University os Trás-os-Montes e Alto Douro, Portugal.

Viamonte, M.J., Ramos, C., Rodrigues, F., & Cardoso, J.C. (2006). ISEM: A Multi-Agent Simulator For Testing Agent Market Strategies. *IEEE Transactions on Systems, Man and Cybernetics – Part C: Special Issue on Game-theoretic Analysis and Stochastic Simulation of Negotiation Agents*, 36(1), 107-113.

Yamamoto, J., & Sycara, K. (2001). A Stable and Efficient Buyer Coalition Formation Scheme for E-Marketplaces. *Proceedings of the Fifth International Conference on Autonomous Agents*, pp. 237-288.

Chapter IX
Semantic Web for Media Convergence:
A Newspaper Case

Ferran Perdrix
Universitat de Lleida, Spain & Diari Segre Media Group, Spain

Juan Manuel Gimeno
Universitat de Lleida, Spain

Rosa Gil
Universitat de Lleida, Spain

Marta Oliva
Universitat de Lleida, Spain

Roberto García
Universitat de Lleida, Spain

ABSTRACT

Newspapers in the digitalisation and Internet era are evolving from mono-channel and static communication mediums to highly dynamic and multi-channel ones, where the different channels converge into a unified news editorial office. Advanced computerised support is needed in order to cope with the requirements arising from convergent multimedia news management, production and delivery. Such advanced services require machines to be aware of a greater part of the underlying semantics. Ontologies are a clear candidate to put this semantics into play, and Semantic Web technologies the best choice for Web-wide information integration. However, newspapers have made great investments in their current news management systems so a smooth transition is required in order to reduce implementation costs. Our proposal is to build an ontological framework based on existing journalism and multimedia standards and to translate existing metadata to the Semantic Web. Once in a semantic space, data integration and news management and retrieval are facilitated enormously. For instance, Semantic Web tools are being developed in the context of a media house that are capable of dealing with the different kinds of media managed in the media house in an integrated and transparent way.

CURRENT SITUATION

Web news publishing is evolving fast, as the majority of Internet services, and nowadays this service is trying to adapt information to a way that best fits users' interests in order to increase its use. With that, newspapers are expecting to profit more from their news sites. In parallel, many of the newspaper companies are changing into news media houses. They own radio stations and video production companies that produce content unsupported by traditional newspapers, but that is delivered by Web newspapers or new mobile services. Initially, Web news was a mere reproduction of those in the printed edition. Nowadays, they are constantly updated and provide new services for those users interested on reaching this information as soon as possible and enjoying new ways of interaction with them (Eriksen & Ihlström, 2000; Lundberg, 2002; Ihlström, Lundberg, & Perdrix, 2003).

Consequently, news industry communication model is changing from the traditional one shown on the left of Figure 1 to the one shown in the right. In the former, each channel is considered separately (press, TV, radio, Internet, mobile phones…) and implies his way creating his own message, transmitting over this channel and using his own interface in order to show the message to the receivers. On the other hand, the latter is based on an information convergence flux. In this model, transmitters make information in collaboration with other transmitters and produce messages that include as media as it is necessary (video, text, audio, images…). Finally, receivers choose the channel that best fits their needs in order to get access to messages.

The previous situation is the one faced in the context of the Diari Segre Media Group[1], which is a journalism holding that in the last years has been facing this convergence trend. This holding started 25 years ago with a newspaper edition. Today produces three press editions in two languages, three radio stations, six television regional channels and several Internet Websites. Nowadays, all the editorial staff is applying the convergence of information flux approach during news generation and management. Therefore, they are required to be versatile journalists because they cannot be specialized in any concrete media. They must deal with video, image and text edition. Moreover, they must write in different ways, for instance for press news or for radio or TV voiceover.

On the other hand, the Diari Segre archive system is changing to a new repository build from the combination of text, images, video and audio files. In this sense, archive management is becoming a big issue and it requires deep improvements in terms of content search, relations among news (e.g. historical relations among news items) or information retrieval interfaces. The archive system must be a very productive and comprehensive tool in order to assist journalists while they create new content. This business case details how Semantic Web technologies are being explored in the context of the Diari Segre Media Group in order to face this new challenges.

In general, it has been observed that media houses must adapt to the requirements imposed by this new model. First of all, there are changes in how they reach consumers. News are build up from a combination of different content types (video, audio, the traditional text plus images, etc.) and are delivered to users through different channels and adapted to many kinds of devices (PC, PDA, smart phones, etc.). Therefore, formats must be selected and adapted according to the device and connection the user is using. These operations include transcoding of formats, resizing of images or recoding for higher levels of compression. Moreover, multi-channel distribution must take into account that for each channel one must define its own content, aesthetic and interaction model. These characteristics define what an interactive channel is (McDonald, 2004).

However, changes are not just restricted to the relation with consumers. Digital media eliminates

Figure 1. Traditional news information flux (left) and the new trend of convergent news flux (right)

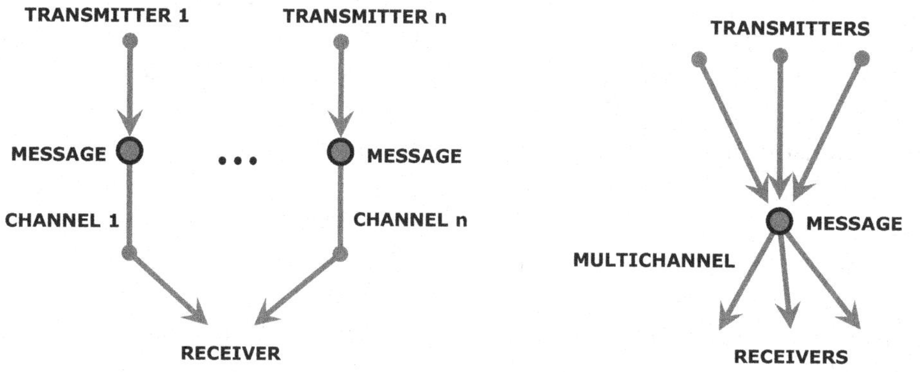

many time and space restrictions and changes editorial team routines. Moreover, all different media converge into a unified news object that is produced by interdisciplinary teams. Consequently, more efficient and effective means for news management are needed in order to facilitate coordination and production of these multimedia assets.

The news industry is currently using content management solutions for these means, but the additional requirements of a convergent editorial office stress the need for advanced knowledge management and information retrieval. Currently, there are specific standardisation efforts in the journalism domain, together with more generic ones in the multimedia domain, which carry some uniformity to the newspaper content management systems. However, as it is introduced in the following subsections, they just provide data structures and schemas that facilitate systems interoperability. They do not facilitate knowledge management and information retrieval tasks. These tasks are currently carried out mainly by the documentation department, who is in charge of the news archival process using legacy tools.

Journalism Metadata

One of the main standardization frameworks in the journalism domain is the International Press Telecommunications Council[2], an international consortium of news agencies, editors and newspapers distributors. IPTC has developed standards like the Information Interchange Model[3], NewsCodes[4] (formerly the Subject Reference System), the News Industry Text Format[5] or NewsML[6].

Currently, almost all of them have evolved towards XML-based standards to represent and manage news along their whole lifecycle, including their creation, exchange and consumption. For instance, NewsML is used to represent news as multimedia packages and NITF deals with document structure, i.e. paragraphs, headlines, etc. On the other hand, the Subject Reference System (SRS), now part of IPTC NewsCodes, is a subject classification hierarchy with three levels and seventeen categories in its first level.

Moreover, a new family of these journalism standards has been just proposed, expanding the range of available metadata. The new suite, known as the IPTC G2, is actually a series of specifications and XML components that can be shared among all IPTC G2 components for maximum efficiency.

IPTC G2 Standards make possible the integration of any news item with text, photos, graphics, video or other media. The News Architecture model (NAR) is used in order to package any combination of these items. Moreover, it makes stronger use of IPTC's robust metadata taxonomy suite, which is based on NewsCodes, and better interacts with other IPTC-G2 standards.

This standard contains hooks for managing news items, and its flexibility allows news providers to choose whether to support all of the IPTC G2-standards XML tags or a compact subset. It's the cost-effective way of managing news, whether for a Web site, news aggregator, newspaper, radio or television station.

Multimedia Metadata

All the previous initiatives are centred on the journalism specific aspects of a semantic newspaper. However, as has been pointed out, newspapers are evolving towards the digital multimedia domain. Therefore, they stress more and more their multimedia management requirements.

In the multimedia metadata domain, as it is extensively shown in the literature (Hunter, 2003; Einhoff, Casademont, Perdrix, & Noll, 2005), the MPEG-7 (Salembier, & Smith, 2002) standard constitutes the greatest effort for multimedia description. It is divided into four main components: the Description Definition Language (DDL, the basic building blocks for the MPEG-7 metadata language), Audio (the descriptive elements for audio), Visual (those for video) and the Multimedia Description Schemes (MDS, the descriptors for capturing the semantic aspects of multimedia contents, e.g. places, actors, objects, events, etc.).

In addition to MPEG-7, which concentrates on content description, MPEG-21 defines an open framework for multimedia delivery and consumption. This standard must be also considered because it focuses on the content management issues for full delivery and consumption chain, from content creators' applications to end-users' players. The different MPEG-21 parts deal with diverse aspects like Digital Rights Management or Digital Items, the definition of a fundamental content unit for distribution and transaction very useful for convergent media management.

Problem Statement

As has been pointed out in the description of the current situation in many media houses, archivists classify news using a proprietary hierarchical thesaurus while journalists search this information when they need to inform themselves on subjects, histories or events. This search can be performed in extreme situations, e.g., lack of time, or lack of knowledge in relation to the archive system. This is reflected in the way journalists formulate their queries. The gap between archivists' and journalists' mental models implies that more flexible content categorization and search systems are needed. This trend is even bigger when we consider cross-media content production and coordination in order to get multimedia and multichannel news.

Therefore, in order to take advantage of the possibilities offered by the digital medium to exploit a newspaper archive, the aspects that can be improved include:

- Keyword search falling short in expressive power
- Weak interrelation between archive items: users may need to combine several indirect queries manually before they can get answers to complex queries
- Lack of a commonly adopted standard representation for sharing archive news across newspapers
- Lack of internal consensus for content description terminology among reporters and archivists
- Lack of involvement of journalist in the archiving process

These shortcomings are difficult to deal with if the existing standards are used as provided. The main standards that have been presented, both in the journalism and multimedia domains, are based on XML and specified by XML Schemas. The more significant case is the MPEG-7 one. It is based on a set of XML Schemas that define 1182 elements, 417 attributes and 377 complex types. NewsML and NITF are also very big standards, they define more than 100 elements, and the NewsCodes hierarchy of subjects defines more than one thousand different subjects.

The complexity of these standards makes it very difficult to manage them. Moreover, the use of XML technologies implies that a great part of the semantics remains implicit. Therefore, each time an application is developed, semantics must be extracted from the standard and re-implemented.

For instance, if we use XQuery in order to retrieve MPEG-7 SegmentType descriptions from an XML database, we must be aware of the hierarchy of segment types and implement an XQuery that has to cover any kind of multimedia segment, i.e. VideoSegmentType, AnalyticClipType, AudiSegmentType, etc.

If the intended interpretation of the segments structure was available for computerised means, semantic queries would benefit from the corresponding formal semantics. Consequently, a semantic query for SegmentType will retrieve all subclasses without requiring additional developing efforts. This is not possible with XML tools because, although XML Schemas capture some semantics of the domain they model, XML tools are based on syntax. The captured semantics remain implicit from the XML processing tools point of view. Therefore, when an XQuery searches for a SegmentType, the XQuery processor has no way to know that there are many other kinds of segment types that can appear in its place, i.e. they are more concrete kinds of segments.

The previous example only illustrates one kind of difficulty derived from the use of just syntax-aware tools. Another example is that the lack of explicit semantics makes MPEG-7 very difficult to extend in an independent way, i.e. third party extensions. The same applies for MPEG-21 or the journalism standards. Moreover, standards from both worlds share many concepts so it would be possible, and easier, to integrate them once their implicit semantics are available from a computer processing point of view.

PROPOSED SOLUTION

In this chapter, we explore Semantic Web technologies (Berners-Lee, Hendler & Lassila, 2001) as a way to overcome many of the challenges of digital and convergent media houses. The size and complexity of the stored information, and the time limitations for cataloguing, describing and ordering the incoming information, make newspaper archives a relatively disorganised and difficult to manage corpus. In this sense, they share many of the characteristics and problems of the World Wide Web, and therefore the solutions proposed in the Semantic Web vision are pertinent here.

In order to implement more advanced newspaper content management applications, they should be more informed about the content they are managing. They are not just files with some weak interrelations. There is a lot of knowledge embedded in these pieces of content and in their interrelationships. In order to make computers aware of it, their implicit semantics must be formalised, for instance using ontologies. Semantic Web technologies facilitate the building blocks for Web ontologies, which add the facilities for Web-wide ontology sharing and integration. The latter is a key feature for convergent and globalised media houses.

In order to build an ontological infrastructure for the Semantic Newspaper, it is important to consider the state of the art of the metadata initiatives in the journalism domain, which have been introduced in the current situation description section. Additionally, digital newspapers have stressed the requirements of multimedia management. Digital news is managed as multimedia packages that integrate text, images, video, audio, etc. Therefore, it is also important to consider the current situation in the more general multimedia metadata domain.

We have undertaken the application of the Semantic Web proposals to the newspapers world by following a smooth transition strategy (Haustein, & Pleumann, 2002). This strategy advises about keeping compatibility, at least initially, with current newspaper content management systems and journalism and multimedia standards. Consequently, we have rooted our proposed approach on existing journalism and multimedia standards and provide a methodology to move them, together with existing data, to the Semantic Web domain.

Objectives

The objective is then to design a Semantic Web-based platform that is an extension of previously working systems in mass media companies, particularly in the context of the Diari Segre Media Group. The manual creation of semantic instances for news items, at a regular daily pace, is indeed a feasible goal as long as this process is integrated into existing systems and it just causes a slightly greater work load while producing observable benefits. Consequently, the introduction of new semantic documentation tools requires a careful work of analysis, design, testing and balancing of the additional burden that such tools may impose on archivists, journalists or readers.

In order to produce a semantic platform that seamlessly integrates into newspapers content management systems, the first objective is to develop an ontological framework based on existing standards. Once this ontological infrastructure based on existing journalism and multimedia standards is developed, the objective is then to put it into practice in the context of an architecture based on Semantic Web tools for semantic integration, querying and reasoning. However, all this effort must end up reaching users through applications that offer to them the extra benefits of semantic metadata while avoiding them the burden of dealing with the underlying extra complexity.

Overview

The proposed solution is detailed in Section 3. First of all, Section 3.1 presents the methodology that produces an ontological framework based on existing standards. This methodology is based on two mappings. The first one from XML Schema, the language used in most of the considered standards, to ontologies based on the Semantic Web language Web Ontology Language (OWL) (McGuinness & Harmelen, 2004). The second one is based on the previous one and makes it possible to map from XML metadata, based on XML Schemas previously mapped to OWL, to Semantic Web metadata, based on the Resource Description Framework (RDF) (Becket, 2004).

The ontologies produced using this methodology constitute the foundation on top of which an architecture based on Semantic Web technologies is built. This architecture, described in Section 3.2, takes profit from the semantics formalised by these ontologies and loads Semantic Web metadata based on them in order to offer services like semantic integration, semantics queries or logic reasoning. These services are used in order to build applications that facilitate managing heterogeneous media repositories and the underlying knowledge. One example of such an application is given in Section 3.3.

The described application builds on top of a text-to-speech and a semantic annotation tool. The generated annotations are based on existing standards ontologies and loaded into the proposed semantic architecture, which makes it possible to manage audio, audiovisual and text content in an integrated way. However, the key point here is to offer all the semantic services to users in a usable and accessible way. To this end, the application is based on a user interface that provides an object-action interaction paradigm best suited for heterogeneous information spaces. The interface does not solely facilitate content management, it also allows browsing the underlying domain knowledge, formalised using specialised ontologies, and constitutes a useful tool in media houses in order to facilitate news tracking and producing new content.

SOLUTION DETAILS

This section provides a detailed description of the proposed solution. The different modules are described in the following subsections starting from the methodology used in order to benefit from existing standards and produce ontologies that formalise them. These ontologies make possible to develop an architecture that takes profit from their semantics in order to offer advanced services like semantic integration, querying and reasoning. Finally, these services are used in order to build an application that makes the benefits emerging from semantic metadata and ontologies available for end users.

XML Semantics Reuse Methodology

In order to put into practice the smooth transition strategy, the first step has been to reuse existing standards in the journalism and multimedia fields, which have been for long very active in standardization.

However, as has been highlighted in current situation analysis, all the more recent standards are based on XML and lack formal semantics that facilitate applying a Semantic Web approach. Therefore, in order to facilitate the transition from current standards and applications to the semantic world, we have applied the XML Semantics Reuse methodology (García, 2006).

The main caveat of semantic multimedia metadata is that it is sparse and expensive to produce. If we want to increase the availability of semantic multimedia metadata and, in general, of semantic metadata, the more direct solution is to benefit from the great amount of metadata that has been already produced using XML, which is extensively used by many newspaper content management systems.

There are many attempts to move metadata from the XML domain to the Semantic Web. Some of them just model the XML tree using the RDF primitives (Klein, 2002). Others concentrate on modelling the knowledge implicit in XML languages definitions, i.e. DTDs or the XML Schemas, using Web ontology languages (Amann, Beer, Fundulak, & Scholl, 2002; Cruz, Xiao, & Hsu, 2004). Finally, there are attempts to encode XML semantics integrating RDF into XML documents (Lakshmanan, & Sadri, 2003; Patel-Schneider, & Simeon, 2002).

However, none of them facilitates an extensive transfer of XML metadata to the Semantic Web in a general and transparent way. Their main problem is that the XML Schema implicit semantics are not made explicit when XML metadata instantiating this schemas is mapped. Therefore, they do not benefit from the XML semantics and produce RDF metadata almost as semantics-blind as the original XML. Or, on the other hand, they capture these semantics but they use additional ad-hoc semantic constructs that produce less transparent metadata.

Therefore, we propose the XML Semantics Reuse methodology, which is implemented by the ReDeFer project[7] as an XML Schema to OWL plus and XML to RDF mapping tool. This methodology combines an XML Schema to Web ontology mapping, called XSD2OWL, with a transparent mapping from XML to RDF, XML2RDF. The ontologies generated by XSD2OWL are used during the XML to RDF step in order to generate semantic metadata that makes XML Schema semantics explicit. Both steps are detailed next.

XSD2OWL Mapping

The XML Schema to OWL mapping is responsible for capturing the schema implicit semantics. This semantics are determined by the combination of XML Schema constructs. The mapping is based on translating these constructs to the OWL ones that best capture their semantics. These translations are detailed in Table 1.

The XSD2OWL mapping is quite transparent and captures a great part XML Schema semantics. The same names used for XML constructs are used for OWL ones, although in the new namespace defined for the ontology. Therefore, XSD2OWL produces OWL ontologies that make explicit the semantics of the corresponding XML Schemas. The only caveats are the implicit order conveyed by xsd:sequence and the exclusivity of *xsd:choice*.

For the first problem, *owl:intersectionOf* does not retain its operands order, there is no clear solution that retains the great level of transparency that has been achieved. The use of RDF Lists might impose order but introduces ad-hoc constructs not present in the original metadata. Moreover, as has been demonstrated in practise, the element ordering does not contribute much from a semantic point of view. For the second problem, owl:unionOf is an inclusive union, the solution is to use the disjointness OWL construct, *owl:disjointWith*, between all union operands in order to make it exclusive.

To conclude, one important aspect is that the resulting OWL ontology may be OWL-Full depending on the input XML Schema. This is due to the fact that, in some cases, the XSD2OWL translator must employ *rdf:Property* for those xsd:elements that have both data type and object type ranges.

XML2RDF Mapping

Once all the metadata XML Schemas are available as mapped OWL ontologies, it is time to map the XML metadata that instantiates them. The intention is to produce RDF metadata as transparently as possible. Therefore, a structure-mapping approach has been selected (Klein, 2002). It is also possible to take a model-mapping approach (Tous, García, Rodríguez, & Delgado, 2005).

XML model-mapping is based on representing the XML information set using semantic tools. This approach is better when XML metadata is semantically exploited for concrete purposes.

Table 1. XSD2OWL mappings from XML Schema building blocks to OWL ones plus an explanation of why they are interpreted as equivalent modelling constructs

XML Schema	OWL	Explanation
element | attribute	rdf:Property owl:DatatypeProperty owl:ObjectProperty	Named relation between nodes or nodes and values
element@substitutionGroup	rdfs:subPropertyOf	Relation can appear in place of a more general one
element@type	rdfs:range	The relation range kind
complexType|group |attributeGroup	owl:Class	Relations and contextual restrictions package
complexType//element	owl:Restriction	Contextualised restriction of a relation
extension@base | restriction@base	rdfs:subClassOf	Package concretises the base package
@maxOccurs @minOccurs	owl:maxCardinality owl:minCardinality	Restrict the number of occurrences of a relation
sequence choice	owl:intersectionOf owl:unionOf	Combination of relations in a context

However, when the objective is semantic metadata that can be easily integrated, it is better to take a more transparent approach.

Transparency is achieved in structure-mapping models because they only try to represent the XML metadata structure, i.e. a tree, using RDF. The RDF model is based on the graph so it is easy to model a tree using it. Moreover, we do not need to worry about the semantics loose produced by structure-mapping. We have formalised the underlying semantics into the corresponding ontologies and we will attach them to RDF metadata using the instantiation relation *rdf:type*.

The structure-mapping is based on translating XML metadata instances to RDF ones that instantiate the corresponding constructs in OWL. The more basic translation is between relation instances, from *xsd:elements* and *xsd:attributes* to *rdf:Properties*. Concretely, *owl:ObjectProperties* for node to node relations and *owl:DatatypeProperties* for node to values relations.

However, in some cases, it would be necessary to use *rdf:Properties* for *xsd:elements* that have both data type and object type values. Values are kept during the translation as simple types and RDF blank nodes are introduced in the RDF model in order to serve as source and destination for properties. They will remain blank for the moment until they are enriched with semantic information.

The resulting RDF graph model contains all that we can obtain from the XML tree. It is already semantically enriched due to the *rdf:type* relation that connects each RDF properties to the *owl:ObjectProperty* or *owl:DatatypeProperty* it instantiates. It can be enriched further if the blank nodes are related to the *owl:Class* that defines the package of properties and associated restrictions they contain, i.e. the corresponding *xsd:complexType*. This semantic decoration of the graph is formalised using *rdf:type* relations from blank nodes to the corresponding OWL classes.

At this point we have obtained a semantics-enabled representation of the input metadata. The instantiation relations can now be used to apply OWL semantics to metadata. Therefore, the semantics derived from further enrichments of the ontologies, e.g. integration links between different ontologies or semantic rules, are automatically propagated to instance metadata due to inference.

However, before continuing to the next section, it is important to point out that these mappings have been validated in different ways. First, we have used OWL validators in order to check the resulting ontologies, not just the MPEG-7 Ontology but also many others (García, Gil, & Delgado, 2007; García, Gil, Gallego, & Delgado, 2005). Second, our MPEG-7 ontology has been compared to Hunter's (2001) and Tsinaraki's ones (2004).

Both ontologies, Hunter's and Tsinaraki's, provide a partial mapping of MPEG-7 to Web ontologies. The former concentrates on the kinds of content defined by MPEG-7 and the latter on two parts of MPEG-7, the Multimedia Description Schemes (MDS) and the Visual metadata structures. It has been tested that they constitute subsets of the ontology that we propose.

Finally, the XSD2OWL and XML2RDF mappings have been tested in conjunction. Testing XML instances have been mapped to RDF, guided by the corresponding OWL ontologies from the used XML Schemas, and then back to XML. Then, the original and derived XML instances have been compared using their canonical version in order to correct mapping problems.

Ontological Infrastructure

As a result of applying the XML Semantics Reuse methodology, we have obtained a set of ontologies that reuse the semantics of the underlying standards, as they are formalised through the corresponding XML Schemas. All the ontologies related to journalism standards, i.e. NewsCodes NITF and NewsML, are available from the Semantic Newspaper site[8]. This site also contains some of the ontologies for the MPEG-21 useful for news modelling as convergent multimedia units. The MPEG-7 Ontology is available from the MPEG-7 Ontology site[9]. These are the ontologies that are going to be used as the basis for the semantic newspaper info-structure:

- **NewsCodes subjects ontology:** An OWL ontology for the subjects' part of the IPTC NewsCodes. It is a simple taxonomy of subjects but it is implemented with OWL in order to facilitate the integration of the subjects' taxonomy in the global ontological framework.
- **NITF 3.3 ontology:** An OWL ontology that captures the semantics of the XML Schema specification of the NITF standard. It contains some classes and many properties dealing with document structure, i.e. paragraphs, subheadlines, etc., but also some metadata properties about copyright, authorship, issue dates, etc.
- **NewsML 1.2 ontology:** The OWL ontology resulting from mapping the NewsML 1.2 XML Schema. Basically, it includes a set of properties useful to define the news structure as a multimedia package, i.e. news envelope, components, items, etc.
- **MPEG-7 ontology:** The XSD2OWL mapping has been applied to the MPEG-7 XML Schemas producing an ontology that has 2372 classes and 975 properties, which are targeted towards describing multimedia at all detail levels, from content based descriptors to semantic ones.
- **MPEG-21 digital item ontologies:** A digital item (DI) is defined as the fundamental unit for distribution and transaction in MPEG-21.

System Architecture

Based on the previous XML world to Semantic Web domain mappings, we have built up a system architecture that facilitates journalism and multimedia metadata integration and retrieval. The architecture is sketched in Figure 2. The MPEG-7 OWL ontology, generated by XSD2OWL, constitutes the basic ontological framework for semantic multimedia metadata integration and appears at the centre of the architecture. In parallel, there are the journalism ontologies. The multimedia related concepts from the journalism ontologies are connected to the MPEG-7 ontology, which acts as an upper ontology for multimedia. Other ontologies and XML Schemas can also be easily incorporated using the XSD2OWL module.

Semantic metadata can be directly fed into the system together with XML metadata, which is made semantic using the XML2RDF module. For instance, XML MPEG-7 metadata has a great importance because it is commonly used for low-level visual and audio content descriptors automatically extracted from its underlying signals. This kind of metadata can be used as the basis for audio and video description and retrieval.

In addition to content-based metadata, there is context-based metadata. This kind of metadata higher level and it usually, in this context, related to journalism metadata. It is generated by the system users (journalist, photographers, cameramen, etc.). For instance, there are issue dates, news subjects, titles, authors, etc.

This kind of metadata can come directly from semantic sources but, usually, it is going to come from legacy XML sources based on the standards' XML Schemas. Therefore, in order to integrate them, they will pass through the XML2RDF component. This component, in conjunction with the ontologies previously mapped from the corresponding XML Schemas, generates the RDF metadata that can be then integrated in the common RDF framework.

This framework has the persistence support of a RDF store, where metadata and ontologies reside. Once all metadata has been put together, the semantic integration can take place, as shown in the next section.

Figure 2. News metadata integration and retrieval architecture

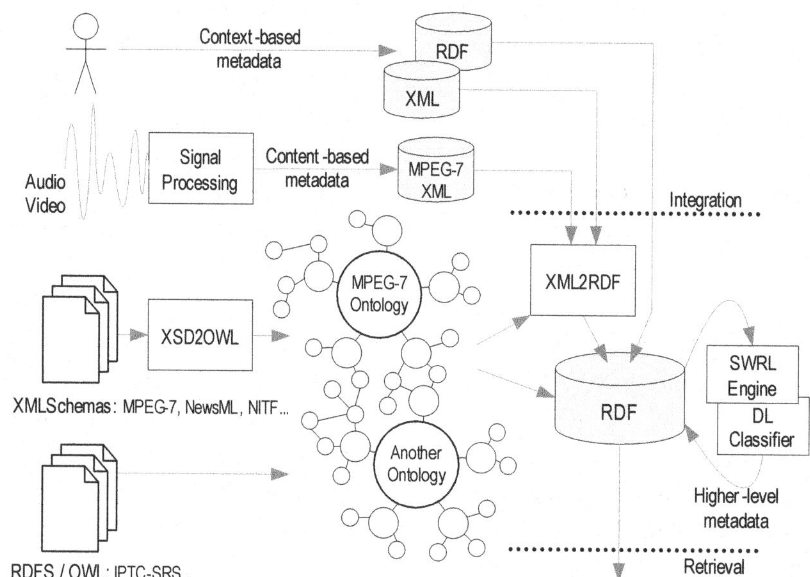

Semantic Integration Outline

As mentioned in the introduction, one of the main problems in nowadays media houses is that of heterogeneous data integration. Even within a single organization, data from disparate sources must be integrated. Our approach to solve this problem is based on Web ontologies and, as the focus is on multimedia and journalism metadata integration, our integration base are the MPEG-7, MPEG-21 and the journalism ontologies.

In order to benefit from the system architecture presented before, when semantic metadata based on different schemes has to be integrated, the XML Schemas are first mapped to OWL. Once this first step has been done, these schemas can be integrated into the ontological framework using OWL semantic relations for equivalence and inclusion: *subClassOf*, *subPropertyOf*, *equivalentClass*, *equivalentProperty*, *sameIndividualAs*, etc. These relations allows simple integration relations, for more complex integration steps that require changes in data structures it is possible to use Semantic Web rules (Horrocks, Patel-Schneider, Boley, Tabet, Grosof, & Dean, 2004).

These relationships capture the semantics of the data integration. Then, once metadata is incorporated into the system and semantically-decorated, the integration is automatically performed by applying inference. Table 2 shows some of these mappings, performed once all metadata has been moved to the semantic space.

First, there are four examples of semantic mappings among the NITF Ontology, the NewsML Ontology and the IPTC Subjects Ontology. The first mapping tells that all values for the *nitf:tobject.subject* property are from class *subj:Subject*. The second one that the property *nitf:tobject.subject.detail* is equivalent to *subj:explanation*. The third one that all *nitf:body* instances are also *newsml:DataContent* instances and the fourth one that all *newsml:Subject* are *subj:Subject*. Finally, there is also a mapping that is performed during the XML to RDF translation. It is necessary in order to recognise an implicit identifier, *nitf:tobject.subject.refnum* is mapped to rdf:ID in order to make this recognise this identifier in the context of NITF and make it explicit in the context of RDF.

Table 2. Journalism and multimedia metadata integration mapping examples

Semantic Mappings
∀ nitf:tobject.subject . subj:Subject
nitf:tobject.subject.detail ≡ subj:explanation
nitf:body ⊆ newsml:DataContent
newsml:Subject ≡ subj:Subject
XML2RDF Mappings
nitf:tobject.subject.refnum → rdf:ID

SEMANTIC MEDIA INTEGRATION FROM HUMAN SPEECH

This section introduces a tool, build on top of the ontological infrastructure described in the previous sections, geared towards a convergent and integrated news management in the context of a media house. As has been previously introduced, the diversification of content in media houses, who must deal in an integrated way with different modalities (text, image, graphics, video, audio, etc.), carries new management challenges. Semantic metadata and ontologies are a key facilitator in order to enable convergent and integrated media management.

In the news domain, news companies like the Diari Segre Media Group are turning into news media houses, owning radio stations and video production companies that produce content not supported by the print medium, but which can be delivered through Internet newspapers. Such new perspectives in the area of digital content call for a revision of mainstream search and retrieval technologies currently oriented to text and based on keywords. The main limitation of mainstream text IR systems is that their ability to represent meanings is based on counting word occurrences, regardless of the relation between words (Salton, & McGill, 1983). Most research beyond this limitation has remained in the scope of linguistic (Salton, & McGill, 1983) or statistic (Vorhees, 1994) information.

On the other end, IR is addressed in the Semantic Web field from a much more formal perspective (Castells, Fernández, & Vallet, 2007). In the Semantic Web vision, the search space consists of a totally formalized corpus, where all the information units are unambiguously typed, interrelated, and described by logic axioms in domain ontologies. Such tools enabled the development of semantic-based retrieval technologies that support search by meanings rather than keywords, providing users with more powerful retrieval capabilities to find their way through in increasingly massive search spaces.

Semantic Web based news annotation and retrieval has already been applied in the Diari Segre Media Group in the context of the Neptuno research project (Castells, Perdrix, Pulido, Rico, Benjamins, Contreras, & Lorés, 2004). However, this is a partial solution as it just deals with textual content. The objective of the tool described in this section is to show how these techniques can also be applied to content with embedded human-speech tracks. The final result is a tool based on Semantic Web technologies and methodologies that allows managing text and audiovisual content in an integrated and efficient way. Consequently, the integration of human speech processing technologies in the semantic-based approach extends the semantic retrieval capabilities to audio content. The research is being undertaken in the context of the S5T research project[10].

As shown in Figure 3, this tool is based on a human speech recognition process inspired by

Figure 3. Architecture for the Semantic Media Integration from Human Speech Tool

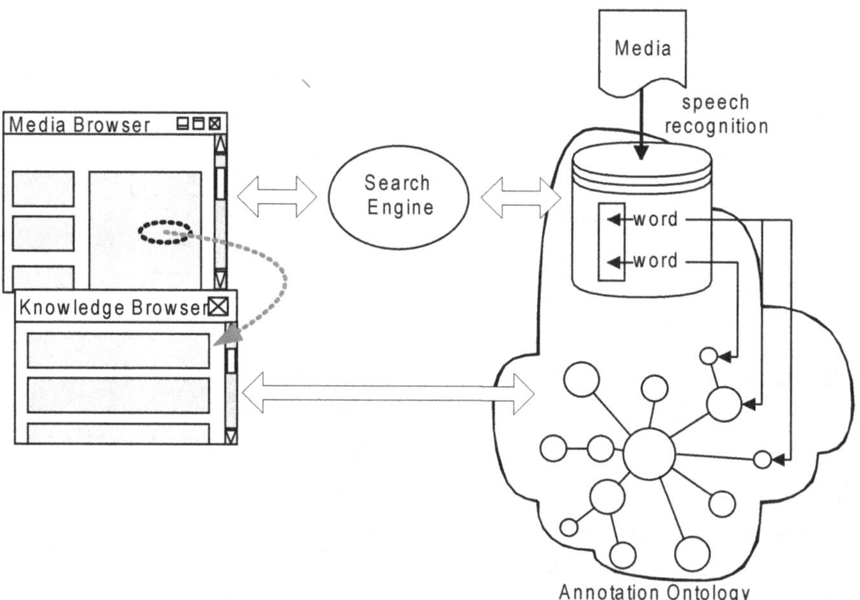

(Kim, Jung, & Chung, 2004) that generates the corresponding transcripts for the radio and television contents. From this preliminary process, it is possible benefit from the same semi-automatic annotation process in order to generate the semantic annotations for audio, audiovisual and textual content. Keywords detected during speech recognition are mapped to concepts in the ontologies describing the domain covered by audiovisual and textual content, for instance the politics domain for news talking about this subject. Specifically, when the keyword forms of a concept are uttered in a piece of speech, the content is annotated with that concept. Polysemic words and other ambiguities are treated by a set of heuristics. More details about the annotation and semantic query resolution processes are available from (Cuayahuitl, & Serridge, 2002).

Once audio and textual contents have been semantically annotated (Tejedor, García, Fernández, López, Perdrix, Macías, et al., 2007), it is possible to provide a unified set of interfaces, rooted on the semantic capabilities provided by the annotations. These interfaces, intended for journalists and archivist, are shown on the left of Figure 3. They exploit the semantic richness of the underlying ontologies upon which the search system is built. Semantic queries are resolved, using semantic annotations as has been previously described, and retrieve content items and pieces of these contents. News contents are packaged together using annotations based on the MPEG-21 and MPEG-7 ontologies, as it is described in Section 3.3.1. Content items are presented to the user through the Media Browser, detailed in Section 3.3.2, and the underlying semantic annotations and the ontologies used to generate these annotations can be browsed using the Knowledge Browser, described in Section 3.3.3.

Semantic News Packaging Using MPEG Ontologies

Actually, in an editorial office there are a lot of applications producing media in several formats. This is an issue that requires a common structure to facilitate management. The first step is to treat each unit of information, in this case each new, as a single object. Consequently, when searching something upon this structure, all related content is retrieved together.

Another interesting issue is that news can be linked to other news. This link between news allows the creation of information threads. A news composition metadata system has been developed using concepts from the MPEG-21 and MPEG-7 ontologies. It comprises three hierarchical levels as shown in Figure 4.

The lower level comprises content files, in whatever format they are. The mid level is formed by metadata descriptors (what, when, where, how, who is involved, author, etc.) for each file, mainly based on concepts from the MPEG-7 ontology generated using the methodology described in Section 3.1. They are called the Media Digital Items (Media DI).

These semantic descriptors are based on the MPEG-7 Ontology and facilitate automated management of the different kinds of content that build up a news item in a convergent media house. For instance, it is possible to generate semantic queries that benefit from the content hierarchy defined in MPEG-7 and formalised in the ontology. This way, it is possible to pose generic queries

Figure 4. Content DI structure

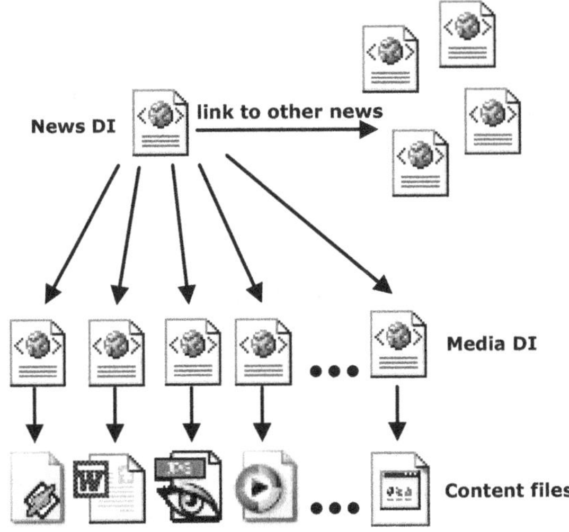

for any kind of segment (e.g. *AudioSegmentType*, *VideoSegmentType*...) because all of them are formalised as subclasses of *SegmentType* and the implicit semantics can be directly used by a semantic query engine.

Table 3 shows a piece of metadata that describes an audio segment of a Diari Segre Media Group news item used in the S5T project. This semantic metadata is generated from the corresponding XML MPEG-7 metadata using the XML to RDF mapping and takes profit from the MPEG-7 OWL ontology in order to make the MPEG-7 semantics explicit. Therefore, this kind of metadata can be processed using semantic queries independently from the concrete type of segment. Consequently, it is possible to develop applications that process in an integrated and convergent way the different kinds of contents that build up a new.

The top level in the hierarchy is based on descriptors that model news and put together all the different pieces of content that conform them. These objects are called News Digital Items (News DI). There is one News DI for each news item and all of them are based on MPEG-21 metadata. The part of the standard that defines digital items (DI) is used for that. DI is the fundamental unit defined in MPEG-21 for content distribution and transaction, very useful for convergent media management. As in the case of MPEG-7 metadata, RDF semantic metadata is generated from XML using the semantics made explicit by the MPEG-21 ontologies. This way, it is possible to implement generic processes also at the news level using semantic queries.

On top of the previous semantic descriptors at the media and news level, it is possible to develop an application for integrated and convergent news management in the media house. The application is based on two specialised interfaces described in the next subsections. They benefit from the ontological infrastructure detailed in this chapter, which is complemented with ontologies for the concrete news domain. However, the application remains independent from the concrete domain.

Media Browser

The Media Browser, shown in Figure 5, takes profit from the MPEG-21 metadata for news and MPEG-7 metadata for media in order to implement a generic browser for the different kinds of media that constitute a news item in a convergent newspaper. This interface allows navigating them and presents the retrieved pieces of content and the available RDF metadata describing them. These descriptions are based on a generic rendering of RDF data as interactive HTML for increased usability (García, & Gil, 2006).

The multimedia metadata is based on the Dublin Core schema for editorial metadata and IPTC News Codes for subjects. For content-based metadata, especially the content decomposition depending on the audio transcript, MPEG-7 metadata is used for media segmentation, as it was shown in Table 3. In addition to the editorial metadata and the segments decomposition, a specialized audiovisual view is presented. This view allows rendering the content, i.e. audio and video, and interacting with audiovisual content through a click-able version of the audio transcript.

Two kinds of interactions are possible from the transcript. First, it is possible to click any word in the transcript that has been indexed in order to perform a keyword-based query for all content in the database where that keyword appears. Second, the transcript is enriched with links to the ontology used for semantic annotation. Each word in the transcript whose meaning is represented by an ontology concept is linked to a description of that concept, which is shown by the Knowledge Browser detailed in the next section. The whole interaction is performed through the user Web browser using AJAX in order to improve the interactive capabilities of the interface.

For instance, the transcript includes the name of a politician that has been indexed and modelled in the ontology. Consequently, it can be clicked in order to get all the multimedia content where the name appears or, alternatively, to browse all the knowledge about that politician encoded in the corresponding domain ontology.

Table 3. MPEG-7 Ontology description for a audio segment generated from XML MPEG-7 metadata fragment

```
<?xml version="1.0"?>
<rdf:RDF
  xmlns:mpeg7="http://rhizomik.net/ontologies/2006/03/Mpeg7-2001.owl#">
  <mpeg7:AudioType rdf:about="http://rhizomik.net/audio/2007-01-13.mp3">
    <mpeg7:Audio>
      <mpeg7:AudioSegmentType>
        <mpeg7:MediaTime>
          <mpeg7:MediaTimeType>
            <mpeg7:MediaTimePoint
              rdf:datatype="&xsd;time">01:27.0</mpeg7:MediaTimePoint>
            <mpeg7:MediaDuration
              rdf:datatype="&xsd;time">P5S</mpeg7:MediaDuration>
          </mpeg7:MediaTimeType>
        </mpeg7:MediaTime>
      </mpeg7:AudioSegmentType>
    </mpeg7:Audio>
  </mpeg7:AudioType>
</rdf:RDF>
```

Figure 5. Media Browser interface presenting content metadata (left) and the annotated transcript (right)

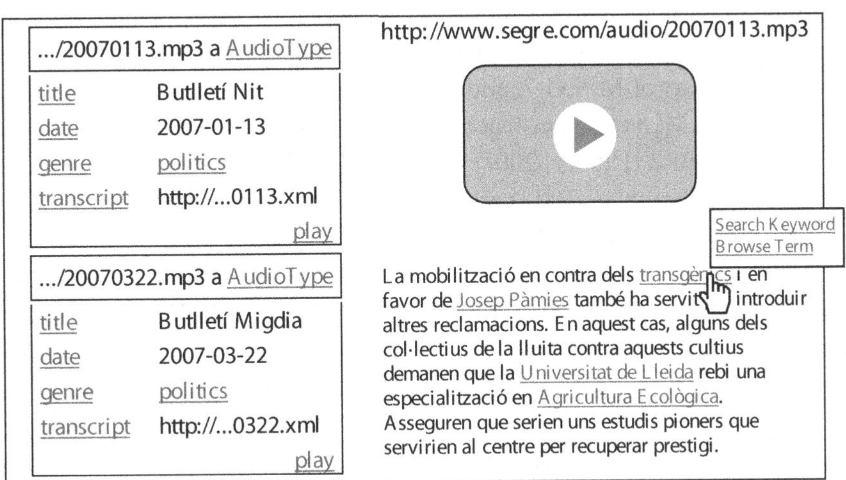

Knowledge Browser

This interface is used to allow the user browsing the knowledge structures employed to annotate content, i.e. the underlying ontologies. The same RDF data to interactive HTML rendering used in the Media Browser is used here. Consequently, following the politician example in the previous section, when the user looks for the available knowledge about that person and interactive view of the RDF data modelling him is shown. This way, the user can benefit from the modelling effort and, for instance, be aware of the politician party, that he is a member of the parliament, etc.

This interface constitutes a knowledge browser so the link to the politician party or the parliament can be followed and additional knowledge can be retrieved, for instance a list of all the members of the parliament. In addition to this recursive navigation of all the domain knowledge, at any browsing step, it is also possible to get all the multimedia content annotated using the concept currently being browsed. This step would carry the user back to the Media Browser.

Thanks to this dual browsing experience, the user can navigate through audiovisual content using the Media Browser and through the underlying semantic models using the Knowledge Browser in a complementary an inter-weaved way. Finally, as for the Media Browser, the Knowledge Browser is also implemented using AJAX so the whole interactive experience can be enjoyed using a Web browser.

ALTERNATIVES

There are other existing initiatives that try to move journalism and multimedia metadata to the Semantic Web world. In the journalism field, the Neptuno (Castells, Perdrix, Pulido, Rico, Benjamins, Contreras, et al., 2004) and NEWS (Fernández, Blázquez, Fisteus, Sánchez, Sintek, Bernardi, et al., 2006) projects can be highlighted. Both projects have developed ontologies based on existing standards (IPTC SRS, NITF or NewsML) but from an ad-hoc and limited point of view. Therefore, in order to smooth the transition from the previous legacy systems, more complex and complete mappings should be developed and maintained.

The same can be said for the existing attempts to produce semantic multimedia metadata. Chronologically, the first attempts to make MPEG-7 metadata semantics explicit where carried out, during the MPEG-7 standardisation process, by Jane Hunter (2001). The proposal used RDF to formalise a small part of MPEG-7, and later incorporated some DAML+OIL construct to further detail their semantics (Hunter, 2001). More recent approaches (Hausenblas, 2007) are based on the Web Ontology Language (McGuinness & Harmelen, 2004), but are also constrained to a part of the whole MPEG-7 standard, the Multimedia Description Scheme (MDS) for the ontology proposed at (Tsinaraki, Polydoros, & Christodoulakis, 2004).

An alternative to standards-based metadata are folksonomies (Vanderwal, 2007). Mainly used in social bookmarking software (e.g. del.icio.us, Flickr, YouTube), they allow the easy creation of user driven vocabularies in order to annotate resources. The main advantage of folksonomies is the low entry barrier: all terms are acceptable as metada, so no knowledge of the established standards is needed. Its main drawback is the lack of control over the vocabulary used to annotate resources, so resource combination and reasoning becomes almost impossible. Some systems combine social and semantic metadata and try to infer a formal ontology from the tags used in the folksonomy (Herzog, Luger & Herzog, 2007). In our case we believe that it is better to use standard ontologies both from multimedia and journalism fields than open and uncontrolled vocabularies.

Moreover, none of the proposed ontologies, for journalism of multimedia metadata, is accompanied by a methodology that allows mapping existing XML metadata based on the corresponding standards to semantic metadata. Consequently, it is difficult to put them into practice as there is a lack of metadata to play with. On the other hand, there is a great amount of existing XML metadata and a lot of tools based on XML technologies. For example, the new Milenium Quay[11] cross-media archive system from PROTEC, the worldwide leadership in cross-media software platforms, is XML-based. This software is focused on flexibility using several XML tags and mappings, increasing interoperability with other archiving systems. The XML-based products are clearly a trend in this scope. Every day, new products from the main software companies are appearing, which deal with different steps in all the news life-cycle, from production to consumption.

Nowadays, commercial tools based on XML technologies constitute the clear option in newspaper media houses. Current initiatives based on Semantic Web tools are constrained due to the lack of "real" data to work with; they constitute a too abrupt breaking from legacy systems. Moreover, they are prototypes with little functionality. Consequently, we do not see the semantic tools as an alternative to legacy systems, at least in the short term. On the contrary, we think that they constitute additional modules that can help dealing with the extra requirements derived from media heterogeneity, multichannel distribution and knowledge management issues.

The proposed methodology facilitates the production of semantic metadata from existing legacy systems, although it is simple metadata as the source is XML metadata that is not intended for carrying complex semantics. In any case, it constitutes a first and smooth step toward adding semantic-enabled tools to existing newspaper content management systems. From this point, more complex semantics and processing can be added without breaking continuity with the investments that media houses have done in their current systems.

COST AND BENEFITS

One of the biggest challenges in media houses is to attach metadata to all the generated content in order to facilitate management. However, this is easier in this context as in many media houses there is a department specialized in this work, which is carried out by archivists. Consequently, the additional costs arising from the application of Semantic Web technologies are mitigated due to the existence of this department. It is already in charge of indexation, categorization and content semantic enrichment.

Consequently, though there are many organizational and philosophy changes that modify how this task is currently carried out, it is not necessary to add new resources to perform this effort. The volume of information is another important aspect to consider. All Semantic Web approaches in this field propose an automatic or semi-automatic annotation processes.

The degree of automation attained using Semantic Web tools allows archivists spending less time in the more time consuming and mechanical tasks, e.g. the annotation of audio contents which can be performed with the help of speech-to-text tools as in the S5T project example presented in Section 3.3. Consequently, archivists can spend their time refining more concrete and specific metadata details and leave other aspects like categorization or annotation to partially or totally automatic tools. The overall outcome is that, with this computer and human complementary work, it is possible to archive big amounts of content without introducing extra costs.

Semantic metadata also provides improvements in content navigability and searching, maybe in all information retrieval tasks. This fact implies a better level of productivity in the media house, e.g. while performing event tracking through a set of news in order to produce a new content. However, it is also important to take into account the gap between journalists' and archivists' mental models, which is reflected in the way archivists categorise content and journalist perform queries.

This gap is a clear threat to productivity, although the flexibility of semantic structures makes it possible to relate concepts from different mental models in order to attain a more integrated and shared view (Abelló, García, Gil, Oliva, & Perdrix, 2006), which improves the content retrieval results and consequently improves productivity.

Moreover, the combination of semantic metadata and ontologies, together with tools like the ones presented for project S5T, make it possible for journalists to navigate between content metadata and ontology concepts and benefit from an integrated and shared knowledge management effort. This feature mitigates current gaps among editorial staff that seriously reduce the possibilities of media production.

Another point of interest is the possibility that journalists produce some metadata during the content generation process. Nowadays, journalists do not consider this activity part of their job. Consequently, this task might introduce additional costs that have not been faced at the current stage of development. This remains a future issue that requires deep organisational changes, which are not present yet in most editorial staffs, even if they are trying to follow the media convergence philosophy.

To conclude, there are also the development costs necessary in order to integrate the Semantic Web tools into current media houses. As has been already noted, the choice of a smooth transition approach reduces the development costs. This approach is based on the XSD2OWL and XML2RDF mappings detailed in Section 3.1.

Consequently, it is not necessary to develop a full newspaper content management system based on Semantic Web tools. On the contrary, existing systems based on XML technologies, as it is the common case, are used as the development platform on top of which semantic tools are deployed. This approach also improves interoperability with other media houses that also use XML technologies, though the interoperation is performed at the semantic level once source metadata has been mapped to semantic metadata.

RISK ASSESSMENT

In one hand we can consider some relevant positive aspects from the proposed solution. In fact, we are introducing knowledge management into the newspaper content archive system. The proposal implies a more flexible archive system with significant improvements in search and navigation. Compatibility with current standards is kept while the archive system allows searching across media and the underlying terms and domain knowledge. Finally, the integrated view on content provides seamless access to any kind of archived resources, which could be text, audio, video streaming, photographs, etc. Consequently, separate search engines for each kind of media are no longer necessary and global queries make it possible to retrieve any kind of resources.

This feature represents an important improvement in the retrieval process but also in the archiving one. The introduction of a semi-automatic annotation process produces changes in the archivist work. They could expend more time refining semantic annotation and including new metadata. Existing human resources in the archive department should spend the same amount of time than they currently do. However, they should obtain better quality results while they populate the archive with all the semantically annotated content. The overall result is that the archive becomes a knowledge management system.

On other hand, we need to take into account some weaknesses in this approach. Nowadays, Semantic Web technologies are mainly prototypes under development. This implies problems when you try to build a complete industrial platform based on them. Scalability appears as the main problem as it was experienced during the Neptuno research project (Castells et al., 2004) also in the journalism domain.

There is a lack of implementations supporting massive content storage and management. In other words, experimental solutions cannot be applied to real system considering, as our experience has shown, more than 1 million of items, i.e. news, photos or videos. This amount can be generated in 2 or 3 months in a small news media company. A part from the lack of implementations, there is also the lack of technical staff with Semantic Web development skills.

Despite all these inconveniences, there is the opportunity to create a platform for media convergence and editorial staff tasks integration. It can become an open platform that can manage future challenges in media houses and that is adaptable to different models based on specific organizational structures. Moreover, this platform may make it possible to offer new content interaction paradigms, especially through the World Wide Web channel.

One of these potential paradigms has already started to be explored in the S5T project. Currently, it offers integrated and complementary browsing among content and the terms of the underlying domain of knowledge, e.g. politics. However, this tool is currently intended just for the editorial staff. We anticipate a future tool that makes this kind of interaction available from the Diari Segre Web site to all of its Web users. This tool would provide an integrated access point to different kinds of contents, like text or news podcasts, but also to the underlying knowledge that models events, histories, personalities, etc.

There are some threats too. First of all, any organizational change, like changing the way the archive department works or giving unprecedented annotation responsibilities to journalists, constitutes an important risk. Changes inside an organization never be easy and must be well done and follow very closely if you want to make them successful. Sometimes, the effort-satisfaction ratio may be perceived as not justified by for some journalist or archivists. Consequently, they may react against the organisational changes required in order to implement rich semantic metadata.

FUTURE TRENDS

The more relevant future trend is that the Semantic Web is starting to be recognised as a consolidated discipline and a set of technologies and methodologies that are going to have a great impact in the future of enterprise information systems (King, 2007). The more important consequence of this consolidation is that many commercial tools are appearing. They are solid tools that can be used in order to build enterprise semantic information systems with a high degree of scalability.

As has been shown, the benefits of semantic metadata are being put into practice in the Diari Segre Media Group, a newspaper that is becoming a convergent media house with press, radio, television and a World Wide Web portal. As has been detailed, a set of semantics-aware tools have been developed. They are intended for journalist and archivists in the media house, but they can be also adapted to the general public at the portal.

Making the Diari Segre semantic tools publicly available is one of the greatest opportunities and in the future, with the help of solid enterprise semantic platforms, is the issue where the greatest effort is going to be placed. In general, a bigger users base puts extra requirements about the particular needs that each user might have. This is due to the fact that each user may have a different vision about the domain of knowledge or about searching and browsing strategies. In this sense, we need some degree of personalisation beyond the much more closed approach that has been taken in order to deploy these tools for the editorial staff.

Personalisation ranges from interfaces, to processes or query construction approaches applying static or dynamic profiles. Static profiles could be completed by users in when they first register. Dynamic profiles must be collected by the system based on the user system usage (Castells et al., 2007). Per user profiles introduce a great amount of complexity, which can be mitigated building groups of similar profiles, for instance groups based on the user role.

Moreover, to collect system usage information while users navigate through the underlying conceptual structures makes it possible to discover new implicit relations among concepts with some semantic significance, at least from the user, or group to which the user belongs, point of view. If there are a lot of users following the same navigation path between items, maybe it would be better to add a new conceptual link between the initial and final items. Currently, this kind of relations can only be added manually. In the near future, we could use the power of Semantic Web technologies in order to do this automatically. This would improve user experience while they search or navigate as the underlying conceptual framework would accommodate the particular user view on the domain.

To conclude this section, it is also important to take into account the evolution of the standards upon which the ontological framework has been build. On the short range, the most import novelty is the imminent release of the NewsML G2 standard (Le Meur, 2007). This standard is also based on XML Schemas for language formalisation. Therefore, it should be trivial to generate the corresponding OWL ontologies and to start mapping metadata based on this standard to semantic metadata. More effort will be needed in order to produce the integration rules that will allow integrating this standard into existing legacy systems augmented by Semantic Web tools.

CONCLUSION

This research work has been guided by the need for a semantic journalism and multimedia metadata framework that facilitates semantic newspaper applications development in the context of a convergent media house. It has been detected, as it is widely documented in the bibliography and professional activity, that IPTC and MPEG standards are the best sources for an ontological framework that facilitates a smooth transition from legacy to semantic information systems. MPEG-7, MPEG-21 and most of the IPTC standards are based on XML Schemas and thus they do not have formal semantics.

Our approach contributes a complete and automatic mapping of the whole MPEG-7 standard to OWL, of the media packaging part of MPEG-21 and of the main IPTC standard schemas (NITF, NewsML and NewsCodes) to the corresponding OWL ontologies. Instance metadata is automatically imported from legacy systems through a XML2RDF mapping, based on the ontologies previously mapped from the standards XML schemas. Once in a semantic space, data integration, which is a crucial factor when several sources of information are available, is facilitated enormously.

Moreover, semantic metadata facilitates the development of applications in the context of media houses that traditional newspapers are becoming. The convergence of different kinds of media, that now constitute multimedia news, poses new management requirements that are easier to cope with if applications are more informed, i.e. aware of the semantics that are implicit in news and the media that constitute them. This is the case for the tools we propose for archivists and journalists, the Media Browser and the Knowledge Browser. These tools reduce the misunderstandings among them and facilitate keeping track of existing news stories and the generation of new content.

REFERENCES

Abelló, A., García, R., Gil, R., Oliva, M., & Perdrix, F. (2006). Semantic Data Integration in a Newspaper Content Management System. In R. Meersman, Z. Tari, & P. Herrero (Eds.), *OTM Workshops 2006*. LNCS Vol. 4277 (pp. 40-41). Berlin/Heidelberg, DE: Springer.

Amann, B., Beer, C., Fundulak, I., & Scholl, M. (2002). Ontology-Based Integration of XML Web Resources. *Proceedings of the 1st International Semantic Web Conference*, ISWC 2002. LNCS Vol. 2342 (pp. 117-131). Berlin/Heidelberg, DE: Springer.

Becket, D. (2004). RDF/XML Syntax Specification. World Wide Web Consortium Recommendation. Retrieved from http://www.w3.org/TR/2004/REC-rdf-syntax-grammar-20040210.

Berners-Lee, T., Hendler, J., & Lassila, O. (2001). The Semantic Web. *Scientific American*, 284(5), 34-43.

Castells, P., Fernández, M., & Vallet, D. (2007). An Adaptation of the Vector-Space Model for Ontology-Based Information Retrieval. *IEEE Transactions on Knowledge and Data Engineering*, 19(2), 261-272.

Castells, P., Perdrix, F., Pulido, E., Rico, M., Benjamins, R., Contreras, J., et al. (2004). Neptuno: Semantic Web Technologies for a Digital Newspaper Archive. In C. Bussler, J. Davies, D. Fensel, & R. Studer, (Eds.), *The Semantic Web: Research and Applications: First European Semantic Web Symposium*, ESWS 2004, LNCS Vol. 3053 (pp. 445-458). Berlin/Heidelberg, DE: Springer.

Castells, P., Perdrix, F., Pulido, E., Rico, M., Benjamins, R., Contreras, J., & Lorés, J. (2004). *Neptuno: Semantic Web Technologies for a Digital Newspaper Archive*. LNCS Vol. 3053 (pp. 445-458).Berlin/Heidelberg, DE: Springer.

Cruz, I., Xiao, H., & Hsu, F. (2004). An Ontology-based Framework for XML Semantic Integration. *Proceedings of the Eighth International Database Engineering and Applications Symposium*, IDEAS'04, (pp. 217-226). Washington, DC: IEEE Computer Society.

Cuayahuitl, H., & Serridge, B. (2002). Out-of-vocabulary Word Modelling and Rejection for Spanish Keyword Spotting Systems. *Proceedings of the 2nd Mexican International Conference on Artificial Intelligence.*

Einhoff, M., Casademont, J., Perdrix, F., & Noll, S. (2005) ELIN: A MPEG Related News Framework. In M. Grgic (Ed.), *47th International Symposium ELMAR: Focused on Multimedia Systems and Applications* (pp.139-142). Zadar, Croatia: ELMAR.

Eriksen, L. B., & Ihlström, C. (2000). Evolution of the Web News Genre - The Slow Move Beyond the Print Metaphor. In *Proceedings of the 33rd Hawaii international Conference on System Sciences.* IEEE Computer Society Press.

Fernández, N., Blázquez, J.M., Fisteus, J.A., Sánchez, L., Sintek, M., Bernardi, A., et al. (2006). NEWS: Bringing Semantic Web Technologies into News Agencies. *The Semantic Web - ISWC 2006*, LNCS Vol. 4273 (pp. 778-791). Berlin/Heidelberg, DE: Springer.

García, R. (2006). XML Semantics Reuse. In *A Semantic Web Approach to Digital Rights Management*, PhD Thesis (pp. 116-120). TDX. Retrived from http://www.tdx.cesca.es/TDX-0716107-170634.

García, R., & Gil, R. (2006). Improving Human-Semantic Web Interaction: The Rhizomer Experience. *Proceedings of the 3rd Italian Semantic Web Workshop*, SWAP'06, Vol. 201 (pp. 57-64). CEUR Workshop Proceedings.

García, R., Gil, R., & Delgado, J. (2007). A Web ontologies framework for digital rights management. *Artificial Intelligence and Law*, 15(2), 137-154.

García, R., Gil, R., Gallego, I., & Delgado, J. (2005). Formalising ODRL Semantics using Web Ontologies. In R. Iannella, S. Guth, & C. Serrao, Eds., *Open Digital Rights Language Workshop*, ODRL'2005 (pp. 33-42). Lisbon, Portugal: ADETTI.

Hausenblas, M., Troncy, R., Halaschek-Wiener, C., Bürger, T., Celma, O., Boll, et al. (2007). *Multimedia Vocabularies on the Semantic Web.* W3C Incubator Group Report, World Wide Web Consortium. Available from http://www.w3.org/2005/Incubator/mmsem/XGR-vocabularies-20070724.

Haustein, S., & Pleumann, J. (2002). Is Participation in the Semantic Web Too Difficult? In *Proceedings of the First International Semantic Web Conference on The Semantic Web*, LNCS Vol. 2342 (pp. 448-453). Berlin/Heidelberg: Springer.

Herzog C., Luger M., & Herzog M. (2007). Combining Social and Semantic Metadata for Search in Document Repository.Bridging the Gap Between Semantic Web and Web 2.0. *International Workshop at the 4th European Semantic Web Conference* in Insbruck, Austria, June 7, 2007.

Horrocks, I., Patel-Schneider, P.F., Boley, H., Tabet, S., Grosof, B., & Dean, M. (2004). *SWRL: A Semantic Web Rule Language Combining OWL and RuleML.* W3C Member Submission, World Wide Web Consortium. Retrieved from http://www.w3.org/Submission/SWRL

Hunter, J. (2001). Adding Multimedia to the Semantic Web - Building an MPEG-7 Ontology. *Proceedings of the International Semantic Web Working Symposium* (pp. 260-272). Standford, CA.

Hunter, J. (2003). Enhacing the Semantic Interoperability of Multimedia through a Core Ontology. *IEEE Transactions on Circuits and Systems for Video Technology*, 13(1), 49-58.

Ihlström, C., Lundberg, J., & Perdrix, F. (2003) Audience of Local Online Newspapers in Sweden, Slovakia and Spain - A Comparative Study. In *Proceedings of HCI International* Vol. 3 (pp. 749-753). Florence, Kentucky: Lawrence Erlbaum Associates.

Kim, J., Jung, H., & Chung, H. (2004). A Keyword Spotting Approach based on Pseudo N-gram Language Model. *Proceedings of the 9th Conf. on Speech and Computer*, SPECOM 2004 (pp. 256-259). Patras, Greece.

King, R. (2007, April 29). Taming the World Wide Web. *Special Report, Business Week*. Retrieved from http://www.businessweek.com/technology/content/apr2007/tc20070409_248062.htm

Klein, M.C.A. (2002). Interpreting XML Documents via an RDF Schema Ontology. In *Proceedings of the 13th International Workshop on Database and Expert Systems Applications*, DEXA 2002 (pp. 889-894). Washington, DC: IEEE Computer Society.

Lakshmanan, L., & Sadri, F. (2003). Interoperability on XML Data. *Proceedings of the 2nd International Semantic Web Conference*, ICSW'03, LNCS Vol. 2870 (pp. 146-163). Berlin/Heidelberg: Springer.

Le Meur, L. (2007). How NewsML-G2 simplifies and fuels news management. Presented at *XTech 2007: The Ubiquitous Web*, Paris, France.

Lundberg, J. (2002). *The online news genre: Visions and state of the art*. Paper presented at the 34th Annual Congress of the Nordic Ergonomics Society, Sweden.

McDonald, N. (2004). Can HCI shape the future of mass communications. *Interactions,* 11(2), 44-47.

McGuinness, D.L., & Harmelen, F.V. (2004). *OWL Web Ontology Language Overview*. World Wide Web Consortium Recommendation. Retrieved from http://www.w3.org/TR/owl-features

Patel-Schneider, P., & Simeon, J. (2002). The Yin/Yang Web: XML syntax and RDF semantics. *Proceedings of the 11th International World Wide Web Conference*, WWW'02 (pp. 443-453). ACM Press.

Salembier, P., & Smith, J. (2002). Overview of MPEG-7 multimedia description schemes and schema tools. In B.S. Manjunath, P. Salembier, & T. Sikora (Ed.), *Introduction to MPEG-7: Multimedia Content Description Interface*. John Wiley & Sons.

Salton, G., & McGill, M. (1983). *Introduction to Modern Information Retrieval*. New York: McGraw-Hill.

Sawyer, S., & Tapia, A. (2005). The sociotechnical nature of mobile computing work: Evidence from a study of policing in the United States. *International Journal of Technology and Human Interaction*, 1(3), 1-14.

Tejedor, J., García, R., Fernández, M., López, F., Perdrix, F., Macías, J.A., et al. (2007). Ontology-Based Retrieval of Human Speech. *Proceedings of the 6th International Workshop on Web Semantics*, WebS'07 (in press). IEEE Computer Society Press.

Tous, R., García, R., Rodríguez, E., & Delgado, J. (2005). Arquitecture of a Semantic XPath Processor. In K. Bauknecht, B. Pröll, & H. Werthner, Eds., *E-Commerce and Web Technologies: 6th International Conference*, EC-Web'05, LNCS Vol. 3590 (pp. 1-10). Berlin/Heidelberg, DE: Springer.

Tsinaraki, C., Polydoros, P., & Christodoulakis, S. (2004). Integration of OWL ontologies in MPEG-7 and TVAnytime compliant Semantic Indexing. In A. Persson, & J. Stirna, Eds., *16th International Conference on Advanced Information Systems Engineering*, LNCS Vol. 3084 (pp. 398-413). Berlin/Heidelberg, DE: Springer.

Tsinaraki, C., Polydoros, P., & Christodoulakis, S. (2004). Interoperability support for Ontology-based Video Retrieval Applications. *Proceedings of 3rd International Conference on Image and Video Retrieval, CIVR 2004*. Dublin, Ireland.

Vanderwal T. (2007) *Folksonomy Coinage and Definition*. Retrieved from: http://vanderwal.net/folksonomy.html.

Vorhees, E. (1994). Query expansion using lexical semantic relations. *Proceedings of the 17th ACM Conf. on Research and Development in Information Retrieval*, ACM Press.

ADDITIONAL READING

Kompatsiaris, Y., & Hobson, P. (Eds.). (2008). *Semantic Multimedia and Ontologies: Theory and Applications*. Berlin/Heidelberg, DE: Springer.

ENDNOTES

1. http://www.diarisegre.com
2. IPTC, http://www.iptc.org
3. IIM, http://www.iptc.org/IIM
4. http://www.iptc.org/NewsCodes
5. NITF, http://www.nitf.org
6. http://www.newsml.org
7. http://rhizomik.net/redefer
8. http://rhizomik.net/semanticnewspaper
9. http://rhizomik.net/ontologies/mpeg7ontos
10. http://nets.ii.uam.es/s5t
11. Milenium Quay, http://www.mileniumcross-media.com

Chapter X
Ontologically Enhanced RosettaNet B2B Integration

Paavo Kotinurmi
Helsinki University of Technology, Finland

Armin Haller
National University of Ireland - Galway, Ireland

Eyal Oren
Vrije Universiteit Amsterdam, The Netherlands

ABSTRACT

RosettaNet is an industry-driven e-business process standard that defines common inter-company public processes and their associated business documents. RosettaNet is based on the Service-oriented architecture (SOA) paradigm and all business documents are expressed in DTD or XML Schema. Our "ontologically-enhanced RosettaNet" effort translates RosettaNet business documents into a Web ontology language, allowing business reasoning based on RosettaNet message exchanges. This chapter describes our extension to RosettaNet and shows how it can be used in business integrations for better interoperability. The usage of a Web ontology language in RosettaNet collaborations can help accommodate partner heterogeneity in the setup phase and can ease the back-end integration, enabling for example more competition in the purchasing processes. It provides also a building block to adopt a semantic SOA with richer discovery, selection and composition capabilities.

CURRENT SITUATION

Information and communication technologies are increasingly important in the daily operations of organisations. In the current networked business environment most information systems need to interoperate with other internal and external information systems. Such interoperation is not easily achievable and therefore causes significant costs. For example, Brunnermeier & Martin (2002) studied interoperability in the U.S. automotive supply chain and estimated the cost of poor interoperability in product data exchange alone to be around one billion dollar per annum.

Standards such as RosettaNet or ebXML facilitate Business-to-Business (B2B) integration (Shim et al., 2000). These standards support electronic commerce over existing Internet standards and lead to cost and extensibility benefits. The aim of B2B standards is to facilitate integration with less implementation effort for each e-business partner organisation. Many B2B standards employ XML technologies and the Internet to standardise document exchange and ease the implementation effort of collaborations (Nurmilaakso & Kotinurmi, 2004; Shim et al., 2000). However, there are many competing B2B standards that are not mutually interoperable. So the choice for a particular B2B standard also forms a potential integration bottleneck.

Emerging Semantic Web technologies enable a business integration that is more adaptive to changes that might occur over the lifetime of B2B integrations (Fensel, 2003; Trastour, Preist, & Coleman, 2003). This chapter will describe existing B2B standards and focus on an extension of RosettaNet that uses Semantic Web technologies. The usage of this extension for B2B integration and the added flexibility that is gained with it will be demonstrated in a practical integration scenario.

EXISTING STANDARDS FOR B2B INTEGRATION

Many relevant standards have been introduced to alleviate B2B integration issues such as data heterogeneity and process heterogeneity. We describe XML and RosettaNet, and explain the remaining issues in practical B2B integrations even when using these standards.

XML and RosettaNet

XML (Extensible Markup Language) is a language for describing and exchanging data. Before the introduction of XML, business partners needed to accommodate various file formats, such as flat files or different EDI (Electronic Data Interchange) versions, and setup a parsing/management infrastructures for each format used by a partner. The introduction of XML lowered the integration barriers between organisations, as partners could reuse their XML infrastructure for all exchanged documents between all partners. The main two schema languages associated to the XML standard are DTD (Document Type Definition language) and XSD (XML Schema Definition language). These schema languages enable business partners to validate whether incoming and outgoing documents conform to a required structure.

The use of XML as such does not resolve interoperability issues in B2B integrations, since the exchange of XML documents does not mean that the documents are understood similarly. Therefore, standards are needed that guide how XML is used in B2B integrations. RosettaNet[1] is one such XML-based B2B standard; already in 2004, RosettaNet had over 3000 documented implementations (Damodaran, 2004). Other common B2B standards include OAGIS[2], ebXML[3] and UBL[4].

RosettaNet is an industry-driven consortium that aims to create, implement, and promote open B2B integration standards. The member organisations represent the information technology, electronic components, semiconductor manufacturing, telecommunications, and logistics industries. The most important components in RosettaNet are Partner Interface Processes (PIPs), dictionaries and the RosettaNet Implementation Framework (RNIF). All three are described in the following paragraphs.

RosettaNet Partner Interface Processes (PIPs)

RosettaNet Partner Interface Processes (PIPs) define cross-organisational processes (choreographies), which define the message exchange patterns occurring in different business collaborations. Each PIP contains a specification document, a set of document schemas and message guidelines to help to interpret these schemas. RosettaNet processes are not directly executable, but are manually mapped by trading partners onto their internal systems (Aalst & Kumar, 2003). RosettaNet PIPs are organised into eight clusters, denoted by numbers, which are further subdivided into segments, denoted by letters. For example, cluster 3 deals with "Order Management"; it is divided into four segments including for example PIP 3A "Quote and Order Entry".

The specification document in a PIP defines the message exchange sequence using Unified Modeling Language (UML) activity diagrams, sequence diagrams and textual descriptions; the specification document also describes, in English, the roles of the partners and the conditions to initiate a collaboration. The document schema and the accompanying message guidelines define the valid PIP business document structure and content. The message guidelines introduce additional constraints and explanations, such as the meaning of a modification date and the representation and interpretation of date values. Similarly, the meanings of business codes that can appear in a document are specified.

Historically, PIPs have been expressed using DTD-based schemas. New PIPs, developed after 2004, use XML Schemas for documents and the ebXML Business Process Specification Schema (Clark et al., 2001) for the process descriptions. Since XML Schema is more expressive than DTD, some of the constraints in the message which have been described before only textually can now be represented formally. However, still in early 2008, many PIPs are specified in DTD-based schemas and thus contain many constraints in accompanying descriptions in plain English only.

Common terms used in all PIPs are defined in the global RosettaNet dictionaries. In addition to dictionaries, global RosettaNet identifiers are used, such as Data Universal Numbering System (DUNS) codes to identify companies and the Global Trade Identification Number (GTIN) to identify product types.

RosettaNet Implementation Framework (RNIF)

The RosettaNet Implementation Framework (RNIF) specifies secure messaging over the Internet. It defines the RosettaNet business message that contains the business document specified by the schemas and the necessary headers and security features needed to process the messages. RNIF also defines how attachments are encoded in the RosettaNet business messages and uses e.g. MIME and S/MIME for packing and encryption.

RNIF defines exception-handling mechanisms and ensures that the delivery is non-repudiated, so neither the sender nor the receiver can later deny having sent or received the RosettaNet business message. Many vendors, such as BEA and Microsoft, support RNIF in their products. The currently widely used RNIF version 2.0 does not use Web Service standards such as SOAP or WSDL. However, the RosettaNet Multiple Messaging Services specification, published in 2006, defines how RosettaNet PIPs can be sent using ebXML Messaging Services, Web Services or AS/2 specification.

Problems in RosettaNet Integrations

The standardised business processes described by RosettaNet simplify cross-organisational collaboration and B2B integration. The degree of standardisation offered still requires considerable manual effort during the setup of B2B collaborations (Trastour, Bartolini, & Preist, 2003). This manual effort is necessary given the modelling freedom left by weakly defined document schemas. As a consequence interoperability challenges are only partly addressed by the introduction of standardised PIPs and B2B integrations still suffer from long set up times and high costs (Damodaran, 2005; Preist et al., 2005).

To detail the challenges in a practical B2B integration situation, we present a quoting and purchasing scenario based on RosettaNet PIPs "3A1 Request for Quote (RFQ)" and "3A4 Request Purchase Order (PO)". Figure 1 shows the overall choreography including the message exchange of a Buyer (requester) and a Seller (provider) using BPMN[5] notation. The white coloured activity boxes denote parts of the internal computational steps, dotted boxes are placeholders for possibly many computation steps performed internally, whereas the dark coloured boxes represent the public behaviour according to PIP 3A1 and PIP 3A4 respectively. The process message boxes here include RosettaNet-specific RNIF behaviour related to validating and acknowledging incoming messages.

The scenario presented in Figure 1 contains interaction with only one Seller. When the Buyer wants to introduce competition by receiving multiple quotes from different sellers, the following interoperability challenges arise:

- **Business process alignment:** The Buyer's internal processes have to be adjusted to the introduction of a new Seller. Although all processes should conform to the same com-

Figure 1. RosettaNet B2B Collaboration in a quoting and purchasing process

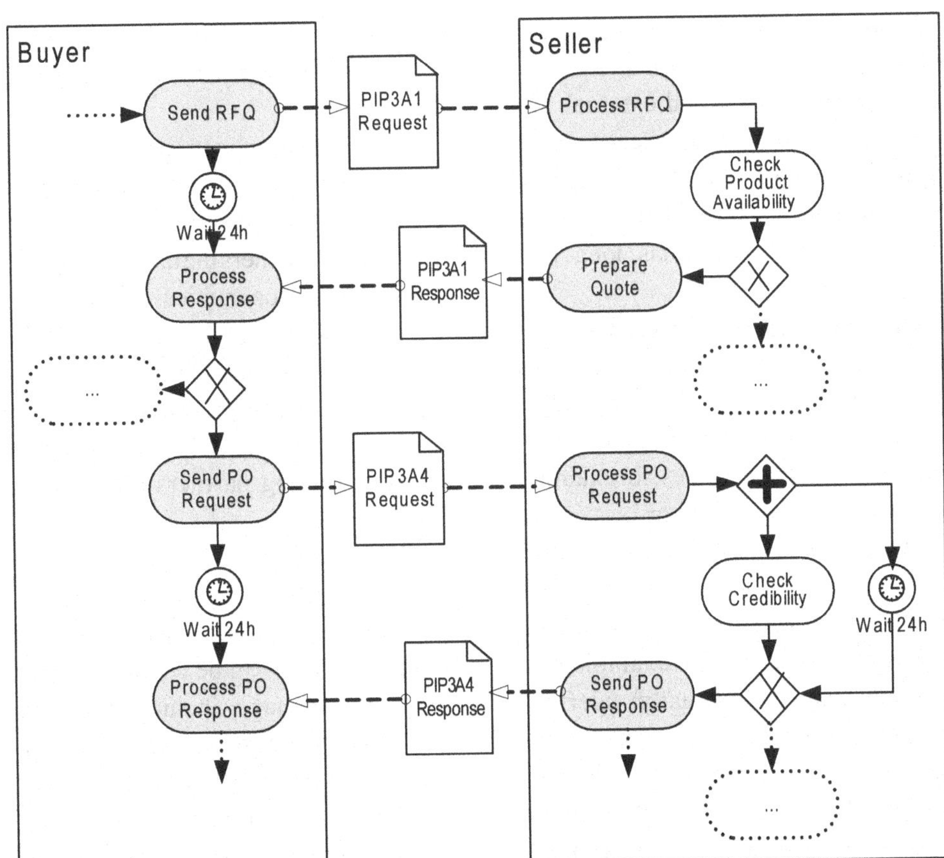

mon PIP, manual alignment is still necessary, since the PIPs business process definitions are informal and lack process details.

- **Expressive power:** The schema languages (DTD and XML Schema) lack expressive power to capture all necessary constraints and do not make all document semantics explicit. This lack of expressive power in the current RosettaNet specification has been acknowledged by RosettaNet experts (Damodaran, 2004, 2005). For example, the RosettaNet business dictionary defines a finite set of enumerated values for certain elements in a PIP message but does not describe the relationship between these values. This leads to heterogeneity in the messages as for example EU sellers typically use Euro values for quotation and the metric system for units of measurement, whereas U.S.-based companies quote in Dollars and inch-pound units.
- **Repetition:** Current schema languages have limited support for information reuse through reference, rules, and external imports. As a consequence, messages contain a high amount of repetition since all implicit information must be stated explicitly. These repetitions make the schemas long and complex to interpret.
- **Ambiguous message definitions:** PIP message definitions are ambiguous: partners can use the same PIP messages in different ways. Logically similar information can be represented in many different places, for example on the level of "total order" or on "order-line item" level, and many elements within a schema definition for a PIP are optional and not implemented by every company. As a consequence, in our example the Buyer might need to (manually) interpret additional information sent by a newly introduced Seller. For example, a new Seller might typically offer substitutable products in its responses which the Buyer can not handle without changes to the RosettaNet solution.
- **Context-dependent constraints:** PIP processes expressed in XSD schemas are highly nested and the same elements may appear in several documents exchanged during an interaction. In fact, the nesting is an advantage over DTD-based PIPs which are self-contained and duplicate the same schema information in every PIP. However, as identified by Trastour, Preist, & Coleman (2003), constraints on a class in RosettaNet depend on its deployment context, including the PIP document being used, the trading partner and its role (buyer or seller) and the business process in which the messages are exchanged. In current B2B integrations, developers have to manually aggregate contextual constraints into refined XML schemas or into informal documents. Such manual integration is inefficient and leads to interoperability problems when partners apply different constraints.

When the number of partners increases, these limitations become increasingly important, especially for companies that are not in a position to dictate their partners the usage terms of PIPs. Since resolving heterogeneities on a case-by-case basis is expensive, in practice the choice of integration partners is limited and restricted at design-time. As a consequence, B2B integrations typically do not support competitive arrangements in which multiple trading partners compete, at runtime, for best offers.

To overcome these challenges, we introduce semantic technologies to B2B integrations. As such the information exchanged in the RosettaNet messages can be encoded in a formal Web ontology language, including definitional facts that make the dependencies between elements defined in the RosettaNet business dictionary explicit. A semantic Service-oriented architecture to communicate and mediate between the RosettaNet-enabled business partners and the internal back-end systems is applied as a proof-of-concept implementation for our ontologically-enhanced RosettaNet approach.

THE ONTOLOGICALLY-ENHANCED ROSETTANET SOLUTION

The objective of ontologising RosettaNet is to ease the integration to sellers and thus introduce more competition. The solution should be flexible to adding new partners and new collaborative processes and support coping with inevitable variations that come when working with multiple partners. A quick integration process, reuse of existing solutions and powerful discovery, selection, composition, validation and mediation capabilities are important objectives for the proposed solution. Companies have invested considerable amounts of money and resources to implement current B2B integrations based on existing B2B standards, and they have the supporting infrastructure largely in place. In our scenario, only the buyer adopts semantic technologies internally, enabling to manage integration with multiple sellers using current B2B standards. The Ontologically-enhanced RosettaNet solution shows how existing RosettaNet challenges can be solved using semantic technologies.

Semantic Technologies for B2B Integration

Semantic Web technologies and Semantic Web Services have been proposed to achieve more dynamic partnerships (Bussler et al., 2002) and constitute one of the most promising research directions to improve the integration of applications within and across organisations.

Several standardisation efforts, such as OWL-S (Martin et al., 2004), WSMO (Roman et al., 2005) and SWSF (Battle et al., 2005), define frameworks and formal language stacks for Semantic Web Services. Semantic Web Services employ ontologies for semantic annotation of B2B integration interfaces. Such semantic annotation enables (semi-)automated mediation of heterogeneous message content and more flexible service discovery, composition and selection (McIlraith et al., 2001).

Our solution demonstrates how a Service-oriented architecture (SOA) capable of handling semantic technologies can tackle some of the interoperability challenges with RosettaNet-based B2B integrations related to purchasing processes involving multiple partners.

We demonstrate our ontologically-enhanced RosettaNet solution using WSMO. The choice has been made on the fact that we require a more expressive language than RDF(s), but also a framework treating services as first-class citizen in its metamodel. However, although we have opted to use WSMO and its stack of WSML languages, the ontology could also be defined in OWL and OWL-S.

The WSMO Semantic Web Services Framework

The Web Service Modelling Ontology (WSMO) (Bruijn et al., 2005) is a Semantic Web Services framework consisting of a conceptual model and a language for describing the relevant aspects of services. The goal of such markup is to enable the automation of tasks (such as discovery, selection, composition, mediation, execution and monitoring) involved in both intra- and inter-enterprise integration. The WSMO framework is implemented in a SOA (Haselwanter et al., 2006; Vitvar et al., 2007) that can support RosettaNet integration scenarios (Haller et al., 2007).

The markup of services according to the WSMO conceptual model is expressed in the Web Service Modeling Language (WSML) family of ontology languages. WSML offers a human readable syntax, as well as XML and RDF syntaxes for exchanging data between services. WSML distinguishes conceptual and logical expression syntaxes. The conceptual syntax is used to model the fundamental WSMO concepts (Web Services, ontologies, goals and mediators); the logical expression syntax is used for describing additional constraints and axioms.

WSML consists of a number of variants based on different logical formalisms and correspond with different levels of logical expressiveness, which are both syntactically and semantically layered. These variants are WSML-Core, WSML-DL, WSML-Flight, WSML-Rule and WSML-Full. WSML-Core is the least expressive variant but with the best computational characteristics. WSML-Core is expressively equivalent to Description Logic Programs (Grosof et al., 2003), an intersection of Description Logic and Horn Logic. The WSML-DL, WSML-Flight and WSML-Rule variants extend WSML-Core to provide increasing expressiveness in the direction of Description Logics and Logic Programming. WSML-Full is the union of these two directions, making it the most expressive WSML variant.

RosettaNet Ontology

Ontologies, used for semantic annotation of the B2B integration interfaces, are formal descriptions of the concepts and relationships that can exist in some domain (Gruber, 1993; Uschold & Gruninger, 1996). The RosettaNet specification framework is such a world-view, namely that of the RosettaNet consortium, encompassing an exhaustive definition of the concepts, attributes and relations in the e-business domain.

However, the conceptualisation in form of DTDs and XML Schemas is not rigorously formal and leaves knowledge implicit in natural language. In this section, we show how to translate the PIPs into a formal Web ontology language. By translating the RosettaNet specifications to a richer and formal Web ontology language the constraints on the semantics of the business documents can be captured explicitly.

This section presents a generic RosettaNet ontology. As mentioned earlier, the ontology includes facts that cannot be expressed in the schema languages currently used in the RosettaNet PIPs. The ontology is modelled according to RosettaNet PIP specifications, in our example PIPs 3A1 and 3A4, containing concepts such as *PartnerDescription* or *PhysicalAddress*, and their attributes. Listing 1 shows a snippet of the RosettaNet ontology, describing how the *PartnerDescription* is expressed in the Web Service Modeling Language. The concept definition includes three property definitions and its respective type information and cardinality constraints.

Definitional Facts

In this section we focus on the modelling of implicit knowledge in the RosettaNet specification, which can be made explicit in the ontology. For example, the RosettaNet business dictionary defines an enumerated list of 367 possible values for *units of measurements*, with the logical relation-

Listing 1. Product ontology extract in WSML[6]

```
concept partnerDescription
    nonFunctionalProperties
        dc#description hasValue "The collection of business properties that describe a business identity."
    endNonFunctionalProperties
    globalbusinessidentifier ofType (1 1) _int
    globalsupplychaincode ofType (0 1) _string
    globalpartnerclassificationcode ofType (1 1) globalPartnerClassificationCode
```

ships between the values unspecified. They are directly modelled and constrained in RosettaNet as tokenised strings. All the inherent relations between the individual tokens are left unspecified. We made such logical relations explicit and included these axiomatisations in the ontology.

First, we identified for each tokenised string in the XML Schema its unit type class membership in the Suggested Upper Merged Ontology (SUMO) (Niles & Pease, 2001). SUMO is a richly axiomatised formal ontology created by the merger of multiple existing upper-level ontologies. SUMO is divided into eleven sections whose interdependencies are carefully documented. We are mostly interested in classes from the base ontology, numeric and measurement layer. Other parts of the ontology include among others, temporal, process and class theories. All unit types in the 367 token values can be related to the *PhysicalQuantity* class in SUMO, which itself subclasses *ConstantQuantity, FunctionQuantity* and *UnitOfMeasure*. By using SUMO we derive foundational relations, such as the equivalence of 1 *litre* to 1 *cubic decimetre* and the relation that 4.54609 *litres* are equal to 1 *UnitedKingdomGallon*, all facts defined in the axiom schemata of SUMO. Listing 2 shows the concept definitions in the ontology and its related classes in SUMO. *PoundMass* and *Kilogram* in SUMO are second level subclasses of *ProductQuantity*.

Next, we identified common types in the tokens and modelled them as concepts in the ontology. Examples of similar tokens are a *10 Kilogram Drum*, a *100 Pound Drum* and a *15 Kilogram Drum*. Listing 3 shows the first two tokens in its XML Schema definition and Listing 4 shows its representation in our ontology. We identified the concept *Drum* as being member of a *FluidCon-*

Listing 2. ***UnitOfMeasureTypes*** *in the RosettaNet ontology*

```
ProductQuantity subConceptOf sumo#ProductQuantity concept PoundMass
subConceptOf sumo#PoundMass concept Kilogram subConceptOf
sumo#Kilogram
```

Listing 3. ***UnitOfMeasureTypes*** *extract of XML Schema; Listing 4.* ***UnitOfMeasureTypes*** *extract in the RosettaNet ontology*

```
<xs:simpleType name="UnitOfMeasureContentType">
 <xs:restriction base="xs:token">
  <xs:enumeration value="1KD">
   <xs:annotation>
    <xs:appinfo>
     <urss:Definition>10 Kilogram Drum.</urss:Definition>
    </xs:appinfo>
   </xs:annotation>
  </xs:enumeration>
  <xs:enumeration value="1PD">
   <xs:annotation>
    <xs:appinfo>
     <urss:Definition>100 Pound Drum.</urss:Definition>
    </xs:appinfo>
   </xs:annotation>
  </xs:enumeration>
 </xs:restriction>
</xs:simpleType>
```

```
concept ProductQuantity subConceptOf sumo#
    ProductQuantity
  hasTokenValue ofType _string
  hasUnitQuota ofType _float
  hasUnitType ofType ProductQuantity

concept Drum subConceptOf {sumo#FluidContainer,
    ProductQuantity}

instance _10KilogramDrum memberOf Drum
  hasTokenValue hasValue "1KD"
  hasUnitQuota hasValue 10
  hasUnitType hasValue Kilogram

instance _100PoundDrum memberOf Drum
  hasTokenValue hasValue "1PD"
  hasUnitQuota hasValue 100
  hasUnitType hasValue PoundMass
```

tainer in SUMO and it inherits similarly to all other converted unit types the *hasTokenValue*, *hasUnitSize* and *hasUnitType* attributes from its parent concept (*Quantity*).

This style of modelling allows us to further include semantic relations between instances of the same unit type concept. To define the numerical dependencies between different *UnitOfMeasureContentType* we add equivalence relations similar to the one shown in Listing 5. It states that a *Quantity* instance with a certain amount ?z of "100 Pound Drum" unit types equals 4.5359237 times *10 Kilogram Drums*. Since we have derived a subsumption hierarchy, this axiom applies to all sub-classes of *Quantities*, such as *ProductQuantity*, the fourth most used type in the RosettaNet schema.

Since RosettaNet does not and can not model all domain knowledge, such as the actual product and partner identification, measurement types or currency types, other specifications (ontologies) have to ensure the uniform understanding of the elements within a message. RosettaNet publishes guidelines which standards to use, but does not reference or integrate ontologies to homogenise their usage.

ProductIdentification and *PartnerIdentification*, two element types highly used throughout the RosettaNet specifications (see Haller et al. (2008) for detailed statistics on the occurrence of schema types within RosettaNet) reference for example one of the following identifier types: *uat:identifiertype*, *ulc:AlternativeIdentifier*, *udt:GTIN*, *udt:DUNS*, *udt:DUNSPlus4* and *udt:GLN*.

The role of these identifiers is to describe products (GTIN), companies (DUNS) and locations (GLN or DUNSPlus4 for company location) uniquely. When, for example, ordering a hammer, it is easier to refer to an identifier, such as the 14-digit GTIN "55566677788899", than specifying "Tool, hammer, hand tool, Fiskars,..." in every message. Alternative identifiers can also be used, typically for buyer identification. Using differing identification schemas creates a mapping challenge where ontologies can help to state similarity between different identifiers for a product.

Since an n-to-n mapping between identifiers is unfeasible even in an ontology, we propose to map to an existing product classification such as the eCl@ss classification (code \AAA374002" for hammer). By specifying this semantic detail and referring to the existing eClassOwl-ontology[7] (Hepp, 2005b), it is possible to provide information on similar products, such as hammers produced by other manufacturers. Further benefits materialise when respective UN/SPSC classifications are mapped to eCl@ss categories. This enables companies that map their identifier codes to a category to provide substitutable products and increase their chance of realising sales.

Domain-Specific Rules

Each collaboration requires the setup of additional domain-specific rules to capture any data heterogeneity that is not resolved by the definitional facts in the domain ontology.

Listing 5. Equivalence relation between 100 Pound Drum and 10 Kilogram Drum

```
axiom _1PD1KDDependency
    definedBy
        ?x memberOf Quantity and ?x[hasUnitType hasValue _100PoundDrum] and ?y[hasNumericalValue hasValue ?z]
        equivalent
        ?x memberOf Quantity and ?x[hasUnitType hasValue _10KilogramDrum] and ?y[hasNumericalValue hasValue
            wsml#numericMultiply(?z1,?z,4.5359237)].
```

These domain specific rules define how attribute values in the different ontology instances are related. One such example is given in Listing 6. It defines a constraint how a unit price relates to the *financialAmount* and *productQuantity* properties and how from a given instance a per-unit price can be calculated. The constraint can be used by the requester to implement a price comparison between competing offers received from different partners. The dependencies between the different packaging sizes and its corresponding values are made explicit in the ontology. This simple illustrative example shows how two partners can agree on the interpretation of the *financialAmount* in a PIP 3A1 message instance, since the amount can refer to different quantities of the product. The RosettaNet specification includes many more elements where the relation between values is not as straightforward as in the unit price example such as the payment terms, shipment terms or tax types to just mention some of the under-specified elements in a RosettaNet PIP 3A1.

Language Expressivity Advantages in Ontologised RosettaNet

This section presents our transformation methodology to translate traditional XML Schema and DTD-based RosettaNet messages to our ontological schema; this methodology can be used to non-obtrusively introduce the solution to existing B2B collaborations.

The DTD versions of PIP 3A1 and PIP 3A4 support two different kinds of product identifiers; the Global Trade Identification Number (GTIN), recommended by RosettaNet, and company-specific identifiers. The extract in Listing 7 shows the definition of product identifiers in the PIP 3A1 (and 3A4). The PIP3A1 DTD is very long so only the relevant lines (291-304) are shown.

Listing 6. Unit price constraint

```
relation unitPrice (ofType financialAmount, ofType productQuantity, ofType _decimal)
  nfp
    dc#relation hasValue unitPriceDependency
  endnfp

axiom unitPriceDependency
  definedBy
    !- unitPrice(?x,?y,?z) and wsml#numericDivide(?z,?x,?y).
```

Listing 7. PIP 3A1 DTD extract

```
291  <!ELEMENT ProductIdentification
292    (GlobalProductIdentifier?,
293     PartnerProductIdentification*)>
294
295  <!ELEMENT GlobalProductIdentifier'
296    (#PCDATA)>
297
298  <!ELEMENT PartnerProductIdentification
299    (GlobalPartnerClassificationCode,
300     ProprietaryProductIdentifier,
301     revisionIdentifier?)>
302
303  <!ELEMENT ProprietaryProductIdentifier
304    (#PCDATA)>
```

RosettaNet message guidelines for PIP 3A1 add a *natural language constraint* for *ProductIdentification* that the DTD's expressive power does not capture: *Constraint: One instance of either GlobalProductIdentifier or PartnerProductIdentification is mandatory.* Without this constraint, a valid *ProductIdentification* could be without any identifiers as both identifications are optional. PIP 3A1 is not yet available as XML Schema, where such constraint can be expressed.

Listing 8 shows such an XML Schema version of PIP 3A4. The namespaces and annotations are dropped for brevity as XML Schemas take more space than DTDs. The XML Schemas name PIP elements differently to DTDs. The XML Schema also allows arbitrary authorities to specify the identification schemes, which introduces another mapping challenge.

In the Web Service Modeling Language such constraints can be easily expressed as shown in this section. The product identifier information in our ontology is presented in Listing 9. The GTIN is handled as any other identification authority/qualifier (*qualificationAgency*) and the RosettaNet DTD and XML Schema product identification information can be presented in this ontology including the natural language constraints. The qualification agency can be for example the *buyer's, seller's*

Listing 8. PIP 3A4 XML Schema extract

```
<xs:element name="ProductIdentification" type="ProductIdentificationType" />
<xs:complexType name="ProductIdentificationType">
 <xs:complexContent><xs:sequence>
   <xs:element name="ProductName" type="xs:string" minOccurs="0" />
   <xs:element name="Revision" type="xs:string" minOccurs="0" />
   <xs:choice>
     <xs:element ref="AlternativeIdentifier" maxOccurs="unbounded" />
     <xs:element ref="GTIN" />
   </xs:choice>
 </xs:sequence></xs:complexContent>
</xs:complexType>
<xs:element name="AlternativeIdentifier" type="AlternativeIdentifierType" />
<xs:complexType name="AlternativeIdentifierType">
 <xs:sequence>
   <xs:element name="Authority" type="xs:string" />
   <xs:element name="Identifier" type="xs:string" />
 </xs:sequence>
</xs:complexType>
```

Listing 9. Product identification in the RosettaNet ontology

```
concept productIdentification
      nonFunctionalProperties
            dc#description hasValue "Collection of business properties describing identifiers."
      endNonFunctionalProperties
      productIdentifier ofType (1 1) _string
      qualificationAgency ofType (1 1) _string
      revision ofType (0 1) _string

axiom qualificationAgencyConstraint
      nonFunctionalProperties
            dc#description hasValue "The valid list of agencies who have defined product identifiers."
      endNonFunctionalProperties
      definedBy !- ?x[qualificationAgency hasValue ?type] memberOf productIdentification
            and (?type = "GTIN" or ?type = "Manufacturer" or ?type = "Buyer"
                 or ?type = "Seller" or ?type = "EN" or ?type = "BP").
```

or *original equipment manufacturer's identifier* or any other identification scheme provider. The constraint in Listing 9 ensures that the value of *qualificationAgency* is among those supported by the Buyer. The benefit of applying a more expressive Web ontology language such as WSML is that it allows the description of logical relationships between the elements. This information can subsequently be applied for better validation of the message contents. Furthermore, with ontologies it is straightforward to specify that a given product belongs to certain classification class and this information can be utilised to offer suitable substitutable products. Hepp et al., 2005 present a product classification schema in a Web Ontology language which can be used for this purpose.

A SEMANTIC ROSETTANET INTEGRATION ARCHITECTURE

In this section we outline how RosettaNet collaborations are currently implemented in Service-oriented architectures and what additional functionality is required when introducing Semantic Web Services.

Service-Oriented Architecture (SOA)

Service-oriented architecture is an approach to the development of loosely-coupled, protocol-independent and distributed software applications as collections of well-defined autonomous services in a standardised way, enhancing re-usability and interoperability. The SOA paradigm intends to model the business as a collection of services that are available across the enterprise that can be invoked through standard protocols. SOAs are often realised through Web Services technologies (Papazoglou & Heuvel, 2007).

The idea of SOA is to use documents as loosely-coupled interfaces and thereby hiding implementation details (Glushko & McGrath, 2005). Therefore, the RosettaNet PIPs form natural services based on standard protocols. For instance, in the PIP 3A4 Purchase Order (PO) process, the seller provides a service that receives a PIP 3A4 PO request messages. After internally checking the PO, the seller sends the PIP 3A4 PO confirmation as the response to the request. The PO message information is extracted and saved to the back-end systems that need to expose some sort of service interfaces to support those interactions. In this collaboration, the standard RosettaNet messages are the common standard protocol.

The current RosettaNet-based integrations often utilise SOA associated products. These products, offered by many of the major software companies (e.g. Microsoft BizTalk, TIBCO BusinessWorks, Oracle BPEL Process Manager etc.), support Web Service technologies and B2B standards such as RosettaNet (Medjahed et al., 2003). They have functionality related to design the private and public processes of a collaboration participant and to define the mapping between different schemas. They also contain adapters to popular packaged application to facilitate interoperability with those applications.

Semantic Service-Oriented Architecture

The notion of a semantic service-oriented architecture (sSOA) (Haller et al., 2005) has been introduced to capture the additional requirements on the execution of Semantic Web Services. In order to avail of the benefits of ontologised RosettaNet messages we propose a light-weight adoption of the WSMX architecture (Haselwanter et al., 2006).

We introduce the following services to a traditional SOA architecture; a knowledge base replacing the service repository in a traditional SOA, ontology adapters ensuring the lifting and lowering of traditional XML Schema based messages to an ontological level and a reasoner service for query answering over the knowledge base, see Figure 2.

Knowledge Base

Similar to traditional SOAs the knowledge base is a mechanism that handles the persistence of distributed data. However, in an sSOA the data is stored in ontology language documents. In the RosettaNet collaboration these documents include the ontology schemas as well as runtime instances generated by the adapter after the receiving of PIP messages. The knowledge base is used by the reasoner service to perform information retrieval and query-answering functionality.

Reasoner Service

The reasoner is required to perform query answering operations on the knowledge base, including the collaboration instance data during execution. Reasoning is an important functionality throughout the execution process and it is used by the adapters to perform data mediation. It can further be used by a decision support system after and during the execution for the selection of a provider based on the domain specific rules included in the ontology.

The type of reasoner required is dependent on the variant of WSML to be used for the semantic descriptions. The reasoner service offers an abstraction layer (WSML2Reasoner[8]) on top of several reasoners. Depending on the variant used, the queries are passed to the appropriate underlying reasoning engine. Since the current RosettaNet ontology falls into the WSML-Rule variant, we use IRIS[9] and Flora-2 (Yang et al., 2003) for reasoning services.

Adapter Framework

The integration of the Buyer's back-end applications and the B2B standards of each Seller require specific mapping functionality. The role of the adapters is to translate the non-WSML data formats to WSML. The adapters act as the actual service provider for the semantic B2B gateway.

Figure 2. Overview of the integration architecture

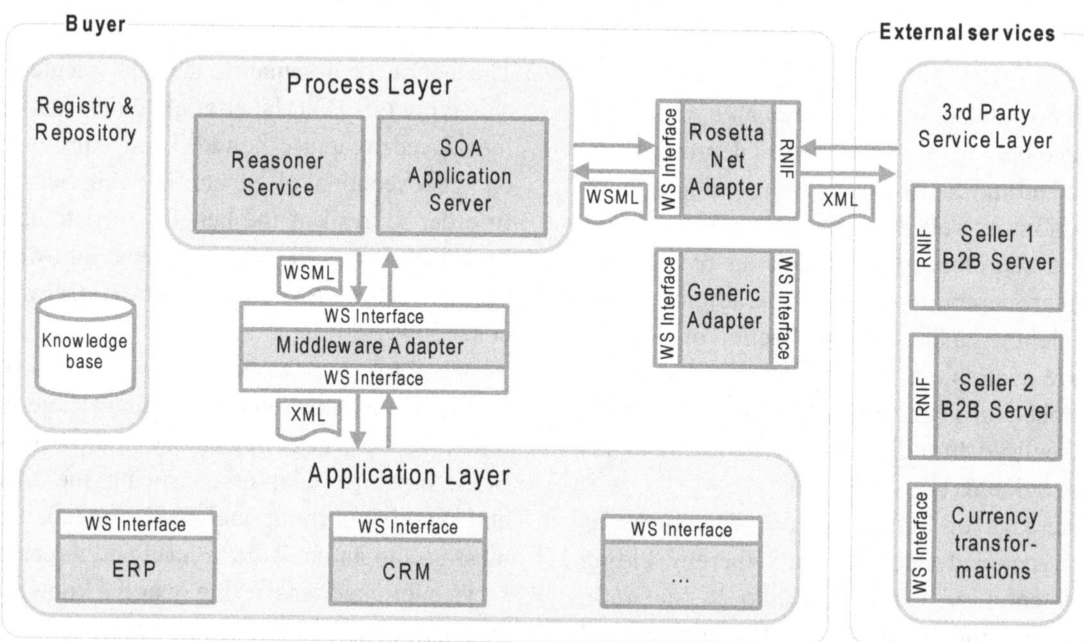

The service interface of the adapter is used by the sSOA to invoke the provider functionality instead of directly invoking the RosettaNet service endpoint of the partner. Thus, essentially the adapter functionality is registered as a service with the system. Further, the sSOA only operates on the choreography of the adapter (c.f. left part of Figure 4), which maps between the choreography of the partner's (c.f. right part of Figure 4) e-business environment and the choreography registered with sSOA. The choreography definition is part of the WSMO description of a service and specifies the input and output operations as well as transition rules and constraints on the states in the communication.

RosettaNet adapters The basic functionality of the RosettaNet adapter involves the functionality related to enveloping, encrypting and decrypting and validation of RosettaNet messages. Here, the existing B2B gateway functionality can be used if the organisation already has a product for RNIF communication. Tikkala et al. (2005) present a system with such a functionality, which can handle the RNIF 2.0 related tasks.

When working with sSOA, the mapping rules need to be defined for the runtime phase to lift RosettaNet XML instance messages to the WSML ontology and lower it back to the XML level respectively (c.f. Figure 3).

In our scenario described in section 2.2 mapping rules for PIPs 3A1 and 3A4 are required. We lift the messages to the domain ontology and essentially implement the mediation in the adapter using XSLT style sheets. Listing 10 contains a snippet of such an example mapping from a DTD-based PIP to WSML. Listing 11 shows the same mappings, but for the XML Schema version PIP. We assume that Seller 1 uses the XML Schema version of RosettaNet PIP 3A4. The mapping lifts the GTIN number to the uniform identification scheme in the ontology. In the lowering of messages, by knowing that a GTIN identifier and company-specific identifiers point to the same product, the mapping can provide an identifier needed by the given partner. As the product information definitions in all DTD and XML Schema based PIPs are similar, these mapping templates can be reused with all the PIPs. With small modification it is easy to create templates for other B2B standards as well.

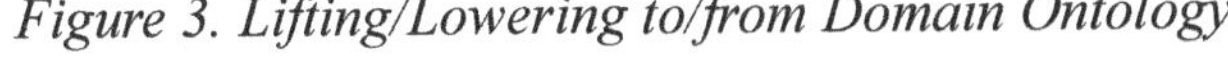
Figure 3. Lifting/Lowering to/from Domain Ontology

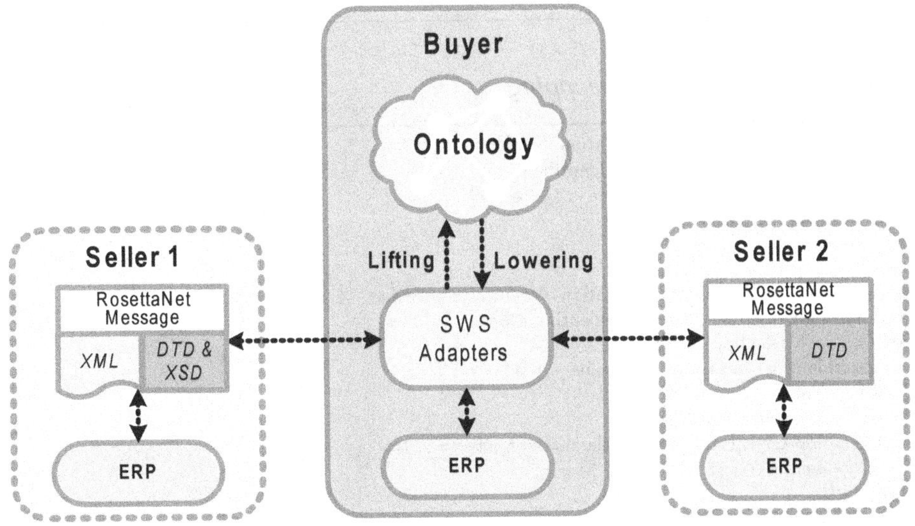

Figure 4 shows the RosettaNet adapter execution flow in a PIP process of RFQ request and response messages as described in the motivating example. The execution flow is logically identical with PIP 3A4:

- The sSOA first sends the WSML message to the RosettaNet adapter as a WSML RFQ message.
- The adapter receives the RFQ and translates it to a RosettaNet RFQ XML message.
- The adapter creates an RNIF 2.0 envelope for this message and signs the message using certificates and sends it to the endpoint of a Seller (certificate as well as endpoint information are implemented in the adapter). As a result, a confirmation that the message has been received is sent back to sSOA. This information is used to start the 24h countdown during which the Seller has time to answer with a quote response.
- The sSOA subsequently expects an acknowledgment message by the Seller in form of an RNIF 2.0 signal message. The acknowledgement needs to arrive in 2 hours or the original RFQ is sent again as indicated in the PIP.
- After receiving the acknowledgment, the adapter is waiting for the Quote response from the Seller.
- The adapter receives the Quote response and translates it using an XSLT script to WSML

Listing 10. DTD-based XSLT mapping

```
<xsl:for-each select="ProductIdentification/GlobalPartnerClassificationCode">
  instance localUID memberOf productIdentification
    productIdentifier hasValue <xsl:value-of select="."/>
    qualificationAgency hasValue GTIN
</xsl:for-each>

<xsl:for-each select="ProductIdentification/PartnerProductIdentification/">
  instance localUID memberOf productIdentification
    <xsl:for-each select="ProprietaryProductIdentifier">
      productIdentifier hasValue <xsl:value-of select="."/>
    </xsl:for-each>
    <xsl:for-each select="GlobalPartnerClassificationCode">
      qualificationAgency hasValue <xsl:value-of select="."/>
    </xsl:for-each>
</xsl:for-each>
```

Listing 11. XML-Schema-based XSLT mapping

```
<xsl:for-each select="ProductIdentification/GTIN">
  instance localUID memberOf productIdentification
    productIdentifier hasValue <xsl:value-of select="."/>
    qualificationAgency hasValue GTIN
</xsl:for-each>

<xsl:for-each select="ProductIdentification/AlternativeIdentifier/">
  instance localUID memberOf productIdentification
    <xsl:for-each select="Identifier">
      productIdentifier hasValue <xsl:value-of select="."/>
    </xsl:for-each>
    <xsl:for-each select="Authority">
      qualificationAgency hasValue <xsl:value-of select="."/>
    </xsl:for-each>
</xsl:for-each>
```

Figure 4. RosettaNet Adapter

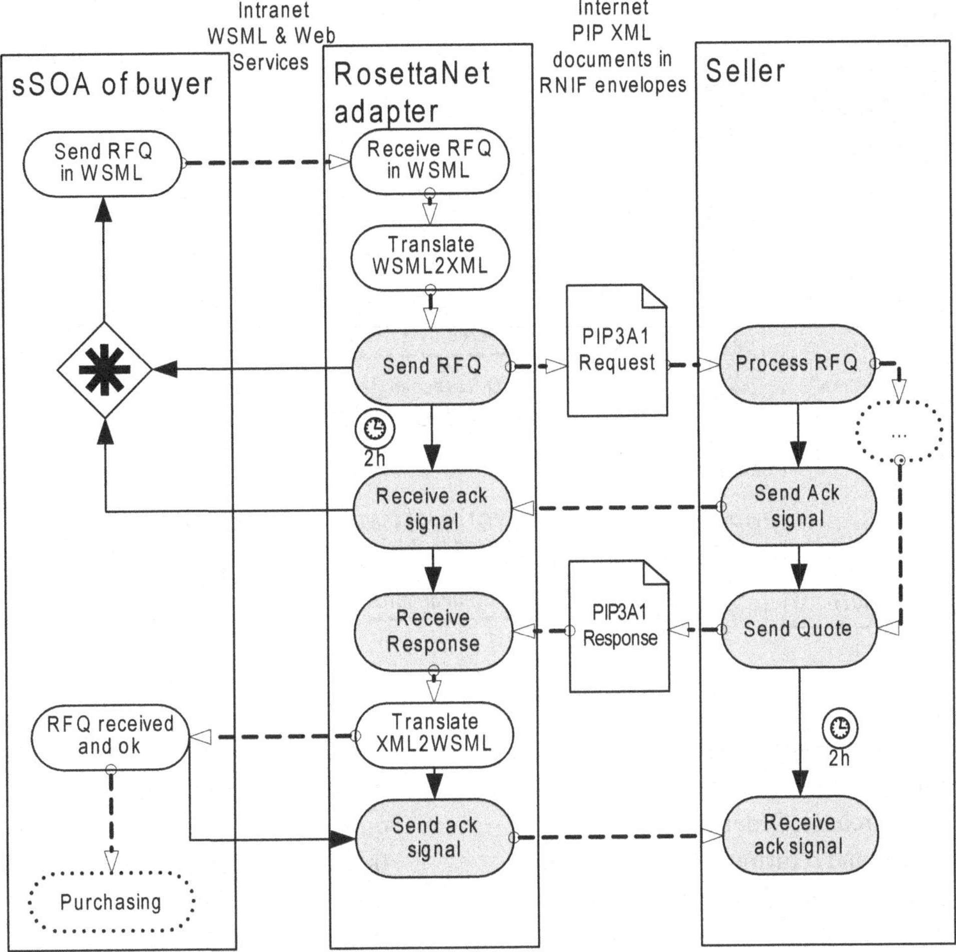

and sends it to the sSOA to check that the response does not violate the axioms of the ontology. This response is processed in the sSOA and sent to the back-end applications. The sSOA also forwards an acknowledgment signal indicating that their Quote response was received at the adapter, which sends the acknowledgment signal back to the Seller.

Back-End Adapters. Likewise to the RosettaNet adapter, specific adapters to integrate various back-end systems are required. The messages used within the back-end system (e.g. XML or flat-file) have to be mapped to/from the domain ontology. The back-end system adapters are required to perform the lifting/lowering of the internally used messages between the back-end systems and the sSOA.

Description of the Complete Message Flow with Heterogeneous Sellers

This section introduces example runtime behaviour when interacting with two sellers. We describe the execution process and interactions in the sSOA according to the scenario: (1) initiation of a request for specific parts by the back-end systems, (2)

Figure 5. Runtime behaviour of the proposed solution

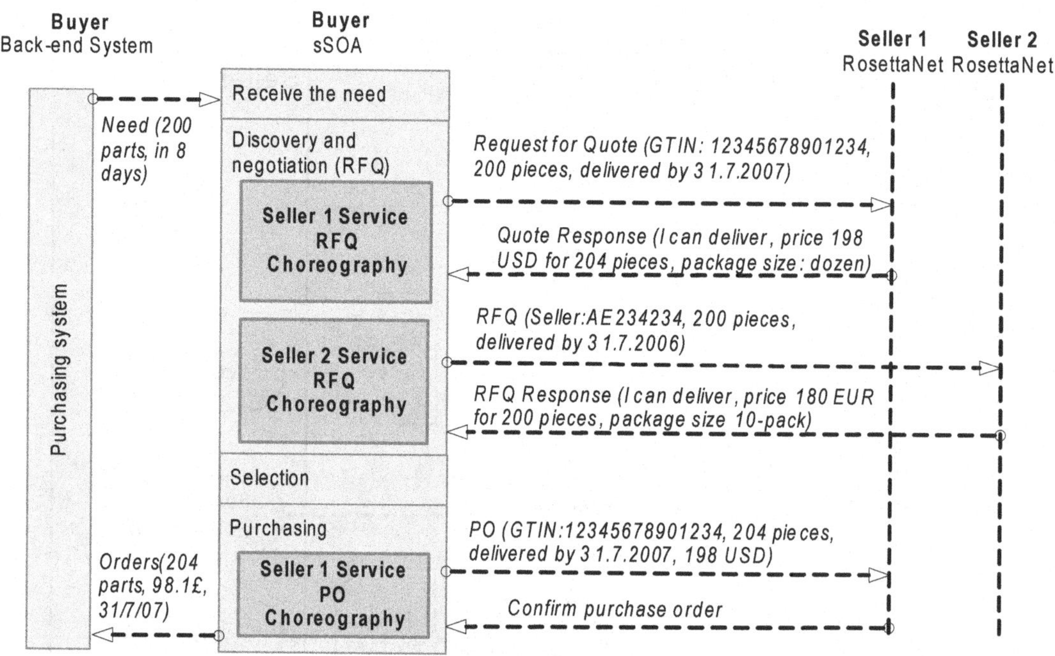

requesting quotes from potential sellers for price and availability, (3) selecting the best quote, (4) initiating the Purchase Order process with the selected supplier and returning the details to the back-end system. Figure 5 shows the run-time behaviour of the solution:

- **Getting the service need:** The buyer's back-end system issues a request in its proprietary format to the back-end adapter. The request is *to get 200 parts delivered to the plant within 8 days*. The adapter translates the request into a request in WSML, the format required by the sSOA for matching potential services.
- **Requesting quotes:** All services in the sSOA repository that match the request are found. In our case the services of Sellers 1 and 2 are discovered as potential suppliers for the requested part. The PIP 3A1 "Request for Quote" choreography (RFQ) is initiated with both Sellers to identify whether they can indeed deliver the required product within the given schedule and to discover their quoted price. The two sellers offer quotes that differ in packaging sizes, currencies and part identifiers. These heterogeneities in the request and response messages are automatically mediated by the RosettaNet adapter which translates all exchanged messages as described previously in Figure 4. For reference, extracts[10] of the sellers' PIP 3A1 "Quote response messages" in XML and in WSML are shown in Listing 12.
- **Selection:** Once both sellers provided their quotes and the messages are received and lifted to WSML, rules defined at design-time and rules defined in the RosettaNet ontology ensure that facts are inserted during reasoning to obtain homogenous ontology instances. These facts are used for comparison to select the best supplier for the requested service. In our scenario, the selection is performed according to the

Listing 12. Extract of Seller 1's PIP 3A1 response in XML (left) and WSML (right)

```
<GlobalTransportEventCode>Dock</
    GlobalTransportEventCode>
  <ProductQuantity>204
  </ProductQuantity>
<GlobalProductUnitOfMeasureCode>dozen
</GlobalProductUnitOfMeasureCode>
<SubstituteProductReference>
  <GlobalProductSubstitutionReasonCode>
    Better product
  </GlobalProductSubstitutionReasonCode>
</SubstituteProductReference>
<totalPrice>
  <FinancialAmount>
    <GlobalCurrencyCode>USD
    </GlobalCurrencyCode>
    <MonetaryAmount>198
    </MonetaryAmount>
  </FinancialAmount>
</totalPrice>
```

```
instance QuoteLineItem1 memberOf
    rfq#quoteLineItem
  rfq#globalProductUnitOfMeasurementCode
    hasValue "dozen"
instance quantitySchedule1 memberOf
    core#quantitySchedule
  core#productQuantity hasValue "204"
instance substituteProductReference1 memberOf
    core#substituteProductReference
  core#GlobalProductSubstitutionReasonCode
    hasValue "Better product"
instance totalPrice1 memberOf core#totalPrice
  core#financialAmount
    hasValue FinancialAmountTot
instance FinancialAmountTot memberOf
    core#FinancialAmount
  core#globalCurrencyCode hasValue USD
  core#monetaryAmount hasValue "198"
```

cheapest price per unit. Since currency rates are volatile, the transformations cannot be expressed in logical axioms; instead, an external Web service is invoked at runtime. To find the cheapest price, a conversion of the different currencies and packaging sizes used in the quotes is performed inside the sSOA through an appropriate currency transformation service and packaging unit transformation service. In this case, Seller 1 offers the cheaper quote and is therefore selected.

- **Purchasing:** The "purchase order" process (PO) is initiated by the sSOA with the selected Seller 1. The process is similar to the "Request for Quote" process except that the message exchange follows PIP3A4 instead of PIP3A1.

After receiving the PO response from Seller 1, the sSOA performs again the necessary data mediation for product identifiers and currencies; after mediation the translated PO response is returned to the initial back-end system (using a format and structure native to the back-end's interface).

ALTERNATIVES

Anicic et al. (2006) present how two XML Schema-based automotive standards, AIAG and STAR, are translated from XML to an OWL-based ontology using XSLT. The authors use a two-phase design and runtime approach. Their approach focuses on the conceptual lifting of XML Schemas to OWL.

Brambilla et al. (2006) present a prototype solution based on ontologies designed in the Web Service Modeling Language to tackle the factitious requirements defined in the Semantic Web Service challenge[11]. The system uses a software engineering approach and utilises a commercial visual modelling tool.

Dogac et al. (2006) present Artemis, a system to semantically enrich Web Services in the healthcare domain. The work discusses how healthcare data defined in domain standards, such as HL7 and CEN, can be formally represented and how these formal representations are used in the execution of Semantic Web Services. The presented architecture clearly distinguishes between the functional Web Service interfaces and the application data.

Foxvog & Bussler (2006) describe how EDI X12 can be presented in the WSML, OWL and CycL ontology languages. The work focuses on issues encountered when building a general-purpose B2B ontology.

Khalaf (2007) describes an implementation applying the Business Process Specification Language (BPEL) to RosettaNet PIPs. The objective is to allow the partners to exchange details about their business processes. The evaluation is done by presenting the solution to the RosettaNet board and the BPEL Technical Committee in OASIS. In the test setup, the author deployed multiple servers running different instances representing different companies. The implementation used Web Services instead of RNIF to demonstrate easier agreement of choreography details. PIPs 3A2 and 3A4 were used in the demonstration.

Preist et al. (2005) present a prototype solution covering all phases of a B2B integration life-cycle, starting from discovering potential partners to performing integrations including mediations. The work also addresses issues in translating messages to RDF. The demonstrator uses XML, RDF and OWL-DL. Back-end integration or security aspects are not addressed in this work.

Trastour, Bartolini, & Preist (2003) and Trastour, Preist, & Coleman (2003) augment RosettaNet PIPs with partner-specific DAML+OIL constraints and use agent technologies to automatically propose modifications if the partners use messages differently.

RosettaNet is used in many of the solutions described above, but none of them applies a RosettaNet ontology in combination with external business ontologies to automatically homogenise the message content from different providers and select services based on the most competitive offer. All solutions including the one described in this chapter are still use case based and lack evaluations in production settings.

COST AND BENEFITS

The current long and expensive setup of B2B integrations has lead to business models with simple public processes in which long term rigid partnerships are established between organisations. In RosettaNet collaborations there is often no competition in the request for quotes, as usually the default partner is selected directly for purchasing using long-term contracts (Kotinurmi et al., 2006). This is partly due to the overhead to manage multiple partner specific quoting and purchasing integrations.

The presented solution shows how heterogeneities, caused by the introduction of new partners to the supply chain, are reduced and how more competitive arrangements can be organised. The quoting and purchasing scenario highlights some of the problems currently observed in RosettaNet collaborations. For example, accepting suppliers from different countries causes heterogeneities, as the partners are likely to use different currencies, different measurement units or different packaging units. The current DTD-based PIPs even enforce organisations to implement additional validation means. However, even with the introduction of XSD based PIPs, one can represent the same information within two message instances based on the same schema in different ways. For example, some PIPs allow time durations to be specified either using "starting time and duration" or "starting time and ending time". Such freedom in the specification requires both partners to agree on the particular representation and its implementation. Any changes to the way information is represented according to the schema causes additional costs in the setup.

The benefits of resolving such heterogeneities for the buyer result from decreased costs of purchasing as the best value deals can be selected on the basis of the best quotes. The sellers benefit from being able to integrate to multiply buyers without making potentially costly changes to their current interfaces. Only declarative rules defining how to interpret incompatible message instances have to be added. Contrary to traditional B2B collaborations where functions are developed on a point-to-point basis, the explicitly modelled relations between concepts in the RosettaNet ontology help to resolve data heterogeneities globally and are thus reusable in every partner integration. The relations between the elements in the RosettaNet specification are not specified by the current schemas as they are not expressive enough to present such relations.

Being able to handle the heterogeneities caused by the freedom in the specifications is particularly important for companies that cannot dictate the use of B2B standards to their partners. Additional partners are introduced more easily to the supply chain and the possibility to have more competitive partnerships benefits the buyers. The solutions provided have potential use in a significant portion of all RosettaNet PIPs, of which roughly half contain currency and measurement unit information. According to McComb (2004), more than half of the 300 billion dollars annually spent on systems integration is spent on resolving such semantic issues.

The costs associated with the presented solution are characterised by two distinctive features; high ontology engineering costs, but low subsequent setup costs. The high costs associated with the ontology engineering can be compared with the development of the RosettaNet framework. Highly skilled knowledge engineers are required to ontologise the full semantics implicit to the current RosettaNet specifications. Following a bottom-up approach the solution presented takes the existing schema definitions and gradually introduces formal semantics for different kind of heterogeneity sources. It is a time-consuming knowledge engineering task to encompass all RosettaNet business documents in the ontology, but it is a one-time effort. We presented an approach to automatically derive a core RosettaNet ontology in Haller et al. (2008). Similar ontologisation efforts are undertaken in multiple domains, such as the CyC ontology[12] for general knowledge, the Geonames ontology[13] for geospatial information, uniProt[14] for protein sequences and the Gene Ontology[15] describing gene and gene product attributes in any organism. As discussed by Preist et al. (2005), the use of dynamic integration via semantic descriptions and generic e-business ontologies is expected to become an important industrial technique in the near future; an example of such a generic e-business ontology is the eClassOWL[16] ontology, an ontologised taxonomy of product and service categories (Hepp, 2005a,b; Hepp et al., 2005).

Similarly to traditional B2B integrations (Bussler, 2003) adapters are required for the communication on the application layer as well as the service layer. The behaviour of the RosettaNet adapter concerning RNIF is identical in all RosettaNet PIPs and thus needs to be defined just once. Adapters for different partners at the service layer in an ontologically enhanced RosettaNet solution have the advantage over schema matching approaches that the semantic relations are reusable. Instead of partner-specific point-to-point XSLT transformations, semantic relations are specified only once, but reused in many collaborations. Multiple approaches exist to automatically (Aumueller et al., 2005; Hu et al., 2006; Tang et al., 2006) or semi-automatically (Maedche et al., 2002; Mocan & Cimpian, 2007; Noy & Musen, 2000) derive such semantic relations between two ontologies. However, even if the mappings have to be added manually to the ontology, they are easier to create, since the schema (ontology) makes all data semantics explicit.

RISK ASSESSMENT

Several publications on semantic integrations (Anicic et al., 2006; Cabral et al., 2006; Preist et al., 2005; Trastour, Preist, & Coleman, 2003; Vitvar et al., 2007) have shown that conceptually, B2B integrations can benefit from semantic technologies. However, all documented implementations are prototypical and all mapping and mediation capabilities are on a use case basis. Recently, more standardised evaluation procedures have been initiated in the context of the Web Service[17] and Semantic Web Service[18] challenges. These initiatives are a first step towards a unified and realistic evaluation framework.

In terms of a migration strategy for existing infrastructure and processes, the solution presented in this chapter does not mandate changes to the infrastructure of the business partners. Rather, the solution builds on top of existing B2B standards: business partners can still utilise their existing infrastructure, while the buyer profits from applying Semantic Web technologies.

In terms of performance and scalability issues, these have not yet been addressed in current evaluations. Especially the lifting and lowering of message instances to their ontological representations in the adapters requires additional computational resources as compared to existing solutions. Since production PIP instances have been reported to be even hundreds of megabytes large (Damodaran, 2004), scalability and performance are obvious concerns in such settings. Further testing is needed to evaluate scalability and performance, as for example done with RosettaNet technologies (Tikkala et al., 2005). However, in the presented architecture, reasoning is only performed at design time, since only one partner uses message ontologies. Thus, no runtime ontology mediation is required and instead all mapping logic is coded into the back-end and RosettaNet adapters. Even current SOA implementations are said to "think SOA and implement high-performance transaction system" to address similar concerns with basic Web Service technologies (Bussler, 2007).

The strengths, weaknesses, opportunities and threats of the Ontologically-enhanced RosettaNet solution are analysed in Table 1.

- **Strengths:** The main strengths are the possibility to increase competition in the supply chain by simplifying runtime integration with multiple service providers, the lowered integration costs since many manual integration and alignment tasks (e.g. measurement unit translation and currency alignment) can be automated; and the possibility to automatically validate incoming business messages against ontologised business constraints (which are currently only informally documented at best).
- **Weaknesses:** The main weaknesses are the required skills in ontological modelling which might not be available in organisations given the young age of semantic technologies; the computational overhead in lifting and lowering XML messages, and the

Table 1. SWOT analysis of the Ontologically-enhanced RosettaNet solution

Strengths	Weaknesses
• increased competition	• ontology modeling skills required
• lower integration costs	• overhead in message lifting/lowering
• automatic validation	• high initial ontology development costs
Opportunities	**Threats**
• ontology reuse (CyC, eClassOWL)	• highly volatile environment
• automation in integration testing	• unclear technology uptake
• solution reuse	• immature tool support

required investment in the initial development of domain ontologies. On the other hand, like any other standardisation effort, the costs of ontology development can be shared by the entire business domain and development costs can be relatively low due to a high level of potential ontology reuse.

- **Opportunities:** The main opportunities are the reuse of existing top-level and e-commerce ontologies such as SUMO, Cyc and eClassOWL and the benefits gained by their reuse. Reuse is central to ontology development and offers significant business opportunities and savings through accumulated network effects. Further, the explicit formal semantics of ontologised RosettaNet messages offer opportunities for automated testing of integration solutions, which currently have to be verified manually. Finally, as in any innovative technology, an opportunity exists for early adopters to master the solution and reuse it across other domains, or even to become solution providers for other organisations in the B2B integration marketplace.
- **Threats:** The main threats are the highly volatile environment of organisations which may hamper technology that requires some setup time. The uptake of semantic technologies is still limited and the tool support for semantic technologies is immature.

Overall, the presented approach is best suited for organisations that encounter multiple heterogeneity issues and cannot dictate their partners the B2B integration details. If an organisation is able to dictate the B2B integration details onto their partners, the benefits of semantically enriched messages are limited since such an organisation can achieve homogeneity through its mandate. Similarly, for organisations with only a limited number of partner relationships the introduction of ontologised RosettaNet messages might be an overhead.

FUTURE RESEARCH DIRECTIONS AND ADDITIONAL READING

Current approaches to enterprise application integration (Erasala et al., 2003; Linthicum, 1999) and B2B integration (Bussler, 2003) are still based on static binding to services and partners. One of the major trends in enterprise information system development is model-driven design (Brown, 2004). The promise is to create business-driven IT solutions quickly and reduce the gap between business experts and technology experts. SOA and business process management standards are one step towards this goal. Ultimately, the models in an sSOA should span from formal data representations to formal business process models. Different abstraction levels should be supported such that the business analyst can use a modelling environment on a high abstraction level, but still the resulting process model can be used by the implementer as a scaffolding model. However, currently data models are still disconnected from process models and business process models on different abstraction levels, such as solution maps and business process execution language (Andrews et al., 2003) based models, are disconnected. Several recent research projects[19] and publications (Haller et al., 2006; Hepp & Roman, 2007) are trying to tackle the issue of relating different abstraction levels of business process modelling.

Other research topics related to formal process models in sSOA are the automatic composition of services and processes (Milanovic & Malek, 2004). Based on a formal model it is possible to generate a plan (process model) automatically. Most approaches to service composition are related to AI planning (McIlraith & Son, 2002; Wu et al., 2003), deductive theorem proving (Rao et al., 2006) and model checking (Berardi et al., 2005; Bultan et al., 2003). The general assumption is that every Web Service can be specified by its preconditions and effects in the planning context.

An important step towards a dynamic integration, both within and across enterprise boundaries, is a scalable and ultimately fully mechanised approach to service discovery. Automatically locating services to achieve a certain business goal can considerably reduce the development costs of B2B integrations. Providers can be dynamically selected based on the service they provide and on the properties associated with the services, such as its cost, the trust relation, security, etc. For instance, in the context of our motivating example the discovery based on the product's classification category enables a meaningful way to compare substitutable products with the initially requested items.

The solution presented in this chapter does not avail of dynamic service selection. However, as a promising research direction multiple efforts are dedicated to solve its challenges (Keller et al., 2005; Ran, 2003; Sycara et al., 2004).

CONCLUSION

The scenario discussed in this chapter on quoting and purchasing highlights the problems currently observed in RosettaNet collaborations. RosettaNet represents the current state-of-the-art in B2B integration, and its usage of XML is an improvement compared to more traditional integration solutions. However, setting up integrations using RosettaNet still requires considerable manual effort due to the heterogeneity that arises from the interpretation freedom in the RosettaNet specification.

Specifically, RosettaNet integrations still suffer from interoperability challenges in aligning the business processes of the partners, message heterogeneity due to the lack of expressive power in the schemas, and ambiguity in the type definitions, again due to the low expressivity of the schema languages used in RosettaNet.

As a consequence of the required manual integration effort, current business models in B2B integration are still simple and integration of new partners is difficult, limiting the possibility of introducing more competition in the supply chain. For example, interacting with suppliers from different countries introduces heterogeneities, since the suppliers are likely to use different currencies, different measurement units or different packaging unit. Due to the current type definitions in RosettaNet, manual effort is needed to overcome these heterogeneities.

The ontologically-enhanced RosettaNet solution presented in this chapter helps tackling heterogeneities in RosettaNet interactions. The solution relies upon a formalised RosettaNet ontology to capture otherwise implicit knowledge and rules to resolve data heterogeneities. The ontology captures definitional facts, such as the relation between measurement units or product category memberships. Such information is currently not modelled in RosettaNet. The solutions provided in this chapter have potential use in significant portions of all RosettaNet Partner Interface Processes (PIPs). Furthermore, ontologising RosettaNet messages provides support for better discovery, selection and composition of PIPs and PIP parts for other situations.

By automatically resolving such heterogeneities, the buyer gains benefits through decreased costs of purchasing as the best value deals can be selected based on the best quotes. The sellers benefit from being able to easier integrate to the buyer without having to make potentially costly changes to their current integration interfaces. The ontologically enhanced RosettaNet solution enables scalable, fast and easy to monitor processes eliminating unnecessary repetitive manual work and enabling people to concentrate on value-adding activities. Furthermore, many testing tasks can be avoided, since formal algorithms can check the quality of the processes such as the existence of data transformation from the buyer's schemas into the seller's schemas.

ACKNOWLEDGMENT

This material is based upon works supported by the Science Foundation Ireland under Grant No. SFI/04/BR/CS0694 and Grant No. SFI/02/CE1/I131 and by the Finnish Funding Agency for Technology and Innovation. The authors wish to thank Dr. Tomas Vitvar for his research participation and commenting the chapter.

REFERENCES

Aalst, W. M. van der, & Kumar, A. (2003). XML-Based Schema Definition for Support of Interorganizational Workflow. *Information Systems Research, 14* (1), 23-46.

Andrews, T., Curbera, F., Dholakia, H., Goland, Y., Klein, J., Leymann, F., et al. (2003, May). *Business Process Execution Language for Web Services, v1.1.*

Anicic, N., Ivezic, N., & Jones, A. (2006). An Architecture for Semantic Enterprise Application Integration Standards. In D. Konstantas, J.-P. Bourrires, M. Lonard, & N. Boudjlida (Eds.), (pp. 25-34). London, UK: Springer.

Aumueller, D., Do, H. H., Massmann, S., & Rahm, E. (2005). Schema and ontology matching with COMA++. In *Proceedings of the ACM SIGMOD International Conference on Management of Data* (pp. 906-908). Baltimore, Maryland, USA.

Battle, S., Bernstein, A., Boley, H., Grosof, B., Gruninger, M., Hull, R., et al. (2005). *Semantic Web Services Framework (SWSF) Overview* (Member Submission). W3C. (Available from: http://www.w3.org/Submission/SWSF/)

Berardi, D., Calvanese, D., Giacomo, G. D., Lenzerini, M., & Mecella, M. (2005). Automatic Service Composition Based on Behavioral Descriptions. *Int. J. Cooperative Inf. Syst., 14* (4), 333-376.

Brambilla, M., Celino, I., Ceri, S., Cerizza, D., Valle, E. D., & Facca, F. M. (2006). A Software Engineering Approach to Design and Development of Semantic Web Service Applications. In *Proceedings of the 5th International Semantic Web Conference.* Athens, GA, USA: Springer.

Brown, A. (2004). An Introduction *to Model Driven ArchitecturePart I: MDA and Todays Systems* (Tech. Rep.). IBM. (Available from: http://www.ibm.com/developerworks/rational/library/3100.html)

Bruijn, J. de, Bussler, C., Domingue, J., Fensel, D., Hepp, M., Keller, U., et al. (2005). *Web Service Modeling Ontology (WSMO)* (Member Submission). W3C. (Available from: http://www.w3.org/Submission/WSMO/)

Brunnermeier, S. B., & Martin, S. A. (2002). Interoperability costs in the US automotive supply chain. *Supply Chain Management: An International Journal, 7* (2), 71-82.

Bultan, T., Fu, X., Hull, R., & Su, J. (2003). Conversation specification: a new approach to design and analysis of e-service composition. In *Proceedings of the 12th international conference on World Wide Web* (pp. 403-410). New York, NY, USA: ACM Press.

Bussler, C. (2003). *B2B integration: Concepts and Architecture.* Springer.

Bussler, C. (2007). The Fractal Nature of Web Services. *IEEE Computer, 40* (3), 93-95.

Bussler, C., Fensel, D., & Maedche, A. (2002). A Conceptual Architecture for Semantic Web Enabled Web Services. *SIGMOD Record, 31* (4), 24-29. ACM Press.

Cabral, L., Domingue, J., Galizia, S., Gugliotta, A., Tanasescu, V., Pedrinaci, C., et al. (2006). IRS-III: A Broker for Semantic Web Services Based Applications. In *Proceedings of the 5th International Semantic Web Conference.* (pp. 201-214). Athens, GA, USA:Springer.

Clark, J., Casanave, C., Kanaskie, K., Harvey, B., Clark, J., Smith, N., et al. (2001). *ebXML Business Process Specification Schema (Version 1.01).* ebXML. (Available from: http://www.ebxml.org/specs/ebBPSS.pdf/)

Damodaran, S. (2004). B2B integration over the Internet with XML: RosettaNet successes and challenges. In *Proceedings of the 13th International World Wide Web Conference on Alternate track papers & posters.* (pp. 188-195). New York, NY, USA: ACM Press.

Damodaran, S. (2005). RosettaNet: Adoption Brings New Problems, New Solutions. In *Proceedings of the XML 2005 Conference.* (pp. 1-14). Atlanta, USA: IDE Alliance.

Dogac, A., Laleci, G. B., Kirbas, S., Kabak, Y., Sinir, S. S., Yildiz, A., et al. (2006). Artemis: Deploying semantically enriched Web services in the healthcare domain. *Information Systems, 31* (4-5), 321-339.

Erasala, N., Yen, D. C., & Rajkumar, T. M. (2003). Enterprise Application Integration in the electronic commerce world. *Computer Standards & Interfaces, 25* (2), 69-82.

Fensel, D. (2003). *Ontologies: A Silver Bullet for Knowledge Management and Electronic Commerce.* Springer.

Foxvog, D., & Bussler, C. (2006). Ontologizing EDI Semantics. In *Proceedings of the Workshop on Ontologising Industrial Standards.* (pp. 301-311). Tucson, AZ, USA: Springer.

Glushko, R. J., & McGrath, T. (2005). Document engineering: analyzing and designing the semantics of business service networks. In *Proceedings of the IEEE EEE05 international workshop on business services networks.* (pp. 9-15). Piscataway, NJ, USA: IEEE Press.

Grosof, B. N., Horrocks, I., Volz, R., & Decker, S. (2003). Description logic programs: combining logic programs with description logic. In *Proceedings of the 12th International World Wide Web Conference* (pp. 48-57). New York, NY, USA: ACM Press.

Gruber, T. R. (1993). Towards Principles for the Design of Ontologies Used for Knowledge Sharing. In N. Guarino & R. Poli (Eds.), *Formal Ontology in Conceptual Analysis and Knowledge Representation.* Deventer, The Netherlands: Kluwer Academic Publishers.

Haller, A., Cimpian, E., Mocan, A., Oren, E., & Bussler, C. (2005). WSMX - A Semantic Service-Oriented Architecture. *In Proceedings of the 3rd International Conference on Web Services,* (pp. 321-328). Orlando, Florida, USA: IEEE Computer Society.

Haller, A., Gontarczyk, J., & Kotinurmi, P. (2008). Towards a complete SCM Ontology - The Case of ontologising RosettaNet. In *Proceedings of the 23rd ACM symposium on applied computing* (SAC2008). Fortaleza, Ceara, Brazil. (to appear)

Haller, A., Kotinurmi, P., Vitvar, T., & Oren, E. (2007). Handling heterogeneity in RosettaNet messages. In *Proceedings of the 22rd ACM symposium on applied computing* (SAC2007). Seoul, South Korea. (pp..1368-1374). ACM.

Haller, A., Oren, E., & Kotinurmi, P. (2006). m3po: An ontology to relate choreographies to workflow models. In *Proceedings of the 3rd international conference on services computing,* (pp. 19-27). Chicago, Illinois, USA: IEEE Computer Society.

Haselwanter, T., Kotinurmi, P., Moran, M., Vitvar, T., & Zaremba, M. (2006). WSMX: A Semantic Service Oriented Middleware for B2B integration. In *Proceedings of the International Conference on Service-Oriented Computing,* (pp. 477-483). Springer.

Hepp, M. (2005a). eClassOWL: A fully-fledged products and services ontology in OWL. In

Proceedings of the International Semantic Web Conference (ISWC).

Hepp, M. (2005b). A methodology for deriving OWL ontologies from products and services categorization standards. In *Proceedings of the 13th European Conference on Information Systems* (ECIS2005), (pp. 1-12).

Hepp, M., Leukel, J., & Schmitz, V. (2005). A Quantitative Analysis of eCl@ss, UNSPSC, eOTD, and RNTD Content, Coverage, and Maintenance. In *Proceedings of the IEEE ICEBE 2005 Conference*, (pp. 572-581).

Hepp, M., & Roman, D. (2007). An Ontology Framework for Semantic Business Process Management. In *Proceedings of the 8th International Conference Wirtschaftsinformatik* 2007.

Hu, W., Cheng, G., Zheng, D., Zhong, X., & Qu, Y. (2006). The Results of Falcon-AO in the OAEI 2006 Campaign. In *Proceedings of the 1st International Workshop on Ontology Matching*. Athens, GA, USA.

Keller, U., Lara, R., Lausen, H., Polleres, A., & Fensel, D. (2005). Automatic Location of Services. In *Proceedings of the 2nd European Semantic Web Conference*, (pp. 1-16). Heraklion, Crete, Greece: Springer.

Khalaf, R. (2007). From RosettaNet PIPs to BPEL processes: A three level approach for business protocols. *Data and Knowledge Engineering, 61* (1), 23-38.

Kotinurmi, P., Vitvar, T., Haller, A., Richardson, R., & Boran, A. (2006). Semantic Web Services Enabled B2B integration. In J. Lee, J. Shim, S. goo Lee, C. Bussler, & S. S. Y. Shim (Eds.), *DEECS* (pp. 209-223). Springer.

Linthicum, D. (1999). *Enterprise Application Integration*. Reading, MA: Addision-Wesley Longman.

Maedche, A., Motik, B., Silva, N., & Volz, R. (2002). MAFRA - A MApping FRAmework for Distributed Ontologies. In *Proceedings of the 13th International Conference on Knowledge Engineering and Knowledge Management. Ontologies and the Semantic Web*, (pp. 235-250). Springer.

Martin, D., et al. (2004). *OWL-S: Semantic Markup for Web Services* (Member Submission). W3C. (Available from: http://www.w3.org/Submission/OWL-S/)

McComb, D. (2004). *Semantics in Business Systems: The Savvy Manager's Guide*. San Francisco: Morgan Kaufmann.

McIlraith, S. A., & Son, T. C. (2002). Adapting Golog for Composition of Semantic Web Services. In *Proceedings of the 8th International Conference on Principles and Knowledge Representation and Reasoning*. Toulouse, France.

McIlraith, S. A., Son, T. C., & Zeng, H. (2001). Semantic Web Services. *IEEE Intelligent Systems, 16* (2), 46-53.

Medjahed, B., Benatallah, B., Bouguettaya, A., Ngu, A. H. H., & Elmagarmid, A. K. (2003). Business-to-business interactions: issues and enabling technologies. *VLDB Journal, 12* (1), 59-85.

Milanovic, N., & Malek, M. (2004). Current Solutions for Web Service Composition. *IEEE Internet Computing, 8* (6).

Mocan, A., & Cimpian, E. (2007). An Ontology-Based Data Mediation Framework for Semantic Environments. *International Journal on Semantic Web and Information Systems (IJSWIS)*, 3 (2).

Niles, I., & Pease, A. (2001). Towards a standard upper ontology. In *Proceedings of the international conference on formal ontology in information systems*, (pp. 2-9). New York, NY, USA.

Noy, N. F., & Musen, M. A. (2000). PROMPT: Algorithm and Tool for Automated Ontology

Merging and Alignment. In *Proceedings of the 7th National Conference on Artificial Intelligence,* (pp. 450-455). Austin, Texas, USA.

Nurmilaakso, J.-M., & Kotinurmi, P. (2004). A Review of XML-based Supply-Chain Integration. *Production Planning and Control, 15* (6), 608-621.

Papazoglou, M. P., & Heuvel, W.-J. van den. (2007). Service-Oriented Architectures: approaches, technologies and research issues. *VLDB Journal, 16* (3), 389-415.

Preist, C., Cuadrado, J. E., Battle, S., Williams, S., & Grimm, S. (2005). Automated Business-to-Business Integration of a Logistics Supply Chain using Semantic Web Services Technology. In *Proceedings of 4th International Semantic Web Conference,* (pp. 987-1001). Springer.

Ran, S. (2003). A model for Web services discovery with QoS. *SIGecom Exch., 4* (1), 1-10.

Rao, J., Kungas, P., & Matskin, M. (2006). Composition of Semantic Web services using linear logic theorem proving. *Information Systems, 31* (4), 340-360.

Roman, D., Keller, U., Lausen, H., Bruijn, J. de, Lara, R., Stollberg, M., et al. (2005). Web Service Modeling Ontology. *Applied Ontologies, 1* (1), 77-106.

Shim, S. S. Y., Pendyala, V. S., Sundaram, M., & Gao, J. Z. (2000). Business-to-Business E-Commerce Frameworks. *IEEE Computer, 33* (10), 40{47.

Sycara, K. P., Paolucci, M., Soudry, J., & Srinivasan, N. (2004). Dynamic Discovery and Coordination of Agent-Based Semantic Web Services. *IEEE Internet Computing, 8* (3), pp. 66-73.

Tang, J., Li, J., Liang, B., Huang, X., Li, Y., & Wang, K. (2006). Using Bayesian decision for ontology mapping. *Journal of Web Semantics, 4* (4), 243-262.

Tikkala, J., Kotinurmi, P., & Soininen, T. (2005). Implementing a RosettaNet Business-to- Business Integration Platform Using J2EE and Web Services. In *Proceedings of the 7th IEEE International Conference on E-Commerce Technology* , (pp. 553-558). IEEE Computer Society.

Trastour, D., Bartolini, C., & Preist, C. (2003). Semantic Web support for the business-to-business e-commerce pre-contractual lifecycle. *Computer Networks, 42* (5), 661-673.

Trastour, D., Preist, C., & Coleman, D. (2003). Using Semantic Web Technology to Enhance Current Business-to-Business Integration Approaches. In *Proceedings of the 7th International Enterprise Distributed Object Computing Conference,* (pp. 222-231). IEEE Computer Society.

Uschold, M., & Gruninger, M. (1996). Ontologies: principles, methods, and applications. *Knowledge Engineering Review, 11* (2), 93-155.

Vitvar, T., Mocan, A., Kerrigan, M., Zaremba, M., Zaremba, M., Moran, M., et al. (2007). Semantically-enabled Service-Oriented Architecture: concepts, technology and application. *Service Oriented Computing and Applications, 2* (2), 129-154.

Wu, D., Parsia, B., Sirin, E., Hendler, J. A., & Nau, D. S. (2003). Automating DAML-Sweb Services Composition Using SHOP2. In *Proceedings of the 2nd International Semantic Web Conference,* pp. 195-210. Sanibel Island, FL, USA: Springer.

Yang, G., Kifer, M., & Zhao, C. (2003). Flora-2: A rule-based knowledge representation and inference infrastructure for the Semantic Web. In *Proceedings of the Coopis, doa, and odbase - otm confederated international conferences, On the move to meaningful internet systems 2003.* Catania, Sicily, Italy.

ENDNOTES

1 http://www.RosettaNet.org/
2 http://www.openapplications.org/
3 http://www.ebxml.org/
4 http://www.oasis-open.org/committees/ubl/
5 http://www.bpmn.org/
6 For understanding the syntax, see http://www.WSMO.org/WSML/WSML-syntax
7 See http://ontologies.deri.org/eclass/5.1/#C_AAA374002
8 See http://tools.deri.org/WSML2reasoner/
9 http://iris-reasoner.org/
10 The full examples are available at http://www.m3pe.org/ontologies/RosettaNet/
11 http://sws-challenge.org/
12 http://www.opencyc.org/
13 http://www.geonames.org/ontology/
14 http://dev.isb-sib.ch/projects/uniprot-rdf/
15 http://www.geneontology.org/
16 http://www.heppnetz.org/eclassowl/
17 http://ws-challenge.org/
18 http://sws-challenge.org/
19 http://www.ip-super.org/, http://www.m3pe.org/

Chapter XI
Towards an Operational REA Business Ontology

Frederik Gailly
Ghent University, Belgium

Geert Poels
Ghent University, Belgium

ABSTRACT

It is widely recognized that ontologies can be used to support the semantic integration and interoperability of heterogeneous information systems. Resource Event Agent (REA) is a well-known business ontology that was proposed for ontology-driven enterprise system development. However, the current specification is neither sufficiently explicit nor formal, and thus difficult to operationalize for use in ontology-driven business information systems. In this chapter REA is redesigned and formalized following a methodology based on the reengineering extension of the METHONTOLOGY framework for ontology development. The redesign is focused on developing a UML representation of REA that improves upon existing representations and that can easily be transformed into a formal representation. The formal representation of REA is developed in OWL. The chapter discusses the choices made in redesigning REA and in transforming REA's UML representation into an OWL representation. It is also illustrated how this new formal representation of the REA-ontology can be used to support ontology-driven supply chain collaboration.

CURRENT SITUATION

The last 10 years there has been an increased interest in generic models that describe parts of a business or the activities of a business. These so called "business ontologies" have been proposed to support requirements elicitation, modeling and engineering of e-commerce application, enterprise systems and e-collaboration systems (Assmann, Zchaler, & Wagner, 2006; Baida, Gordijn, Saele, Morch, & Akkermans, 2004; Dietz, 2005; Grunninger, 2003). For instance, in ontology-driven business modeling, they are used to constrain the contents and structure of business models, thereby helping to identify and organize relevant objects, relationships and other knowledge (Guarino, 1997). The use of ontologies at run-time (i.e. ontology-driven systems instead of ontology-driven development - Guarino, 1997) also offers great potential for business ontologies. Specifically in and between enterprises ontology-driven information systems can be used to create interoperability at different enterprise levels: shop-floor, intra-enterprise and inter-enterprise level.

The two oldest business ontologies are TOVE (Fox, 1992) and the Enterprise ontology (Ushold, King, Moralee, & Zorgios, 1998) and were developed by some early ontology researchers. The major contribution of their work was not the ontologies themselves but the ontology engineering methodology which was used to develop the ontologies. More recent business ontologies like the Resource Event Agent business ontology (REA-ontology) (Geerts & McCarthy, 2002), E^3-value ontology (Gordijn, 2002) and e-BMO (Osterwalder, 2004) have their origin in some kind of business theory and where developed by information system researchers and not ontology researchers. The main problems with the more recent developed business ontologies is that they were developed in ad hoc manner without taking into account some basic ontology engineering principles which results in a series of problems: the applicability of these ontologies is limited because the intended use is not always clear, the conceptualization of the ontology is not clear and is divided over different sources, and these ontologies do in most cases not have a formal representation. On the contrary these ontologies have a strong theoretical background and are in most cases better understood by business practitioners which have the same background as the developers. As a result they offer real opportunities for businesses which are currently not realized and which can be realized if new Semantic Web technologies are used.

Problem Statement

The REA-ontology is an example business ontology that has been proposed for ontology-driven enterprise systems development. The origin of REA is an accounting data model (McCarthy, 1982) that has been extended first into an enterprise information architecture and later into a full-scale enterprise ontology. This development followed an ad-hoc process rather than being guided by an Ontology Engineering methodology. The REA developers focused more on the theoretical background of the ontology (events accounting and Micro-Economic theories) than on the representation, formalization and computational correctness of the ontology (although they did perform in Geerts & McCarthy, 2002 an ontological analysis using Sowa's classification (Sowa, 1999)). As a consequence, there is no formal representation of REA. Furthermore, the available literature sources on REA (e.g. Dunn, Cherrington, & Hollander, 2005; Geerts & McCarthy, 2005, 2006; Hruby, Kiehn, & Scheller, 2006) present different views on the REA conceptualization of an enterprise and use a variety of different formats (including text, tables and diagrams) to specify the ontology. The lack of a generally accepted conceptualization and a uniform, complete and formal representation of the ontology causes imprecision in its definition and ambiguity in its interpretation. For instance, in (Gailly & Poels, 2006) we showed that the ontological concepts and the relations between the concepts are not strictly defined and that the ontological axioms, only informally defined in text, are confusing (mixing up types and instances of concepts). There have been attempts to formalize REA (e.g. Bialecki, 2001; Chou, 2006), but the results obtained were highly dependent on the researchers' subjective interpretation of REA.

REA-Ontology

As an 'event ontology' (Allen & March, 2006), REA focuses on the events occurring within the

Table 1. Definitions of the basic REA concepts

Concept	Definition
Economic Resource	A thing that is scarce and has utility for economic agents and is something users of business applications want to plan, monitor and control.
Economic Agent	An individual or organization capable of having control over economic resources, and transferring or receiving the control to or from other individuals or organizations.
Economic Event	A change in the value of economic resources that are under control of the enterprise.
Commitment	A promise or obligation of economic agents to perform an economic event in the future
Contract	A collection of increment and decrement commitments and terms.

realm of a company, their participating agents, affected resources, and regulating policies. REA can be used as a reference for modeling a single business cycle (e.g. sales-collection) or a chain of business cycles, connected through resource flows. REA specifies five basic concepts (*Economic **R**esource, Economic **E**vent, Economic **A**gent, Commitment, Contract*) in terms of which an enterprise is described. These five concepts (defined in Table 1) are the ontological primitives upon which the other ontological elements (e.g. specialized concepts, typified concepts, relations) are built and in terms of which domain axioms are defined. We also assume these definitions when redesigning the conceptual representation of REA.

In (Geerts & McCarthy, 2002) a knowledge layer has been proposed on top of the previous described operational business concepts. The typification abstraction is used to provide concept descriptions that apply to a kind of objects (e.g. describing the characteristics of different kind of sales like cash sales, credit sales, etc). The type images of the operational concepts are named *Economic Resource Type, Economic Agent Type, Economic Event Type, Commitment Type* and *Contract Type*.

REA further defines and names a number of relations between the basic concepts. For instance, *Economic Resources* are associated with the *Economic Events* that cause their *inflow* or *outflow* (*stockflow relations*). *Economic Events* that result in resource *inflows* (e.g. purchases) are paired by *Economic Events* that result in resource *outflows* (e.g. cash disbursements) (*duality relations*). *Participation relations* identify the *Economic Agents* involved in *Economic Events*. A *Commitment* will eventually be related to an *Economic Event* of the specified type by a *fulfillment relation*. *Reciprocity relations* are analogous to *duality relations*, but relate *Commitments* instead of *Economic Events*. *Specify relations* exists between *Commitments* and the *Economic Agents Types* that are scheduled to participate in some type of *Economic Event*. They also exist between *Commitments* and the *Economic Resource Types* that are needed or expected by future *Economic Events*.

These and other concept relations are defined informally in text or are depicted as relationships in ER diagrams, UML class diagrams or other graphical formalisms that provide a partial view on the ontology. Implicitly they introduce a number of derived concepts like specializations of basic concepts (e.g. *Economic Events* that cause an inflow (*Increment Economic Events*) versus *Economic Events* that cause an outflow (*Decrement Economic Events*)) and type images (e.g. *Economic Event Type*), as well as constraints (e.g. if Commitments A and B are linked by *reciprocity*, and *Economic Events* C and D *fulfill* respectively A and B, then C and D must be linked by *duality*). Apart from type images (described extensively in (Geerts & McCarthy, 2006)) these inferred concepts and constraints are underspecified.

Also a minimal set of ontological axioms is defined, again informally. The definitions of axioms 1 and 2 are literally copied from (Geerts & McCarthy, 2005). Axiom 3 is based on (Hruby et al., 2006) and is more precisely formulated than its equivalent in (Geerts & McCarthy, 2005):

- ***Axiom1:*** At least one inflow event and one outflow event exist for each economic resource; conversely inflow and outflow events must affect identifiable resources.
- ***Axiom2:*** All events effecting an outflow must be eventually paired in duality relationships with events effecting an inflow and vice-versa.
- ***Axiom3:*** Each economic event needs to have at least one provide and one receive relationship with an economic agent.

The main problem with these definitions is that it not always clear whether the axioms apply to instances or types. For instance, an enterprise can own an economic resource that it has produced or acquired (e.g. a car) but not sold, used or consumed yet. Clearly the existence of a decrement event for every economic resource under the control of a company is not an axiom. However, following economic rationale (i.e. value creation), we could say that for every type of economic resource there exists at least one type of decrement economic event (e.g. a car manufacturer produces cars to sell them). Axiom 3 further introduces specializations of the *participation* relation: *provide* and *receive*.

REA Applications

REA application is defined here in a very broad sense and refers to applications that make use of or benefit somehow from the ontology. Some of these applications are only theorized and not actually put into practice but exploring these applications can help us in illustrating the current problems that arise when trying to use the REA-ontology in a business context. We limit ourselves largely to applications that have been proposed or developed after the publication of the REA extensions (Geerts & McCarthy, 2002; Geerts & McCarthy, 1999). Applications that are mainly based on the original REA model as in (McCarthy, 1982) are not discussed.

Ontology-Driven Software Engineering

Using the REA-ontology makes the development of the application more straightforward and software applications based on REA should contain more and more correct business knowledge. In this context the REA-ontology can be used for different purposes. It can be used as a language ensuring unambiguous communication and understanding among all participants of the software development process. Similar REA can be used as a reference model thereby helping to identify and organize relevant objects, relationships and other knowledge (Gailly & Poels, 2007). Finally more ambitious the REA-ontology can be used in the model-driven development of systems (Borch, Jespersen, Linvald, & Osterbye, 2003; Hruby, 2005a, 2005b; Hruby et al., 2006). More precisely the Model-Driven Architecture (MDA) describes the use of a Computation Independent Model (CIM) as an abstraction of the system from the end-user's viewpoint. The CIM is a representation of the problem domain focusing on systems requirements and can be developed by using the REA-ontology as a reference.

Supply Chain Collaboration

Using the REA-ontology should make it easier to establish supply chain collaboration via internet technologies. The REA-ontology is used for supporting interoperability within and between enterprises. It provides an ontological framework for specifying the concepts and relations involved in business transactions and scenarios (Haugen & McCarthy, 2000; Hofreiter, Huemer, Liegl, Schuster, & Zapletal, 2006; ISO, 2006). E-collaboration can be realized by the REA-ontology by providing standard business scenarios and the necessary services to support them in order to establish quickly and cost effectively short term relationships between businesses. In this context the REA developers have been very active in different international standardization efforts for e-collaboration systems (e.g. ISO Open-EDI initiative, UN/CEFACT, OAG, eBTWG). REA was the basis for the business process ontology in the UMM business process and information model construction methodology (UN/CEFACT, 2003), the ECIMF system interoperability enabling methodology (ECIMF, 2003) and the Open-EDI business transaction ontology which is part of the ISO/IEC 15944-4 standard.

Knowledge Representation and Search

Finally, ontologies can also be used for knowledge representation and search. By adding semantics into the business applications additional information can be more easily extracted from the business. Enterprise applications can use the operational REA-ontology at run-time for adding semantics to the enterprise schema and data (Geerts, 2004; Geerts & McCarthy, 2000). These additional semantics make it easier to find the correct information. Because of the accountant background of REA, applications that use REA as a knowledge representation offer additional auditing and internal control (e.g. SOX compliance checking) mechanisms (Geerts & McCarthy, 2006).

This short overview of the REA applications provides some proof that REA can be used for a wide series of applications: education, business modeling, software engineering, knowledge representation, information retrieval and various e-collaboration applications. Apart from inter/intra-enterprise modeling, many of the proposed applications are only theorized or implemented with an illustrative (toy) example rather than providing a convincing proof of concept. It is clear that in order to fully exploit the potential of REA as a business domain ontology, a generally accepted, explicit and formal specification of the REA ontology is needed which is reusable across different types of business applications.

The degree of formalization required depends of course on the type of application. In order to make a formal and explicit specification of the REA-ontology also usable for application contexts which do not require a high degree of formality, the formal representation should be easily transformable into a graphical, semi-formal and easy-to-understand representation. A general agreement about a formal and explicit specification of the REA-ontology will also make the realization of the currently theorized applications more straightforward and can make the REA-ontology more useful for application areas which are currently not explored by the REA-ontology community.

PROPOSED SOLUTION

For many years now, ontology research has been a growing research domain in Knowledge Engineering and Artificial Intelligence. Ontologies can be used to represent explicitly the semantics of structured and semi-structured information enabling automatic support for maintaining and accessing information (Fensel, 2001). In this chapter we use existing ontology research in order to make the REA-ontology more applicable for ontology-driven system development and ontology-driven information systems.

Objectives

As currently REA is not formally represented, not sufficiently explicit, and not based on a demonstrable shared conceptualization, it needs improvement before it can be applied on a wide scale in ontology-driven systems. The aim of this chapter is to facilitate the operationalization of REA (i.e. increasing its applicability to be used at run-time) by making it more explicit and formal. We first present the development of a new graphical UML representation of REA that presents a unified and consistent view on the ontology's concepts, relations and axioms. This new conceptual representation is subsequently used as the basis for a more formal representation of REA in OWL. Improving the conceptual and formal representations of REA makes the ontology more understandable, easier to compare to alternative business ontologies, easier to analyse (e.g. for consistency), and more operational (e.g. executable). This chapter focuses on representation and formalization aspects, but not on the contents of REA. The new representations will not make REA more accepted per se (in the sense of a having a conceptualization that is widely shared in the business community). However, they do facilitate ontological analysis and the evaluation whether there is agreement upon the ontological definitions and axiomatization.

It is our position that the reengineering of business ontologies to improve their applicability should be guided by proven Ontology Engineering principles and techniques. The two REA reengineering activities presented in this chapter are part of a more encompassing business ontology reengineering methodology which is based on the METHONTOLOGY framework (Gómez-Pérez & Rojas, 1999) and which we are currently refining specific for business domain ontologies.

Overview

REA as it stands can be characterized as a lightweight ontology (Lassila & McGuiness, 2001). To formalize a lightweight ontology a specification is needed that provides a complete view of the conceptualization with as much explicit semantics as possible. Preferably such a specification is developed in a language that can easily be mapped onto an ontology language but at the same time allows for ontology modeling.

Recently, Ontology Engineering researchers have proposed the use of conceptual modeling languages (ER, UML, ORM, ...) for modeling ontologies (Kogut et al., 2002; Spaccapietra, Parent, Vangenot, & Cullot, 2004; Spyns, 2005). Most conceptual modeling languages propose graphical representations with well-defined syntax and semantics that are close to how humans perceive the world (Mylopoulos, 1998). Specifically in a business context, the diagrammatic techniques offered by conceptual modeling languages are known (or can easily be learned) by business domain experts (Davies, Green, Rosemann, Indulska, & Gallo, 2006). Conceptual modeling languages therefore provide a more suitable basis for the analysis and refinement of the content of an ontology than the more formal knowledge representation languages, as the resulting representation of the ontology will be more natural and hence easier to understand for the domain experts.

REA uses a combination of informal text, table definitions and diagrams. These definitions and diagrams can be found in different sources by different authors. To facilitate the formalization of REA we first developed a representation of REA that unifies these partial (and often imprecise) definitions into a single coherent view with explicit semantics. In case of doubt we referred to the 'official' version of the ontology as described by the REA developers in their most recent papers (i.e. (Geerts & McCarthy, 2005, 2006)). We developed this new representation in UML (using a class diagram) and refer to it as the *conceptual* representation of REA because its intended users are humans and not machines. UML was chosen as ontology modeling language because it provides a standard and tool-supported notation. Furthermore, the Ontology Definition Metamodel (ODM) request for proposal of the Object Management Group (OMG) has resulted in the proposal of semantically correct mapping rules in both directions between UML and the ontology languages RDF and OWL (OMG, 2006).

The development of the new UML representation of REA corresponds roughly to the reverse engineering and restructuring steps in the METHONTOLOGY reengineering process. The currently available representations of REA had to be gathered, analyzed and combined to recover to the best possible extent the original conceptualization (i.e. reverse engineering). Unifying the existing definitions, resolving inconsistencies and explicitly representing the recovered semantics in a UML class diagram can be seen as a restructuring activity. The result should however be seen as a redesigned representation of REA rather than a redesigned conceptualization as no fundamental changes to the intended content of the ontology were proposed. The proposed reengineering methodology is intended as an iterative process and in future iterations the new conceptual representation can be used for in-depth analysis of REA's conceptualization of business and subsequent discussion and refinement. In this first iteration, the UML class diagram was primarily meant as a starting point for the formalization of REA.

The purpose of the formalization activity is to map the conceptual representation into a *formal* representation, meaning a machine-readable representation (i.e. the intended users are machines and not humans). The ontology language chosen was OWL because of its wide acceptance as a Web ontology language. Also, the availability of ontology tools that support OWL (e.g. Description Logic reasoners) will make it easier to experiment with REA-driven business applications.

Solution Details

Redesigned REA-Ontology Representation

The new conceptual representation that we propose for REA is shown in Figure 1. REA concepts are shown as classes, concept relations are shown as associations or association classes, and axioms are specified by means of multiplicities. At this stage multiplicities are sufficient to represent the current axioms. It is possible that in the future other UML constructs or OCL will be needed to represent additional axioms. For a more detailed and complete account of the shortcomings in the current REA representations and how we resolve them in our UML class diagram, we refer to (Gailly & Poels, 2007).

The two main improvements are:

- The explicit specification of specializations of basic REA concepts and their type images: *Increment Economic Event, Decrement Economic Event, Increment Commitment, Decrement Commitment, Increment Economic Event Type,* and *Decrement Economic Event Type.* Less commonly used in UML is the specialization of association classes (that are used to represent concept relations): *inflow* and *outflow* as specializations of the *stockflow* relation and *provide* and *receive* as specializations of the *participation* relation. These new classifications add formerly implicit semantics to the conceptual representation. The diagram shows, for instance, that *inflows* relate *Increment Events* to *Resources, outflows* relate *Decrement Events* to *Resources, Increment Events fulfil Increment Commitments*, and *Decrement Events fulfil Decrement Commitments.* Note that *Contract* is not shown in the diagram, though it can be added by reifying the *reciprocity* relation. Further, both *Contract* and *Commitment* can be typified (again not shown in Figure 1).
- The extensions make it also possible to specify the REA axioms by means of multiplicities. For instance, the first part of axiom 1 can now be stated more precisely by enforcing the participation of every *Economic Resource Type* object in at least one

Figure 1. Conceptual representation of REA as a UML class diagram

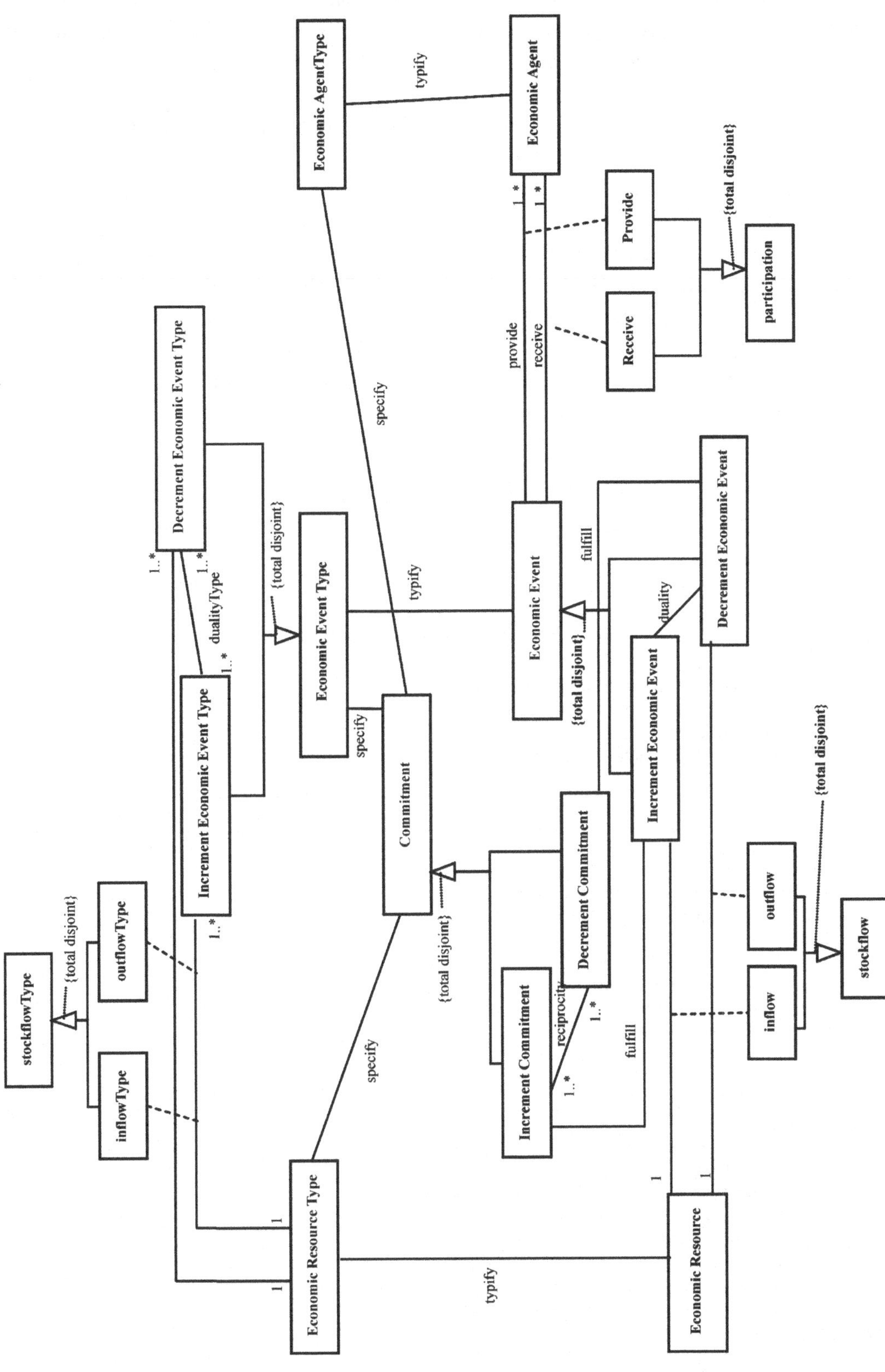

inflowType link and at least one *outflowType* link. It is however not required that every *Economic Resource* object is related to at least one *Economic Increment Event* and one *Economic Decrement Event.* Other multiplicities than the ones shown in Figure 1 can be specified, but for the sake of clarity we only included the multiplicities that correspond to the three basic axioms. There is only one exception; the multiplicities shown for the *reciprocity* relation imply that every *increment commitment* must be paired with at least one *decrement commitment,* and vice versa (i.e. the economic reciprocity principle of capitalist market economies that underlies every written or unwritten contract). This example shows that additional domain axioms can easily be integrated into the conceptual representation.

REA-Ontology Formalization

Different authors have stipulated guidelines for transforming UML class diagrams into a formal representation in an ontology language (Kogut et al., 2002; Spaccapietra et al., 2004) and vice versa (Brockmans et al., 2006). In the absence of a uniform approach, the recently adopted ODM proposal (OMG, 2006) is used to guide the formalization of REA in OWL. All classes, relation-

Table 2. Transformations UML to OWL (UML class, UML association (class))

UML elements	OWL elements
Class	Class, disjointWith

```
<owl:Class rdf:ID="Economic_Agent">
<owl:disjointWith rdf:resource="#Economic_Agent_Type"/>
<owl:disjointWith rdf:resource="#Economic_Event"/>
<owl:disjointWith rdf:resource="#Economic_Resource_Type"/>
<owl:disjointWith rdf:resource="#Economic_Resource"/>
    <owl:disjointWith rdf:resource="#Economic_Event_Type"/>
    <owl:disjointWith rdf:resource="#Commitment"/>
</owl:Class>
```

UML elements	OWL elements
Binary association	ObjectProperty, domain, range, inverseOf

```
<owl:ObjectProperty rdf:ID="fulfill">
    <rdfs:domain rdf:resource="#Economic_Event"/>
    <rdfs:range rdf:resource="#Commitment"/>
    <owl:inverseOf rdf:resource="#inverse_of_fulfill"/>
</owl:ObjectProperty>
<owl:ObjectProperty rdf:ID="inverse_of_fulfill">
    <rdfs:domain rdf:resource="#Commitment"/>
    <rdfs:range rdf:resource="#Economic_Event"/>
    <owl:inverseOf rdf:resource="#fulfill"/>
</owl:ObjectProperty>
```

UML elements	OWL elements
Association class	ObjectProperty, domain, range, inverseOf

```
<owl:ObjectProperty rdf:ID="stockflow">
    <rdfs:domain rdf:resource="#Economic_Resource"/>
    <rdfs:range rdf:resource="#Economic_Event"/>
    <owl:inverseOf rdf:resource="#inverse_of_stockflow"/>
</owl:ObjectProperty>
<owl:ObjectProperty rdf:ID="inverse_of_stockflow">
    <rdfs:domain rdf:resource="#Economic_Event"/>
    <rdfs:range rdf:resource="#Economic_Resource"/>
    <owl:inverseOf rdf:resource="#stockflow"/>
</owl:ObjectProperty>
```

ships and constraints presented in the UML class diagram (Figure 1) are transformed into OWL by mapping them to OWL constructs. In most cases these transformations are straightforward but some of them require additional explanation. One of the problems with the ODM specification is that sometimes for the same UML construct different mapping rules can be used and that for some UML constructs no appropriate OWL construct exists. As a result the mapping from UML to OWL depends to some extent on the transformation choices made. The used UML to OWL transformations and corresponding examples are shown in Tables 2, 3, 4 and 5.[1]

In Table 2, the UML classes *Economic Event (Type)*, *Economic Agent (Type)*, *Economic Resource (Type)* and *Commitment* are mapped onto disjoint OWL classes (i.e. disjoint subclasses of `owl:Thing`). The binary associations and association classes (but not their sub-classes) in Figure 2 are represented by OWL properties (using the ObjectProperty construct). In OWL a property name has a global scope, while in UML the association name scope is limited to the class and subclasses of the class on which it is defined. As a result we have decided to give all associations a unique name. The transformation from UML binary association to OWL properties follows the approach taken in the ODM specification which states that every bidirectional binary association must be translated into a pair of properties where one is inverseOf the other. For an association class the same approach is followed.

UML specializations can be very straightforward transformed into OWL by using the subclass construct for specialized classes (subClassOf) and the subproperty construct for properties (subPropertyOf) for specialized association classes (Table 3 and 4). In UML specialization structures can be declared as being disjoint, meaning each member of a superclass may be a member of no more than one subclass. In OWL this constraint is added by declaring that the subclass must be disjoint with the other subclasses.

Notice that also the *stockflow* and *participation* relations are specialized in disjoint 'sub-relations'. The corresponding association classes in the UML class diagram are represented by means of the OWL ObjectProperty construct. The current specification of OWL does not allow declaring

Table 3. Transformations UML to OWL (total disjoint subclasses)

UML elements	OWL elements
Total disjoint subclasses	disjointWith, unionOf, subClass

```
<owl:Class rdf:ID="Economic_Event">
    <rdfs:subClassOf>
    <owl:Class>
    <owl:unionOf rdf:parseType="Collection">
    <owl:Class rdf:about="#Decrement_Economic_Event"/>
    <owl:Class rdf:about="#Increment_Economic_Event"/>
    </owl:unionOf>
    </owl:Class>
    </rdfs:subClassOf>
</owl:Class>
<owl:Class rdf:ID="Decrement_Economic_Event">
    <rdfs:subClassOf rdf:resource="#Economic_Event"/>
    <owl:disjointWith rdf:resource="#Increment_Economic_Event"/>
</owl:Class>
<owl:Class rdf:ID="Increment_Economic_Event">
    <rdfs:subClassOf rdf:resource="#Economic_Event"/>
    <owl:disjointWith rdf:resource="#Decrement_Economic_Event"/>
</owl:Class>
```

subproperties as being disjoint (this issue will probably be solved by the OWL 1.1 extensions). A solution could be reifying the *stockflow* and *participate* relations (i.e. declaring them as OWL classes and next declaring disjoint subclasses). A drawback of this approach is that additional OWL properties are needed to represent all associations between the reified associations and the original classes. These additional OWL properties will have no direct counterpart in the REA conceptual representation, so it might be hard to give them meaningful names. That is why we preferred not to reify them. The UML constraints on the specializations in Figure 1 are also total or complete, meaning that all members of a superclass must be members of at least one subclass. This can be formalized be defining a covering axiom on the superclass which states that the superclass is the union of the subclasses.

The formalization of the REA axioms is less straightforward and different approaches can be followed. Based on the ODM proposal we decided to formalize the multiplicities on the association ends by means of OWL minimum and maximum cardinality restrictions (see Table 5). In OWL

Table 4. Transformations UML to OWL (total disjoint subrelations)

UML elements	OWL elements
Total disjoint 'subrelations'	subPropertyOf

```
<owl:ObjectProperty rdf:ID="inflow">
    <rdfs:domain rdf:resource="#Economic_Resource"/>
    <rdfs:range rdf:resource="#Increment_Economic_Event"/>
    <owl:inverseOf rdf:resource="#inverse_of_inflow"/>
    <rdfs:subPropertyOf rdf:resource="#stockflow"/>
</owl:ObjectProperty>
<owl:ObjectProperty rdf:ID="inverse_of_inflow">
    <rdfs:domain rdf:resource="#Increment_Economic_Event"/>
    <rdfs:range rdf:resource="#Economic_Resource"/>
    <owl:inverseOf rdf:resource="#inflow"/>
    <rdfs:subPropertyOf rdf:resource="#inverse_of_stockflow"/>
</owl:ObjectProperty>
```

Table 5. Transformations UML to OWL (multiplicities)

UML elements	OWL elements
Multiplicities	maxCardinality, minCardinality

```
<owl:Class rdf:ID="Increment_Economic_Event">
<rdfs:subClassOf>
    <owl:Restriction>
    <owl:onProperty rdf:resource="#inverse_of_inflow"/>
    <owl:minCardinality
            rdf:datatype="&xsd;int">1</owl:minCardinality>
    </owl:Restriction>
</rdfs:subClassOf>
<rdfs:subClassOf>
    <owl:Restriction>
    <owl:onProperty rdf:resource="#inverse_of_inflow"/>
    <owl:maxCardinality
            rdf:datatype="&xsd;int">1</owl:maxCardinality>
    </owl:Restriction>
</rdfs:subClassOf>
</owl:Class>
```

cardinality restrictions are property restrictions used in class descriptions or definitions.

An alternative solution for specifying a maximum cardinality of one is to declare a property as functional. A property is functional if for a given individual, there can be at most one individual that is related to this individual via the property. Being functional is a characteristic of a property and is not a property restriction used in class descriptions or definitions. Although the effect of declaring a property as functional and defining a maximum cardinality restriction for the property of one is the same, we prefer the use of the maximum cardinality restriction because it is shown explicitly in the class description whereas the functional characteristic of the property is not. Cardinality restrictions provide an explicit formalization of the REA axioms and are as such easier to trace back to the informal REA axioms they intend to formalize than a more implicit formalization using functional properties. To specify a minimum cardinality of one we could also use an existential quantifier restriction for the property instead of a minimum cardinality restriction of one. As the range of all properties is specified there is no difference between these alternatives. Both types of property restriction are also shown explicitly in the class description so we do not prefer one form above the other. Here minimum cardinality restrictions are used because we also use maximum cardinality restrictions.

It should be noted that OWL considers cardinalities as restrictions and not as constraints as in UML. Specified cardinalities are not checked but are used to infer the existence or equality of individuals. The interpretation as restrictions that can be used for inference might be appropriate for applications that involve reasoning. However, for applications in the field of conceptual modeling, software engineering and database design, cardinalities should be interpreted as constraints that must be satisfied by models. A practical solution enforcing the interpretation of the OWL cardinality restrictions as constraints is to use the Unique Naming Assumption (UNA) implying that when two individuals have different names then they are different individuals. Similarly, the range of a property (or alternatively the use of a universal quantifier restriction) does not impose a constraint in OWL but is used for inferring class membership. However, since we have declared all classes as disjoint, the range specification is actually used as a constraint because an individual can only belong to one class. So if for a given individual, there is an individual that is related to this individual via the property and the individual belongs to another class than the one specified in the range of the property, then this results in an inconsistency. In applications where class membership needs to be inferred by a reasoner it makes sense to eliminate some of the disjointness declarations (but not disjointness that results from disjoint specialisations).

REA-Driven Supply Chain Collaboration

The new conceptualization and accompanying formalization makes the use of the REA-ontology much more straightforward. In (Gailly, Laurier, & Poels, 2007; Gailly & Poels, 2007) we illustrate how the reengineered REA ontology can be used for ontology-driven business modeling and requirement elicitation. The redesigned REA representation is uniform (using a single representation formalism), unified (including definitions of concepts, concept relations and axioms) and more useful. The proposed UML class diagram makes the semantics of the REA-ontology explicit and thus represents an understandable reference model for business modelers. It acts as a generic business model for generating and validating concrete business models. Instantiating this generic model constrains the business subjective interpretation of business reality and assures the basic business laws are respected in the generated models.

In this chapter we will illustrate how the REA formalization can be used for creating enterprise application interoperability. To illustrate this we consider a purchase order mediation problem (based on the Semantic Web Service Challenge[2]) which involves two actors: a purchaser (company A) which orders products and a supplier (company B) which accepts orders from company A. Company A has an send-order system which sends an XML message to their suppliers which corresponds to a specific XML-schema. Company B has a legacy order system which is programmed in Cobol and has recently adopted a service-oriented approach. This means that the java application server has been used as integration middleware solution in order to make the functionalities of the legacy order system available as a Web service. The messages that are accepted by the Web service are described in a WSDL document and are based on the Rosetta standards. The introduction of the Java application server makes it possible for company A to send an order to company B by using SOAP message for the communication. However this approach still does not overcome message level heterogeneities between the service requestor and the service provider. This problem has been generally recognised in literature. Adding a semantic layer to the Web service architecture is generally seen as a solution for this mediation problem and is the core concept behind Semantic Web Services. Different approaches have been proposed for implementing Semantic Web services (OWL-S, WSMO, WSDL-S).

In this illustration we will show how the semantic REA-model of an order process can be used for adding semantic information to the different messages. Figure 2 gives a general overview of how SAWSDL (Farell & Lausen, 2007) which is the successor of WSDL-S, is used to annotate WSDL fragments with an REA semantic model of an order and payment process. We will use the SAWSDL because this makes it very easy to use existing formal ontologies that have been described in OWL or even in UML. In the next paragraphs the semantic annotations are described in more detail.

The messages used by the two companies can be extended with semantic annotations. For example Table 6 and 7 show examples of how respectively the outgoing order message from company A and the incoming message from the Web service of company B are annotated with semantic data from the REA order model in Figure 2. The examples show that the REA Order ontology can be used to indicate that the coreProductIndetification concept of company A en the articleId of company B correspond to the REA order productTypeIdentifier. Previous annotations are very straightforward because of the existence of one to one relation between the different concepts. However in some cases the mappings are more complex and the schema mapping mechanism of SAWSDL will be needed to relate different concepts. Table 8 shows the semantic annotation of the Physical Address concept of Company A with the Address concept of the REA Order ontology and uses the XSLT mapping of Table 9.

This example only shows conceptually how the messages are semantically annotated but we do not show how these annotations can be used for data mediation. The available semantic annotations in the XML-schema's of the different messages need to be used for automatically transforming a message from company A into the different messages accepted by the Web service from company B. A semantic engine can use the semantic annotations for matching the messages by parsing and reasoning over this semantic model. It should also be further investigated how these semantic annotations can be used for process integration purposes. The order process consists of different steps and dependent on the outcome of one of the previous steps, other steps must be taken. For example it could be that the each order registration also results in changes for the inventory system and accounting system. This means that the order process results should result in an automatically discovery of other services which should be invocated.

Figure 2. Semantic REA order model and association to WSDL elements

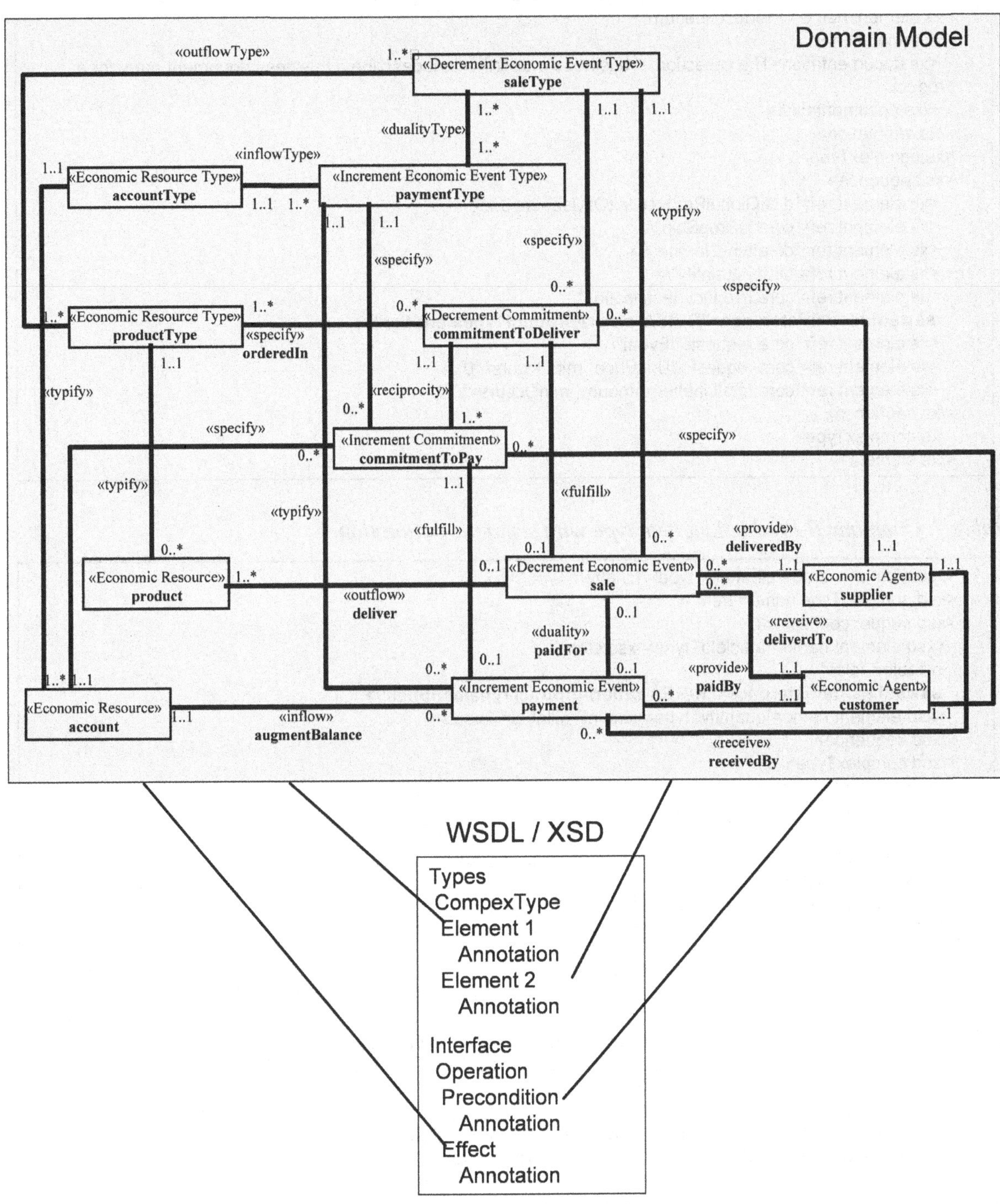

Table 6. Company A ProductLineItem XML-schema Data type descriptions with semantic annotation

```
<xs:element name="ProductLineItem">
<xs:annotation>
  <xs:documentation>The collection of business properties that describe a business document entry for a
product.
  </xs:documentation>
</xs:annotation>
<xs:complexType>
<xs:sequence>
  <xs:element ref="dict:GlobalProductUnitOfMeasureCode"/>
  <xs:element ref="core:isDropShip"/>
  <xs:element ref="core:LineNumber"/>
  <xs:element ref="OrderQuantity"/>
  <xs:element ref="core:ProductIdentification"
   sawsdl:modelReference="R-REA-order#productTypeIdentifier"/>
  <xs:element ref="core:requestedEvent"/>
  <xs:element ref="core:requestedUnitPrice" minOccurs="0"/>
  <xs:element ref="core:totalLineItemAmount" minOccurs="0"/>
</xs:sequence>
</xs:complexType>
</xs:element>
```

Table 7. Company B ProductLineItem type with semantic annotation

```
<xsd:element name="LineItem" type="LineItemType"/>
<xsd:complexType name="Item">
<xsd:sequence>
  <xsd:element name="articleId" type="xsd:string"
  nillable="false"
  sawsdl:modelReference="R-REA-order#productTypeIdentifier"/>
  <xsd:element name="quantity" type="xsd:int" nillable="false"/>
</xsd:sequence>
</xsd:complexType>
<xsd:complexType name="LineItemType">
<xsd:sequence>
  <xsd:element name="authToken" type="xsd:string" nillable="false"/>
  <xsd:element name="orderId" type="xsd:long" nillable="false"
   sawsdl:modelReference=
   "R-REA-order#commitmentToDeliverIdentifier"/>
  <xsd:element name="item" type="Item" nillable="false"/>
</xsd:sequence>
</xsd:complexType>
```

Table 8. Company A PhysicalAddress type with semantic annotation

```
<xs:element name="PhysicalAddress">
<xs:complexType
  sawsdl:modelReference="R-REA-Order#OrderConfirmation"
  sawsdl:liftingSchemaMapping="companyA-address.xslt">
<xs:sequence>
  <xs:element ref="addressLine1" minOccurs="0"/>
  <xs:element ref="cityName" minOccurs="0"/>
  <xs:element ref="dict:GlobalCountryCode" minOccurs="0"/
  <xs:element ref="NationalPostalCode" minOccurs="0"/>
</xs:sequence>
</xs:complexType>
</xs:element>
```

Table 9. Company A PhysicalAddress type mapping

```
<?xml version='1.0' ?>
<xsl:transform version="2.0"
  xmlns:xsl="http://www.w3.org/1999/XSL/Transform"
  xmlns:rdf="http://www.w3.org/1999/02/22-rdf-syntax-ns#">
<xsl:template match="/">
 <Address rdf:ID="Address1">
  <has_StreetAddress rdf:datatype="xs:string">
    <xsl:value-of select="PhysicalAddress/addressLine1"/>
  </has_StreetAddress >
  <has_City rdf:datatype="xs:string">
    <xsl:value-of select="PhysicalAddress/cityName"/>
  </has_City>
  <has_ZipCode rdf:datatype="xs:string">
    <xsl:value-of select="PhysicalAddress/NationalPostalCode"/>
  </has_ZipCode>
  <has_Country rdf:datatype="xs:string">
    <xsl:value-of select="PhysicalAddress/dict:GlobalCountryCode"/>
  </has_Country>
 </Address>
</xsl:template>
</xsl:transform>
```

ALTERNATIVES

In this chapter different choices had to be made for which meaningful alternatives exist. The first choice was the use of UML class diagrams for the graphical representation of the REA-ontology. Using a conceptual modeling language like UML helps conceptualizing the ontology (i.e. creating a conceptual representation) because they offer representations that are close to how humans perceive the world (Mylopoulos, 1998) and there exist mapping rules in both directions between UML and the knowledge representation languages RDF and OWL (OMG, 2006). The formalization of an ontology's conceptual representation will therefore be facilitated if UML is used as the ontology modeling language. Another clear advantage of using specifically UML class diagrams for the conceptualization of the REA ontology is the availability of UML tools and the wide acceptance of the language in a business environment. However using UML for ontology also results in some problems because of the difference in background between conceptual modelling and ontology engineering (de Bruyn, Lara, Polleres, & Fensel, 2005). For example in some case UML is not rich enough to represent all concepts, relations and axioms of the ontology and in other cases the formal representation languages in not rich enough to represent all UML constructs. Even more problematic is the fact that some constructs (e.g. multiplicities) are interpreted in a different way by the different research communities (see formalization of the axioms). Alternatives are ontology specific representation languages (which are in most cases used by other business ontologies) but this makes it difficult to compare different ontologies. A promising approach is the OWL UML profile proposed by the ODM which use the UML profile mechanism for developing a graphical representation language which corresponds to OWL. This OWL profile will certainly prove to be very useful if we want to use the REA-ontology in a conceptual modelling context because it provides a clear linkage between the REA conceptualization and domain specific modelling in a model-driven engineering context.

A second important decision was the use of OWL as a formal representation language. This choice comes from the availability of the UML to OWL mappings provided by the ODM. However, it is not always clear that OWL is the best language for some of the applications theorized by the REA-ontology research community. The OWL representation language is very well suited for the REA-ontology knowledge representation application but for ontology-driven business modelling applications OWL is probably not the best solution because for example OWL contains no meta-classes and also follows its description logics background which works with restrictions and not constraints. Additionally for the supply-chain collaboration problem described in previous section the WSMO Semantic Web service approach also uses another ontology representation languages (WSML) because of some shortcomings of OWL for this purpose.

Thirdly, there are alternatives for the Semantic Web service approach used for the purchase order mediation problem. The solution described used SAWSDL for adding a semantic layer to Web services but it seems like other approaches like WSMO in combination with WSMX will be more useful if the ontology is not only used to solve a data mediation problem but also a process mediation problem. This will be further investigated in future research. At is clear that different alternative languages can be used for the conceptualization and formalization of the REA-ontology and no best solution exists. The choice depends on the type of application for which the ontology will be used and as a result it should be easy to transform from one language into another.

COST AND BENEFITS

Different trends and technologies such as an Enterprises Service Bus (ESB), Enterprise application platforms, Web Services (WS) and Service-oriented architecture (SOA) have been proposed to address the different interoperability barriers which make the integration and cooperation of different business application within and between enterprises a difficult task. It is our opinion that they provide all very useful solutions for the technological barriers which exists because of the incompatibility of the different technologies used (hardware, architecture, platform, languages, standards, ...) but does not address the semantic differences between the different data sources. A clear proof of this is the large amount of human intervention and maintenance that is still needed by these systems. A lot of this human intervention is invested in solving the syntactic differences as well as semantic differences between heterogeneous sources. At this stage it is hard to assess if these new Semantic Web technologies are actually useful for real business applications and provides a better solution for the interoperability problems. A lot of researchers claim that ontologies can be used for creating interoperability but it is seldom proved that these new solutions actually are better than the old solutions.

The success of ontology-driven business integration applications depends in large extent on the available technologies and tools but also on the quality of the conceptual backbone: the business domain ontology. A clear benefit of using the REA is the strong theoretical background of the ontology but also the availability of a big REA community. As a result REA can acts as a perfect vehicle for non Semantic Web experts to get to know new technologies and recognising the importance of adding semantics in different type of applications. However a lot of work still needs to be done in order to make REA a generally accepted business ontology.

RISK ASSESSMENT

The limitation of this research is its focus on representation and formalization issues. Existing ontology engineering techniques are used for improving the representation and formalization of the REA-ontology and we explore how this new reengineered version improves the applicability of the ontology. However future research is needed to validate REA and to address ontological content rather than just form. An ontological analysis with respect to an upper-level ontology (e.g. SUMO, Dolce, GFO, BWW, SOWA, ...) is part of this validation. Additionally the usefulness of the REA-ontology should be empirically tested and not only illustrated by using a toy example. Further exploring the REA applications will expose additional shortcomings about the ontology but will also provide new opportunities for the REA-ontology. A more detailed analysis of how REA is used in existing standardization efforts can also help in improving the ontological content of the REA ontology.

Semantic Web research is still a relatively new research domain where changes and new insights are proposed at an enormous tempo. This makes it very hard for business people who want to make use of these new technologies to keep up and this research domain will probably not stabilize in the near future. This stands in strong contrast with the information systems domain which is more mature and which contains some research topics (conceptual modelling, databases) which were heavily investigated the last 25 years and are currently more stable. The difference between these domains and also the difference in background results in series of problems that must be solved in the near future in order to make the Semantic Web technologies useful for business practitioners. Initiatives like the OMG's ODM are therefore very important and should be further evaluated with actual implementations.

FUTURE TRENDS

In order to make ontologies successfully used in real world applications different challenges have to be addressed (Hepp, 2007). In this chapter we try to improve the interplay between human understandable visualizations of ontologies and machine-readable formalization. For business people and information system researchers it is hard to keep up all technologies that are introduced by the Semantic Web technology. However some of the challenges are probably better know by people outside of the Semantic Web research community.

The use of formal representation languages for conceptual modeling purposes is very hard because differences in background between formal ontology languages and conceptual modeling languages which results in different interpretation problems. In the future these differences must be solved in order to make Semantic Web technologies useful for the conceptual modeling domain. Additionally these two research domains also need to find each other much more because a lot of research is overlapping each other. For example a lot of the concepts defined in the Model driven engineering approach to software engineering are very similar to ontology concepts (Assmann et al., 2006).

A lot of the Semantic Web researchers are also not familiar with the business ontologies mentioned in this chapter. The Semantic Web services research community recognises the importance of using business ontologies but to our knowledge there has been no research on how existing business ontologies which are based on economic theory can be used in the Semantic Web service architectures developed by the Semantic Web service research community.

In the future real test cases should be developed which show how business people and information systems researchers can use ontologies to solve realistic business problems. On the other hand these business cases should also convince Semantic Web researchers of the importance of theoretically sound ontologies and the necessity of these ontologies in order to fully exploit the potential of the proposes Semantic Web technologies.

CONCLUSION

This chapter presents the development of two new representations of the Resource Event Agent (REA) business ontology. This development addresses shortcomings in the current specification that are likely to impede REA's use as a run-time ontology supporting semantic integration and interoperability of heterogeneous business applications and enterprise systems. The first representation is a UML class diagram that can be used by human users as an explicit, unified and uniformly represented specification of REA's conceptualization of business. The second representation is a formal, machine-readable specification obtained by applying UML to OWL mappings. The OWL formalization of REA, which would not be possible without first redesigning its conceptual representation, will facilitate its operationalization in ontology-driven systems as it makes REA executable. This is illustrated by means of supply chain collaboration problem where REA is used to add semantic annotations to the messages that are being sent from purchaser to supplier and vice versa.

The research contribution of the chapter is the embedding of the REA redesign and formalization activities into a comprehensive business ontology reengineering methodology. Other activities suggested by this methodology, such as ontological evaluation and synthesis, can readily be performed based on the proposed conceptual representation. This new UML representation of REA may also serve as an improved basis to compare REA to other business ontologies and to evaluate the degree to which this business conceptualization is shared in the business community. The OWL representation of REA is of practical value for those wishing to explore the use of REA as a run-time ontology. It also allows for formal ontology evaluation, for instance verifying the consistency of the concept definitions using a Description Logic reasoner.

REFERENCES

Allen, G. N., & March, S. T. (2006). The effects of state-based and event-based data representation on user performance in query formulation tasks. *MIS Quarterly, 30*(2), 269-290.

Assmann, U., Zchaler, S., & Wagner, G. (2006). Ontologies, Meta-Models, and the Model-Driven Paradigm. In C. Calero, F. Ruiz & M. Piattini (Eds.), *Ontologies for Software Engineering and Software Technology*.

Baida, Z., Gordijn, J., Saele, H., Morch, A. Z., & Akkermans, H. (2004). Energy services: A case study in real-world service configuration. *Lecture Notes in Computer Science*, 3084, 36-50

Bialecki, A. (2001). *REA ontology*. http://www.getopt.org/ecimf/contrib/onto/REA/

Borch, S.E., Jespersen, J.W., Linvald, J., & Osterbye, K. (2003). A Model Driven Architecture for REA based systems. *Workshop on Model Driven Architecture: Foundations and Applications*. University of Twente, Enshede, The Netherlands

Brockmans, S., Colomb, R., Haase, P., Kendal, E., Wallace, E., Welty, C.,et al. (2006). A Model Driven Approach for building OWL DL and OWL Full Ontologies. *Lecture Notes in Computer Science*, 4273.

Chou, C.-C. (2006). *Using ontological methodology in building the accounting knowledge model – REAP*. Paper presented at the 2006 AAA mid-year meeting - 2006 AI/ET Workshop

Davies, I., Green, P., Rosemann, M., Indulska, M., & Gallo, S. (2006). How do practioners use conceptual modeling in practice? *Data & Knowledge Engineering, 58*(3), 358-380.

de Bruyn, j., Lara, R., Polleres, A., & Fensel, D. (2005). *OWL DL vs. OWL Flight: Conceptual Modeling and Reasoning for the Semantic Web*. Paper presented at the World Wide Web Conference (WWW 2005).

Dietz, J. L. G. (2005). *System Ontology and its role in Software Development.* Paper presented at the Advanced Information Systems Engineering wokshops (CAiSE 2005), Porto, Portugal.

Dunn, C. L., Cherrington, J. O., & Hollander, A. S. (2005). *Enterprise Information Systems: A Pattern Based Approach*: McGraw-Hill.

ECIMF. (2003). *E-Commerce Integration Meta-Framework. Final draft.* ECIMF Project Group.

Farell, J., & Lausen, H. (2007). *Semantic Annotations for WSDL and XML Schema*: W3C.

Fensel, D. (2001). *Ontologies: A Silver Bullet for Knowledge Management and Electronic Commerce*: Springer-Verlag.

Fox, M. S. (1992). *The TOVE Project: Towards a common-sense Model of the Enterprise.*

Gailly, F., Laurier, W., & Poels, G. (2007). *Positioning REA as a Business Domain Ontology.* Paper presented at the Resource Event Agent -25 Conference (REA-25).

Gailly, F., & Poels, G. (2006). *Towards a Formal Representation of the Resource Event Agent Pattern.* Paper presented at the International Conference on Enterprise Systems and Accounting (ICESAcc 2006).

Gailly, F., & Poels, G. (2007). Ontology-driven Business Modelling: Improving the Conceptual Representation of the REA-ontology. *Lecture Notes in Computer Science 4801*, 407-422.

Geerts, G. (2004). An XML Architecture for Operational Enterprise Ontologies. *Journal of Emerging Technologies in Accounting, 1*, 73-90.

Geerts, G., & McCarthy, W. (2002). An Ontological Analysis of the Economic Primitives of the Extended-REA Enterprise Information Architecture. *International Joural of Accounting Information Systems, 3*(1), 1-16.

Geerts, G., & McCarthy, W. E. (1999). An Accounting Object Infrastructure for Knowledge Based Enterprise Models. *IEEE Intelligent Systems and Their Applications, 14*(4), 89-94.

Geerts, G., & McCarthy, W. E. (2000). Augmented Intensional Reasoning in Knowledge-Based Accounting Systems. *Journal of Information Systems, 14*(2), 127.

Geerts, G., & McCarthy, W. E. (2005). *The Ontological Foundation of REA Enterprise Information Systems* - Working Paper.

Geerts, G., & McCarthy, W. E. (2006). Policy-Level Specification in REA Enterprise Information Systems. *Journal of Information Systems, Fall.*

Gómez-Pérez, A., & Rojas, M. D. (1999). *Ontological Reengineering and Reuse.* Paper presented at the 11th European Workshop on Knowledge Acquisition, Modeling and Management, Dagstuhl Castle, Germany.

Gordijn, J. (2002). *Value based requirements engineering: Exploring innovative e-commerce ideas.* Vrije Universiteit Amsterdam.

Grunninger, M. (2003). Enterprise Modelling. In P. Bernus, L. Nemes & G. Schmidt (Eds.), *Handbook on Enterprise Architecture*: Springer.

Guarino, N. (1997). Understanding, building and using ontologies. *International Journal of Human-Computer Studies, 46*(2-3), 293-310.

Haugen, R., & McCarthy, W.E. (2000). REA: A Semantic Model for Internet Supply Chain Collaboration. *Proceedings of the Business Objects and Component Design and Implementation Workshop VI: Enterprise Application Integration.*

Hepp, M. (2007). Ontologies: State of the art, Business Potential, and grand challenges. In M.

Hepp, P. De Leenheer, A. De Moor & Y. Sure (Eds.), *Ontology Management: Semantic Web, Semantic Web Services, and Business Applications* (pp. 3-22): Springer.

Hofreiter, B., Huemer, C., Liegl, P., Schuster, R., & Zapletal, M. (2006). UN/CEFACT'S Modeling Methodology (UMM): A UML Profile for B2B e-Commerce. *Lecture Notes in Computer Science*, 4231, 19-31.

Hruby, P. (2005a). *Ontology-based Domain-Driven Design*. Paper presented at the OOPSLA Workshop on Best Practices for Model Driven Software Development.

Hruby, P. (2005b). *Role of Domain Ontologies in Software Factories.* Paper presented at the OOPSLA Workshop on Software Factories, San Diego, California.

Hruby, P., Kiehn, J., & Scheller, C. V. (2006). *Model-driven design using business patterns.* New York: Springer.

ISO. (2006). *Information technology -- Business Operational View -- Part 4: Business transaction scenarios -- Accounting and economic ontology* (ISO/IEC 15944-4).

Kogut, P., Cranefield, S., Hart, L., Dutra, M., Baclawski, K., Kokar, M. K., et al. (2002). UML for ontology development. *Knowledge Engineering Review, 17*(1), 61-64.

Lassila, O., & McGuiness, D. L. (2001). *The Role of Frame-Based Representations on the Semantic Web.* Stanford, California: Knowledge System Laboratory, Stanford University.

McCarthy, W. (1982). The REA Accounting Model: A Generalized Framework for Accounting Systems in A Shared Data Environment. *The Accounting Review, july*, 554-578.

Mylopoulos, J. (1998). Information modeling in the time of the revolution. *Information Systems, 23*(3-4), 127-155.

OMG. (2006). *Ontology Definition Metamodel: OMG Adopted Specification (ptc/06-10-11)*: Object Management Group.

Osterwalder, A. (2004). *The Business Model Ontology - a proposition in a design science approach.* University of Lausanne, Lausanne.

Sowa, J. (1999). *Knowledge Representation: Logical, Philosophical, and Computational Foundations*: Pacific Grove, Brooks/Cole.

Spaccapietra, S., Parent, C., Vangenot, & C., Cullot, N. (2004). On Using Conceptual Modeling for Ontologies. *Lecture Notes in Computer Science*, 3307, 22-23.

Spyns, P. (2005). Object Role Modelling for ontology engineering in the DOGMA framework. *Lecture Notes in Computer Science*, 3762, 710-719.

UN/CEFACT. (2003). *UN/CEFACT Modeling Methodology (UMM) User Guide* (No. CEFACT/TMG/N093).

Ushold, M., King, M., Moralee, S., & Zorgios, Y. (1998). The Enterprise Ontology. *The Knowledge Engineering Review: Special Issue on Putting Ontologies to Use, 13*(1), 31-89.

ADDITIONAL READING

Abecker, A., & van Elst, L. (2004). Ontologies for Knowledge Management. In S. Staab & R. Studer (Eds.), *Handbook on Ontologies*: Springer.

Andersson, B., Bergholtz, M., Edirisuriya, A., Ilayperuma, T., Johannesson, P., Grégoire, B., et al. (2006). *Towards a Reference Ontology for Business Models.* Paper presented at the Conceptual Modeling (ER 2006), Tucson, AZ, USA.

Borgo, S., & Leitao, P. (2004). *The Role of Foundational Ontologies in Manufacturing Domain Applications.* Paper presented at the OTM Confederated International Conferences, ODBASE 2004, Ayia Napa, Cyprus.

Bramer, m., & Terziyan, V. (2005). *Industrial Applications ofSemantic Web* (Vol. 188): Springer-Verslag.

Bussler, C. (2003). The role of Semantic Web technology in EAI. *The Bulletin of the IEEE Computer Society Technical Committee on Data Engineering*.

Bussler, C. (2005). Business-to-business integration technology. *Data Management in a Connected World*, 3551, 235-254.

Calero, C., Ruiz, F., & Piattini, M. (2006). *Ontologies for software engineering and software technology* (1st ed.). New York: Springer.

Ciocoiu, M., Gruninger, M., & Nau, D. S. (2000). Ontologies for Integrating Engineering Applications. *Journal of Computing and Information Science in Engineering*, 1(1), 12-22.

Fensel, D. (2001). *Ontologies: A Silver Bullet for Knowledge Management and Electronic Commerce*: Springer-Verslag.

Gasevic, D. (2006). *Model driven architecture and ontology development* (1st ed.). New York: Springer.

Gómez-Pérez, A., Fernández-López, M., & Corcho, O. (2004). *Ontological Engineering*: Springer-Verlag.

Gordijn, J. (2002). *Value based requirements engineering: Exploring innovative e-commerce ideas*. Vrije Universiteit Amsterdam.

Gruninger, M., Atefi, K., & Fox, M. S. (2000). Ontologies to Support Process Integration in Enterprise Engineering. *Computational and Mathematical Organization Theory*, 6(4), 381-394.

Guarino, N. (1998). *Formal Ontology and Information Systems*. Paper presented at the International Conference on Formal ontology in Information Systems (FOIS'98), Trento, Italy.

Guizardi, G. (2007). On Ontology, ontologies, Conceptualizations, Modeling Languages, and (Meta)Models. In O. Vasilecas, J. Edler & A. Caplinskas (Eds.), *Frontiers in Artificial Intelligence and Applications, Databases and Information Systems IV*. Amsterdam: IOS press.

McComb, D. (2004). *Semantics in business systems : the savvy manager's guide. The discipline underlying Web services, business rules, and the Semantic Web*. San Francisco, CA: Morgan Kaufmann Publishers.

Newcomer, E. (2002). *Understanding Web services : XML, WSDL, SOAP, and UDDI*. Boston: Addison-Wesley.

Stuckenschmidt, H., & Harmelen, F. v. (2005). *Information Sharing on the Semantic Web*: Springer.

ENDNOTES

1 The complete OWL formalization of the conceptual REA representation developed in this chapter can be downloaded from http://purl.org/REA/REAontology.owl

2 http://sws-challenge.org/wiki/index.php/Main_Page

Chapter XII
Towards Semantic Business Processes:
Concepts, Methodology, and Implementation

Muhammad Ahtisham Aslam
University of Leipzig, Germany & COMSATS Institute of Information Technology, Pakistan

Sören Auer
University of Leipzig, Germany & University of Pennsylvania, USA

Klaus-Peter Fähnrich
University of Leipzig, Germany

ABSTRACT

The business process execution language for Web services (BPEL4WS, shortly BPEL) is one of the most popular languages and de facto standard for modelling business processes as Web services compositions. However, it only allows using hard-coded syntactical interfaces for partners and the process itself, i.e. semantic descriptions of services cannot be used within a process model. The lacks of an ontological description of the process elements cause limitations in the ways services are used within a process. A service providing the same functionality as the one referenced in the process model, but via a different syntactical interface, cannot be used instead. As a result, a process model cannot find an alternate service that performs the same functionality but exposes a different interface and can crash. Also, another drawback of such business processes is that they expose syntactical interfaces and cannot be discovered and composed dynamically by other semantic enabled systems slowing down the process of interaction between business partners. OWL-S on the other hand is suite of OWL ontologies and can be used to describe the compositions of Web services on the basis of matching semantics as well as to expose semantically enriched interfaces of business processes. Consequently, translating BPEL process descriptions to OWL-S suite of ontologies can overcome syntactical limitations of BPEL processes enabling them to 1) edit and model the composition of Web services on the basis of matching semantics 2) provide semantically enriched information of business processes. This semantically enriched information helps for dynamic and automated discovery, invocation and composition of business processes as Semantic Web services. Describing an approach and its implementation that can be used to enable business processes for semantic based dynamic discovery, invocation and composition by translating BPEL process descriptions to OWL-S suite of ontologies is the aim of this chapter.

SWSS TECHNOLOGY EMERGENCE AND CURRENT STATUS

Investigating capabilities and limitations of Semantic Web, Semantic Web languages, SWSs and SWSs languages that can be used to overcome syntactical limitations of process modeling languages (e.g. BPEL (Francisco, et. al., 2003; Matjaz, et. al. 2004)) is the preliminary step to understand the problem and to navigate through possible solutions. Here, we describe that how different workflow modeling languages (e.g. BPEL) can be used to model business processes as compositions of multiple services and what are limitations of such syntax based compositions of Web Services. Then we describe the vision of the Semantic Web and provide a short overview of Semantic Web languages (e.g. RDF (Graham & Jeremy, 2004), RDF-S (Dan, et al., 2004) and OWL (Deborah, & Frank, 2004)). Then we provide some technical details about Semantic Web language (i.e. Web ontology language (OWL)) and how OWL ontologies can be used to provide machine understandable meanings of data. We also describe that how SWS community makes use of Semantic Web language (i.e. OWL) to provide machine understandable meanings of Web services. We also provide short technical descriptions of SWS languages (e.g. OWL-S (David et. al., 2006), WSDL-S (Rama et. al., 2006), WSMO (Sinuhe, 2005)) and compare them with respect to their semantic and workflow modeling capabilities. By analyzing and comparing existing SWS languages we argue that semantic and process modeling capabilities of OWL-S are much batter as compare to other SWS languages and it can be used to address syntactical limitations of traditional process modeling languages (e.g. BPEL) by translating BPEL process descriptions to OWL-S suite of ontologies.

Workflow Modeling

Different workflow languages like Web Services flow language (WSFL) (Frank, 2001), MS XLANG (Satish, 2001) and business process execution language for Web services (BPEL4WS, shortly (BPEL)) (Francisco, et. al., 2003; Matjaz, et. al. 2004) have been developed to define workflows. WSFL from IBM addresses workflow on two levels: (1) it takes a directed-graph model approach for defining and executing business processes (2) it defines public interfaces that allows business processes to advertise as Web services (Jun et. al. 2006). XLANG is an XML based business process language that can be used to orchestrate Web services. An XLANG service description is a WSDL (David, & Canyang, 2007) service description with an extension element that describes the behaviour of the service as a part of a business process. MS XLANG is the language that is used in MS BizTalk Server (Microsoft's business process modeling tool). However, processes modelled in BizTalk server can easily be exported and imported to BPEL (an industry wide accepted standard for modeling business processes).

BPEL4WS

BPEL4WS is a mature business process modeling language and is industry wide accepted standard for modeling business processes as Web services compositions. A BPEL process consumes Web services operations to perform a specific business tasks by defining control flow and data flow between these Web services operations with in process. A BPEL process can itself be exported as a Web service. BPEL supports the implementation of any kind of business process in a very natural manner and has gradually become the basis of a standard for Web service description and composition (Jun, et., al., 2006). Several characteristics of BPEL make it language of choice for modeling business processes. For example, BPEL is a language that combines workflow capabilities of IBM WSFL and structural constructs of MS XLANG. Most of process modeling tools (e.g. MS BizTalk Server, IBM WebSphere, SAP NetWeaver etc.) provides support for importing and exporting BPEL processes from one framework to other. In presence of all these capabilities it has many shortcomings resulting in limitations for seamless interoperability of business processes. These limitations can be addressed successfully by getting across semantic gap between process modeling languages and upcoming Semantic Web and SWSs languages. Figure 1 gives an overview of evolution and relation between these syntax and semantic based languages.

Semantic Web

Semantic Web is an extension to the current Web (WWW) to present more meaningful data that is easily and efficiently process able and understandable for machines. It aims at providing common formats for exchanging data and languages for describing relations between data objects. For this purpose different languages (e.g. RDF, RDF-S and OWL) have been presented. resource description framework (RDF) was developed to provide a standard way to model, describe, and exchange information about resources. Providing information as RDF triples was not enough for the vision of Semantic Web to become true. The further development resulted in resource description framework Schema (RDF-S). RDF-S is semantic extension to RDF, as it enhances the information description capabilities of RDF by describing the groups of related resources and relationship between these resources. Lacks of information expression capabilities of RDF-S (e.g. defining properties of properties, necessary and sufficient conditions for class membership, or equivalence or disjointness of class) resulted in

Figure 1. Evolution and relation between Web services, workflow, Semantic Web and SWSs languages

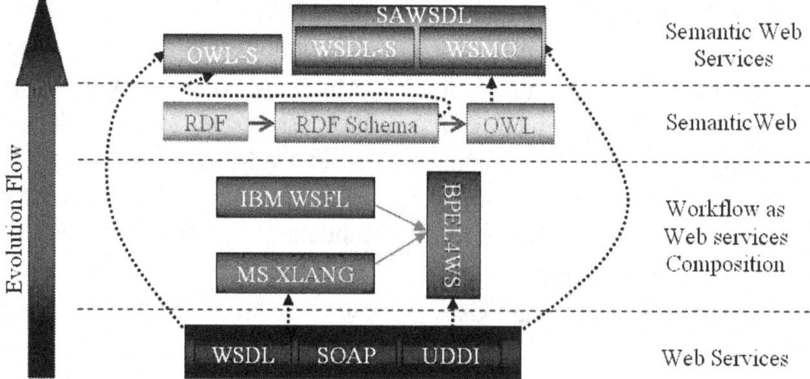

more expressing Semantic Web language (i.e. Web Ontology Language (OWL)). OWL is intended to be used when the information contained in documents need to be processed by applications, as opposed to the situations where the content only needs to be presented to humans (Deborah, & Frank, 2004). Figure 2 (taken from Evren Sirin's talk "using Web ontologies for Web Services Composition") gives a very interesting example of an OWL ontology. This sample ontology defines relation of a student with his geographical location, university, course etc.

Emerging Semantic Web Services Languages

Different efforts are going on to develop SWSs languages (e.g. WSDL-S, WSMO and OWL-S). All of these SWSs languages working groups are using OWL to provide domain specific semantics of a Web service.

WSDL-S

WSDL-S is a SWS development language that is jointly developed by the University of Georgia and IBM. WSDL-S extends WSDL *operation* and *message* tags by annotating them with domain ontologies to provide semantics. In addition with extending WSDL, WSDL-S also adds new tags (i.e. *LSDISExt:precondition* and *LSDISExt:effect*) to WSDL specifications to describe pre-conditions and effects of a Web service operation. Figure 3 summarizes WSDL-S approach. Also, WSDL-S concepts are being fed to upcoming SWS language (i.e. Semantic Annotation for WSDL (SAWSDL) (Joel, & Holger, 2006)) as a joint effort of WSDL-S and WSMO working groups. Since, WSDL-S concepts are being implemented as major of the SAWSDL approach therefore, we do not discuss it separately.

WSMO

Web Service Modeling Ontology (WSMO) is part of ongoing research to achieve dynamic, scalable and cost-effective infrastructure for transaction and collaboration of business services. Web Service Modeling Language (WSML) (Joel, et. al., 2006) is formal language used to describe WSMO services. The Web Service Execution Environment (WSMX) (Christoph, et. al. 2005) is execution environment for dynamic discovery, invocation and composition of WSMO services.

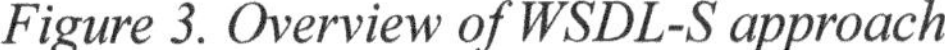

Figure 3. Overview of WSDL-S approach

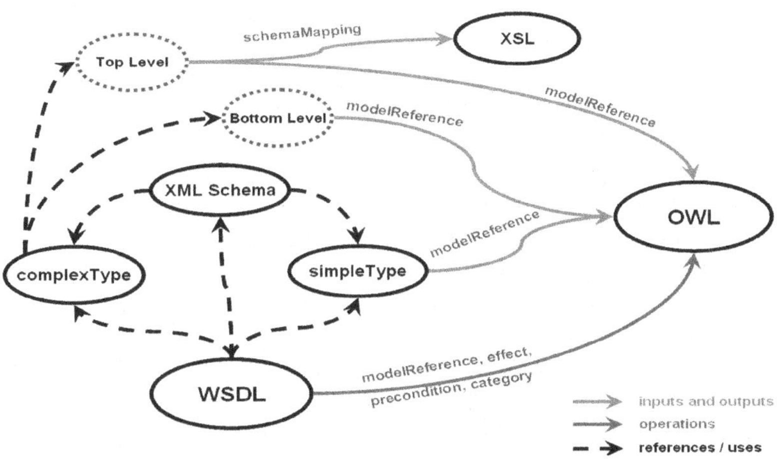

OWL-S

OWL-S is another language being developed to provide Web services semantics to facilitate dynamic and automated discovery, invocation and composition of Web services. OWL-S is suite of OWL ontologies (i.e. *Profile*, *Process Model* and *Grounding* ontologies). *Profile* ontology provides semantically enriched information about Web service capabilities that helps in semantic based publishing and discovery of Web services. *Process Model* ontology describes how to use a service and can be used for semantic based composition modeling of complex services. *Grounding* ontology describes how to access a service. OWL-S uses OWL ontologies to provide universally unique meaning of a service by annotating its *inputs, outputs* with domain ontologies and by describing its *pre-conditions* and *effects*. Also, *Process Model* ontology has very expressive capabilities to model composition of multiple Web services like workflow languages but based on their semantic descriptions. Two major reasons for choosing OWL-S to semantically describe BPEL process models are (1) *Profile* ontology can be used to provide semantically enriched meaning of a process as OWL-S SWS (2) *Process Model* ontology of OWL-S suite can be used to edit and model compositions of multiple SWSs (like a workflow language). Table 1 describes a comparison of these SWSs languages.

Problem Scenario

In order to understand the problems raised due to semantic limitations of BPEL we consider an example scenario of Web services composition (i.e. a BPEL process). The example scenario helps to realize needs for establishing correspondence between syntax based and semantic based composition of Web services.

To keep the complexity of scenario within limitations we consider a simple *Translator and Dictionary* process example ('.bpel' of the process and '.owl' files of mapped OWL-S service and *atomic* processes are available with the tool download). The *Translator and Dictionary* process is modelled in MS BizTalk Server as syntax-based composition of two services (i.e. the *Translator* service and the *Dictionary* service). The *Translator*

service is a Web service that can be used to translate a string from one language to another supported language by using its operation *getTranslation*. The *Dictionary* service is a Web service that can be used to get the meaning of an English word in English (i.e. the only English language is supported by the *Dictionary* service)

Table 1. Comparison of SWSs languages

	OWL-S	WSMO	WSDL-S
Language	OWL	WSML	WSDL with Extensions
Multiple Interfaces	Supported	Supported	Not supported
Service Semantics	Supported	Supported	Not Supported
Operational Semantics	Not Supported	Not Supported	Supported
Composite Processes	Supported	Not Supported	BPEL with Extensions
Simple Process	Supported	Not Supported	Not Supported
Invocation	WSDL Grounding	WSDL Grounding	WSDL
Development Tool	Available	Available	Available

by using its operation *getMeaning*. Now we define two problem scenarios (tasks) that cannot be performed by anyone of these two services (i.e. the *Translator* Service or the *Dictionary* Service). To perform these tasks we need to model a BPEL process as composition of these two Web services. These two scenarios are:

- How we can get meaning of a *German* word in *English*? Because the *Dictionary* service supports only meaning of an *English* word in *English*, not the meaning of a *German* word in *English*.
- How we can get the meaning of a *German* word in *German*? Because the *Translator* service only translates string from one language to other language (not give the meaning of a word) and the *Dictionary* service gives meaning of only *English* words in *English*.

In both of above scenarios none of a single Web service is able to perform required task. As a solution we model a BPEL process as composition of these services to perform required tasks. In first problem scenario we can define a workflow (as shown in Figure 4) as composition of the *Translator* service and the *Dictionary* service and consists of the following steps.

- Process accepts input string (*German* word) from user (a user may be a human user or another service).
- Transfers this string as an input to the *Translator* service to translate the string from *German* to *English*.
- Output of the *Translator* service is given as an input to the *Dictionary* service.
- As a last step of the process, the *Dictionary* service returns the meaning of the input string.

Similarly task pointed in second scenario (i.e. getting meaning of the *German* word in *German*) can be accomplished by enhancing process model of Web services composition by following steps (as shown in Figure 5):

- Process accepts the input string (i.e. the *German* word) from the user.
- Transfers this string as an input to the *Translator* service to translate the string from *German* to *English*.

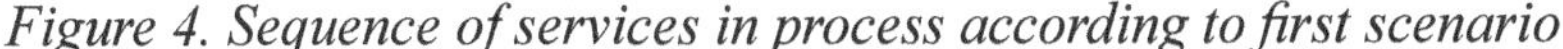

Figure 4. Sequence of services in process according to first scenario

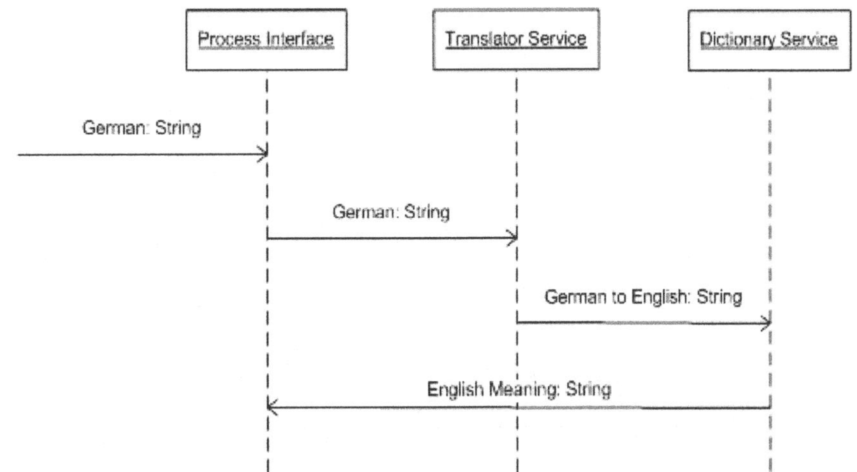

- The output of the *Translator* service (i.e. the *English* translation of the input string) is given as an input to the *Dictionary* service.
- The output of the *Dictionary* service (i.e. the meaning of the word) is given as input to the *Translator* service to translate it back from *English* to *German.*
- As a last step of the process the *Translator* service translates the string (i.e. the meaning of the word) back from *English* to *German.*

If we analyze the process (composition of Web services) more at semantic level then following issues are identified:

- When the process is exported as a Web service, it has same syntactical limitations as traditional WSDL services resulting in clampdown of process for dynamic discovery, invocation and composition.
- If we want to extend the process (as shown in Figure 4) in a semantic environment to perform the task pointed in second scenario (as shown in Figure 5) then we will realize that:
    - o Web services with in composition provide no information for semantic based editing and modeling of process. For example, consider the input message (as shown in Example 1) required by the *Translator* service. This message provides no semantic information about message parts (i.e. *inputString, inputLanguage* and *outputLanguage*).
    - o Semantic limitations of Web services with in process restrict to dynamically discover and compose (on the basis of matching semantics) a Semantic Web service (e.g. semantic based *Translator* service).

Bridging the semantic gap between syntax based and semantic based composition of Web services can help to address above discussed problems. Example 2 shows annotation of input message part (i.e. *inputLanguage*) with ontology concept (i.e. *SupportedLanguage*) defined in appropriate domain ontology. Providing such semantic information can help to:

- Provide machine understandable meaning of the process as an OWL-S composite service

Figure 5. Sequence of services in process according to second scenario

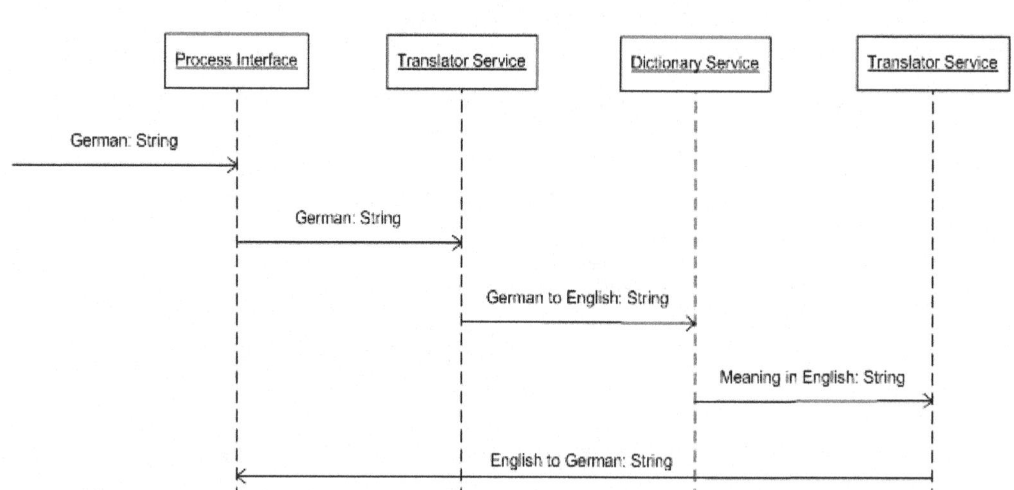

Example 1. A sample WSDL syntax based message

```
<wsdl:message name="TranslatorRequest">
 <wsdl:part name="inputString" type="s:string" />
 <wsdl:part name="inputLanguage" type="s:string" />
 <wsdl:part name="outputLanguage" type="s:string" />
</wsdl:messag
```

Example 2. Semantically Enriched Message

```
<process:Input rdf:ID="inputLanguage">
 <process:parameterType rdf:datatype="&xsd;#anyURI">
  &this;#SupportedLanguage</process:parameterType>
 <rdfs:label>Input Language</rdfs:label>
</process:Input>
```

that can help in dynamic discovery, invocation and composition of BPEL process as an OWL-S Semantic Web service.

- Shift the process from syntax-based to semantic based composition providing semantically enriched information about each service involved with in composition.
- Edit and model the composition on the basis of matching semantics rather than relying just on syntactical information.
- Defining abstract process (semantics for a required service) with in composition to dynamically discover and compose a service on the basis of matching semantics defined in abstract process (according to approach discussed in (Evren, et., al., 2005)).
- Using an AI planning for automated composition by mapping OWL-S *composite* and *atomic* processes to tasks and operators of the planning language (e.g. HTN planning).

In above discussed simple but extensive example we have just considered inputs and outputs of different services for the purpose of composition. In actual scenarios we can use other information related to a Web service (e.g. service provider, response time, geographical location, defining data flow and control flow between services etc.) for more accurate and efficient composition of Web services. *One thing to note* at this point is that we have provided two example scenarios for modeling processes as Web services compositions. For first scenario we modeled a BPEL process in MS BizTalk Server as syntax based composition of two services (i.e. the *Translator* service and the *Dictionary* service). Then we highlighted limitations of such syntax based process modeling. In Sections 2 and 3 we provide detail analysis of BPEL process models and OWL-S SWSs and then on the basis of this analysis we define specifications to translate BPEL process descriptions to OWL-S suite of ontologies. In remaining chapter we use this BPEL process (please note that the '.bpel' of the process and the '.owl' files of mapped OWL-S service and *atomic* processes are available with the tool download) to provide some code samples of mapping specifications. In evaluation section (i.e. Section 5) whole BPEL process is mapped to OWL-S service. Then we use this mapped OWL-S service to answer the problem questions (i.e. 1) semantic based composition editing and modeling of services 2) semantically enriched interface of the BPEL process as OWL-S SWS). In our evaluation section we enhance the *Process Model* ontology of mapped OWL-S service in semantic environment (e.g. Protégé (John, et., al., 2003) (OWL-S Editor) (Daniel, et., al., 2005) or even with simple editor like Note pad to develop SWS for scenario 2 (as shown in Figure 5).

MAPPING CONSTRAINTS

Mapping constraints create the base of mapping specifications and provide analysis of BPEL process model and OWL-S SWS and their components. Here, we do not mean to provide complete description of these languages as their specifications cover them very well but analytical description of BPEL process models and OWL-S suite of ontologies helps to categorize and to specify that which part of a process should be mapped to which construct of OWL-S.

Analysis of BPEL Process Model

A BPEL process model is set of *primitive* and *structured* activities. Here, we describe functional behavior of BPEL processes and its activities on the basis of which we have defined mapping specifications.

Processes

BPEL allows describing business processes in two ways:

- **Executable Processes** are used to model interaction between participants (Web services) of a business process. The logic and state of the process determine the nature and sequence of Web services interactions conducted at each business partner, and thus the interaction protocol (Francisco, et al., 2003).
- **Abstract Processes** are not typically executable. They are meant to couple Web service interface definition with behavioral specifications that can be used to both constrain the implementation of business roles and define in precise terms the behavior that each party in a business protocol can expect from others (Matjaz, et al., 2004).

Primitive Activities

A BPEL process is a set of activities (*primitive* and *structured* activities). *Primitive* activities are used to perform basic tasks of a process. Some important BPEL *primitive* activities and their behavioral characteristics are as under:

- **Invoke** (*<invoke>*) activity is used to invoke a Web service by sending it some input message and probably by receiving some output message (Example 3 shows a sample *invoke* activity). In a BPEL process *invoke* activity can have dual behavior i.e. (1) it can be used to perform a Web service operation (2) it can be used to create the interface of an asynchronous BPEL process. Due to its different behavior mapping of *invoke* activity to OWL-S also varies (as discussed in Sections 3.1.2 and 3.2).
- **Receive** (*<receive>*) activity receives a message from a Web service probably to start a process. Like an *invoke* activity, a *receive* activity also has dual behavior i.e. (1) it can act as an interface of a BPEL process (2) it can be used to receive a message from a Web service in response to an asynchronous Web service operation.
- **Reply** (*<reply>*) activity is used to reply a message in response to a *receive* activity.
- **Assignment** (*<assign>*) activity is used to assign values to message variables. In a

Example 3. ***invoke*** *activity that performs the Web service operation (i.e.* ***getMeaning*** *operation)*

```
<invoke partnerLink="To_Translation_Service_Port_1"
    portType="q2:TranslatorPortType" operation="getTranslation"
    inputVariable="Message1_To_Translation_Service"
    outputVariable="Message1_From_Translation_Service" />
```

BPEL process the Assignment activity can be used to initialize input message of a Web service operation.

Primitive activities are used to perform small tasks within a complex process. Different activities can be combined and their order of execution can be defined by using some *structured* activities.

Structured Activities

BPEL *structured* activities are used to define control flow between sub*primitive* and *structured* activities within a process. Some major structured activities with their functional behavior are described below:

- **Sequence** (<*sequence*>) activity is used to define a set of activities that are performed in a sequence. A *sequence* completes when its last child activity has been performed.
- **Flow** (<*flow*>) activity is used to invoke child activities concurrently. A *flow* activity completes when all activities within *flow* activity have completed.
- **Switch-Case** (<*switch*>) activity is used to perform child activities under some conditional aspects. A *switch* activity can have one or more conditional branches defined by *case* elements. A *case* may have optional *otherwise* branch that is performed when condition statement becomes false.
- **While** (<*while*>) is used to repeatedly perform a child activity. The child activity under the *while* activity is performed as long as the *while* condition holds true.

Some Additional Activities

- **Wait** (<*wait*>) activity is used to wait for some time.
- **Throw** (<throw>) activity is used for throwing exceptions and indicating faults.
- **Terminate** (<*terminate*>) activity is used to terminate a process.

In this section we provided analytical description of BPEL processes and functional constraints of BPEL activities. With such analytical description of functional constraints of BPEL processes and activities it becomes easier to specify that which BPEL activities have matching behavior to which OWL-S CCs. Table 2 summarizes BPEL process components with their short functional description.

Analysis of OWL-S Ontologies

OWL-S is being developed to describe SWSs. Here, we analyze functional constraints of OWL-S suite and its CCs that can help to specify that which activities of BPEL process can be mapped to which OWL-S CCs on the basis of their matching behavior.

Table 2. BPEL process model activities and their description

Activities	Description
Primitive Activities	
Invoke	Performs WS operation or create process interface
Receive	Receives process input message or response of synchronous WS operation
Reply	Replies in response of some Receive activity
Assignment	Assigns message values
Structured Activities	
Sequence	Performs sub-activities in sequence
Flow	Synchronizes sub-activities
Case-switch	Shows conditional behavior
While	Repeatedly performs a task
Some Other Activities	
Wait	Waits for some time
Throw	Throws exceptions and errors
Terminate	Terminates a process

Note: WS stands for Web service.

OWL-S: Technical Overview

OWL-S is suite of OWL ontologies (i.e. *Profile*, *Process Model* and *Grounding* ontologies). *Profile* ontology is used to present semantically enriched interface of a process as SWS. Like a workflow language, the *Process Model* ontology can be used to model composition of multiple *atomic* and *composite* processes (services). Figure 6 provides an overview of the OWL-S *Process Model* ontology and relation of *Process* class with child classes. *Grounding* ontology describes about how to access a service by specifying message formats, protocols and transport. *Service* ontology actually acts as an organizer for the *Profile*, *Process Model* and *Grounding* ontologies. Each OWL-S service has one instance of the *Service* class.

Processes

OWL-S has three kinds of processes:

- **Atomic Processes** are processes that can be executed in a single step and they have no sub process. *Atomic* processes are somehow like Web services operations that can be performed in a single step. An *atomic* process is described by using the class *AtomicProcess* that is sub class of the *Process* class (as shown in Figure 6).
- **Simple Processes** may be used either to provide a view of (a specialized way of using) some *atomic* process, or a simplified representation of some *composite* process (for purposes of planning and reasoning) (David, et., al., 2006, p. 1).
- **Composite Processes** are processes that can have sub *atomic* and *composite* processes. Like a workflow modeling language we can use *composite* processes to model the composition of multiple atomic and composite processes. A *composite* process allows defining the control flow between sub *atomic* and *composite* processes by using different CCs (e.g. *sequence, split, split-join* etc.).

Figure 6. OWL-S process model ontology

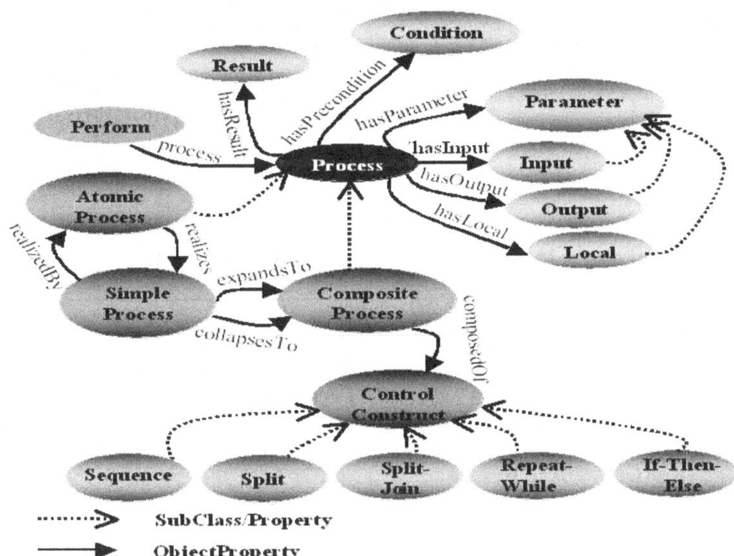

Control Constructs

OWL-S defines a number of CCs that can be used to define control flow between sub processes within *Process Model* ontology. Discussion about capabilities of these CCs is necessary because they are used to define control flow of BPEL process in the mapped OWL-S service. OWL-S defines many CCs that can be used to define control flow between process components. Some of these CCs are as under:

- **Sequence:** Components of a *Sequence* CC are performed in a sequence. *Sequence* class is sub class of the class *ControlConstruct* (as shown in sample code below) that holds other CCs as sub classes:

```
<owl:Class rdf:ID="Sequence">
 <rdfs:subClassOf rdf:resource="#ControlConstruct"/>
  ..........
 </rdfs:subClassOf>
</owl:Class>
```

- **Split** CC is used to perform its process components in parallel. Also, a *Split* CC completes as soon as all of its process components are scheduled for execution.
- **Split-Join** CC is used for concurrent execution of process components with partial synchronization. A *Split-Join* CC completes as soon as all of its process components have been performed.
- **If-Then-Else** CC can be used to implement conditional behavior within a *composite* process. It has three properties (i.e. *ifCondition, then, else*). Execution of *then* and *else* depends on either *ifCondition* is true or false (i.e. if *ifCondition* is true, perform *then* part and if *ifCondition* is false then perform *else*).
- **Repeat-While** CC is used to repeatedly perform its process component (i.e. as long as *Repeat-While* condition holds true). Condition is important part of OWL-S CCs (e.g. *If-Then-Else, Repeat-While, Repeat-Until* CCs).

Table 3. Analytical description of OWL-S ontology constructs

OWL-S	Description
Profile	
Input/Output	Provides functional semantics of service as inputs and outputs
Pre-condition/effect	Describes functional semantics as conditions before and after service execution
Result	Conditional output of service
Service category, provider, location	Non-functional semantics
Process Model	
Atomic process	Executes in single step
Simple process	Gives multi view of same process
Composite process	Executes in multiple steps
Sequence	Performs process components in sequence
Split	Concurrently executes process components
Split-Join	Synchronizes process components
If-Then-Else	Shows conditional behavior
Repeat-While	Repeatedly perform sub component
Grounding	
WsdlGrounding	Describes process grounding
hasAtomicProcessGrounding	Provides reference of atomic process grounding
xsltTransformationString	Transform XML document to other

Some Other OWL-S Mapping Constraints

Some other constraints that need to be addressed while mapping BPEL process descriptions to OWL-S are follows:

- **Performing Individual Processes:** Since *composite* process is a composition of sub *atomic* and *composite* processes, these processes can be performed by using *Perform* CC. The invocation of a process is indicated by an instance of the *Perform* class. The *process* property of class *Perform* indicates the process to be performed.
- **Condition Expressions:** We use SWRL (Peter, 2005) expressions being the most recommended standard to define conditions for OWL-S CCs. OWL-S API (Evren, 2006) (developed by MIDSWAP Lab) also supports the execution of conditions defined by using the SWRL.
- **Data Flow and Parameter Binding:** OWL-S defines a class *Binding* for the data flow between process components. OWL-S specifications allow to define hard coded values (e.g. 5, "hello" etc.) as inputs of processes.
- **Parameters and Results:** In OWL-S specifications, parameters are what we call variables in general programming languages. Parameters can be expressed by using *Parameter* class.

Table 3 summarizes important components of OWL-S ontology and their analytical description. On the basis of capabilities and limitations of components of BPEL and OWL-S we define mapping specifications for shifting BPEL process model to OWL-S ontology.

TRANSLATING BPEL PROCESS DESCRIPTIONS TO OWL-S

In previous section (i.e. Section 2), we have discussed in detail about process modeling and semantic capabilities of BPEL and OWL-S and components of these languages. Since, OWL-S is suite of three ontologies (i.e. *Profile, Process Model* and *Grounding* ontologies) therefore, we describe the translation (mapping) of BPEL process descriptions to OWL-S at three levels (i.e. mapping of BPEL process model to OWL-S *Profile, Process Model* and *Grounding* ontologies). Table 4 describes specification for mapping BPEL process to OWL-S. The specifications describe from abstract level to components and activities level translation of BPEL process to OWL-S service. Areas, where direct mapping is not possible or needs some additional work from the end user, are also discussed in detail.

Algorithm 1 provides a very abstract level description of the recursive algorithm used for extracting OWL-S suite from BPEL process model. It traverses *bpelfile* objects tree as long as activities in *bpelfile* come to end. An important thing to note is that when an activity is not an I/O *primitive* activity then it is mapped to *perform* CC (as described in Lines 13 and 33 of Algorithm 1) to perform relevant *atomic* process. In next section we describe the extraction of *Process Model* ontology from BPEL process model.

Translation to the OWL-S Process Model Ontology

In this section we describe how a BPEL process model is mapped to OWL-S *Process Model* on-

Table 4. Summary of BPEL4WS to OWL-S mapping specifications

Ontology	BPEL4WS	OWL-S
Profile		
	Receive (message variable)	Input parameters
	Invoke (input message variable)	Output parameters
	Invoke (input/output message variable)	Input/Output parameters
	Reply (message variable)	Output parameters
Process Model		
	Executable process	Composite process
	Primitive activity (operation)	Atomic process
	Primitive activity (Invoke)	*Perform* CC
	Sequence	Sequence
	Flow	Split-Join
	Switch-case	Sequence(If-Then-Else)
	While	Repeat-While
	Condition statement	SWRL expression
	Assignment	Data flow specifications
	Terminate	Note
	Throw	Note
	Wait	Note
Grounding		
	Primitive activity (operation)	hasAtomicProcessGrounding
	Complex Message	xsltTransformationString

Note: No equivalent control construct is available in OWL-S for direct mapping.

tology with defined control and data flow. The *Process Model* mapping specifications describe about how BPEL *primitive* and *structured* activities, condition statements, input/output data passing between different activities, variables etc. are mapped to OWL-S relevant control constructs, SWRL expression and parameters respectively. We also provide some code example of mapping of BPEL activities to OWL-S CCs. The whole process of translating BPEL process descriptions to OWL-S depends on functional characteristics of BPEL and OWL-S components as described in Section 2. During discussion of mapping specifications we consider the translation of BPEL process (i.e. *Translator and Dictionary* process), which is mapped to OWL-S service. Now we describe step by step translation of BPEL process components to OWL-S CCs.

Process Level Translation

BPEL process model is composition of multiple Web services with defined control and data flow

Algorithm 1. Abstract level definition of mapping algorithm

```
   Input: Tree view list of BPEL process and WSDL services
   Output: OWL-S suite of ontologies
1  begin
2      Extract BPEL activity from tree
3      Map structured activity to OWL-S CC (Algorithm 2)
4      Get child activities
5      while child activities exist do
6          if activity is not structured activity then
7              if activity is assignment activity then
8                  while activity is assignment activity do
9                      Traverse activity list
10                 end
11                 if activity is non-I/O primitive activity (i.e. invoke activity) then
13                     Map it to perform CC to perform atomic process
14                     Create data flow
15                     Add reference of atomic process Grounding
16                 end
17             end
18             if activity is not assignment activity then
19                 if activity is I/O receive activity then
20                     Create composite process input
21                     Create Profile input parameters
22                 else
23                     if activity is I/O reply activity then
24                         Create composite process output
25                         Create Profile output parameters
26                     else
27                         if activity is I/O invoke activity then
28                             Create composite process output
29                             Create Profile output parameters
30                         else
31                             if activity is non-I/O invoke activity then
33                                 Map it to perform CC to perform atomic process
34                                 Create data flow
35                                 Add reference of atomic process Grounding
36                             end
37                         end
38                     end
39                 end
40             end
41         end
42         if child activity is structured activity then
43             Map structured activity to OWL-S CC (Line 3)
44         end
45     end
46 end
```

to perform a joint task. A BPEL process model is mapped to OWL-S *composite* process that is a semantic based composition of multiple *atomic* and *composite* processes. Control flow and data flow between different Web services operations within a BPEL process model is mapped to control flow and data flow between process components of an OWL-S composite service. An *atomic* process within a *composite* process is result of mapping of a Web service operation that is performed by a *primitive* activity.

We discussed before that a BPEL process is composition of Web services operations that can be performed in a single step. Each Web service operation within a BPEL process is mapped to OWL-S *atomic* process. The mapped *atomic* process consists of complete OWL-S suite of ontologies (i.e. *Profile*, *Process Model* and *Grounding* ontologies). Since, actual tasks within a BPEL process are performed by executing Web service operations therefore, a successful and useful mapping of BPEL process model to OWL-S is intimately dependent on translation of each Web service operation involved within a BPEL process to OWL-S *atomic* process. As much as we know, till now there has no effort been done which supports the mapping of a BPEL process to OWL-S and translates Web services operations within a BPEL process to OWL-S *atomic* processes. Each Web service operation that is mapped to OWL-S atomic process is stored in a separate OWL file. We can also execute these *atomic* processes by using some execution engines (e.g. OWL-S API) or by importing and executing them in SWS development tool (e.g. Protégé (OWL-S Editor)). Since, our sample *Translator and Dictionary* process uses two Web services operations (i.e. *getTranslation* and *getMeaning*, as discussed in Section 1.4) therefore, these Web services operations are translated to OWL-S *atomic* processes (i.e. *getTranslationProcess* and *getMeaningProcess*) and stored in *getTranslation.owl* and *getMeaning.owl* files (as shown in Figure 7).

Activities and Control Flow Translation

In above section we have discussed that a Web service operation performed by a *primitive* activity is mapped to OWL-S *atomic* process. The *primitive* activity that performs Web service operation is mapped to OWL-S *Perform* CC to perform that *atomic* process within mapped OWL-S service. For example, consider the *primitive* activity (i.e. *invoke* activity as shown in Example 3) that

Figure 7. Web services operations translated to OWL-S ***atomic*** *processes and stored in* ***owl files***

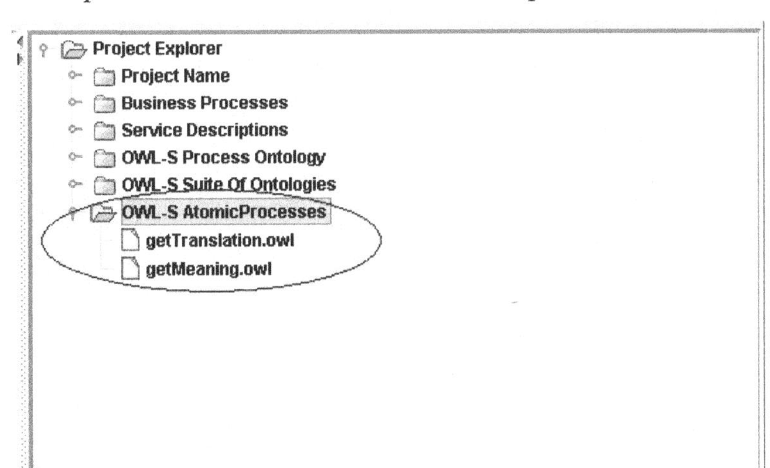

is used to perform Web service operation (i.e. *getTranslation* operation). The *primitive* activity is mapped to *Perform* CC to perform the process *getTranslationProcess* (as shown in sample code below), where *getTranslationProcess* is *atomic* process created in above step (i.e. in Section 3.1.1) and stored in *getTranslation.owl* file:

```
<process:process rdf:resource="http://examples.org/
DummyURI.owl#getTranslationProcess"/>
```

BPEL *structured* activities are used to define control flow between different child activities. OWL-S provides a number of CCs (e.g. *Sequence*, *Split* etc.) for defining control flow between sub processes. Table 4 summarizes mapping of BPEL *structured* activities to OWL-S control constructs on the basis of their matching behavior and Algorithm 2 their mapping from implementation perspective. We have discussed in detail about behavioral characteristics of BPEL *structured* activities and OWL-S CCs in Sections 2.1.3 and 2.2.3. As sample of mapping these activities we describe translation of two *structured* activities (i.e. *flow* and *switch*) to relevant OWL-S CCs (i.e. *Split-Join* and *sequence* of (*If-Then-Else* CCs)), because mapping of these activities is a little bit tricky.

Synchronization between sub activities and process components is important for defining workflows especially in complex business process integration scenarios. BPEL uses *flow* activity to define synchronization between sub activities. "*A Flow activity completes when all of its sub activities are completed*". OWL-S CCs (e.g. *Split* and *Split-Join*) are used to define synchronization between process components. "*Split-Join completes when all of its process component have completed*". Where as capabilities of *Split* are expressed as: "*Split completes as soon as all of its process components have been scheduled for execution*". Even though both *Split* and *Split-Join* CCs are used for concurrent execution of process components but we map *Flow* activity to *Split-Join* CC on the basis of their matching functional characteristics.

A *switch structured* is used to describe conditional behavior and consists of a list of one or more conditional branches defined by using *case* elements. A *case* element has a *condition* attribute to define its condition and can have an optional *otherwise* branch that is executed if the *case* condition becomes false. The *switch* activity is mapped to *Sequence* CC of OWL-S specifications and each *case* element listed under *switch* activity is mapped to *If-Then-Else* CC. The *condition* part of each *case* element is translated to SWRL expression (discussed in next section (i.e. Section 3.1.3)) and *otherwise* part of *case* element is mapped to *else* part of *If-Then-Else* CC. We can summarize

Algorithm 2. Algorithm to map BPEL structured activities to OWL-S CCs

```
Input: structured activity
Output: OWL-S CC
begin
    if activity equal to sequence then
        Map to Sequence CC
    else
        if activity equal to flow then
            Map to Split-Join CC
        else
            if activity equal to while then
                Map to Repeat-While CC
            else
                if activity equal to switch then
                    Map switch activity to Sequence of If-Then-Else CCs
                end
            end
        end
    end
end
```

mapping of *switch* activity with a list of *case* elements as a sequence (*Sequence*) of *If-Then-Else* CCs mapped with optional *else* part.

Translating Condition Statements

Conditions are an important part of BPEL activities (e.g. *switch*, *while* etc.) and OWL-S CCs (e.g. *If-Then-Else*, *Repeat-While* etc.). Without mapping *condition* statements, only mapping of BPEL activities, which depend on conditions to OWL-S CCs, is not useful. We have implemented an efficient algorithm that translates *condition* statements of BPEL activities to SWRL expressions, which are supported by OWL-S specifications. The mapped SWRL expressions can be parsed and executed by execution engines (e.g. OWL-S API). Mapping *condition* statements to SWRL expressions supports all conditional operators (e.g. =, !=, <, >, <=, >= etc.).

Before having a look on condition mapping algorithm we should keep in mind that complexity of *condition* statement could vary with complexity of message variables being used in *condition* statement. The reason is that extracting message variables and message parts of an *atomic* process that are being used in *condition* statement is a complex task (especially when message variables of complex message types are involved). However, our algorithm handles the translation of *condition* statements to SWRL expressions carefully and efficiently by parsing and tracking the list of *atomic* processes and their messages.

Data Flow Translation

We can discuss the mapping of data flow at two levels; one is defining input and output of a *composite* process, second level of defining data flow is passing messages between process components within *composite* process.

To understand data flow definition at first level, consider a BPEL process in which *receive* activity receives a message from outer world to start a process. Such a message that initiates a process is defined as input message of *composite* process within *Process Model* ontology of mapped OWL-S service. In remaining process this message is referred as a message that belongs to the process *TheParentPerform* to pass this message as input of sub processes. Similarly such situations are also possible in which the output of a sub process becomes the output of *composite* process. In such cases output of sub process is also defined as output of the process *TheParentPerform*.

We have also discussed that within a BPEL process model output of one Web service operation can be used as input of the next Web service operation. During the mapping of a BPEL process to OWL-S service, passing messages (data) between sub processes within a *composite* process is addressed by using the *Binding* class.

Variables and Local Parameters Translation

Like traditional programming languages, we can also declare variables in a BPEL process to store and share data between different activities within a process. Such variables within a BPEL process are mapped to local variables (*LocalVariable*) in OWL-S. These local variables can be used to manipulate and share data between sub *atomic* and *composite* processes. In Section 3.1.3 we have discussed that how these local variables are used in *condition* expressions to store and compare values with inputs and outputs of sub *atomic* and *composite* processes. Local variables can be connected with processes by using the property *hasLocal* of the *process* class.

In this section we have discussed the translation of BPEL process model to OWL-S *Process Model* ontology. We also described the logic of translation of BPEL activities to OWL-S CCs on the basis of mapping constraints (discussed in Section 2). Translation of some of BPEL ac-

Algorithm 3. Algorithm to parse ***condition*** *statement and to generate SWRL expression*

```
Input: condition statement
Output: SWRL expression
begin
    Parse condition statement
    Extract left hand operands of condition statement ( i.e. message1_Name, variable1_Name and
    part1_Name )
    if variable1_Name equal to null and part1_Name equal to null then
        while list of Local Variables not ended do
            if local_Variable_Name equal to message_Name then
                Save reference of local variable as local_Variable1_Name
            end
        end
    end
    Find condition operator
    if right hand operand is message variable of an atomic process then
        Find index of "and" operator or "or" operator
        if "and" operator exists or "or" operator exists then
            Display message "Multiple conditions are not supported"
            Extract right hand operand of condition statement
        end
        Extract right hand operand of condition statement ( i.e. message2_Name, variable2_Name
        and part2_Name )
        if variable2_Name equal to null and part2_Name equal to null then
            while list of Local Variables (local_Variable_Name) not ended do
                if local_Variable_Name equal to message_Name then
                    Save reference of local variable as (local_Variable2_Name)
                end
            end
        end
    end
    Extract right hand operand (i.e. expression)
    if (local_Variable1_Name equal to null and local_Variable2_Name equal to null ) or (
    local_Variable1_Name equal to null and expression equal to null ) then
        while condition operands not end do
            while list of atomic processes not ends do
                if operand equal to atomic process input then
                    Save reference of atomic process input
                end
                if operand not equal to atomic process input then
                    Find operand in output list of atomic processes and save its reference
                end
            end
        end
    end
    Generate SWRL expression;
end
```

tivities to OWL-S CCs have been described with their syntactical information to describe mapping aspects with respect to their language specifications. The mapped *Process Model* ontology can be used to further edit and model more complex service in a semantic environment (as discussed in Section 5 to evaluate our approach).

Translation to the OWL-S Profile Ontology

Profile ontology is used to describe semantically enriched information about capabilities of a BPEL process when it is mapped to OWL-S SWS. Semantically enriched information about capabilities of mapped process model is described as (1) *inputs* required by the service (2) *outputs* generated by the service (3) *pre-conditions* required to use a service (4) *effects* that service produces in surrounding world after its execution. Semantics of these input/output parameters, pre-conditions and effects are provided by annotating them with domain ontologies defined in a separate OWL files. Since, BPEL process model provide no semantic information about a process therefore, *Profile* ontology parameters of mapped OWL-S service are automatically annotated by the mapping tool with dummy ontological concepts (URIs). Since, semantic information about a service capabilities can vary from user to user therefore, it is not possible to judge a user requirements automatically, generate domain ontologies according to that requirements and annotate *Profile* ontology parameters with these ontological concepts. Maximum process of generating *Profile* ontology from BPEL process is performed automatically by the mapping tool but end user can provide semantic of mapped service by annotating input/output parameters of *Profile* ontology with their required domain concepts. In short user can finish up with *Profile* ontology by performing following tasks:

- Developing domain ontologies by using some Semantic Web development tool (e.g. Protégé).
- Annotating *Profile* ontology parameters with these domain ontology concepts.

How to develop domain ontologies (Matthew, et., al., 2004), edit (annotate) and develop SWSs with these domain ontologies ? is not the aim of this chapter. However, we explain these topics to some extent so that the end user can get more clear idea and understanding that how the *Profile* ontology of mapped OWL-S service can be extended to enable it for semantic based publishing and discovering. First of all, we describe the criteria that we used to extract *Profile* ontology from a BPEL process model and automatic annotation of *Profile* ontology parameters with domain ontologies. Then we give a short description about how to develop domain ontologies and to use them to annotate *Profile* ontology parameters of mapped OWL-S service.

Extracting the Profile Ontology

In Section 2.1.2 we have already discussed that *primitive* activities can have dual behavior i.e. (1) to perform a Web service operation (2) to interact with the outer world (i.e. to create interface of BPEL process model). Mapping of *primitive* activities that are used to perform Web services operations with in a BPEL process has been discussed in Sections 3.1.1 and 3.1.2. Here we are concerned with *primitive* activities that can be used to create interface of BPEL process model. A BPEL process can have one or more *primitive* activities (i.e. *receive, invoke* and *reply* activities) that are used to interact with outer world. Such activities are declared as input/output (I/O) activities during mapping process. Message parts of these I/O activities messages are used to create input and output parameters of *Profile* ontology. For example if a process has a *receive* activity which receives a message from user to start a process then this activity is declared as I/O activity and message parts of the message received by this activity are used to create input parameters of resulting *Profile* ontology. Again, consider a *primitive* activity (*<receive>*) and its message that has three parts (i.e. *input_Lang, output_Lang* and *input_Str*). These message parts are used to create input parameters of resulting *Profile* ontology (as shown in Example 6).

A *reply* activity can be used to send a message to the outer world in response to a *receive* activity. If a *receive* activity has corresponding *reply* activity then message parts of the message of such *reply* activity are used to create output parameters of mapped *Profile* ontology. It is also possible that a *receive* activity does not has corresponding *reply* activity (as you can see in some example BPEL processes available with the tool

*Example 6. An example of mapped **Profile** ontology*

```
<profile:Profile rdf:about="&bpel4ws2owls;#TestProfile">
<profile:textDescription>This Profile is created by BPEL2OWLS Tool
</profile:textDescription>
<profile:hasInput>
 <process:Input rdf:about="&bpel4ws2owls;#inputStr">
  <process:parameterType rdf:datatype="xsd:anyURI">&xsd;:string
  </process:parameterType>
 </process:Input>
</profile:hasInput>
<profile:hasInput>
............... other input/output parameters
<rdfs:label>BPEL2OWLS Profile</rdfs:label>
<service:presentedBy rdf:resource="&bpel4ws2owls#TestService"/>
</profile:Profile>
```

download) and BPEL process uses *invoke* activity to send output message to the outer world. In this case message of the *invoke* activity is parsed in corresponding WSDL file and its message parts are used to create output parameters of *Profile* ontology of mapped OWL-S service.

So far, we explained that how *primitive* activities are used to create interface of BPEL process and how we use message parts of these I/O activities to create input/output parameters of mapped *Profile* ontology. One more thing that needs to be clarified is that among dual role of BPEL *primitive* activities how a *primitive* activity is declared as an I/O activity so that its message parts can be used to create input/output parameters of *Profile* ontology. The criteria that we used for this purpose is that if a *receive* activity is being used as an initial activity to start a BPEL process and its *portType* and *operation* is supported by BPEL's corresponding WSDL file.

Another important issue that we think is important to highlight is that mapping specifications support to extract one *Profile* ontology from a BPEL process model. It means that if a BPEL process has multiple activities that act as an interface of BPEL process, only two *primitive* activities are declared as I/O activities and their message parts are used to create input/output parameters of *Profile* ontology of mapped OWL-S service. Even though OWL-S specification support to create multiple *Profile* ontologies for one *Process Model* ontology the automatic translation of BPEL process description to OWL-S extracts one *Profile* ontology for one *Process Model*.

Developing and Annotating with Domain Ontologies

In above section we have described in detail that how a *Profile* ontology is extracted from a BPEL process model. If we have a deeper look at sample *Profile* ontology (i.e. Example 6) provided in previous section, we see that input/output parameters of *Profile* ontology are mapped to dummy URIs. These dummy URIs need to be replaced with user defined domain ontological concepts (Figure 8 provides a conceptual view of annotating *Profile* ontology parameters with domain ontological concepts). Such annotation provides semantically

*Figure 8. Annotating **Profile** ontology with domain ontology concepts*

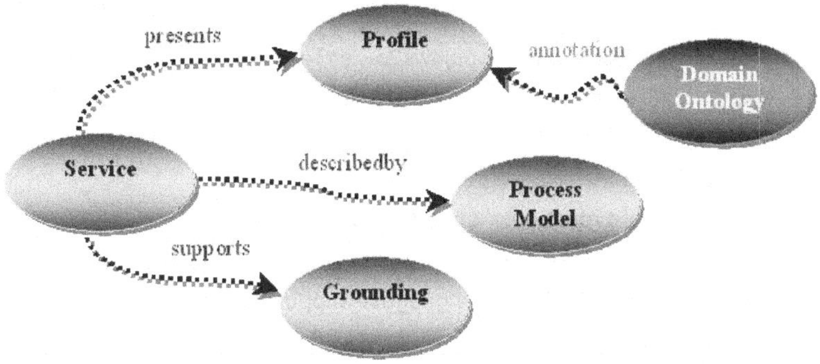

*Example 7. Sample **Language** ontology*

```
<owl:Class rdf:ID="SupportedLanguage">
 <rdfs:comment>Languages supported by the BabelFish translator is an
    enumerated set of the following languages</rdfs:comment>
 <owl:oneOf rdf:parseType="Collection">
  <factbook:Language rdf:about="&factbook;#English"/>
  <factbook:Language rdf:about="&factbook;#Dutch"/>
  <factbook:Language rdf:about="&factbook;#French"/>
  <factbook:Language rdf:about="&factbook;#German"/>
  ..........
  .......... (list of supported languages)
 </owl:oneOf>
</owl:Class>
```

enriched information about capabilities of mapped OWL-S service.

Since, OWL-S specifications support to define multiple *Profile* ontologies for one *Process Model* ontology therefore, end user can also define multiple *Profile* ontologies for one *Process Model* ontology to provide different meaning of same service. Protégé with its OWL plugin (Holger, et., al., 2004) is an ideal framework for developing domain ontologies. Example 7 gives a simple example of the *Language* ontology that we can use to annotate input/output parameters of our mapped *Profile* ontology to provide semantically enriched information of mapped service.

Suppose that above language ontology is defined at following address *http:www.uni-leipzig.de/Languages.owl*} (shortly &languages). Then the mapped *Profile* ontology (as shown in Example 6) after annotating its parameters with domain ontology looks like Box 1.

Translation to the OWL-S Grounding Ontology

Grounding ontology of the OWL-S service describes that how to access a service. Access details include information about protocol, transport and message formats. These details enable *Grounding*

*Box 1. Mapped **Profile** ontology, annotated with domain ontology*

```
<profile:Profile rdf:about="&bpel4ws2owls#TestProfile">
 <profile:textDescription>This Profile is created by BPEL2OWLS Tool
 </profile:textDescription>
  <profile:hasInput>
   <process:Input rdf:about="&bpel4ws2owls#inputStr">
    <process:parameterType rdf:datatype="http://www.w3.org/2001/
     XMLSchema#anyURI">&languages#SupportedLanguage
    </process:parameterType>
   </process:Input>
  </profile:hasInput>
    ..........
    .......... (other input/output parameters)

 <rdfs:label>BPEL2OWLS Profile</rdfs:label>
 <service:presentedBy rdf:resource="&bpel4ws2owls#TestService"/>
</profile:Profile>
```

to provide concrete level specifications needed to access a service. Concrete level definition of inputs/outputs of *atomic* processes in some transmittable format is provided in *Grounding* ontology. For this purpose original WSDL services are referred in *Grounding* to access real implementation of services. When a Web service operation within a BPEL process is mapped to OWL-S *atomic* process (during the mapping process) then input/output messages of Web service operation are defined as set of inputs/outputs in the *Grounding* ontology of that *atomic* process. That's why in Section 3.2 we have seen that input/output messages of I/O activities are not directly used to create *Profile* ontology but message parts of these messages are used as set of inputs and outputs in *Profile* ontology. These inputs and outputs when annotated with domain ontologies provide Web service semantics.

Now about types of messages and message parts: there are two possibilities (1) the message is a complex message of some OWL class type (2) the message is of other usual data type (e.g. string, int etc.). In first case, in which message is of some OWL class type; we need to give the definition of OWL class. This definition can be given within the same document[1] or can be defined in separate OWL file and can be referred in the type parameter[2].

An OWL-S service *Grounding* is an instance of the *Grounding* class that has sub class *WsdlGrounding*. Each *WsdlGrounding* class contains a list of *WsdlAtomicProcessGrounding* instances that refers to *Grounding* of *atomic* process. *WsdlAtomicProcessGrounding* has properties (e.g. *wsdlInputMessage, wsdlInput, wsdlOutputMessage, wsdlOutput* etc.). *wsdlInputMessage* and *wsdlOutputMessage* objects contain mapping pairs for message part of WSDL input/output messages and is presented by using an instance of *WsdlInputMessageMap*. If a message part is of some complex type (e.g. some OWL class) then XSLT Transformation property gives an XSLT script that generates message part from an instance of the *atomic* process. As an example consider grounding (as shown in Box 2) of mapped OWL-S service.

The sample code in Box 2 gives an example of grounding of mapped composite service (i.e. *TestService*), where *getTranslationAtomicProcessGrounding* and *getMeaningAtomicProcessGrounding* are groundinges of two *atomic* processes which are sub processes within mapped *composite* process. The sample ontology shown in Box 3 gives an example of *Grounding* ontology of the *getTranslation atomic* process.

Implementation of Mapping Tool

We have developed a tool (i.e. BPEL4WS 2 OWL-S Mapping Tool[3]) that can be used to translate existing BPEL processes to OWL-S services. The BPEL4WS 2 OWL-S Mapping Tool is an open source project and has hundreds of download since the time it has been uploaded to open source project directory (sourceforge.net).

Architecture

The overall architecture of BPEL4WS 2 OWL-S Mapping Tool consists of three components (i.e. WSDL Parser, BPEL Parser and OWL-S Mapper) as shown in Figure 9. As it is clear from name that WSDL Parser parses each WSDL file with in mapping project and creates their object view. An important feature of WSDL Parser is that it extracts information about operations supported by a Web services and send this information to OWL-S Mapper which maps each Web service operation to OWL-S *atomic* process. OWL-S Mapperwrites the generated OWL-S *atomic* process in a separate OWL file and saves it in atomic processes directory of mapping project. Atomic processes are used with in *composite* process to define control flow and data flow between process components with in OWL-S composite service.

BPEL Parser traverse through BPEL file and creates object view of process activities. It parses *primitive* activities and sends information about these activities to OWL-S Mapper. Before sending information to OWL-S Mapper, BPEL parser declares either a *primitive* activity is an I/O activity or not (Section 3.2 describes in detail that how an activity is declared and mapped as an I/O activity). If a *primitive* activity is declared as an I/O activity then OWL-S Mapper uses message part of this activity to create input/output of parameters of *composite* process, which ultimately are used to create the *Profile* ontology parameters. If a *primitive* activity is non I/O activity then OWL-S Mapper maps it to *Perform* CC to perform related *atomic* process. Also, BPEL Parser parses *structured* activities in defined control flow of input BPEL process and sends information about these activities to OWL-S Mapper. The OWL-S Mapper translates them to relevant CCs to define

Box 2. Grounding of mapped OWL-S service

```
<grounding:WsdlGrounding rdf:about="&bpel4ws2owls#TestGrounding">
 <service:supportedBy rdf:resource="&bpel4ws2owls#TestService"/>
 <grounding:hasAtomicProcessGrounding rdf:resource="&dummyURI
        #getTranslationAtomicProcessGrounding"/>
 <grounding:hasAtomicProcessGrounding rdf:resource="&dummyURI
        #getMeaningAtomicProcessGrounding"/>
</grounding:WsdlGrounding>
```

control flow of mapped OWL-S composite service. If BPEL Parser sends information to OWL-S Mapper about *Assignment* activity then OWL-S Mapper traverse through list of existing *atomic* processes to extract input/output parameters of these processes matches them with *<copy> <to>* and *<copy> <from>* parameters of *Assignment* activity and creates data flow between relevant process components. If a BPEL parser comes to some conditional *structured* activity then it simply sends condition string to OWL-S Mapper which creates corresponding SWRL expression (as explained in Section 3.1.3).

OWL-S Mapper is actually responsible for writing resulting OWL-S service according to defined mapping specifications. It uses OWL-S API developed by Mindswap lab to write resulting OWL-S composite service. OWL-S API is set of APIs that can be used to *read*, *write* and *execute* OWL-S services. Since, OWL-S API uses a third party reasoner (e.g. Jena reasoner) to reason the mapped OWL-S ontology therefore, our tool also uses Jena reasoner (as default reasoner) for such reasoning purposes.

User Interface

The BPEL4WS 2 OWL-S Mapping Tool provides very easy to use interface which consists of four major parts (i.e. Project Explorer, Object Explorer,

Box 3. ***Grounding*** *ontology of the* ***getTranslation atomic*** *process.*

```
<grounding:WsdlGrounding rdf:about="#getTranslationGrounding">
 <grounding:hasAtomicProcessGrounding>
  <grounding:WsdlAtomicProcessGrounding
         rdf:ID="getTranslationAtomicProcessGrounding"/>
 </grounding:hasAtomicProcessGrounding>
 <service:supportedBy rdf:resource="#getTranslationService"/>
</grounding:WsdlGrounding>

<grounding:WsdlAtomicProcessGrounding
        rdf:about= "#getTranslationAtomicProcessGrounding">
 <grounding:wsdlInputMessage
        rdf:datatype="xsd:#anyURI">&wsdlFileAddress#TranslatorRequest
 </grounding:wsdlInputMessage>
  <grounding:wsdlInput>
   <grounding:WsdlInputMessageMap>
    <grounding:wsdlMessagePart "http://www.w3.org/2001/
           XMLSchema#anyURI">&wsdlFileAddress#inputLanguage
    </grounding:wsdlMessagePart>
    <grounding:owlsParameter rdf:resource="&wsdlFileAddress#inputLanguage"/>
   </grounding:WsdlInputMessageMap>
  </grounding:wsdlInput
  ..........
  .......... (other message parts)
</grounding:WsdlAtomicProcessGrounding>
```

Figure 9. Architecture of the mapping tool

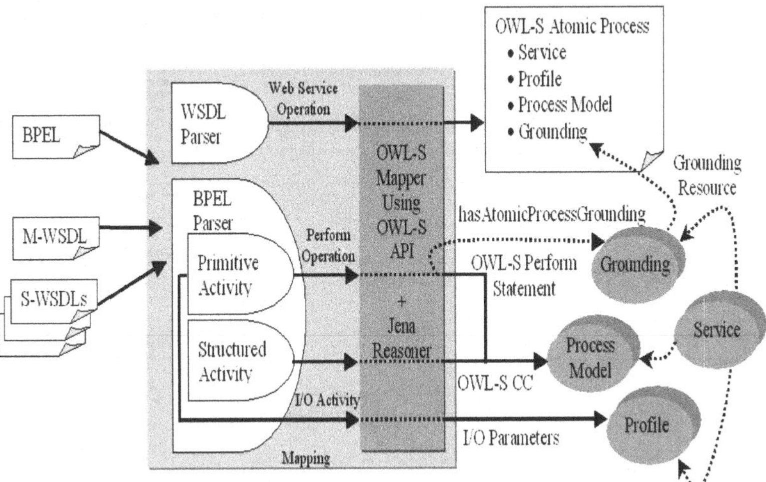

Content Window and Output Window) and a *Toolbar* and *Menu bar* as shown in Figure 10.

Project Explorer can be used to see project input and output files. Object Explorer provides object view of input BPEL and WSDL files. Content window can be used to see contents of any of the input/output files. User can simply select a file in the Project Explorer to see its contents in the Content Window. Output of different actions performed (e.g. Validate, Build and Map) can be seen in the Output Window.

RELATED WORK

Translating business process descriptions to OWL-S ontologies is a very efficient and cost effective way for enabling business processes with semantics to facilitate dynamic interaction between business partners. Several efforts have already been done to address semantic limitations of process modeling languages. For example, the METEOR-S research group at LSDIS Lab is working on extending BPEL with semantics to compose Web services (i.e. WSDL-S services) on the basis of matching semantics. The work discussed in (Jun et., al., 2005; Jun., et., al., 2006} describes mapping of BPEL process model to OWL-S *Process Model* ontology. We have already criticized and pointed out drawbacks of this approach in our work Aslam., et., al., 2006. Major drawback of(Jun., et., al., 2006; Jun., et., al., 2005) are that they do not support the *Profile* and the *Grounding* ontologies. Without *Profile* ontology, mapped BPEL process model cannot be advertised as OWL-S SWS that can be discovered, invoked and composed dynamically. The work discussed in (Massimo, et., al., 2003) describes a good effort to map WSDL services to DAML-S (updated to OWL-S) services. Another effort (Gayathri, & Yun-Heh, 2007) has been done by a joint group of researchers from University of Edinburgh and School of Informatics to address semantic limitations of Fundamental Business Process Modeling Language (FBPML) by mapping it to OWL-S *Process Model* ontology. The work discussed in (Gayathri, & Yun-Heh, 2007) also supports only the mapping of FBPML process model to OWL-S *Process Model*. It does not support the mapping of *Profile* and *Grounding* ontologies. The work discussed in (Gayathri, & Yun-Heh, 2007) has almost same limitations as that of the work discussed in (Jun., et., al. 2006; Jun., et., al., 2007) and which is criticized in (Aslam, et., al.,

Figure 10. Overview of BPEL4WS 2 OWL-S Mapping Tool.

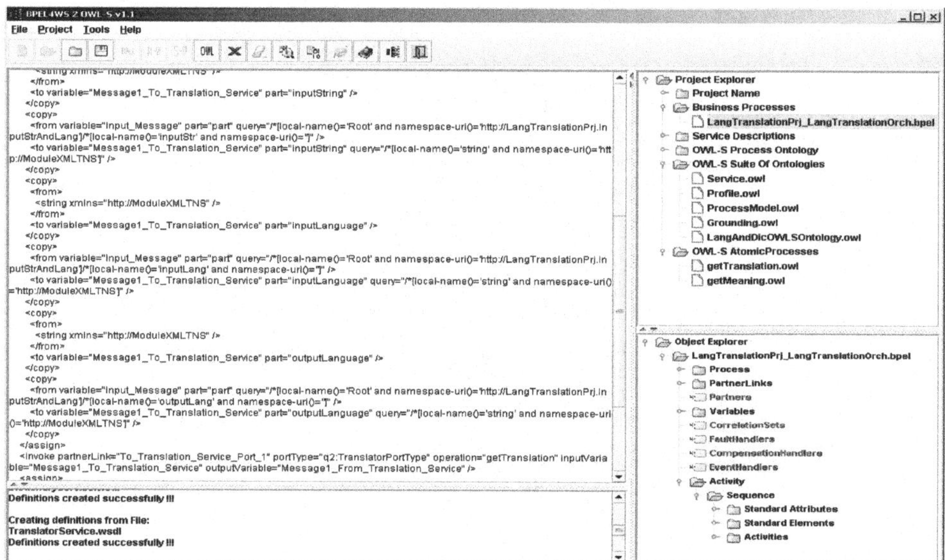

2006). We can summarize that there have many efforts been done to address semantic limitations of process modeling languages by mapping them to Semantic Web services languages (e.g. OWL-S) but none of these efforts provide expressive and consistent solution. Our work is unique with these aspects that it supports to the BPEL process descriptions to complete OWL-S suite of ontologies. We have also well addressed the issues (e.g. conditions mapping, support for complex messages, mapping of *atomic* processes etc.) that have not been addressed by any other research group. Another uniqueness of our work is that we use the OWL-S API in our tool to write the resulting OWL-S service due to which it becomes consistent with execution engines like OWL-S API and Semantic Web services development tool (i.e. OWL-S Editor).

EVALUATION AND BENEFITS

In Section 1.4 we defined two problem scenarios (as show in Figures 4 and 5) and modeled a BPEL process to perform the task defined in first scenario (Figure 4). Then we analyzed BPEL and OWL-S processes and their components and defined step-by-step translation of BPEL process to OWL-S SWS. Till the end of Section 3 the whole BPEL process was mapped to OWL-S SWS with each Web service operation within the BPEL process model mapped to OWL-S *atomic* process.

As a first step to edit the mapped OWL-S service to perform the task defined in second scenario (Figure 5), we replace dummy URIs of input and output parameters of mapped *atomic* and *composite* processes with domain ontologies (as discussed in Section 3.2). The annotation of input/output parameters can be performed by opening the mapped OWL files (atomic and composite processes) in OWL-S Editor (even though some compatibility issues between OWL-S Editor and our tool still need to be addressed, as discussed in conclusion and future work section (i.e. Section 7)) or in any other editor (e.g. Notepad). Annotating input/output parameters helps to edit and extend the *composite* process by defining data flow between sub processes on the basis of matching semantics. Mapped OWL-S service takes *inputString, inputLang* and *outputLang* as inputs of the OWL-S service. The first *atomic* process (*getTranslationProcess*) translates the input string from input language (i.e. *German*) to output language (i.e. *English*) and the second *atomic* process (*getMeaningProcess*) provides the meaning of input word in *English* language. From here we start editing the mapped service and add one more atomic process (i.e. *getTranslation-Process*) within the *Sequence* CC of *composite* process. This *atomic* process is used to perform the additional task defined in second scenario (Figure 5) (i.e. to translate the meaning of the *German* word back from *English* to *German*). For this purpose we define data flow for this newly added *atomic* process (i.e. *getTranslationProcess*). The *getTranslationProcess* process takes as input *inputLang* (*English*), *outputLang* (*German*) and *inputStr* (output of *atomic* process *getMeaning-Process*). The data flow can be defined by using data binding between *atomic* processes (as discussed in Section 2.2) on the basis of matching semantics.

In Section 1.4 we defined two major problems of BPEL process i.e. (1) syntactical interface (2) syntax based process modeling (i.e. Web services composition). We address both of these problems by translating BPEL process description to OWL-S suite of ontologies. *Profile* ontology of mapped OWL-S service provides semantically enriched information about BPEL process as OWL-S SWS and can be used for dynamic discovery, invocation and composition of BPEL process as OWL-S service. Mapped OWL-S service is edited and extended on the basis of matching semantic information rather than syntactical information to solve the problem defined in second scenario (Figure 5).

With rapidly growing rate of e-shopping it is becoming very important for e-business companies to keep their business processes and services alive with upcoming Semantic Web technologies. Adding semantics will enable existing business processes and services for dynamic co-operation with business partners and for dynamic interaction with end users. But developing semantic enabled business process and services from scratch is very cost effective and time consuming for both small and large organizations. Our approach provides a very efficient solution with respect cost and time to shift existing business process to SWSs enabling them for dynamic discovery, invocation and composition by other semantic enabled systems.

RISK ASSESSMENT

Although, the goal of automatic translation is very appealing, the intention may have some threats in practice for a number of reasons. One of them is that OWL-S with respect to its process modeling capabilities is not as mature as BPEL and mapping of block-structured BPEL to semantic based OWL-S is challenging. Since, BPEL is syntactical language and provides no semantic information therefore, in case of complex business processes it may become hectic to develop domain ontologies from scratch and to annotate mapped OWL-S service parameters with these domain ontologies.

Modelling BPEL processes is supported by a number of tools (e.g. MS BizTalk Server, IBM WebSphere, SAP NetWeaver etc.). None of them support to export BPEL processes to OWL-S services. Integrating BPEL4WS 2 OWL-S Mapping Tool with these process modeling tools can enable them to export BPEL processes as OWL-S services but this functionality will neither be fully automated nor support full semantics. End user involvements will be necessary to add meaning to each of the process elements and make them machine-readable and understandable. In addition, it will also allow for reasoning on the process descriptions as OWL-S services. Once, BPEL process is mapped to OWL-S SWS and edited to add semantics, will make it possible to automatically assign Web service (or their composition) to each task and to generate final service that can be deployed and executed by SWS execution engines (e.g. OWL-S API).

CONCLUSION AND FUTURE ASPECTS

In this chapter we have presented an approach leading towards semantic business processes. The concept behind the proposed approach is that traditional business processes (e.g. BPEL processes) due to their semantic limitations cannot be dynamically discovered, invoked and composed by other semantic enabled systems. These semantic limitations slow down the process of integration between business partners, business organizations and customers. The methodology that we have used to address these limitations of process modeling languages (e.g. BPEL) consists of mapping constraints and specifications that can be used translate BPEL process descriptions to OWL-S suite of ontologies (i.e. OWL-S SWSs). The resulting OWL-S services are semantic based compositions of child services and expose semantically enriched interfaces. As a result they can be edited on the basis of matching semantics to model more complex services as well as can be dynamically discovered, composed and invoked by other semantic enabled systems. We have implemented our approach as a mapping tool (i.e. *BPEL4WS 2 OWL-S Mapping Tool*) that can be used to map (translate) BPEL process descriptions to OWL-S services. Critical mapping issues (e.g. mapping of *condition* statements, translating activities to CCs, generating *Profile* ontology parameter from complex I/O messages etc.) have been addressed by implementing efficient parsing and mapping algorithms in mapping process. Since, OWL-S is not as mature as BPEL therefore, we have also highlighted different areas where direct mapping is not supported. In order to implement direct translation of BPEL activities (e.g. terminate, fault handling etc.) we need more consistent specifications of OWL-S to address these issues. We have also highlighted areas where user needs some manual work (e.g. changing parameter type by annotating input/output parameters with domain ontologies etc.).

It will be much useful to perform more consistent mapping by addressing limitations that we have described in our mapping specifications with upcoming OWL-S specifications. Also, making the tool part of some larger framework like Protégé will be more useful for end user. Such an effort will enable the end user to directly import BPEL processes as OWL-S services in Protégé (OWL-S Editor). It will also become easier for end users to develop domain ontologies and to annotate *Profile* ontology parameters with domain concepts while working in the same framework (i.e. Protégé). We are working on making our tool part of Protégé as *BPEL4WS 2 OWL-S Import Plugin* for Protégé (OWL-S Editor).

ACKNOWLEDGEMENT

Funding for the research leading to these findings is provided by the Higher Education Commission (HEC) of Pakistan under the scheme "Partial Support Scholarship for PhD Studies Abroad".

REFERENCES

Aslam, M., A., Sören, A., Jun S., & Michael, H. (2006). Expressing business process model as owl-s ontologies. In E. Dustdar (Ed.), *Proceedings of the 2nd International Workshop on Grid and Peer-to-Peer based Workflows in conjunction with the 4th International Conference on Business Process Management,* Volume 4103/2006 (pp. 400-415), Vienna, Austria.

Christoph, B., Emilia, C., Dieter, F., Juan, M., G., Armin, H., Thomas, H., Michael, K., Adrian, M., Matthew M., Eyal, O., Brahmananda, S., Ioan, T., Jana, V., Tomas, V., Maciej, Z., & Michal,

Z. (2005). *Web service execution environment (wsmx)*. Retrieved April 20, 2007, from http://www.w3.org/Submission/WSMX/

Dan, B., & Ramanathan, V., G. (2004). *RDF vocabulary description language 1.0: RDF schema*. Retrieved May 22, 2007, from http://www.w3.org/TR/2004/REC-rdf-schema-20040210/.Daniel, E., Grit, D., David, M., Fred, G., John, K., Shahin, S., & Rukman, S. (2005). The OWL-S editor - A development tool for Semantic Web services. In A. Gomez-Perez & J. Euzenat (Eds.), *The Semantic Web Research and Applications, 2nd European Semantic Web Conference*, Volume 3532 (pp. 78-92), Heraklion, Crete, Greece.

David, B., & Canyang, K., L. (2006). *Web services description language (WSDL) version 2.0 part 0: Primer*. Retrieved April 11, 2007, from http://www.w3.org/TR/2006/CR-wsdl20-primer-20060327

David, M., Mark, B., Jerry H., Ora, L., Drew, M., Sheila, M., Srini, N., Massimo, P., Bijan, P., Terry, P., Evren, S., Naveen, S., & Katia, S. (2006). *Owl-S: Semantic markup for Web services*. Retrieved April 10, 2007, from http://www.ai.sri.com/daml/services/owl-s/1.2/overview/, March 2006.

Deborah, L., M., & Frank V., H. (2004). *OWL Web ontology language overview*. World Wide Web Consortium, Recommendation REC-owl-features. Retrieved April 17, 2006, from http://www.w3.org/TR/owl-features/

Evren, S. (2006). *Owl-S api*. Retrieved May 20, 2006, from http://www.mindswap.org/2004/owl-s/api/

Evren, S., Bijan P., & James, H. (2005). Template-based composition of Semantic Web services. In *AAAI Fall Symposium on Agents and the Semantic Web*, Virginia, USA.

Francisco, C., Hitesh, D., Yaron, G., Johannes, K., Frank L., Kevin, L., Dieter, R., Doug, S., Siebel, S., Satish, T., Ivana, T., Sanjiva, W. (2003). *Business process execution language for Web services*. Retireved April 5, 2007, from ftp://www6.software.ibm.com/software/developer/library/ws-bpel11.pdf

Frank, L. (2001). *Web Services Flow Language (WSFL 1.0)*. Retrieved May 14, 2007, from http://www-306.ibm.com/software/solutions/webservices/pdf/WSFL.pdf

Gayathri, N, & Yun-Heh, C. (2007). Translating Fundamental Business Process Modelling Language to the Web Services Ontology through Lightweight Mapping. *IET Software Journal*, 1, 1-17.

Graham, K., & Jeremy, J., C. (2004). *Resource description framework (RDF): Concepts and abstract syntax*. Retrieved May 25, 2007, from http://www.w3.org/TR/2004/REC-rdf-concepts-20040210

Holger, K., Mark, A., M., & Alan, L., R. (2004). Editing description logic ontologies with the Protégé OWL plugin. In V. Haarslev and R. Moller (Eds.), *Proceedings of the 2004 International Workshop on Description Logics*, volume 104 (pp. 70-78), Whistler, BC, Canada.

Joel, F., & Holger, L. (2006). *Semantic annotations for wsdl*. Retrieved March 26, 2007, from http://www.w3.org/TR/2006/WD-sawsdl-20060928/

John, H., G., Mark, A., M., Ray, W., F., William, E., G., Monica, C., Henrik, E., Natalya, F., N., & Samson, W., T., (2003). The evolution of protégé: an environment for knowledge-based systems development. *International Journal of Human-Computer Studies*, 58(1), 89-123.

Jos D., B., Holger, L., Axel, P., Dieter, F. (2006). The Web service modeling language WSML: An overview. In Y. Sure and J. Domingue (Eds.), *Proceedings of 3rd European Semantic Web Conference*, Volume 4011 (pp. 590-604). Budava, Montenegro.

Jun, S., Georg, G., Yun, Y., Markus, S., Michael, S., Thomas, R. (2006). Analysis of business process integration in Web service context. *International Journal of Grid Computing: Theory, Models and Applications*, 23 (3), 283-294.

Jun, S., Yun, Y., Chengang, W., & Chuan, Z. (2005). From BPEL4WS to OWL-S: Integrating E-business process descriptions. In *Proceedings of International Conference on Services Computing*, Volume 1 (pp. 181-190), Orland, FL, USA.

Massimo, P., Naveen, S., Katia, P., S., & Takuya, N. (2003). Towards a semantic choreography of Web services: From WSDL to DAML-S. In L. Zhang, (Ed.), *Proceedings of the International Conference on Web Services* (pp. 22-26), Las Vegas, Nevada, USA.

Matjaz J., Benny, M., & Poornachandra, S. (2004). *Business Process Execution Language for Web Services: A Practical Guide to Orchestrating Web Services Using BPEL4WS.* PACKT Publishing.

Matthew, H., Holger, K., Alan, R., Robert, S., & Chris, W. (2004). *A practical guide to building owl ontologies using the protege-owl plugin and co-ode tools edition 1.0.* The University of Manchister, UK and Stanford University, USA.

Nigel, S., Tim, B., & Wendy, H. (2006). The Semantic Web revisited. *IEEE Intelligent Systems*, 21(3),96-101.

Peter, F., P., (2005). Requirements and non-requirements for a Semantic Web rule language. In *Rule Languages for Interoperability.*

Satish, T. (2001). *XLANG Web services for business process design.* Retrieved May 1st, 2007, from http://xml.coverpages.org/XLANG-C-200106.html

Sinuhe, A., Emilia, C., John, D., Cristina, F., Dieter, F., Birgitta, K., Holger, L., Axel, P., & Michael, S. (2005). *Web service modeling ontology primer.* Retrieved June 12, 2007, from http://www.w3.org/Submission/WSMO-primer/

ENDNOTES

1. http://www.mindswap.org/2004/owl-s/services.html BabelFish Translator service provide such example.
2. http://www.mindswap.org/2004/owl-s/services.html Find Cheaper Book Price service provide such example.
3. http://bpel4ws2owls.sourceforge.net/

Chapter XIII
Experiences in Building Mobile E-Business Services:
Service Provisioning and Mobility

Ivano De Furio
AtosOrigin Italia S.p.A., Italy

Giovanni Frattini
AtosOrigin Italia S.p.A., Italy

Luigi Romano
AtosOrigin Italia S.p.A., Italy

ABSTRACT

Organizations in all sectors of business and government are pursuing service-oriented architecture (SOA) initiatives in response to their need for increased business agility. This is particularly true for mobile telecommunications companies. That is why mobile telecom operators need to research new and innovative sources of revenue. Innovation is not an easy task. It requires embracing a new way of doing business, where new technologies are fundamental. SOA architecture and Web services technology are proposed by IT industry as the best solution to create a network of partnership and new services, but despite software producer claims, interoperability issues arise with service composition. Such a problem can be significantly reduced by adopting a semantic approach in service description and service discovery. Our research is focused on new methods and tools for building high personalized, virtual e-business services. A new service provisioning architecture based on Web services has been conceived, taking into account issues related to end-user mobility. The following pages deal with a proposal for creating real localized, personalized virtual environments using Web services and domain ontologies. In particular, to overcome interoperability issues that could arise from a lack of uniformity in service descriptions, we propose a way for controlling and enforcing annotation policies based on a Service Registration Authority. It allows services to be advertised according to guidelines and domain rules. Furthermore, this solution enables enhanced service/component discovery and validation, helping software engineers to build services by composing building blocks and provision/deliver a set of personalized services.

CURRENT SITUATION

Today's telecom operators live in a rapidly changing environment. The revenues per minutes from voice traffic have steadily decreased in the last 10 years (see Figure 1). The Value Added Service (VAS) revenues are following the reverse path: the growth ratio is almost 35% per year.

This is the main reason that drives telecommunications industries to invest in new value added services. Actually, Value Added Services revenues come mostly from content provisioning. Typical services are based on the download of contents like: logos, ring tones, games. The value chain for VAS is shown in Figure 2.

Mobile operators are in the middle of the value chain and control provisioning and billing processes. It means that, if goods vendors want to sell a product using the mobile network payment system, they are completely dependant on the operator.

A Telecommunication business model is mostly based on an operator-centric approach.

Legal barriers have strengthened the position of the mobile operators in the value chain limiting, as a consequence, the growth of the mobile

Figure 1. Average Revenue Per User (ARPU) for Voice is slowly decreasing while VAS is constantly increasing their importance (Italian case. Source: Assinform)

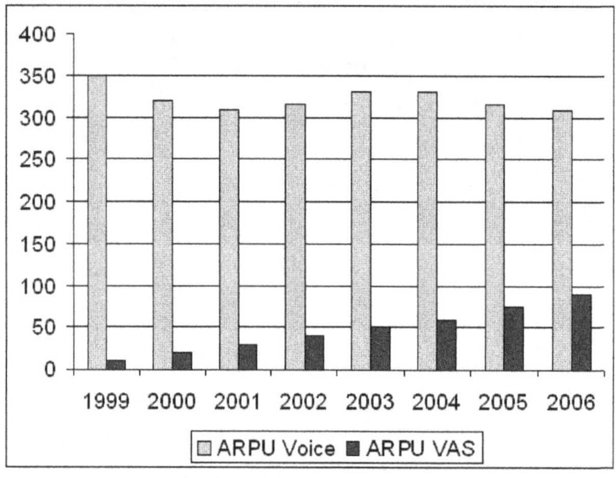

Figure 2. Today's value chain. Operators are in full-control of the delivery process

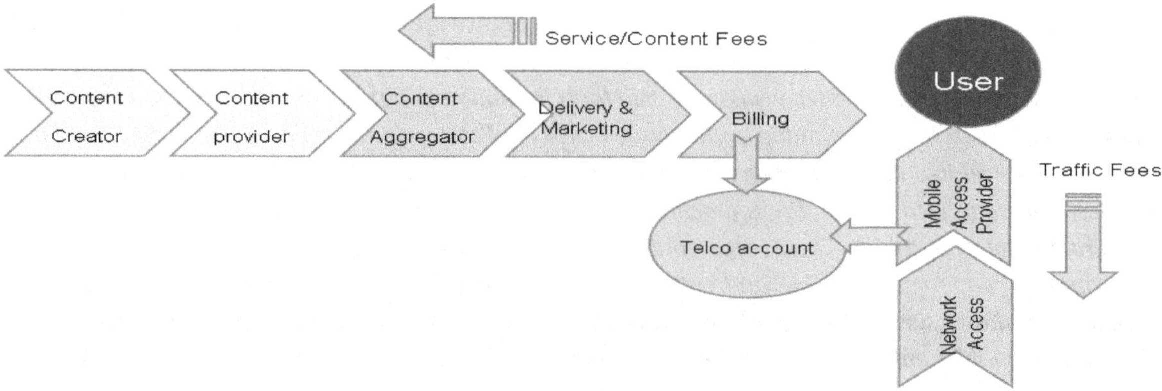

service offering. Technology issues also have contributed to enforce a closed business model approach, despite the market demands for a more open and collaborative business approach.

In the latest years telecommunications monopolies have been abolished in Europe. Telecommunications operators are facing increasingly fierce competition with new operators. It has become imperative for such companies to reinvent themselves and adopt the nimbleness that makes their new competitors so successful. Innovation requires embracing a new way of doing business (open garden), where spotting and cultivating new technologies is fundamental. This includes the systematic identification of new technologies and business models, detailed evaluation, aggressive prototyping, and, last but not least, implementation and operations.

For example, the next generation of services should take localization into account. In other words: services are increasingly based on *user position*. An efficient mobile-ticketing service, where a user can buy, for instance, bus tickets using its telecom account, should allow user mobility from both a geographical and a service provider point of view. Imagine users routinely traveling within his town by metro or bus and paying via mobile-ticketing service. When users move to another country, the same operator should offer the same service localized in the new town or should have a service roaming agreement with a local operator that allows users to access the service in the same way (interface and procedures) they are accustomed. Notice that in this case roaming is used in a wider sense: it is not referred just to the core services of the network operator, but it also covers service processes. Addressing the problem of roaming services to a higher level of abstraction is a first step turned towards opened business models. Furthermore, in almost all the European countries, telecommunications operators generally offer services that are strictly related to their core business, and services like mobile-ticketing are not widely deployed.

The tailoring of services to customers' preferences and profiles is a key success factor for the service offerings of mobile network operators and service providers. Indeed, mobile users have shown their interest in mobile phone customization by buying colored covers, personal logos and ring tones. The next step is the personalization of services: content adaptation to terminal capabilities, context and location based services and content filtering on the basis of user preferences.

This scenario leads us to the Virtual Home Environment (VHE) concept. Basically it means that telecommunications companies users can access services with the same personalized features and

Figure 3. Today services are based on telecommunications accounts. Future services must be billed differently

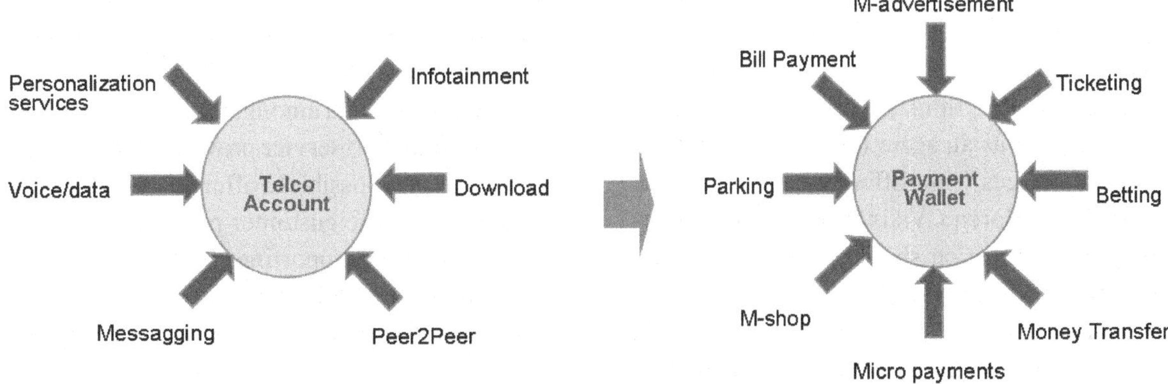

user interface customization in whatever network, whatever terminal (within the capabilities of the terminal and the network) and wherever the user may be located.

3GPP (3rd Generation Partnership Project) has defined the concept of a Virtual Home Environment. Its key features are network and protocol independence (achievable through standard abstract interfaces), terminal independence (via standard execution environments on terminal, Mobile Execution Environment, MExE, specifications) and an abstract data structure for expressing customer personal profiles. It is not specified, however, how to roam high level applications, built on top of a virtualized network, from one geographical region to another. Neither it is specified how to extend the home environment to services based on collaborating partners that cannot export customers' personal data.

The VHE concept, thus, should be extended. Voice, SMS, etc. are services that are always independent on the serving network and position of the user. The same could apply to services like ticketing, m-shopping, etc, provided that a system for making them independent from the user position exists.

In order to address customer mobility, e-business (or better an m-business) solution should follow the terminal capabilities evolutions. Most of the commercial handsets on the market are able to run applications. It is especially relevant for the diffusion of phones supporting Java technologies, (Java 2 Mobile Edition, J2ME) compared to other available development environments (notably, Symbian OS, Microsoft Mobile Edition/CE, Linux).

It is possible to think about services based on a client acting as an agent for mediating among different devices with different communication capabilities (Moreno, Valls & Viejo 2003). User-friendlier application should take into account dynamics in content and services (e.g. the possibility to update service menus as well as accessing dynamic content), the interaction among mobile devices and smart cards and the possibility to interact with other networks. In other words, in a mobile service environment, devices should be able to interact with local networks as well as with usual (and expensive) cellular network connection, using protocols like ZigBee, IEEE 802.11x, Bluetooth, using, where possible, a single, uniform approach.

Actually, techniques that provide users with services and information that are adapted to individual needs (according to user specific preferences and interests) are still at a early stage.

Our experience suggests that Web services are a good solution to support transparent service roaming (extending the concept of roaming that is traditionally referred to network services like pre-paid accounts, connectivity and voice services) and localized services. In general, methods and technologies for building a flexible service oriented delivery platform is a key challenge for software industry. Web services have a great potential as an enterprise application integration technology. They can be also used to streamline business-to-business processes that in turn could foster service provider coalition and could enable service-level roaming.

Problem Statement

Let us consider a mobile bus ticketing service. Generally this kind of service is localized: a local bus company operates in a specific geographical area. What happens when a mobile-ticketing service user leaves, for some reason, its "home" location and moves to another area? He would not be able to use the service. But, if we assume a business agreement among, for example, different public transport service providers ("roaming" agreement), it is possible to offer the same service independent of the customer position, provided that a platform for supporting cooperation among partners exists. Enabling flexible mobile business, in other words, means that service roaming, as known to every mobile user, must be enhanced in a wider sense, preserving customer preferences (user should feel at "home" using the services while roaming). The key idea is that services should have a "standard behaviour" while user is roaming from one provider to another. Just like the handset can automatically choose the best network based on signal power, an ad-hoc service environment should be automatically set up based on a user profile.

A key issue in service roaming is establishing the best service provider, within a set of providers, with a given customer profile (including user's location information).

Since the number of services and service providers increase, automated service discovery is a key feature for service provisioning. Service discovery should enable users to automatically discover and use services through their devices. Furthermore, a mechanism for advertising newly delivered services must be provided to Service Providers.

Semantic Web and Semantic Web technologies offer a new approach to managing information and processes, by means of semantic metadata, that can significantly improve service discovery.

Using Semantic Web technologies brings several benefits. Considering semantic reasoning capabilities, first of all, a reasoning system could extend an existing knowledge-base by making new inferences and could highlight semantic ambiguity in service description (allowing, in this way, a safer publishing method and an advanced and effective service discovery). Semantically defined services are more clearly defined, allowing a reasoning system to mitigate interoperability issues that can arise in a traditional, text-based service matchmaking system, due to ambiguous descriptions. Indeed, matchmaking approaches based on syntactic service description are not able to express the semantics of service functionality but just their signature. Several matchmaking approaches based on semantic descriptions have been proposed. Ontologies have been identified as a core technique for semantic aspects of these descriptions. Moreover if services are provided with metadata describing their function and context, then services can be automatically selected and invoked. Thus, such a semantic description is likely to become a key factor for large-scale SOA implementations.

In the second place, we can organise and find information based on meaning, not just text. Through semantics, systems could understand that different words are semantically equivalent. When searching for 'Garibaldi', for example, in a semantic search engine we may be provided with an equally valid document referring to 'Hero of the Two Worlds'. Conversely it can distinguish where the same word is used with different meanings. When searching for references to 'Garibaldi' in the context of Travel Ticketing, the system can disregard historical references to the Italian patriot and soldier of the Risorgimento and propose travel options referring to the Garibaldi Square railway station. When not much can be found on the subject of a search, the system can try instead to locate information on a semantically related subject.

Last but not least, personalized services matching user preferences with service descriptions can be delivered. Using semantic matchmaking a more efficient selection could remove from consideration services that do not fit the user profiles. Services could be delivered mediating among different devices, personalizing content delivery further, by prioritizing information to be displayed and delivering the one predicted to be most pertinent first.

To enable such a roaming mechanism, semantics is not the only ingredient. Even if services could be presented to the user using standard environments (WAP), the use of applications for presenting menus and contents in the most appropriate way should be taken into account. Such an approach ensures the highest service usability (service environment designed following usability methodologies) and avoids inappropriate network interactions (saving money that the user does not want to pay). Furthermore, as discussed above, services that are geographically localised must interact with the local environment in most of the business scenarios (e.g. for passing through an automatic barrier). These are requirements that must be taken into account for building effective mobile business services.

SOLUTION DESCRIPTION

As we mentioned before, the VAS market demands for new services and new business models that require new architectural and technological solutions for building highly personalized, mobile virtual service environments. Next generation services should implement business processes that tightly integrate actors in the value chain from a business point of view, while keeping them loosely coupled from a technological point of view. The proposed solution, based on SOA and Web Service technology (Booth et al. 2004), enhanced with semantic support (De Furio and Frattini 2006), best fits these needs.

Let us consider the possible roles that a telecommunications operator can play within a collaborative business model. The telecommunications operator could be the ideal actor for mediating among its subscribers and service providers. It is better able to control the heterogeneity of the terminals and customer preferences and, at the same time, it can act as a technology provider for a large variety of business actors, no matter the market segment they are working in.

According to Gisolfi (2001), a telecommunications operator can play different business roles in SOA:

- **Service requestor:** Also called consumer, the service requestor could be a company needing a specific service.
- **Service provider:** The entity that implements a service specification or description.
- **Registry:** A software entity that acts a service locator. It implements the discovery and order functions for the requestor for a specific service, and where new services are published and delivered.
- **Broker:** A special service that can pass service requests to other service providers. In service-oriented architectures, service description and metadata play a central role in maintaining a loose coupling between service requestors and service providers. The role of the broker extends the registry, as it offers additional metadata about the partners' services and, based on this metadata, the functionality for searching and classification of services. In addition, industry-specific taxonomy data helps the customers find service providers and enables service providers to describe service offerings precisely.

Figure 4. Telecommunications operator like mediator

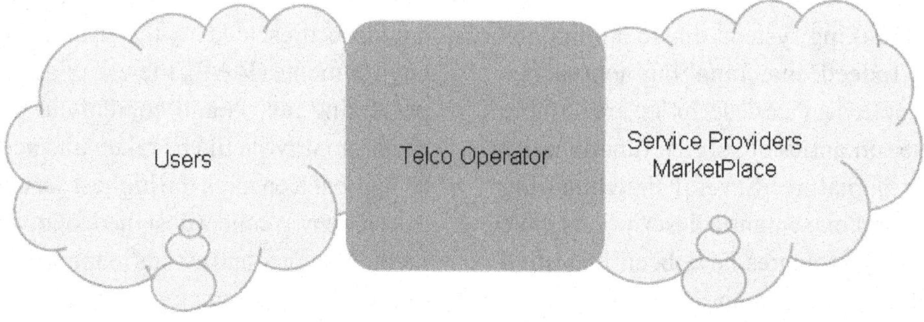

- **Aggregator/Gateway:** This extends the capabilities of the broker by the ability to describe actual policy, business processes and binding descriptions that form the standard way of operation on the marketplace, and which are fulfilled by service-providing partners. It would be the logical place to find standard Web Service interface definitions for common business processes in the industry. Marketplace customers then can use these as a reference to use the services.

In our solution, the telecommunications operator plays the role of a service broker, collecting requests coming from other business entities and providing services offered by its partners. More specifically, the broker interacts with the partners in order to offer composite services to the customers, and therefore can be seen as an intermediary providing service aggregation. It also offers context-support. Semantic technology is fundamental as long as it provides methods and tools for representing information that can be used for effective service discovery and composition.

Acting as a mediator between service users and providers, the operator could offer a standardized way of interacting with the required services. In other words, the mediator should be able to hide the heterogeneity of interacting with different service providers, which makes service usage easier for the customers and, at the same time, offers flexibility in choosing the most suitable provider. Services from multiple parties can be compounded to form comprehensive service bundles.

A mobile telecommunications operator can personalise services considering the terminal features and the customer profiling.

The role of the broker extends the registry, as it offers additional metadata about the partners' services and, based on this metadata, the functionality for searching and classification of services. In addition, industry-specific taxonomy data helps the customers find service providers and enables service providers to describe service offerings precisely.

Objectives

The proposed solution faces some critical issues such as: dealing with different devices and with different capabilities; delivery of dynamic contents and services to the telecom operator's customers (e.g. the possibility to update services menus as well as accessing dynamic contents), fulfil the interaction with other networks and service providers in order to realize a service-level VHE.

In building a flexible service delivery/provisioning platform, the additional benefits that semantics can add are:

- Better access to all relevant information and functionality, due to the semantic service registry.
- Better quality of business services, due to standardization in service descriptions and publishing.
- Semantic user profiles representing the current working context of the user which can be used to guide service searching, browsing, filtering and alerting.
- Faster response to market changes, due to component reuse.
- Savings in resources, time, and money, as processes will be modelled and run automatically, and centralized computer assisted management capabilities.

Until now, a fully semantic approach has been far from viable. However, it is possible to combine semantic technology with standard tools in order to exploit the additional features it offers.

Figure 5 represent a typical case in which a company B must set-up an agreement with other companies with a similar business, geographically bounded to specific regions, in order to achieve effective service roaming.

Figure 5. The service roaming scenario

The fundamental processes that must be considered are:

- Agreement setup
- Service localization upon explicit customer update
- Run-time service discovery and presentation
- Run-time service delivery
- Billing the service

The agreement setup in turn involves (or could involve) the following steps:

- The new partner downloads the technical specification.
- Off-line implementation of the Web services that will be published to the external world following the specification.
- Once ready it will come back to the system and declare its availability:
    - The system, according to the domain ontology, asks for additional information (e.g. rating information, terminal class supported, multimedia formats supported, location area for the service, etc.).
    - Test the whether the Web service enforces the interoperability rules (as described in the technical specification).
    - Insert the information into the metadata repository.
    - Activate the partner.

In other words a service provider must first register itself, declaring its availability to collaborate with the others according to collaboration rules, and during the provisioning phase insert all the additional information that the system requires. This additional information will be used during the run-time operations for service delivery.

Thus, our approach to semantics includes the introduction of a semantic-enabled validation layer to check the advertisement of new services and the extension of the standard discovery mechanisms exploiting the additional information that such a publishing environment allows. Furthermore, in order to make the knowledge manageable, we lay out some boundaries to ontology management, its evolution and target domain complexity. We assume that an enterprise, possibly the telecommunications operator, playing the role of broker in the value chain, defines its own business ontology model and that every partner of software services is required to adopt it. This constraint greatly simplifies the discovery and composition of services while reducing interoperability problems.

A thorough domain analysis is necessary in order to devise a suitable ontology model. Such a model encompasses the enterprise vocabulary, the main concepts, the service and operations taxonomy up to the level of detail for which properties, attributes and operational constraints about each service are defined.

A contract must be defined for each operation, specifying the operation and the messages it can exchange. Defining a contract for each available operation ensures interoperability between all instances of that operation category so that a service that satisfies the search criteria will also meet all interoperability requirements.

When a set of domain ontologies has been defined, Web services can be formally described by using common meanings from that pool. Services can then be published in registries according to interoperability constraints, thereby becoming available for process composition.

In order to do that, we use our front-end, the Service Registration Authority (SRA). It has to be used by both external service providers and internal publishers, indifferently.

The SRA allows them to advertise their services according to fixed guidelines and domain rules. The SRA also allows publishers to navigate the domain ontology and proposes service category slots available for publishing. By using the SRA, any publisher can download service/component technical specifications, implementation instructions, and all the required technical documents (e.g. WSDL template and required business data such as XML schemas). SRA also informs the publisher about the properties and attributes that can be or must be provided to correctly annotate the service/component. It also transparently generates the semantic annotation according to the domain ontologies and validates the service annotation highlighting both syntactic and semantic errors. Finally, the service description is published on a standard SOA registry, UDDI (2004) or ebXML (2005), and synchronized with the metadata store.

This kind of publishing of Web services delivers interoperable business services, which means that services will exhibit consistent accessibility to any composite business process that wishes to use it.

Thanks to SRA, the service providers are not forced to invest in tools or people reskilling for using semantic technologies. What they see and use are always well known Web pages.

A telecommunications operator, working on a pool of loosely-coupled, homogenously and well annotated Web Services is able to aggregate services and switch among similar services according to end-user requests, avoiding any human intervention. This greatly simplifies the service delivery processes. Services participating in a composite process are now selected from common pools (service registries). Business processes are composed and executed at a higher semantic (abstract) level.

Once a common repository of semantics has been established, inclusive of user profiles, device profiles, etc., it will be possible to apply personalization to Service Discovery. This will allow optimization of the service itself, as only the relevant services will be presented to the user, according to his context and preferences.

Overview

The general architecture we adopted is shown in Figure 6. It is a general reference model widely adopted when analysing telecom oriented new generation service delivery platforms. The picture underlines how every software layer must be used by means of interfaces (Service Provider Interface).

The solution fits the needs of an effective partner management (service provider management layer) as well as the customer requests for the delivery of the services (service platform).

It is important to stress the role of the client side for implementing the concept of VHE for high-level services: the client must be able to act as an access point for the local service environment. This role can be enabled using the technology we have developed and concisely described below. Thus, the client is a fundamental part of the VHE architecture we have implemented.

Figure 6. Reference architecture

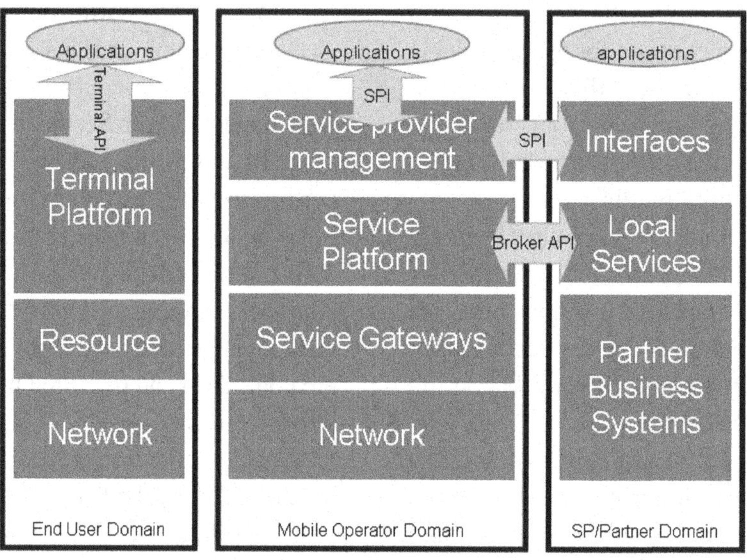

Figure 7. Terminal domain modules and server side specific services

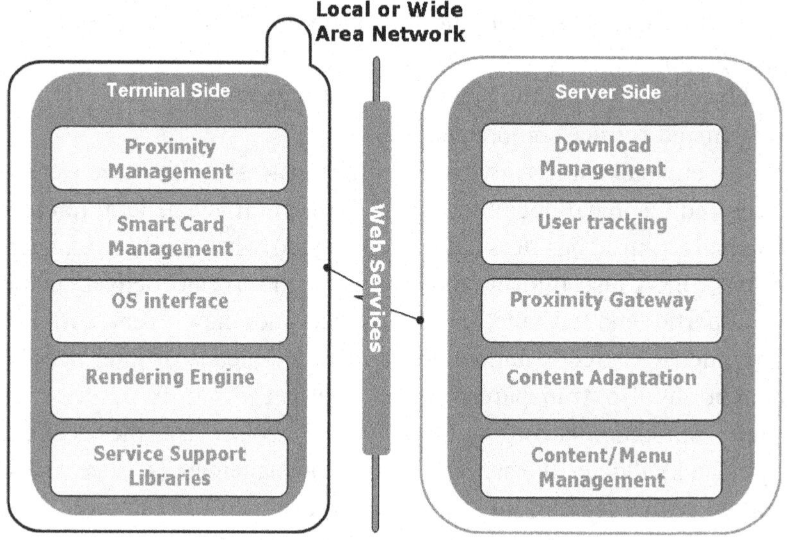

The Terminal Domain

We have designed and developed a solution for enabling inexpensive, customizable, usable and secure vertical services. Figure 7 shows the terminal domain subsystem.

As shown in Figure 7, we have developed several software modules. We will not discuss them one by one, but we will show a few characteristics. In the m-commerce arena, where the bandwidth of mobile devices is low and large data transfers would not be possible, the discovery of new information and retrieval techniques that would filter through thousands of services or millions of pages to return only relevant information is a key element.

Figure 8. Architectural view of the Service Platform

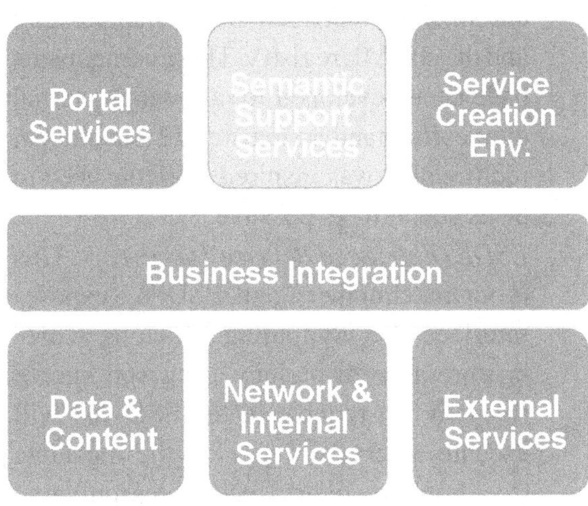

We have focused our attention on these main directions:

1. Simplify as much as possible the mark-up for service, trying to identify the minimal set of information needed for an optimal navigation.
2. Abstracting as much as possible application from the mark-up, to achieve a higher degree of flexibility.
3. Selecting the best rendering mechanism, to avoid as much as possible unwanted network accesses.
4. Maximum exploitation of the terminal short range communication capabilities, for both service access and service security.
5. Combining keyword queries with ontology, in order to achieve better and more effective query formation.

Terminal technologies are evolving continuously and more and more attention is dedicated to the definition of service environments designed by considering special usability issues. It is likely that in the near future technologies like J2ME (Java FX)[1] and/or Mobile Ajax[2] will aid in implementing new and more usable mobile applications. Furthermore, both mobile operators and terminal manufactures are working to new proximity protocols for interacting with local service point. These are facts that must be taken into account for building next generation services.

The Mobile Operator/Service Aggregator Domain

In Figure 8 gives a view of the main platform modules. Even though it could be interesting to discuss all the modules, we will concentrate our attention on Semantic Support Services, the ones for managing the service lifecycle, using semantic annotation.

The type of semantic information that would be useful in describing a Web Service encompasses the concepts defined by the Semantic Web community in OWL-S (Martin et al., 2004) and other efforts METEOR-S (Rajasekaran, Miller, Verma and Sheth 2004), WSMO (Roman, Keller and Lausen 2004). The idea is to extend service descriptions by adding context information, (i.e. what the service does, how it behaves, security policies, etc.). The potential benefits of Semantic Web Services (SWS) include better usability by means of a more expressive Web service description, and it is well-known how it enables the automated Web service discovery, execution, composition and interoperation.

Ontologies provide a large extent of flexibility and expressiveness, the ability to express semi-structured data, constraints, and support types and inheritance. The industry's Web service standards, however, provide better manageability, scalability, and modularization. We moved towards an evolutionary approach to Web Service architecture that combines the two worlds and their potential benefits. So we designed a delivery platform that tries to benefit from both technologies.

SEMANTIC SUPPORT SERVICES: DETAILS

This subsystem can be decomposed into several components. All these components have been designed for ensuring interoperability with existing solutions, enabling an efficient service creation mechanism.

Figure 9 depicts the layout of the semantic subsystem. The main components of the system are:

- The *Registry/Repository*: As our component repository we chose the ebXML Registry/ Repository. In fact, the ebXML registry provides a persistent layer for service description, supporting a wide variety of objects and metadata.
- The *Metadata Store subsystem* manages metadata expressed in XML format. Furthermore, this subsystem handles the domain ontology in OWL format and the service annotations extracted from the main repository (ebXML). Some reasoning is pre-computed for improving performances. For that we use Jena[3] extensively. Jena is a Java framework for building Semantic Web applications developed at HP Bristol's laboratory.
- *Sync tools*: Tools are provided to export part of the OWL domain conceptualization to ebXML taxonomies, ensuring compatibility with a standard ebXML service discovery. We have also developed tools for data synchronization between the metadata-store and the ebXML registry. These components have been developed for allowing external queries to a standard registry. This additional requirement was inspired from the need to be as standard as possible.
- *ESDL (Enhanced Service Discovery)*: This is our matchmaker agent. ESD-WS exposes interfaces for computing matching scores on a pre-agreed ontology using well-known rules. When requested, the ESD-WS will execute a service query on the metadata store applying query-specific reasoning.
- *ReAL (REgistry Abstraction Layer)*: This software layer allows, in perspective, the reuse of the overall architecture using a different registry (e.g. UDDI).
- *SRA (Service Registration Authority)*: Has been shortly described in the previous sections. In brief, it allows publishers to navigate the domain ontology and proposes service category slots available for publishing. By using the SRA, any publisher can download service/component technical specifications, instructions to implement it, and all the needed technical documents (e.g. WSDL template and required business data as XML schemas). The SRA also informs the publisher about the properties and attributes that can be or must be provided to annotate the service/component correctly. It also transparently generates the semantic annotation according to the upper domain ontology and validates the service annotation highlighting both syntactic and semantic errors. Finally, the service description is published on an ebXML registry and synchronized with an external metadata store.
- *CDG (Component Description Generator)*: The goal of the CDG is to create an application that assists the user in semantically annotating components already available

Figure 9. Semantic subsystem layout

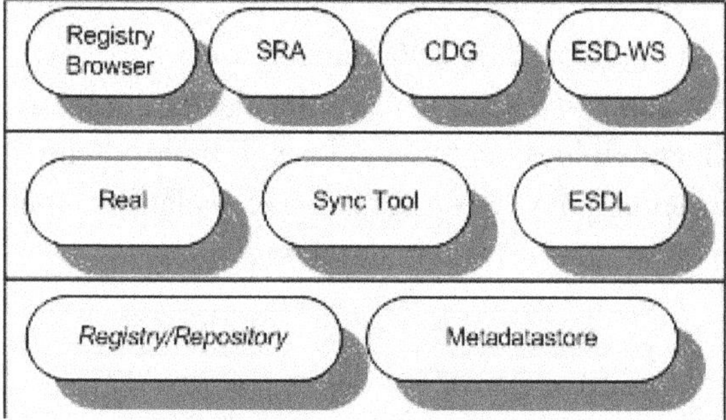

in the customer organization like legacy components. CDG using a point-and-click interface (Figure 10) enables the user to semantically annotate pre-existing Web Services, but also other software components (Plain Old Java Objects (POJO), EJBs, etc.). The key feature of CDG is the ability to suggest which ontological class to use to annotate each element of the component description. The recommendations are based on a machine learning algorithm like in Heß, Johnston, and Kushmerick (2004).

This modular architecture is backward compatible with standard ebXML registries in order to ensure interoperability with existing solutions. A core component of the architecture is an authority whose role is to enforce the respect of enterprise policies while publishing new services. Furthermore, it has been designed in such a way as to be able to deal not only with Web services, but also with other software components (POJO, EJBs, etc.). This is one of the main reasons for selecting the ebXML registry, being the latter also a repository. We would like to be ready for publishing not only Web services but also annotated components. In other words, we would extend the concept of the semantic enabled registry to a central repository of "servicelet". We define a service let as everything that could be composed and reused for building a service. We believe that semantics could add a huge value in helping enterprises to build new services, reusing existing servicelets - borrowing the same approach used for Web Services. Anyway this paper will not deal with this topic.

Considering that UDDI registries are available on the market with similar capabilities, we have given thought to an abstraction layer for achieving a "registry independence" and eventually plug a different registry whenever requested.

In short, we devised a set of software tools that allow the end user (software designer) to take advantage of the descriptive power of semantic languages and tools, while shielding, at least partially, their complexities.

In the medium term we expect that similar approaches will foster service/component reuse.

Figure 10. Component description generator GUI

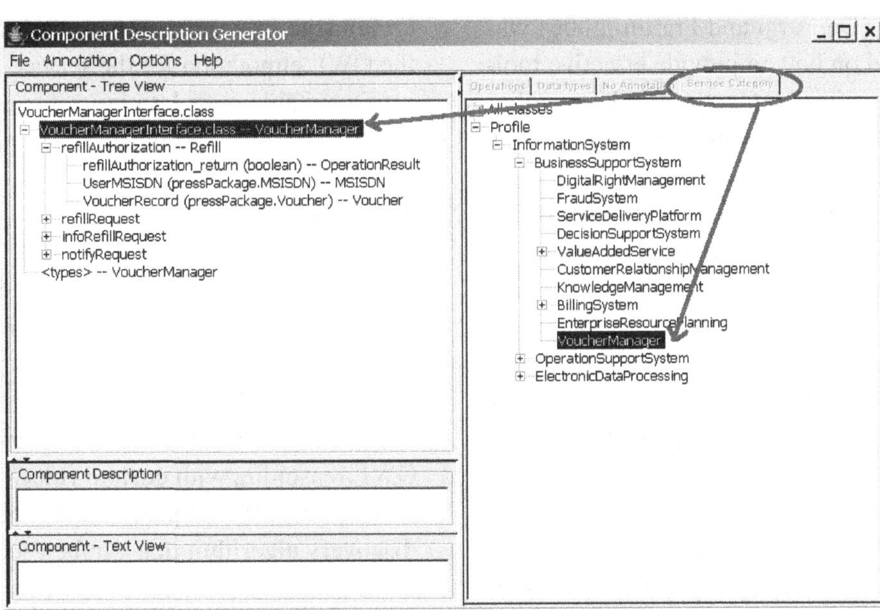

Figure 11. A Semantic SOA

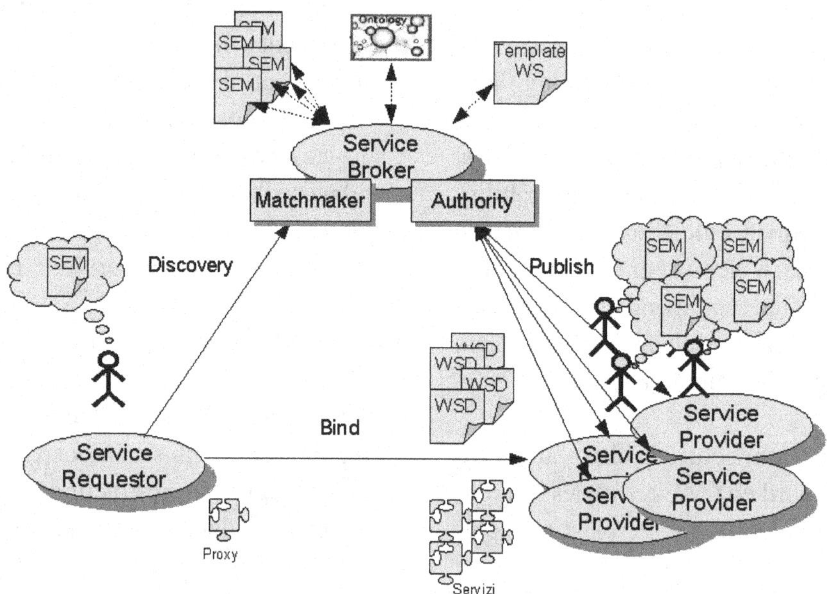

In fact associating services/ components with a significant knowledge body, expressed in standard languages, ensures that such services/components are completely documented and hence much easier to reuse.

The Service Registration Authority

Our research (De Furio and Frattini 2006) was hence focused on how to provide effective tools for annotating (adding semantically relevant information) software services and components while publishing them in the registry. The publishing service manages the domain ontology internally and, thus, it is able to annotate the service by adding semantic annotation.

To ensure interoperability among domains:

- The publisher must first contact an authority in order to obtain (download) the service specifications for any given service category.
- The publisher will have to create the service, conforming to the specifications obtained.
- Finally, the publisher will notify the authority about the availability of the new service.

It is worth noting that the authority will prevent publishing of services not included in the domain taxonomy. Every service to be published will therefore adhere to specific domain policies. Upon confirmation of the success of the publishing operation, the authority will automatically generate the OWL annotation for the service and transfer it to a suitable metadata repository, making the service available for semantic discovery.

The Matchmaker

An Enhanced Service Discovery Web Service (ESD-WS) exposes interfaces for computing matching scores on a pre-agreed ontology using domain rules. The ESD-WS is our matchmaker agent that can resolve service queries applying OWL reasoning with custom rules.

The ESD-WS implements a flexible service discovery algorithm that can be used:

- To resolve business workflow templates at run time, replacing service tasks depicted by criteria for service selection with service instances.
- To substitute a service instance at run time with an equivalent one.
- To compose service menus for terminals matching services with user profiles (preference-dependant), matching services with terminal characteristics (terminal dependant) and matching services with user context (context-aware).

On top of this platform we have built a system for m-ticketing, considering the possibility that a user could roam from a city to another, accessing seamlessly to the same service, providing just its position. The system enables two or more hypothetical transportation companies to establish a relationship that enables the service virtualization when the user is roaming. The system is able to identify the requested service using its semantic description and, if necessary, it infers the best service given both the customer and the service profile (matchmaking). The ticketing service itself is a Web Service that returns a ticket identifier and its representation as a bar code. When the user is at "home" the "local" ticketing service is invoked; when the user declares a new position the system updates its profile and, at run-time, discovers the external partner service trying to find the one that best matches the customer profile. Other QoS criteria, given the customer profile, could be applied for selecting the best service. It is important to notice that, even if we have implemented the system assuming a central brokering platform (a mobile telecommunications operator), every single local service provider could act as a broker for its roaming customers, keeping control of the customer profile and even of the customer billing.

The system covers all the relevant processes. For avoiding any lack of clarity, in the remainder of this section we describe the relevant phase for complete service provisioning.

Design-Time

The system relies upon a number of design-time activities that must be carried out in order for the system to work correctly at run-time. As depicted before, the actor playing the role of broker must set-up its SRA. As broker, he must define the ontology that will be partially shown as service taxonomy in the SRA (see Figure 12). Furthermore the company must define its specific policies and produce a template for providing its partners a technical specification for interacting with the partner at run-time. Furthermore, the partner downloads a specification of the specific message exchange pattern for correctly interacting with the other parties.

Considering the fact that only services respecting the domain policies are enabled to participate to business processes, a workflow designer needs to face just two problems: coding the criteria for service selection and invoking the service. Other problems vanish since structural and semantic differences between services are eliminated during the publishing phase.

Publishing-Time

We assume that a commercial relationship exists amongst parties. Once an agreement is signed among the parties, it is possible to set-up the collaboration infrastructure.

The partner connects to the SRA after having obtained the credentials for accessing the Web site. A page presenting the service taxonomy of the services is presented.

When a new service provider (i.e. a new local transportation company) joins the business community, he uses the SRA to select the service category slots available for its business category. By using the SRA, the new partner can download

Figure 12. SRA (a) Technical specification download (b) Aided service annotation

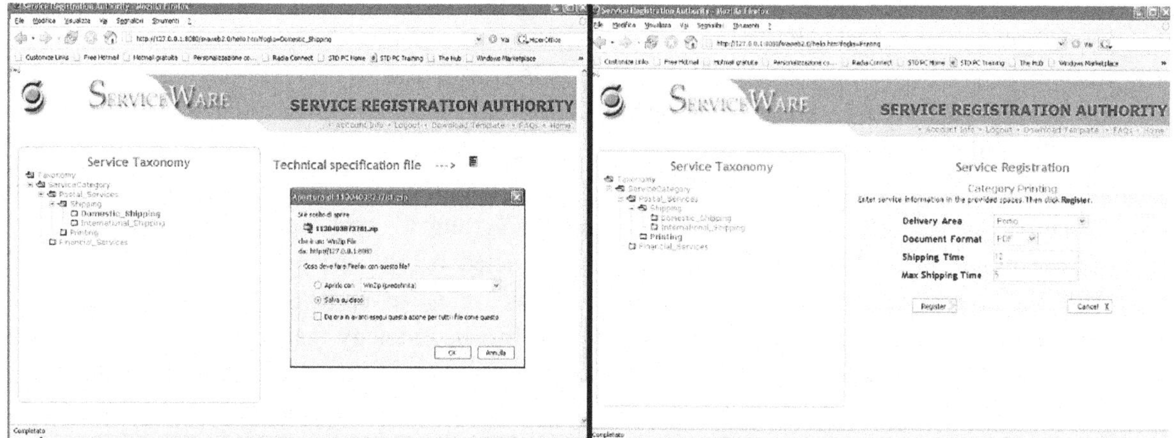

service specifications, instructions to implement it, and all the needed technical documents.

The SRA also informs the publisher about the properties and attributes that can be or must be provided to annotate the service correctly and enable the run-time service provisioning.

The publisher will have to create the service, conforming to the specifications obtained, using standard tools to develop Web Services.

Finally the publisher has to notify the authority about the availability of the new service, completing the registration. The SRA then, transparently, generates the semantic annotation according to the upper domain ontology and validates the service annotation highlighting both syntactic and semantic errors. The service description is published on the registry and synchronized with the metadata store. The publishing workflow could also include the testing of the partner interface in order to avoid run-time fault. At this time, the service is discoverable and it can participate in the business.

The SRA facilitates the discovery of a Web Service that cannot only be based on its name or description; but also has to account for its operational metrics and its interfaces.

In fact the composition of e-workflows cannot be undertaken while ignoring the importance of operational metrics. Trading agreements between suppliers and customers modelled with e-workflow include the specification of QoS items such as products or services to be delivered, deadlines, quality of products, and cost of service. The correct management of such specifications directly impacts both the success of organizations participating in e-commerce and the success and evolution of e-services itself.

Run-Time

A client on a mobile phone using Java technology (J2ME) is allowed to use Web Services for interacting over the Internet (via GPRS) and eventually store data locally, avoiding expensive accesses to the mobile network. In a typical scenario, the java client has been downloaded and installed on the customer mobile phone at the end of his/her service subscription procedure to the service and, thus, that the customer has a service geographical region and a "billing home". When the application on the mobile starts, the client downloads and presents a menu of the "home" services. The user can change the home using the application itself.

In the implemented scenario, having a dedicated client on his/her mobile the user can buy a "home" public transportation ticket. This is only an example of a possible service: the same approach could be easily applied in several different e-business scenarios. A normal ticket acquisition flow encompass: (1) the loading of the customer profile, (2) the calling of an authorization service according to the ticket price (billing), (3) the production of a ticket code, (4) the rendering of the code in a visual format (bi-dimensional bar code), (5) the accounting of the ticket on the home payment system.

To implement the service flow we have used our own orchestration engine. The orchestration engine is able to bind dynamically the components needed for completing the task. So we experienced dynamic selection of the most appropriate services among the available ones, and replacement of services by equivalent ones (i.e. in case of failure). The business designer composes a template workflow where just the selection criteria for the services are coded. At run time a workflow engine will discover services suitable for the assigned task. The construction of dynamic services is, thus, simplified due to the fact that equivalent services have the same interfaces. The registration procedures, mediated using the SRA are, thus, very effective for enabling such a degree of dynamicity.

After receiving an "update position" command, the system executes the following tasks: (1) loading the user profile, (2) acquire terminal position depending on the user selection (real GPS position, cell-ID or a string), (3) update the service menu on the mobile phone. Since the user profile contains also the current service localization (e.g. Milan-company A) every change must be tracked. When the user requests an update location, the system tries to solve the request by matching the user profile against the metadata store, trying to find the best service providers against the user preferences and position. If a service provider exists the system retrieves an appropriate service menu, downloads it on the customer device and updates the user service profile for taking into account the updates.

The flow for a ticket request, during a roaming, does not differ from the normal one except for the Web Services invocation that is transparent for the user: the ticket code is produced remotely according to its internal rules and, finally, the accounting service is both local and remote (for reconciliation purposes). Thus, exploiting the metadata stored during the publishing phase, creating partnerships is very simple and has very small impacts on the business: the system does not have to adapt messages or calls to the partners since they have been forced to comply to the domain policies: as in the "home" flow, the system loads the user profile, evaluates the ticket cost and asks for authorization to the home payment system. Then, the system requests a valid ticket identifier to the remote partner, commits the payment transaction, and notifies the partner for future reconciliation.

It is worth noting that the customer data, including sensible data, are always in the home environment: the agreement among the companies allows a transparent service roaming. In other words, the roaming mechanisms that every mobile user knows very well for telecommunications services, are reproduced for other kind of services. The key ingredients are: Web Services; ontologies for describing accurately the service, the user profile and the user context; and a platform for building an effective client environment, based on dynamically reconfigurable service menus.

ALTERNATIVES

The growth of Web services and service oriented architecture (SOA) offers attractive basis for realizing dynamic architectures, which mirrors the dynamic and ever changing business environment. With the help of industry wide acceptance of standards like Business Process Execution Language for Web Services (BPEL4WS), Web Service Description Language (WSDL) and Simple Object Access Protocol (SOAP), Web Services offers the potential of low cost and immediate integration with other applications and partners.

Several commercial platforms are available for building Web Service enabled SOA, like IBM WebSphere, webMethods Fabric, BEA WebLogic Enterprise Platform and others. All these products have in common that they do not facilitate semantic annotation of the published services. All these products are based on a pure syntactical approach. This implies that the corresponding Web service architectures built on Web Service SOA exhibit little flexibility and expressiveness and that restrict the usability of Web services mostly to human users rather than machine agents. However, SOAs will not scale without significant automation of service discovery, service adaptation, negotiation, service composition, service invocation, and service monitoring; and data and process mediation. For the latter one would need, e.g., Web service description languages that support semi-structured data, constraints, types and inheritance.

The Semantic Web is fundamental to enabling the services and applications outlined above by providing a universally accessible platform that allows data to be shared and processed by automated tools, and by providing the machine-understandable semantics of data and information that will enable automatic information processing and exchange. Experts have already developed a range of mark-up frameworks and languages, notably the revised Resource Description Framework (RDF) and the Ontology Web Language (OWL) which mark the emergence of the Semantic Web as a broad-based, commercial-grade platform.

Combination and enhancement of Semantic Web and Web Service technologies is expected to produce a new technology infrastructure — Semantic Web Services.

Several research initiatives focused on mechanisms to applying semantics in annotation, quality of service, discovery, composition, execution with Web services like OWL-S (Martin et al., 2004), METEOR-S (Rajasekaran, Miller, Verma and Sheth 2004), WSMO (Roman, Keller and Lausen 2004), European Semantic Systems Initiative (ESSI 2007) , and OASIS Semantic Execution Environment (OASIS 2007). The idea is to extend service descriptions by adding context information (i.e. what the service does, how it behaves, security policies, etc.), that add semantics to service descriptions.

Some other effort has been spent by the international community to apply Semantic Web technology to Business architecture, for example in (Werthner, Hepp, Fensel and Dorn 2006), it is discussed a B2B architecture that uses intelligent mobile agents to provide automatic negotiation with less cost and time within open and heterogeneous environments like the Internet.

The mentioned research can be exploited to automate Web services-related tasks, like discovery, selection, composition, mediation, monitoring, and invocation, thus enabling seamless interoperation between them while keeping human intervention to a minimum. Nevertheless many major challenges still need to be addressed and solved in this field to allow a real-world implementations of SWS applications, so until now, a fully semantic approach has been far from being viable. Academic and research institutions worldwide are strongly supporting this effort but some other research work needs to be done before the Semantic Web Services vision can make a reality. However, it is possible to combine it with standard tools in order to exploit the additional features it offers.

We propose an open modular architecture that enables an efficient service creation mechanism, a publishing method for fully semantic annotated services, and enhanced service discovery using OWL reasoning. This modular architecture is backward compatible with standard ebXML registries in order to ensure interoperability with existing solutions. A core component of the architecture is an authority whose role is to enforce respect of enterprise policies while publishing new services. Furthermore, it has been designed in such a way as to be able to deal not only with Web services but also with other software components (POJO, EJBs, etc.).

In short, we devised a set of software tools that allows the software designer to take advantage of the descriptive power of semantic languages and tools, while shielding, at least partially their complexities .

In the medium term we expect that similar approaches will foster services/components reuse. In fact associating services/ components with a significant knowledge body expressed in a standard language ensures that such services/ components are completely documented and hence much easier to reuse.

COST AND BENEFITS

As discussed in section 1, telecommunications operators are facing a strong competition due to new entrant. This simple fact implies that they need to reduce costs.

As stated in Duke and Richardson (2006):

The costs of integration, both within an organisation and with external trading partners, are a significant component of the IT budget. A Forrester survey (Koetzle, 2001) found that average spending on integration by the top 3500 global companies was $6.3 million and 31% was spent on integrating with external trading partners.

Service oriented architectures are particularly suitable for implementing VAS, since they reduce the integration costs for both internal and external systems. Especially for integrating external partners using Web services, a big problem is to enforce integration rules. Integrating every single potential partner could imply changes to the security rules, business logic (especially when aggregating recursively services). Thus, in a market that is increasingly federated, due both to regulatory pressures and to companies' attempts to catch market opportunities with tailored, bundled services, a solution for controlling possible integration complexity explosions is more than necessary. The solution we propose addresses this problem, considering the position of telecommunications operator in the value chain: they are always the first user point of contact and they can play a central role in building new Value Added Services. Furthermore, services like m-ticketing are built aggregating equivalent service providers. Ontology is the best way for describing service providers equivalence class, and, at the same time, for managing efficiently information that cannot be simply included in the service description language selected (generally WSDL). The service provider ontology, thus, can be efficiently

As introduced above, most of IT decision makers are sceptics with respect a massive introduction of semantics in their software architectures. The solution we propose tries to overcome this problem. This solution, while using semantics for expressing additional knowledge on services, tries to shield both Telecom operators, playing the role of brokers/aggregators in the business ecosystem, and service providers, whose main objective is to exploit the best new marketing channels, from the need to invest in tools and training.

It is important to notice that the concepts like service level VHE are fundamental for implementing m-business services. The bus ticketing example is again very representative: a user does not need to use its mobile for buying a bus ticket, changing his habits from one day to another. A normal user is likely to use its mobile while travelling: this would really help him. Implementing such a mechanism, while theoretically possible using standard technologies, would create huge interoperability problems and introduce costs for aggregating/adapting potential partners to let them participate to the business. On the other hand, a service provider, such as a mass transportation company, whose core business is not IT intensive, does not want to invest in new software systems; what they want is something easy. Apart from the example of bus ticketing, this is true for many other business categories: m-shopping, event ticketing (cinema, theatre, etc.), m-advertising, m-couponing, amongst others. It is important to find a solution that makes it as easy as possible to participate and, at the same time to offer a service that is there when needed.

RISK ASSESSMENT

Semantics and all the related technologies are not well known in the IT environment. Most of the IT people day by day problems are related to the maintenance of their platforms and services. That is why introducing new technologies is always difficult. This is particularly true for semantics since it is perceived as still immature: few big players are now marketing semantic enabled products.

Nevertheless, the telecom market is asking for innovation. A simple internet like approach to mobility does not face the real problems related to user mobility. Our solution tries to face some of the relevant issues: usability, usefulness, simplicity, service benefit/cost ratio boosting. We are absolutely conscious that many factors could influence the market: political decision could enlarge the possibility to pay for goods and services using telecommunications accounts, terminal manufacturers could enable new proximity mechanisms enabling new business scenarios, new telecommunications operators could introduce new business models. A strategic analysis is difficult since most of the IT and Telecom market big players could influence the future and take advantage from their dominant position in the market. At the moment, real revenues are coming from traditional services: logo, ring-tone, games, etc. Since an investment for creating a network of service providers could be large and the estimation of the return of investment (ROI) not easy, most of the big players are delaying decisions. Furthermore the IT big players are concentrated in marketing service oriented solutions, keeping eventual more advanced solutions in their lab. In other words, at the moment, we suggest to keep moving very carefully. That is one of the reason for introducing semantic technologies gradually, masking it to operational people. In other words, considering the value that semantics could add, it is easier to introduce new solutions starting from real issues: governance, total cost of ownership reduction, new revenue streams. Hence, even if it is still felt as unsafe to apply semantic technologies in an open environment where domain knowledge is uncontrollable and ontology is not pre-defined and agreed upon, it is possible to focus on internal service life cycle, where even operational people could appreciate the benefit of an improved IT governance. Thus, the idea we have followed aims to exploit semantic annotation in a restricted domain in order to improve service oriented architectures as currently implemented using standard tools and products: from service creation and publishing, to service discovery mechanisms

We would like also to suggest paying attention to scalability issues and, thus, to consider carefully what are the customer requisite. Some of the technologies we have used for implementing our trial system are not able to scale enough for serving a large number of concurrent users (e.g. Using Jena it is not possible to open more than a single connection while updating). Nevertheless, this is not the major problem: it is of fundamental importance to implement semantic enabled architectures reusing as much as possible products having strong market penetration in the telecommunications worlds (especially for what concern RDBMS). This will open new real marketing perspectives. It is possible to use alternatives solutions reusing software products usually well known by IT people (e.g. rule engines) without renouncing to an ontological representation of the domain.

FUTURE TRENDS

In the last few months new investment in the telecommunications market are coming from Mobile Virtual Network Operators. This is a relatively new phenomenon: they are well known all over the world. What is really new is that some of these new players are financial institutions (e.g. *Rabobank* in Holland, *Poste Italiane* in Italy). It is likely that they will exploit their core business for enabling payments using mobile terminals. M-payment is not new and by itself is relatively interesting: what is really new is the fact that new services will be enabled by a single business actor. This could create the conditions for an explosion of the m-business market, considering that at least one of the barriers is falling. This would be the ideal condition for proposing a new, more flexible architecture for semantic enabled service provisioning like the one we dealt with in this chapter.

The need for new research is huge. Our research group will further proceed by extending the set of tools needed to support services/components along all their lifecycle. More specifically, we intend to develop visual tools for reusing components/services using an intelligent service/component environment. This should improve the service creation phase allowing non technical people to create services reusing as much as possible the existing software component and services. The idea is to use the Service Registration Authority as a front-end for a configuration management system, enabling one to keep track not only of the software components/services but also of their meaning. This system should improve the service creation process and enable large companies to save large amounts of money.

Moreover, a more direct link to enterprise architecture methodologies and tools must be studied and developed. We believe that in the near future enterprise software architectural models will have to include domain ontologies. Thus tools for simplifying this prominent design task will become an absolute priority for the software research community.

It could be said that, from our point of view, the new frontier of the IT industry is strictly related to semantics. This is the main way to really introduce innovation and to justify future investment in this sector.

CONCLUSION

We have presented a solution for enabling a more effective service provisioning all along the service lifecycle. We started from considering the need to open the mobile operator business, trying to identify a solution for enabling a more flexible service publication mechanism and a more effective service discovery. Such a platform can be used for enabling a higher level of service personalisation, allowing service roaming among a coalition of business partners, reproducing the well-known concept of roaming at a higher abstraction level. The core subsystem of the overall infrastructure is the Service Registration Authority, a component based on a pre-engineered domain ontology, which plays the role of entry point for publishing new partner services. The idea underneath the SRA could be used for improving the service creation process, enabling the reuse of services and components for creating new value-added services.

The market is evolving rapidly and signs of a wide adoption of semantic enabled services architecture are more and more frequent. We have adopted an approach that mixes together semantic annotation along with traditional tools aiming to overcome some of the cultural barriers that could frighten conservative IT people.

REFERENCES

Booth D., Haas H., McCabe F., Newcomer E., Champion M., Ferris C., & Orchard D. (2004)

Web Services architecture. From: http://www.w3.org/TR/ws-arch/, Retrieved February 2004

De Furio, I. & Frattini, G. (2006) *A Semantic Enabled Service Provisioning Architecture* in Proceedings of the 6th Business Agents and the Semantic Web (BASeWEB) Workshop, Hakodate, Japan, May 2006

Duke, A. & Richardson, M., (2006) *"A Semantic Service-Oriented Architecture for the Telecommunications Industry"*, in *"Semantic Web Technologies: Trends and Research in Ontology-based Systems"* J. Davies, R. Studer, P. Warren, John Wiley & Sons

EbXML (2005) *OASIS ebXML RegRep Standard*. Available at http://docs.oasis-open.org/regrep/v3.0/regrep-3.0-os.zip

ESSI (2007), *The European Semantic Systems Initiative Site*, Last access June 2007 http://www.essi-cluster.org/

Gisolfi, D. (2001). *Web services architect, Part 2: Models for dynamic e-business*. Retrieved January 2007 from http://www-128.ibm.com/developerworks/webservices/library/ws-arc2.html.

Heß, A., Johnston, E. & Kushmerick, N., (2004) *ASSAM: A Tool for Semi-Automatically Annotating Semantic Web Services* © Springer Verlag, Lecture Notes in Computer Science 3rd International Semantic Web Conference (ISWC 2004)

Koetzle L. (2004) *IT Spends Follows Organizational Structure*. From Forrester Research http://www.forrester.com/

Martin, D. , Burstein, M., Hobbs, J., Lassila, O., McDermott, D., Mcllraith, S., Narayanan, S., Paolucci, M., Parsia, B., Payne, T., Sirin, E., Srinivasan, N., & Scycara K. (2004) *OWL-S: Semantic Markup for Web Services, version 1.1* available at http://www.daml.org/services/owl-s/1.1/overview/

Moreno, A., Valls,A. & Viejo,A. (2003) *Using JADE-LEAP to implement agents in mobile devices. TILAB "EXP in search of innovation"*; Italy from http://jade.tilab.com/papers/EXP/02Moreno.pdf

OASIS (2007), *The OASIS Semantic Execution Environment TC Site* , Last access June 2007 http://www.oasis-open.org/committees/tc_home.php?wg_abbrev=semantic-ex

Rajasekaran, P., Miller, J., Verma, K., & Sheth, A., (2004) *Enhancing Web Services Description and Discovery to Facilitate Composition*, International Workshop on Semantic Web Services and Web Process Composition, proceedings of SWSWPC2004 available at http://lsdis.cs.uga.edu/lib/download/swswpc04.pdf

Roman, D. , Keller, U. , & Lausen, H. (2004) *Web Service Modeling Ontology - Standard (WSMO - Standard), version 0.2* available at http://www.wsmo.org/2004/d2/v1.0

UDDI Version 3.0.2. (2004). *OASIS Standard*. Available at http://www.oasis-open.org/committees/uddi-spec/doc/tcspecs.htm#uddiv3.

Werthner, H., Hepp, M., Fensel, D., & Dorn, J. (2006) *Semantically-enabled Service-oriented Architectures: A Catalyst for Smart Business Networks*, Proceedings of the Smart Business Networks Initiative Discovery Session, June 14-16, Rotterdam, The Netherlands

ADDITIONAL READING

Akkiraju, R. & Goodwin R. (2004). Semantic Matching in UDDI, External Matching in UDDI, in the *proceedings of IEEE International Conference on Web Services* (ICWS) July 2004. San Diego. USA

Davies, J., Studer, R. & Warren, P. (2006.) *Semantic Web Technologies: trends and research in ontology-based systems*. West Sussex: Wiley Publishing, John Wiley & Sons

Dogac, A., Laleci, G. B., Kabak, Y., Cingil, I., (2002) Exploiting Web Service Semantics: Taxonomies vs. Ontologies, *IEEE Data Engineering Bulletin*, Vol. 25, No. 4, December 2002.

Dogac, A., Kabak, Y., Laleci, G., (2004) Enriching ebXML Registries with OWL Ontologies for Efficient Service Discovery, in *proc. of RIDE'04*, Boston, March 2004.

Mahmoud, Q. (2005). *Service-oriented architecture (SOA) and Web services: The road to enterprise application integration (EAI)*. Technical Articles, Sun Development Network. Retrieved October 19, 2005, from http://java.sun.com/developer/technicalArticles/WebServices/soa/

Salam, A.F. and Stevens, J. R., (2006) *Semantic Web Technologies and E-Business: Toward the Integrated Virtual Organization and Business Process Automation.* Idea Group Publishing, Hershey US.

Sivashanmugam, K., Verma, K., Sheth, A. P. and Miller, J. A. (2003) Adding Semantics to Web Services Standards. *ICWS 2003*: 395-401

ENDNOTES

1 See java.sun.com/javafx/

2 AJAX (Asynchronous JavaScript and XML), or Ajax, is a Web development technique used for creating interactive Web applications. The intent is to make Web pages feel more responsive by exchanging small amounts of data with the server behind the scenes so that the entire Web page does not have to be reloaded each time the user requests a change. Some of the commercial mobile browser are able to support Ajax. The idea is to overcome some of the issues related to mobile application usability using the Ajax approach. One of the issues that Ajax solve is the latency of the over-the-air communication (12-15 sec for UMTS networks)

3 See http://jena.sourceforge.net/

Chapter XIV
Towards the Use of Networked Ontologies for Dealing with Knowledge-Intensive Domains:
A Pharmaceutical Case Study

Germán Herrero Cárcel
ATOS Origin SAE, Spain

Tomás Pariente Lobo
ATOS Origin SAE, Spain

ABSTRACT

Knowledge intensive sectors, such as the pharmaceutical, have typically to face the problem of dealing with heterogeneous and vast amounts of information. In these scenarios integration, discovery and an easy access to knowledge are the most important factors. The use of semantics to classify meaningfully the information and to bridge the gap between the different representations that different stakeholders have is widely accepted. The problem arises when the ontologies used to model the domain become too large and unmanageable. The current status of the technology does not allow to easily working with this type of ontologies.In this chapter we propose the use of networked ontologies to solve these problems for the particular case scenario of the nomenclature of products in the pharmaceutical sector in Spain. Instead of using a single ontology, the idea is to break the model in several meaningful pieces and bind them together using a networked ontology model for representing and managing relations between multiple ontologies. The semantic nomenclature is a case study that is currently under development in the EC funded FP6 project NeOn[1]. Among the main objectives of the case study, are helping in the systematization of the creation, maintenance and keeping up-to-date drug-related information, and to allow an easy integration of new drug resources. In order to do that, the case study tackles the engineering of a drug Reference Ontology, the provision of easy mechanisms for discovery, model and mapping of drug resources in a collaborative way, and the ability to reason on the context of user and ontologies to ease the mapping and retrieving processes.

CURRENT SITUATION

One of the most important issues in the pharmaceutical sector regarding the description of medicines is that of having a common and unified nomenclature. Steps in that direction have been taken by different international bodies and organizations. A number of classifying systems, thesauri, taxonomical classifications and even ontologies have arisen in the last years. However, the current scenario is that there is no unified way of naming and work with drug-related information. In the next paragraphs a quick overview of the most used international classification schemas and nomenclatures are depicted.

The Anatomical Therapeutic Chemical Classification System (2007) (ATC classification) is one of the most widely used classifications of drugs. It is controlled by the WHO[2] Collaborating Centre for Drug Statistics Methodology, and was first published in 1976. Medicinal products are classified according to the main therapeutic use of the main active ingredient, on the basic principle of only one ATC code for each pharmaceutical formulation (i.e. similar ingredients, strength and pharmaceutical form).

SNOMED (Systematized Nomenclature of Medicine) is a systematically organised computer processable collection of medical terminology covering most areas of clinical information such as diseases, findings, procedures, microorganisms and pharmaceuticals. The design of this Nomenclature is based on Description Logics. SNOMED CT is one of a suite of designated data standards for use in U.S. Federal Government systems for the electronic exchange of clinical health information (College of American Pathologists, 2007).

Medical Subject Headings (MeSH) is a huge controlled vocabulary (or metadata system) for the purpose of indexing journal articles and books in the life sciences including drugs and pharmaceutical preparations. Created and updated by the United States National Library of Medicine (NLM), it is used by the MEDLINE article database and by NLM's catalogue of book holdings. MeSH contains around 23.000 subject headings which are arranged in a hierarchy and could be viewed as a thesaurus (National Library of Medicine, 2007a).

Also, the globalisation in the marketing of drugs and sharing information among pharmaceutical professionals, the competent authorities and laboratories has contributed to the creation of terminologies as MedDRA. This terminology is used mainly in pharmacovigilance, due to MedDRA has a high number of terms for coding diseases, symptoms, diagnosis...

There are more thesauruses, taxonomical classifications, or medical languages as the Unified Medical Language System (UMLS) (National Library of Medicine, 2007b). UMLS is a controlled compendium of many vocabularies, not only about pharmaceutical products, such as LOINC, RxNORM, HL7, NCI and other, which also provides a mapping structure between them.

Some medical ontologies such as Galen[3], OpenCyC[4] or the NCI thesaurus[5] define the concept of pharmaceutical product and attempt to classify different categories of drug-related information. But the current status is that there is a limited set of ontologies focused specifically on drugs, particularly in the description of pharmaceutical products.

Meanwhile, the Spanish governmental organizations are working in improving their Nomenclature providing their information about drugs in the Spanish market following mostly the ATC classification. Figure 1 shows the main actors of the pharmaceutical sector in Spain, depicting the main life-cycle relationships. The main actors represented in the figure are:

- The Ministry of Health edits and provides two official databases (*Digitalis, Integra*) with information about pharmaceutical products in Spain every month. *Digitalis* is the nomenclature officially used in the invoicing of prescriptions and contains

Figure 1. Overview of the Spanish Pharmaceutical sector main stakeholders

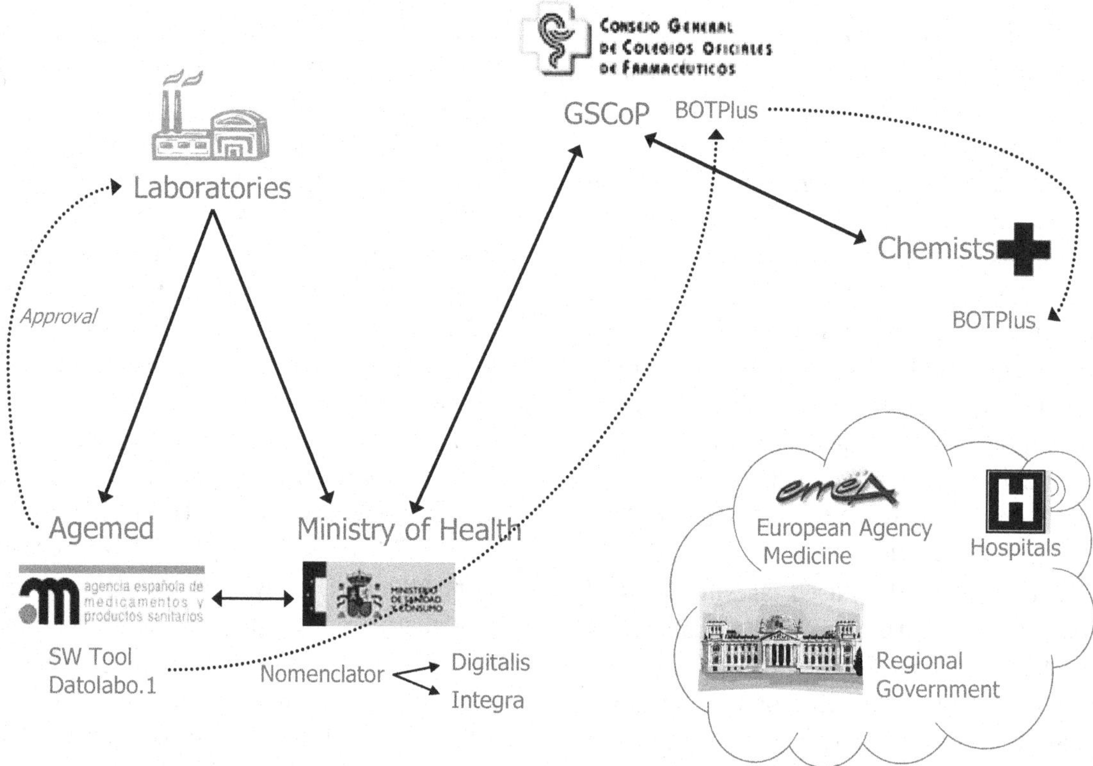

data such as the identification of the pharmaceutical product, prices, composition of the medicine, etc. *Integra* stores information about pharmaceutical products consumed (and assimilated) in the hospital field.

- The Spanish General Agency of Drugs and Sanitary Products (Agemed[6]) provides a SW tool (*Datolabo*) with the information about all pharmaceutical specialities for human-use authorized or in process to be licensed. Reports and alerts about the products.
- Some other Regional governmental bodies have responsibilities for managing the drug market in their region delegated by the central government.
- The European Agency of Medicine is in charge of setting European-wide rules and recommendations in the pharmaceutical sector. EudraPharm is intended to be a source of information on all medicinal products for human or veterinary use that have been authorised in the European Union (EU).
- Among the responsibilities of the General Spanish Council of Pharmacists (GSCoP), are the representation, coordination and enabling co-operation among the pharmacy profession in Spain. GSCoP provides to its members the Health Information Data Base (*BOTPlus*) for having access to harmonised, updated information on medicines, patients, diseases, treatments, etc. It includes around 140.000 pharmaceutical products.
- Laboratories and wholesalers provide legacy systems and resources with descriptions about their own products.

The number available of drugs today in the Spanish pharmaceutical domain is enormous. The vast amount of information related with these drugs is difficult to gather, combine and comprehend. There are several lists of information about drugs available to the professionals, but the interoperability and easy cross-checking is far from being achieved. Using a standardized outline format would be desirable, but is not the current situation.

On the other hand, the information must be kept up-to-date. Thus the inclusion, modification or withdrawal of drugs is subject to a workflow or life-cycle that involves most of the stakeholders and it is performed according to the Spanish and European regulations.

In November 2004, the Spanish Ministry of Health published a strategic plan[g] where some actions to promote the sharing of information about medicines between the professionals of the sector was proposed. One of the main goals of this plan was to reduce the costs derived from the promotion and searching of information, because these costs have a direct influence on the price of the medicines. A new nomenclature (widely called "vademecum" in Spain) with more advanced features would be of great help to achieve this objective.

In summary, there is a clear lack of systematization for the creation, maintenance and update of the drug-related information. Moreover, there is no reasoning involved in management of this information, and the interoperability is far from being achieved.

Problem Statement

The past decade has seen the rapid development of ontologies applied to the medical sector. There are some efforts devoted to develop ontologies in the pharmaceutical domain, but these ontologies are far from being mature and have not reached the Spanish sector at all (Gómez-Pérez, Pariente, Daviaud, & Herrero, 2006).

One of the tasks of the W3C is to establish recommendations for generic technologies on the World Wide Web that operate between the underlying transport layer and the applications specific to individual industrial sectors. We can read from (W3C, 2007):

For classifying symptoms, diagnoses, treatments and drugs, medicine abounds with indexing systems and controlled vocabularies. The Resource Description Framework (RDF) language from W3C is an XML application that supports the representation of controlled vocabularies, thesauri and term lists where the relations between the terms are weakly defined. Built on top of this is the OWL language to represent ontologies. An ontology is a conceptual model of a domain of discourse, it is not just a thesaurus or a term list. The relations between items in an ontology are defined much more strictly than in a simple term list or thesaurus. This enables more precise reasoning to weed out erroneously defined terms, and to dynamically generate new concepts and their definitions that can be derived from those already included. In the medical domain thesauri such as UMLS and ontologies such as UK Drug Ontology can be represented in these languages and then interact with the XML representations of other documents.

However, as stated before, there is a clear lack on ontologies tackling the description of pharmaceutical products. Besides, the number of drugs available today is enormous and the Spanish pharmaceutical sector is a very complex, heavily regulated sector. According to the GSCoP, this sector is even more complex and opaque than it seems. There are several stakeholders interacting with each other, but the communication and sharing of drug-related information is very limited. In fact, in the opinion of the GSCoP, a high confidentiality leads to a lack of communication and brings difficulties in the exchange of information between the different stakeholders. As one of the activities promoted by the Spanish Ministry of Health, as it is stated in the law, is the collaboration and exchange of information about pharmaceutical products between the stakeholders, helping to solve this issue is critical.

The complexity of the sector has a reflection in the technological problems they face. Each stakeholder maintains the information in their own format. When an actor requires information from others, in the best case scenario the information is provided partially and in a different format. Consequently the data has to be reformatted and completed by digging on different sources. That means that not all information is obtained in an electronic format. For instance the AGEMED sends monthly a list of the new pharmaceutical products in paper to the GSCoP, containing a brief description of each product (around eight attributes). With this information, the GSCoP have to contact other actors to obtain complementary information. Depending on the stakeholder, the contact is made using different means of communication (fax, telephone, e-mail, etc.). Finally, once the information is retrieved, it takes 2-3 hours of a technician's time to update the pharmaceutical database. In some cases it is obvious that the information is obtained depending on the technician's abilities and experience in persuading laboratory and government workers to facilitate the required information.

This scenario suggests that there is a place for a platform that would allow different actors with diverse, complex and heterogeneous interests to develop a collaborative environment, in which the information and the processes, enriched with underlying semantics, will provide an improvement in the quality of service presented to the different stakeholders.

PROPOSED SOLUTION

The need to share diverse knowledge and information with other applications already built has given rise up to a growing interest in research on ontologies. But, what is an ontology? *While* a variety of definitions of the term ontology have been suggested, *we* will use the definition first suggested by Studer, Benjamins and Fensel (1998) *"... an ontology is a formal specification of a shared conceptualization..."* Through the representation of domain-specific knowledge, ontologies provide a way of sharing and reusing knowledge among people and heterogeneous applications. So, ontologies are one of the core resources in any Semantic Web application enabling semantic interoperability and integration of data and processes.

In recent years, studies published by Gartner Group (Jacobs & Linden, 2002) ranks ontologies as third in their list of the top 10 technologies. According to this study, we are now entering a phase of knowledge system development, in which ontologies are produced in larger numbers and exhibit greater complexity.

High-intensive knowledge sectors, like the pharmaceutical, are the objective of the ontologies in order to build a new generation of Semantic Web applications which can deal easiness with large volumes of data and large and reusable resources which are complex to deal with them with other technologies.

This new generation of applications will thus reflect the fact that new ontologies are embedded in a network of already existing ontologies and that ontologies and metadata have to be kept-up-to-date with the changing application environments, sector and users' needs.

Based on this scenario, semantic integration by means of one global semantic model is probably unmanageable. In contrast, a solution for the semantic integration based on a network of contextualized ontologies provides more facilities for maintaining a set of ontologies locally consistent and it is clearly easier to manage.

However, in order to work with several interlinked ontologies a set of new tools, methodologies and techniques are needed. The NeOn project addresses this challenge, offering a set of methodologies and technologies for realizing this new generation of semantic applications, from foundational research for contextualised networked ontology environments to application-level demonstration of collaborative ontology creation, population, maintenance and access. Consequently, the Semantic Nomenclature case study will use NeOn as foundations.

Objectives

As is described before, there is no common model or significant development on ontologies of drugs in the Pharmaceutical sector in Spain. One of objectives of this scenario is cover this lack, where our proposal is to create, from existing sources and schemas, a common reference model of the Semantic Nomenclature valid for all the stakeholders. In simpler words, Semantic Nomenclature consists of the creation of a reference model for a Semantic Nomenclature that complements typical pharmaceutical compendium characteristics by giving flexible, extensible and reliable information about drugs to the users of the Pharmaceutical domain.

Overview

NeOn provides the following definition:

Network of Ontologies is a collection of ontologies related together via a variety of different relationships such as mapping, modularization, version, and dependency relationships. We call the elements of this collection Networked Ontologies. (Haase, Rudolph, Wang, & Brockmans, 2006)

NeOn also defines four main ontology assumptions: *Dynamic* (ontologies will evolve), *Networking* (ontologies are interconnected via mappings or by means of reuse), *Shared* (ontologies are shared by people and applications), and *Contextualized* (ontologies are dependent of the context in which are built or are used) (Sabou et al., 2006).

The Reference Ontology model of the Semantic Nomenclature will be based in this definition. In this sense, the Reference Ontology model is developed based on the schemas of the main sources of information about drugs in Spain: Integra, Digitalis, BOTPlus and in the ATC Classification. Moreover this reference model will be mapped to external sources of the same or similar domain, such as Snomed, connecting the reference model with other international medical vocabularies.

Based on this solution, the case study provides a collaborative scenario to ease the communication between the stakeholders, including an application that allows users to query and process all this information in order to get and make use of all this knowledge and infer new one.

The first version of the Reference Ontology, plus a set of core ontologies (Digitalis, BOTPlus, Integra and ATC), was developed in 2007. In 2008 the ontology network will evolve and will be mapped with other ontologies, such as Snomed, MedDRA, EudraPharm, etc.

The aim of the Semantic Nomenclature application is to improve the medical product information management within the Spanish pharmaceutical domain which is presently decentralized in several data bases and repositories. The application uses the pharmaceutical ontology network, which contains the Pharmaceutical Reference Ontology, which centralizes the key medical product information and links the rest of ontologies each others. This ontology network is especially useful for allowing a more complex information retrieval as well as resolving medical product identification and different classification alignments. In spring of 2008, the first version of the Semantic Nomenclature prototype application for the end users will be provided.

SOLUTION DETAILS

Ontology Development

Methodology Followed

The realization of real-life applications in the Semantic Web requires the ability to deal with

Figure 2. Reference ontology model and drug data sources

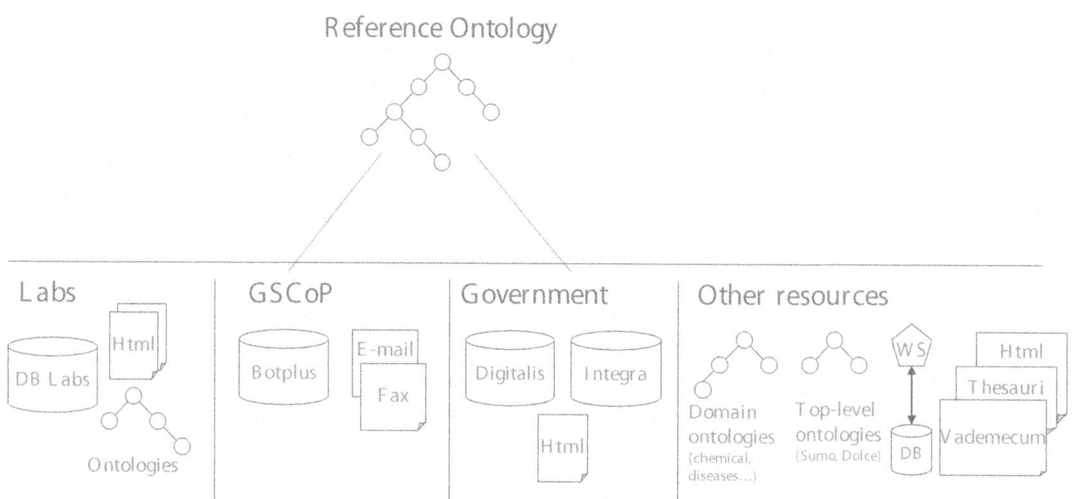

heterogeneous ontologies fragmented and distributed over multiple autonomous nodes.

Next generation semantic applications will be characterized by several ontologies linking each other and networking and sharing knowledge. The aim of NeOn project is to create the first ever service-oriented, open infrastructure, and associated methodology, to support the development life-cycle of such a new generation of semantic applications that will rely in a network of contextualized ontologies.

As is described before, a *Network of Ontologies is a collection of ontologies related together via a variety of different relationships such as mapping, modularization, version, and dependency relationships.* So with the help of networking ontologies and methodologies, technologies and tools provided by NeOn, we aim to fulfil the requirements posed by the pharmaceutical sector. We will be able to carry out the development of a new generation semantic applications able to achieve a better management, integration and exploitation of the large quantity of knowledge required by this particular sector and also provide new functionalities and services to the business.

Using Networked Ontologies instead of a single, centralized one, will allow to the different stakeholders of the pharmaceutical sector to maintain their current models (formalised as ontologies), while the NeOn infrastructure and modular framework takes care of their interlinking and mapping.

Currently there is not a methodology to work with Networked Ontologies. NeOn will provide methodology to support the collaborative construction and dynamic evolution of Networked Ontologies in distributed environments (Gomez-Perez & Suarez, 2008). In the mean time this case study is following the Methontology guidelines.

It was decided that the best method to adopt for this investigation was to use the recommendations and suggestions coming from NeOn to develop Networked Ontologies in a distributed scenario. This methodology is an extension of the Methontology (Fernandez, Gomez-Perez, & Juristo, 1997) more dedicated to Networked Ontologies and the new generation of Semantic Web applications. In broad terms, the proposed methodology describes different activities and tasks identified in the ontology lifecycle development and each simple

Figure 3. NeOn methodology

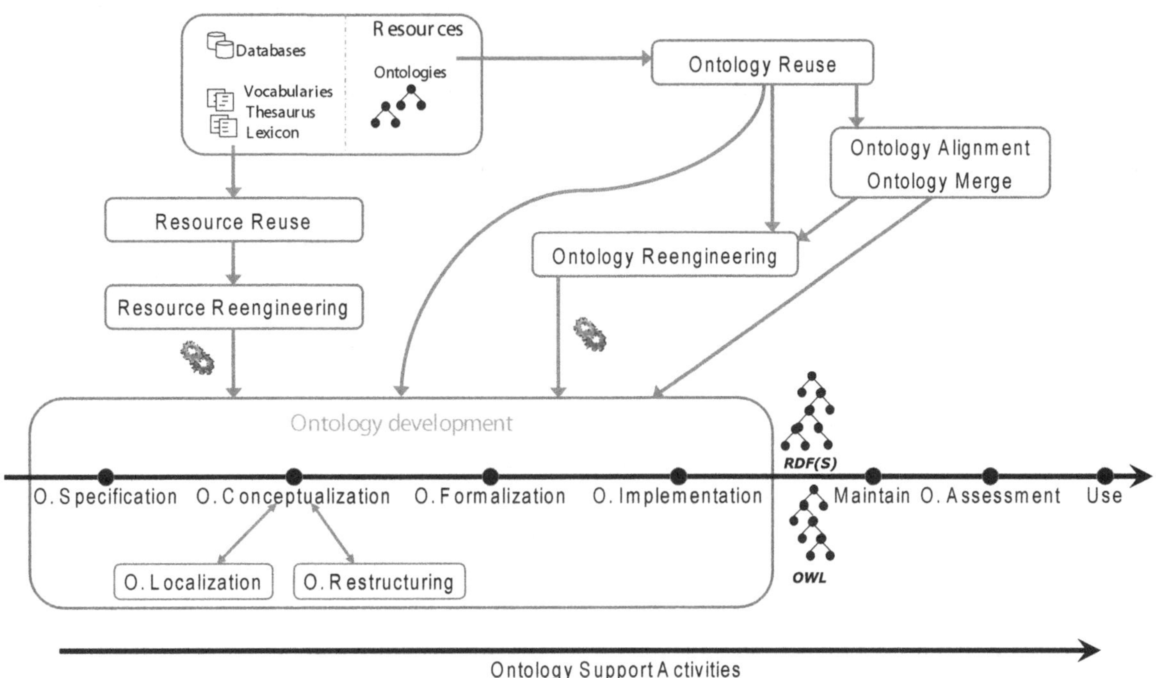

scenario is an instance of the needed activities needed in each specific scenario.

According to the methodology, first, the ontology engineer must specify the needs that the ontology has to satisfy in the new application, their intended uses and which are the users of the ontology. For this preliminary task, the methodology suggests to specify different competency questions in order to help in solve the first doubts, and identify the objects of the discourse of the domain. In the Semantic Nomenclature scenario these objects of discourse are medical products, active ingredients, substances, laboratories, pharmaceutical forms, administration method, etc. After this specification, the ontology expert should identify terms that belong to common ontologies like terms related with time, geographical information, etc.

In parallel, the methodology recommends a review of the inventory of resources needed in the scenario, such as standards and classifications, thesaurus, vocabularies, taxonomies or ontologies that could be reused. The goal of this study is the reusability of resources. The ontology engineer searches, evaluates and selects the most appropriate resources. The nature of the resource will lead to include the ontology in the Networked Ontologies, or perform ontology reengineering tasks.

Finally, the ontology expert should carry out the conceptualization of the objects of the discourse of the domain, considering tasks such as of ontology localization and modularization, pruning, etc. Then the ontology is formalized and implemented and ready to be used and maintained in the new semantic application.

Around this ontology lifecycle, the methodology suggests different ontology support activities that should be taken into account, like configuration management, documentation, elicitation, evaluation, etc.

Towards a Semantic Nomenclature Reference Ontology

It has conclusively been shown that the Spanish pharmaceutical sector lacks of a ontology that encompasses the description of pharmaceutical products. According to the characteristics of the scenario and the recommendations of the methodology, the use of a network of ontologies for representing the Reference Ontology in the pharmaceutical sector seems to be a good solution.

This Reference Ontology model should be a compilation of the main terms and objects related to drugs, the general aspects of them and classify this pharmaceutical terms according to the ATC classification, since it's the WHO recommendation and is followed by the pharmaceutical experts in Spain (Europe).

Also, this Reference Ontology model is connected with the ontology models of the main databases which contain the information about the pharmaceutical products available in the Spanish market as Digitalis or BOTPlus. In the end, the Reference Ontology could be linked with the main medical vocabularies used in the world and should facilitate the integration of new resources or ontologies that will appear in the evolved scenario.

The Semantic Nomenclature Network of Ontologies

For the purpose of developing a network of ontologies for the Semantic Nomenclature scenario, we followed the modular approach suggested by the NeOn methodology. The development of the Reference Ontology and the Nomenclature network ontology is motivated by scenarios presented to the end-user application that will use the ontology network.

The ontology network lifecycle model decided was the iterative/incremental model. This decision was taken up based first on the decision tree provided by the NeOn methodology suggested in (Gomez-Perez & Suarez, 2008), but also from the identification of requirements of the Semantic Nomenclature Ontology network, and on past experiences developing ontologies.

The main motivation of this decision is that the pharmaceutical scene is more or less static in their models, the pharmaceutical sector has a low frequency of change at the model level (not at data level). From that we deduced that there will not be many changes in the ontology network requirements. Other reason that motivated this decision is that it is planned to produce different versions of the Networked Ontologies and application during the next months

Following the methodology described before, first of all, several competency questions were defined. Specific competency questions related with the Pharmacist are for instance: What is the drug commercial name? What is its Spanish national code? Which one is the drug therapeutic WHO group? etc.

From the competency questions, we extracted the terminology that is formally represented in the ontology by means of concepts, attributes and relations. Terms (also known as predicates) and the objects in the universe of discourse (instances) are identified.

From this terminology, we checked that some of the terms (dates related with pharmaceutical product, dosage of the drugs, location of the laboratory manufacturers, etc), were related to common domains such as time, geographical or measure. Accordingly, we reviewed existing ontologies on these domains, and evaluated them. The result was mapped to the Reference Ontology.

The next steps were studying standards and resources, evaluate them and start defining the domain ontologies of the model. Starting from the basis of the glossary and terminology extracted, the pharmaceutical reference model was modeled, based on the main schemas and the ATC classification.

In parallel, the selected standards and pharmaceutical classification systems, thesaurus, taxonomies and vocabularies were reengineered in order to provide a semantic enrichment before reusing them in the model. These resources are the main databases in Spain (Digitalis, Integra, BOTPlus). The ATC classification and Snomed vocabulary are considered as the most important de facto standards that connect and the Nomenclature network ontology.

Finally, the main source of knowledge and data in this scenario, the pharmaceutical databases, were reengineered and modelled as ontologies. In this phase, Digitalis, Integra and BOTPlus are modelled as ontologies and populated their models from the databases. Concepts from these models are networked with the Nomenclature ontology network, integrating their information.

Other resources suggested by pharmaceutical professionals were the online vademecum (vademecum,es), and medical vocabularies. Thesaurus and taxonomies (UMLS, MedDRA) from international bodies related with pharmacy were analyzed trying to find how the pharmaceutical products are described in order to find connections between them and our models.

Figure 4 shows the Semantic Nomenclature Ontology Network. The pharmaceutical Reference Ontology model is enriched with the general ontologies (Time, Location, Units...), and connected via mappings with the ontology models as Digitalis or BOTPlus. In addition, the pharmaceutical Reference Ontology is related with the most important classification system ontologies as the ATC or Snomed (in grey meaning that is due for a second stage of the network). Finally, in new iterations of the lifecycle model, the pharmaceutical Reference Ontology should integrate new resources or ontologies related with the main medical vocabularies used in the world.

This ontology network outlined in this chapter is aligned with the goals and expectations

Figure 4. The Reference Ontology as a network of ontologies

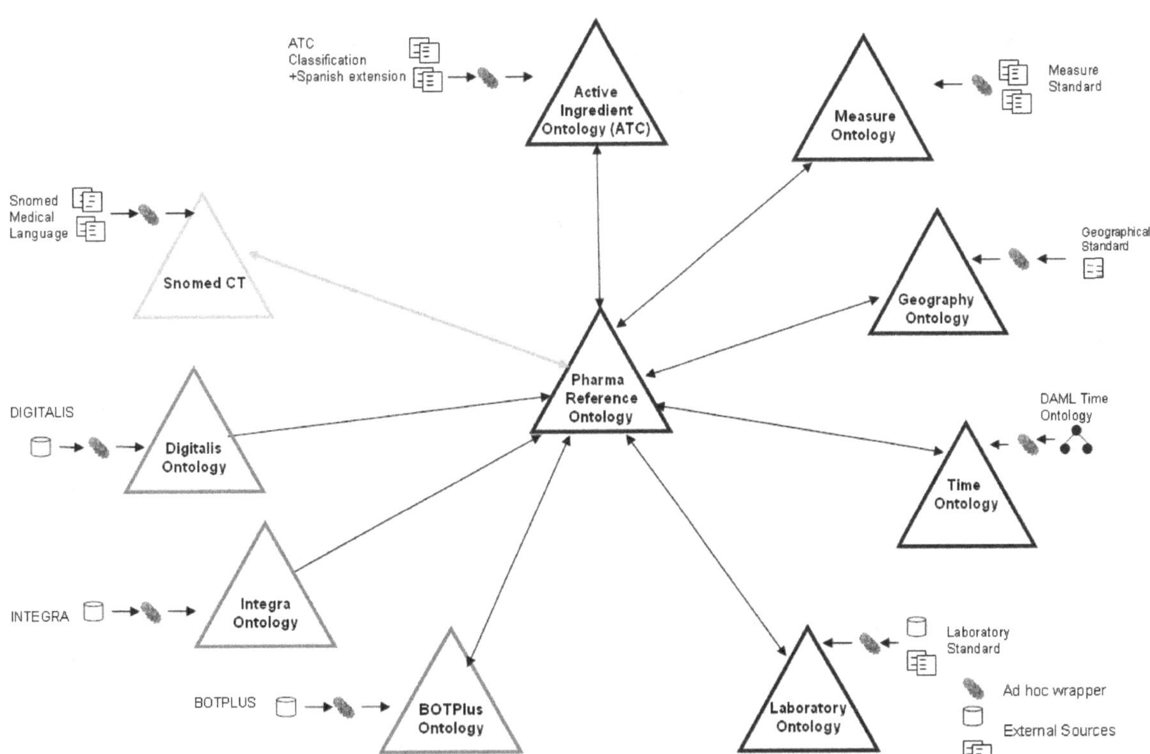

extracted from the pharmaceutical scenarios depicted before: integration of existing pharmaceutical resources. The ontology network architecture facilitates the aggregation of drug-related information, because the Reference Ontology is mapped and related with a set pharmaceutical ontologies at different levels. This network will be useful as well as foundation of one of the Semantic Nomenclature application objectives: The update of the BOTPlus database. This is a perfect scenario to show the possible business impact of Networked Ontologies. The pharmaceutical product information gathered in the Networked Ontologies is an added value to bodies such as the GSCoP in order to improve their commercial database reducing their updating process effort and complementing typical pharmaceutical compendium characteristics by giving flexible, extensible and reliable information about drugs to the users of the Pharmaceutical domain.

Architecture of the Semantic Nomenclature Network of Ontologies

The Nomenclature Ontology Network is organized in three levels: the Pharmaceutical domain ontologies, the Application domain ontologies and the General ontologies. Figure 5 shows the levels of the Nomenclature Ontology Network based on reusability and usability of the levels.

The representation ontology language (OWL) is at the base of the pyramid showed in the previous figure. On top of it, the reused vocabulary is depicted.

In the domain ontology level the ontologies or ontology modules which define several notions and concepts of the pharmaceutical domain that are substantial in the sector are included. The Pharmaceutical Reference Ontology is a compilation of the main terms and objects related with pharmaceutical products and the general aspects of them. Also, in this level ontologies are included, which provide a classification or vocabulary of these pharmaceutical terms, in this case, the ATC classification (because of the fact that is the WHO recommendation and is followed by the pharmaceutical experts in Spain and Europe) or the Snomed vocabulary.

The common ontology level groups the ontologies needed in the ontology network for describing any sort of real world objects and things, which could be of interest in some areas of discourse. Here are included ontologies as Time ontology, Geography ontology, Units ontology, etc.

Figure 5. Modular approach for ontology construction

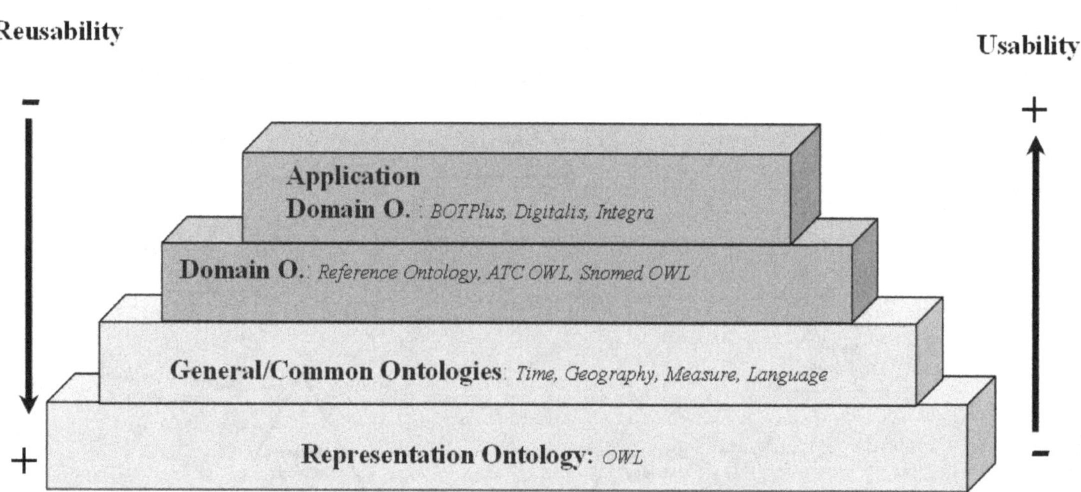

At a top level, the application domain ontologies are grouped. These ontologies are specialized in representing the knowledge of the real-world resources, in other words, they are the ontology models of the main databases which contain the information about the pharmaceutical products available in the Spanish market, as Digitalis or BOTPlus.

Architecture of the Case Study

The Semantic Nomenclature and the NeOn Architecture

The Semantic Nomenclature application is based on the NeOn architecture and the functionalities that NeOn provides. The general architecture of NeOn is ordered into three layers. The layering is done according to the level of abstraction of the data and the process flow between the components.

In the lowest layer, called Infrastructure services, are classified the basic services like repository service, reasoner...needed by any semantic application. In the middle layer are included all the ontology engineering components developed in NeOn. These components realized their tasks over the infrastructure services, and they are differentiated between tightly coupled components (editors, mapping, visualization algorithms, etc), and loosely coupled services, such as annotation or collaboration support.

The GUI components are placed at the top level of the NeOn architecture. In this layer this components are user front-ends for the engineering components and for the infrastructure services.

NeOn provides a number of services which allow managing and supporting the entire ontology lifecycle, from design to exploitation. The main properties of the NeOn architecture are its adaptability and extensibility. These two properties are crucial for the use and deployment of the NeOn infrastructure in the context of the pharmaceutical scenario, where NeOn infrastructure will be customized to support specific user requirements.

Figure 7 describes the Semantic Nomenclature architecture, where different blocks with different functionality can be distinguished. These blocks

Figure 6. NeOn (Toolkit) architecture (Waterfeld & Weiten, 2007)

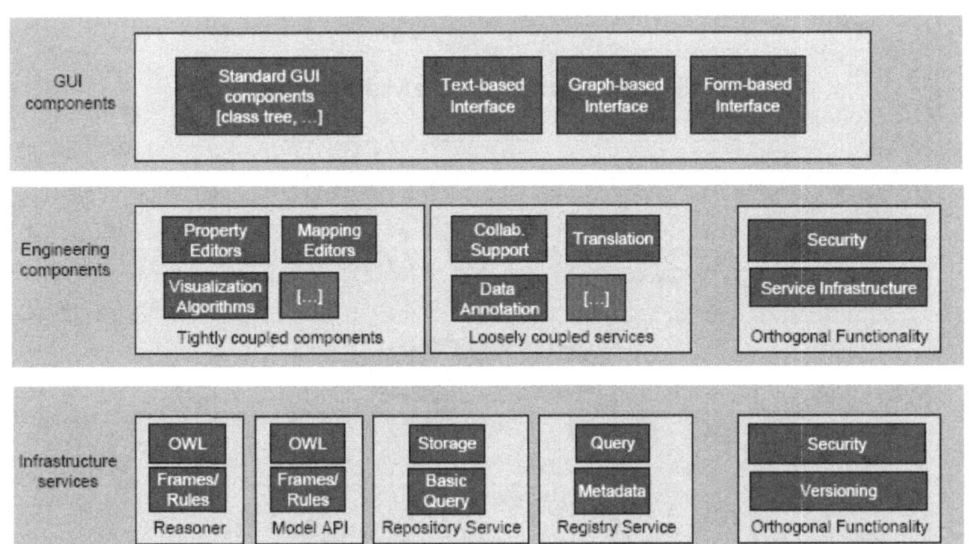

are related to the three layers differentiated in NeOn architecture.

At the infrastructure block, the Semantic Nomenclature is supported by the services provided by NeOn, such as the model API, a repository service, a reasoner, etc. Above this block, the application contains the engineering components needed for the purpose of the network of ontologies and the semantic application. In our case, we identified services for ontology experts, such as the mapping service, annotation service, etc. Also services for the end-user (pharmacist) such as the query service, population service, etc., were identified.

The Semantic Nomenclature middleware is located between the GUI and the engineering layers. This block manages the communication between the visualization and engineering components blocks. The visualization components interact and link to the different services across the Semantic Nomenclature middleware and provide to the users a graphical view of these services. With these services, the users will interact with the different resources stored in the infrastructure services and can create/modify them. This block is the one which manage all the workflow of the different scenarios identified.

The visualization block contains the user interfaces that interact and show to the end user (ontology experts & pharmacists) the services to edit ontologies and visualize, browse and validate the pharmaceutical knowledge.

The Architecture for Ontology Engineers

Based on the problems detected on the pharmaceutical scenario and the solution proposed, two

Figure 7. Semantic Nomenclature architecture

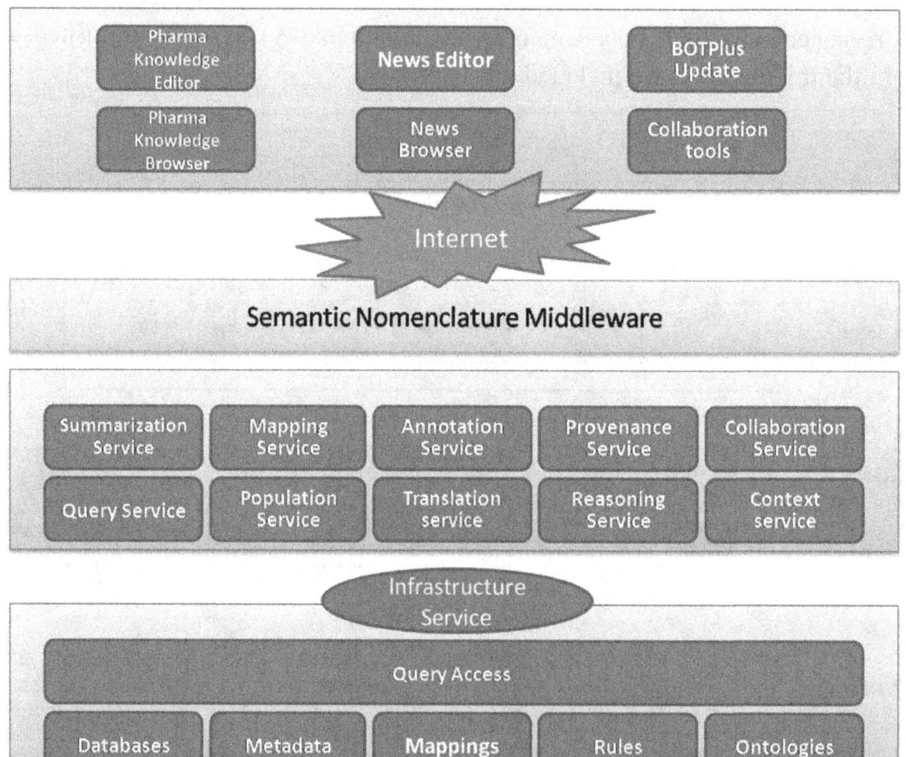

sub-scenarios can be differentiated according to the nature of the tasks to be developed and the users involved. On the one side, ontology engineers need an architecture that allows them to develop and support the entire network ontology lifecycle and on the other side a Semantic Web application which allow pharmacists browse, query and reason over the Nomenclature Network ontology and keep update their databases has to be provided.

In the first scenario, the ontology engineer need all the components required to support building and maintaining the network of ontologies. Derived from the scenario, different functionalities as ontology edition, mapping edition, annotations, population and contextualization of ontologies are needed to develop the scenario. These functionalities are provided and covered by the NeOn toolkit. Also, NeOn Toolkit provides different visualization components are identified in the scenario to facilitate these tasks to the ontology engineers and show the results. Moreover, the infrastructure services provide a repository and access services to the engineering components for the different resources of the Nomenclature Networked Ontologies.

The Architecture for End-Users

Services needed by domain experts are related with searching, querying, navigating and updating information about drugs. To fulfil this scenario the architecture should provide different functionalities than the previous one. End-users are not ontology experts, so they need a user interface that should provide a higher level of abstraction of the underlying ontologies

The end-user will interact and navigate with the Semantic Nomenclature network ontology in order to search and select information related with the Spanish pharmaceutical medicines. The engineering components provide functionalities such as summarizing the content and rating the provenance of the sources, querying the network of ontologies about the latest changes in the pharmaceutical domain, reasoning services, and population and updating of databases.

Figure 8. Semantic Nomenclature Ontology Engineers architecture

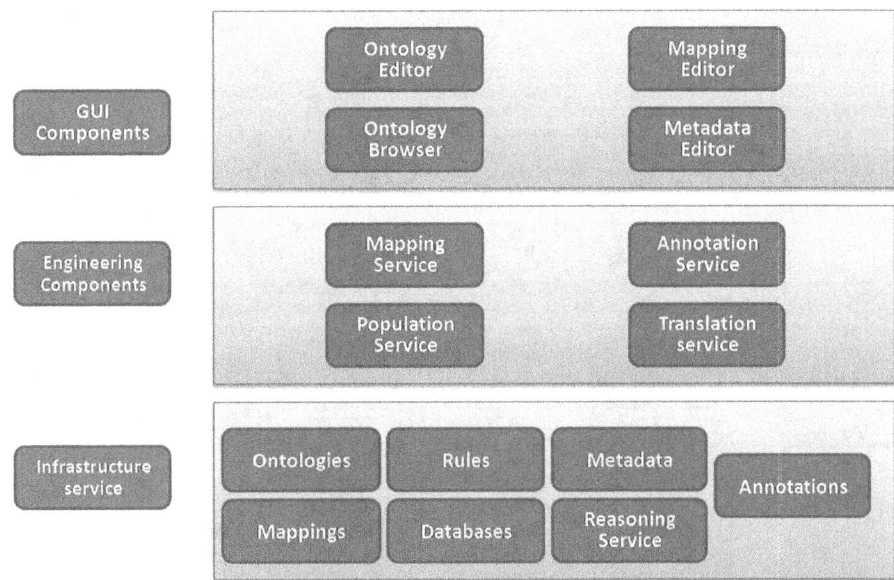

Implementation

Usage and Adaptation of the NeOn Toolkit to the Semantic Nomenclature

The different services, components and functionalities identified in the three layers of the architecture are covered by different tools and services of the NeOn toolkit, mainly at ontology engineering components and infrastructure services.

In the first sub-scenario, one of the most important services is a GUI component for creating and editing the Nomenclature network ontology. This GUI is provided by the NeOn toolkit, which evolved from the latest versions of Ontostudio[h], allowing ontology engineering in OWL format. Moreover, the NeOn toolkit provides other tool for model ontologies called Ontogen, a system based on machine learning and text mining techniques (Fortuna, Grobelnik, & Mladenic, 2006). Ontogen suggests concepts and relations extracted from a large and mass quantity of documents provided by the user at the beginning of the construction process.

Other important issue in the scenario is the mapping functionality. This functionality is crucial for the ontology engineer in the development and lifecycle of the networked model. The NeOn toolkit provides an Alignment Server (Euzenat, 2007) for discovering and suggesting mappings based in their context between two ontologies in an automatic way. Also, NeOn toolkit provides a mapping metamodel and graphical means for draw mappings manually between different models.

Other important aspect of the solution is the connection between the main databases and the ontology models. For this purpose, NeOn toolkit and the UPM provide a technology called R2O & ODEMapster (Barrasa, Corcho & Gomez-Perez, 2007). This technology is based on the declarative description of mappings between relational and ontology elements and in an exploitation of mappings by a domain independent processor. R20 & ODEMapster is a useful framework to

Figure 9. Semantic Nomenclature end-users architecture

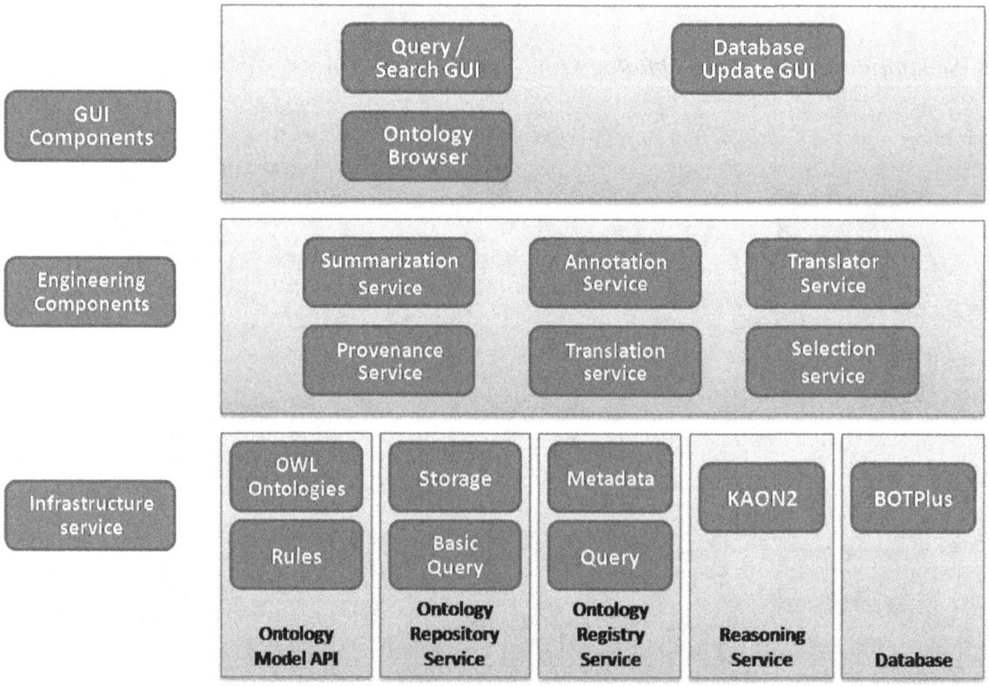

upgrade relational legacy data (databases) to the ontologies.

For ontology annotation, NeOn provides two tools for this purpose. Magpie is an annotation tool that uses the ontology infrastructure to semantically mark-up Web documents on-the-fly (Domingue, Dzbor & Motta 2004). Magpie tool aims to identify and filter out the concepts-of-interest from any webpage it is given. The other annotation tool called GATE provides an easy to use interface for indicating which pieces of text denote which of your concepts of your ontologies, doing the annotation manually or automatically (Kenter & Maynard, 2005). In the pharmaceutical scenario annotation is clearly identified and used when some source of knowledge are identified as reports or documents from the government about alerts, news or recommendations about the drugs and their content should be annotated into one ontology model of the Nomenclature network ontology.

Other functionalities identified as the translation service or multilinguality of the model are covered by the multilinguality model provided by NeOn and the TermTranslator tool. Summarization, provenance and trust service are supported by the NeOn toolkit in order to help ontology engineers and end-users in their analysis of the purpose of the ontologies and data in the application.

The Infrastructure services block will be in charge of storing all the data the system needs. It stores ontologies, metadata, annotations, mappings, queries, rules that the users have designed and the most relevant databases in the Spanish pharmaceutical domain. For the end-users, NeOn provides Query service, a registry to access all the elements and Reasoning service at infrastructure level. The Query service is quite important scenario. In the Semantic Nomenclature application we provide searching facilities to the users, in order to find the information in a faster and more accurate way. This Query service attack the infrastructure services and resources in order to find this information to the user, and should provide facilities to build queries in natural language or similar. This natural language query functionality is beyond the repository service of

Figure 10. Instantiation of NeOn architecture for Semantic Nomenclature (I)

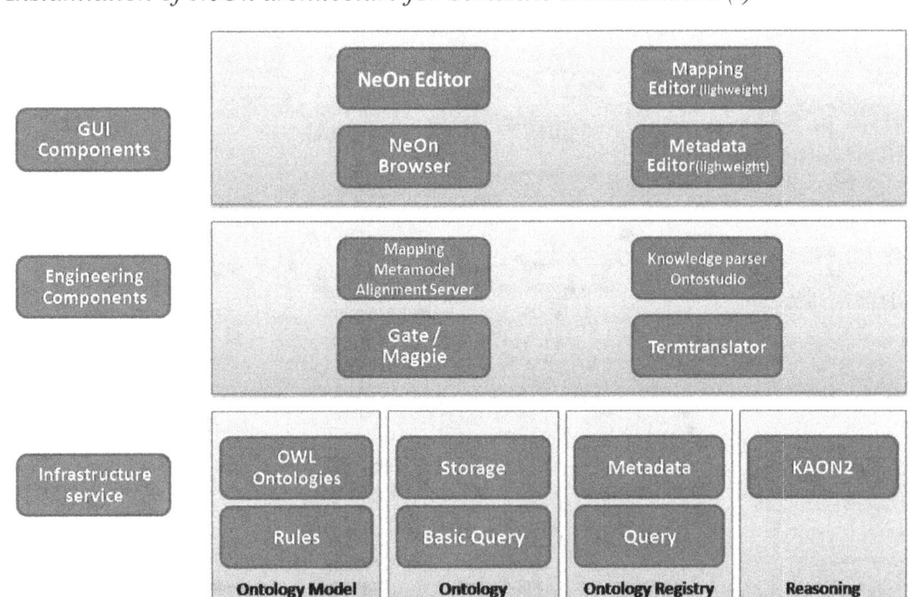

the basic NeOn infrastructure, and it is not one of the main priorities of the case study. ORAKEL, an engineering component from University of Karlsruhe tackles this functionality (Cimiano, Haase, Heizmann, & Mantel, 2007).

The reasoning service is a crucial service in the case study. Using this service, the Semantic Nomenclature can check the Semantic Nomenclature system when a new pharmaceutical resource is added, or can search about new resources provided by the Networked Ontologies in order to add it to the system or find new information and pharmaceutical data across the different information sources in order to update the BOTPlus database. NeOn includes KAON2 as reasoning service[i]. KAON2 is an infrastructure for managing OWL-DL, SWRL, and F-Logic ontologies. The main features of the infrastructure are an API for programmatic management of OWL-DL, SWRL and F-Logic ontologies, a stand-alone server providing access to ontologies in a distributed way, an inference engine for answering queries expressed in SPARQL syntax, and a module for extracting ontology instance from relational databases. The main relevance for the Semantic Nomenclature scenario is the KAON2 ontology management, inference service (in order to search new drug information across the ontologies) and the module for extract ontology instances from the main pharmaceutical databases in Spain (BOTPlus, Digitalis, Integra).

The communication between the GUI components and the services will be based on HTTP and Web services for the loosely coupled services like the "Pharmaceutical Browser" and a tightly coupled client. The application will be Web-based.

Business Case Implementation of the Case Study

There are four main application functionalities and services that the Semantic Nomenclature will provide to end-users: drug knowledge alert system, news service, collaboration tools and update service.

One relevant functionality is the Drug knowledge alert system. The Semantic Nomenclature

Figure 11. Instantiation of NeOn architecture for Semantic Nomenclature (II)

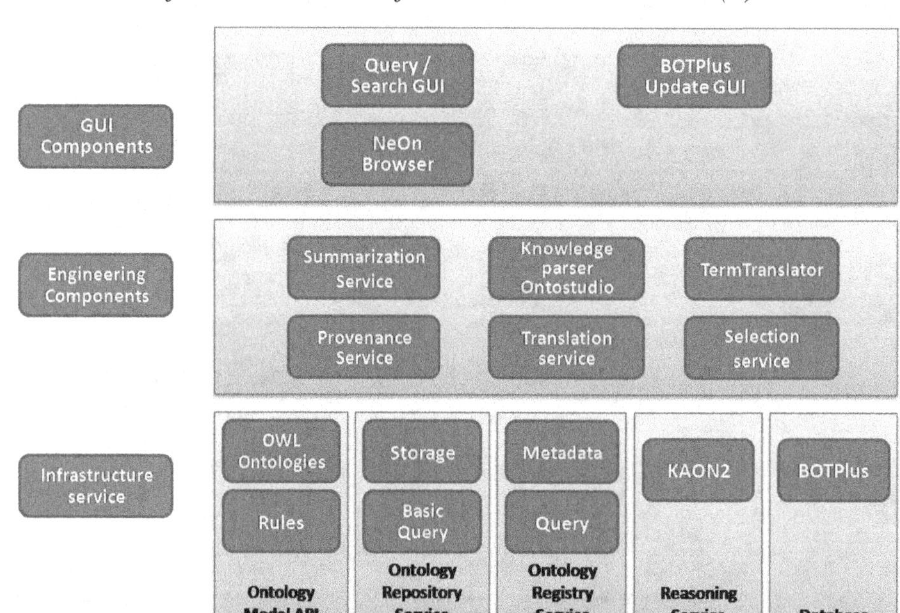

application will select relevant drug information and pharmaceutical alerts to inform to the pharmacists, taking into account their preferences and experience. As a result of that, the pharmacists could access to the latest information provided by the main information sources (government, laboratories and professional entities).

The News Service provides to the users additional information and news about pharmaceutical extracted from Web pages, documents, and other resources related with the pharmaceutical professional and suggested by the end-users.

Other relevant and innovative functionality is the collaborative scenario through a social network among professionals for a better communication between the pharmaceutical stakeholders. The collaborative tools could provide to the pharmaceutical community a new way of sharing knowledge. A Semantic Nomenclature wiki could be very useful for the end-users, because this tool could provide accurate content and the pharmacists could use it in their everyday work. Furthermore, the end-users have the chance to edit the content, validate it, exchange and share experiences and subscribe to their topics of interest. Moreover, this collaborative tools and the information provided by the pharmacists could be used to analyzed and processed by the Semantic Nomenclature in order to annotate this information to the correspondent elements in the ontology network. These annotations could be offered as added-value to the knowledge of the Nomenclature network.

The Update service is one of the core facilities provided to particular actors to update their legacy systems with the latest information. The main pharmaceutical actors and end-users of the information can take advantage of the Nomenclature network of ontologies in order to gather information about the pharmaceutical products from different sources it and incorporate into their legacy systems. This information is checked and provided with a provenance rating and the end-user can validate it before update their legacy. We aim to implement an example of this service during the NeOn project life-span.

ALTERNATIVES

As it was explained before, the vast amount of information related with drugs in the Spanish pharmaceutical sector is difficult to gather, combine and comprehend, but the interoperability and easy cross-checking is far from being achieved. Besides, they are not several alternatives for solving the lack of communication between the main actors in the pharmaceutical business scenario.

As is described in the beginning of the chapter, in recent years the Spanish Ministry of Health published a strategic plan (Ministerio de Sanidad, 2004) where some actions to promote the sharing of information about medicines between the professionals in order to reduce the costs derived from the promotion and searching of information. A new nomenclature with more advanced features would be of great help to achieve this objective.

The main competitors in the Spanish case study are the current applications already available, as BOTPlus or vademecum on-line. These resources are the typical compendium of characteristics of the pharmaceutical products, but these applications not cover the lack of communication and integration of the information. In both cases, the tools are not free of charge, although some information and searches are publicly available in throughout the Web.

At Semantic Web technology level there are not real competitors in Spain or Europe. In the USA market, Snomed and UMLS are the most important vocabularies, largely used by the official entities in their applications. But the penetration on the European market and mainly in Spain is not significant.

COST AND BENEFITS

The Semantic Nomenclature focuses on a real domain with information heterogeneity problems that have direct economical impact on the pharmaceutical sector. The main result of the Semantic Nomenclature application is the Nomenclature network ontology. The potential of the Networked Ontologies would serve as a proof of concept for the pharmaceutical sector.

However, all the previously mentioned solution and technologies suffer some costs. Although the case study software will be delivered as open source, in order to develop a fully-fledged application, there will be several steps with associated costs.

Although much of the NeOn toolkit is free of licensing costs, there will be a number of engineering components and services that will be exceptions. At the present time, NeOn is a project in progress, so these issues will be further clarified during the duration of the project.

Also, just as the pharmaceutical sector and market evolve, the prototype should be customized for the real client needs. That would mean for instance review the requirements of the pharmacists, reengineer the network of ontologies, add new ontologies or create new software modules.

Another problem with this approach is that is needed some time for personnel training for ontology engineers, dedicated personnel to the management of the resources (finding new resources, rating information, reengineering the ontologies in case the systems evolves, etc.) and specially for end-users which are not related with the Semantic Web technologies.

In contrast, the Semantic Nomenclature provides some different benefits for the pharmaceutical scenario. The two main concepts of the solution provided for the scenario are integration of diverse systems together and interoperability of the information used by the different actors of the pharmaceutical sector. Networked Ontologies is the better way of dealing with information coming from multiple resources and allow to the actors develop and maintain their own heterogeneous models, mapping one to other, integrate and exchange information in a dynamic view. Moreover, this solution reduces costs for all stakeholders, against trying to solve their problems of integration with one of each of the other stakeholders separately.

Other benefit is that the Nomenclature Reference ontology will serve the purpose of bridging the gap between different classifications and nomenclatures. Instead of oblige everybody to follow the same vocabulary (with has proven to be difficult), the Semantic Nomenclature bridges the gap between vocabularies encompassing current and future resources.

Another important finding is the better and new semantic-based search facilities. Against other traditional types of searching mechanisms, the idea of "personalized search" actually requires semantic capabilities and provides facilities to build queries in natural language or similar.

Interestingly, the most striking result to emerge from this business scenario is that the Semantic Nomenclature prototype is a clear example of how to improve the process of updating a private stakeholder (GSCoP). This organization could keep their legacy system because it is described abstractly in an ontology, connecting it with other models, enable NeOn infrastructure and Semantic Nomenclature business prototype as a bridge between models and integration solution.

RISK ASSESSMENT

In this business scenario and solution, different types of risks need to be taken into account, including technological risks, resources risks and market and exploitation risks.

At technological level, NeOn should reach a wide technical community in order to enrich its platform and to be accepted as a good ontology development toolkit. Technology changes and evolves requiring redesign of NeOn architecture/ tools adapting the NeOn toolkit to them.

To take a stance against the market and exploitation risks, the Semantic Nomenclature must be presented in pharmaceutical events to create awareness to the solution and review the needs and requirements of the end-users in order to adapt them into the prototype. In this line, finding a client to test the solution is of great interest, although the risk is not as high as the previous ones. Also, we must take into account the GSCoP opinion about the difficulties sharing information and in the communication between the main actors in the pharmaceutical sector.

In this SWOT Analysis (Table 1) the strengths and weaknesses of the current Spanish pharmaceutical scenario in relation with the Semantic Nomenclature are depicted. This SWOT analysis has been conducted with respect to the foreseen NeOn technology innovations.

FUTURE TRENDS

According to Tim Berners-Lee – the inventor of the World Wide Web (WWW) – data integration is the Web´s next leap forward (Berners-Lee, 2007): "Progress towards better data integration will happen using the same basic technology that has made the World Wide Web so successful in the first place: *the link*. Nevertheless, the Semantic Web will derive its power through linking data instead of documents as the current Web does."

The current global business environment, which is evolving swiftly, brings to the different companies research and innovate new habits managing information in order to be more competitive.

According to these two premises, the use of semantics to classify meaningfully the information and to bridge the gap between the different representations that different stakeholders have is widely accepted. The Semantic Web provides tools and technologies (RDF, OWL, AJAX...) in order to facilitate the integration of distributed and heterogeneous sources.

The current situation in the lifecycle of Semantic Web applications, technologies and ontologies is anchored and need mature and dive into a new step more robust, where new methodologies and tools are supported and ready to be used by the community for the new challenges as integration tools. In this aspect, the NeOn project takes advantage and provides support in the lifecycle of the new generation of Semantic Web applications.

Nowadays, each company has their own legacy systems, databases, formats... and just as is described before, companies should integrate and share their knowledge with others in order to exploit their data. In order to facilitate these tasks, the Semantic Web community should provide mechanisms to structure some relevant unstructured information of companies (emails, reports, HTML...) or semi-structured (databases) that the companies manage in their work. Also, it will be useful provide to the end-users the possibility of reasoning over the aggregated information.

Other steps of the Semantic Web technology is provide augmentation of the information on the Web. With this feature, semantics provides more inference and automation on the decisions or steps done by computers inside business workflows. This will provide reduce the off-line human decisions and lead to faster overall completion of workflow. This results in saving money and greater productivity, and this is why "semantics" is important to business (Roth, 2007).

The solution presented in this chapter for the Spanish pharmaceutical sector, people from industry observes that Networked Ontologies are useful for dealing with heterogeneous and shared knowledge. Networked Ontologies adds a level of intelligence into the knowledge of the companies and provides to the end-users a new way of sharing and mapping knowledge with people in related activities.

Market predictions for knowledge technologies from companies like Gartner are based on

Table 1. Semantic Nomenclature SWOT analysis

	POSITIVE	NEGATIVE
INTERNAL	**Strengths** • No solution currently offers software that allows semantic interoperability of different pharmaceutical vocabularies. • BOTPlus is being developed and maintained by ATOS. This issue give us a good understanding of this tool, apart from the possibility of future interaction.	**Weaknesses** • No real client available. • The work to be done is too much for the time of the project. Simplification of the ontologies. • There are other non-semantic tools (BOTPlus, vademecum on-line) that offers reasonable functionality in the Spanish market. • The Nomenclature model has a slowly evolution, low frequency of changes.
EXTERNAL	**Opportunities** • The need of sharing information among stakeholders is clear and is fostered by the government action plans. • There is a clear need of improving the interoperability between drugs vocabulary. • A Semantic Nomenclature could be a very useful tool for the set of actors of this sector. • There is a good quantity of resources and legacy systems about pharmaceutical area, but in a few years are going to be more and more complex and specific in the pharmaceutical and health environment. • No semantic competitors in the Spanish market for this technology.	**Threats** • Semantic technology is not very well known by the stakeholders. • The complexity of the sector may derive in a difficult implementation in real stakeholders. • There is a governmental initiative for developing an integrated Nomenclature in Spain. It is not based on semantic technologies. • Failure of NeOn in delivering the promising technology • Not good Semantic Nomenclature Reference Ontology development • Lack of awareness: o Failure in dissemination and adoption of the NeOn technology. o Failure in the dissemination of the Semantic Nomenclature prototypes among the pharmaceutical stakeholders in Spain.

market pull, and assume the existence of mature technology. Nowadays, is depicted that the state of Semantic Web applications are not mature and at the early adopter stage focused on the knowledge management area. The challenge faced in the coming years is to "cross the chasm" to the early majority of the mainstream market, and extend the area to more business to business situations.

CONCLUSION

This chapter introduced the Semantic Nomenclature case study of the NeOn project as a solution to cover the profound lack of systematization for creating, maintaining and updating drug-related information in the Spanish pharmaceutical sector. The main contributions of the case study could be identified in different sides. The pharmaceutical scenario is a good test bed for the Networked Ontologies and their benefits against one large ontology.

In other hand, the main contribution of the Semantic Nomenclature is the development of a set of ontologies about the main drug information repositories and resources in the pharmaceutical Spanish sector, networked between them and also provides a Reference Ontology. Currently, there is no common model or significant development on ontologies of drugs in the Pharmaceutical sector in Spain. This reference model for the Semantic Nomenclature complements typical pharmaceutical compendium characteristics by giving flexible, extensible and reliable information about drugs to the users of the Pharmaceutical domain.

Semantic Nomenclature and NeOn technologies will contribute in several ways to solving the mentioned business problems in the Spanish pharmaceutical scenario. Through Networked Ontologies we hope to facilitate the consensus forming process required by such a large-scale initiative. With the technology provided, only partial consensus needs to be achieved; the rest would be automatically managed by the ontological infrastructure. Second, using automatic annotation and mapping techniques, we significantly reduce the cost of joining the initiative. We aim at zero cost for inclusion: any organization may join and maintain its actual information interchange format, while the technology takes care of mapping its internal format to the agreed-upon ontology network. And also, we will provide more added-value services as a news service and a better exploitation of the information stored in a distributed way in several repositories.

The main benefits expected when these large ontologies are created and networked are made their knowledge more robust and redundant, reasoning in order to obtain new aggregated knowledge, provide more functionalities and faster information to the customer.

The direction of the future work is to continue to develop the networked ontology model for the pharmaceutical scenario in Spain. A middleware to interact with the services provided by the NeOn toolkit will be developed, and services to the pharmaceutical sector will be delivered on top of it.

REFERENCES

Anatomical Therapeutic Chemical Classification System. (2007). Wikipedia, the free encyclopedia. Retrieved from http://en.wikipedia.org/wiki/Anatomical_Therapeutic_Chemical_Classification_System

Barrasa, J., Corcho, O., & Gomez-Perez, A. (2007). *R2O, an extensible and semantically database-to-ontology mapping language.*

Berneers-Lee, T. (2007). Welcome to the Semantic Web. *The Economist*, 21, The World in 2007, p. 146.

Cimiano, P., Haase, P., Heizmann, J., & Mantel, M. (2007). *ORAKEL: A portable Natural Language Interface to Knowledge Bases.*

College of American Pathologists. (2007). *SNOMED CT User Guide – January 2007 Release.* Retrieved August 7, 2007, from http://www.ihtsdo.org/fileadmin/user_upload/Docs_01/Technical_Docs/snomed_ct_user_guide.pdf

Domingue, J., Dzbor, M., & Motta E. (2004). *Magpie: Supporting Browsing and Navigation on the Semantic Web.*

Euzenat, J. (2007). MATChing ontologies for context. NeOn deliverable D3.3.1.

Fernandez, M., Gomez-Perez, A., & Juristo, N. (1997). METHONTOLOGY: From Ontological Art to Ontological Engineering. *Workshop on Ontological Engineering. Spring Symposium Series. AAAI'97.*

Fortuna, B., Grobelnik, M., & Mladenic, D. (2006). Semi-automatic Data-driven Ontology Construction System. In *Proceedings of the 9th International multi-conference Information Society IS-2006*, Ljubljana, Slovenia.

Gomez-Perez, A., & Suarez, M.C. (2008). NeOn methodology for building contextualized ontology networks. NeOn Deliverable D5.4.1.

Gómez-Pérez, J.M., Pariente, T., Daviaud, C., Herrero G. (2006). Analysis of the pharma domain and requirements. NeOn Deliverable D8.1.1.

Haase, P., Rudolph, S., Wang, Y., & Brockmans, S. (2006). Networked Ontology Model. NeOn Deliverable D1.1.1.

Jacobs, J., & Linden, A. (2002). Semantic Web Technologies Take Middleware to Next Level. Retrieved August 7, 2007 from http://www.gartner.com/DisplayDocument?doc_cd=109295

Kenter, T., & Maynard, D. (2005). Using Gate as an Annotation tool.

Ministerio de Sanidad. (2004). Plan estratégico de Política Farmacéutica para el Sistema Nacional de Salud Español. Retrieved August 7, 2007 from http://www.anisalud.com/ficheros/Plan.pdf

National Library of Medicine. (2007). MeSH factsheet. Retrieved August 7, 2007 from http://www.nlm.nih.gov/pubs/factsheets/mesh.html

National Library of Medicine. (2007). UMLS factsheet. Retrieved August 7, 2007 from http://www.nlm.nih.gov/pubs/factsheets/umls.html

Roth, B. (2007). Semantic Web the next big thing? Retrieved August 7, 2007 from http://www.web-2journal.com/read/407403.htm

Sabou, M. et al. (2006). NeOn Requirements and Vision Deliverable.

Studer, R., Benjamins R., & Fensel D. (1998). Knowledge engineering: principles and methods. *Data Knowledge Engineering*, 25, 161-197.

W3C. (2007). W3C and the Medical Sector. Retrieved August 7, 2007 from http://www.w3c.rl.ac.uk/QH/WP5/handouts/health_w3c.html

Waterfeld, W., & Weiten, M. (2007). Design of NeOn architecture. NeOn Deliverable D6.2.1.

ENDNOTES

1. NeOn Project, http://www.neon-project.org
2. WHO: World Health Organization, http://www.who.int
3. http://www.opengalen.org
4. http://www.opencyc.org
5. http://www.cancer.gov
6. AGEMED - Agencia Española de Medicamentos y Productos Sanitarios
7. http://www.anisalud.com/ficheros/Plan.pdf
8. http://ontoedit.com/content/index_eng.html
9. KAON 2 – Ontology Management for the Semantic Web http://kaon2.semanticweb.org

Chapter XV
Semantic Competence Pull: A Semantics-Based Architecture for Filling Competency Gaps in Organizations

Ricardo Colomo-Palacios
Universidad Carlos III de Madrid, Spain

Marcos Ruano-Mayoral
Universidad Carlos III de Madrid, Spain

Juan Miguel Gómez-Berbís
Universidad Carlos III de Madrid, Spain

Ángel García-Crespo
Universidad Carlos III de Madrid, Spain

ABSTRACT

Despite its considerable growth and development during the last decades, the software industry has had to endure several significant problems and drawbacks which have undoubtedly had negative effects. One of these aspects is the lack of alignment between the curricula offered by Universities and other kinds of education and training centres and the professional profiles demanded by companies and organizations. This problem defines the objective of this work: to provide a set of mechanisms and a solution to allow companies to define and express their competency gaps and, at the same time, allow education centres to analyse those gaps and define the training plans to meet those needs.

INTRODUCTION

The software industry has become one of the main streams of development all around the world. In Spain, the information technology market generated a volume of 17,716 million € in 2006, which represents an increase of 7.8% with respect to the market volume in 2005 (MITC, 2007). The information services submarket experienced the highest rate of increase at 10.5%, representing 4 975 million €, and the software market sector volume was 1,600 million € (MITC, 2007). Traditionally, the information technology market demonstrated an insufficient number of practitioners due to the increasing demand for information technology professionals. Nowadays, demand continues to be relevant but it has experienced a deceleration accompanied by the appearance of market niches with unstable demand rates. Due to the scarce barriers to entry for practitioners (Joseph, 2005) work teams are formed by people from many different educational backgrounds and with diverse academic levels and training profiles (McConnell, 2003): bachelor and master graduates in Computer Science, graduates in other disciplines, licensed practitioners and undergraduate and unlicensed practitioners. During the 1990s, the demand for IT professionals exceeded the supply of qualified persons for several years (Koong, Liu & Liu, 2002). In 1999, there were 722,158 unfilled IT jobs in the United States. It was predicted that the shortage would grow to about 846,901 jobs by 2002 (Goodwin, 2000). While it is true that the economy has slowed down since the last quarter of 2000, many companies are still hiring persons with critical IT skills while other workers are being laid off (Armour, 2001; Gladwin, 2001).

Additionally, the software industry has been characterized by a problem that was first identified at the beginning of the 1970s (Brooks, 1987). This problem is the inability to finish and deliver software products within the established time schedule, and not being able to remain within the planned budget, and was referred to as the 'software crisis' (Nauer, 1969). Latter analyses of the problem and the related literature have confirmed the clear difficulty in building software (Brooks, 1987) and have redefined the crisis as a breakdown or a chronic disease (Gibbs, 1994). Several key elements have been established to combat the effects of the crisis (Pressman, 2005): Project, Product, Development process and Personnel. Regarding the latter, human factors, considered by many authors as *Peopleware* (DeMarco, 1987), are proving as crucial aspects in the field of software development.

Boehm (1981) points out that subsequent to the size of the product, personnel factors have the most important influence on the total effort necessary for the development of a software project, and that personnel characteristics and human resources related activities constitute the most relevant source of opportunities for improving software development (Boehm, 2000). On the same issue, some other authors state that inadequate competence verification of software engineers is one of the principal problems when it comes to carrying out any software development project (McConnell, 2003).

In the information and communications technologies (ICT) field, software is a critical element. Failure rates associated with software projects are really high, and the personnel included in software development teams is one of the most decisive aspects for projects and their deficiencies (Pressman, 2005). The teams should be comprised of practitioners having heterogeneous education and experience (McConnell, 2003) and human resources management systems should be easily able to identify and assess the engineers' professional training with the objective of improving the workforce's competence level (Curtis, 2001).

Current Labour Market Situation

This section presents both the current situation and the evolution of the labour market from the point of view of the demand for practitioners and their competency profiles. Historically, employment in the field of Information Technologies has been impacted by several crises such as the bankruptcy of *dotcom* companies, the delays in the adoption of new technologies and the worldwide economical crisis (Zamorano, 2003). These circumstances lead to a wave of dismissals and factory closures (Zamorano, 2003) and to an intense modification of the competences demanded in practitioners. The volume of the workforce required and the reorganization of labour markets define a constantly changing environment shifting towards an increase of the competency level. This consequently instigates a deceleration of the increase in salaries (Mallet, 1997), which forces the practitioners to improve their education and training.

Historically, the professional environment in the Information Technologies labour market has been characterized by a strong lack of qualified practitioners (Casanovas, 2004). In 2003, according to AETIC (Asociación de Empresas de Electrónica, Tecnologías de la Información y Telecomunicaciones, Spanish Association of Electronics, Information Technologies and Telecommunications Companies), the ICT market grew 6%, up to a volume of 75,818 million €. However, direct employment in the sector showed a recession of 4.1% and there was an 8,000 reduction in the number of jobs (Ruiz, 2004). In 2004 the ICT market grew 9% up to 82,535 million € (MITC, 2005); and direct employment displayed an increase, however, the growth was trivial. The contribution of the ICT sector to production in that year represented 11.811 million €, growing 4.7%. This indicates that the sector underwent a smaller growth compared to the overall activity in Spain, whose GDP was 6.6%. These figures, viewed in the international economic context, show that the ICT sector in Spain rather grows at a higher rate than the European average (2.8%), although at an inadequate pace for conformance with the convergence plans for the relevance of the sector in the European economy.

An overview of the current situation of labour markets is provided by the RENTIC report (Fernández, 2002). This report shows the results obtained from an analysis of the job vacancies in ICT sector published in relevant Spanish newspapers. The analysis was focused on the specific ICT knowledge profile required in the offers, as well as some other complementary requirements such as languages, degree, and behaviour competences. The study was carried out using 249 published job offers. Such a reduced data population does not allow a detailed analysis of its conclusions, but it should be noted that the relevance granted by the study to 'personal competences' is a reflection of the general (De Ansorena, 1996) or generic (González & Wagenaar, 2003) competences required. The report concludes that there is an evident interest on hiring personnel with both technical and general competences, and a requirement for education and training centres to meet companies' requests. Lastly, the author remarks that there is an insufficient description of competences in the curriculums of candidates.

Some of the conclusions provided by the RENTIC report show latent similarities with the analysis provided by the Bureau of Labor Statistics. This report discusses the tendency of hiring IT practitioners with strong technical, interpersonal and business skills in a labour market in which software engineering is projected to be one of the fastest-growing occupations from 2004 to 2014 (Bureau of Labor Statistics, 2006). This scene should result in very good opportunities for those college graduates with at least a bachelor's degree in computer engineering or computer science.

Another significant trend with implications in both the business and labour market is the two-way flow of foreign project contracts and software-skilled immigrants. On the one hand, firms may aim to cut costs by shifting operations to lower wage foreign countries with highly educated workers who have strong technical skills (Bureau of Labor Statistics, 2006). On the other hand, countries like India, where about 100,000 English-speaking software professionals graduate per year, can be a source of practitioners to compensate for the lack of qualified resources in developed countries.

In short, the labour market situation for ICT, and particularly Software Engineering, situation is significantly changing. Additionally, this knowledge area shows an extremely rapid evolution: its knowledge doubles every three years, and competences have a mean lifetime of two and a half years (Ang, 2000). The proliferation of new areas will continue to grow from rapidly evolving technologies such as e-commerce, WWW applications, cyber security, mobile technologies, and wireless networks, among others (Bureau of Labor Statistics, 2006). The combination of these two facts forces practitioners to retrain almost constantly and, thus, organizations must implement mechanisms to measure the evolution of the competences of their personnel, and establish policies to allow the monitoring of the evolution of recently acquired competences.

Problem Statement

In the previous sections, a labour market situation has been described which indicates a clear misalignment between the demand for qualified staff and supply of college graduates. Organizations require either the hiring of skilled practitioners, or the training of their personnel in order to comply with business changes, improve productivity or start new projects. Moreover, traditional education channels are slow and rarely specific; there is no connection between the organisation's needs and the educational content, and if a connection exists, its effects are trivial (McConnell, 2003).

The lack of specification with respect to defining and fulfilment of professional careers can hinder the adaptation of graduates' professional competencies to the requests of labour markets. This circumstance is threatening countries' prosperity (Career Space, 2001) and is forcing organizations to create and finance "Corporate Universities" (Casanovas, Colom, Morlán, Pont & Sancho, 2004). This not only delays the incorporation of professionals to development projects, but also implies an increase in costs for organizations.

Considering this scenario, corporate universities are not the solution, since they combine the characteristics of both businesses and educational centres, and they are usually created and based upon non formal contacts between organizations. Moreover, according to the point of view of LifeLong learning, "enterprises need lifelong learning – that is, studies that one pursues during life and particularly during one's working career. It includes basic education, further and continuous education, graduate and postgraduate studies, work/job-related and general studies, and a general interest in trying to understand the evolution of society and of work. Lifelong learning is a way to update and upgrade competence systematically; in fact, it is a form of "human recycling", especially in situations where employees move from one job to another (Otala, 1994, pp. 13).

The integration of the concepts of a pull strategy and LifeLong learning allows the creation of a solution to the problem described in this work, with which organizations will be able to fulfil their competency gaps. At the same time, it will allow professionals to follow a progressive development of their competences during their careers and adapt this development to specific market and emerging requirements as fast and precisely as possible.

PROPOSED SOLUTION

This section presents a novel and promising architecture that applies and takes advantage of the best capabilities of semantics in the field of competence management. The objectives of the research and an overview of the architecture will be discussed.

Objectives

Semantic Competence Pull has been defined as one main objective, which is comprised of a set of inherent sub objectives. The main objective is to minimize the misalignment between educational centres and organizations' competency needs by determining competency gaps in the organizations, defining the training plan to fill in those gaps, and thus identifying the necessary personnel with the required competency profile.

In order to fulfill this objective, organizations should be able to express and define their professional profiles and competency needs by means of a unified mechanism, and training centres and education systems should be able to define the profiles of their graduates in an equivalent way.

Another interesting objective is the implementation of a mechanism to allow the exchange of information between both organizations and training centres so that they can establish a fluent and productive communication.

Overview

An overview of *Semantic Competence Pull* is presented in Figure 1. The figure shows organizations which represent any enterprise or company with competency gaps in their personnel. These gaps can originate from market or technology changes, new business lines, new commercial relationships, or other economic or business factors. By means of a description based on competences, the organizations express their needs in terms of training current workers or hiring trained professionals. On the other side of the system, *Semantic Competence Pull* allows education and training centres to analyse the gaps existing in the organizations and consequently determine, or design if necessary, the training plans constructed to fulfil the competency requirements of the organizations.

The next section provides a detailed definition of the components of *Semantic Competence Pull* that permit the implementation of the aforementioned functions.

SOLUTION DETAILS

In this section, we present a novel and promising architecture and a set of algorithms to provide a potential solution to the situation depicted in the previous section. We propose a tailor-made value-adding technological solution which addresses the aforementioned challenges and solves the integration problem with respect to searching, finding, and integrating heterogeneous sources through semantic technologies.

Figure 1. Semantic competence pull overview

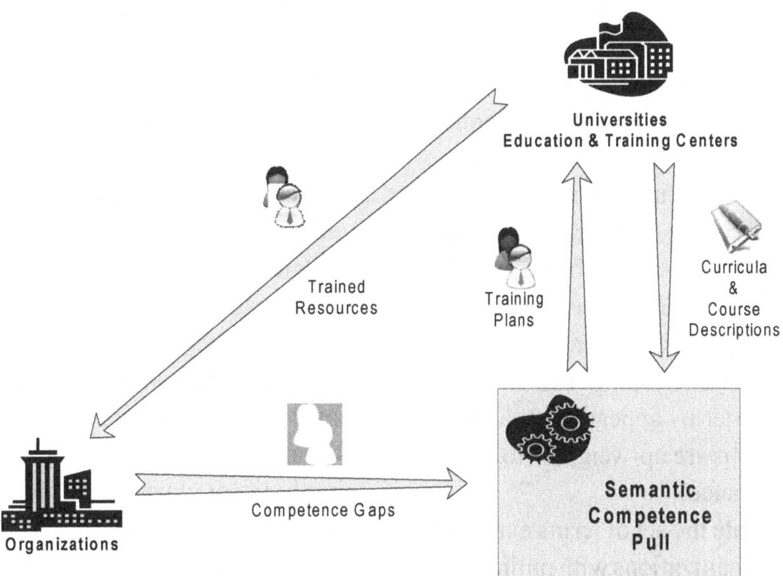

Knowledge-Extraction Algorithms

First of all, we propose the application of a set of algorithms and knowledge extraction techniques to the various sources of information, where we obtain the semantic descriptions of each and every organization involved. These algorithms are usually applied in Information Retrieval, so their use in this domain is a novel contribution of the work presented. The first algorithm is the Vector Space Model (Salton, Wong & Yang, 1975), an algebraic model used for information filtering, information retrieval, indexing and relevancy rankings. It represents natural language documents (or any objects, in general) in a formal manner through the use of vectors (of identifiers, such as, for example, index terms) in a multi-dimensional linear space. Documents are represented as vectors of index terms (keywords). The set of terms is a predefined collection of terms, for example the set of all unique words occurring in the document corpus. Relevancy rankings of documents in a keyword search can be calculated, using the assumptions of document similarities theory, by comparing the deviation of angles between each document vector and the original query vector, where the query is represented as the same type of vector as the documents. The second algorithm applies Latent Semantic Analysis (LSA) (Deerwester, Dumais, Furnas, Landauer & Harshman, 1990), an algorithm for analyzing relationships between a set of documents and the terms they contain by producing a set of concepts related to the documents and terms. LSA uses a term-document matrix which describes the occurrences of terms in documents. A typical example of the weighting of the elements of the matrix is the TF-IDF (Term Frequency–Inverse Document Frequency): the element of the matrix is proportional to the number of times the terms appear in each document, where rare terms are up-weighted to reflect their relative importance.

Finally, we validate the set of terms extracted from the different organizations with online lexical resources, such as Wordnet. Dictionaries are generally considered as a valuable and reliable source containing information about the relationships among terms (e.g. synonyms). Also, Wordnet can add conceptual meaning to the tags, and there is an RDF transcript available.

Functional Architecture

Competency gaps can be expressed as a set of instances, belonging to a particular organization whereby the organization to which it belongs to and the role it plays are clearly defined in a specific ontology. Each role has a particular policy (or policies). A Policy (P) represents a conceptual feature reserved for each role in a community and expressed through a set of Rules ($R_1,R_2,...,R_n$). Essentially a Rule is a function that takes an access request as input and results in an action (permit, deny or not-applicable). A rule is composed of the triple Subject (S), Resource (R) and Action (A) that must be fulfilled for a rule to apply to a given request. In the proposed conceptualization, Subjects are the identities that play specific Roles such as project leader, IT Supervisors, Customer Relationship Management (CRM) expert and sales manager. A resource is the organizations' training resources such as deliverables, documents etc. So, the Rule is simplified as:

$$R = \{S,R,A\}$$

If "Mark Maedche" is an expert on formal methods for software validation and verification and a particular organization is interested in this knowledge, he might be subject of a training "call for experts" of that organization. Rules are then defined by means of Subject ("Mark Maedche"), Resource ("Software V&V expertise") and Action ("Call for Experts"). Obviously, Policies are defined over the Rule, so an organization could simply list or cluster a number of organizational competences of interest. These Policies will imply a set of Rules that can be inferred by means of an underlying logical formalism.

The framework presented would not have any real use if the inference capability of the framework were not taken into account. Defining the needs of an organisation according to Policies and Rules encapsulates a body of knowledge which represents the structure of the requirements of the organisation. Thus, further knowledge can be inferred from the established relationships to describe both the organisation and the application of the knowledge. Languages defined for providing Semantics give great support for reasoning properties, since when they were defined, requisites were established to guarantee enough expressive power and reasoning support. Any ontology language for Semantic Web is based on formal semantics, which means that the ontologies semantics defined by the language are not influenced by either subjective intuitions or open interpretations (Antoniou & Van Harmelen, 2004). This has particular relevance to mathematical logic, since it allows one-way inference from the knowledge expressed in a non explicit manner.

The ontologies inference capacity also allows the identification of any instance with a class although it is not directly declared in it. For instance, if an employee has hierarchical relationships with other employees, we can deduce that he is a boss. In summary, automatic reasoning allows the verification of more cases that can be checked manually, since it evaluates all the ontology singularities and the characteristics declared in it. Consequently, the framework domain can establish relationships which are a closer representation of the real organization based on logical relationships. Unfortunately, an ontology language's inference capacity and its expressivity are two divergent questions. The greater the expressive capacity of the language, the less inference, since the computationality cannot be guaranteed. Because of this, OWL language (W3C, OWL Web Ontology Language Overview, 2004), nowadays the most widespread ontology Semantic Web language, offers three language versions that differ in their expressivity capacity: OWL Full, OWL DL and OWL Lite. OWL can be considered as being comprised of three sub-languages with increasing expressivity capacities (Gasevic, Djuric, & Devedzic, 2006). OWL Lite gives support to hierarchical constructions and simple restrictions. However, OWL DL offers maximum expressivity, based on Description Logics that can guarantee the ontologies computability, which means that it can be processed in a finite time. OWL Full offers maximum possible expressivity, based on First-Order-Logic, and a syntactic freedom, however, it does not guarantee ontology computability nor decidability.

In the present context, the maximum expressivity capacities are intended since we need an ontology which most closely reflects the real world. In contrast, inference capacities cannot be affected since they are highly needed to infer privileges. Due to the inference restrictions of OWL Full, it has to be discarded, OWL Lite is also discarded since it places too many limitations on the expressivity of ontologies. However, OWL DL offers enough expressive power, guaranteeing the inference capacity for the framework.

The ontology languages expressivity shows inherent limitations due to their tree-like structure. Some logic suppositions cannot be inferred natively; for example, if a person has a brother and a son, the uncle-nephew relationship cannot be inferred. This limitation is solved by applying horn logic languages on top of ontologies. Horn Logic languages are Rule-like languages where knowledge is defined by:

$$A_1,\dots,A_n \rightarrow B$$

where $\{A_i$ and $B\}$ are atomic formulas that can understood as, if $\{A_1 \dots A_n\}$ are true, then B is also true. These languages are the perfect complement to the logic offered by ontology languages. Horn Logic and Predicate Logic are orthogonal between them, which means that none of the logics is subset of the other. Languages based on Horn Logic have been defined to lie on an upper layer of ontology languages, integrating both expressivity and reasoning power. However, the decidability guarantee in Horn Logic languages needs to impose some restrictions on its expressiveness (W3C, SWRL: A Semantic Web Rule Language, 2004) and adds some additional complexity to the framework.

In this section, a logics-based knowledge-enriched functional architecture has been outlined, which fully supports formally the approach and conceptual model for the *Semantic Competence Pull*. In the following section, the actual software architecture underlying the functional architecture will be discussed.

Software Architecture

Our architecture is a service oriented architecture (SOA), which is a software system consisting of a set of collaborating software components with well-defined interfaces that combined perform a task. These components may be distributed and executed in different network locations, connected through different communication protocols. Also, these components can be plugged-in and plugged-out from the system. The *Semantic Competence Pull* Architecture is composed by a number of components depicted in Figure 2. These components will now be described:

- **Competence-oriented semantic descriptions:** Competences are stored by means of semantic descriptions, which are based on the fundamental traits of the competencies. Particularly, Policies and Rules originating from the different organizations.
- **RDF repository:** The RDF repository is a semantic data store system that allows semantic querying and offers a higher abstraction layer to enable fast storage and retrieval of large amounts of RDF, while maintaining a lightweight architecture approach. An example of such a system is the OpenRDF Sesame RDF Storage system (Open RDF Sesame, http://www.openrdf.org), which deals with data integration. The advantages of using RDF as a "lightweight" ontology language partially rely on Faceted Search and Browsing techniques. These techniques will be analyzed at the end of this section.
- **GUI:** This is the component that interacts with the user. It collects the users request and presents the results obtained. In our particular architecture, the GUI will collect requests pertaining to search criteria, such as, for example, "competences related to Information Systems". The GUI communicates with the Manager component providing the user request and displays the results provided as a response from the Manager component.

Figure 2. Semantic competence pull architecture

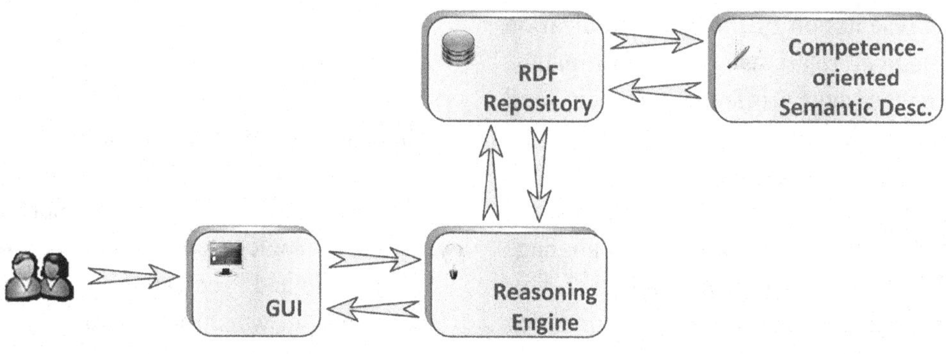

- **Reasoning engine:** The Reasoning Engine component uses Description Logics, which can guarantee the ontologies computability. As previously stated, this allows the processing of queries in a finite time. The selected reasoning engine is Pellet, a Java-based DL reasoning engine.

The workflow of the different components of the architecture is supported by the Functional Architecture described in the previous sections. Fundamentally, organizations define their core competencies using the Policies, Rules and Subject (S), Resource (R), Action (A) model. These descriptions can be extracted using the knowledge-extraction set of algorithms depicted previously, and they are stored by means of semantics in the Storage Component. Organizations interested in bridging their competencies gap can browse and search (by means of faceted search or browse or structured search, for example) the competencies of their organizations using *Semantic Competence Pull*. Since their needs in terms of competencies are also defined using the Policies- Rules model, inference serves as a basis for recommendation, and the *Semantic Competence Pull* provides a well-defined architecture providing matching functionality.

Example: Using Semantic Competence Pull

Finally, we would like to illustrate the use of *Semantic Competence Pull* with a real-world case study scenario which demonstrates the breakthroughs of our system. Enterprise Inc. needs to fill twenty Software Engineering positions. The profile of the required professionals must include expertise in the Software Engineering Management knowledge area of SWEBOK (Abran & Moore, 2004). The competence level of the professionals should be above the level specified by SWEBOK for software engineers having four years of experience. Given this situation, Enterprise Inc. establishes a complete competence description of the desired professional profile, paying special attention to the competency gap existing in Software Engineering Management, and more specifically in Software Process Planning. This necessity is defined by means of *Semantic Competence Pull.* The system would perform a careful analysis of the competency profile to determine, in this case, that professionals with a specific undergraduate level in Software Process Planning are required. The next step is a search in the system's repository to retrieve those courses with competence specifications equivalent to those demanded by Enterprise Inc. At this point there are two possible situations: there are courses matching the established criteria or there are not. In the first case, the system would return the list of retrieved courses, so that education and training centres could satisfy the competency needs, contributing professionals which match the desired requirements. In the latter case, *Semantic Competence Evaluation* would propose the description of a specific course to the training centres. Upon receiving the request, those centres interested in teaching the course and having the necessary personnel, would design and implement the course, would enrol students fulfilling the aforementioned requirements, and the correct termination of the course would be contingent upon the subsequent hiring of the professionals by Enterprise Inc.

ALTERNATIVES

Semantic Competence Pull confronts the problem of competency gaps by providing organizations with specifically trained practitioners to make up for their lack of competences in certain areas. Thus, the solution offered to solve the problem is unique and innovative. However, there are other alternatives to deal with these kinds of situations or similar ones. A set of possible alternatives is presented in this section.

One of the most relevant solutions to produce professionals which conform perfectly to companies' needs is the creation of tailored and specific degrees by means of joint ventures between academic institutions and the companies. The degrees are usually an adaptation of official or widespread degrees which include some tracks or sets of elective courses designed and given by the companies and that include those areas and topics of interest to them. These kinds of educational solutions can only be afforded by relevant companies which periodically need large groups of people with a certain profile. Additionally, if the designed degree is very distinct from the official one it may cause accreditation problems to graduates, with consequent loss of interest in the course.

Some companies opt for the creation of their own corporate universities. In this way they can design, establish and implement the training plans they consider necessary. Similar to the previous alternative, this solution can only be afforded by large corporations. Even so, the construction of the necessary structures to finance the school signifies a major economic and investment effort for the companies, which may make it highly unprofitable. Corporate Universities have been subjected to numerous studies and have received considerable investments since the foundation of Disney University (Solomon, 1989). The importance of this phenomenon is highlighted by specific studies carried out in the USA (Prince & Stewart, 2002), China (Sham, 2007), Germany (Andresen & Lichtenberger, 2007) and worldwide (Holland & Pyman, 2006). The Universities-Companies collaboration has been identified as one of the key factors for business development regardless as full integration or achieved by the new capacities provided by the Internet (Hilse & Nicolai, 2004).

Another possibility for the integration of hiring and training processes is the creation of a new generation of employment positions from the adaptation of currently existing ones, for example, those offered by Monster, among others. The offer of these portals should be an aggregation of job positions and the training options that candidates should follow to improve their fit to the positions and, hence, increase the probability of being hired. Dixon (2000), pointed out that generally, e-recruiters come in two varieties: corporate recruiters and third-party recruiters. Third-party recruiters do not restrict the types of jobs posted by the employers or select specific job seekers résumés. They function as a centre for all sorts of employment. Niche recruiters which focus on smaller market segments are aimed towards more specialised types of employment. However, the major players are the executive recruiters, high-tech recruiters, and medical recruiters.

One common characteristic of the solutions presented so far, including *Semantic Competence Pull*, is that all of them seek the incorporation of new human resources to the organization. Nevertheless, in order to meet companies' competency needs, it may not be necessary to contract additional practitioners. This is the approach proposed by *Prolink* (Gómez-Berbís, Colomo-Palacios, Ruiz-Mezcua & García-Crespo, 2008), which considers the creation of a social network with semantic characteristics to share and reuse knowledge, expertise and lessons learned from previously conducted projects.

COST AND BENEFITS

This section presents an overview of the costs associated with the implementation of the *Semantic Competence Pull* solution. The cost analysis has been performed taking into account development, infrastructure, operation and maintenance costs.

Due to the size of the problem, the development costs have been estimated to be similar to an average COCOMO II project (Boehm et al., 2000) with a temporal cost of 14,500 man-hours.

This cost can be assumed as a differential cost of implementing the solution.

Infrastructure and operation costs of adopting *Semantic Competence Pull* could be integrated into the current infrastructure and operation costs, because the solution could be added to the existing structure of the organisation. The only requirement with respect to infrastructure is that the solution should be accessible via Web, and the connection should have enough capacity to withstand the traffic generated by the system.

Maintenance tasks for *Semantic Competence Pull* entail a significant human cost. There should be personnel dedicated to the addition, modification and maintenance of the information processed within the system. This information includes professional profiles, course plans, competence descriptions and needs, etc., and the tasks should be performed at both sides of the solution: the organizations as well as the training and education centres.

In summary, the economic costs for implementing and adopting *Semantic Competence Pull* are not significantly excessive. However the adoption of such a solution must be accompanied by a modification of the traditional way of working in the organizations and the educational bodies, mainly because of the adaptation of the current profiles and requirements for the competency paradigm.

RISK ASSESSMENT

A risk analysis of the implementation and adoption of *Semantic Competence Pull* has been made by means of a SWOT analysis.

The strengths of the solution stem from the combination of two solid foundations. On the one hand, the application of the most novel academic recommendations which focus their efforts on the definition of professional profiles, academic degrees and training plans in terms of competences; and which are fully aligned with the emerging standardised educational framework in Europe. On the other hand, the adaptation of a set of widespread standards and tools (HR-XML, OpenRDF Sesame, YARS, Semantic Web…) that perfectly complement the architecture contribute to the construction of this solution.

When considering those aspects which might hinder the successful implantation of *Semantic Competence Pull*, two features should be outlined. The first one is the possible inability of the organizations to express and define professional roles and needs in terms of competences. This fact implies a profound change in the traditional structure of those organizations which have historically defined their needs according to legacy, stovepipe frameworks. In other words, defining competences in a static way, without their integration into the IT infrastructure of the organisation. The second issue is representative of the same weakness, but on the academic supply side. Universities and official education centres must adopt the competency paradigm into their models because of the standardisation of the European Higher Education Area. Non-official private centres should adopt the aforementioned paradigm in order to be able to use *Semantic Competence Pull*.

Undoubtedly, the implantation of *Semantic Competence Pull* can take advantage of the current economic situation which promotes a buoyant labour market which will welcome the solution presented in this research. Moreover, the novelty of *Semantic Competence Pull*, in terms of technology and methodology, must be definitely considered as a positive aspect. Lastly, the intensive increase in the utilization of Internet and Semantic Web technologies paves the way for the globalization of the resources.

Finally, two closely related threats to *Semantic Competence Pull* should be discussed. The first one is the evident shortage of training and education in the Information Technologies market, which is directly linked to the lack of consciousness of IT practitioners with respect to continuous improvement, education and training.

The risk assessment performed in this section is summarized in Figure 3.

FUTURE RESEARCH DIRECTIONS

The definition of new academic initiatives for university degrees incorporating competences descriptions has been a widespread trend across Europe since the advent of the European Higher Education Area. According to the guidelines established by the European directive and the academic initiatives sponsored by the IEEE/ACM joint initiative, the creation of undergraduate and master university degrees oriented to the verification of semantic scenarios such as those presented in this work have been proposed.

Secondly, it would be interesting to define and create career paths incorporating specific suggestions with regard to competency levels and the necessary courses and accreditations to reach all the defined levels. According to McConnell (2003), organizations currently do not provide career paths for ICT workers and Software Engineers. However, this aspect has proven to be a characteristic feature of mature professions (Ford & Gibbs, 1996).

Taking into account previous works on Competence Management, from the perspective of either ontology creation (Sicilia, 2005), the construction of integrated systems for specific organizations (Lindgren, Stenmark & Ljungberg, 2003), or their exchange among isolated systems via HR-XML, the definition and development of competences must be performed not only following their verification for a specific position or project, but should enrich learning organizations in an strategic way, providing a sound basis upon which to build a long term competitive advantage. This competitive advantage is achieved, in the case of the cited works, by means of the classification and management of the competences in organizations and, in the case of our work, by the collaboration between the providers and receivers of knowledge and those who harness it.

CONCLUSION

Semantic Competence Pull, the technological solution introduced in this chapter represents a tailor-made value adding contribution aimed to the fulfilment of competency gaps in organizations, encompassing the distinctive features of semantic technologies.

Figure 3. SWOT analysis

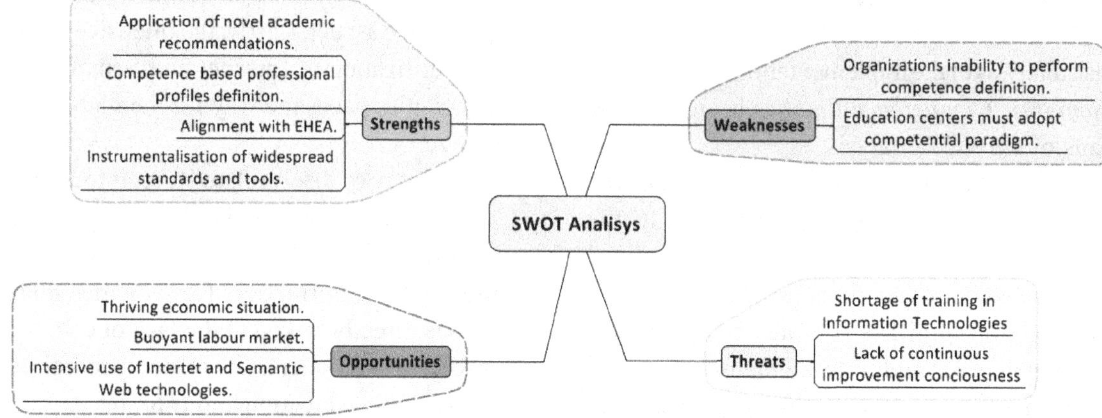

The solution comprises the software architecture of an information system supporting this solution. The main contribution of *Semantic Competence Pull* is the integration of a novel and promising architecture and the concept of real-time alignment of the necessities of companies with the possibilities of training professionals in education centres. The main objective of the presented solution is to fulfil competency needs in the fastest and most precise way as possible; which subsequently reduces the elapsed time for the incorporation of new subjects and courses to curricula. This is particularly interesting at master and specialization courses level because it increases the knowledge that training centres have about companies' requirements. On the other hand, *Semantic Competence Pull* exhibits an evident drawback due to the fact that its implantation could imply a profound modification in the stakeholders' way of working. Nevertheless, the significant benefits that it can produce for all parties identify it as an attractive solution to be adopted and supported.

REFERENCES

Abran, A. & Moore, J.W. (2004). *Guide to the Software Engineering Body of Knowledge*: 2004 Version. IEEE Computer Society Press.

Andresen, M. & Lichtenberger, B. (2007). The corporate university landscape in Germany. *Journal of Workplace Learning* Vol. 19 (2) (pp. 109-123).

Ang, S. & Slaughter, S. (2000). The Missing Context of Information Technology Personnel: A Review and Future Directions for Research. In: Zmud, R.W. (Ed.), *Framing the Domains of IT Management: Projecting the Future through the Past.* Pinnaflex Educational Resources, Cincinnati, Ohio.

Antoniou, G. & Van Harmelen, F. (2004). *A Semantic Web Primer.* MIT Press.

Armour, S. (2001). Companies Hire Even As They Lay Off. *USA Today.* May 15, A1.

Bureau of Labor Statistics. (Ed.). (2006). Computer Software Engineers. *Occupational Outlook Handbook, 2006-07 Edition.* U.S. Department of Labor. Retrieved August 01, 2007 from http://www.bls.gov/oco/ocos267.htm.

Boehm, B. W. (1981). *Software Engineering Economics.* Prentice Hall, Englewood Cliffs, New Jersey.

Boehm, B.W., Horowitz, E., Madachy, R., Reifer, D., Clark, B.K., Steece, B., Brown, A.W., Chulani, S. & Abts, C. (2000). *Software Cost Estimation with COCOMO II.* Prentice Hall, Upper Saddle River, New Jersey.

Brooks, F.P. (1987). No Silver Bullet: Essence and Accidents of Software Engineering. *Computer.* 20 (4), 10-19.

Career Space (Ed.). (2001). *Directrices para el desarrollo curricular. Nuevos currículos de TIC para el siglo XXI: el diseño de la educación del mañana.* International Co-operation Europe Ltd, Luxembourg.

Casanovas, J, Colom, J.M., Morlán, I., Pont, A. & Sancho, M.R. (2004). *Libro Blanco sobre las titulaciones universitarias de informática en el nuevo espacio europeo de educación superior.* Proyecto Eice, ANECA.

Curtis, B., Hefley, W. E. & Miller, S. A. (2001). *People Capability Maturity Model (P-CMM®) Version 2.0.* CMU/SEI-2001-MM-01.

De Ansorena, A. (1996). *15 pasos para la selección de personal con éxito. Métodos e instrumentos.* Paidos, Barcelona.

Deerwester, S. Dumais, Furnas, G. W. Landauer, T. K. Harshman, R. (1990). Indexing by Latent Semantic Analysis. *Journal of the Society for Information Science*, Vol. 41 (6). (pp 391-407).

DeMarco, T & Lister, T. R. (1987). *Peopleware: Productive Projects and Teams.* Dorset House, New York.

Dixon, P. (2000). *Job Searching Online for Dummies.* IDG Books Worldwide Inc., Boston, MA.

Fernández Sanz, F. (2002). *Estudio de la oferta de empleo en Nuevas Tecnologías de la Información y de las Comunicaciones.* Requisitos para el empleo. Universidad Europea de Madrid.

Ford, G., Gibbs, N.E. (1996). *A Mature Profession of Software Engineering.* Software Engineering Institute, Technical Report CMU/SEI-96-TR-004 ESC-TR-96-004.

Gaaevic, D., Djuric, D., Devedzic, V. & Selic, B. (2006). *Model Driven Architecture and Ontology Development.* Springer-Verlag.

Gladwin, L. (2001). Dot-Com Bust A Mixed Bag for IT Staffing. *Computerworld* (39), May 7, p. 38.

Gibbs, W. (1994). Software's Chronic Crisis. *Scientific American*, Vol. 271 (3) (pp. 72-81).

Gomez, J.M., Colomo Palacios, R., Ruiz Mezcua, B. & García Crespo, A. (2008). ProLink: A Semantics-based Social Network for Software Project. *International Journal of Information Technology and Management*, Vol.7(4) (pp. 392 - 404).

González, J. & Wagenaar, R. (2003). *Tuning Educational Structures in Europe.* Universidad de Deusto. Bilbao.

Goodwin, B. (2000). Government Slashes Red Tape to Let in Overseas IT Workers. *Computer Weekly*, May 11.

Harth, A. & Decker, S. (2005). Optimized Index Structures for Querying RDF from the Web. *Proceedings of the 3rd Latin American Web Congress.*

Hilse, H., Nicolai, A.T. (2004). Strategic learning in Germany's largest companies: empirical evidence on the role of corporate universities within strategy processes. *Journal of Management Development,* Vol. 23 (4) (pp.374-400).

Holland, P. & Pyman, A. (2006). Corporate universities: a catalyst for strategic human resource development? *Journal of European Industrial Training,* Vol. 30 (1) (pp. 19-31).

Joseph, D., Ang, S. & Slaughter, S. (2005). Identifying the prototypical career paths of IT professionals: a sequence and cluster analysis. *Proceedings of the 2005 ACM SIGMIS CPR Conference on Computer Personnel Research* (pp. 94-96).

Koong, K.S. and Liu, L.C. and Liu, X. (2002). A Study of the Demand for Information Technology Professionals in Selected Internet Job Portals. *Journal of Information Systems Education.* Vol. 13 (1) (pp. 21-28).

Lindgren, R., Stenmark, D., & Ljungberg, J. (2003). Rethinking competence systems for knowledge-based organizations. *European Journal of Information Systems*, Vol. 12(1) (pp. 18-29).

Mallet, L. (1997). *Títulos y Mercado de trabajo: resultados y cuestiones.* Ágora de Salónica. CEDEFOP.

Ministerio de Industria, Turismo y Comercio (MITC). (2005). *Gabinete de prensa.*

Ministerio de Industria, Turismo y Comercio (MITC). (2007). *Las tecnologías de la información en España, 2006.* Centro de Publicaciones.

McConnell, S. (2003). *Professional Software Development.* Addison-Wesley, Boston.

Nauer, P. & Randall, B. (Eds.). (1969). *Software Engineering.* NATO Scientific Affairs Division, Brussels.

Otala, L. (1994). Industry-University Partnership: Implementing Lifelong Learning. *Journal of European Industrial Training*, Vol. 18 (8) (pp. 13-18).

Pressman, R.S. (2005). *Software Engineering: A practitioner's approach*. McGraw Hill, 6th edition, New York.

Prince, C. and Stewart, J. (2002). Corporate universities – an analytical framework. *Journal of Management Development*, Vol. 21(10) (pp. 794-811).

Prud'hommeaux, E. & Seaborne, A. (2004). *SPARQL Query Language for RDF*. World Wide Web Consortium.

Ruiz Antón, F. (in press). (2004). *La Gaceta de los negocios*.

Salton, G. Wong, A. and Yang, C. S. (1975). A Vector Space Model for Automatic Indexing. *Communications of the ACM*, Vol. 18(11) (pp 613–620).

Sham, C. (2007). An exploratory study of corporate universities in China. *Journal of Workplace Learning*, Vol. 19 (4) (pp. 257-264).

Sicilia, M. A. (2005). Ontology-based competency management: Infrastructures for the knowledge- intensive learning organization. In M. D. Lytras and A.Naeve (Eds.), *Intelligent learning infrastructures in knowledge intensive organizations: A Semantic Web perspective* (pp. 302-324). Hershey, PA: Idea Group.

Solomon, C.M. (1989). How does Disney do it? Personnel Journal, Vol. 68(12) (pp. 50-57).

Yee, K. P, Swearingen, K., Li, K. & Hearst, M. (2003). Faceted metadata for image search and browsing. In *Proceedings of the ACM SIGCHI Conference on Human Factors in Computing Systems* (CHI '03), Fort Lauderdale, FL, USA, April 5 – 10. New York. ACM Press.

Zamorano, P. (in press). (2003). *Empleo y tecnología, dos términos antagónicos*. Diario Expansión.

Chapter XVI
Using Semantic Web Services in E-Banking Solutions

Laurent Cicurel
iSOCO, Spain

Jesús Contreras
iSOCO, Spain

José Luis Bas Uribe
Bankinter, Spain

José-Manuel López-Cobo
iSOCO, Spain

Sergio Bellido Gonzalez
Bankinter, Spain

Silvestre Losada
iSOCO, Spain

ABSTRACT

Offering public access to efficient transactional stock market functionalities is of interest to all banks and bank users. Traditional service oriented architecture (SOA) technology succeeds at providing reasonable, good Web-based brokerage solutions, but may lack extensibility possibilities. By introducing Semantic Web Services (SWS) as a way to integrate third party services from distributed service providers, we propose in this chapter an innovative way to offer online real-time solutions that are easy-to-use for customers. The combined use of ontologies and SWS allows different users to define their own portfolio management strategies regardless of the information provider. In deed the semantic layer is a powerful way to integrate the information of many providers in an easy way. With due regard for more development of security technological issues, research on SWS has shown that the deployment of the technology in commercial solutions is within sight.

INTRODUCTION

When operating on the stock market, investors make their decisions on the basis of huge amount of information about the stock evolution, economic and politic news, third parties recommendation and other kind of sources. Thanks to the proliferation of the Internet banks the profile of an average investor is changing from a financial expert to common people making small investments on the online stock market. In addition to the business generated around the stock market operations, banks use their online stock market application to attract new and to reinforce the customer commitment.

Banks, as any other commercial organization, needs to optimize the deployment of new products and services to the market. The deployment time of new services or applications is an important issue in a highly competitive market, since it defines the future market share and revenues. Online banks are looking for technologies and architectural paradigms that would allow them to design, implement and deploy new services on a low cost basis and in a short time period. New services often imply integration of many already existing applications, some of them internal and others external to the organization.

This is the case of online stock brokerage solutions adopted by online banks. An online stock brokerage application proposes to the user to buy and sell its stock options via a computerized network. Banks are willing to offer an easy to use application including as much information and as many options as possible without incurring large development costs. We will show that the use of the Semantic Web technology, combined with a service-oriented architecture (SOA), greatly reduces the cost and effort of developing and maintaining an online stock brokerage solution.

A broker based on a semantic service oriented architecture has all the advantages of a service oriented architecture (e.g. modularity, reusability) combined with the advantages of Semantic Web technologies. Semantic Web technology main advantage is to give a clear semantic inside (and eventually outside) the enterprise which reduces the communication confusions (technical or human). This also leads to higher maintainability of the products and to a better automatisation of the system mechanisms. These advantages applied to SOA will be extended in the proposed solution of this chapter. Next section will first exposes the current situation of brokerage applications based on classical SOA.

CURRENT SITUATION: BROKERAGE APPLICATION BASED ON WEB SERVICES

Banking companies have invested heavily in the last few years to develop brokerage solutions based on a new dominant paradigm in the IT World: service oriented architecture (SOA). The concept of this paradigm is not new: propose a loosely coupled distributed system architecture where independent services provide functionality, so that the difficulty is divided which leads to reduce the development cost and improve the reusability. But the technologies to implement this paradigm are relative new. Web Services are one of the solutions that appeared a couple of years ago and that made the success of this paradigm. For this reason Web Services are often confused with the SOA paradigm.

In this section we first present in more detail the business case for the brokerage application that we propose. We will then explain why a service oriented architecture implemented using Web Services technologies is a suitable solution. The solution properties will be detailed and it will be shown that this kind of architecture is suitable for brokerage application. We then present what the benefits of such an architecture are from both, a technical and a business point of view.

Web-Based Brokerage Applications

Introduction

As a major interface between the financial world and the non-financial world, banks always try to improve their services related to the stock market. As the Internet represents one of the most interesting communication channels of recent years, banks are interested in using this channel to improve the quality of their service and thus increase their image and revenue. Such banks or bank departments have been called eBanks or online banks.

We have identified three different strategies for online Banking:

- **Technological leader profile:** Banks that focus their strategy on technology and consider the Internet an opportunity to improve their markets. Also, the Internet specialized banks, usually recently founded banks (not subsidiaries) that have earn a significant market share, even though they do not offer their clients a wide range of products.
- **Follower banks profile:** Banks that first considered the Internet as a threat. When the market has matured, they changed their strategy from a defensive position to a competitive attitude towards those who were the first leaders in Internet banking. In some cases, subsidiary entities were created so as not to cannibalize their own market share.
- **Non "internetized" banks:** Banks that did not invest in the Internet because of their small size, their strategy or other reasons. However, they are a minority in terms of market share.

In these days, banks that already have Web-based brokerage application in place choose the technological leader strategy, while those banks that are only now considering developing their own applications follow the second strategy. Other mediums are also possible:

- **Branches:** Too expensive for Banks. Only for high end clients.
- **Phone banking service:** Expensive for banks. Only for selected clients
- **Mobile services (SMS, mobile phone applications):** Cheap for banks, usually free or at a small fee per service usage.

However, the Internet medium, as a cheap and universal way to perform banking operations is the highlighted solution of this business case.

In current brokerage solutions banks usually only offer the service of making the operations (buy, sell) but rarely integrate the search of relevant information to make the transaction decision. The delivery of this 'hard to integrate' functionality search, is, however, a useful to provide to the end user, who wants to buy and sell stock knowing the most relevant and current information. The user usually searches this information on external pages independently of the bank services. Some of these are free services which propose information of the stock market in real-time or with a minimum delay. Web pages such as Yahoo Finance (http://finance.yahoo.com/), Google Finance (http://finance.google.com), Reuters UK (http://uk.reuters.com/home), Xignite (http://preview.xignite.com/), Invertia (http://www.invertia.com) are good examples of financial information from different providers with different degrees of quality.

However, the need to search the information on several Web pages and then navigate to the brokerage application to execute the transaction is a waste of time and adds unwanted complexity to the end user. The idea is to build an online broker that merges and provides a unified or single point of access to information and operational services. In that way, the user will have an unified environment which integrates most of the tools required to fulfil his/her wishes of buying and selling stocks. A comparison of a traditional brokerage application interaction and the new interaction we proposed is showed in Figure 1. In the traditional interaction, the user must retrieve the information from each Data Provider (Yahoo Finance, etc.) independently and only then do the brokerage action (i.e. buy or sell). In the unified environment we propose, all the interactions are performed through the brokerage application and the brokerage application take care of showing the best data information regarding the user context (user profile, portfolio of the user, etc.).

In the next section we define the functional and non-functional requirements of our business

Figure 1. Brokerage application interaction comparison

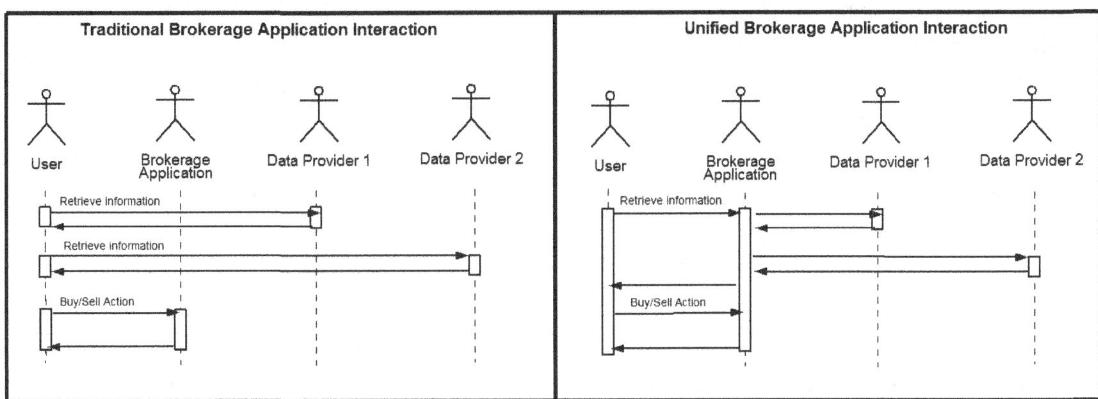

case. The following sections present one relatively new but already commonly used way of using a service oriented architecture (SOA) to implement these requirements. This solution, however, has some problems exposed later on that we resolve exposing a new and innovative way using SOA combined with Semantic Web Technologies.

Functional Requirements

The functional requirements the brokerage application must support in order to fulfil the business case are summarised below:

- **Stock market consultation functionalities:** The application should be able to retrieve information about the stock market such as the price of a share, volume of a share, historical information, etc. Several sources can be used to obtain the information necessary to the supply the user with the information they require to make the trade.
- **Customer information consultation functionalities:** The application should be able to obtain easily the customer information such as his portfolio, buy and sell history and recent searches by the user.
- **Operational functionalities:** Invocation of operations on the stock market using the bank services: buy, sell.
- **Complex conditional queries:** Possibility to write a complex order in terms of conditions such as "if the stock value of Cisco is higher than X and its volume is lower than Y, ..." that may use different source of information. Logical combinations of the conditions should be possible.
- **Simple entry point of all services:** Complete integration of the conditional queries and operational functionalities within one simple entry point.

Non Functional Requirements

The non-functional requirements that the brokerage application must fulfil are:

- **Highly maintainable:** As the stock market is an entity subject to rapid change, it must be possible to maintain the application in an optimal way.
- **Usability:** The application is aimed at non-expert end users. The application should as usable as possible in order to present to the end user a friendly and easy-to-use interface.
- **Extensibility of the information source:** Possibility to easily add and change the providers of the banking information services.

And to extend and choose the categories of information that the user wants to see. For example, if the user is executing a buy or sell transaction the user may want to see different sets of information.

Solution Based on SOA/Web Services

Introduction

During the last four decades, software design has been prone to many changes. After abstracting software code from the hardware infrastructure, computer scientists thought to write code in so called black-boxes and invented function oriented software design. The next big revolution was object oriented software design, in which data was intended to be packaged in objects where objects are metaphors of real world entities. Objects were then abstracted in components in order to manage the problem of the increasing number of objects. A component can be defined as a set of objects that has a coherent meaning as a standalone entity. What is the next level of abstraction? A composition of components will always be a component if we only focus on the data that these components contain. The composition must then be thought of a set of components that fulfil a given task. By doing so the packaging is no longer data-oriented but service-oriented, the set of components does no more contain information and methods to access to this information but is a black-box that offers one specific service. The services can then be composed in more abstract services and be part of the entire system, a service-oriented system.

Choosing service-oriented applications allows the clear separation of the users (commonly called 'consumers') from the service implementation (commonly called 'producers'). By having this distinction, the application can then be distributed on several platforms and possibly across networks. Each platform can have its own technology and can be located in any physical place. The software design has fundamentally changed in system design.

The Organization for the Advancement of Structured Information Standards (OASIS) defines the service oriented architecture as follows (MacKenzie et al, 2006):

A paradigm for organizing and utilizing distributed capabilities that may be under the control of different ownership domains. It provides a uniform means to offer, discover, interact with and use capabilities to produce desired effects consistent with measurable preconditions and expectations.

In this definition a service is designed as an entity with on one hand measurable preconditions and on the other hand measurable expectations. It can be reformulated as the input and output of a function in a typical programming paradigm, but in a service the input (precondition) and the output (expectation) are no data but state of the world or effect on the world.

We must clearly separate the architecture from the underlying technology that can be implemented. The Web Services made the fame of the SOA, but there exists other technologies which are totally suitable to be used in a Service-oriented Architecture such as: RPC, DCOM, CORBA, or WCF (Donani, 2006).

In the following subsection we present a standard SOA for a brokerage application using Web Services as the underlying technology.

Architecture

An overview of the architecture of a brokerage application based on a SOA/Web Service architecture (Booth et al., 2004) is described in Figure 2.

The Web Services are physically located in either the service provider such as Bankinter or

Figure 2. SOA Architecture of a brokerage application

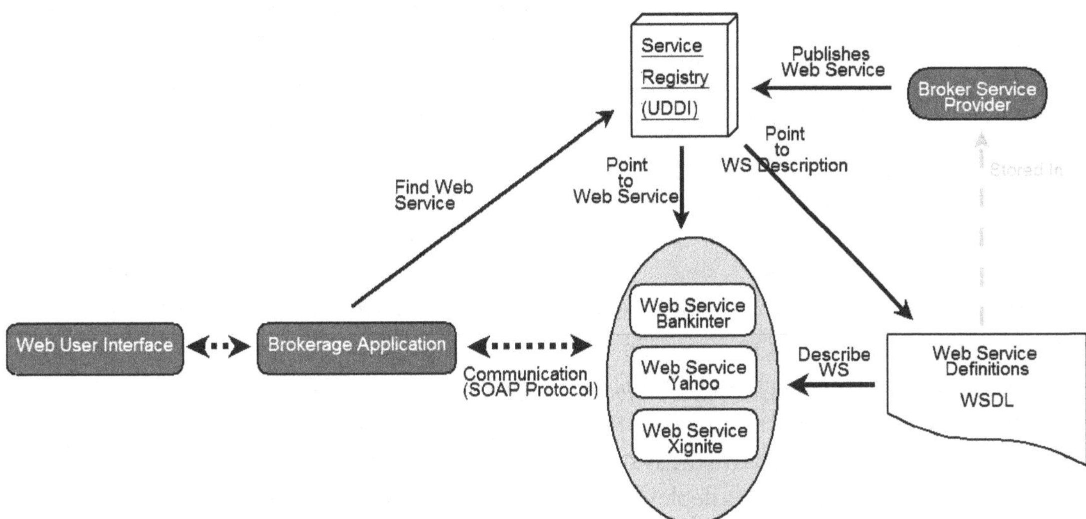

Xignite that provides their own Web Services, or in a specific Web Service container in the case that the Web Service provider does not provide a Web Service Interface and some wrapping mechanisms are needed. This is the case with the above yahoo based Web Service in which analysis (wrapping) of the Web page is needed to extract the right information.

The Web Service Descriptions are stored inside a Broker Service Provider which publishes all the descriptions and is in charge in managing the publication inside a Service Registry.

Through this registry, Web Services can be found and communication between the application and the Web Service is done using the SOAP.

This quite simple and elegant architecture has a lot of advantages that are explained in the following subsections on a technical and business perspective.

Benefits of SOA on a Technical Perspective

SOA is finding increased adoption across more and more business domains. This evolution can be explained by a set of technical benefits. The two most important ones are the following:

- **Reuse:** By decentralizing the systems in self contained atomic Web Services, a SOA allows the redundancy inside the system to be reduced since the Web-services can be used more than once for different purposes. This allows also delivering new functionalities in shorter time.
- **Loosely-coupled:** In a loosely-coupled system, each entity (Web Services) makes its requirements explicit and makes few assumptions about other entities. This permits not being aware where we locate the Web Services and thus increases the IT efficiency (critical Web Services can have an adapted hardware framework), improve the Quality of Service and reduce the costs. Another advantage of a loosely-coupled system is to have standard interfaces. This way there is no need for technical people to know about the whole details of the system and allows a strategically organisational separation of skills inside the project team.

Benefits of SOA on a Business Perspective

As many times the decision of choosing an architecture is done on a business level, it is important for an architecture type to have good benefits on a business perspective. The main SOA advantages are:

- **Business effectiveness:** If one word could be chosen to describe a SOA, it would be the word "agility". By using loosely-coupled services, the responsiveness to market is highly increased. Each process of the system is better controlled and allowed a deployment of resources based on the business needs.
- **Cost efficiency:** Service-oriented architectures Enables reduction of the development costs by separating the skills and efforts in specific development areas. The separation in services allows putting the resources in the technical areas that correspond best to their skills and thus reduce the costs of training or hiring new resources. The maintenance costs of such systems are also highly reduced because of well separated services and technology and location independence. Last cost reduction is the price/performance optimization based on the freedom to select the adequate platform.
- **Risk reduction:** Dividing problems in smaller parts always has the advantage to reduce the risk of a project, thus SOA is based on this division, we can say that the risk of projects based on SOA are inherently reduced. Another point is the risk reduction of the system deployment which can be done incrementally.

Problem Statement

We have presented the benefits of using a SOA based on Web Services to develop brokerage applications. However, there are a number of points in which the standard SOA is unable to respond:

- **Web services heterogeneity:** In the Web Service technologies, the information is described at a syntactical level. For example, in WSDL XML Schema technology is used to describe what the interchanged objects are. However, this kind of technology only allows describing the type of the objects: string, date, integer etc. The semantic of what the objects are is missing. This adds inside the project development a lot of potential problems:
  - Misunderstanding of what is interchanged (if the documentation is badly done, errors can be quickly done)
  - Integration problems due to different type definition (for example, one service could describe an address with different fields while the service consumer use an unique string)
- **Poor visibility:** As defined by the standardization group OASIS inside the OASIS SOA Reference Model, the visibility *refers to the capacity for those with needs and those with capabilities to be able to see each other* (MacKenzie, 2006. In standard SOA, the visibility is mainly provided by means of a registry which lists the available services. By having only a syntactic description of the Web Service, the visibility is highly reduced and more efforts in terms of search and analysis are needed by any entity that wants to consume a Web Service.
- **Manual work:** In standard SOA system, an important effort of Web Services integration is needed in order to develop the entire system. The orchestration (composition) of the necessary Web Services corresponds to one the highest effort time spent inside the project due to the mostly manual work that these efforts imply. Middleware is often used in order to solve the orchestration. Mediation

(data conversion) is on this topic the major problem. The previously cited visibility problem also implies a lot of effort time because of the manual effort spent during the localization of each Web Service.

All these points constitute the problems of actual brokerage application based on pure SOA. However, as discussed earlier SOA has a lot of advantages. This encourages us to re-use this solution and improve it. The proposed solution of the next section aims at solving these problems of the actual solution by adding semantic technologies to this SOA paradigm.

SOLUTION: BROKER BASED ON SEMANTIC WEB SERVICES

As seen in the previous section, SOA technology provides a number of powerful concepts that when applied to brokerage applications allow us to construct flexible and easily extensible systems. However, problems have been identified with this kind of technical approach; those problems are responsible for an important part of the cost of such applications. The identified problems were *vocabulary heterogeneity*, *poor visibility* of the services and *manual work* needed in the development and maintenance phases. If we succeed developing a homogeneous vocabulary for Web Services, then we would increase the visibility and reduce the manual work. Three solutions were proposed in (Verma et al., 2007):

- **Pre-agree on all terms (operation name, parameters):** This implies a high oral communication between the development team and a lot of documentation writing. Pre-agreeing on the terms with no formally technical structure implies a high risk for any company due to the risk of losing common knowledge or getting integration problems.
- **Comment all aspects of a service:** In this solution, the comments are added inside the IT components. Each service contains the description of what the service proposes to do. Operation names and the semantic of the parameters are described in natural language.
- **Semantic descriptions:** This solution envisages a formal description of the services, called annotation. The services are not described using natural language but with the proper mechanism of the chosen technology.

This last solution, called Semantic Web Service (SWS), is the one that we propose in this section because it represents the most advanced and thus suitable of these three solutions. The annotation is done by using so called semantic technologies, in which the components of the system (here Web services) are formally described by using semantic resources (usually ontologies). This technology is the base of the vision of Tim Berners-Lee who put the base of a Web where the computer will be able to optimally understand and compute the information (Berners-Lee, 2001). We will explain how the use of ontologies, which is the base of most semantic system, adds visibility to the components by homogenizing the vocabulary used. We will also point out how this enhancement leads to a reduction of manual work and thus a reduction of cost.

Powerful Functionalities

The aim of annotating Web Services is not only to add clarity in the Web Service definitions but also to allow the Web Service to be read by machines. This machine-readability makes the power of the SWS by adding to the system the following functionalities:

- **Power to reason:** The machine is able to "understand" what the Web Service is doing. It is able to interpret the messages that are interchanged. The messages are no more only pure data structure but are structured in such a way that the data can be analyzed and transformed (mediated). For example, if a SWS receives information of a "client" but expected a "person", he is able to infer that a client is a person and is able to extract the right information. The whole information space is structured and coherent. Axioms are responsible of maintaining this space coherent and reasoners are the medium to do this. As described in the functional requirements, the brokerage system needs a system that is able to handle a unique point entry. The reasoning capabilities given by SWS fit perfectly to these requirements, the queries can be interpreted by the system and the system can identify what the user's wishes are. Additionally, as the machine is able to interpret what the input of the user is, it is able to help the user at the moment of maintaining the system. For example, a company has a brokerage application that allows the user to buy stocks. However, for marketing purposes the number of times that the customer can buy depends on the profile of the customer. In this case, the maintainer of the brokerage system could want to add a new type of client. With a SWS-based system, this is highly simple, as the only action to do is to add the concept of this new type in the ontology and add the information on how many operations he can do. No additional development efforts are needed and no risk of adding errors in the application is run. If the maintainer makes an error in adding the information inside the ontology, the reasoner will warn him before he put it in production.

- **Automatic discovery:** Formally describing what each Web Service does adds the functionality of automatically discovering them. This means that a query written in a formal language can be interpreted so that the correct Web Services with the appropriate functionalities and Quality of Service parameters are found. This allows a better decoupling between: what the user wants and what the system proposes. By separating these two parts, the system gets more flexible. This SWS functionality responds to the functional requirements about the processing of complex queries. The user expresses a complex query in Natural Language or through a Web Interface, this query is translated into the corresponding formal language and this formal query can then be used to retrieve the best Web Services. More than one Web Service can be accessible for the same functionality; the system takes care at choosing the more adapted one. In terms of maintainability, the separation of the SWS is also important in the sense that adding new duplicated SWS of other providers does not require modifying the application. If new types of SWS are added, some extents must be added to the query generation functionality of the brokerage application. But this task remains relatively easy because of the use of ontologies which takes care of the coherence of the system. The automatic discovery responds to the non functional property of the "extensibility of the information source".
- **Automatic orchestration:** SWS support the automatic orchestration or composition of Web services (Medjahed, 2003). By orchestration, we mean the composition of the Web Services in order to provide a more complex service. As Semantic Web Services are semantically annotated, the system has enough information to handle a user query and respond to it by assembling the Web Services. Automatic orchestration provides an easy way to combine a usable interface to the user, with one entry point that provides the three main requirements: stock market consulta-

tion, costumer information consultation and operational invocation.

SWS Technologies

The Semantic Web Service technologies have been in the last few years under intensive research world-wide. In the actual states, two approaches have been developed. Each one of these approach were part of research projects and their validity was proven by the deployment of concrete use-cases. The two approaches are:

- **Pure Semantic Web Services:** These technologies represent a way to write pure Semantic Web Services. By pure, we mean that they are written directly in a formal language and are independent from any non-Semantic Web Services. Of course, all SWS technologies need to be able to be connected with non-Semantic Web Services (called grounding) in order to support any already developed Web service system. But the idea is to be able to build new Semantic Web Services that will not carry on the "old" non semantic technologies. There are two main technologies based on this approach: OWL-S (Martin et al, 2003) based on the OWL ontology language and WSMO (Fensel et al., 2007) (de Brujin, Bussler et al. , 2005)based on the WSML (de Brujin, Fensel et al., 2005) ontology language. The first is mainly a North American development effort, while the second one has been developed within EU-funded projects (Sekt, DIP, Knowledge Web, ASG and SUPER projects). They both are submitted to the W3C and have the necessary specification, development tools and execution engines.
- **Semantic Annotation of Web Services:** The second approach consists in directly annotating the WSDL with semantic information. Two main specification efforts are actually done: WSDL-S (Akkiraju et al. , 2005) that is at the Member Submission stage in W3C and SAWSDL(Farell et al., 2007) that is a W3C proposed recommendation. Main advantage of these approaches is that the annotation is done directly in the WSDL / XML Schema. Thus, the evolution of existing systems is facilitated. Other advantage is that these specifications are ontology language independent, thus execution engine can be developed for any chosen ontology language. Both languages have the necessary development tools.

Tools already exist and are operational to model and run Semantic Web Services. Most of them were part of a research project and are freely available on the Internet.

For modelling SWS, the following tools are available:

- **WSMO Studio[1]:** A SWS and semantic Business Process Modelling Environment. Also support SAWSDL. As described by the name, this tool supports the WSMO Framework. It is Eclipse-based and the last version is 0.7.2 released on 29/11/2007 (in the moment that this chapter is written: end of 2007)
- **Web Service Modelling Toolkit (WSMT)[2]:** A lightweighted framework for the rapid creation and deployment of the tools for SWS. It supports WSMO Framework. It is Eclipse-based and the last version is 1.4.1 released on 13/09/2007 (in the moment that this chapter is written: end of 2007)
- **Radiant (Gomadam, 2005)[3]:** A WSDL-S / SAWSDL Annotation Tool developed by the University of Georgia. The annotation is made using OWL ontologies. It is Eclipse-based and the last version is 0.9.4beta released on 29/05/2007 (in the moment that this chapter is written: end of 2007).
- **ODE SWS (Corcho, 2003)[4]:** A toolset for design and composition of SWS. It is based

on UMPL and some work has been done to integrate OWL-S.

- **OWL-S IDE (Srinivasan, 2006)[5]:** A development environment supporting a SWS developer through the whole process from the Java generation, to the compilation of OWL-S descriptions, to the deployment and registration with UDDI. The last version is 1.1 released on 26/07/2005 (in the moment that this chapter is written: end of 2007).
- **OWL-S Editor (Elenius, 2005)[6]:** A Protégé Ontology Editor plugin for a easy creation of SWS. The last version was released on 04/11/2004 (in the moment that this chapter is written: end of 2007).

The following SWS Engines are available:

- **WSMX[7]:** The reference implementation of WSMO
- **Internet Reasoning Service III (IRS-III)[8]** (Domingue et al, 2004)**:** A SWS framework, which allows applications to semantically describe and execute Web services.
- **OWL-S tools:** A series of tools WSDL2OWL-S, Java2OWL-S, OWL-S2UDDI, etc. are available at: http://www.daml.ri.cmu.edu/tools/details.html

Through these tools represent good proofs of the viability of the technology. That said, further development would be required to adapt them to the needs of real world system. Professional benchmarks would be needed to identify efficiency and security lacks and allow the development of professional SWS frameworks.

We gave a short overview of the existing SWS technologies and we explain now how these technologies can be applied to brokerage applications.

Approach and Architecture

The approach taken for creating a brokerage application with SWS is to use the SWS engine as a central component of the architecture. By taking advantage of the reasoning capacities of the SWS engine, it is possible to build a simple and extendible Brokerage Application. New Semantic Web Services are added directly in the engine and we minimize the development costs of managing new services. The SWS engine "understands" the semantic of the new added SWS and only few modifications are needed inside the Brokerage Application itself. This approach has been proven during the DIP project on a use-case (see the two screenshots Figure 3 And 4) that simulated a brokerage application with Bankinter and external Web Services.

The user can enter a complex query composed of several conditions and one action to be taken. The conditions are connected with logical operators (AND/OR). The conditions can be of the types:

- *If the price of a specific stock is higher than a given price.*
- *If the value of an index is lower than a given value.*
- *If the expert recommendation is equal to a specified one.*
- *If the variation of the value of a given stock is higher.*

For each information that needs to be retrieved, the SWS Engine is responsible for discovering the best suitable Semantic Web Service, eventually by composing multiple Semantic Web Services (orchestration) and invoke the one (/ones) that correspond to the given Quality of Services parameters (time to respond, localization, etc.). If a Semantic Web Services is grounded on some other service systems (like normal Web Services), it is in charge of getting the information and converting it into the semantic language. The Brokerage application then returns the result of the execution to the Web Interface.

Figure 5 shows the architecture that implements this approach.

Figure 3. First screenshot of the SWS based brokerage prototype

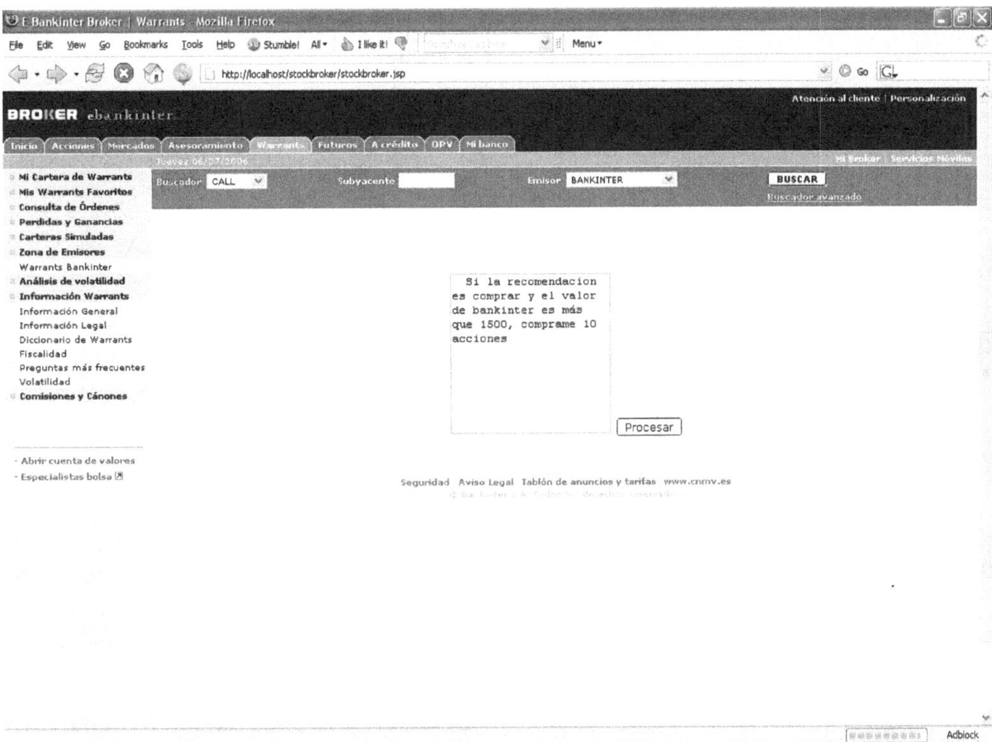

Figure 4. Second screenshot of the SWS based brokerage prototype

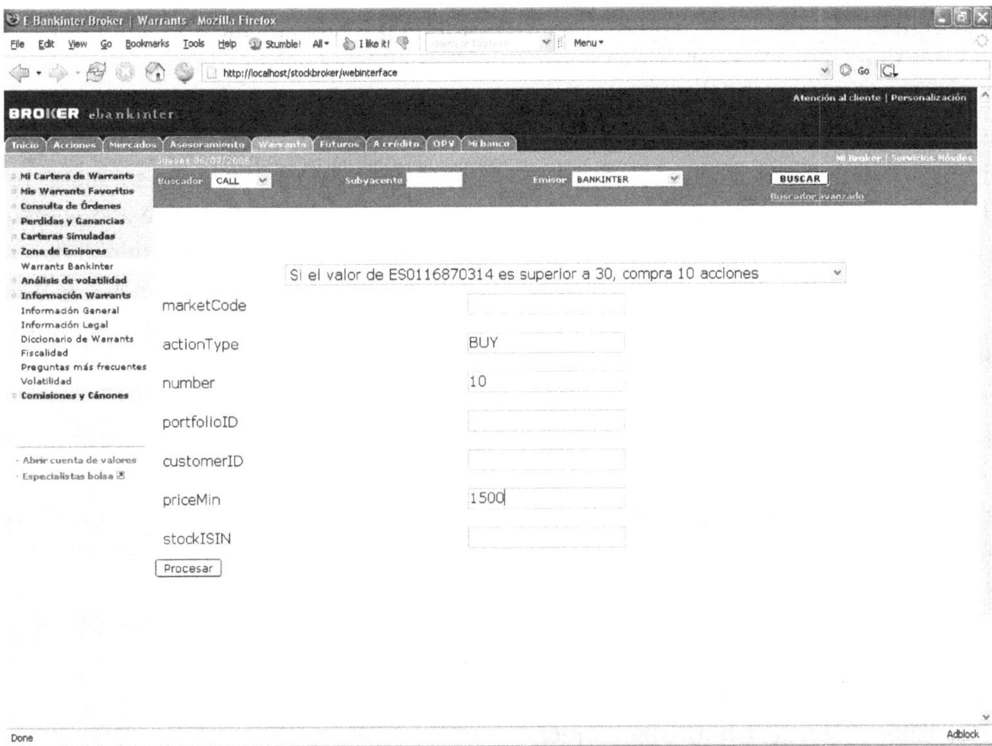

Figure 5. Brokerage application architecture

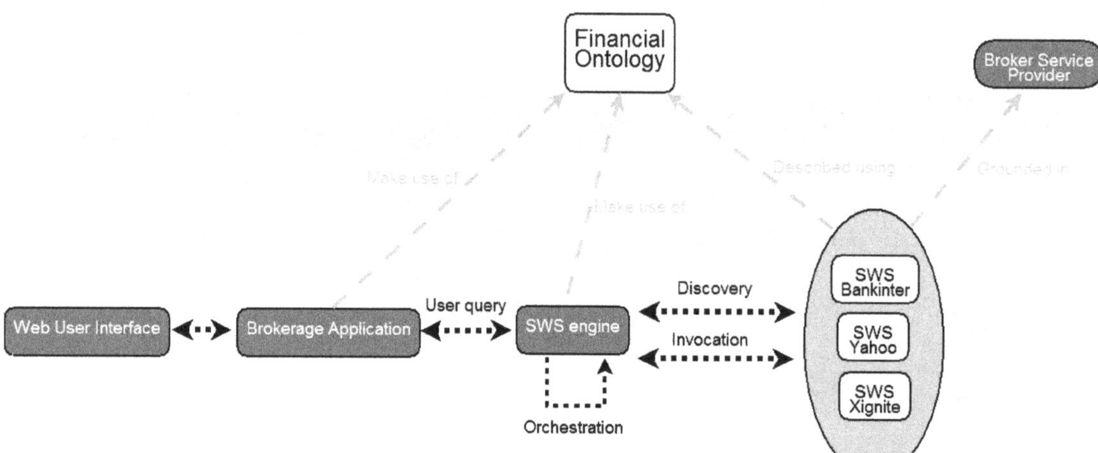

The three main components are:

- The Web User Interface that should respond to the Usability non-functional requirement.
- The Brokerage Application that should support all the functional requirements and that is in charge of the communication with the SWS Engine.
- The SWS Engine that is in charge of managing the semantic resources: discovering, invoke and orchestrate the SWS.

The brokerage application prototype developed in DIP has been developed using J2EE technologies. The application makes use of Natural Language Processing technologies to offer a simplified interface to the user. Receiving one sentence as input, the brokerage application is able to identify what is the user intention and automatically retrieve the information that it needs to invoke the SWS. These parameters are used to generate a WSMO goal (de Brujin, 2005) formally describing the user intention. This goal is the entry point to the SWS Engine.

As SWS Engine, WSMX (Bussler et al., 2005)[9] was chosen over IRIS-III (Domingue et al., 2004) (Cabral et al., 2006)[10] in order to prove the correct implementation of this SWS Engine inside the research project. From the input goal provided by the brokerage application and some optional Quality of Service parameters, the SWS engine discovers the necessary SWS and invokes the retrieved SWS in the right order (orchestration). The brokerage application can then have access to all the information it needs to check the condition provided by the user and if the conditions are validated execute the buy/sell order through another call to the SWS engine.

The Financial ontology, exhaustively described in (López-Cobo, 2008) plays a major role in all the tasks of the SWS engine and is the pillar of the whole brokerage application. It describes the vocabulary of the application and is used to annotate the SWS on both levels: the functionality description (capability) and the interface (message exchange).

By using an architecture based on the Financial ontology and the SWS engine, we provide a flexible and maintainable application and provide to the brokerage system the whole benefits of using SWS technologies.

In the next section, we describe in a higher level the cost and benefits of adopting such architecture.

COST AND BENEFITS

From a business point of view, the profits of the proposed solution must not be focused on new incomes neither on costs, although they both exist. The resulting application is intended to create a new product, by giving new options to manage their portfolio. These options could have been developed using a more traditional approach but, due to the complex and usually mature architectures used by the financial institutions, the costs would have been significantly higher, both the development and the future sub-applications costs.

Also, a more traditional approach (i.e. without semantic technologies) would have implied agreements with the information providers (data formats, relevant data, how to provide the information, how to access to the data, etc), which will usually implied a one-by-one Trading Partner Agreement (TPA). The semantic layer gives us the ability to smartly read the provided data and therefore to manage it easily. It is also easy to add new providers with this approach. Finally, data is accessed when required and if required, making use of the Web Service advantages.

The costs and benefits, from the technical point of view, must be also considered. The Cost/Benefits ratio in terms of adapting actual systems, although not trivial, is not as dramatic change as the one that was performed in the transition to the Internet era.

Banks were usually based on main frame architectures. The scenario in these last 10-20 years has changed from a exclusive main-frame scenario, where only the bank employees had access to the IT transactional systems, to a Web Based scenario where virtually any customer, anywhere at anytime could be using the bank transactional. This transition meant high investments on scaling the main frame architecture to a 24*7 architecture adding several layers: Web servers, application servers, database servers, security layers...

Fortunately a Web Service scenario is more natural in the actual client-servers environment, therefore, in terms of cost/benefits the investment is lower. The same reasoning can be applied to a SWS scenario, where besides the new Web Service layer to be added, semantic pieces appear to complete the puzzle.

Therefore, taking the chance of adding semantic layers to an existing bank architecture implies low economical risk since no major implications are needed to expand the current architecture.

As a result, and taking into account the business opportunity, the small amount of effort required to create and maintain the service, and the technical prerequisites, the SWS approach emerges as a smart solution to create the new service at a reasonable level of cost, both for the developer and, which is more important, for the final user.

RISK ASSESSMENT

From a business point of view, alternatives are almost always more expensive but it could depend on how each Financial Institution manage its own Stock Market Services. What is more, in several cases the solution could be so complex that it could be considered as 'nearly impossible' to develop without studying in depth what is going to be modified, (Stock Market applications are critical tasks for Financial Institutions due to the volatility of the market and the quality assurance that is required in this specific market).

At the same time, the new proposed service is intended to give better utilities to the clients. These kinds of services are actually free, although the final user must manage with them. So the price of the service for the final clients could not be high and thus, it has to be developed at a reasonable cost.

There are some risks when the use of SWS is considered:

- **Security issues:** No doubt this is the major functional risk to be considered when deploying SWS technologies. On banking environments security is the mayor column on which all the architecture must be built. All the security issues must be clarified and solved before any transactional application using real customer banking data is deployed to the real world. If this milestone is not achieved all the SWS-based applications will be forced to handle only with public data and the real value of semantic applications will remain as a proof-of-concept not as a real-world-application.
- **Evolution issues:** SWS techniques are in their first steps of use in business environments. As these techniques become more familiar they will evolve and this evolution could mean scalability issues that should be treated as any other scalability issues inside any corporation environment. Although the semantic techniques are mature their wide use could imply changes that would mean changes on the semantic platform. However these two evolution issues are natural to any IT development or to the deploy of any new technology. The IT business, no matter if it is the banking business or any other, has got enough experience to handle these potential risks.

FUTURE TRENDS

The evolution of the Stock Market and its associated services must be forecasted as part of the global social tendencies: people (and investors) are requiring more and more sophisticated products and services allowing them to make their own decisions. If we consider that information aggregators are the Internet 'killer applications' (i.e.: Google, Yahoo, You Tube, etc) investors are expected to make use of Stock Market data aggregators (in fact, the actually use them: Yahoo! Finances, Invertia, etc), making their own buying/selling decisions and finally performing them in their favourite Stock Market site.

None of these services are designed to perform automatic operations that completely fulfil the investor requirements, nor of them are prepared to perform a personalised strategy when data aggregation is required. There are several solutions for professional investors but they are available at a high cost, thus they are only interesting when high volumes are regularly performed (high volume both in terms of number of transactions and in terms of money invested). But there they are not an option for individuals.

Our tests[11] reveal that people usually make use of at least two Stock Market services just to fulfil their information requirements. The SWS is intended to aggregate them and, in the near future, to automatically perform the actions according to the investor strategy, combining sources and retrieving specific data form them.

CONCLUSION

Responding to the need of maintainable and efficient brokerage applications, we have presented in this chapter a novel approach that combines the SOA architecture and the semantic technologies. By using the proposed solution, we resolve the three identified problems of a non-semantic SOA solution: heterogeneity of the vocabulary used in the services which reduces the maintainability and possibilities of evolution of the application, the poor visibility which reduces the possibility for automatic discovery and the lot of manual work that is generated by this poor visibility and the lack of automatic composition possibilities.

We exposed the advantages of a solution based on Semantic Web services: reasoning functionalities, automatic discovery and automatic orchestration. Such functionalities allow us to build an architecture centralized on the SWS engine and have a really flexible system.

The feasibility to build such brokerage application has been demonstrated during the European project called DIP. The output of these projects is a framework called WSMO associated with an ontology language (WSML) and execution engines (WSMX and IRS-III). The European Commission continues to invest money in the research in Semantic Web Services for example in the SUPER project which aims to take advantage of the Semantic Web Services in order to improve Business Process Management Systems. A lot of research is also done in other technologies such as OWL-S. The high activity of these research projects reflects the important interest that should have industrial investor in such technology. The Semantic Web services are ready and continue to be improved.

Companies should consider the benefits of SWS on two levels: the strategic level and the tactical one. On the strategic level, the SWS give the possibility to build highly maintainable applications and profits from a loosely coupled architecture. On a tactical level, a company should see the benefits on other projects where the ontologies that have been created for the SWS are reused and form a common base for the applications. Using such Semantic technologies is interesting for companies because it promotes the homogeneity of the systems inside the company. The intra-company and inter-company applications are then much easier integrable.

REFERENCES

Akkiraju R., Farrell J., Miller J., Nagarajan M., Schmidt M., Sheth A., Verma K. (2005) *Web Service Semantics - WSDL-S,* from: http://www.w3.org/Submission/WSDL-S/, retrieved November 2005.

Berners-Lee T., Hendler J., Lassila O. (2001). *The Semantic Web.* Scientific Amarican, 284, 34-43

Booth D., Haas H., McCabe F., Newcomer E., Champion M., Ferris C., Orchard D. (2004) *Web Services architecture.* From: http://www.w3.org/TR/ws-arch/, Retrieved February 2004

Bussler C., Cimpian E., Fensel D., Gomez J.M., Haller A., Haselwanter T., Kerrigan M., Mocan A., Moran M., Oren E., Sapkota B., Toma I., Viskova J., Vitvar T., Zaremba Maciej, Zaremba Michal (2005). *Web Service Execution Environment (WSMX).* From: http://www.w3.org/Submission/WSMX/, retrieved November 2007.

Cabral, L., Domingue, J., Galizia, S., Gugliotta, A., Norton, B., Tanasescu, V., and Pedrinaci, C. (2006) *IRS-III: A Broker for Semantic Web Services based Applications,* The 5th International Semantic Web Conference (ISWC 2006), Athens, GA, USA,

Corcho, O., Fernández-López, M., Gómez-Pérez, A., and Lama, M. (2003). *ODE SWS: A Semantic Web Service Development Environment.* VLDB-Workshop on Semantic Web and Databases, 203-216. Berlin, Germany.

de Brujin J., Bussler C., Domingue J., Fensel D., Hepp M., Keller U., Kifer M., König-Ries B., Kopecky J., Lara R., Lausen H., Oren E., Polleres A., Roman D., Scicluna J., Stollberg M. (2005). *Web Service Modeling Ontology (WSMO).* From: http://www.w3.org/Submission/WSMO/, retrieved November 2007.

de Brujin J., Fensel D., Keller U., Kifer M., Lausen H., Krummenacher R., Polleres A., Predoiu L. (2005). *Web Service Modeling Language (WSML).* From: http://www.w3.org/Submission/WSML/, retrieved November 2007.

Domingue J., Cabral L., Hakimpour F., Sell D., Motta E (2004). IRS-III: A platform, and infrastructure for creating WSMO-based Semantic Web services. In *Proc. Of the Workshop on WSMO Implementations.* CEUR Workshop Proceedings

Donani M.H. (2006). SOA 2006: State Of The Art. *Journal of Object Technology*, 5.

Elenius D., Denker G., Martin D., Gilham F., Khouri J., Sadaati S., and Senanayake R., The OWL-S editor- A Development Tool for Semantic Web Services. In *The Semantic Web: Research and Applications*. Series: Lecture Notes in Computer Science , Vol. 3532, 78-92. Springer Berlin / Heidelberg 2005. ISBN: 978-3-540-26124-7

Farell J., Lausen H. (2007) *Semantic Annotations for WSDL and XML Schema*. From: http://www.w3.org/TR/sawsdl/ , retrieved July 2007.

Fensel D., Lausen H., Polleres A., Brujin J.d., Stollberg M. Romand D., Domingue J. (2007). *Enabling Semantic Web Services – The Web Service Modelin Ontology*. Springer.

Gomadam K., Verma K., Brewer D., Sheth A. P., Miller J. A. (2005) Radiant: A tool for semantic annotation of Web Services, *ISWC 2005*.

López-Cobo J.M., Cicurel L., Losada S., *Ontology Management in eBanking applications*. In *Ontology Management. Semantic Web, Semantic Web Services, and Business Applications*. Series: Semantic Web and Beyond , Vol. 7. Hepp, M.; De Leenheer, P.; de Moor, A.; Sure, Y. (Eds.) 2008, Approx. ISBN: 978-0-387-69899-1

MacKenzie M, Laskey K., McCabe F., Brown P.F., Metz R. (2006) *Reference Model for Service Oriented Architecture 1.0*. From: http://docs.oasis-open.org/soa-rm/v1.0/soa-rm.html , Retrieved October 2006.

Martin D., Burstein M., Hobbs J., Lassila O., McDermott D., McIraith S., Narayanan S., Paolucci M., Parsia B., Payne T., Srinivasan N., Sycara K. (2003). *OWL-S: Semantic Markup for Web Services*. From: http://www.w3.org/Submission/OWL-S/, retrieved November 2007.

Medjahed B., Bouguettaya A. and Elmagarmid A. K.(2003). Composing Web services on the Semantic Web. *VLDB J.*, 12(4), 333-351.

Srinivasan, N., Paolucci, M., and Sycara, K. (2006). Semantic Web Service Discovery in the OWL-S IDE. In *Proceedings of the 39th Annual Hawaii international Conference on System Sciences - Volume 06* (January 04 - 07, 2006). HICSS. IEEE Computer Society, Washington, DC, 109.2.

Verma K., Sheth A. (2007). Semantically Annotating a Web Service. *IEEE Computer Society*, March/April 2007, 11, 83-85.

ENDNOTES

1 http://www.wsmostudio.org/download.html

2 https://sourceforge.net/projects/wsmt/

3 http://lsdis.cs.uga.edu/projects/meteor-s/downloads/index.php?page=1

4 http://kw.dia.fi.upm.es/odesws/

5 http://projects.semwebcentral.org/projects/owl-s-ide/

6 http://owlseditor.semwebcentral.org/

7 http://www.wsmx.org/

8 http://kmi.open.ac.uk/projects/irs/

9 http://www.wsmx.org

10 http://kmi.open.ac.uk/projects/irs/

11 Done inside the DIP (http://dip.semanticweb.org/) project, Deliverable 10.10.

Chapter XVII
Formal Ontology for Media Rights Transactions

Adam Pease
Articulate Software, USA

Godfrey Rust
Rightscom/Ontologyx, UK

ABSTRACT

Rightscom (a UK-based media and rights consultancy), is working with Articulate Software (a formal ontology consultancy) and with another system developer to create a large-scale metadata integration and transaction management system, founded on an ontology-based metamodel. Previous versions of this system have utilized lightweight schema and conventional Semantic Web technologies such as OWL. This has become unwieldy, and does not take advantage of latest technologies. Our current version employs formal ontology development in the logical language of SUO-KIF and involves reuse of an extension of a large formal ontology – the Suggested Upper Merged Ontology (SUMO) - and its associated ontology management system, called Sigma. In particular, integration with a large ontology will give the Rightscom model greater coverage of more domains and expand business opportunities to supporting more kinds of transaction management applications. By utilizing an open source technology core, Rightscom will be able to leverage a larger and more robust set of technologies for our clients than would be possible with a proprietary system developed entirely in house. A key challenge in this work is maintaining customer-specific vocabularies and descriptions that are more appropriate in different contexts than the generic explanations in SUMO, that also conform to the central SUMO model.

CURRENT SITUATION

The 21st century has already seen a revolution in the provision of media content in digital form. In many domains, from academic articles to teenage rock band recordings, on-line delivery has become the method of choice for the consumer, and therefore the producer. In most other domains it seems certain to follow before the century is a quarter through.

This seismic shift away from the physical to the virtual has created an identity crisis in the content industries, and a corresponding headache for systems developers. Businesses such as record companies, journal and book publishers which for decades (and in some cases, centuries) have dealt with the creation and distribution of physical products, typically specializing in one particular mode such as print or audio, are inhabiting a strange new world which challenges every commercial assumption and operates at increasingly frightening levels of granularity. In a domain where anyone anywhere can produce and exploit media of any type in any combination then everyone in the value chain is – to some degree - a multimedia producer, rights controller, aggregator and provider. A parallel identity crisis is overshadowing the library world.

In this situation there is a rapidly growing need for formal ontology. The scope of content metadata – whether for workflow, description or rights management – has burst the banks of traditional methodologies.

Rightscom[1] is a content/media industry consultancy providing advice and technology in this marketplace. It has developed a data architecture (the Contextual Ontologyx Architecture or COA) to meet the requirement for flexible and extensible metadata management. Rightscom's ontology-based solutions operate under the brand name Ontologyx.

The COA evolved from earlier work in the <indecs> project[2], particularly concerned with establishing interoperability in multi-media rights and policy metadata. However, its MetaModel is not domain specific.

The COA is based on a conceptual data model (the Context Model) extensible to any level of granularity into domain ontologies. The COA approach aims to combine the best principles of data modelling, taxonomy and formal ontology. The expression of COA which is used as the basis of application and ontologies is the COA MetaModel, which extends the Context Model with a number of standard attribute types.

With the COA MetaModel as its basis, Rightscom has developed a large ontology (or more accurately, a group of integrated ontologies) covering media, "content" and rights.

COA is being applied in three main ways. The first is in industry messaging standards. The music industry's DDEX[3] message standards (for reporting online music content, usage and accounting) are managed by Ontologyx through a COA ontology. The prototype text industry licensing messages (ONIX For Licensing Terms[4]) is based on the COA MetaModel. The MPEG21 Rights Data Dictionary, ISO 21000-6 (ISO 21000-6, 2005) is based on an earlier iteration of the indecs/COA modelling.

Secondly, the COA MetaModel and ontology is used as a basis for systems design. The use case referenced in this chapter is for the design of a new rights management system an international multimedia rights and product licensing organization to be implemented in 2008. The client has office in four continents, licensing the use of music, text and other media such as audio and video clips and printed music to a variety of organizations and institutions. Its market is primarily business to business but with some movement into direct consumer services. The scope and complexity of its business is growing steadily.

Thirdly, the MetaModel and ontology is used as a basis for a 'Translator' tool providing many-to-many transformations between different metadata schemas. This tool is also used in the current client implementation[5].

The client in this use case is an archetypal "rights intermediary": an organization managing the exploitation of rights, most but not all of which have been acquired from others. The systems requirement they face is characteristic of all rights intermediaries in the digital age, and can be summarised as the requirement to be able to manage any kind of right in any kind of resource at any level of granularity under any commercial (or non-commercial) terms in any period, place or context. In other words: make available anything, to anyone, anytime, anywhere, to anyone for any purpose under any terms (or none), and ensure everyone who needs to gets paid.

For an enterprise of this kind (and this can include "non-commercial" organizations such as libraries or archives as well as those in commerce) the requirement is for a metadata system that can cope with the fact that the client doesn't know what the detailed system requirements are going to be in even in the medium term, and may hardly know what some of the general system requirements are in the long term.

The COA has been developed for such complex situations. Note though that while the current use case is for media content and rights management, the MetaModel is generally agnostic about the knowledge domain in which it is applied, and the system being built should work for most metadata management requirements when supported by an appropriate ontology. Note also that although COA will accommodate all the normal commercial and institutional metadata requirements that Rightscom has yet encountered, it would falter in more esoteric domains which use quantum or non-serial models of time, or which do not recognize 3D concepts of space, etc.

One of the chief goals of this approach is substantial use of ontological inference in the everyday processing of the system, and harnessing the power of theorem provers to commercial and institutional computing. In rights management, for example, the computation of exactly which parties are entitled to issue licenses for particular uses of a resource in a given time and place can result in a query of serious complexity involving a network of subclass, partial and disjoint relations. This was meat and drink to theorem provers – could we give them something practical to chew on?

In undertaking this work (which has been in planning for several years), Rightscom partnered in 2007 with Articulate Software[6], the primary developers of the open source Suggested Upper Merged Ontology SUMO[7] (Niles & Pease 2001) and the open source ontology management and development system called Sigma[8] (Pease 2003).

We characterize the domain as "policy management" rather than the narrower "rights management": it is concerned with the widest possible interpretation of *policies*: that is, parties declaring what *may, may not* or *must* be done about whatever it is they have a concern with. Whether such policies are determined by agreements (including licenses) or whether they are imposed as business rules is simply another variable. Rightscom has major clients in the commercial, educational, library and governmental sectors, and has found that the nature of requirements for both policy and metadata management are common across the spectrum. Although the domain is policy management, the metadata issues we are dealing with are generic, so it is not the purpose of this use case to explain in any detail (except with some illustrative examples) the application of the COA model or SUMO to policy management *per se:* a review of metadata for policy management is a book in itself.

Problem Statement

There are two parts to the problem statement. The first is this: what language works best for the formal axiomatization of COA and its ontologies? The second is this: how to build the bridges between that ontology language and to the client's relational database system so that the client can benefit from the ontology and its inferential capability without their software developers having to become formal ontologists themselves.

By 2007 Ontologyx had reached a critical point in its development that required some choices being made. It had developed its COA ontology using entirely un-ontological tools – MSExcel and MSSQL Server - with some XML and HTML glue and representations. The ontology was a triple store, but written in a native language so that it was not encumbered in its early development by the limitations of specific formalisms like OWL or RDF or tools such as Protégé (especially as these formalisms were themselves in relatively early stages). It has its own terms covering the OWL relations, and other rule structures besides. COA and its associated client ontologies was by now very large (over a million triples), and had developed a good deal of processing sophistication, but it could not routinely be validated or reasoned with since the language was informally defined in its native form and required rendering out into one or more fully defined formalisms before such work could be carried out.

This was clearly a roadblock to any integration with customer systems. COA needed full, native ontological formalization.

Secondly, customers would need a user-friendly ontology management system themselves, sooner rather than later. To date, Ontologyx had managed the development and maintenance of COA ontologies, but this was not viable as the sole business model – with the ontology being of such potential importance, customers wanted to be hands-on and not tied a particular supplier. Excel, which had been ideal through a development phase, and remains an excellent platform for rapid development of large sets of terms and ontologising complex "composite" constructs like schemas, was reaching the end of its manageable life as a comprehensive user interface. That said, Excel (or a similar spreadsheet) has many features which make it ideal for certain aspects of ontology creation or editing, not least that it is readily available and familiar to users. Rightscom's experience with it, and the relatively unsophisticated functionality of existing ontology editors for manipulation of blocks of data, has led us to retain Excel as a component of the ontology management system for the longer term.

Thirdly, the solution must lend itself to the possibility of inference on substantial quantities of instance data, both for querying and transformation, if the goals releasing the inferential potential of the ontology into the system are to be realized.

The task was to find a formalism and toolset that would fit the bill for expressiveness, flexibility and computation. Ideally a solution would also be open source, to save customers the burden of relying on another supplier with costs and licenses. Finally it should not be technically over-sophisticated or arcane, or too "state of the art" so that a conventional IT department could understand and maintain it.

The choice made was for SUMO/SUO-KIF/Sigma, but as this book is focussed on the Semantic Web, consideration needs to be given to the rejection of RDF, OWL and related tools as core technology for this particular application.

OWL representations of some COA ontologies have been produced by Ontologyx and used for limited validation purposes. However, the broader Ontologyx requirements highlighted a further set of more general issues for ontology within the Semantic Web initiative. A COA ontology makes heavy use of "composites" – that is, sets of terms used as "allowed value sets" or to represent the message or database schemas of the client systems it supports. The binary approach of RDF and OWL is unwieldy for set-based axioms.

The lack of a general facility of expressing rules is restrictive, and OWL-DL provides inadequate support for higher order axioms (in particular, the Class/Instance dichotomy, which is a significant weakness for systems such as those being supported by Ontologyx which rely heavily on "allowed value sets" of classes of classes). This can be done using OWL-Full, of course, but then the availability of reasoners is a problem.

For example, lacking a facility for expressing rules (ignoring the development for the moment of SWRL), there is no way to have restrictions between pairs of instances, such as that if John has Bob as a sibling then Bob must share a mother and father. Of course, for every such rule we could imagine defining a new kind of type restriction in a frame language like OWL. But there are an infinite number of such possible restrictions. Relying on OWL forces one to have either a massive language specification that still prevents new constraints from being expressed by a user of the language, or a language that is so minimal that many things can't be said. For some cases, there is a workaround that is arguably just inelegant. Take the case of wanting to say that John does not have a sibling named Bob. We could define a slot called `notSibling`. However, since we could conceivably want to express the opposite of most any slot, that would force us to define a second "not-X" slot for every slot. This becomes rather inefficient. This limitation is present even if one combines SWRL with OWL.

Another limitation of frame languages (and another not overcome by current proposed additions to OWL, such as SWRL) is the inability to handle relations among three or more things without a rather inelegant workaround that will be discussed later. Imagine that one wants to state that the letter "B" is between "A" and "C". A logical language would simply state `(between B A C)`. If one has only a frame, a slot and a value we have the slot relating two things: the frame and the slot value. The workaround is to decompose the ternary relations (a relation among three things) into a set of binary relations. This becomes:

```
(between1 A betweenness1)
(between2 B betweenness1)
(between3 C betweenness1)
```

Modelling this conventionally in OWL, we are forced to create three new binary relations, which in this case we have called `between1`, `between2` and `between3` to capture the three arguments. We are also forced to create a new term that is the "instance" of betweenness, to which we can relate the three arguments. If the original input is in logical form we would also have to create several additional statements to define how `between1` is related to the first argument of the original statement. There are, of course, a variety of approaches that can be used to work around this inherent weakness of a triple-based system, but the sheer volume of such constructs in COA makes this very unattractive as a canonical form. The domains in which Ontologyx works commonly involve complex multi-argument relations, which with COA are grouped in contexts (if they are "knowledge") or in composites (if they are syntactic data structures). Compactness of expression is a key issue if ontology creators (those who are not computer scientists) are to understand the ontology they are writing. The insistence of the Semantic Web initiative on RDF, and its fundamental restriction to binary relations as the underpinning of everything is an unhelpful constraint.

The rejection of a "Semantic Web" solution was a practical choice, not a rejection of Semantic Web solutions in principle, which are larger than the particular set of current implementations of the Semantic Web concept. We regard the ability to express our ontologies and data in RDF and OWL as essential for interoperability purposes, and in future probably for making use of other tools and applications. But, like most practitioners in this space, we find ourselves at the leading edge on several different fronts. We also suspect that as other practitioners realize that the current limitations of OWL are untenable for large scale knowledge representation it will decouple from RDF and evolve to be just another syntax for full first order logic.

The second part of the problem concerns the "translation" of data and rules from an ontological language into a more conventional relational environment, in a way that is seamless from the user's point of view, but does not require users to use the language or structures of the underlying ontology. In this case the challenge is a big one, as practically all the "intelligence" of the system is held in the ontology and its rules, not in procedural code. The ontology controls all aspects of the data relationships. The client system has a very simple database (as described below) and a "rules engine" into which constraints and processing rules are ingested from the ontology, and updated when necessary.

The main aspect of this problem is that the constraints or "axioms" of the client system are related to, but not identical to, the "knowledge" axioms of the ontology. For example, the underlying ontology states that there are dozens of kinds of creations, organized in class hierarchies. However, the client wishes in his system only to explicitly recognize a certain arbitrary number of these for a specific purpose (for example, manual data entry), but a larger arbitrary number, including superclasses, for other purposes (for example, data analysis and reporting). In addition, superclasses and subclasses may be mixed arbitrarily in specific user dropdown lists. Further, terms may be present with names in different languages with different documentation according to the regions or departments making use of the system.

This means that as well as dealing with conventional knowledge management, the underlying ontology must be capable of recognizing rules and constraints that apply only within the domain of the client system, and should be capable of supporting these. Such rules will not be inconsistent with the more general axioms of the underlying ontology, but will be more specialized.

It also means that the underlying ontology must be capable of automatically translating ontologically efficient data into less "efficient", relational or other structures in a way that retains semantic consistency.

In this context it is worth noting that the COA requirements for an ontology management system go well beyond what any ontology editor we have seen can currently offer. In this use case we are expecting the ontology to be maintained, in the long term, by the client's developers and trained users. Accordingly we will be enhancing Sigma's capabilities substantially, and integrating it with MS Excel as a data preparation tool for dealing with high volume ontology creation and mapping. Ontologyx already has its own mapping tool with which it creates COA mappings of any XML or database schema, and outputs from this will also be integrated into SUMO/SUO-KIF/Sigma.

PROPOSED SOLUTION

Objectives

Our technical objectives are:

- To create a metadata management system configured by an ontology rather than procedural code.
- To add formality to the COA model which will support full logical inference, to enable and enhance the overall system with query capability, rule validation and the ability to update and deploy system rules.
- To provide customers with a user-friendly ontology editor so that they can maintain the ontology and rules for themselves after deployment.
- To add a broader set of definitions that will allow greater degrees of database integration, as well as expansion into new markets.
- To leverage the work of others, in order to make our work more efficient and deliver greater value for the customer.
- To exercise SUMO and Sigma in real business applications as a way to increase robustness of the formal model and software, and motivate expansion of features and scope.

As a general objective, we need to go beyond the restrictions in knowledge representation imposed by the most popular current Semantic Web technologies. We also hope that by showing how a richer representation solves problems in current approaches, we may motivate richer representations in the Semantic Web.

For Ontologyx the business objective is twofold: a successful client implementation, and a generic system productized for use by others.

Overview

Our solution is to integrate the COA MetaModel and its ontologies into SUMO, expressing it in SUO-KIF using the Sigma ontology environment. Significant enhancements to SUMO, SUO-KIF and Sigma itself will not only enable them to meet the client system requirements, but also provide new tools and features for other users of SUMO and Sigma.

The initial "merger" is implemented in four broad stages:

1. The expression of COA relations and a number of classes in SUO-KIF, including a lightweight mapping to SUMO, so that this becomes the canonical form of expression of COA. This has required some enhancements to SUMO, primarily in the area of describing hierarchical data structures such as XML. This effort was complete at the time of writing (January 2008).
2. A number of enhancements are made to Sigma to support the maintenance of COA and its various Excel, HTML, XML and SQL inputs and outputs, and the expressions of client-specific system rules. At this point the management of COA and the production and maintenance of client ontologies can be transferred to Sigma. Although further refinements in this area are planned, this work was largely complete at the time of writing.
3. A comprehensive mapping of COA into SUMO. This will result in significant enhancements to both. This effort had begun in earnest with approximately 250 new terms and 3500 new formal axioms at the time of writing.
4. The development of a client-specific view of Sigma, enabling a client to use it for maintenance of the ontology. A prototype of this interface has been developed and deployed as part of the Sigma server that is available to the general public for browsing SUMO.

SOLUTION DETAILS

Overall Architecture

The system being built is split into three distinct parts:

- Procedural code to support client data management
- Ontology of terms and rules created by the client and Ontologyx
- SUMO/Sigma ontology and management tool

The software comprises a generic metadata management system. It is not fundamentally a rights management or royalty distribution system. This system is configured by the ontology and rules to create the particular applications required by the client. The two parts are independent of one another, so that a different ontology and set of rules written for a different organization (for example, a healthcare business, a library or a motor spares dealer) could use the same software for a quite different range of business activities.

The software will enable a user to perform a range of generic functions, including:

- Create data entities, and create and amend their attributes and links to other entities, by both manual and automated means.
- Comprehensively search, query and report on data.
- Carry out appropriate financial calculations.
- Output data in various forms for machine or human consumption.
- Establish the authority for all data.
- Retain a complete audit trail of all metadata activity.

- Manage workflow and internal/external messaging.

The ontology will be managed through the Sigma-based toolset. The system will be updated whenever terms or rules are added to or amended. In return, data from the system will be passed to Sigma for "offline" complex querying and inference, with results being fed back to the system or reported otherwise.

Application of the COA MetaModel

The client system's data structure is configured or parameterized by data which are stored as classes, axioms and rules in the ontology, reducing the procedural code to be written to a minimum. In this use case, the SQL database has a very simple "two table" structure ("Entity" and "Relationship"). All other database constraints, the bulk of the user interface and screen design parameters and the data processing rules are all expressed within the ontology in SUO-KIF, from which the system is "compiled" whenever changes are required. There are in fact a few specific SQL tables for authority and audit data, but these are specializations for performance reasons where functionality is predictably limited.

The client ontology is built (as with all COA-based developments) as an extension of the COA MetaModel. The rules are stored in a triple-based rules engine in the client's system, having been translated from SUO-KIF. This rules engine is used to drive many of the conventional maintenance, querying and reporting functions, but not for the more complex inference which Sigma/SUMO/SUO-KIF provides. The SUMO mapping then provides a platform for interoperability with other ontologies: although none is required for this use case at this stage, we anticipate this will be a very significant longer-term benefit.

The data architecture of the client's system is determined by the ontology which identifies the set of core metadata elements, shown in Tables 1 and 2.

Links between Entity types are specialized by the use of relators which can be expressed in COA in the form of Role-pairs (e.g. Source/Adaptation, Creator/Creation, PublishingEvent/PlaceOfPublication) or Relators (isSourceOf, hasCreator, hasPlace etc). Each Attribute has a specific generic structure of component elements. These element structures are "hard-coded" into the client system: this is one of the few areas where procedural code is written to implement data structure. A small number of standard specializations (for example, for Personal Name or Postal Address structures) are also defined in the COA MetaModel and can be hard-coded into the database structure, purely for performance optimization (though these are not being used in the current client implementation.

Note that Attributes are Entities in their own right and can therefore have their own Links and Attributes. They are specialized only in (a) their special element structures and (b) that they are wholly-owned by a single Entity.

The client's system also makes a modest move out of metadata and into the domain of content management with an item such as a song lyric.

These elements are not particular to this client but would apply to any organization using this system. For example, in the MetaModel a resource may have many different kinds of relationship with other resources according to their respective types. A sound recording, say, may be a remix of another sound recording; a track on various CDs, cassettes and DVDs; contained in various types of digital download or streaming service; it may contain samples of other sound recordings; it may be a manifestation of one or more compositions; it may have related audiovisual products and clips; sleeve artwork; DVD chapters; text blurbs and descriptions; reviews; associated still photos; and so on. The level of complexity in multimedia relationships of this type is as limitless as the methods of creating, adapting, aggregating and disseminating content (and the relationships exemplified here are only descriptive, and do not yet touch on the rights or permissions metadata which may be implied by any of them).

The COA approach is to create an ontology as an integral component of the system, so that changes to the schema are "soft coded" in the ontology, and their impact mediated automatically in the system through changes in ontological axioms rather than procedural code. The relational schema should therefore require little or no updating (and in the case, with a "two-table" model, none at all).

Because the MetaModel is highly generic, its structures apply to all entity and attribute types – rules for managing licenses, resources, parties, places or even workflow tasks are expressed using the same few primitives and building blocks.

The MetaModel therefore provides a rich but relatively simple data structure which is then specialized or "parameterized" by terms which are classes or properties in an ontology (subclasses or subproperties of the Context Model entities). The semantics of the system are therefore almost completely to be found in the supporting ontology.

Suggested Upper Merged Ontology

The Suggested Upper Merged Ontology (SUMO) (Niles & Pease, 2001) is a free, formal ontology of about 1000 terms and 4000 definitional statements. It is provided in the SUO-KIF language (Pease, 2003), which is a first order logic with some second-order extensions, and also translated into the OWL Semantic Web language (which is a necessarily lossy translation, given the limited expressiveness of OWL). SUMO has also been extended with a number of domain ontologies, which together number some 20,000 terms and 70,000 axioms (see Figure 1). SUMO has been

Table 1. Entities

COA name/ SUMO name[9]	Informal description
Resource/ Entity	Anything which is made, e.g. a song, songbook, CD, leadsheet, video clip, document
Party/ Agent	A person, group or organization
Place/ Region	A geographical place (e.g. a city or postal place) or a "virtual" place (eg a Website, email account or bank account)
Time/ TimePosition	A point or period of time
Context/ Process	An event or state (e.g. an agreement, use of a creation, publishing event, death of a party, control of a right)
Link/ Relation	A relationship between any two entities (e.g. person X is the composer of song Y, lyric B is a part of work C)

Table 2. Attributes/Properties

COA name/ SUMO name	Informal description
Name/ name	A name by which an entity is referenced
Identifier/ uniqueIdentifier	A unique name of an entity (including addresses, email addresses and phone numbers)
Annotation/ documentation	A description, comment or other informative text about an entity
Category/ subclass	A type or quality of an entity
Flag/ truth	A binary Category (True/False)
Quantity/ measure	A measurement of some aspect of an entity

mapped to the WordNet lexicon (Fellbaum, 1998) of over 100,000 noun, verb, adjective, and adverb word senses (Niles & Pease, 2003), which not only acts as a check on coverage and completeness, but also provides a basis for work in natural language processing (Pease & Murray, 2003) (Elkateb et al, 2006) (Scheffczyk et al, 2006). SUMO is now in its 75th free version; having undergone six years of development, review by a community of hundreds of people, and application in expert reasoning and linguistics. Various versions of SUMO have been subjected to formal verification with an automated theorem prover.

A key portion of SUMO for Media Rights is its model of semiotics (Pease&Niles 2002). Semiotics is the theory of signs, and it has aroused considerable interest in a wide range of fields, including linguistics, anthropology, literary criticism, political science, and philosophy. The SUMO semiotics content was developed to represent and relate items such as the following:

- The fictional character Hamlet
- An edition of Shakespeare's play "Hamlet"
- A copy of the play "Hamlet"
- A performance of "Hamlet"
- A performance of "2Hamlet" captured on video
- The timeless informational content of the play "Hamlet"

Distinctions of these kinds are central to media rights and policy management, as the explosion in digital content has been accompanied by a parallel explosion in the granularity of content and rights identification. To the above list can be added items such as:

- An original master recording of a production of "Hamlet"
- A digital file containing an adapted copy of the master of a recording of a performance of "Hamlet"
- An image file containing a representation of a photograph of a painting of Hamlet
- A journal article about "Hamlet"
- A specific copy of a digital file of a journal article about "Hamlet" in a university library,

Figure 1. SUMO structure

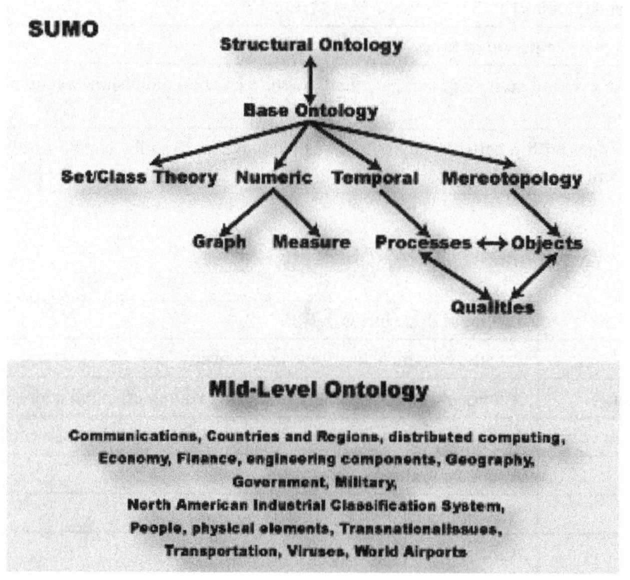

available under free use terms to students of the university but not others

And so on. The identities of these creations and the rights in them which are controlled (or not) are subject to complex semantic distinctions and relationships for which only ontology offers the promise of really effective management. Note that by "management" we do not here mean in support of restriction or commercial control: quite the opposite, in fact. The challenge facing the intellectual property community (that is, the users of the Internet) is that in the absence of effective means of identification and policy expression, rights controllers will always go for the "lowest common denominator" – which in rights management is "when in doubt, the answer is No".

SUMO Mid-Level and Domain Ontologies

The Mid-Level Ontology (MILO) is the most significant of the lower level ontologies. Rather than being driven by a specific application, it was developed largely as a by-product of the WordNet mapping effort. We guided the MILO development by using a version of the Brown corpus (Kucera&Francis 1967) that was manually annotated with fully disambiguated WordNet word senses. We started with the most frequently appearing senses and progress through to all senses that appeared at least three times in the corpus. If there was an existing SUMO concept that was equivalent to each word, we simply recorded the mapping equivalence. If there was not an equivalent concept however, we attempt to create a new formal concept. While this resulted in some new concept in SUMO proper, and some very domain specific concepts that clearly belonged in a domain ontology, there were many others that equally clearly applied to many domains and therefore were placed in MILO.

Several domain ontologies were created in attempt to ontologize the CIA World Factbook (Brasseys 1997). The ontologies that resulted were Communications, Government, Geography, People, TransnationalIssues, Transportation, Economy, and Finance. However in the subsequent years to that project those files have been considerably expanded. The CountriesAndRegions ontology is largely a list of facts one would find in an atlas, such as that France is a Nation. The Distributed Computing ontology was developed in the course of a large project that was focused on distributed operating systems and other system-level computing issues. In order to perform automated system configuration it was beneficial to have a formal ontology that could support a decision support system. Most of this ontology is highly specific. The Engineering Components ontology was developed by Michal Sevcenko (Sevcenko, 2002). Various military ontology projects have motivated the general purpose Military ontology and its subontologies of MilitaryProcesses, MilitaryPersons, and MilitaryDevices. The North American Industrial Classification system ontology was an initial and rather shallow attempt to convert the NAIC taxonomy standard into an ontology. Only the first level of the taxonomy has been properly integrated and defined. This effort did however motivate a number of additions to MILO for occupations and retail products. The Physical Elements ontology is a simple collection of facts about the fundamental physical elements, such as that lead has an atomic weight of 207. The Viruses ontology was developed by Mike Pool of IET while working on a project to represent information about biological warfare. The World Airports ontology is also a simple collection of facts about the airports in the world.

A great deal of domain specific ontology has been added to SUMO in the course of working with Rightscom. This consists of holidays, religious practices, print media artefacts, digital media artefacts, and media content creation even types. Even more content will need to be created before SUMO covers the full semantics of COA. Adding this content with full formal axioms also points out issues with the current COA representation, thereby enriching both models.

The SUO-KIF Language

SUO-KIF, the Standard Upper Ontology Knowledge Interchange Format (Pease, 2004) was created as a variant of the KIF language (Genesereth, 1991) and designed to support the SUMO project. It retains the LISP-like syntax of the original KIF, but simplifies the language somewhat by including only logical operators in the language itself, leaving any ontology that employs the language to define and handle issues such as class and instance declarations and the difference between necessary and sufficient definitions (if any). It has a relatively "free" syntax, allowing higher-order constructs such as variables in the predicate position, quantification over formulas, and no restrictions such as prohibiting predicates and instances sharing names. On the other hand, the syntax is more restricted than some other variants of KIF in that constructs that have little use in common sense knowledge representation, such as empty conjunctions, are not allowed. Variables are denoted by a leading "?" character, and universal quantification, existential quantification, implication, and biimplication are shown as "forall", "exists", "=>" and "<=>", respectively. Quantifier lists are delimited by parentheses and quantified variables have no explicit sort syntax.

Sigma

The Sigma system (Pease 2003) was designed to integrate several different kinds of tools for working with knowledge in first order logic and to be as independent of a particular ontology as possible. There are however many features that become available in Sigma when SUMO is used as the upper ontology. Current features are primarily to do with error checking. Knowing a standard method for defining argument type restrictions, class-subclass relations and documentation allows us to alert the user when such statements are conflicting or not present.

The Sigma system contains several different sorts of browsers for viewing formal knowledge bases. The most basic component is a term browser, which presents all the statements in which a particular term appears. The statements are sorted by argument position and then the appearance of the term in rules and non-rule statements are then shown. All the statements are hyperlinked to the terms that appear in them.

Two types of tree browser are provided. One provides an automatic graph layout. Another

Figure 2. System architecture

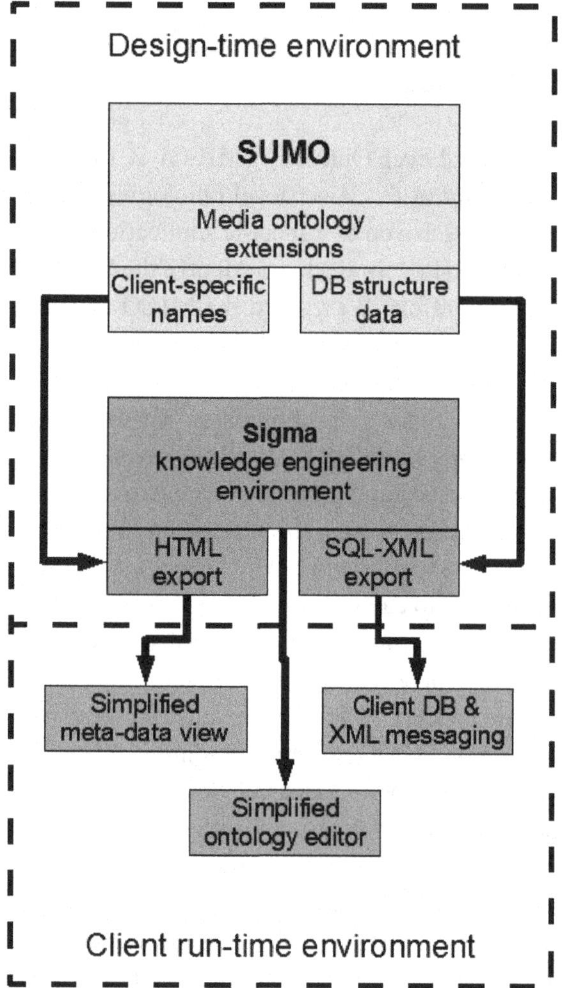

shows a textual hierarchy. The user can chose the term to start with, the number of "levels" that should be presented from the term, and the binary relation to choose as the predicate that links the different nodes in the graph. For example, if the user asks for a graph of the term `IntentionalProcess` and for the subclass relation, the system will go "up" the graph to display the term `Process`, and down the graph to display the terms `Keeping`, `Guiding`, `Maintaining`, etc. The user can ask for more levels up or down the graph. Note that any relation can be chosen so for example a presentation of partonomies, or attribute hierarchies is also supported by choosing the relations `part` and `subAttribute` respectively. Work with Rightscom resulted in the development of a simplified browsing and graphing view suitable for non-logicians. Essential for this feature has been the long-term development of a natural language paraphrasing capability for logical axioms. Coupled with translation "templates" developed for languages as diverse as Hindi, Chinese, Tagalog, French, German and English, it enables non-logicians to see paraphrases of complex logical expressions in their native language.

Sigma includes several options for proof presentation. It includes textbook-style linear proofs and also proof trees. Recent work with University of Miami (Pease&Sutcliffe, 2007) has resulted in an interface with the TPTP theorem proving suite, which gives Sigma the option to try proofs with a variety of different theorem provers, each of which have different performance in different situations. That work has also resulted in SUMO-based tests being included in the yearly CASC theorem proving competition[10], and announcement of a cash prize[11] by Articulate Software to help motivate performance on practical SUMO-based queries.

An important area for proofs in policy management lies in determining whether or not competing claims for rights ownership are consistent. Having theorem proving available for examining complex legal issues in rights ownership is a potentially significant advance, as representing legal agreements requires the full power of formal axioms.

Integrating COA and SUMO/Sigma

The outline of the approach of the target system is that all ontology content will be defined as part of SUMO (see Figure 1). Sigma, with a number of enhancements, is then used as the ontology management tool.

Each Ontologyx client has its own ontology. Each has a proprietary set of local term names and informal definitions that correspond directly to terms and definitions in SUMO, but which are worded in language that is more comfortable for and specific to the client. The set of client terms determine which portions of SUMO are considered of interest and which will be exported to define a database. A set of mapping metadata controls the physical expression of the declarative content in the database, including the arrangement into tables, foreign keys, whether to use XML attributes or subtags, and the hierarchical arrangement of tags. Processes in Sigma use the formal ontology, the client specific wording, and the mapping metadata to produce XML and SQL representations. The client installation will include not only a database, but a simplified representation of the ontology, and an ontology editor, so that Ontologyx will not need to be involved in most incremental updates to the client ontology.

The medium-term aim is for the client's Sigma-mediated ontology to be fully integrated into the policy management system itself. This will enable two main things:

- Changes made to the terms and rules in the ontology will allow the parameters of the policy management system itself to be reconfigured without intervention by development staff.
- Sigma will be used for querying and inference on instance data

The COA approach to semantics brings a different, user-based emphasis to the deployment of ontology, and as such will have broaden out the capabilities of SUO-KIF and Sigma in a number of ways, including the following:

- As it is user-focused, COA places importance on the documentation and user interface aspects of an ontology. Terms may have multiple names of different types, languages and a range of supporting comments and examples, many shared between multiple terms.
- A COA ontology incorporates complete schemas, such as XML message schemas and database schemas, so that all terms and documentation can be fully integrated. SUMO has been extended to incorporate these "composite" elements.
- The incorporation of schemas into an ontology creates the need for contextual documentation of terms when appearing in different schemas.
- Namespaces as well as languages become very important: COA client ontologies each have their own "native" naming conventions, and within a client ontology there will normally be multiple namespaces representing different systems or schemas, where the same term name may be employed to use different things.
- Sigma's input has been supplemented to allow for SUO-KIF representations to be created from a number of different Excel and XML inputs. Ontologyx is not scrapping Excel input but will continue to use it for a number of purposes, including the creation and management of schemas, the initial preparation of new ontologies "in bulk" (many of which re-use existing COA terms); and in particular for the generation of its "Context Families", where dozens, sometimes even hundreds, of class and relation terms are created in relation to a single verb.
- Sigma has been extended to support a range of new output representations of ontology, including graphic and tabular views of some or all elements, and to re-create Excel input sheets to support maintenance.

Sigma, with a number of enhancements, is then used as the ontology management tool. Sigma is also used as a "query database" to undertake complex offline queries in full first order logic whose results are then reported or fed back into the active relational database. Sigma does not perform inference directly on the SQL database (although that is direction in which we are heading) but data is extracted from the database into Sigma for this purpose. Because the client system is wholly based on a COA ontology there are no semantic issues involved in this transformation, which is purely syntactic. It may be argued that a more integrated solution to this would be achieved, say, by using an RDF triple store in the client system database. However, this would introduce the limitations to which we have referred above, and also expose a technologically conservative client to unacceptable risk at this point in the maturity of RDF-based tools for their main day-to-day systems. The use of Sigma "off line" for inference adds considerable value without much risk at this point.

The SUMO mapping then provides a platform for interoperability with other ontologies: although none is required for this particular client at this stage, we anticipate this will be a very significant longer-term benefit.

We have three approaches to XML and SQL generation that take into account legacy and third party interfaces. First, the current Ontologyx approach is to create a lightweight representation in Excel spreadsheets that specifies the structure and content of these outputs. This allows for a straightforward interface to existing schema, such as DDEX, which is an XML standard that is maintained independently of the current Ontologyx system as well as the transition target of Sigma. Sigma now includes a simple routine to generate XML data from the contents of a knowledge base. There are several challenges in this. XML is strictly a syntax for data, and says nothing about semantics. Further, it is very flexible, and many entirely reasonable representations could be created from any given knowledge base formalism. A well-axiomatized formal knowledge base typically has a directed graph structure, which is a different structure that the hierarchical arrangement that XML typically exhibits. As a result, we take a simple approach of having a very "flat" structure in the automatically created XML output. Each instance in the knowledge base is collected, along with every ground (i.e. not having variables) relation that holds on that instance. Each instance becomes a top level entity with a series of subordinate relation entities that contain the name of the relation and its value on the particular instance. The approach for generating SQL table structures is similar.

Secondly, and more interesting, is support for users to specify the structure of XML schema and SQL database schema by employing "meta"-information within the knowledge-base to guide a generation system. Each term can be designated as a database table or XML schema element. A term can also be designated as subordinate to another in an XML schema. Database data types can also be specified, although it should be straightforward to determine these automatically in a future version of the database generator. This supports the expansion of an ontology to be not only an enterprise data dictionary but also, potentially, the repository for an enterprise's entire data architecture.

The third interface is an existing XML mapping tool with which a schema can be mapped to COA semantics. Once a COA mapping ("COAM") has been created this can be used by the Translator tool to generate triples whose relations conform to the COA MetaModel. This data is then available for processing by the client system and by Sigma.

The initial focus of our work is on the integration of ontology and ontology tools to meet immediate and real business needs. However, in the longer term the integration of the COA MetaModel and SUMO promises some interesting and potentially powerful developments. In a sense, these are two "upper ontologies" being integrated. The COA MetaModel "upper ontology" is a non-mathematical but well-tested and rigorous applied contextual model, while SUMO rests on a complex Web of formal relations. Each will borrow from the other to the extent that it is useful to do.

ALTERNATIVES

Broadly, there are three alternatives to the approach being taken:

1. Stick with conventional object-relational methodologies. This is always tempting, and can be called the "boiled frog" approach. A frog placed in water that is slowly heated won't notice the change in temperature until too late. Without a shock to the system, many companies continue to extend their current process, making their long term situation ever more vulnerable. Change can be difficult, but as data models become much larger, there is no sensible alternative to massive reuse of data models that are far more formally specified than most are today. The problem of the explosion of granularity in content and content relationships is, in practical terms, not solvable with conventional object-relational data modelling alone. Up to date media organizations and rights management intermediaries have had, in general, to deal with reasonable static markets in fairly stable, physically-based content in a defined industry – printed books,

academic journals, Music CDs, video films, and TV programmes. Now every serious "publisher", "studio" or "record company" (including the range of parties involved in media who can play all such roles now, from Google at one extreme to the teenager on YouTube or MySpace at the other), is both a creator and acquirer of media and rights in all content types to be made available in a constantly expanding range of media and commercial models, at ever increasing levels of fragmentation. The result is a crisis in the specification of requirements: for most enterprises their requirement is for a system that can cope with the fact that they can no longer accurately predict even their short-term requirements. Frogs are reaching boiling point quite rapidly.

2. Implement a lightweight approach. This is a reasonable characterization of most of the work being conducted in the Semantic Web community. Models are created largely from scratch rather than through comprehensive reuse. Models are typically done in OWL-DL, often not even using most of the facilities available in that already restricted language. This sort of approach can achieve significant benefits. It's easy to learn, and not disruptive to most programmers and data modelers. There is often a significant improvement in any software implementation simply in trying to code it a second time. Recoding even without any change in fundamental technology application or approach can yield a real benefit. The problem is that the long term prospects are largely unaltered with such efforts: semantic tools alone don't fit the modelling and meaning gaps. Without significant reuse of a broad upper model, a new data model will be just as limited by simplifying assumptions as the old. With little formalization of terms beyond taxonomic and role filler constraints the potential for misinterpretation remains high, and the possibilities for automated consistency checking remain low.
3. A third alternative might be to follow the current formal ontology approach, but with a different upper ontology. There are three significant formal ontologies in existence, SUMO, Cyc and DOLCE. Cyc (Lenat, 1995) is the largest, and has been the subject of the longest research program. However, it has remained proprietary, with only the taxonomic information and a few dozen rules being released to the public as of the time of this writing, and therefore not subject to open peer review. While the taxonomic information may be useful, it is the rules that give the terms most of their actual meaning, and make Cyc useful for inference. It has been mapped to a small subset of WordNet, which numbers only some 12,000 out of 117,000 word meanings. There would be significant licensing cost to adopting a proprietary solution, and Ontologyx would not have control over the derivative product. A proprietary approach would also prevent the leveraging of effort from business partners, academic partners and standards bodies on improving and applying the ontology. Finally, the Cyc ontology critically depends on the proprietary Cyc editor and inference engine, rather than an open source system, which further limits distribution, use and cooperative development. DOLCE (Gangemi et al, 2002) is the newest effort of the three. It is public, but much smaller than either SUMO or Cyc, with a few hundred terms and axioms. It has also been mapped to only a small portion of WordNet. As such, it would offer limited additional formalization, and therefore little additional benefit, beyond continuing to develop COA from scratch, and independently of an upper ontology.

A further observation is worth making here. Semantic Web approaches tend to assume a degree (sometimes a frightening degree) of uncertainty about the meaning of terms in the data being referenced. This is reasonable when confronted with Web data *en masse*. Ontology is therefore viewed as bringing order and structure to bear on a mass of semantically doubtful data, and so anything will be seen as an improvement. "A little semantics goes a long way", as Jim Hendler has said[12].

This is fine, but Ontologyx clients face a somewhat different problem: the need for very precise class/role semantics for use within or between organizations, where inaccurate definition can result in significant human cost and error, with content being licensed (or not) in error, with the wrong people being paid, or no-one being paid at all, for the use of content. The challenge they face is to express and manage those semantics in a profitable way. It remains to be seen how far "a little semantics" can actually help with this set of problems. With any semantic integration or transaction system, where significant money and legal liability depend on having systems that understand terms in precisely the same way at a high level of granularity, "a little semantics" is clearly not enough. Those who follow a lightweight approach may be - to mix metaphors - like a frog jumping out of the boiling pan into the fire.

COST AND BENEFITS

We believe that there is no additional cost to the client as the implementation technologies will initially be equivalent to, or perhaps less than, prior implementations, and eventually a good deal cheaper: this appears to be so in our current client use case. The key in this case is the simplicity of the underlying COA data model. Much development complexity and cost stems from the complexity of an underlying database schema. The more it can be simplified, the more generic the software becomes. The current use case employs a database which is more or less a triple store.

There is also a significant cost saving likely in adopting a comprehensive existing data model, rather than (as now) developing a data model as part of the requirements process. The client receives a higher quality database and system design at potentially lower cost than would otherwise be possible. For Ontologyx there is some cost in transitioning the main technical business process of the company to a different ontology management system, but even in that regard it is anticipated that real savings will be made as resources are being redirected from active development on the prior technical approach to one based on SUMO and Sigma. The rate of technology investment is the same, but by adopting an existing powerful toolset that is also open source, there is no license cost, but a large benefit from all the prior investment in SUMO and Sigma. Additionally, since they are open source, all ongoing work and investment at improving these tools from universities and government research will also be available to Ontologyx and its clients at no cost.

For the client, the benefits are simple: cost savings and increased opportunity. We believe it is the latter which is the main driver. Taking the current client as an example, with their current systems they simply cannot expand to take the opportunities offered to them. A conventional, proprietary approach would enable them to take some of them, but with significant constraints. The COA-SUMO approach gives them, in principle, the opportunity to define their future data requirements in any way they need.

RISK ASSESSMENT

The risks to this approach are relatively low, and generally involve potential of disruption to the current process during transition to the new formal ontology system. This is being mitigated by developing the new system in parallel with maintenance of the existing system. At least initially, the implementation of the run-time system will be done using entirely conventional technologies – a relational database and procedural software. The main payoffs of the new technology approach, although they impact the correctness of the run time system, are realized at design time. Ontologyx already uses a large ontology developed in house that largely contains the same sort of frame information as in an OWL-based solution. By utilizing SUO-KIF and SUMO, a greater degree of automated consistency checking is possible for system meta-data, which should actively *decrease* risks, including that of data corruption during execution. Note that this processing can be done off-line, eliminating performance and scaling risk and run-time checking can still be effectively constrained in the current approach that compiles out the ontology into a database.

Scalability is a risk in terms of performance, as the "two-table" SQL database model results in very large database tables and higher levels of indirection in database reads. However, tests indicate this should not be a serious problem, and the risk is also likely to be mitigated by some limited specialization of the model to retain distinct tables for audit and authority purposes. One aspect of the COA approach is that it permits for every statement to be supported by a data event (who created it, when and why) and by one or more assertions or authority (who says that it is true). This "metadata of metadata" will be larger in size than the primary metadata itself, and so collapsing their relationships into distinct tables is prudent.

The performance risks on inference are mitigated by limiting Sigma's role to offline queries which are not time critical. The client database, though large, is not enormous in commercial terms: less than a million "creations" are referenced.

One possible risk is in the usability of the resulting metadata definition system for the target customers. Ontologyx does not want to be the party solely responsible for the maintenance of customer ontology (indeed, no client would commit to such a dependency), and needs to be able to push down this primary responsibility to the customers, and simply support ongoing system maintenance with expert consulting services, while focusing on the more challenging value-added activity of system development and implementation. Customers are currently presented with simplified metadata tables generated automatically from the spreadsheet-based ontology. A prototype has been implemented in Sigma that generates HTML pages in the same simplified format as currently. A challenge remains however to present enough of SUMO in a way which supports understanding of the full formal semantics of each term, without overwhelming and confusing the customer.

The open source development model significantly limits business risk for the client, as the technologies can be deployed and redistributed without license fees. Should any developer be unavailable, the client may also freely modify the system, as the source code is completely open. There is some business risk to Articulate Software and Ontologyx in having such an open system, because a client could continue development without the benefit of further consulting once the system is deployed and IT personnel are trained in its maintenance. However, we believe the highest value for our services is the expert application of the technology, rather than its incremental maintenance once an application is developed, and we would prefer the client take over that effort. Additionally, there is a business risk that another consultancy could start selling SUMO and Sigma-based services. However, we believe that is unlikely in the near term, and longer term, the market for the application of formal ontology is so large that having other players will have a greater positive impact in promoting our solutions than any lost opportunities.

FUTURE TRENDS AND CONCLUSION

In summary, Ontologyx's business has been growing along with its installed customer base. Their current approach of using a proprietary ontology developed from scratch, and limited ontology management automation based on spreadsheets was becoming increasing untenable. A solution based on the most common current Semantic Web approach of employing OWL, tools such as Protege, and continuing to use an application-specific ontology was considered and rejected in favor of a broader and more sophisticated approach. Reusing the formal semantics of SUMO will result in an ontology that has much greater rigor and much broader scope of application than would have been possible with an application ontology built from scratch. Using SUO-KIF, rather than OWL, has allowed of statements that require a level of expressiveness closer to English than frame representations support, and resulted in definitions with much greater degree of precision and resistance to confusion and misinterpretation. Use of the Sigma system has the benefits of a much greater degree of automation in the ontology management process than was possible with a process based on generic spreadsheet technology. Also, the sophisticated first-order inference capabilities of Sigma hold the promise of conducting powerful inferences not possible in a frame based language, and certainly beyond the ad-hoc approaches applicable to spreadsheet-based meta-data management.

The trend to reuse large amounts of ontology content has arguably not appeared yet in the commercial world outside of this present effort, but we believe it will be evident soon. There is no alternative to large scale reuse of information models in the same way that there is no alternative in modern software development to the reuse of operating systems, device drivers, database systems, and software language libraries.

The trend towards more sophisticated and expressive languages is clear. As databases become larger, the potential for ambiguity and inconsistency in definition and use of metadata is increasing significantly. Informal specifications in English can only go so far to address this problem, as they necessarily require human assessment of conformance. Only automated consistency checking using some sort of formal methods is likely to scale.

In working with clients, one of the consequences of this approach is that the ontology becomes central to the enterprise's operations. Where (as in this use case) the system being built is enterprise-wide, the process of defining the ontology becomes one of defining the whole scope of the enterprise. Users and business managers are therefore actively engaged with its development: it becomes the enterprise data dictionary. By transferring much of the processing logic to the ontology, users can take more direct control of their system. The governance of the ontology (in this client's case, through a review committee of users, analysts and developers, to be led by a designated ontology manager) therefore becomes a central corporate function rather than the province of an IT specialist. This has implications for the tools to be used: ontology is being out of the perceived ivory tower of academia and into the mainstream of business administration.

Another consequence is that the ontology itself contains the definitions of the schemas and rules and messages required by the system. This extends the scope of the ontology well beyond what a conventional "knowledge representation" role into the realm of data/schema representation in which complex data elements such as database or XML schemas are modeled. Syntactic as well as semantic mappings from an external schema (such as a legacy system or incoming message).

In a traditional development, analysts would first establish user requirements and later develop a data model to support the system to be built. In the COA approach the data model is provided up front, and it is then specialized through the development of the ontology as requirements are identified. Functional requirements are therefore expressed *in the terms of the ontology*, minimising the ubiquitous risk of meaning being "lost in translation" between the user, the analyst and the programmer; and with the aid of SUMO and Sigma the results can be deployed directly to the system itself. Users become ontologists, and ontologies become code-generators.

REFERENCES

Brasseys, I., (1997) *The World Factbook: 1997-98*. Central Intelligence Agency, Washington, D.C. https://www.cia.gov/library/publications/the-world-factbook/

Hillmann, D., Coyle, K., (2007). Resource Description and Access (RDA) Cataloging Rules for the 20th Century. *D-Lib Magazine* January/February 2007 Volume 13 Number 1/2 ISSN 1082-9873

Elkateb, S., Black, W., Rodriguez, H, Alkhalifa, M., Vossen, P., Pease, A. and Fellbaum, C., (2006). Building a WordNet for Arabic, in *Proceedings of The Fifth International Conference on Language Resources and Evaluation* (LREC 2006).

Fellbaum, C. (ed.) *WordNet: An Electronic Lexical Database*. MIT Press, 1998.

Gangemi, A., N. Guarino, C. Masolo, A. Oltramari, and L. Schneider. (2002). Sweetening ontologies with DOLCE. In *Proceedings of the 13th International Conference on Knowledge Engineering and Knowledge Management* (EKAW02), volume 2473 of LNCS, page 166 ff, Sig uenza, Spain, Oct. 1-4, 2002.

Genesereth, M., (1991). Knowledge Interchange Format', In *Proceedings of the Second International Conference on the Principles of Knowledge Representation and Reasoning*, Allen, J., Fikes, R., Sandewall, E. (eds), Morgan Kaufman Publishers, pp 238-249.

Hickey, Thomas B., Edward T. O'Neill, and Jenny Toves. 2002. Experiments with the IFLA Functional Requirements for Bibliographic Records (FRBR). *D-Lib Magazine* 8, 9 (September).

ISO 21000-6 (2005). *International Organisation for Standardisation/Organisation Internationale de Normalisation iso/iec jtc 1/sc 29/wg 11 coding of moving pictures and audio*. Available at http://www.chiariglione.org/mpeg/technologies/mp21-rdd/index.htm

Kucera and Francis, W.N. (1967). *Computational Analysis of Present-Day American English*. Providence: Brown University Press.

Lenat, D. (1995). Cyc: A Large-Scale Investment in Knowledge Infrastructure. *Communications of the ACM* 38, no. 11 (November).

Niles, I & Pease A., (2001). Towards A Standard Upper Ontology. In *Proceedings of Formal Ontology in Information Systems (FOIS 2001)*, October 17-19, Ogunquit, Maine, USA, pp 2-9. See also http://www.ontologyportal.org

Niles, I., and Pease, A. (2003) Linking Lexicons and Ontologies: Mapping WordNet to the Suggested Upper Merged Ontology. *Proceedings of the IEEE International Conference on Information and Knowledge Engineering*, pp 412-416.

Pease, A., (2003). The Sigma Ontology Development Environment. In *Working Notes of the IJCAI-2003 Workshop on Ontology and Distributed Systems*. Volume 71 of CEUR Workshop Proceeding series. See also http://sigmakee.sourceforge.net

Pease, A., (2004). *Standard Upper Ontology Knowledge Interchange Format*. Unpublished language manual. Available at http://sigmakee.sourceforge.net/

Pease, A., and Murray, W., (2003). An English to Logic Translator for Ontology-based Knowledge Representation Languages. In *Proceedings of the 2003 IEEE International Conference on Natural*

Language Processing and Knowledge Engineering, Beijing, China, pp 777-783.

Pease, A., and Niles, I., (2002), Practical Semiotics: A Formal Theory. *Proceedings of the IEEE 2002 International Conference on Information and Knowledge Engineering*, Las Vegas, NV, pp 3-7.

Pease, A., and Sutcliffe, G., (2007) First Order Reasoning on a Large Ontology, in *Proceedings of the CADE-21 workshop on Empirically Successful Automated Reasoning on Large Theories* (ESARLT).

Riazanov A., Voronkov A. (2002). The Design and Implementation of Vampire. *AI Communications*, 15(2-3), pp. 91—110.

Sevcenko, M., (2002). *Engineering ontology for the KSMSA project*. Unpublished SUO-KIF file. See http://sigmakee.cvs.sourceforge.net/*checkout*/sigmakee/KBs/engineering.kif

Sutcliffe G., Suttner C.B. (1998), The TPTP Problem Library: CNF Release v1.2.1, *Journal of Automated Reasoning* 21(2), 177-203.

ENDNOTES

1 http://www.rightscom.com

2 http://www.indecs.org/project.htm

3 http://www.ddex.net

4 http://www.bisg.org/onix/index.html

5 Further information on the COA can be found at www.rightscom.com.

6 http://www.articulatesoftware.com

7 http://www.ontologyportal.org

8 http://sigmakee.sourceforge.net

9 The mappings shown here are not all precise, but show mapping to the nearest existing SUMO term at the commencement of the project. Sub- or superclasses are being added to SUMO or changes made to COA where required to ensure exact equivalence.

10 http://www.cs.miami.edu/~tptp/CASC/J4/Design.html

11 http://www.ontologyportal.org/reasoning.html

12 http://research.microsoft.com/workshops/SemGrail2007/Papers/JimH_Position.doc

Compilation of References

1720/1999/EC. *Decision of the European Parliament and of the Council* of 12 July 1999

2004/387/EC. (2004). *Decision of the European Parliament and of the Council on Interoperable Delivery of pan-European Services to Public Administrations.*

Aalst, W. M. van der, & Kumar, A. (2003). XML-Based Schema Definition for Support of Interorganizational Workflow. *Information Systems Research, 14* (1), 23-46.

ABA Task Force on Electronic Commerce and Alternative Dispute Resolution. *Final Report.* (2002)

Abecker, A., & van Elst, L. (2004). Ontologies for Knowledge Management. In S. Staab & R. Studer (Eds.), *Handbook on Ontologies*: Springer.

Abelló, A., García, R., Gil, R., Oliva, M., & Perdrix, F. (2006). Semantic Data Integration in a Newspaper Content Management System. In R. Meersman, Z. Tari, & P. Herrero (Eds.), *OTM Workshops 2006.* LNCS Vol. 4277 (pp. 40-41). Berlin/Heidelberg, DE: Springer.

Aberer, K., Datta, A., & Hauswirth, M. (2005). A decentralized public key infrastructure for customer-to-customer e-commerce. *International Journal of Business Process Integration and Management*, 1, 26-33.

Abran, A. & Moore, J.W. (2004). *Guide to the Software Engineering Body of Knowledge*: 2004 Version. IEEE Computer Society Press.

Agnesund, M. (1997). Representing culture-specific knowledge in a multilingual ontology. *Proceedings of the IJCAI-97 Workshop on Ontologies and Multilingual NLP.*

Akkiraju R., Farrell J., Miller J., Nagarajan M., Schmidt M., Sheth A., Verma K. (2005) *Web Service Semantics - WSDL-S,* from: http://www.w3.org/Submission/WSDL-S/, retrieved November 2005.

Akkiraju, R. & Goodwin R. (2004). Semantic Matching in UDDI, External Matching in UDDI, in the *proceedings of IEEE International Conference on Web Services* (ICWS) July 2004. San Diego. USA

Allen, G. N., & March, S. T. (2006). The effects of state-based and event-based data representation on user performance in query formulation tasks. *MIS Quarterly, 30*(2), 269-290.

Amann, B., Beer, C., Fundulak, I., & Scholl, M. (2002). Ontology-Based Integration of XML Web Resources. *Proceedings of the 1st International Semantic Web Conference*, ISWC 2002. LNCS Vol. 2342 (pp. 117-131). Berlin/Heidelberg, DE: Springer.

Anatomical Therapeutic Chemical Classification System. (2007). Wikipedia, the free encyclopedia. Retrieved from http://en.wikipedia.org/wiki/Anatomical_Therapeutic_Chemical_Classification_System

Andersson, B., Bergholtz, M., Edirisuriya, A., Ilayperuma, T., Johannesson, P., Grégoire, B., et al. (2006). *Towards a Reference Ontology for Business Models.* Paper presented at the Conceptual Modeling (ER 2006), Tucson, AZ, USA.

Andresen, M. & Lichtenberger, B. (2007). The corporate university landscape in Germany. *Journal of Workplace Learning* Vol. 19 (2) (pp. 109-123).

Andrews, T., Curbera, F., Dholakia, H., Goland, Y., Klein, J., Leymann, F., et al. (2003, May). *Business Process Execution Language for Web Services, v1.1.*

Ang, S. & Slaughter, S. (2000). The Missing Context of Information Technology Personnel: A Review and Future Directions for Research. In: Zmud, R.W. (Ed.), *Framing the Domains of IT Management: Projecting the Future through the Past.* Pinnaflex Educational Resources, Cincinnati, Ohio.

Anicic, N., Ivezic, N., & Jones, A. (2006). An Architecture for Semantic Enterprise Application Integration Standards. In D. Konstantas, J.-P. Bourrires, M. Lonard, & N. Boudjlida (Eds.), (pp. 25-34). London, UK: Springer.

Ankolenkar A., Paolucci M., Srinivasan N., and Sycara K., (2004). *The owl services coalition, owl-s 1.1 beta release*. Technical report, July 2004.

AnsiX12 (n.d.). *National Standards Institute Accredited Standards Committee X12.*

Antoniou G., Baldoni M., Baroglio C., Baumgartner R., Bry F., Eiter T., Henze N., Herzog M., May W., Patti V., Schindlauer R., Tompits H., Schaffert S. (2004). Reasoning Methods for Personalization on the Semantic Web. *Annals of Mathematics, Computing & Telefinformatics*, 2(1), 1-24.

Antoniou, G. & Van Harmelen, F. (2004). *A Semantic Web Primer.* MIT Press.

Antoniou, G., Kehagias, A. (2000). *A note on the refinement of ontologies*, International Journal of Intelligent Systems 15(7), pp. 623-632.

Armour, S. (2001). Companies Hire Even As They Lay Off. *USA Today.* May 15, A1.

Aslam, M., A., Sören, A., Jun S., & Michael, H. (2006). Expressing business process model as owl-s ontologies. In E. Dustdar (Ed.), *Proceedings of the 2nd International Workshop on Grid and Peer-to-Peer based Workflows in conjunction with the 4th International Conference on Business Process Management*, Volume 4103/2006 (pp. 400-415), Vienna, Austria.

Assmann, U., Zchaler, S., & Wagner, G. (2006). Ontologies, Meta-Models, and the Model-Driven Paradigm. In C. Calero, F. Ruiz & M. Piattini (Eds.), *Ontologies for Software Engineering and Software Technology.*

Aumann, R.J. (1976). Agreeing to Disagree. *The Annals of Statistics*, 4(6) 1236–1239.

Aumueller, D., Do, H. H., Massmann, S., & Rahm, E. (2005). Schema and ontology matching with COMA++. In *Proceedings of the ACM SIGMOD International Conference on Management of Data* (pp. 906-908). Baltimore, Maryland, USA.

Baida, Z., Gordijn, J., Saele, H., Morch, A. Z., & Akkermans, H. (2004). Energy services: A case study in real-world service configuration. *Lecture Notes in Computer Science*, 3084, 36-50

Barillot C., Amsaleg L., Aubry F., Bazin J-P., Benali H., Cointepas Y., Corouge I., Dameron O., Dojat M., Garbay C., Gibaud B., Gros P., Inkingnehun S., Malandain G., Matsumoto J., Papadopoulos D., Pélégrini M., Richard N., Simon E. (2003). Neurobase: Management of distributed knowledge and data bases in neuroimaging. *Human Brain Mapping*, 19, 726-726, New-York, NY.

Barrasa, J., Corcho, O., Gomez-Pérez, A. (2004). *R2O, an extensible and semantically based database-toontology mapping language.* In: Second International Workshop on Semantic Web and Databases.

Battle, S., Bernstein, A., Boley, H., Grosof, B., Gruninger, M., Hull, R., et al. (2005). *Semantic Web Services Framework (SWSF) Overview* (Member Submission). W3C. (Available from: http://www.w3.org/Submission/SWSF/)

Becket, D. (2004). RDF/XML Syntax Specification. World Wide Web Consortium Recommendation. Retrieved from http://www.w3.org/TR/2004/REC-rdf-syntax-grammar-20040210.

Benatallah B., Hacid M. S., Léger A., Rey C., Toumani F. (2005). On automating Web services discovery. *VLDB Journal* 14(1): 84-96.

Berardi, D., Calvanese, D., Giacomo, G. D., Lenzerini, M., & Mecella, M. (2005). Automatic Service Composition Based on Behavioral Descriptions. *Int. J. Cooperative Inf. Syst., 14* (4), 333-376.

Berneers-Lee, T. (2007). Welcome to the Semantic Web. *The Economist*, 21, The World in 2007, p. 146.

Berners-Lee, T (1998). *The Fractal Nature of the Web*, working draft.

Berners-Lee, T., Hendler, J., & Lassila, O. (2001). The Semantic Web. *Scientific American*, 284(5), 34-43.

Bialecki, A. (2001). *REA ontology.* http://www.getopt.org/ecimf/contrib/onto/REA/

Billig A. and Sandkuhl K. (2002). Match-making based on semantic nets: The xml-based approach of baseweb. *1st workshop on XML-Technologien fur das Semantic Web*, 39–51.

Bizer, C., Heese, R., Mochol, M., Oldakowski, R., Tolksdorf, R., Eckstein, R. (2005). *The Impact of Semantic Web Technologies on Job Recruitment Processes.* Proc of the 7. Internationale Tagung Wirtschaftsinformatik 2005, Bamberg, Germany.

Boehm, B. W. (1981). *Software Engineering Economics.* Prentice Hall, Englewood Cliffs, New Jersey.

Boehm, B.W., Horowitz, E., Madachy, R., Reifer, D., Clark, B.K., Steece, B., Brown, A.W., Chulani, S. & Abts, C. (2000). *Software Cost Estimation with COCOMO II.* Prentice Hall, Upper Saddle River, New Jersey.

Bonifacio M. and Molani A. (2005). Managing Knowledge needs at Trenitalia. *Proceedings of the Second European Semantic Web Conference* ESWC 2005, Industry Forum proceedings. http://www.eswc2005.org/industryforum.html

Bonino, D., Corno, F., Farinetti, L., Ferrato, A. (2004). Multilingual Semantic Elaboration in the DOSE platform. *ACM Symposium on Applied Computing, SAC'04.* Nicosia, Cyprus. March.

Booth D., Haas H., McCabe F., Newcomer E., Champion M., Ferris C., Orchard D. (2004) *Web Services architecture.* From: http://www.w3.org/TR/ws-arch/, Retrieved February 2004.

Borch, S.E., Jespersen, J.W., Linvald, J., & Osterbye, K. (2003). A Model Driven Architecture for REA based systems. *Workshop on Model Driven Architecture: Foundations and Applications.* University of Twente, Enshede, The Netherlands.

Borgo, S., & Leitao, P. (2004). *The Role of Foundational Ontologies in Manufacturing Domain Applications.* Paper presented at the OTM Confederated International Conferences, ODBASE 2004, Ayia Napa, Cyprus.

Brambilla, M., Celino, I., Ceri, S., Cerizza, D., Valle, E. D., & Facca, F. M. (2006). A Software Engineering Approach to Design and Development of semantic Web Service Applications. In *Proceedings of the 5th International Semantic Web Conference.* Athens, GA, USA: Springer.

Bramer, M., & Terziyan, V. (2005). *Industrial Applications of Semantic Web* (Vol. 188): Springer-Verslag.

Brasseys, I., (1997) *The World Factbook: 1997-98.* Central Intelligence Agency, Washington, D.C. https://www.cia.gov/library/publications/the-world-factbook/

Brickley, D and Guha, R (2004). *RDF Vocabulary Description Language 1.0: RDF Schema*, W3C. http://www.w3.org/TR/rdf-schema/

Brockmans, S., Colomb, R., Haase, P., Kendal, E., Wallace, E., Welty, C., et al. (2006). A Model Driven Approach for building OWL DL and OWL Full Ontologies. *Lecture Notes in Computer Science*, 4273.

Brooks, F.P. (1987). No Silver Bullet: Essence and Accidents of Software Engineering. *Computer.* 20 (4), 10-19.

Brown, A. (2004). An Introduction *to Model Driven ArchitecturePart I: MDA and Todays Systems* (Tech. Rep.). IBM. (Available from: http://www.ibm.com/developerworks/rational/library/3100.html)

Bruijn, J. de, Bussler, C., Domingue, J., Fensel, D., Hepp, M., Keller, U., et al. (2005). *Web Service Modeling On-*

tology (WSMO) (Member Submission). W3C. (Available from: http://www.w3.org/Submission/WSMO/)

Brunnermeier, S. B., & Martin, S. A. (2002). Interoperability costs in the US automotive supply chain. *Supply Chain Management: An International Journal, 7* (2), 71-82.

Brunschweig B. and Rainaud J.F. (2005). Semantic Web applications for the Petroleum industry. *Proceedings of the 2nd European Semantic Web Conference,* ESWC 2005 Industry Forum http://www.eswc2005.org/industryforum.html

Bryan, M. (eds.) (2001). MULECO -Multilingual Upper-Level Electronic Commerce Ontology. MULECO draft CWA. *The CEN/ISSS Electronic Commerce Workshop.*

BT plc. (2006). *Open Source Discussion.* Retrieved July 30th, 2007, from http://www.btplc.com/Innovation/Strategy/Open/Open.pdf

Bultan, T., Fu, X., Hull, R., & Su, J. (2003). Conversation specification: a new approach to design and analysis of e-service composition. In *Proceedings of the 12th international conference on World Wide Web* (pp. 403-410). New York, NY, USA: ACM Press.

Bureau of Labor Statistics. (Ed.). (2006). Computer Software Engineers. *Occupational Outlook Handbook, 2006-07 Edition.* U.S. Department of Labor. Retrieved August 01, 2007 from http://www.bls.gov/oco/ocos267.htm.

Bussler C., Cimpian E., Fensel D., Gomez J.M., Haller A., Haselwanter T., Kerrigan M., Mocan A., Moran M., Oren E., Sapkota B., Toma I., Viskova J., Vitvar T., Zaremba Maciej, Zaremba Michal (2005). *Web Service Execution Environment (WSMX).* From: http://www.w3.org/Submission/WSMX/, retrieved November 2007.

Bussler, C. (2003). *B2B integration: Concepts and Architecture.* Springer.

Bussler, C. (2003). The role of Semantic Web technology in EAI. *The Bulletin of the IEEE Computer Society Technical Committee on Data Engineering.*

Bussler, C. (2005). Business-to-business integration technology. *Data Management in a Connected World,* 3551, 235-254.

Bussler, C. (2007). The Fractal Nature of Web Services. *IEEE Computer, 40* (3), 93-95.

Bussler, C., Fensel, D., & Maedche, A. (2002). A Conceptual Architecture for Semantic Web Enabled Web Services. *SIGMOD Record, 31* (4), 24-29. ACM Press.

Cabral, L., Domingue, J., Galizia, S., Gugliotta, A., Tanasescu, V., Pedrinaci, C., et al. (2006). IRS-III: A Broker for semantic Web Services Based Applications. In *Proceedings of the 5th International Semantic Web Conference.* (pp. 201-214). Athens, GA, USA:Springer.

Calero, C., Ruiz, F., & Piattini, M. (2006). *Ontologies for software engineering and software technology* (1st ed.). New York: Springer.

Cardoso J. and Sheth A. (2003). Semantic e-workflow composition. *Journal of Intelligent Information Systems,* 21(3): 191–225. Technical description of the composition of a workflow.

Career Space (Ed.). (2001). *Directrices para el desarrollo curricular. Nuevos currículos de TIC para el siglo XXI: el diseño de la educación del mañana.* International Co-operation Europe Ltd, Luxembourg.

Casanovas, J, Colom, J.M., Morlán, I., Pont, A. & Sancho, M.R. (2004). *Libro Blanco sobre las titulaciones universitarias de informática en el nuevo espacio europeo de educación superior.* Proyecto Eice, ANECA.

Castells, P., Fernández, M., & Vallet, D. (2007). An Adaptation of the Vector-Space Model for Ontology-Based Information Retrieval. *IEEE Transactions on Knowledge and Data Engineering,* 19(2), 261-272.

Castells, P., Perdrix, F., Pulido, E., Rico, M., Benjamins, R., Contreras, J., et al. (2004). Neptuno: Semantic Web Technologies for a Digital Newspaper Archive. In C. Bussler, J. Davies, D. Fensel, & R. Studer, (Eds.), *The Semantic Web: Research and Applications: First European Semantic Web Symposium,* ESWS 2004, LNCS Vol. 3053 (pp. 445-458). Berlin/Heidelberg, DE: Springer.

Castells, P., Perdrix, F., Pulido, E., Rico, M., Benjamins, R., Contreras, J., & Lorés, J. (2004). *Neptuno: Semantic Web Technologies for a Digital Newspaper Archive*. LNCS Vol. 3053 (pp. 445-458).Berlin/Heidelberg, DE: Springer.

Chalabi, C. (1998). Sakhr Arabic-English Computer-Aided Translation System. *AMTA'98*. pp. 518–52.

Chan May K.S., Bishop Judith and Baresi Luciano (2006). *Survey and Comparison of Planning Techniques for Web Services Composition*. Technical Report.

Charlet J., Cordonnier E., Gibaud B. (2002). Interopérabilité en médecine: quand le contenu interroge le contenant et l'organisation. *Revue Information, interaction, intelligence*, 2(2), 37-62.

Cho, Y., Im, I., Hiltz, S., Fjermestad, J. (2002). An Analysis of Online Customer Complaints: Implications for Web Complaint Management. *Proceedings of the 35th Annual Hawaii Int. Conf. on System Sciences*. Vol. 7.

Chou, C.-C. (2006). *Using ontological methodology in building the accounting knowledge model – REAP*. Paper presented at the 2006 AAA mid-year meeting - 2006 AI/ET Workshop

Christoph, B., Emilia, C., Dieter, F., Juan, M., G., Armin, H., Thomas, H., Michael, K., Adrian, M., Matthew M., Eyal, O., Brahmananda, S., Ioan, T., Jana, V., Tomas, V., Maciej, Z., & Michal, Z. (2005). *Web service execution environment (wsmx)*. Retrieved April 20, 2007, from http://www.w3.org/Submission/WSMX/

Cimiano, P., Haase, P., Heizmann, J., & Mantel, M. (2007). *ORAKEL: A portable Natural Language Interface to Knowledge Bases*.

Cimpian E, Mocan A (2005). *Process Mediation in WSMX*. WSMO Working Draft D13.7 v0.1. http://www.wsmo.org/TR/d13/d13.7/v0.1/

Cimpian, E., Mocan, A. (2005). *WSMX Process Mediation Based on Choreographies*. In: Business Process Management Workshops. 130–143

Ciocoiu, M., Gruninger, M., & Nau, D. S. (2000). Ontologies for Integrating Engineering Applications. *Journal of Computing and Information Science in Engineering*, 1(1), 12-22.

Claes, F., Wernerfelt, B. (1987). Defensive Marketing Strategy by Customer Complaint Management: A Theoretical Analysis. *Journal of Marketing Research*, No. 24. November pp. 337–346

Clark & Parsia LLC (2007). *Pellet: The Open Source OWL DL Reasoner*. http://pellet.owldl.com/

Clark, J., Casanave, C., Kanaskie, K., Harvey, B., Clark, J., Smith, N., et al. (2001). *ebXML Business Process Specification Schema (Version 1.01)*. ebXML. (Available from: http://www.ebxml.org/specs/ebBPSS.pdf/)

College of American Pathologists. (2007). *SNOMED CT User Guide – January 2007 Release*. Retrieved August 7, 2007, from http://www.ihtsdo.org/fileadmin/user_upload/Docs_01/Technical_Docs/snomed_ct_user_guide.pdf

Corcho, O., Fernández-López, M., Gómez-Pérez, A., and Lama, M. (2003). *ODESWS: A Semantic Web Service Development Environment*. VLDB-Workshop on Semantic Web and Databases, 203-216. Berlin, Germany.

Cordonnier E., Croci S., Laurent J.-F., Gibaud B. (2003). Interoperability and Medical Communication Using "Patient Envelope"-Based Secure Messaging. *Medical Informatics Europe Congress*, 95, 230-235.

CrosswaterSystems. (2003). *Der Virtuelle Arbeitsmarkt der Bundesanstalt für Arbeit. Anspruch und Wirklichkeit - das Millionengrab*.

Cruz, I., Xiao, H., & Hsu, F. (2004). An Ontology-based Framework for XML Semantic Integration. *Proceedings of the Eighth International Database Engineering and Applications Symposium*, IDEAS'04, (pp. 217-226). Washington, DC: IEEE Computer Society.

Cuayahuitl, H., & Serridge, B. (2002). Out-of-vocabulary Word Modelling and Rejection for Spanish Keyword Spotting Systems. *Proceedings of the 2nd Mexican International Conference on Artificial Intelligence*.

Cuel R., Deleteil A., Louis V., Rizzi C. (2008). *Knowledge Web Technology Roadmap: The Technology Roadmap of the Semantic Web*. To appear early 2008.

Curtis, B., Hefley, W. E. & Miller, S. A. (2001). *People Capability Maturity Model (P-CMM®) Version 2.0.* CMU/SEI-2001-MM-01.

Damodaran, S. (2004). B2B integration over the Internet with XML: RosettaNet successes and challenges. In *Proceedings of the 13th International World Wide Web Conference on Alternate track papers & posters.* (pp. 188-195). New York, NY, USA: ACM Press.

Damodaran, S. (2005). RosettaNet: Adoption Brings New Problems, New Solutions. In *Proceedings of the XML 2005 Conference.* (pp. 1-14). Atlanta, USA: IDE Alliance.

Dan, B., & Ramanathan, V., G. (2004). *RDF vocabulary description language 1.0: RDF schema.* Retrieved May 22, 2007, from http://www.w3.org/TR/2004/REC-rdf-schema-20040210/.Daniel, E., Grit, D., David, M., Fred, G., John, K., Shahin, S., & Rukman, S. (2005). The OWL-S editor - A development tool for semantic web services. In A. Gomez-Perez & J. Euzenat (Eds.), *The Semantic Web Research and Applications, 2nd European Semantic Web Conference*, Volume 3532 (pp. 78-92), Heraklion, Crete, Greece.

Dasgupta, P., & Das, R. (2000). Dynamic Service Pricing for Brokers in a Multi-Agent Economy. *Proceedings of the Third International Conference for Multi-Agent Systems* (ICMAS), pp. 375-76.

Dasiopoulou S., Saathoof C., Mylonas Ph., Avrithis Y., Kompatsiaris Y., Staab S. (2007). Introducing Context and Reasoning in Visual Content Analysis: An Ontology-based Framework. In Paola Hobson, Ioannis Kompatsiaris (Editors), *Semantic Multimedia and Ontologies: Theories and Applications.* Springer-Verlag.

David, B., & Canyang, K., L. (2006). *Web services description language (WSDL) version 2.0 part 0: Primer.* Retrieved April 11, 2007, from http://www.w3.org/TR/2006/CR-wsdl20-primer-20060327

David, M., Mark, B., Jerry H., Ora, L., Drew, M., Sheila, M., Srini, N., Massimo, P., Bijan, P., Terry, P., Evren, S., Naveen, S., & Katia, S. (2006). *Owl-S: Semantic markup for web services.* Retrieved April 10, 2007, from http://www.ai.sri.com/daml/services/owl-s/1.2/overview/, March 2006.

Davies, I., Green, P., Rosemann, M., Indulska, M., & Gallo, S. (2006). How do practioners use conceptual modeling in practice? *Data & Knowledge Engineering, 58*(3), 358-380.

Davies, J., Studer, R. & Warren, P. (2006.) *Semantic Web Technologies: trends and research in ontology-based systems.* West Sussex: Wiley Publishing, John Wiley & Sons

De Ansorena, A. (1996). *15 pasos para la selección de personal con éxito. Métodos e instrumentos.* Paidos, Barcelona.

de Bruijn, J., Ehrig, M., Feier, C., Martìns-Recuerda, F., Scharffe, F., Weiten, M. (2006b). *Ontology Mediation, Merging, and Aligning* In: Semantic Web Technologies: Trends and Research in Ontology-based Systems. John Wiley & Sons, Ltd. 95–113

de Bruijn, J., Lausen, H., Polleres, A., Fensel, D. (2006). *The Web Service Modeling Language: An overview.* In: Proceedings of the 3rd European Semantic Web Conference (ESWC2006), Budva, Montenegro, Springer-Verlag

de Brujin J., Bussler C., Domingue J., Fensel D., Hepp M., Keller U., Kifer M., König-Ries B., Kopecky J., Lara R., Lausen H., Oren E., Polleres A., Roman D., Scicluna J., Stollberg M. (2005). *Web Service Modeling Ontology (WSMO).* From: http://www.w3.org/Submission/WSMO/, retrieved November 2007.

de Brujin J., Fensel D., Keller U., Kifer M., Lausen H., Krummenacher R., Polleres A., Predoiu L. (2005). *Web Service Modeling Language (WSML).* From: http://www.w3.org/Submission/WSML/, retrieved November 2007.

de Bruyn, j., Lara, R., Polleres, A., & Fensel, D. (2005). *OWL DL vs. OWL Flight: Conceptual Modeling and Reasoning for the Semantic Web.* Paper presented at the World Wide Web Conference (WWW 2005).

De Furio, I. & Frattini, G. (2006) *A Semantic Enabled Service Provisioning Architecture* in Proceedings of the 6th Business Agents and the Semantic Web (BASeWEB) Workshop, Hakodate, Japan, May 2006

Deborah, L., M., & Frank V., H. (2004). *OWL web ontology language overview*. World Wide Web Consortium, Recommendation REC-owl-features. Retrieved April 17, 2006, from http://www.w3.org/TR/owl-features/

Deerwester, S. Dumais, Furnas, G. W. Landauer, T. K. Harshman, R. (1990). Indexing by Latent Semantic Analysis. *Journal of the Society for Information Science*, Vol. 41 (6). (pp 391-407).

Della Valle, E., Cerizza, D. (2005). *The mediators centric approach to automatic web service discovery of glue*. In: MEDIATE2005. Volume 168 of CEUR Workshop Proceedings., CEUR-WS.org 35–50

Della Valle, E., D., Cerizza, I. Celino, J. Estublier, G. Vega, M. Kerrigan, J. Ramirez, B. Villazon-Terrazas, P. Guarrera, G. & Zhao G. (2007). *Monteleone: SEEMP: a Semantic Interoperability Infrastructure for e-government services in the employment sector*, Proc. of the 4th European Semantic Web Conference (ESWC).

DeMarco, T & Lister, T. R. (1987). *Peopleware: Productive Projects and Teams*. Dorset House, New York.

Description Logics for Information Integration, (2002). *Computational Logic: Logic Programming and Beyond*. LNCS; Vol. 2408, pp 41 – 60. London, UK: Springer-Verlag.

Dhamankar R., Lee Y., Doan A., Halevy A., Domingos P. (2004). iMAP: Discovering complex semantic matches between database schemas. *Proceedings of the 2004 ACM SIGMOD international conference on Management of data*, pages 383 – 394.

Di Noia T., Di Sciascio E., Donini F. M., Mongiello M. (2003). A system for principled matchmaking in an electronic marketplace. *Proceedings of the 12th international conference on World Wide Web*, WWW 2003, 321–330.

Dickinson, I (2005). *HOWTO use Jena with an external DIG reasoner.* http://jena.sourceforge.net/how-to/dig-reasoner.html

Dietz, J. L. G. (2005). *System Ontology and its role in Software Development.* Paper presented at the Advanced Information Systems Engineering wokshops (CAiSE 2005), Porto, Portugal.

Direct Employers. (2006). *Recturing Trends Survey.*

Dixon, P. (2000). *Job Searching Online for Dummies*. IDG Books Worldwide Inc., Boston, MA.

Do H.H. and Rahm E. (2002). COMA - a system for flexible combination of schema matching approaches. In *Proceedings of Very Large Databases* VLDB 2002, 610–621.

Dogac, A., Kabak, Y., Laleci, G., (2004) Enriching ebXML Registries with OWL Ontologies for Efficient Service Discovery, in *proc. of RIDE'04*, Boston, March 2004.

Dogac, A., Laleci, G. B., Kabak, Y., Cingil, I., (2002) Exploiting Web Service Semantics: Taxonomies vs. Ontologies, *IEEE Data Engineering Bulletin*, Vol. 25, No. 4, December 2002.

Dogac, A., Laleci, G. B., Kirbas, S., Kabak, Y., Sinir, S. S., Yildiz, A., et al. (2006). Artemis: Deploying semantically enriched Web services in the healthcare domain. *Information Systems, 31* (4-5), 321-339.

Dolog P., Stuckenschmidt H., & Wache H.. (2006). *Robust query processing for personalized information access on the semantic web.* In 7th International Conference on Flexible Query Answering Systems (FQAS 2006), Nr. 4027 in LNCS/LNAI, Springer, Milan, Italy.

Domingue J., Cabral L., Hakimpour F., Sell D., Motta E (2004). IRS-III: A platform, and infrastructure for creating WSMO-based semantic web services. In *Proc. Of the Workshop on WSMO Implementations.* CEUR Workshop Proceedings

Domingue, J., Dzbor, M., & Motta E. (2004). *Magpie: Supporting Browsing and Navigation on the Semantic Web.*

Donani M.H. (2006). SOA 2006: State Of The Art. *Journal of Object Technology*, 5.

Dou D., McDermott D., Qi P. (2005). Ontology translation on the Semantic Web. *Journal on Data Semantics*, 3360, 35–57.

Duke, A. & Richardson, M., (2006) *"A Semantic Service-Oriented Architecture for the Telecommunications Industry"*, in *"Semantic Web Technologies: Trends and Research in Ontology-based Systems"* J. Davies, R. Studer, P. Warren, John Wiley & Sons

Dumitru Roman, Uwe Keller, Holger Lausen, Jos de Bruijn, Ruben Lara, Michael Stollberg, Axel Polleres, Cristina Feier, Christoph Bussler, Dieter Fensel (2005). *Web Service Modeling Ontology, Applied Ontology Journal*, Volume 1, Number 1, Pages 77-106

Dunn, C. L., Cherrington, J. O., & Hollander, A. S. (2005). *Enterprise Information Systems: A Pattern Based Approach*: McGraw-Hill.

E. Della Valle, D. Cerizza, and I. Celino, J. Estublier, G. Vega, M. Kerrigan, J. Ramirez, B. Villazon, P. Guarrera, G. Zhao and G. Monteleone (2007) *SEEMP: an Semantic Interoperability Infrastructure for e-government services in the employment sector* – In Proceedings of 4th European Semantic Web Conference, ESWC 2007, LNCS 4519, Innsbruck, Austria

E. Della Valle, D. Cerizza, and I. Celino, J. Estublier, G. Vega, M. Kerrigan, J. Ramirez, B. Villazon, P. Guarrera, G. Zhao and G. Monteleone (2007) *SEEMP: Meaningful Service-based Collaboration Among Labour Market Actors* – In Proceedings of 10th International Conference on Business Information Systems, BIS 2007, LNCS 4439, Poznan, Poland

E. Della Valle, M.G. Fugini, D. Cerizza, I. Celino, P. Guarrera, G. Zhao, G. Monteleone, A. Papageorgiou, J. Estublier, J. Ramìrez, B. Villazon, M. Kerrigan (2007) *SEEMP: A marketplace for the Labour Market* - In Proceedings of e-challenges 2007, 24 - 26 October 2007, The Hague, The Netherlands

EbXML (2005) *OASIS ebXML RegRep Standard*. Available at http://docs.oasis-open.org/regrep/v3.0/regrep-3.0-os.zip

EC (2004). European Communities: *European interoperability framework for pan-european e-government services*. Technical report, Office for Official Publications of the European Communities.

ECIMF. (2003). *E-Commerce Integration Meta-Framework. Final draft.* ECIMF Project Group.

EDIFACT. ISO 9735. (2002). *Electronic data interchange for administration, commerce and transport (EDIFACT) – Application level syntax rules*. International Standards Organisation.

Ehrig M. and Staab S. (2004). QOM: Quick ontology mapping. *Third International Semantic Web Conference*, ISWC 2004, LNCS 3298, 683–697.

Einhoff, M., Casademont, J., Perdrix, F., & Noll, S. (2005) ELIN: A MPEG Related News Framework. In M. Grgic (Ed.), *47th International Symposium ELMAR: Focused on Multimedia Systems and Applications* (pp.139-142). Zadar, Croatia: ELMAR.

Elenius D., Denker G., Martin D., Gilham F., Khouri J., Sadaati S., and Senanayake R., The OWL-S editor- A Development Tool for Semantic Web Services. In *The Semantic Web: Research and Applications*. Series: Lecture Notes in Computer Science , Vol. 3532, 78-92. Springer Berlin / Heidelberg 2005. ISBN: 978-3-540-26124-7

Elkateb, S., Black, W., Rodriguez, H, Alkhalifa, M., Vossen, P., Pease, A. and Fellbaum, C., (2006). Building a WordNet for Arabic, in *Proceedings of The Fifth International Conference on Language Resources and Evaluation* (LREC 2006).

Erasala, N., Yen, D. C., & Rajkumar, T. M. (2003). Enterprise Application Integration in the electronic commerce world. *Computer Standards & Interfaces, 25* (2), 69-82.

Eriksen, L. B., & Ihlström, C. (2000). Evolution of the Web News Genre - The Slow Move Beyond the Print Metaphor. In *Proceedings of the 33rd Hawaii international Conference on System Sciences*. IEEE Computer Society Press.

ESSI (2007), *The European Semantic Systems Initiative Site* , Last access June 2007 http://www.essi-cluster.org/

Estublier, J., Vega, G. (2005). *Reuse and variability in large software applications.* In: ESEC/SIGSOFT FSE. 316–325

European Commission (2002). *EC Regulation 1400/2002; Application of Article 81(3) of the Treaty to categories of vertical agreements and concerted practices in the motor vehicle sector.* http://ec.europa.eu/comm/competition/car_sector/distribution/

European Commission (2004). *Proposal for a Directive of the European Parliament and of the Council amending Directive 98/71/EC on the Legal Protection of Designs.* Extended Impact Assessment. http://register.consilium.eu.int/pdf/ en/04/st12/st12555-ad01.en04.pdf

European Commission (2004). The European Automotive Industry: Competitiveness, Challenges, and Future Strategies, *European Competitiveness Report 2004*, http://ec.europa.eu/enterprise/library/lib-competitiveness/doc/european_competitiveness_report%202004_en.pdf

Euzenat J. and Shvaiko P. (2007). *Ontology Matching.* Springer-Verlag.

Euzenat J. and Valtchev P. (2004). Similarity-based ontology alignment in OWL-lite. *Proceedings of European Conference on Artificial Intelligence* ECAI 2004, 333–337.

Euzenat, J. (2007). MATChing ontologies for context. NeOn deliverable D3.3.1.

Evans, D., Milham, D., O'Sullivan, E. & Roberts, M. (2002). Electronic Gateways — Forging the Links in Communications Services Value Chains. *The Journal of The Communications Network*, 1, Part 1.

Evans-Greenwood P, Stason M (2006). Moving Beyond Composite Applications to the Next Generation of Application Development: Automating Exception-Rich Business Processes. *Business Integration Journal*, May/June 2006.

Evren, S. (2006). *Owl-S api.* Retrieved May 20, 2006, from http://www.mindswap.org/2004/owl-s/api/

Evren, S., Bijan P., & James, H. (2005). Template-based composition of semantic web services. In *AAAI Fall Symposium on Agents and the Semantic Web*, Virginia, USA.

Farell J., Lausen H. (2007) *Semantic Annotations for WSDL and XML Schema.* From: http://www.w3.org/TR/sawsdl/ , retrieved July 2007.

Fatima, S., Wooldridge, M., & Jennings, N. (2004). An agenda-based framework for multi-issue negotiation. *Artificial Intelligence*, 152(1), 1-45.

Fellbaum, C. (ed.) *WordNet: An Electronic Lexical Database.* MIT Press, 1998.

Fensel D., Lausen H., Polleres A., Brujin J.d., Stollberg M. Romand D., Domingue J. (2007). *Enabling Semantic Web Services – The Web Service Modelin Ontology.* Springer.

Fensel, D. (2001). *Ontologies: A Silver Bullet for Knowledge Management and Electronic Commerce*: Springer-Verlag.

Fensel, D., Hendler, J.A., & Lieberman, H. (2005). *Spinning the Semantic Web. Bringing the World Wide Web to Its Full Potential.* MIT Press.

Fensel, D., Kifer, M., de Bruijn, J., Domingue, J. (2005). *Web service modeling ontology (wsmo) submission.* w3c member submission.

Fensel, D., Lausen, H., Polleres, A., de Bruijn, J., Stollberg, M., Roman, D., Domingue, J. (2006). *Enabling Semantic Web Services – The Web Service Modeling Ontology.* Springer

Fernández Sanz, F. (2002). *Estudio de la oferta de empleo en Nuevas Tecnologías de la Información y de las Comunicaciones.* Requisitos para el empleo. Universidad Europea de Madrid.

Fernández, M., Cantador, I., Castells, P. (2006). *CORE: A Tool for Collaborative Ontology Reuse and Evaluation*, Proc. of the 4th International Evaluation of Ontologies for the Web (EON2006) Workshop located at the 15th International World Wide Web Conference WWW 2006.

Fernandez, M., Gomez-Perez, A., & Juristo, N. (1997). METHONTOLOGY: From Ontological Art to Ontological Engineering. *Workshop on Ontological Engineering. Spring Symposium Series. AAAI'97.*

Fernández, N., Blázquez, J.M., Fisteus, J.A., Sánchez, L., Sintek, M., Bernardi, A., et al. (2006). NEWS: Bringing Semantic Web Technologies into News Agencies. *The Semantic Web - ISWC 2006*, LNCS Vol. 4273 (pp. 778-791). Berlin/Heidelberg, DE: Springer.

Ferris G.R., Hochwarter W.A., Buckley M.R., Harrell-Cook G., Frink D.D. (1999). Human resources management: some new directions. *Journal of Management*, 25(3), pp. 385-415.

Ford, G., Gibbs, N.E. (1996). *A Mature Profession of Software Engineering.* Software Engineering Institute, Technical Report CMU/SEI-96-TR-004 ESC-TR-96-004.

Fortuna, B., Grobelnik, M., & Mladenic, D. (2006). Semi-automatic Data-driven Ontology Construction System. In *Proceedings of the 9th International multi-conference Information Society IS-2006*, Ljubljana, Slovenia.

Fox, M. S. (1992). *The TOVE Project: Towards a common-sense Model of the Enterprise.*

Foxvog, D., & Bussler, C. (2006). Ontologizing EDI Semantics. In *Proceedings of the Workshop on Ontologising Industrial Standards.* (pp. 301-311). Tucson, AZ, USA: Springer.

Francisco, C., Hitesh, D., Yaron, G., Johannes, K., Frank L., Kevin, L., Dieter, R., Doug, S., Siebel, S., Satish, T., Ivana, T., Sanjiva, W. (2003). *Business process execution language for web services.* Retireved April 5, 2007, from ftp://www6.software.ibm.com/software/developer/library/ws-bpel11.pdf

Frank, L. (2001). *Web Services Flow Language (WSFL 1.0).* Retrieved May 14, 2007, from http://www-306.ibm.com/software/solutions/webservices/pdf/WSFL.pdf

Gaaevic, D., Djuric, D., Devedzic, V. & Selic, B. (2006). *Model Driven Architecture and Ontology Development.* Springer-Verlag.

Gailly, F., & Poels, G. (2006). *Towards a Formal Representation of the Resource Event Agent Pattern.* Paper presented at the International Conference on Enterprise Systems and Accounting (ICESAcc 2006).

Gailly, F., & Poels, G. (2007). Ontology-driven Business Modelling: Improving the Conceptual Representation of the REA-ontology. *Lecture Notes in Computer Science 4801*, 407-422.

Gailly, F., Laurier, W., & Poels, G. (2007). *Positioning REA as a Business Domain Ontology.* Paper presented at the Resource Event Agent -25 Conference (REA-25).

Gangemi, A., N. Guarino, C. Masolo, A. Oltramari, and L. Schneider. (2002). Sweetening ontologies with DOLCE. In *Proceedings of the 13th International Conference on Knowledge Engineering and Knowledge Management* (EKAW02), volume 2473 of LNCS, page 166 ff, Sig uenza, Spain, Oct. 1-4, 2002.

García, R. (2006). XML Semantics Reuse. In *A Semantic Web Approach to Digital Rights Management*, PhD Thesis (pp. 116-120). TDX. Retrived from http://www.tdx.cesca.es/TDX-0716107-170634.

García, R., & Gil, R. (2006). Improving Human-Semantic Web Interaction: The Rhizomer Experience. *Proceedings of the 3rd Italian Semantic Web Workshop*, SWAP'06, Vol. 201 (pp. 57-64). CEUR Workshop Proceedings.

García, R., Gil, R., & Delgado, J. (2007). A web ontologies framework for digital rights management. *Artificial Intelligence and Law*, 15(2), 137-154.

García, R., Gil, R., Gallego, I., & Delgado, J. (2005). Formalising ODRL Semantics using Web Ontologies. In R. Iannella, S. Guth, & C. Serrao, Eds., *Open Digital Rights Language Workshop*, ODRL'2005 (pp. 33-42). Lisbon, Portugal: ADETTI.

Garg S., Goswami A., Huylebroeck J., Jaganathan S., Mullan P. (2005). MediaCaddy - Semantic Web Based On-Demand Content Navigation System for Entertainment. *Proceedings of the 4th International Semantic Web Conference*, ISWC 2005. LNCS 3729, 858 – 871.

Gasevic, D. (2006). *Model driven architecture and ontology development* (1st ed.). New York: Springer.

Gayathri, N, & Yun-Heh, C. (2007). Translating Fundamental Business Process Modelling Language to the Web Services Ontology through Lightweight Mapping. *IET Software Journal*, 1, 1-17.

Geerts, G. (2004). An XML Architecture for Operational Enterprise Ontologies. *Journal of Emerging Technologies in Accounting, 1*, 73-90.

Geerts, G., & McCarthy, W. (2002). An Ontological Analysis of the Economic Primitives of the Extended-REA Enterprise Information Architecture. *International Joural of Accounting Information Systems, 3*(1), 1-16.

Geerts, G., & McCarthy, W. E. (1999). An Accounting Object Infrastructure for Knowledge Based Enterprise Models. *IEEE Intelligent Systems and Their Applications, 14*(4), 89-94.

Geerts, G., & McCarthy, W. E. (2000). Augmented Intensional Reasoning in Knowledge-Based Accounting Systems. *Journal of Information Systems, 14*(2), 127.

Geerts, G., & McCarthy, W. E. (2005). *The Ontological Foundation of REA Enterprise Information Systems* - Working Paper.

Geerts, G., & McCarthy, W. E. (2006). Policy-Level Specification in REA Enterprise Information Systems. *Journal of Information Systems, Fall.*

Genesereth, M., (1991). Knowledge Interchange Format', In *Proceedings of the Second International Conference on the Principles of Knowledge Representation and Reasoning*, Allen, J., Fikes, R., Sandewall, E. (eds), Morgan Kaufman Publishers, pp 238-249.

Gibbs, W. (1994). Software's Chronic Crisis. *Scientific American*, Vol. 271 (3) (pp. 72-81).

Gilarranz, J., Gonzalo, J., Verdejo, F. (1997). Language-independent text retrieval with the EuroWordNet multilingual semantic database. *The 2nd WS on Multilinguality in the Software Industry.*

Gisolfi, D. (2001). *Web services architect, Part 2: Models for dynamic e-business*. Retrieved January 2007 from http://www-128.ibm.com/developerworks/webservices/library/ws-arc2.html.

Giunchiglia F. and Shvaiko P. (2003). Semantic matching. *Knowledge Engineering Review Journal*, 18(3), 265–280.

Giunchiglia F., Shvaiko P., Yatskevich M. (2004). S-Match: an algorithm and an implementation of semantic matching. In *Proceedings of the First European Semantic Web Symposium*, ESWS2004, LNCS 3053, 61–75.

Giunchiglia, F. & Shvaiko, P. (2004). Semantic Matching. *Knowledge Engineering Review*, 18(3), pp. 265–280.

Gladwin, L. (2001). Dot-Com Bust A Mixed Bag for IT Staffing. *Computerworld* (39), May 7, p. 38.

Glushko, R. J., & McGrath, T. (2005). Document engineering: analyzing and designing the semantics of business service networks. In *Proceedings of the IEEE EEE05 international workshop on business services networks.* (pp. 9-15). Piscataway, NJ, USA: IEEE Press.

Gomadam K., Verma K., Brewer D., Sheth A. P., Miller J. A. (2005) Radiant: A tool for semantic annotation of Web Services, *ISWC 2005.*

Gomez, J.M., Colomo Palacios, R., Ruiz Mezcua, B. & García Crespo, A. (2008). ProLink: A Semantics-based Social Network for Software Project. *International Journal of Information Technology and Management*, Vol.7(4) (pp. 392 - 404).

Gómez-Pérez, A., & Rojas, M. D. (1999). *Ontological Reengineering and Reuse.* Paper presented at the 11th European Workshop on Knowledge Acquisition, Modeling and Management, Dagstuhl Castle, Germany.

Gomez-Perez, A., & Suarez, M.C. (2008). NeOn methodology for building contextualized ontology networks. NeOn Deliverable D5.4.1.

Gomez-Perez, A., Fernandez-Lopez, M., & Corcho, O. (2004). Ontological Engineering – with examples from the areas of Knowledge Management, e-Commerce and the Semantic Web. *Advanced Information and Knowledge Processing.* Springer.

Gomez-Pérez, A., Fernandez-Lopez, M., Corcho, O. (2003). *Ontological Engineering*. Springer Verlag

Gómez-Pérez, J.M., Pariente, T., Daviaud, C., Herrero G. (2006). Analysis of the pharma domain and requirements. NeOn Deliverable D8.1.1.

González, J. & Wagenaar, R. (2003). *Tuning Educational Structures in Europe*. Universidad de Deusto. Bilbao.

Goodwin, B. (2000). Government Slashes Red Tape to Let in Overseas IT Workers. *Computer Weekly*, May 11.

Gordijn, J. (2002). *Value based requirements engineering: Exploring innovative e-commerce ideas*. Vrije Universiteit Amsterdam.

Graham, K., & Jeremy, J., C. (2004). *Resource description framework (RDF): Concepts and abstract syntax*. Retrieved May 25, 2007, from http://www.w3.org/TR/2004/REC-rdf-concepts-20040210

Grosof, B. N., Horrocks, I., Volz, R., & Decker, S. (2003). Description logic programs: combining logic programs with description logic. In *Proceedings of the 12th International World Wide Web Conference* (pp. 48-57). New York, NY, USA: ACM Press.

Gruber, R.T. (1995). Toward principles for the design of ontologies used for knowledge sharing. *International Journal Hum.-Comput. Stud.*, 43(5-6), pp. 907–928.

Grund, C. (2006). Mitarbeiterrekrutierung über das Internet. *Marktanalyse und empirische Untersuchung von Determinanten und Konsequenzen für die Arbeitnehmer, 76*(5), pp. 451-472.

Grüninger M. & Fox M. (1995). *Methodology for the Design and Evaluation of Ontologies*. Proc. of the Workshop on Basic Ontological Issues in Knowledge Sharing, IJCAI95.

Gruninger, M., Atefi, K., & Fox, M. S. (2000). Ontologies to Support Process Integration in Enterprise Engineering. *Computational and Mathematical Organization Theory*, 6(4), 381-394.

Grunninger, M. (2003). Enterprise Modelling. In P. Bernus, L. Nemes & G. Schmidt (Eds.), *Handbook on Enterprise Architecture*: Springer.

Guarino N., Masolo C., Vetere G. (1999). OntoSeek: Content-Based Access to the Web. *IEEE Intelligent System*, 14(3), 70-80, (May 1999).

Guarino, N. (1997). Understanding, building and using ontologies. *International Journal of Human-Computer Studies, 46*(2-3), 293-310.

Guarino, N. (1998). *Formal Ontology and Information Systems*. Paper presented at the International Conference on Formal ontology in Information Systems (FOIS'98), Trento, Italy.

Guizardi, G. (2007). On Ontology, ontologies, Conceptualizations, Modeling Languages, and (Meta)Models. In O. Vasilecas, J. Edler & A. Caplinskas (Eds.), *Frontiers in Artificial Intelligence and Applications, Databases and Information Systems IV*. Amsterdam: IOS press.

Haarslev V., Moller R., Wessel M. (1999-2007). *RACER: Semantic middleware for industrial projects based on RDF/OWL, a W3C Standard*. http://www.sts.tu-harburg.de/~r.f.moeller/racer/

Haase, P., Rudolph, S., Wang, Y., & Brockmans, S. (2006). Networked Ontology Model. NeOn Deliverable D1.1.1.

Halevy A. (2001). Answering Queries Using Views: A Survey. *VLDB Journal*, Vol. 10, Issue 4.

Halevy A., Rajaraman A., Ordille J. (2006). Data Integration: The Teenage Years. 10-year best paper award. *VLDB*.

Haller, A., Cimpian, E., Mocan, A., Oren, E., & Bussler, C. (2005). WSMX - A Semantic Service-Oriented Architecture. *In Proceedings of the 3rd International Conference on Web Services*, (pp. 321-328). Orlando, Florida, USA: IEEE Computer Society.

Haller, A., Gontarczyk, J., & Kotinurmi, P. (2008). Towards a complete SCM Ontology - The Case of ontologising RosettaNet. In *Proceedings of the 23rd ACM symposium on applied computing* (SAC2008). Fortaleza, Ceara, Brazil. (to appear)

Haller, A., Kotinurmi, P., Vitvar, T., & Oren, E. (2007). Handling heterogeneity in RosettaNet messages. In *Proceedings of the 22rd ACM symposium on applied computing* (SAC2007). Seoul, South Korea. (pp..1368-1374). ACM.

Haller, A., Oren, E., & Kotinurmi, P. (2006). m3po: An ontology to relate choreographies to workflow models. In *Proceedings of the 3rd international conference on services computing*, (pp. 19-27). Chicago, Illinois, USA: IEEE Computer Society.

Halpin, T. (1989). *A logical analysis of information systems: static aspects of the data-oriented perspective*. PhD thesis, University of Queensland, Brisbane. Australia.

Halpin, T. (2001). *Information Modeling and Relational Databases*. 3rd edn. Morgan-Kaufmann.

HarmoNet (2008). HarmoNET - the Harmonisation Network for the Exchange of Travel and Tourism Information. Retrieved January 11, 2008, from the World Wide Web: http://www.etourism-austria.at/harmonet.

Harth, A. & Decker, S. (2005). Optimized Index Structures for Querying RDF from the Web. *Proceedings of the 3rd Latin American Web Congress.*

Haselwanter, T., Kotinurmi, P., Moran, M., Vitvar, T., & Zaremba, M. (2006). WSMX: A Semantic Service Oriented Middleware for B2B integration. In *Proceedings of the International Conference on Service-Oriented Computing*, (pp. 477-483). Springer.

Haugen, R., & McCarthy, W.E. (2000). REA: A Semantic Model for Internet Supply Chain Collaboration. *Proceedings of the Business Objects and Component Design and Implementation Workshop VI: Enterprise Application Integration.*

Hausenblas, M., Troncy, R., Halaschek-Wiener, C., Bürger, T., Celma, O., Boll, et al. (2007). *Multimedia Vocabularies on the Semantic Web.* W3C Incubator Group Report, World Wide Web Consortium. Available from http://www.w3.org/2005/Incubator/mmsem/XGR-vocabularies-20070724.

Haustein, S., & Pleumann, J. (2002). Is Participation in the Semantic Web Too Difficult? In *Proceedings of the First International Semantic Web Conference on The Semantic Web*, LNCS Vol. 2342 (pp. 448-453). Berlin/Heidelberg: Springer.

Heese, R., Mochol, M., Oldakowski, R. (2007). Semantic Web Technologies in the Recruitment Domain, in *Competencies in Organizational E-Learning: Concepts and Tools.*

Heinecke, J. and Cozannet, A. (2003). Ontology-Driven Information Retrieval. a proposal for multilingual user requests. *Workshop on Ontological Knowledge and Linguistic Coding at the 25th annual meeting of the German Linguistics*, Feb. 26-28, 2003.

Hepp, M. (2005). eClassOWL: A fully-fledged products and services ontology in OWL. In *Proceedings of the International Semantic Web Conference* (ISWC).

Hepp, M. (2005). A methodology for deriving OWL ontologies from products and services categorization standards. In *Proceedings of the 13th European Conference on Information Systems* (ECIS2005), (pp. 1-12).

Hepp, M. (2007). Ontologies: State of the art, Business Potential, and grand challenges. In M. Hepp, P. De Leenheer, A. De Moor & Y. Sure (Eds.), *Ontology Management: Semantic Web, Semantic Web Services, and Business Applications* (pp. 3-22): Springer.

Hepp, M. (2007). Possible Ontologies: How Reality Constrains the Development of Relevant Ontologies. *IEEE Internet Computing*, 11(7), 96-102.

Hepp, M., & Roman, D. (2007). An Ontology Framework for Semantic Business Process Management. In *Proceedings of the 8th International Conference Wirtschaftsinformatik* 2007.

Hepp, M., Leukel, J., & Schmitz, V. (2005). A Quantitative Analysis of eCl@ss, UNSPSC, eOTD, and RNTD Content, Coverage, and Maintenance. In *Proceedings of the IEEE ICEBE 2005 Conference*, (pp. 572-581).

Herzog C., Luger M., & Herzog M. (2007). Combining Social and Semantic Metadata for Search in Document Repository.Bridging the Gap Between Semantic Web and Web 2.0. *International Workshop at the 4th European Semantic Web Conference* in Insbruck, Austria, June 7, 2007.

Heß, A., Johnston, E. & Kushmerick, N., (2004) *ASSAM: A Tool for Semi-Automatically Annotating Semantic Web Services* © Springer Verlag, Lecture Notes in Computer Science 3rd International Semantic Web Conference (ISWC 2004)

Hibbard, J. (1997). Knowledge management-knowing what we know. *Information Week* (October 20).

Hickey, Thomas B., Edward T. O'Neill, and Jenny Toves. 2002. Experiments with the IFLA Functional Requirements for Bibliographic Records (FRBR). *D-Lib Magazine* 8, 9 (September).

Hillmann, D., Coyle, K., (2007). Resource Description and Access (RDA) Cataloging Rules for the 20th Century. *D-Lib Magazine* January/February 2007 Volume 13 Number 1/2 ISSN 1082-9873

Hilse, H., Nicolai, A.T. (2004). Strategic learning in Germany's largest companies: empirical evidence on the role of corporate universities within strategy processes. *Journal of Management Development,* Vol. 23 (4) (pp.374-400).

Hitzler P., & Sure Y. (2007) *Semantic Web.* Grundlagen, Springer.

Hofreiter, B., Huemer, C., Liegl, P., Schuster, R., & Zapletal, M. (2006). UN/CEFACT'S Modeling Methodology (UMM): A UML Profile for B2B e-Commerce. *Lecture Notes in Computer Science*, 4231, 19-31.

Holger, K., Mark, A., M., & Alan, L., R. (2004). Editing description logic ontologies with the Protégé OWL plugin. In V. Haarslev and R. Moller (Eds.), *Proceedings of the 2004 International Workshop on Description Logics*, volume 104 (pp. 70-78), Whistler, BC, Canada.

Holland, P. & Pyman, A. (2006). Corporate universities: a catalyst for strategic human resource development? *Journal of European Industrial Training,* Vol. 30 (1) (pp. 19-31).

Horrocks, I., Patel-Schneider, P.F., Boley, H., Tabet, S., Grosof, B., & Dean, M. (2004). *SWRL: A Semantic Web Rule Language Combining OWL and RuleML.* W3C Member Submission, World Wide Web Consortium. Retrieved from http://www.w3.org/Submission/SWRL

Hruby, P. (2005). *Ontology-based Domain-Driven Design.* Paper presented at the OOPSLA Workshop on Best Practices for Model Driven Software Development.

Hruby, P. (2005). *Role of Domain Ontologies in Software Factories.* Paper presented at the OOPSLA Workshop on Software Factories, San Diego, California.

Hruby, P., Kiehn, J., & Scheller, C. V. (2006). *Model-driven design using business patterns.* New York: Springer.

Hu, W., Cheng, G., Zheng, D., Zhong, X., & Qu, Y. (2006). The Results of Falcon-AO in the OAEI 2006 Campaign. In *Proceedings of the 1st International Workshop on Ontology Matching.* Athens, GA, USA.

Huhns, M. N., & Singh, M. P. (1997). *Readings in Agents.* San Francisco, CA: Morgan Kaufmann Publishers.

Hull R. and Su J. (2005). Tools for composite Web services: A short Overview. *ACM SIGMOD Record*, Vol. 34, 2.

Hull R., (1997), Managing Semantic Heterogeneity in Databases: A Theoretical Perspective, Tutorial at *PODS 1997.*

Hunter, J. (2001). Adding Multimedia to the Semantic Web - Building an MPEG-7 Ontology. *Proceedings of the International Semantic Web Working Symposium* (pp. 260-272). Standford, CA.

Hunter, J. (2003). Enhacing the Semantic Interoperability of Multimedia through a Core Ontology. *IEEE Transactions on Circuits and Systems for Video Technology,* 13(1), 49-58.

IDABC and Capgemini (2004). *Architecture for delivering pan-European e-Government services*

Ihlström, C., Lundberg, J., & Perdrix, F. (2003) Audience of Local Online Newspapers in Sweden, Slovakia and Spain - A Comparative Study. In *Proceedings of HCI International* Vol. 3 (pp. 749-753). Florence, Kentucky: Lawrence Erlbaum Associates.

ISO 21000-6 (2005). *International Organisation for Standardisation/Organisation Internationale de Normalisation iso/iec jtc 1/sc 29/wg 11 coding of moving pictures and audio*. Available at http://www.chiariglione.org/mpeg/technologies/mp21-rdd/index.htm

ISO. (2006). *Information technology -- Business Operational View -- Part 4: Business transaction scenarios -- Accounting and economic ontology* (ISO/IEC 15944-4).

ISO/IEC 11179-5:2005. *Information technology -- Metadata registries (MDR) -- Part 5: Naming and identification principles.* http://www.iso.org/iso/iso_catalogue/catalogue_tc/catalogue_detail.htm?csnumber=35347

ISO/IEC 14662:2004. *Information technology -- Open-edi reference model.* http://www.iso.org/iso/iso_catalogue/catalogue_tc/catalogue_detail.htm?csnumber=37354

Jacobs, J., & Linden, A. (2002). Semantic Web Technologies Take Middleware to Next Level. Retrieved August 7, 2007 from http://www.gartner.com/DisplayDocument?doc_cd=109295

Jarrar, M. & Meersman, R. (2008, in press). Ontology Engineering -The DOGMA Approach. (Chapter 3). *Advances in Web Semantic.* Volume 1, IFIP2.12. Springer.

Jarrar, M. (2005). *Towards Methodological Principles for Ontology Engineering.* PhD thesis, Vrije Universiteit Brussel.

Jarrar, M. (2005). Modularization and Automatic Composition of Object-Role Modeling (ORM) Schemes. In *OTM 2005 Workshops, proceedings of the International Workshop on Object-Role Modeling (ORM'05).* Volume 3762, LNCS, Pages (613-625), Springer. ISBN: 3540297391.

Jarrar, M. (2006). Towards the Notion of Gloss, and the Adoption of Linguistic Resources in Formal Ontology Engineering. *Proceedings of the 15th International World Wide Web Conference (WWW2006).* Edinburgh, Scotland. Pages 497-503. ACM Press. ISBN: 1595933239.

Jarrar, M. (2007). Mapping ORM into the SHOIN/OWL Description Logic- Towards a Methodological and Expressive Graphical Notation for Ontology Engineering. *OTM workshops (ORM'07).* Portogal. Volume 4805, LNCS, Pages (729-741), Springer. ISBN: 9783540768890.

Jarrar, M. (2007). Towards Automated Reasoning on ORM Schemes. -Mapping ORM into the DLR_idf description logic. *Proceedings of the 26th International Conference on Conceptual Modeling (ER 2007).* Volume 4801, LNCS, Pages (181-197), Springer. ISBN:9783540755623. New Zealand.

Jarrar, M., & Eldammagh, M. (2007, August). *Reasoning on ORM using Racer.* Technical Report. STAR Lab, Vrije Universiteit Brussel, Belgium.

Jarrar, M., & Heymans, S. (2006). Unsatisfiability Reasoning in ORM Conceptual Schemes. *Proceeding of International Conference on Semantics of a Networked World.* Germany. Volume 4254, LNCS, Pages (517-534), Springer. ISBN: 3540467882.

Jarrar, M., & Heymans, S. (2008). Towards Pattern-based Reasoning for Friendly Ontology Debugging. *Journal of Artificial Tools*, Volume 17, No.4. World Scientific Publishing.

Jarrar, M., & Meersman, R. (2002). Formal Ontology Engineering in the DOGMA Approach. In *proceedings of the International Conference on Ontologies, Databases, and Applications of Semantics (ODBase 2002).* Volume 2519, LNCS, Pages: 1238-1254, Springer. ISBN: 3540001069.

Jarrar, M., Demey, J., & Meersman, R. (2003). On Using Conceptual Data Modeling for Ontology Engineering. *Journal on Data Semantics, Special issue on Best papers from the ER/ODBASE/COOPIS 2002 Conferences,* 2800(1):185-207. Springer, ISBN: 3540204075.

Jarrar, M., Keet, M., & Dongilli, P. (2006). *Multilingual verbalization of ORM conceptual models and axiomatized ontologies.* Technical report. STARLab, Vrije Universiteit Brussel.

Jarrar, M., Lisovoy, A., Verlinden, R., & Meersman, R. (2003). *OntoForm Ontology based CCForms Demo.* Deliverable D6.8, The CCFORM Thematic Network (IST-2001-34908), Brussels.

Jarrar, M., Verlinden, R., & Meersman, R. (2003). Ontology-based Customer Complaint Management. *OTM 2003 Workshops, proceedings of the 1st International Workshop on Regulatory Ontologies and the Modeling of Complaint Regulations*. Italy. Volume 2889, LNCS, pages: 594-606, Springer. ISBN: 3540204946.

Jena – A Semantic Web Framework for Java. http://jena.sourceforge.net/

Joel, F., & Holger, L. (2006). *Semantic annotations for wsdl*. Retrieved March 26, 2007, from http://www.w3.org/TR/2006/WD-sawsdl-20060928/

John, H., G., Mark, A., M., Ray, W., F., William, E., G., Monica, C., Henrik, E., Natalya, F., N., & Samson, W., T., (2003). The evolution of protégé: an environment for knowledge-based systems development. *International Journal of Human-Computer Studies*, 58(1), 89-123.

Jos D., B., Holger, L., Axel, P., Dieter, F. (2006). The web service modeling language WSML: An overview. In Y. Sure and J. Domingue (Eds.), *Proceedings of 3rd European Semantic Web Conference*, Volume 4011 (pp. 590-604). Budava, Montenegro.

Joseph, D., Ang, S. & Slaughter, S. (2005). Identifying the prototypical career paths of IT professionals: a sequence and cluster analysis. *Proceedings of the 2005 ACM SIGMIS CPR Conference on Computer Personnel Research* (pp. 94-96).

Jun, S., Georg, G., Yun, Y., Markus, S., Michael, S., Thomas, R. (2006). Analysis of business process integration in web service context. *International Journal of Grid Computing: Theory, Models and Applications*, 23 (3), 283-294.

Jun, S., Yun, Y., Chengang, W., & Chuan, Z. (2005). From BPEL4WS to OWL-S: Integrating E-business process descriptions. In *Proceedings of International Conference on Services Computing*, Volume 1 (pp. 181-190), Orland, FL, USA.

Keim, T. et al. (2004). *Recruiting Trends 2004*. Working Paper No. 2004-5. efinance Institut. Johann-Wolfgang-Goethe-Universität Frankfurt am Main.

Keim, T. et al. (2005). *Recruiting Trends 2005*. Working Paper No. 2005-22. efinance Institut. Johann-Wolfgang-Goethe-Universität Frankfurt am Main.

Keller, U., Lara, R., Lausen, H., Polleres, A., & Fensel, D. (2005). Automatic Location of Services. In *Proceedings of the 2nd European Semantic Web Conference*, (pp. 1-16). Heraklion, Crete, Greece: Springer.

Kenter, T., & Maynard, D. (2005). Using Gate as an Annotation tool.

Kerremans, K., Temmerman, R. and Tummers, J. (2003). Representing multilingual and culture-specific knowledge in a VAT regulatory ontology: support from the termontography approach. *OTM 2003 Workshops*.

Kerrigan, M., Mocan, A., Tanler, M., and Fensel, D. (2007). *The Web Service Modeling Toolkit - An Integrated Development Environment for Semantic Web Services (System Description)*, Proceedings of the 4th European Semantic Web Conference (ESWC2007), June 2007, Innsbruck, Austria

Khalaf, R. (2007). From RosettaNet PIPs to BPEL processes: A three level approach for business protocols. *Data and Knowledge Engineering, 61* (1), 23-38.

Kim, J., Jung, H., & Chung, H. (2004). A Keyword Spotting Approach based on Pseudo N-gram Language Model. *Proceedings of the 9th Conf. on Speech and Computer*, SPECOM 2004 (pp. 256-259). Patras, Greece.

King, R. (2007, April 29). Taming the World Wide Web. *Special Report, Business Week*. Retrieved from http://www.businessweek.com/technology/content/apr2007/tc20070409_248062.htm

Klein, M.C.A. (2002). Interpreting XML Documents via an RDF Schema Ontology. In *Proceedings of the 13th International Workshop on Database and Expert Systems Applications*, DEXA 2002 (pp. 889-894). Washington, DC: IEEE Computer Society.

Klyne, G and Carroll, J (2004). *Resource Description Framework (RDF): Concepts and Abstract Syntax*, W3C. http://www.w3.org/TR/rdf-concepts/

Koetzle L. (2004) *IT Spends Follows Organizational Structure*. From Forrester Research http://www.forrester.com/

Koetzle, L., Rutstein, C., Liddell, H. & Buss, C. (2001). *Reducing Integration's Cost*. Forrester Research Inc. December 2001.

Kogut, P., Cranefield, S., Hart, L., Dutra, M., Baclawski, K., Kokar, M. K., et al. (2002). UML for ontology development. *Knowledge Engineering Review, 17*(1), 61-64.

Kompatsiaris, Y., & Hobson, P. (Eds.). (2008). *Semantic Multimedia and Ontologies: Theory and Applications*. Berlin/Heidelberg, DE: Springer.

Koong, K.S. and Liu, L.C. and Liu, X. (2002). A Study of the Demand for Information Technology Professionals in Selected Internet Job Portals. *Journal of Information Systems Education*. Vol. 13 (1) (pp. 21-28).

Kotinurmi, P., Vitvar, T., Haller, A., Richardson, R., & Boran, A. (2006). semantic Web Services Enabled B2B integration. In J. Lee, J. Shim, S. goo Lee, C. Bussler, & S. S. Y. Shim (Eds.), *DEECS* (pp. 209-223). Springer.

Kucera and Francis, W.N. (1967). *Computational Analysis of Present-Day American English*. Providence: Brown University Press.

Lakshmanan, L., & Sadri, F. (2003). Interoperability on XML Data. *Proceedings of the 2nd International Semantic Web Conference*, ICSW'03, LNCS Vol. 2870 (pp. 146-163). Berlin/Heidelberg: Springer.

Lassila, O., & McGuiness, D. L. (2001). *The Role of Frame-Based Representations on the Semantic Web*. Stanford, California: Knowledge System Laboratory, Stanford University.

Lauser, B., Wildemann, T., Poulos, A., Fisseha, F., Keizer, J., Katz, S. (2002). A Comprehensive Framework for Building Multilingual Domain Ontologies. *Proceedings of the Dublin Core and Metadata*.

Le Meur, L. (2007). How NewsML-G2 simplifies and fuels news management. Presented at *XTech 2007: The Ubiquitous Web*, Paris, France.

Lehtola, A., Heinecke, J., Bounsaythip, C. (2003). Intelligent Human Language Query Processing in mkbeem. Workshop on Ontologies and Multilinguality in User Interface, in the *Proceedings of Human Computer Interface International*, HCII 2003, 4, 750-754.

Lenat, D. (1995). Cyc: A Large-Scale Investment in Knowledge Infrastructure. *Communications of the ACM* 38, no. 11 (November).

Lewis, D. (1969). *Convention: A Philosophical Study*. Oxford: Blackburn

Lindgren, R., Stenmark, D., & Ljungberg, J. (2003). Rethinking competence systems for knowledge-based organizations. *European Journal of Information Systems*, Vol. 12(1) (pp. 18-29).

Linthicum, D. (1999). *Enterprise Application Integration*. Reading, MA: Addision-Wesley Longman.

Lisi, F. A. (2007). *An ILP Approach to Ontology Refinement for the Semantic Web*, Proc. of the 4th European Semantic Web Conference (ESWC2007), Poster Session.

Lopez F. M. (2002). Overview and analysis of methodologies for building ontologies, in *Knowledge Engineering Review*, 17(2).

López-Cobo J.M., Cicurel L., Losada S., *Ontology Management in eBanking applications*. In *Ontology Management. Semantic Web, Semantic Web Services, and Business Applications*. Series: Semantic Web and Beyond , Vol. 7. Hepp, M.; De Leenheer, P.; de Moor, A.; Sure, Y. (Eds.) 2008, Approx. ISBN: 978-0-387-69899-1

Lundberg, J. (2002). *The online news genre: Visions and state of the art*. Paper presented at the 34th Annual Congress of the Nordic Ergonomics Society, Sweden.

MacKenzie M, Laskey K., McCabe F., Brown P.F., Metz R. (2006) *Reference Model for Service Oriented Architecture 1.0*. From: http://docs.oasis-open.org/soa-rm/v1.0/soa-rm.html , Retrieved October 2006.

Maedche, A., Motik, B., Silva, N., & Volz, R. (2002). MAFRA - A MApping FRAmework for Distributed Ontologies. In *Proceedings of the 13th International Conference on Knowledge Engineering and Knowledge*

Management. Ontologies and the Semantic Web, (pp. 235-250). Springer.

Mahmoud, Q. (2005). *Service-oriented architecture (SOA) and Web services: The road to enterprise application integration (EAI)*. Technical Articles, Sun Development Network. Retrieved October 19, 2005, from http://java.sun.com/developer/technicalArticles/WebServices/soa/

Mallet, L. (1997). *Títulos y Mercado de trabajo: resultados y cuestiones*. Ágora de Salónica. CEDEFOP.

Malucelli, A., Rocha, A., & Oliveira, E.. (2004). B2B Transactions enhanced with ontology-based services. *Proceeding of the 1st International Conference on E-business and Telecommunication Networks*. Setúbal, Portugal.

Martin, D. , Burstein, M., Hobbs, J., Lassila, O., McDermott, D., McIlraith, S., Narayanan, S., Paolucci, M., Parsia, B., Payne, T., Sirin, E., Srinivasan, N., & Scycara K. (2004) *OWL-S: Semantic Markup for Web Services, version 1.1* available at http://www.daml.org/services/owl-s/1.1/overview/

Martin, D., et al. (2004). *OWL-S: Semantic Markup for Web Services* (Member Submission). W3C. (Available from: http://www.w3.org/Submission/OWL-S/)

Massimo, P., Naveen, S., Katia, P., S., & Takuya, N. (2003). Towards a semantic choreography of web services: From WSDL to DAML-S. In L. Zhang, (Ed.), *Proceedings of the International Conference on Web Services* (pp. 22-26), Las Vegas, Nevada, USA.

Matjaz J., Benny, M., & Poornachandra, S. (2004). *Business Process Execution Language for Web Services: A Practical Guide to Orchestrating Web Services Using BPEL4WS*. PACKT Publishing.

Matthew, H., Holger, K., Alan, R., Robert, S., & Chris, W. (2004). *A practical guide to building owl ontologies using the protege-owl plugin and co-ode tools edition 1.0*. The University of Manchister, UK and Stanford University, USA.

McCarthy, W. (1982). The REA Accounting Model: A Generalized Framework for Accounting Systems in A Shared Data Environment. *The Accounting Review, july*, 554-578.

McComb, D. (2004). *Semantics in Business Systems: The Savvy Manager's Guide*. San Francisco: Morgan Kaufmann.

McConnell, S. (2003). *Professional Software Development*. Addison-Wesley, Boston.

McDonald, N. (2004). Can HCI shape the future of mass communications. *Interactions,* 11(2), 44-47.

McGuinness D. L., Fikes R., Rice J., Wilder S. (2000). An environment for merging and testing large ontologies. Proceedings of the *Seventh International Conference on Principles of Knowledge Representation and Reasoning* (KR2000), Breckenridge, Colorado, 483–493.

McGuinness, D & van Harmelen, F (2004). *OWL Web Ontology Language Overview*, W3C. http://www.w3.org/TR/owl-features/

McIlraith, S. A., & Son, T. C. (2002). Adapting Golog for Composition of semantic Web Services. In *Proceedings of the 8th International Conference on Principles and Knowledge Representation and Reasoning*. Toulouse, France.

McIlraith, S. A., Son, T. C., & Zeng, H. (2001). Semantic Web Services. *IEEE Intelligent Systems, 16* (2), 46-53.

McKenna, T. (2002). *Telecommunications One-track minds: providers are integrating software to manage service delivery*. Retrieved July 30th, 2007, from http://www.findarticles.com/p/articles/mi_m0TLC/is_5_36/ai_86708476

McIlraith S.A., Son T.C., and Zeng H. (2001). Semantic web services. *IEEE Intelligent Systems, Special Issue on the Semantic Web*, Volume 16, pages 46–53.

Medjahed B., Bouguettaya A. and Elmagarmid A. K.(2003). Composing Web services on the Semantic Web. *VLDB J.*, 12(4), 333-351.

Medjahed, B., Benatallah, B., Bouguettaya, A., Ngu, A. H. H., & Elmagarmid, A. K. (2003). Business-to-business interactions: issues and enabling technologies. *VLDB Journal, 12* (1), 59-85.

Meersman R. (1999). Semantic Ontology Tools in Information System Design. *Proceedings of the ISMIS 99 Conference*, LNCS 1609, Springer Verlag. pp. 30–45

Mena E., Kashyap V., Sheth A., Illarramendi A. (1996). Observer: An approach for query processing in global information systems based on interoperability between pre-existing ontologies. *Proceedings of the First International Conference on Cooperative Information Systems* CoopIS'96, 14–25.

Milanovic, N., & Malek, M. (2004). Current Solutions for Web Service Composition. *IEEE Internet Computing, 8* (6).

Ministerio de Industria, Turismo y Comercio (MITC). (2005). *Gabinete de prensa.*

Ministerio de Industria, Turismo y Comercio (MITC). (2007). *Las tecnologías de la información en España, 2006.* Centro de Publicaciones.

Ministerio de Sanidad. (2004). Plan estratégico de Política Farmacéutica para el Sistema Nacional de Salud Español. Retrieved August 7, 2007 from http://www.anisalud.com/ficheros/Plan.pdf

Mocan, A., & Cimpian, E. (2007). An Ontology-Based Data Mediation Framework for Semantic Environments. *International Journal on Semantic Web and Information Systems (IJSWIS),* 3 (2).

Mocan, A., Cimpian, E., Kerrigan, M. (2006). *Formal model for ontology mapping creation. In: International Semantic Web Conference.* 459–472

Mochol M., Jentzsch A., & Euzenat J. (2006). *Applying an Analytic Method for Matching Approach Selection.* Proc. of the International Workshop on Ontology Matching (OM-2006) collocated with the 5th International Semantic Web Conference (ISWC-2006), Athens, Georgia, USA.

Mochol, M., Jentzsch, A., Wache, H. (2007). *Suitable employees wanted? Find them with semantic techniques*, Making Semantics Work For Business, European Semantic Technology Conference 2007 (ESTC2007), 2007.

Mochol, M., Wache, H., Nixon, L. (2006). *Improving the recruitment process through ontology-based querying*, Proc. of the 1st International Workshop on Applications and Business Aspects of the Semantic Web (SEBIZ 2006), collocated with the 5th International Semantic Web Conference (ISWC-2006).

Mochol, M., Wache, H., Nixon, L. (2007). *Improving the accuracy of job search with semantic techniques*, Proc. of the 10th International Conference on Business Information Systems (BIS2007).

Moreno, A., Valls,A. & Viejo,A. (2003) *Using JADE-LEAP to implement agents in mobile devices. TILAB "EXP in search of innovation"*; Italy from http://jade.tilab.com/papers/EXP/02Moreno.pdf

MYCAREVENT Deliverable D3.2 (2005) *Generic and Integrated Information Reference Model.* http://www.mycarevent.com/Deliverables/DL.3.2_Generic_and_Integrated_Information_Reference_Model_DT_v01.00.pdf

Mylopoulos, J. (1998). Information modeling in the time of the revolution. *Information Systems, 23*(3-4), 127-155.

National Library of Medicine. (2007). MeSH factsheet. Retrieved August 7, 2007 from http://www.nlm.nih.gov/pubs/factsheets/mesh.html

Nauer, P. & Randall, B. (Eds.). (1969). *Software Engineering.* NATO Scientific Affairs Division, Brussels.

Newcomer, E. (2002). *Understanding Web services : XML, WSDL, SOAP, and UDDI.* Boston: Addison-Wesley.

Nigel, S., Tim, B., & Wendy, H. (2006). The semantic web revisited. *IEEE Intelligent Systems*, 21(3),96-101.

Niles, I & Pease A., (2001). Towards A Standard Upper Ontology. In *Proceedings of Formal Ontology in Information Systems (FOIS 2001)*, October 17-19,

Ogunquit, Maine, USA, pp 2-9. See also http://www.ontologyportal.org

Niles, I., and Pease, A. (2003) Linking Lexicons and Ontologies: Mapping WordNet to the Suggested Upper Merged Ontology. *Proceedings of the IEEE International Conference on Information and Knowledge Engineering*, pp 412-416.

Nixon L., Mochol M., Léger A., Paulus F., Rocuet L., Bonifacio M., Cuel R., Jarrar M., Verheyden P., Kompatsiaris Y., Papastathis V., Dasiopoulou S. & Gomez Pérez A. (2004). *Prototypical Business Use Cases*. (Technical report Deliverable 1.1.2), Knowledge Web IST-NoE.

Nixon, L., & Mochol, M. (2005). Prototypical Business Use Cases. Deliverable 1.1.2 in the *Knowledge Web EU Network of Excellence*, pp. 11-15 & 53-56.

Norheim D. and Fjellheim R. (2006). Knowledge management in the petroleum industry. *Proceedings of the 3rd European Semantic Web Conference*, ESWC 2006 Industry Forum. http://www.eswc2006.org/industry.html

Noy, F. & Musen, N. (1999). *An Algorithm for Merging and Aligning Ontologies: Automation and Tool Support*, Proc. of the Workshop on Ontology Management at the Sixteenth National Conference on Artificial Intelligence (AAAI-99). Orlando, FL: AAAI Press.

Noy, N. F., & Musen, M. A. (2000). PROMPT: Algorithm and Tool for Automated Ontology Merging and Alignment. In *Proceedings of the 7th National Conference on Artificial Intelligence*, (pp. 450-455). Austin, Texas, USA.

Nurmilaakso, J.-M., & Kotinurmi, P. (2004). A Review of XML-based Supply-Chain Integration. *Production Planning and Control, 15* (6), 608-621.

OASIS (2007), *The OASIS Semantic Execution Environment TC Site* , Last access June 2007 http://www.oasis-open.org/committees/tc_home.php?wg_abbrev=semantic-ex

Object Management Group (2007) *Unified Modeling Language (UML)*. http://www.omg.org/technology/documents/formal/uml.htm

Obrst, L., Liu, H. & Wray, R. (2003). Ontologies for Corporate Web Applications. *AI Magazine*, 24(3), 49-62.

Oldakowski, R. Bizer, C. (2005). *SemMF: A Framework for Calculating Semantic Similarity of Objects Represented as RDF Graph;* Poster at the 4th International Semantic Web Conference (ISWC 2005), 2005.

OMG. (2006). *Ontology Definition Metamodel: OMG Adopted Specification (ptc/06-10-11)*: Object Management Group.

OntoWeb European Project. (2002). *Successful scenarios for ontology-based applications*.

Osborne, M. J., & Rubinstein, A. (1994). *A Course in Game Theory*. Cambridge, MA: MIT Press.

Osterwalder, A. (2004). *The Business Model Ontology - a proposition in a design science approach*. University of Lausanne, Lausanne.

Otala, L. (1994). Industry-University Partnership: Implementing Lifelong Learning. *Journal of European Industrial Training*, Vol. 18 (8) (pp. 13-18).

Paolucci, M., Sycara, K., Nishimura, T., & Srinivasan, N. (2003). Toward a Semantic Web e-commerce. *Proceedings of the 6th International Conference on Business Information Systems*. Colorado Springs (CO), USA.

Papazoglou M., Traverso P., Dustdar S. and Leymann F. (2006). *Service-oriented computing research roadmap*. Technical report.

Papazoglou, M. P., & Heuvel, W.-J. van den. (2007). Service-Oriented Architectures: approaches, technologies and research issues. *VLDB Journal, 16* (3), 389-415.

Paslaru, E.B. (2005). *Context-enhanced Ontology Reuse*. Doctoral Consortium at the 5th International and Interdisciplinary Conference on Modeling and Using Context CONTEXT05.

Patel-Schneider, P., & Simeon, J. (2002). The Yin/Yang web: XML syntax and RDF semantics. *Proceedings of the 11th International World Wide Web Conference*, WWW'02 (pp. 443-453). ACM Press.

Pease, A., (2003). The Sigma Ontology Development Environment. In *Working Notes of the IJCAI-2003 Workshop on Ontology and Distributed Systems*. Volume 71 of CEUR Workshop Proceeding series. See also http://sigmakee.sourceforge.net

Pease, A., (2004). *Standard Upper Ontology Knowledge Interchange Format*. Unpublished language manual. Available at http://sigmakee.sourceforge.net/

Pease, A., and Murray, W., (2003). An English to Logic Translator for Ontology-based Knowledge Representation Languages. In *Proceedings of the 2003 IEEE International Conference on Natural Language Processing and Knowledge Engineering*, Beijing, China, pp 777-783.

Pease, A., and Niles, I., (2002). Practical Semiotics: A Formal Theory. *Proceedings of the IEEE 2002 International Conference on Information and Knowledge Engineering*, Las Vegas, NV, pp 3-7.

Pease, A., and Sutcliffe, G., (2007) First Order Reasoning on a Large Ontology, in *Proceedings of the CADE-21 workshop on Empirically Successful Automated Reasoning on Large Theories* (ESARLT).

Peter, F., P., (2005). Requirements and non-requirements for a semantic web rule language. In *Rule Languages for Interoperability*.

Petrash G. (1996). Managing knowledge assets for value. *Proceedings of the Knowledge-Based Leadership Conference*, Linkage Inc., Boston, MA, October 1996.

Petridis K., Bloehdorn S., Saathoff C., Simou N., Dasiopoulou S., Tzouvaras V., Handschuh S., Avrithis Y., Kompatsiaris I., Staab S. (2006). Knowledge Representation and Semantic Annotation of Multimedia Content. *IEEE Proceedings on Vision Image and Signal Processing, Special issue on Knowledge-Based Digital Media Processing*, Vol. 153, No. 3, pp. 255-262, June 2006.

Petrini J. and Risch T. (2004). Processing queries over RDF views of wrapped relational databases. In *Proceedings of the 1st International workshop on Wrapper Techniques for Legacy Systems*, WRAP 2004, Delft, Holland, 2004.

Pinto, H., Gómez-Pérez, A., & Martins, J. P. (1999). Some issues on ontology integration. *Proceedings of the Workshop on Ontology and Problem-Solving Methods: Lesson learned and Future Trends at IJCAI'99*, 18, 7.1-7.11.

Pinto, H.S., & Martins, J.P.. (2001) *A methodology for ontology integration*. K-CAP 2001: Proc. of the International Conference on Knowledge capture, ACM Press.

Pistore M., Roberti P., and Traverso P. (2005). Process-Level Composition of Executable Web Services: "On-thefly" Versus "Once-for-all" Composition. The Semantic Web: Research and Applications. *Proceedings of ESWC 2005*, Heraklion, Crete, Greece. LNCS 3532, Springer Verlag.

Poole, J., Campbell, J. A. (1995). A Novel Algorithm for Matching Conceptual and Related Graphs. *Conceptual Structures: Applications, Implementation and Theory, 954*, pp. 293 – 307.

Preguica N., Shapiro M., Matheson C. 2003). Semantics-based reconciliation for collaborative and mobile environments. In *Proccedings of the Eleventh International Conference on Cooperative Information Systems*, CoopIS 2003, LNCS 2888, 38-55.

Preist C, Esplugas-Cuadrado J, Battle SA, Grimm S, Williams SK (2005). Automated Business-to-Business Integration of a Logistics Supply Chain Using Semantic Web Services Technology. In Gil et al. (eds), *Proceedings of the 4th International Semantic Web Conference (ISWC2005)*. Lecture Notes in Computer Science, Volume 3729, Oct 2005, Pages 987-1001

Preist, C., Cuadrado, J. E., Battle, S., Williams, S., & Grimm, S. (2005). Automated Business-to-Business Integration of a Logistics Supply Chain using Semantic Web Services Technology. In *Proceedings of 4th International Semantic Web Conference*, (pp. 987-1001). Springer.

Pressman, R.S. (2005). *Software Engineering: A practitioner's approach*. McGraw Hill, 6th edition, New York.

Prince, C. and Stewart, J. (2002). Corporate universities – an analytical framework. *Journal of Management Development*, Vol. 21(10) (pp. 794-811).

Prud'hommeaux, E & Seaborne, A (2007) *SPARQL Query Language for RDF*, W3C. http://www.w3.org/TR/rdf-sparql-query/

Prud'hommeaux, E. & Seaborne, A. (2004). *SPARQL Query Language for RDF*. World Wide Web Consortium.

Qmair, Y. (1991). *Foundations of Arabic Philosophy*. Dar al-Shoroq. Bairut.

Rahm E. and Bernstein P. (2001). A survey of approaches to automatic schema matching. *Very Large Databases Journal*, 10(4), 334–350, (Dec. 2001).

Rajasekaran, P., Miller, J., Verma, K., & Sheth, A., (2004) *Enhancing Web Services Description and Discovery to Facilitate Composition*, International Workshop on Semantic Web Services and Web Process Composition, proceedings of SWSWPC2004 available at http://lsdis.cs.uga.edu/lib/download/swswpc04.pdf

Ran, S. (2003). A model for web services discovery with QoS. *SIGecom Exch.*, *4* (1), 1-10.

Rao, J., Kungas, P., & Matskin, M. (2006). Composition of semantic web services using linear logic theorem proving. *Information Systems, 31* (4), 340-360.

Riazanov A., Voronkov A. (2002). The Design and Implementation of Vampire. *AI Communications*, 15(2-3), pp. 91—110.

Rodriguez, J.B., Gomez-Pérez, A. (2006). *Upgrading relational legacy data to the semantic web*. In: WWW '06: Proceedings of the 15th international conference on World Wide Web, New York, NY, USA, ACM Press 1069–1070

Roman, D., Keller, U., & Lausen, H. (2004) *Web Service Modeling Ontology - Standard (WSMO - Standard), version 0.2* available at http://www.wsmo.org/2004/d2/v1.0

Roman, D., Keller, U., Lausen, H., Bruijn, J. de, Lara, R., Stollberg, M., et al. (2005). Web Service Modeling Ontology. *Applied Ontologies, 1* (1), 77-106.

Roman, D., Keller, U., Lausen, H., de Bruijn, J. Lara, R., Stollberg, M., Polleres, A., Feier, C., Bussler, C., & Fensel, D. (2005) Web Service Modeling Ontology. *Applied Ontology*, 1(1): 77 - 106, 2005.

Rosenbloom ST, Miller RA, Johnson KB. (2006). Interface terminologies: facilitating direct entry of clinical data into electronic health record systems. *Journal of the American Medical Informatics Association.*

RosettaNet Implementation Framework: Core Specification Version 2.00.01. March 2002. http://www.rosettanet.org/

Roth, B. (2007). Semantic Web the next big thing? Retrieved August 7, 2007 from http://www.web2journal.com/read/407403.htm

Ruiz Antón, F. (in press). (2004). *La Gaceta de los negocios.*

Runyon, K., & Stewart, D. (1987). *Consumer Behavior* (3rd ed.). Merrill Publishing Company.

Russ, T., Valente, A., MacGregor, R., & Swartout, W. (1999). *Practical Experiences in Trading Off Ontology Usability and Reusability.* In Proc. of the KAW99 Workshop.

Sabou, M. et al. (2006). NeOn Requirements and Vision Deliverable.

Salam, A.F. and Stevens, J. R., (2006) *Semantic Web Technologies and E-Business: Toward the Integrated Virtual Organization and Business Process Automation.* Idea Group Publishing, Hershey US.

Salembier, P., & Smith, J. (2002). Overview of MPEG-7 multimedia description schemes and schema tools. In B.S. Manjunath, P. Salembier, & T. Sikora (Ed.), *Introduction to MPEG-7: Multimedia Content Description Interface.* John Wiley & Sons.

Salton, G. Wong, A. and Yang, C. S. (1975). A Vector Space Model for Automatic Indexing. *Communications of the ACM*, Vol. 18(11) (pp 613–620).

Salton, G., & McGill, M. (1983). *Introduction to Modern Information Retrieval.* New York: McGraw-Hill.

Satish, T. (2001). *XLANG web services for business process design*. Retrieved May 1st, 2007, from http://xml.coverpages.org/XLANG-C-200106.html

Sawyer, S., & Tapia, A. (2005). The sociotechnical nature of mobile computing work: Evidence from a study of policing in the United States. *International Journal of Technology and Human Interaction*, 1(3), 1-14.

Semantic Web Case Studies and Best Practices for eBusiness (SWCASE). At *ISWC 2005*, online version http://sunsite.informatik.rwth-aachen.de/Publications/CEUR-WS/Vol-155/

Sevcenko, M., (2002). *Engineering ontology for the KSMSA project*. Unpublished SUO-KIF file. See http://sigmakee.cvs.sourceforge.net/*checkout*/sigmakee/KBs/engineering.kif

Shadbolt, N, Berners-Lee T and Hall, W (2006) The Semantic Web Revisited. *IEEE Intelligent Systems, 21*, pp. 96-101.

Sham, C. (2007). An exploratory study of corporate universities in China. *Journal of Workplace Learning*, Vol. 19 (4) (pp. 257-264).

Shenker, J.L. (2007). Battle for the Future of the Net. *Business Week*. Retrieved July 30th, 2007, from http://www.businessweek.com/globalbiz/content/jul2007/gb20070725_335895.htm

Shim, S. S. Y., Pendyala, V. S., Sundaram, M., & Gao, J. Z. (2000). Business-to-Business E-Commerce Frameworks. *IEEE Computer, 33* (10), 40{47.

Shvaiko P. and Euzenat J. (2005). A survey of schema-based matching approaches. *Journal on Data Semantics* (JoDS) 4, 146–171.

Shvaiko P., Giunchiglia F., Pinheiro da Silva P., McGuinness D. L. (2005). Web explanations for semantic heterogeneity discovery. In *Proceedings of the Second European Semantic Web Conference*, ESWC 2005, 303-317.

Shvaiko P., Léger A., Paulus F., Rocuet L., Nixon L., Mochol M., Kompatsiaris Y., Papastathis V., & Dasiopoulou S. (2004). *Knowledge Processing Requirements Analysis*. Technical report Deliverable D 1.1.3, Knowledge Web IST-NoE.

Shvaiko, P. (2004). *A Classification of Schema-Based Matching Approaches*. Technical Report DIT-04-09, University of Trento. Retrieved, December 2004, from http://eprints.biblio.unitn.it/archive/00000654/01/093.pdf

Sicilia, M. A. (2005). Ontology-based competency management: Infrastructures for the knowledge- intensive learning organization. In M. D. Lytras and A.Naeve (Eds.), *Intelligent learning infrastructures in knowledge intensive organizations: A semantic web perspective* (pp. 302-324). Hershey, PA: Idea Group.

Silva, N., Maio, P., & Rocha J. (2005). An approach to ontology mapping negotiation. *Proceedings of the Third International Conference on Knowledge Capture Workshop on Integrating Ontologies*. Banff, Canada.

Sim, K. M., & Choi, C. Y. (2003). Agents that React to Changing Market Situations. *IEEE Transactions on Systems, Man and Cybernetics*, Part B, 33(2), 188-201.

Sinuhe, A., Emilia, C., John, D., Cristina, F., Dieter, F., Birgitta, K., Holger, L., Axel, P., & Michael, S. (2005). *Web service modeling ontology primer*. Retrieved June 12, 2007, from http://www.w3.org/Submission/WSMO-primer/

Siorpaes, K., & Hepp, M. (2007). myOntology: The Marriage of Ontology Engineering and Collective Intelligence. *Proceedings of the ESWC 2007 Workshop "Bridging the Gap between Semantic Web and Web 2.0"*. Innsbruck, Austria.

Sivashanmugam, K., Verma, K., Sheth, A. P. and Miller, J. A. (2003) Adding Semantics to Web Services Standards. *ICWS 2003*: 395-401

Solomon, C.M. (1989). How does Disney do it? Personnel Journal, Vol. 68(12) (pp. 50-57).

Sowa, J. (1999). *Knowledge Representation: Logical, Philosophical, and Computational Foundations*: Pacific Grove, Brooks/Cole.

Spaccapietra, S., Parent, C., Vangenot, & C., Cullot, N. (2004). On Using Conceptual Modeling for Ontologies. *Lecture Notes in Computer Science*, 3307, 22-23.

Spackman K. A., Dionne R., Mays E., Weis J. Role grouping as an Extension to the Description Logic of Ontylog Motivated by Concept Modeling in SNOMED. *Proceedings of the AMIA Annual Symposium 2002*, San Antonio, Texas, p. 712-6, November, 9-13, 2002.

Spyns, P. (2005). Object Role Modelling for ontology engineering in the DOGMA framework. *Lecture Notes in Computer Science*, 3762, 710-719.

Srinivasan, N., Paolucci, M., and Sycara, K. (2006). Semantic Web Service Discovery in the OWL-S IDE. In *Proceedings of the 39th Annual Hawaii international Conference on System Sciences - Volume 06* (January 04 - 07, 2006). HICSS. IEEE Computer Society, Washington, DC, 109.2.

Staab, S., & Studer R. (2003). *Handbook on Ontologies. (International Handbooks on Information Systems)* Springer.

Stamou G. and Kollias S. (2005), *Multimedia Content and the Semantic Web: Standards, Methods and Tools.* Wiley.

Stamou, Giorgos, Jacco van Ossenbruggen, Jeff Pan and Guss Schreiber. (2006). Multimedia annotations on the Semantic Web. *IEEE Multimedia*, 13(1):86-90.

Stoilos G., Stamou G., Tzouvaras V., Pan J.Z., Horrocks I. (2005). A Fuzzy Description Logic for Multimedia Knowledge Representation. In *Proc. of the International Workshop on Multimedia and the Semantic Web*, pp 12-19, ESWC 2005, Heraklion, Grece, June 2005 .

Strang, C. (2005). Next Generation systems architecture – the Matrix. *BT Technology Journal.* 23(1), 55-68.

Ströbel, M. (2001). Communication Design for Electronic Negotiations on the Basis of XML Schema. *Proceedings of the Ten'th International Conference on World Wide Web.* Hong-Kong, pp. 9-20.

Stuckenschmidt, H., & Harmelen, F. v. (2005). *Information Sharing on the Semantic Web*: Springer.

Studer, R., Benjamins R., & Fensel D. (1998). Knowledge engineering: principles and methods. *Data Knowledge Engineering*, 25, 161-197.

Sure, Y., Maedche, A., & Staab, S. (2000). *Leveraging Corporate Skill Knowledge – From ProPer to OntoProPer.* Proc. of the 3rd International Conference on Practical Aspects of Knowledge Management, 2000.

Sutcliffe G., Suttner C.B. (1998), The TPTP Problem Library: CNF Release v1.2.1, *Journal of Automated Reasoning* 21(2), 177-203.

Sycara, K. P., Paolucci, M., Soudry, J., & Srinivasan, N. (2004). Dynamic Discovery and Coordination of Agent-Based semantic Web Services. *IEEE Internet Computing, 8* (3), pp. 66-73.

T. Berners-Lee, J. Hendler, & O. Lassila. (BeHeLa, 2001) The Semantic Web. *Scientific American*, 284(5), pp. 34–43.

Tang, J., Li, J., Liang, B., Huang, X., Li, Y., & Wang, K. (2006). Using Bayesian decision for ontology mapping. *Journal of Web Semantics, 4* (4), 243-262.

Tejedor, J., García, R., Fernández, M., López, F., Perdrix, F., Macías, J.A., et al. (2007). Ontology-Based Retrieval of Human Speech. *Proceedings of the 6th International Workshop on Web Semantics*, WebS'07 (in press). IEEE Computer Society Press.

Tikkala, J., Kotinurmi, P., & Soininen, T. (2005). Implementing a RosettaNet Business-to- Business Integration Platform Using J2EE and Web Services. In *Proceedings of the 7th IEEE International Conference on E-Commerce Technology* , (pp. 553-558). IEEE Computer Society.

Tous, R., García, R., Rodríguez, E., & Delgado, J. (2005). Arquitecture of a Semantic XPath Processor. In K. Bauknecht, B. Pröll, & H. Werthner, Eds., *E-Commerce and Web Technologies: 6th International Conference*, EC-Web'05, LNCS Vol. 3590 (pp. 1-10). Berlin/Heidelberg, DE: Springer.

Trastour, D., Bartolini, C., & Preist, C. (2003). Semantic Web support for the business-to-business e-commerce pre-contractual lifecycle. *Computer Networks, 42* (5), 661-673.

Trastour, D., Preist, C., & Coleman, D. (2003). Using Semantic Web Technology to Enhance Current Business-to-Business Integration Approaches. In *Proceedings of the 7th International Enterprise Distributed Object Computing Conference*, (pp. 222-231). IEEE Computer Society.

Traverso P. and Pistore M. (2004). Automated composition of Semantic Web services into executable processes. In *Proceedings of the Third International Semantic Web Conference,* ISWC 2004, 380–394, 2004.

Tsinaraki, C., Polydoros, P., & Christodoulakis, S. (2004). Integration of OWL ontologies in MPEG-7 and TVAnytime compliant Semantic Indexing. In A. Persson, & J. Stirna, Eds., *16th International Conference on Advanced Information Systems Engineering*, LNCS Vol. 3084 (pp. 398-413). Berlin/Heidelberg, DE: Springer.

Tsinaraki, C., Polydoros, P., & Christodoulakis, S. (2004). Interoperability support for Ontology-based Video Retrieval Applications. *Proceedings of 3rd International Conference on Image and Video Retrieval, CIVR 2004*. Dublin, Ireland.

Tsvetovat, M., & Sycara, K. (2000). Customer Coalitions in the Electronic Marketplace. *Proceedings of the Fourth International Conference on Autonomous Agents*, pp. 263-264.

UDDI Version 3.0.2. (2004). *OASIS Standard*. Available at http://www.oasis-open.org/committees/uddi-spec/doc/tcspecs.htm#uddiv3.

UN/CEFACT. (2003). *UN/CEFACT Modeling Methodology (UMM) User Guide* (No. CEFACT/TMG/N093).

Uschold M. and Grüninger M. (1996). ONTOLOGIES: Principles, Methods and Applications. *Knowledge Engineering Review*, 11(2).

Uschold M. and Jasper R. (1999). *A Framework for Understanding and Classifying Ontology Applications*. KRR5-99, Stockholm, Sweden.

Uschold, M. & King, M. (1995). *Towards a Methodology for Building Ontologies*. Proceedings Workshop on Basic Ontological Issues in Knowledge Sharing, IJCAI95, 1995.

Uschold, M., & Gruninger, M. (1996). Ontologies: principles, methods, and applications. *Knowledge Engineering Review, 11* (2), 93-155.

Uschold, M., Healy, M., Williamson, K., Clark, P. and Woods, S. (1998). *Ontology Reuse and Application*. Proc. of the International Conference on Formal Ontology and Information Systems - FOIS'98, pp. 179–192.

Ushold, M., King, M., Moralee, S., & Zorgios, Y. (1998). The Enterprise Ontology. *The Knowledge Engineering Review: Special Issue on Putting Ontologies to Use, 13*(1), 31-89.

Van Damme, C., Hepp, M., & Siorpaes, K. (2007). FolksOntology: An Integrated Approach for Turning Folksonomies into Ontologies. *Proceedings of the ESWC 2007 Workshop "Bridging the Gap between Semantic Web and Web 2.0"*. Innsbruck, Austria.

Vanderwal T. (2007) *Folksonomy Coinage and Definition*. Retrieved from: http://vanderwal.net/folksonomy.html.

Vassileva, B., Scoggins, P. (2003). *Consumer Complaint Forms: An Assessment, Evaluation and Recommendations for Complaint Categorization*. Technical report, CCForm Project (IST-2001-34908). Brussels.

Velegrakis Y., Miller R. J., Mylopoulos J. (2005). Representing and querying data transformations. *Proceedings of the 21st International Conference on Data Engineering* ICDE 2005, 81-92.

Verma K., Sheth A. (2007). Semantically Annotating a Web Service. *IEEE Computer Society,* March/April 2007, 11, 83-85.

Viamonte, M.J. (2004). *Mercados Electrónicos Baseados em Agentes – Uma Abordagem com Estratégias Dinâmicas e Orientada ao Conhecimento*. Doctoral dissertation, University os Trás-os-Montes e Alto Douro, Portugal.

Viamonte, M.J., Ramos, C., Rodrigues, F., & Cardoso, J.C. (2006). ISEM: A Multi-Agent Simulator For Testing Agent Market Strategies. *IEEE Transactions on Systems, Man and Cybernetics – Part C: Special Issue on Game-theoretic Analysis and Stochastic Simulation of Negotiation Agents*, 36(1), 107-113.

Vitvar T., Zaremba M., Moran M. (2007a). Dynamic Service Discovery through Meta-Interactions with Service Providers. In *Proceedings of the 4th European Semantic Web Conference* (ESWC2007), Springer-Verlag LNCS series, Innsbruck, Austria.

Vitvar, T. Zaremba M., Moran M., Haller A., Kotinurmi P. (2007b). Semantic SOA to Promote Integration of Heterogeneous B2B Services. *The 4th IEEE Conference on Enterprise Computing, E-Commerce and E-Services* (EEE07), IEEE Computer Society, July, 2007, Tokyo, Japan.

Vitvar, T., Mocan, A., Kerrigan, M., Zaremba, M., Zaremba, M., Moran, M., et al. (2007). Semantically-enabled Service-Oriented Architecture: concepts, technology and application. *Service Oriented Computing and Applications, 2* (2), 129-154.

Vorhees, E. (1994). Query expansion using lexical semantic relations. *Proceedings of the 17th ACM Conf. on Research and Development in Information Retrieval*, ACM Press.

Vossen, P. (ed.) (1998). *EuroWordNet: A Multilingual Database with Lexical Semantic Networks.* Kluwer Academic Publishers, Dordrecht.

W3C. (2007). W3C and the Medical Sector. Retrieved August 7, 2007 from http://www.w3c.rl.ac.uk/QH/WP5/handouts/health_w3c.html

Waterfeld, W., & Weiten, M. (2007). Design of NeOn architecture. NeOn Deliverable D6.2.1.

Werthner, H., Hepp, M., Fensel, D., & Dorn, J. (2006) *Semantically-enabled Service-oriented Architectures: A Catalyst for Smart Business Networks*, Proceedings of the Smart Business Networks Initiative Discovery Session, June 14-16, Rotterdam, The Netherlands

Wiederhold G. (1992). Mediators in the architecture of future information systems. *IEEE Computer*, 25(3), 38-49.

Wiig K. (1997). Knowledge management: where did it come from and where will it go? *Journal of Expert Systems with Applications*, 13(1), 1–14.

Williams SK, Battle SA, Esplugas-Cuadrado J (2006). Protocol Mediation for Adaptation in Semantic Web Services. In Domingue and Sure (eds), *Proceedings of the 3rd European Semantic Web Conference (ESWC2006).* Lecture Notes in Computer Science, Volume 4011, June 2006, Pages 635-649

Wright, P.M., & McMahan, G.C. (1992). Theoretical perspectives for strategic Human resource management. *Journal of Management*, 18, pp. 292-320.

Wu, D., Parsia, B., Sirin, E., Hendler, J. A., & Nau, D. S. (2003). Automating DAML-Sweb Services Composition Using SHOP2. In *Proceedings of the 2nd International Semantic Web Conference*, pp. 195-210. Sanibel Island, FL, USA: Springer.

wwjGbmH. (2005). *Online-Rekrutierung I/2005.*

Yamamoto, J., & Sycara, K. (2001). A Stable and Efficient Buyer Coalition Formation Scheme for E-Marketplaces. *Proceedings of the Fifth International Conference on Autonomous Agents*, pp. 237-288.

Yang, G., Kifer, M., & Zhao, C. (2003). Flora-2: A rule-based knowledge representation and inference infrastructure for the semantic web. In *Proceedings of the Coopis, doa, and odbase - otm confederated international conferences, On the move to meaningful internet systems 2003.* Catania, Sicily, Italy.

Yee, K. P, Swearingen, K., Li, K. & Hearst, M. (2003). Faceted metadata for image search and browsing. In *Proceedings of the ACM SIGCHI Conference on Human Factors in Computing Systems* (CHI '03), Fort Lauderdale, FL, USA, April 5 – 10. New York. ACM Press.

Zamorano, P. (in press). (2003). *Empleo y tecnología, dos términos antagónicos.* Diario Expansi6n.

Zhong J., Zhu H., Li J., Yu Y. (2002). Conceptual graph matching for semantic search. In *Proceedings of the 10th International Conference on Computational Science*, 2393 (2002), 92-106

Zyl J., and Corbett D. (2000). A framework for Comparing the use of a Linguistic Ontology in an Application. *Workshop Applications of Ontologies and Problem-solving Methods*, ECAI'2000, Berlin Germany, August, 2000.

About the Contributors

Roberto García got his MSc in computer science from the Universitat Politècnica de Catalunya (UPC). His MSc thesis, completed the year 2000, developed a distributed knowledge management system using Semantic Web technologies. Then, he completed a Master's in e-commerce and collaborated in the first steps of a web and interactive systems company before returning to the academic world. In 2001 he got a research assistant position at the Universitat Pompeu Fabra (UPF) and carried out his research in Semantic Web based multimedia and digital rights management. These research activities concluded with his PhD thesis in 2006 about a Semantic Web approach to DRM. He is now an assistant professor at the Universitat de Lleida (UdL). He is also member of the GRIHO Human-Computer Interaction and Data Integration research group, where he is combining his previous research lines with trying to get the Semantic Web in touch with "real-world" end-users. More details from http://rhizomik.net/~roberto

* * *

Muhammad Ahtisham Aslam finished his PhD studies in 2007 at the Chair of Business Information Systems at the Department of Computer Science at Universität Leipzig with a thesis on establishing a correspondence between Business Process Execution Language and the Semantic Web Services paradigm. During his MSc studies at Hamdard University, Pakistan he received the All Pakistan Dr. Abdul Qadir Khan Research Laboratories Software Competition Award. His PhD studies at Universität Leipzig were supported by a Scholarship Award for PhD Studies Abroad by the Higher Education Commission (HEC) of Pakistan.

Sören Auer leads the research group Agile Knowledge Engineering and Semantic Web (AKSW) at the Department Business Information Systems (University of Leipzig) and collaborates with the database research group at the University of Pennsylvania, USA. Sören is founder of several high-impact research and community projects such as the Wikipedia semantification project DBpedia, the open-source innovation platform Cofundos.org or the social Semantic Web toolkit OntoWiki. Sören is author of over 50 peer-reviewed scientific publications, co-organiser of several workshops, chair of the first Social Semantic Web conference and member of the advisory board of the Open Knowledge Foundation.

Jose Luis Bas Uribe was born in 1961 in Bilbao (Spain). He holds a degree in economics from the Basque Country University of Bilbao (1982). His professional experience has been focused on both technological and financial areas. His career has been mainly developed in Bankinter (since 1988), where he started working at branches with commercial responsibilities (4 years), and, in order, he was electronic banking product manager in the Bask Country (6 years), electronic banking commercial director for the whole Bank (2 years), SME's commercial director for the whole Bank (1 year), as Internet projects director (3 years) and, at the present time, as applied innovation projects director (for the last 4 years). He was in charge of the e-Banking Case Study Work Package in the DIP Project.

Sergio Bellido González was born in 1975 in Zaragoza (Spain). He holds a degree in mathematics from the Complutense University of Madrid (1993-1998). He has taken PhD courses at the Applied Mathematics Department from the Politécnica University of Madrid (1999-2001) mainly focused on fuzzy logic. His professional experience, besides some teaching during the university years, is in Bankinter, known as one of the most innovative banks in Europe. Nowadays he is a R&D analyst at the innovation department. He has been in charge of many mobile-based projects. He has also been involved in the DIP project as the responsible of the technical side from Bankinter's point of view.

Richard Benjamins is director of innovation and R&D at Intelligent Software Components (iSOCO) in Madrid, Spain, which he co-founded in June 1999. Dr Benjamins has been a part time professor at the Technical University of Madrid. Before working at iSOCO, Dr Benjamins has held positions at the University of Amsterdam, the University of Sao Paulo, Brazil, the University of Paris-South, France, and the Spanish Artificial Intelligence Research Institute in Barcelona. He has published over 100 scientific articles in books, journals and proceedings, covering areas such as knowledge technologies, artificial intelligence, human-computer studies, knowledge management, Semantic Web and ontologies. He has been the guest editor of several journal special-issues and co-chair of numerous international workshops and conferences. He now serves on many international programme committees. He is a member of the editorial board of IEEE Intelligent Systems, Web Semantics (Elsevier), and International Journal on Semantic Web and Information Systems (Idea Group).

Martin Bryan is an ontologist working at CSW on healthcare, pharmaceutical and vehicle knowledge bases. An early exponent of structured markup languages, he wrote his first book on their use, *SGML – An Author's Guide*, as early as 1987. Since then he has been closely involved in the development of markup languages, representing the British Standards Institute on committees developing languages for text formatting (DSSSL), hypermedia (HyTime) and data navigation (Topic Maps) before these became simplified (as XSLT, SMIL and OWL) to form part of the phenomenon now known as the Internet. From 2000 to 2007 Martin chaired the ISO committee tasked with developing the next generation of schema languages, which include RELAX NG, Schematron, NVDL and his own standard, the Data Semantics Renaming Language (DSRL).

Irene Celino graduated in biomedical engineering at Politecnico di Milano in 2003 with a thesis on the impact of ICT on a neonatal intensive care unit. She obtained a post-degree Master title in information technology at CEFRIEL in 2004 with a thesis on Semantic Web portals. Since 2004, she has been working as researcher at CEFRIEL. Her research activities cover the studies on user experience in Web navigation, the application of Semantic Web technologies in the development of web portals, search engines for audio-visual material and Web Services improvement. She is currently participating to the research activities of national projects like NeP4B (FIRB-2005) in the e-business domain and some European projects within FP6, like SUPER (IST-2005-02650, Integrated Project) in business process management area, SEEMP (IST-2005-27347, Specific Targeted Research Project) in e-government domain, and, in the past, COCOON (IST-2002-507126, Integrated Project) in e-healthcare field. She will be involved also in the forthcoming ServiceFinder project (IST-2007-215876, Specific Targeted Research Project) of FP7, in the domain of Web 2.0 and Web services.

Dario Cerizza obtained the graduation in "Ingegneria Informatica" (computer engineering) at Politecnico di Milano in 2001 with a thesis on a multi-channel delivery platform. He has been working since 2001 as researcher at CEFRIEL. His skills have been focused on telemedicine systems. He leaded the developing of a platform for medical teleconsultation and an automatic engine for legal archiving of medical images. He has participated to consulting activities related to distributed regional information system. His research activities focus on software integration and semantic web services technologies. He leaded the researches about a semantic discovery engine for web services and a semantic search engine for multimedia resources. He is leading the SEEMP IST STREP project on e-Gov and the e-Health scenario of the TRIPCOM IST STREP on behalf of CEFRIEL. He is participating to the OASIS standardization effort for the definition of a Semantic Execution Environment for web services (SEE Technical Committee).

Mirko Cesarini is currently working as professor assistant in the Information System Group of the Department of Statistics - University of Milan Bicocca. He is also affiliated to the CRISP Research Center. His research focuses on federated information systems and service science. He has published several papers in refereed journals and in the proceedings of international conferences. He got his PhD in information and communication technologies in 2005 and his Master's degree in computer engineering in 2001, both at the Politecnico di Milano, Milan, Italy.

Jean Charlet is researcher at Assistance Publique – Hôpitaux de Paris and in the unit 872 of French Institute of Health (INSERM). He is also professor at École Centrale Paris and responsible of the French working group on knowledge engineering (http://www.irit.fr/GRACQ). His research focuses on ontologies and digital documents. Jean Charlet works particularly on the construction of ontologies starting from textual corpora and on their relationships with medical thesauri. He studies ontologies epistemology and apply his research to interface ontologies used in medical coding systems. Jean Charlet also works about usage of electronic health records in combination with ontologies. WWW: http://estime.spim.jussieu.fr/~jc

Laurent Cicurel is a young researcher at the R&D department of the company Intelligent Software Components (iSOCO). He has successfully achieved in 2005 a double degree in computer engineering at the National Institute of Applied Science (INSA Lyon, France) and at the University of Karlsruhe (Universität Karlsruhe TH, Germany). After finishing his Master's thesis on word soft-clustering from unstructured texts in the AIFB of the University of Karlsruhe, he entered iSOCO in January 2006 and has participated in natural language processing and Semantic Web related projects. He contributed in the DIP project and continues to work on another European Semantic Web Services related project called SUPER.

Ricardo Colomo has been a faculty member of the Computer Science Department at Universidad Carlos III de Madrid since 2002. His research interests include software process improvement, software project management and information systems. He received his PhD in computer science from the

Universidad Politécnica of Madrid (2005). He also holds a MBA from the Instituto de Empresa (2002). He has been working as software engineer, project manager and software engineering consultant in several companies including Spanish IT leader INDRA.

Jesus Contreras, R&D Director at Intelligent Software Components (iSOCO). PhD computer science (2004) at the Technical University of Madrid, Spain. In 1996 he was an assistant researcher in the Intelligence Systems Research Group (www.isys.dia.fi.upm.es) where he participate in projects oriented towards the development of knowledge based systems and advanced artificial intelligence applications. In 1998 he joined Software A.G. e-business competence center (www.softwareag.com) where he was enrolled in various European projects as software engineer and main researcher. In November 2000 he joined iSOCO in the Innovation Department and participated in knowledge management tasks. Now he is R&D Director of iSOCO, involved in tasks of innovation business development for Semantic Web research results. During his career he published various articles about semantic web, natural language processing and human-computer interaction.

Oscar Corcho is an assistant professor at Universidad Politécnica de Madrid (UPM). He graduated in computer science from UPM in 2000, and received the third Spanish award in computer science from the Spanish Government. He obtained his MSc in software engineering from UPM in 2001, and his PhD in artificial intelligence in 2004. His research activities include ontology languages and tools, the Semantic Web and Grid. He has participated in a large number of European and international projects in these areas, and has published two books, over 50 journal and conference/workshop papers, and reviews papers in many conferences, workshops and journals. He has collaborated in the organisation of conferences like EKAW2002, ESWC2006 and ESWC2008, workshops like the ISWC2003 and ISWC2004 Workshops on Evaluation of Ontology Tools (EON2003, EON2004).

Jay Cousins is a consultant at CSW Group Ltd. Jay works with XML and Semantic Web technologies and specializes in the development of architectures for B2B data interchange, data integration and industry standardization. He has worked in this field since 2000, applying XML and Semantic Web technologies (RDF, Topic Maps, OWL) to projects in the news & media, oil & gas, health, and automotive sectors. Jay has participated in various standardization initiatives, including the development of XML architectures for NewsML and AdsML and Chairing the CEN/ISSS Workshop Modeling for Automotive Repair Information applications - (WS/IMA). Jay graduated from the London School of Economics with an MSc in analysis, design, and management of information systems.

Ivano De Furio achieved the Laurea degree in electronic engineering at the Federico II University of Naples, in March 1996. From July 1994 to March 1996 and from August 1997 to January 2000, he worked in the R&D Centre for Information and Communications Technologies of Bull HN Information Systems Italia SpA, Avellino, Italy. Since February 2000, he has been a research engineer in the Telecom VAS and Media Unit, of Atos Origin Italia S.p.A., Naples, Italy. His research interests include artificial intelligence, rule systems for business agents, semantic web service approaches and architectures. Ivano De Furio has been involved in several research projects, such as HiVDS, SERVICEWARE and WISE and was author of several papers. In March 2007, Ivano De Furio achieved degree cum laude in computer science engineering.

Flavio M. De Paoli, PhD, is associate professor in computer science at the University of Milano Bicocca. He has been visiting researcher at HP Labs (Palo Alto) in 1989, and University of California at Santa Barbara in 1997. His research interests are in software engineering with focus on distributed systems architecture and languages, e-service computing, semantic web-services, multi-agent systems, user-centered cooperative systems and multi-user interaction. He is author of more than 70 papers, 2 books as author and 5 as editor. He is member of ACM and IEEE.

Emanuele Della Valle is program manager of CEFRIEL's Semantic Web Activities, lecturer of "Advanced Information Systems" at Politecnico di Milano, lecturer of "Knowledge Engineering" at Università dell'Insubria and Service Coordinator for "Testbeds and Challenges service" of STI. He is technical manager of the European Project SEEMP. He collaborates to TripCom and SUPER European research projects and to NeP4B FIRB research project. He was deputy technical manager of the European project COCOON. He leaded and participated into several consulting activities related to strategic evolution of distributed information systems, integration of different back-end systems and various feasibility studies for Web portal and document management systems.

Alistair Duke is a principal researcher with Next Generation Web Research Group of British Telecommunications. He graduated from Aston University with a MEng in electronic systems engineering and from Loughborough University with a PhD in collaboration systems for concurrent engineering. His primary interest is the Semantic Web and its application to the fields of knowledge management, service oriented architecture and business systems. He was a member of the EU OnToKnowledge and Semantic Web enabled Web Services (SWWS) projects and a workpackage leader on the EU DIP (where his focus was on applying Semantic Web Services to the telecommunications industry) and SEKT (where he led the Knowledge Access workpackage, developing end-user tools supported by semantic technology) projects.

Jacky Estublier is research director at the French National Research Center (CNRS) in Grenoble, France and holds a PhD on operating systems. He leads since 1984 the software engineering research group in Grenoble university. His research interest was originally on software configuration management. In 1984 one of the early Adele versions was sold to airspace industry for the development of the Airbus and Ariane embedded software. Today about 2000 licenses of the Adele system are on daily industrial production use. Since the early 90s, he focused on process support and process modelling. Since the late 90s, his research activity focused on interoperability and federated applications. This trend of work contributes to the model driven software engineering field through an original approach of model composition. The resulting product, Melusine, is in experimental exploitation, on large scale. He is the coordinator of the French initiative on MDA. He was general chair of various conferences; in particular he was program chair of ICSE 2004, the largest conference in software engineering. He was many times expert for the selection of EU research calls (FP5, FP6), as well as reviewer for different European research projects. He was member of different European projects, in which he was constantly either work package leader or technical director of the project.

Klaus-Peter Fähnrich holds the chair of business information systems at the Department of Computer Science at Universität Leipzig. His main areas of research and teaching are business information systems, software engineering and management, e-business and services science within computer science. He is speaker of the board of directors of the Center for Information, Knowledge and Service-Management, speaker of the Leipziger Informatik-Verbund (LIV) and board member of the Institute for Applied Computer Science (InfAI). He is the author of more than 300 scientific publications and founder of several successful spin-off companies.

Giovanni Frattini achieved his Laurea degree in physics at the University of Naples in 1995. He has worked for several companies with different roles. Since 2000 his focus has been on value added services. He has been delivery unit manager from 2002 to 2004. Currently he is chief architect of several projects providing is contribution to operational and research team. As researcher, his main focus is currently on multimodal mobile services.

Mariagrazia Fugini is associate professor of computer engineering. She received the PhD in computer engineering in 1987 and she was a visiting professor at the University of Maryland, Technical University of Vienna, University of Stuttgart, and University Politecnica de Catalunya. Her research interests are in information system security, software reuse, information retrieval, information systems development and re-engineering, e-government, and ICT for e-science. She participated in the TODOS, ITHACA, F3, WIDE and DEAFIN UE projects, working on information system development and re-engineering, software reuse, data security, information retrieval tools, and workflow and web application design. She is involved in the EU Projects WS-Diamond (Diagnosis in Web Services and Self-Healing Systems) and SEEMP (Single European Employment Market Place), and in some national projects. She is in the editorial board of a few specialized conferences and journals on security and information systems. She is co-author of "Database Security" (Addison-Wesley, 1995).

Frederik Gailly is a doctoral candidate at the Department of Management Information & Operations Management of Ghent University. He holds degrees in applied economics (2001) and applied computer science (2007). His research interests include conceptual modelling, business domain ontologies and semantic web technologies. His doctoral research concerns the representation, formalization and operationalization of business domain ontologies. Mr Gailly has published in *Lecture Notes in Computer Science*. He presented at the International Conferences on Business Information Systems (BIS) and Enterprise Systems and Accounting (ICESAcc) and at workshops organized within the International Semantic Web and CAiSE conferences.

Angel García-Crespo is the head of the SofLab Group at the Computer Science Department in the Universidad Carlos III de Madrid and the head of the Institute for Promotion of Innovation Pedro Juan de Lastanosa. He holds a PhD in industrial engineering from the Universidad Politécnica de Madrid (Award from the Instituto J.A. Artigas to the best thesis) and received an Executive MBA from the Instituto de Empresa. Professor García-Crespo has led and actively contributed to large European Projects of the FP V and VI, and also in many business cooperations. He is the author of more than a hundred publications in conferences, journals and books, both Spanish and international.

Rosa Gil got her degree in physics from the Universitat de Barcelona in 1996. Then, she completed a Master's in environment management in 1997. She worked in the Spanish Research Council until 1998, and afterwards worked in private companies as webmaster before returning to the academic world at the end of 2000. Then, she got a scholarship at the Universitat Pompeu Fabra (UPF) and carried out his research in Semantic Web based multimedia and digital rights management. In 2003 she became assistant professor. These research activities concluded with his PhD thesis in 2005 about agents negotiating in the Semantic Web. He is now an associate professor at the Universitat de Lleida (UdL). She is also member of the GRIHO Human-Computer Interaction and Data Integration research group, where she is combining his previous research lines with trying to get the Semantic Web in touch with "real-world" end-users. More details from http://rhizomik.net/~rosa

Juan Manuel Gimeno got his MSc in computer science from the Universitat Politècnica de Catalunya (UPC). After finishing his degree he became an associate professor in the same university. He was a member of the Artificial Intelligence group working mainly in the areas of machine learning and data mining. In 1998 he got a teaching position at the Universitat de Lleida and now he is an associate professor in programming and software engineering. As a member of the GRIHO Human-Computer Interaction and Data Integration research group, where his main interests are integrating his previous work in improving the usability and applicability of the Semantic Web to real problems.

François Goasdoué is an assistant professor of computer science in the Artificial Intelligence and Inference Systems group of LRI (Computer Science Laboratory) at Univ. Paris-Sud, Orsay, France. He is also a member of the Gemo group (Integration of Data and Knowledge Distributed over the Web) in the Pôle Commun de Recherche en Informatique, a joint lab between INRIA (French National Institute for Research in Computer Science and Control), École Polytechnique, Univ. Paris-Sud, and CNRS (French National Center for Scientific Research). His research interests include knowledge representation and information integration, in particular, description logics, hybrid representation languages, query answering using views, and mediation systems. He received a PhD in computer science from Univ. Paris-Sud. WWW: http://www.lri.fr/~goasdoue

Juan Miguel Gomez is a visiting professor at the Computer Science Department of the Universidad Carlos III de Madrid. He holds a PhD in computer science from the Digital Enterprise Research Institute (DERI) at the National University of Ireland, Galway and received his MSc in telecommunications engineering from the Universidad Politécnica de Madrid (UPM). He was involved in several EU FP V and VI research projects and was a member of the Semantic Web Services Initiative (SWSI). His research interests include semantic web, semantic web services, business process modelling, b2b integration and, recently, bioinformatics.

Asunción Gómez-Pérez is full professor at the Computer Science School at Universidad Politécnica de Madrid, Spain. She is the director of the Ontology Engineering Group since 1995. The most representative projects she is participating are: SEEMP, NeOn, OntoGrid as project coordinator, Knowledge Web NoE acting as scientific vice-director, Esperonto, the OntoWeb thematic network, and also the MKBEEM project. She has published more than 100 papers on the above issues. She is author of one book on ontological engineering and co-author of a book on knowledge engineering. She has been co-director of the summer school on ontological engineering and the Semantic Web in 2003, 2004, 2005, 2006 and 2007. She was program chair of ESWC'05 and EKAW'02. She has been co-organizer of conferences, workshops and tutorials. She acts as reviewer in many conferences and journals.

Armin Haller is research assistant in the Digital Enterprise Research Institute (DERI) and PhD student at the National University Ireland, Galway. Until recently he was co-managing the m3pe project to design a process ontology to formally capture different process execution models. Currently he is involved in the EU funded SUPER project, which aims to extend existing generic models for the representation of processes with semantic information capturing all aspects of system behaviour. His research interests are Business Process Integration and semantic Web Services, where he published some 20 scientific articles in journals, conferences and workshops and co-edited the Business Process Management Workshops Proceedings in 2005. He is the main developer of m3po, a business process integration ontology, semantic RosettaNet, a document standard ontology and has been working in the WSMX initiative, developing the first semantic service-oriented architecture.

Johannes Heinecke is a linguist and a computational linguist who received his MA in 1993 from Heidelberg University and his PhD in 1998 from Potsdam University (Germany). From 1994 to 1999 he worked at the Chair of Computational Linguistics (Department of Linguistics, Humboldt-Universität zu Berlin) on projects on human language processing like VerbModil and syntax and semantic modelling (Dawai, Telex). In 1999 he joined the Natural Language Processing Group at France Telecom R&D in Lannion, where he is also in charge of semantic modelling and semantic analysis of human language. His recent works are about coupling NLP and ontological reasoning as well as aligning ontologies with lexical semantic data.

Germán Herrero Cárcel was born in 1980 in Valencia (Spain). He has a degree in computer & software engineering from the University of Valencia. His technical expertise is in semantic technologies, with strong knowledge in ontology development. He is expert in Java programming. He worked as assistant scholar in the Robotics Institute from the University of Valencia involved in Semantic Web projects. Then, he worked as a software programmer in the computer department of a financial entity. Currently he is working for Atos Origin in the Semantic & Service Engineering Unit of the ARI Department. He is involved on two of the most relevant Semantic Web projects financed by European Union, called NeOn and TAO.

Paola Hobson, manager of personalisation and knowledge at Motorola Labs UK, holds BSc (1984), PhD (1987) and MBA (1999) degrees. Paola has more than 20 years of experience in industrial research since starting her professional career with the UK's Independent Broadcasting Authority in 1987. Paola joined Motorola in 1996, and has for some years managed a group of research engineers and human factors scientists working on a range of projects related to mobile applications. Projects have included transmission of very low bit video over the digital TETRA network, watermarking of images and video for the purposes of tamper detection, and personalisation of content delivery systems. Paola was the co-ordinator of the aceMedia Integrated Project (http://www.acemedia.org) which brings together 13 leading European industrial and academic research labs to create innovative intelligent multimedia applications.

Mustafa Jarrar is a Marie Curie postdoctoral Fellow at the University of Cyprus. Before that he worked as a senior research scientist at STARLab, Vrije Universiteit Brussel in Belgium, where he also completed his Master's (2000) and PhD (2005) in computer science. Jarrar published more than 55 articles and refereed reports in the areas of database, conceptual modeling, ontologies, automated reasoning, and lexical semantics. He chaired 12 international events and workshops, a PC members of more than 55 conferences and journals. Dr. Jarrar served as a project leader in 8 national and international projects, and has recently co-founded the Ontology Outreach Advisory (ontology-advisory.org), which is an international not-for-profit association with the aim of developing strategies for ontology recommendation and standardization, and promoting the ontology technology to industry. Dr. Jarrar is a full member of the IFIP2.6 on Database Semantics, the IFIP2.12 on Web Semantics, the IEEE Learning Standards Committee, and the CEN/ISSS ICT Skills and Curricula. http:www.jarrar.info

Mick Kerrigan is a PhD researcher in the Semantic Technology Institute (STI) located in the University of Innsbruck, Austria. Originally from Dublin, Ireland, Mick holds a BSc from University College Dublin and an MSc from National University of Ireland Galway, both in computer science. Mick's main area of interest is in the software life cycle of Semantic Web services and particularly in supporting the developer throughout the Semantic Web service development cycle. The primary output of his work has been the Web Service Modeling Toolkit (WSMT), an integrated development environment for Semantic Web services, focusing on tools for creating and managing WSMO descriptions. Mick contributes to the WSMO, WSML and WSMX working groups and has been involved in a number of EU funded projects, namely DIP, Knowledge Web, SEEMP and SHAPE. Mick is also a contributor to and the secretary of the OASIS Semantic Execution Environment Technical Committee (SEE-TC).

Paavo Kotinurmi is a researcher and lecturer at the Software Business and Engineering Institute, Helsinki University of Technology. Paavo Kotinurmi received his Doctoral degree in computer science in 2007. His Master's of Science degree was completed in 2001. The PhD topic was applying XML-based standards to solve practical B2B integration problems. In that area, also semantic Web Services technologies have been applied to solve integration problems. As part of that, Dr. Kotinurmi spent nine months in DERI Galway as a visiting researcher. His current research interests include combining XML-based B2B standards, service-oriented architectures and semantic technologies. His current research targets helping companies and healthcare organisations to setup service-oriented architectures utilising B2B standards, ontologies and semantic technologies where appropriate. Dr. Kotinurmi has published around twenty articles in international conferences and journals.

Alain Léger (Ing 71, Master's 82, PhD 87, Habilitation 07-08) is senior scientist. He was director of research program in "Knowledge Processing and Data Analysis" in direction of research at FT R&D (1996-2006) and is now in a sabbatical year. He was head (94-96) of the department on Mediation Services for Telecommunication Applications and deputy-head (91-94) of an R&D department on Telematics and Audiovisual Hypermedia Document. He chaired many international teams and was deeply involved in the standardization field (ISO, IUT-T, CEPT/ETSI) and for picture coding (Head of the JPEG algorithm, (85-88). He received with the JPEG-MPEG team the 1996 EMMI technology and engineering award. He has been actively involved in FIPA for standards in ontology services for intelligent agents (97-98). He is author of 90 international papers. He taught to Master's students multimedia coding and temporal Petri nets (89-96), in High Engineering schools (ESE, ENST) and in Universities. In the European IT co-operation domain he was acting as the scientific manager of the ACTS - ABROSE (cooperative filtering for multi-agent systems). He was scientific coordinator of the IST - MKBEEM (Multilingual Knowledge-Based E-Commerce marketplace). He was leading industry related activities in IST OntoWeb. He was co-leading (2004-2007) Industry in IST NoE Knowledge Web.

José-Manuel López-Cobo was born in 1972 in Granada (Spain). He holds a degree in computer engineering from the University of Málaga and is currently taking his PhD in the field of SWS. He has been working since 1999 in research projects. He worked at Atos Origin and iSOCO, as technical research manager of the R&D department, being responsible for the management of the projects like SWWS, DIP, Infrawebs, TAO, LUISA or SUPER. Currently he works at iSOCO as research manager sharing his time among research and commercial projects.

Silvestre Losada, born in 1977, BS in software engineering from Universidad Carlos III, Madrid, Spain, September 2003. His Master's thesis was about publishing domain ontologies in a Semantic Web portal. In October 2002 he joined iSOCO working on several projects related to Semantic Web services, business process management (SWWS, DIP, SUPER) and projects on applying Semantic Web technology in software solutions. During his career he published various articles about Semantic Web, Semantic Web services and semantic business process.

Malgorzata Mochol is working as a lecturer and researcher at the Free University of Berlin contributing to different national and international projects (e.g. EU Network of Excellence Knowledge Web, Reisewissen, Wissensnetze). In the cooperation with a German recruitment company she has been working on the development of a prototypical semantic web based job portal. Malgorzata is an author of more than 20 publications in various conferences (WI05, I-KNOW'05 & '06), workshops (OWLED-2005, WebS'06, OM-2006) and journals. She has also contributed to the book "Competencies in Organizational E-Learning: Concepts and Tools". Malgorzata has received her diploma in computer science in September 2003 from the Technical University of Berlin. Her PhD research focuses on semantic matching issues taking into account the reuse aspects of the existing approaches and especially the selection of relevant and suitable matchers. She was involved in the organisation of the Ontology Alignment Evaluation Initiative - 2006 Campaign and ExpertFinder workshops.

Lyndon J B Nixon is a lecturer and researcher at the Networked Information Systems group at the Free University of Berlin. In 2007 he obtained his PhD in computer science in the area of semantic multimedia presentations. He has been industry area co-manager for the EU NoE Knowledge Web as well as in-use track co-chair at the ISWC 2007. He is currently a workpackage leader in the STREP TripCom. He actively publishes on Semantic Web, coordination systems and multimedia as well as co-organizing workshops on the Industry uptake of semantic technologies as well as issues of multimedia semantics. WWW: http://page.mi.fu-berlin.de/nixon

Marta Oliva got her MSc in computer science from the Universitat Politècnica de Catalunya (UPC) in 1991. Then, she started to work as associate professor for technical studies at the Universitat de Lleida (UdL). At 1995 she started her collaboration with the BLOOM (BarceLona Object Oriented Model) Project, at UPC, about cooperative systems to manage heterogeneous databases. She carried out her research, in the BLOOM project, in database security and interoperability. These research activities concluded with her PhD thesis in 2001 about integrating security criteria to achieve access control in a federated heterogeneous database system. In 2005, she moved to the Human-Computer Interaction and Semantic Web disciplines and from then, she is also a member of the GRIHO Human-Computer Interaction and Data Integration research group, where she is trying to get the Semantic Web in touch with "real-world" end-users. More details from http://web.udl.es/usuaris/n7807592

Eyal Oren is a researcher at the Network Institute in the Computer Science and Communication Sciences Departments of the Vrije Universiteit Amsterdam. Eyal Oren received a PhD in computer science from the National University of Ireland, Galway for his thesis on algorithms and components for application development on the Semantic Web. He also holds a MSc degree from the Delft University of Technology in the Netherlands. His research is concerned with techniques for large-scale manipulation and analysis of Semantic Web data and with semantics in workflow management and process management. As part of his research, Dr. Oren has published around thirty articles in international conferences and journals and has spent several months as visiting scholar at Stanford University and at the University of Innsbruck. He now works on information extraction, knowledge representation and formal reasoning techniques for automatic analysis of political news texts.

Tomás Pariente Lobo has a degree of Bachelor in telecommunication engineering by the UPM (Spain). His technical expertise is mainly in semantic technologies, e-government, business process mangement (BPM) and knowledge management. He is expert in Java J2EE. This expertise started in 1987 when he joined the company Indra Sistemas, where he has taken part in multiple commercial and R&D projects. Since June 2006 he works as project manager and technical consultant for EU-based projects in semantic technologies in ATOS Origin. He is involved in several working groups in this technology. He worked on EU projects such as Ontologging, SmartGov, OntoGov, INFRAWEBS and is currently involved in the NeOn, LUISA and SOA4ALL projects.

Adam Pease has led research in ontology, linguistics and formal inference, including development of the Suggested Upper Merged Ontology (SUMO), the Controlled English to Logic Translation (CELT) system, the Core Plan Representation (CPR) and the Sigma knowledge engineering environment. Sharing research under open licenses, in order to achieve the widest possible dissemination and technology transfer has been a core element of his research program and his products have been downloaded by thousands of people around the world.

Ferran Perdrix got his MSc in computer science from the Universitat Politècnica de Catalunya (UPC) in 2001. Actually, has pursuing his PhD in computer science at the Universitat de Lleida (UdL). He combines academic and industry activities. He is part-time professor at the UdL since 2001 and R+D director in the Segre Media Group, which includes TV channels, radio stations, internet websites and newspapers, since 2003. He carried out his research in several Human-Computer Interaction and Semantic Web research projects. He is also a member of the GRIHO Human-Computer Interaction and Data Integration research group, where he is trying to explore how the HCI and Semantic Web approaches can help the future of mass media. More details are available from http://griho.udl.cat/ca/membres/investigadors/membre_ferran.html

Geert Poels is a professor with the rank of lecturer at the Department of Management Information and Operations Management. He holds degrees in business engineering and computer science, and a PhD in applied economic sciences. His research interests include software metrics, conceptual modelling and accounting information systems. Dr Poels has published in *IEEE Transactions on Software Engineering, Data & Knowledge Engineering, Software and Systems Modelling, Information and Software Technology*, and *Lecture Notes in Computer Science*, and presented at conferences such as ER &

CAiSE. In 2002, 2003, 2006 and 2007, he co-organized the IWCMQ/QoIS workshops on conceptual model and information system quality at the ER conference.

J. Ramírez obtained his Bachelor's degree in computer science by the Technical University of Madrid in 1996, and his PhD in artificial intelligence by the Artificial Intelligence Department of the Computer Science School (Technical University of Madrid) in 2002. His research activities mainly have been related to the verification of knowledge base systems, ontological engineering, and the development of intelligent tutoring systems based on virtual reality. Currently, he teaches a course on intelligent virtual environments and several courses on computer programming in the Technical University of Madrid. In addition, he collaborates with the Decoroso Crespo Laboratory and the Ontology Engineering Group (both in Technical University of Madrid) in several research projects.

Marc Richardson is a senior researcher in the Next Generation Web Research group, part of Research & Venturing at British Telecommunications plc. He joined BT in 2001 as a developer of knowledge management applications and was involved in the formation of a successful knowledge management spin-off company Exago, which is now part of Corpora Plc. His work is currently focused on research of the Semantic Web and its application in the Telecommunications domain.

Luigi Romano achieved his Laurea degree in physics at the University of Naples in 1996. In 1997 he attended the Pre-Doctoral School in Communication Systems at the Swiss Federal Institute of Technology Lausanne (EPFL). Since 1997 he has been engaged in different roles for several telecommunication operators and in 2000 he started working in the system integration area of Sema Group. In the 2003 he was involved in a research project, in Atos Origin Italia, attempting to ground mobile value added services in innovative architectures. He was involved in other research projects related to multimodal systems and artificial intelligence and he is currently involved in a project aiming to explore the potential of Semantic Grid computing in e-government applications.

Marcos Ruano is a research assistant of the Computer Science Department at Universidad Carlos III de Madrid. He holds a BSc in computer systems from Universidad de Valladolid and a MSc in computer science from Universidad Carlos III de Madrid. He has been involved in several research projects as information management engineer and software consultant.

Godfrey Rust has over twenty years experience of information management in music and copyright. He was principally responsible for the computerisation of the UK music charts, as well as the establishment of the UK National Discography. Godfrey was the director of data services for the music collecting societies MCPS and PRS, and assumed technical lead for the copyright societies' Common Information System Plan and the <indecs> metadata framework. Godfrey is the co-editor of the MPEG-21 Rights Data Dictionary (RDD) on behalf of the contecs:dd consortium and is a long-term metadata consultant to the International DOI Foundation (IDF). Currently, he is working on data modelling and ontology development for various corporate and industry clients. Godfrey is now the principal data architect for Ontologyx, Rightscom's ontology product initiative aimed at providing industrial strength metadata interoperability based on the radical principle of contextual transformation.

Pavel Shvaiko is a postdoc fellow at the Department of Information and Communication Technology (DIT) of the University of Trento (UniTn), Trento, Italy. He obtained his PhD in 2006 at DIT UniTn with the dissertation "Iterative Schema-based Semantic Matching." He has co-authored and co-edited a number of books, contributed to, and published in various international journals, conferences and workshops in the fields of Semantic Web, artificial intelligence, and information systems. He participated in several European, national, and industrial projects. Currently, he is intensively involved in various projects of the European Commission's 6th Framework Programme, such as Knowledge Web and OpenKnowledge. WWW: http://www.dit.unitn.it/~pavel

Nuno Silva is coordinator professor of computer engineering at the School of Engineering of the Polytechnic Institute of Porto. His research interests are information integration, knowledge engineering and the Semantic Web. He received his PhD in electrical engineering from the University of Trás-os-Montes and Alto Douro, Portugal. He is coordinator and technical leader of several research projects.

Elena Simperl is the vice director of the Digital Enterprise Research Institute at the University of Innsbruck, and the education manager of Semantic Technology Institute International. She holds a PhD in computer science from the Free University of Berlin. Elena's primary domain of research is ontology engineering. In particular she is interested in application- and business-oriented aspects of ontology building and management, and approached these topics in various national and European research projects. She is the scientific director of the EU-STREP TripCom and manager of the EU Network of Excellence Knowledge Web. Elena organized scientific workshops addressing the aforementioned research topics at leading conferences in the field (ESWC, ISWC, ESTC) and initiated activities targeted at the supervision and guidance of doctoral students such as the Knowledge Web PhD Symposium series organized at the European Semantic Web Conference ESWC since 2006.

German Vega is a research engineer at the Laboratory of Informatics of Grenoble. His research interests include the use of meta-modeling techniques for the development of specialized software engineering environments. He is particularly interested in building tools to support the complete life cycle of applications based on service-oriented architectures. He received his PhD in computer science from Université Joseph Fourier in Grenoble, France.

Maria João Viamonte is adjunct professor of computer engineering at the School of Engineering of the Polytechnic Institute of Porto. Her research interests are in multi-agent simulation, agent mediated electronic commerce, semantic web technology and decision support systems. She received her PhD in electrical engineering from the University of Trás-os-Montes and Alto Douro, Portugal.

Boris Villazón-Terrazas belongs to Ontology Engineering Group of the Artificial Intelligence Department of the Computer Science School at Universidad Politécnica de Madrid (UPM). He graduated with honours in computer science from Universidad Católica Boliviana in 2002. He is currently PhD student in artificial intelligence in UPM. Previously, he has worked as a junior researcher at the Research Institute of Applied Informatics (RIAI) of Universidad Católica Boliviana. His research activities include Semantic Web and ontological engineering. He is currently participating at the NeOn project and the SEEMP project.

Gang Zhao earned his degrees of MSc and PhD in computer science at the University of Manchester, UK. He has been mostly involved in R&D of intelligent system development. He has been a system programmer, analyst, and architect for such system developments as machine translation, natural language understanding, speech recognition, information extraction, data and text mining, case tools for database modeling, dialogue systems, rule-based inference engines, human resource management system. He has acted as technology lead and project manager in both industrial and academic institutions for both product development and research programs such as IST projects. He has published on computational linguistics and knowledge systems. He is currently consulting to private and public institutions in Belgium on data visualisation, text mining and ontology-based system interoperation in the context of product development and European research programs.

Index

J

K

L

M

N

O

P

R

S

U

V

W

X